UK 2004

The Official Yearbook of the United Kingdom
of Great Britain and Northern Ireland

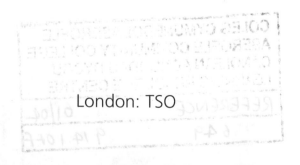

London: TSO

Contact points

We welcome readers' comments and suggestions on this publication:
email   uk.yearbook@ons.gov.uk
telephone   +44 (0)20 7533 5778
or write to
The Editor, UK Yearbook,
Office for National Statistics, Room B5/02,
1 Drummond Gate, London SW1V 2QQ

For general enquiries, contact the National Statistics Customer Contact Centre:
email   info@statistics.gov.uk
telephone   0845 601 3034
                   (UK local rate)
                   +44 (0)1633 812973
                   (International)
                   01633 812399
                   (Minicom number for the Deaf)
fax   +44 (0)1633 652747

or write to
The Customer Contact Centre
Office for National Statistics
Government Buildings
Cardiff Road
Newport
NP10 8XG

You can find National Statistics on the Internet
www.statistics.gov.uk

The UK Yearbook is also available on the National Statistics website
www.statistics.gov.uk/yearbook

About the Office for National Statistics

The Office for National Statistics (ONS) is the government agency responsible for compiling, analysing and disseminating many of the United Kingdom's economic, social and demographic statistics, including the retail prices index, trade figures and labour market data, as well as the periodic census of the population and health statistics. It is also the agency that administers the statutory registration of births, marriages and deaths in England and Wales. The Director of ONS is the National Statistician and the Registrar General for England and Wales.

A National Statistics publication

National Statistics are produced to high professional standards set out in the National Statistics Code of Practice. They undergo regular quality assurance reviews to ensure they meet customer needs. They are produced free from any political interference.

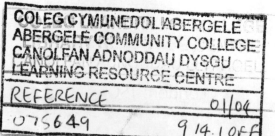

Contents

Contributors

UK 2004 was researched, written and edited by a combination of in-house and freelance authors.

Authors	Anthony Beachey
	Carl Bird
	Ben Bradford
	Simon Burtenshaw
	John Collis
	David Gardener
	David Harper
	Steve Howell
	Henry Langley
	Kylie Lovell
	Matthew Richardson
	Shiva Satkunam
	Dave Sharp
	Conor Shipsey
	Bernadeta Tendyra
	Anna Upson
	Linda Zealey
Review team	Penny Babb
	David Harper
	Nina Mill
Colour pages	Guy Warren
Cover	Michelle Franco
Index	Richard German

Maps	Alistair Dent
	Ray Martin
Picture research	Frances Riddelle
Production	Kate Myers
	Sharon Adhikari
	Lola Akinrodoye
	John Chrzczonowicz
	Sunita Dedi
	Joseph Goldstein
Proof readers	Richard German
	Jane Howard
	Henry Langley
	Jeff Probst
Charts and typesetting	Spire Origination, Norwich
Editors	Carol Summerfield
	Jill Barelli
	Linda Zealey

Acknowledgements

UK 2004 has been compiled with the help of around 250 organisations, including many government departments and agencies. The editors would like to thank all the people from these organisations who have taken so much time and care to ensure that the book's high standards of accuracy have been maintained. Their contributions and comments have been extremely valuable.

Preface

Now in its 55th edition, *UK 2004* is the annual reference book about the United Kingdom. Drawing on a wide range of official and other authoritative sources, it provides a factual and up-to-date overview of Great Britain and Northern Ireland, including the main aspects of government policy, how services are provided, and the organisations involved. Social, economic, cultural, environmental and foreign affairs are all covered. The Yearbook is a widely used work of reference, both in the United Kingdom and overseas, where it is an important element of the information service provided by British diplomatic posts.

This edition has been fully updated and revised to August 2003. The colour pages provide maps and a photographic diary of events, exhibitions, anniversaries and achievements as diverse as the war in Iraq, the opening of the Hadrian's Wall Path National Trail, the 250th anniversary of the British Museum, the Cardiff festival, and the launch of Beagle 2, the British space probe heading for Mars. 2003 was the European Year for Disabled People and this is marked with items of interest throughout the book.

Notes and definitions

1. Figures given in tables and charts may not always sum to the totals shown because of rounding.

2. The full title of the United Kingdom is 'the United Kingdom of Great Britain and Northern Ireland'. 'Great Britain' comprises England, Wales and Scotland.

3. Statistics in this book apply to the United Kingdom as a whole wherever possible. However, data are not always available on a comparable basis, so in some areas information has been given for one or more of the component parts of the United Kingdom. Geographical coverage is clearly indicated.

4. Every effort is made to ensure that the information given in *UK 2004* is accurate at the time of going to press. The text is generally based on information available up to the end of August 2003. Data for the most recent year may be provisional or estimated.

5. The Office for National Statistics released a National Accounts dataset on 30 September 2003 which included revisions back to 1948. The new dataset incorporates the effects of the introduction of annual chain-linking, adjustments for the effect of VAT fraud on imports from within the European Union, other methodological improvements and new information across a range of series. The figures in *UK 2004* were compiled before these new data were fully available.

6. Information about particular companies has been taken from company reports and news releases, or from other publicly available sources. No information about individual companies has been taken from returns submitted in response to ONS statistical inquiries – these remain entirely confidential.

7. Many of the data sources given at the foot of tables and the publications quoted in the further reading lists are available in full on the relevant website.

Symbols and conventions

1 billion = 1,000 million

1 trillion = 1,000 billion

Financial and academic years are shown as 2002/03

Data covering more than one year such as
2000, 2001 and 2002 are shown as 2000–02

The following symbols have been used in tables:
n/a   not available
.   not applicable
–   negligible (less than half the final digit shown)
0   nil

Units of measurement
Area
1 hectare (ha) = 10,000 sq metres = 2.4711 acres
1 square kilometre (sq km) = 100 hectares
= 0.3861 square miles

Length
1 centimetre (cm) = 10 millimetres (mm)
= 0.3937 inches
1 metre (m) = 1,000 millimetres = 3.2808 feet (ft)
1 kilometre (km) = 1,000 metres = 0.6214 miles

Mass
1 kilogram (kg) = 2.2046 pounds (lb)
1 tonne (t) = 1,000 kilograms = 0.9842 long tons (UK)

Volume
1 litre (l) = 1.7598 UK pints = 0.2200 UK gallons
1 cubic metre = 1,000 litres

SI prefixes
hecto (h)	= 100	= 10^2
kilo (k)	= 1,000	= 10^3
mega (M)	= 1 million	= 10^6
giga (G)	= 1 billion	= 10^9
tera (T)	= 1 thousand billion	= 10^{12}

1 The United Kingdom

The United Kingdom of Great Britain and Northern Ireland (UK) was created by the *Act of Union 1800* and constitutes the greater part of the British Isles, a group of islands lying off the north-west coast of Europe. The largest of the islands is Great Britain, which comprises England, Wales and Scotland. Next largest is Ireland, comprising Northern Ireland, which is part of the United Kingdom, and, in the south, the Republic of Ireland.

North-western Scotland is fringed by two large island chains, the Inner and Outer Hebrides. To the north of the Scottish mainland are the Orkney and Shetland Islands. These, along with the Isle of Wight, Anglesey and the Isles of Scilly, have administrative ties with the mainland. The Isle of Man and the Channel Islands are not part of the United Kingdom (see page 7).

Physical features

The oldest rocks, dating back 2.6 billion years, are found in the Scottish Highlands and Outer Hebrides. Metamorphic and igneous rocks are widespread in Wales, the Lake District and southern Scotland, giving rise to mountainous, wild scenery.

Devonian and Carboniferous strata in south-west England have been intruded by granite. The largest granite area is Dartmoor. Carboniferous limestone forms the Mendip Hills and part of the Pennine Chain in the Peak District and around Malham Tarn in North Yorkshire. Deep valleys, such as the Avon gorge, have cut into the limestone and rivers commonly disappear underground where cave networks have developed. The overlying Millstone Grit of the Upper Carboniferous age makes up much of the Pennines, with the Coal Measures forming the lower ground flanking the Pennine Hills. Coal seams are also widespread in the Midlands, South Wales and around Bristol.

Permian and Triassic rocks stretch north-eastwards from Devon to north-west and north-east England, but are at their widest extent across the Midlands, where the sandstones are a major aquifer. Jurassic rocks are dominated by limestone layers, extending from the World Heritage coastline in Dorset, through the Cotswolds and Northamptonshire into Lincolnshire and Yorkshire. Many prominent buildings in London, such as those in Whitehall, are constructed from Jurassic limestone quarried in Dorset.

Cretaceous chalk strata cover wide areas of southern England, such as the South Downs, where they are exposed in white cliffs at Beachy Head and Dover. Younger strata, mainly soft sandstones and clays, are found in east and south-east England and are associated with fertile farmland.

On the Antrim coast in Northern Ireland is the Giants Causeway. At this World Heritage site there are almost 40,000 massive polygonal basalt columns, formed around 60 million years ago from slowly cooling volcanic rock intruded into the surrounding chalk.

In the past 2 million years, ice sheets covered much of the United Kingdom north of a line roughly between the Bristol Channel and London. As the glaciers melted, extensive areas of clay, sand and gravel were deposited, almost entirely obscuring the underlying bedrock of much of East Anglia.

England

England consists of mostly low hills and plains with a 3,200-kilometre coastline cut into by bays, coves and estuaries. Upland regions include the Pennine Chain, known as the 'backbone of England', which splits northern England into western and eastern sectors. The highest point in England is Scafell Pike (978 metres) in the Lake District in the north west, while the north east includes the rugged landscape of the Yorkshire moors.

1

Wales

Wales is on the western side of Great Britain. It is mountainous – around one-quarter is above 305 metres and in the north its highest peak, Snowdon (*Yr Wyddfa*), rises to 1,085 metres. The Welsh coastline stretches for 1,180 kilometres and consists of many bays, beaches, peninsulas and cliffs.

Scotland

Scotland is located in the north of Great Britain. The Scottish Lowlands and Borders are largely areas of gentle hills and woodland, contrasting dramatically with the rugged landscape of the Highlands in the north. A striking physical feature is Glen More, or the Great Glen, which cuts across the central Highlands from Fort William on the west coast for 97 kilometres north-east to

Physical geography of the UK

Area: 242,514 square kilometres

Length and breadth: just under 1,000 kilometres from the south coast to the extreme north of the Scottish mainland and just under 500 kilometres across at the widest point

Highest mountain: Ben Nevis, in the Highlands of Scotland, 1,343 metres

Longest river: the Severn, 354 kilometres, rises in Wales and flows through Shrewsbury, Worcester and Gloucester in England to the Bristol Channel

Largest lake: Lough Neagh, Northern Ireland, 382 square kilometres

Deepest lake: Loch Morar in the Highlands of Scotland, 310 metres deep

Highest waterfall: Eas a'Chual Aluinn, from Glas Bheinn, also in the Highlands of Scotland, with a drop of 200 metres

Deepest cave: Ogof Ffynnon Ddu, Powys, Wales, 308 metres deep

Most northerly point on the British mainland: Dunnet Head, north-east Scotland

Most southerly point on the British mainland: Lizard Point, Cornwall, England

Inverness on the east coast. A string of deep, narrow lochs are set between steep mountains that rise past forested foothills to high moors and remote rocky mountains. Ben Nevis (1,343 metres), is the highest point in the United Kingdom.

Northern Ireland

Northern Ireland's north-east coast is separated from Scotland by the North Channel, only 21 kilometres wide at its nearest point. It has a 488-kilometre border with the Republic of Ireland, forming the only UK land boundary with another Member State of the European Union. The landscape is mainly low hill country. There are two mountain ranges: the Mournes, extending from South Down to Strangford Lough in the east, and the Sperrins in the north-west. Lough Neagh (382 square kilometres) is the largest freshwater lake in the United Kingdom and one of the largest in Europe.

Climate

The climate is generally mild and temperate. Prevailing weather systems move in from the Atlantic, and the weather is mainly influenced by depressions and their associated fronts moving eastwards, punctuated by settled, fine, anticyclonic periods lasting from a few days to several weeks. The temperature rarely rises above 32°C (90°F) or falls below −10°C (14°F). There are four seasons: spring (March to May); summer (June to August); autumn (September to November) and winter (December to February).

Rainfall is greatest in the western and upland areas, where the annual average exceeds 1,100 millimetres; the highest mountain areas receive more than 2,000 millimetres. Over much of lowland central England, annual rainfall ranges from 700 to 850 millimetres. Parts of East Anglia and the south east have the lowest rainfall, just 550 millimetres. Rain is fairly well distributed throughout the year, with February to March generally the driest period and October to January the wettest.

During May, June and July (the months of longest daylight) the mean daily duration of sunshine varies from five hours in northern Scotland to eight hours in the Isle of Wight. During the months of shortest daylight (November, December and January) sunshine is at a minimum, with an average of an hour a day in

Table 1.1 Weather extremes[1] up to August 2003, UK

	England	Wales	Scotland	Northern Ireland
Monthly sunshine				
Maximum	384 hours	354 hours	329 hours	298 hours
	Eastbourne	Dale Fort	Tiree	Mount Stewart
	Jul 1911	Jul 1955	May 1975	Jun 1940
Minimum	0 hours	3 hours	36 minutes	8 hours
	Westminster	Llwynon	Cape Wrath	Silent Valley
	Dec 1890	Jan 1962	Jan 1983	Jan 1996
Rainfall				
Maximum in a day	279 mm	211 mm	238 mm	159 mm
	Martinstown	Rhondda	Sloy Main Adit	Tollymore Forest
	18 Jul 1955	11 Nov 1929	17 Jan 1974	31 Oct 1968
Temperature				
Highest recorded	38°C	35°C	33°C	31°C
	Gravesend	Hawarden Bridge	Dumfries	Shaw's Bridge,
	10 Aug 2003	2 Aug 1990	2 Jul 1908	12 Jul 1983
Lowest recorded	minus 26°C	minus 23°C	minus 27°C	minus 17°C
	Newport	Rhayader	Braemar	Magherally
	10 Jan 1982	21 Jan 1940	10 Jan 1982	1 Jan 1979

1 The recording of weather conditions began at varying points in time, starting with rainfall around 1700.
Source: Met Office

northern Scotland and two hours a day on the south coast of England. Table 1.1 shows weather extremes.

Population

The population at mid-2002 was 59.2 million (see Table 1.2). Official projections, based on 2001 population estimates, suggest that the population will reach nearly 63.2 million by 2026. The population grew by 3.1 per cent between 1991 and 2002, mainly a result of a greater number of births than deaths, although migration is increasingly a factor (see page 92).

The 2001 Census showed that for the first time there were more people aged over 60 than there were children under 16. Northern Ireland had the youngest population in the United Kingdom, with children under 16 representing over 23 per cent of the population, compared with 20 per cent in the United Kingdom as a whole.

The UK population was the third largest in the European Union (EU) in 2001 after Germany (82.4 million) and France (59.2 million – see Table 1.3).

Historical outline

Major events in the development of government in the United Kingdom, together with a brief review of early history, are described below. There is a list of significant dates in appendix B (page 492).

'Britain' derives from Greek and Latin names which probably stem from a Celtic original. Although in the prehistoric timescale the Celts were relatively late arrivals in the British Isles, Britain's recorded history began with them. The term 'Celtic' is often

Liverpool: Capital of Culture 2008
Liverpool defeated bids from five other UK cities to be named European Capital of Culture 2008. The EU's Capital of Culture status will replace the City of Culture programme from 2005. The Liverpool bid promises a year-long festival featuring art, architecture, ballet, comedy, cinema, food, fashion, literature, music, opera, science and theatre. The city hopes to create 14,000 new jobs in the culture sector; to earn £200 million in tourism in the run-up to 2008, which could create a further 3,000 jobs; and to attract public and private sector investment worth some £2 billion.

Table 1.2 Population and area, June 2002, UK

	England	Wales	Scotland	Northern Ireland	United Kingdom
Population (thousands)	49,537	2,919	5,055	1,697	59,207
% population aged:					
under 5	5.8	5.6	5.3	6.6	5.8
5–15	14.1	14.4	13.6	16.5	14.1
16 to pension age[1]	61.8	59.9	62.3	61.1	61.7
above pension age[1]	18.4	20.2	18.8	15.7	18.4
Area (sq km)	130,281	20,732	77,925	13,576	242,514
Population density (people per sq km)	380	141	65	125	244
% population change 1991–2002	3.5	1.6	-0.6	5.6	3.1
Live births per 1,000 population	11.4	10.3	10.1	12.6	11.3
Deaths per 1,000 population	10.1	11.4	11.5	8.6	10.2

1 Pension age is currently 65 for males and 60 for females.
Source: Office for National Statistics; National Assembly for Wales; General Register Office for Scotland; and Northern Ireland Statistics and Research Agency

Table 1.3 Key demographic statistics, 2001, EU

	Population in 2001 (thousands)	% population change 1991–2001	Live births per 1,000 population in 2001	Deaths per 1,000 population in 2001
Austria	8,080	3.4	9.2	9.1
Belgium	10,263	2.6	11.3	10.2
Denmark	5,330	3.4	12.6[1]	10.9[1]
Finland	5,190	3.5	10.8	9.3
France	59,190	3.7	13.2[1]	9.1[1]
Germany	82,360	2.9	9.1	10.0
Greece	10,020	−2.2	11.7[1]	10.5[1]
Irish Republic	3,840	8.7	15.1	7.8
Italy	57,950	2.1	9.3[1]	9.7[1]
Luxembourg	441	14.0	12.4	7.2
Netherlands	16,040	6.4	12.6	8.8
Portugal	10,020	1.5	10.8	10.4
Spain	40,270	3.5	9.9[1]	9.3[1]
Sweden	8,833	2.5	10.2[1]	10.5[1]
United Kingdom[2]	58,837	2.4	11.3	10.2

1 2000 figures.
2 For 2002 mid-year estimate see Table 1.2 above.
Source: *Population Trends, Summer 2003*, Office for National Statistics

used rather generally to distinguish the early inhabitants of the British Isles from the later Anglo-Saxon invaders. After two expeditions by Julius Caesar in 55 and 54 BC, contact between Britain and the Roman world grew, culminating in the Roman invasion of AD 43. Roman rule lasted until about 409, and gradually extended from south-east England to Wales and, for a time, the lowlands of Scotland.

England
When the Romans withdrew from Britain, the lowland regions were invaded and settled by Angles, Saxons and Jutes (tribes from what is now north-western Germany). England takes its name from the first of these. Anglo-Saxon kingdoms were small and numerous, but in time fewer, larger areas of control developed. Eventually the southern kingdom of Wessex became dominant,

mainly because of its leading role in resisting the Viking invasions of the ninth century. Athelstan (who reigned from 924 to 939) used the title of 'King of all Britain', and from 954 there was a single kingdom of England.

The last successful invasion of England took place in 1066. Duke William of Normandy defeated the English at the Battle of Hastings and became King William I, known as 'William the Conqueror'. Many Normans and others from France came to settle; French became the language of the ruling classes for the next three centuries; and the legal and social structures were influenced by those across the Channel. When Henry II, originally from Anjou, was king (1154–89), his 'Angevin empire' stretched from the river Tweed on the Scottish border, through much of France to the Pyreénées. However, almost all of the English Crown's possessions in France were lost during the late Middle Ages.

In 1215 a group of barons demanded a charter of liberties as a safeguard against the arbitrary behaviour of King John. The rebels captured London and the King eventually agreed to their demands. The resulting royal grant was the *Magna Carta*. Among other things, the charter promised that 'To no one will we sell, to no one deny or delay right or justice'. It established the important constitutional principle that the power of the king could be limited.

The Hundred Years War between England and France began in 1337, leading to a period of high taxation. The introduction of a poll tax led to the

Peasants' Revolt in 1381; the most significant popular revolt in English history. The peasants marched on London, executed ministers and won promises of concessions, including the abolition of serfdom, although King Richard II went back on these promises once the peasants had dispersed.

In 1485 Henry Tudor defeated King Richard III at the Battle of Bosworth Field and became King Henry VII. His son, Henry VIII, broke away from the Catholic Church and founded the Church of England. During his reign England and Wales were united. The last of the Tudors, Queen Elizabeth I, was childless. She named James VI of Scotland as her successor, thus uniting the monarchies of Scotland, England and Wales.

Civil war broke out in 1642. The capture and execution of King Charles I changed the balance of power between monarch and Parliament. A leading parliamentarian in the civil war was Oliver Cromwell (1599–1658). He declared England a republic in 1649. As Lord Protector of the Commonwealth from late 1653 until his death, he had supreme legislative and executive power in association with Parliament and the Council of State. The monarchy was restored when King Charles II ascended the throne in 1660.

In 1707 the *Acts of Union* united the English and Scottish Parliaments and the *Act of Union 1800* united Great Britain and Northern Ireland. The 1832 *Reform Act* began dismantling the old parliamentary system and extending the franchise. The *Reform Acts* of 1867 and 1884 gave the vote to a gradually wider section of the population. During the 20th century, the *Representation of the People Acts* took the process further. In 1918, women over the age of 30 who were householders, householders' wives or graduates were enfranchised and in 1928 the *Equal Franchise Act* extended the franchise to women aged 21 or over, giving women the same voting rights as men (see page 33). Universal suffrage for all eligible people over 18 was granted in 1969.

Wales
Wales was a Celtic stronghold ruled by sovereign princes under the influence of England after the Romans left Britain around 409. In 1282 King Edward I brought Wales under English rule; the castles he built in the north remain among the finest UK historic monuments. Edward I's eldest son – later Edward II – was born at Caernarvon in 1284 and became the first English Prince of Wales

Elizabethan celebrations
Celebrations marking the 400th anniversary of the death of Queen Elizabeth I were held during 2003. These included events at Hatfield Palace, where Elizabeth grew up; at the Tower of London, where she was imprisoned during her sister's reign; and at Greenwich, London, where she was born.

Elizabeth succeeded to the throne in 1558. She successfully waged war with Spain; culture flourished with writers and poets such as William Shakespeare and Sir Christopher Marlowe; and voyages of exploration around the world were made. A group of 300 people set up a colony in North America, naming it Virginia after the 'Virgin Queen'.

in 1301. The eldest son of the reigning monarch continues to bear this title, Prince Charles being made Prince of Wales in 1969.

At the beginning of the 15th century Welsh resentment of unjust English laws and administration, and widespread economic discontent, resulted in the nationalist leader Owain Glyndŵr leading an unsuccessful revolt against the English. The Tudor dynasty, which was of Welsh ancestry, ruled England from 1485 to 1603 and during this period the *Acts of Union* (1536 and 1542) united England and Wales administratively, politically and legally.

This situation prevailed until July 1999, when devolution created a National Assembly for Wales with specific powers to make secondary legislation to meet distinctive Welsh needs (see page 15).

Scotland

Evidence of human settlement in what is now Scotland dates from around the third millennium BC. By the time the Romans invaded Britain, many tribes were living in the region. Despite attempts to control them, Roman rule never permanently extended to most of Scotland. In the sixth century, the Scots, a Celtic people from Ireland, settled on the north-west coast of Great Britain, giving their name to the present-day Scotland.

The kingdoms of England and Scotland were frequently at war during the Middle Ages (*c.* 1000–1400). When King Edward I tried to impose direct English rule over Scotland in 1296, a revolt for independence broke out, which ended in 1328 when King Edward III recognised its leader, Robert the Bruce, as King Robert I of Scotland.

The English and Scottish crowns were united in 1603 when James VI of Scotland succeeded Elizabeth I of England. He became James I of England and was the first of the Stuart kings. In 1745 Charles Edward Stuart (also known as 'Bonnie Prince Charlie' or 'The Young Pretender') attempted to retake the British throne, which the Stuarts had lost in 1688. He defeated government forces at Prestonpans and advanced into England, capturing Carlisle, but was turned back at Derby and eventually defeated at the Battle of Culloden, north-east of Inverness, in April 1746.

Politically, England and Scotland remained separate during the 17th century, apart from a period of union forced on them by Oliver Cromwell in the 1650s. In 1707 the English and Scottish Parliaments agreed on a single Parliament for Great Britain to sit at Westminster in London. Nearly 300 years later, in July 1999, power to administer Scottish affairs was devolved to a new Scottish Parliament (see page 20).

Northern Ireland

Henry II of England invaded Ireland in 1169. He had been made overlord of Ireland by the English Pope Adrian IV. Although Anglo-Norman noblemen controlled part of the country during the Middle Ages (*c.* 1000–1400), little direct authority came from England.

During the reign of Elizabeth I (1558–1603) there were several rebellions, particularly in the northern province of Ulster. In 1607, after the rebel leaders had been defeated, Protestant immigrants from Scotland and England settled there.

The English civil war (1642–51) coincided with uprisings in Ireland, which Oliver Cromwell suppressed. More fighting took place after the overthrow of King James II, a Roman Catholic, in 1688. At the Battle of the Boyne in 1690, the Protestant William of Orange (later King William III) defeated James II, who was trying to regain the English throne from his base in Ireland.

In 1782 the Government in London gave the Irish Parliament power to legislate on Irish affairs. Only the Anglo-Irish minority were represented in this Parliament. Following the unsuccessful rebellion of Wolfe Tone's United Irishmen movement in 1798, Great Britain took back control of Ireland under the *Act of Union 1800*. The Irish Parliament was abolished in 1801; Irish interests were represented by members sitting in both Houses of the Westminster Parliament.

The question of 'Home Rule' for Ireland remained one of the major issues of British politics. By 1910 the Liberal Government in London depended for its political survival on support from the Irish Parliamentary Party. The conflict deepened as some unionists and nationalists in Ireland formed private armies. In 1914 Home Rule was approved in the *Government of Ireland Act* but implementation was suspended because of the First World War.

In 1916 a nationalist uprising in Dublin was put down and its leaders executed. Two years later the nationalist Sinn Féin party won a large majority of the Irish seats in the General Election to the Westminster Parliament. Its members refused to attend the House of Commons and instead formed their own assembly – the Dáil Éireann – in Dublin. In 1919 the Irish Republican Army (IRA) began operations against the British administration.

In 1920 a new *Government of Ireland Act* provided for separate Parliaments in Northern and Southern Ireland, subordinate to Westminster. The Act was implemented in Northern Ireland in 1921, giving six of the nine counties of the province of Ulster their own Parliament with powers to manage internal affairs. However, the Act was not accepted in the South and the 26 counties of Southern Ireland left the United Kingdom in 1922.

From 1921 until 1972 Northern Ireland had its own Parliament. The unionists, primarily representing the Protestant community, held a permanent majority and formed the regional government. The nationalist minority was effectively excluded from political office and influence. In the late 1960s and early 1970s, the civil rights movement and reactions to it resulted in serious inter-communal rioting. The British Army was sent in to help the police keep law and order in 1969.

Terrorism and violence continued to increase. In 1972, the UK Government decided to take back direct responsibility for law and order. The Northern Ireland Unionist Government resigned in protest, the regional government was abolished and direct rule from Westminster began; this lasted until devolved powers were given back to a Northern Ireland Assembly in December 1999 (see page 26).

Channel Islands and Isle of Man

The Channel Islands (Jersey, Guernsey, Alderney and Sark being the largest in the group) were part of the Duchy of Normandy in the 10th and 11th centuries and remained subject to the English Crown after the loss of mainland Normandy to the French in 1204. The Isle of Man was under the nominal sovereignty of Norway until 1266, and came under the direct administration of the British Crown in 1765, when it was bought for £70,000.

These territories each have their own legislative assemblies and systems of law, and their own taxation systems. The United Kingdom is responsible for their international relations and external defence. The Isle of Man Parliament, Tynwald, was established more than 1,000 years ago and is the oldest legislature in continuous existence in the world. It also has the distinction of having three chambers: the House of Keys; the Legislative Council; and the Tynwald Court, when the House of Keys and the Legislative Council sit together as a single chamber.

The United Kingdom is a member of the European Union (EU – see page 60) but the Channel Islands and Isle of Man are neither EU Member States in their own right nor part of the UK Member State. EU rules on the free movement of goods and the Common Agricultural Policy broadly apply to the Islands, but not those on the free movement of services or persons. Islanders benefit from the latter only if they have close ties with the United Kingdom.

Further reading

Annual Abstract of Statistics. Office for National Statistics. The Stationery Office.

Population Trends (quarterly publication). Office for National Statistics. The Stationery Office.

Regional Trends (annual publication). Office for National Statistics. The Stationery Office.

Social Trends (annual publication). Office for National Statistics. The Stationery Office.

Websites

British Geological Survey
www.bgs.ac.uk

The Met Office
www.metoffice.com

The National Archives
www.nationalarchives.gov.uk

Office for National Statistics
www.statistics.gov.uk

WWW.

2 England

Population

England's population in 2002 was 49.5 million, nearly 84 per cent of the total population of the United Kingdom, living mainly in the cities and metropolitan areas of London and the South East, South and West Yorkshire, Greater Manchester and Merseyside, the West Midlands, and conurbations on the rivers Tyne, Wear and Tees. Between 1991 and 2002 the population grew by 1.7 million (3.5 per cent). There were big variations between the regions; the falling population in the North East and the North West was more than offset by the rise in population in London, the South West, South East and the East of England (see Table 2.1).

Representation at Westminster and in Europe

There are 529 English parliamentary constituencies represented in the House of Commons (see Table 2.2). The Labour Party's key

Table 2.1 Population and population change, by region[1] June 2002, England

	Population (thousands)	Change in Population 1991–2002 (%)
North East	2,513	−2.8
North West	6,749	−1.4
Yorkshire and the Humber	4,983	0.9
East Midlands	4,215	5.1
West Midlands	5,304	1.4
East of England	5,420	5.8
London	7,355	7.7
South East	8,037	5.3
South West	4,960	5.8
England	**49,537**	3.5

1 These are the areas covered by the Government Offices – see map on page 12.
Source: Office for National Statistics

Table 2.2 Electoral representation, September 2003, England

	UK Parliament (MPs)	European Parliament (MEPs)
Labour	321	24
Conservative	164	33
Liberal Democrats	42	9
UK Independence Party	–	3
Green Party	–	2
Others	2	–
Total seats	**529**	**71**

Source: House of Commons Information Office

support comes mainly from the cities and areas associated with heavy industry, but it also holds many seats that were once 'safe' Conservative constituencies. Conservative support is strongest in suburban and rural areas, and the party has a large number of seats in southern England. The Liberal Democrats, traditionally strong in the South West, now have over a third of their English seats in Greater London and the South East.

A Standing Committee[1] on Regional Affairs consists of 13 Members of Parliament (MPs) sitting for constituencies in England and reflects party representation in the House. Any other MP representing an English constituency may take part in its proceedings, but may not make a motion, vote or be counted in the quorum. During 2002 the Committee considered Regional Development Agencies (see page 344) and the White Paper on the regions (see page 11).

In contrast to Wales, Scotland and Northern Ireland, England has no separate elected national body exclusively responsible for its central administration. Instead a number of government departments look after England's administrative

1 See page 40 for an explanation of Standing Committees.

affairs (see appendix A) and there are nine Government Offices for the Regions (see page 10).

Local government

The structure of local government in England includes shire areas, which have a two-tier council system, and metropolitan areas, unitary authorities and London boroughs, which all have a single-tier system (see map on page 10).

Shire county areas

Most of England is organised into shire areas with two main tiers of local authority – 34 shire county councils and 238 shire district councils, covering 272 out of the 389 elected authorities.

The county councils are responsible for large-scale services in their areas like education, strategic planning, transport, social services, fire services and waste disposal. Each county council area is subdivided into a number of district councils, which are responsible for more local matters like environmental health, housing, local planning applications, local taxation, waste collection, and leisure. Both tiers have powers to provide facilities such as museums and parks, depending on local agreement. Shire areas also have a police authority, made up of local councillors, magistrates and independent members. Police authorities may cover one or more counties.

Metropolitan county areas

The six metropolitan county areas in England – Greater Manchester, Merseyside, South Yorkshire, Tyne and Wear, West Midlands and West Yorkshire – have 36 district councils[2] but no county councils. The district councils are responsible for all services in their areas apart from those that have a statutory authority over areas wider than the individual district. For example, the fire and police services, civil defence, public transport, and waste disposal (in certain areas) are run by joint authorities, which include elected councillors nominated by each district council.

Unitary authorities

There are 47 unitary authorities (including the Isles of Scilly), where the county and district responsibilities are carried out by a single tier of government. Unitary authorities include some of the larger cities, the County of Herefordshire, and the Isle of Wight. Unitary authorities do not have responsibility for the police and the fire and rescue services; these are administered by a police and a fire authority, and usually cover a larger area than the unitary authority.

Greater London

Greater London is made up of 32 boroughs and the City of London, each with a council responsible for most services in its area. Since July 2000 the strategic government of London has been the responsibility of the Greater London Authority (GLA). The GLA is made up of a directly elected Mayor of London,[3] a separately elected Assembly of 25 members, and four functional bodies: the Metropolitan Police Authority; the London Fire and Emergency Planning Authority; Transport for London; and the London Development Agency.

The Mayor of London sets key strategies on a range of London-wide issues, such as transport, economic development, strategic and spatial development, and the environment. The London Assembly scrutinises both the activities of the Mayor and issues of concern to Londoners.

The GLA is the first elected London-wide body since the Greater London Council (GLC) was abolished in 1986. The first elections for the Mayor and the London Assembly were held in May 2000. The Labour Party won nine seats, the Conservatives also won nine, the Liberal Democrats four and the Green Party three. The Mayor stood as an Independent candidate. Subsequent elections will take place every four years. The 2004 GLA elections will be held on the same day as the 2004 elections for Members of the European Parliament.

Parishes

The smallest administrative area in England is the parish. Parishes date from medieval times but have operated in their current form since 1894. Modern parish councils (sometimes called town councils) have two main roles: to represent community views and to deliver local services. There are now around 8,700 parishes in England. During 2002/03, 27 parish councils were created.

---

2 District councils in Metropolitan areas sometimes call themselves borough or city councils.

3 Not to be confused with the Lord Mayor of London, who is the head of the Corporation of London, the local authority for the 'City', also known as the 'Square Mile'.

Local government areas in England

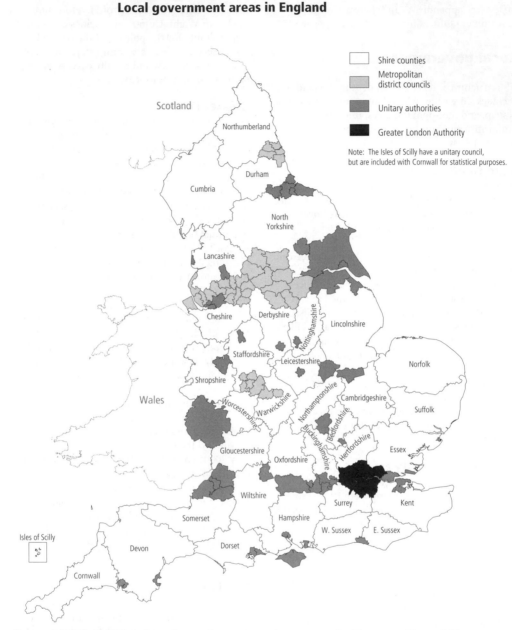

Shire counties

Metropolitan
district councils

Unitary authorities

Greater London Authority

Note: The Isles of Scilly have a unitary council,
but are included with Cornwall for statistical purposes.

Scotland

Northumberland

Durham

Cumbria

North
Yorkshire

Lancashire

Cheshire   Derbyshire

Nottinghamshire

Lincolnshire

Staffordshire

Leicestershire

Norfolk

Shropshire

Wales

Worcestershire   Warwickshire

Northamptonshire

Cambridgeshire

Suffolk

Buckinghamshire

Bedfordshire

Gloucestershire

Oxfordshire

Hertfordshire

Essex

Wiltshire

Surrey

Kent

Somerset   Hampshire

W. Sussex   E. Sussex

Isles of Scilly

Devon   Dorset

Cornwall

The regions of England

Nine Government Offices (GOs) are responsible
for coordinating central government programmes
at a regional level. They bring together the English
regional services for nine government
departments: the Office of the Deputy Prime
Minister; Department of Trade and Industry;
Department for Education and Skills; Department
for Work and Pensions; Department of Health;

Department for Transport; Home Office;
Department for Culture, Media and Sport; and the
Department for Environment, Food and Rural
Affairs. The GOs also work with regional partners,
including local authorities and Regional
Development Agencies (RDAs – see page 344).

The GOs directly manage significant spending
programmes on behalf of these departments. They
oversee budgets and contracts delegated to

A few distinctive facts about England

English law comprises 'common law' (based on ancient custom and previous rulings in similar cases), 'statute law' (parliamentary and European Community legislation) and 'equity' (general principles of justice correcting or adding to common or statute law).

The Church of England broke away from the Roman Catholic Church during the Reformation in the 16th century. The Sovereign is head of the Church of England and appoints its two archbishops and 42 diocesan bishops (see page 212).

England has a diverse natural environment with many unspoilt rural and coastal areas (see chapter 19). Several English regions and counties have inspired writers, artists and musicians over the centuries, including the Lake District (William Wordsworth, poet), Dorset (Thomas Hardy, novelist), Essex and Suffolk (John Constable, landscape painter) and Worcestershire (Edward Elgar, composer).

regional organisations, carry out regulatory functions and sponsor the RDAs. A Regional Coordination Unit represents the GOs in Whitehall and ensures that regional interests are taken into account in the development and evaluation of policy in central government.

Voluntary, multi-party regional chambers have been established in each of the eight English regions outside London. All have adopted the title 'assembly'. They provide a means through which the RDAs can consult on their proposals and give an account of their activities. Local authorities make up 70 per cent of the members of each regional chamber. The remainder are people who work in higher and further education; and representatives from the Confederation of British Industry, the Trades Union Congress, chambers of commerce, small business, the National Health Service, rural and environment groups, and other regional stakeholders.

Proposals for devolution to the English regions

The proposed role of elected regional assemblies was set out in the White Paper, *Your Region, Your Choice: Revitalising the English Regions*, published in May 2002. They would be responsible for setting priorities, delivering regional strategies and allocating funding in key areas such as jobs, planning, housing, transport, culture and environment. Assemblies' functions would be taken from central government and not from local government, which would continue to focus on local service provision and delivery.

The *Regional Assemblies (Preparations) Act 2003* provides for referendums in any region outside London on whether or not to establish an elected assembly. Referendums would only be held in regions that register sufficient interest. The Government held a soundings exercise between December 2002 and June 2003 where individuals and organisations were invited to submit views, information and evidence on the level of interest in their region. More than 8,400 responses were received; over 80 per cent from people responding in a private capacity and the remainder from organisations or individuals like MPs responding in a representative capacity. Sufficient interest in a referendum was registered in three regions: the North East; the North West; and Yorkshire and the Humber.

Before the referendums can be held, the Boundary Committee must carry out a local government review in these three regions to recommend

The English language

English derives primarily from a dialect of Old English (or Anglo-Saxon), itself made up of several Western Germanic dialects brought to Britain in the early fifth century. It has been greatly influenced by other languages, particularly Latin and, following the Norman conquest in 1066, by French.

English is one of the most widely used languages in the world. Estimates suggest that around 326 million people speak it as their first language, with a similar number speaking it as a second language. It is the official language of air traffic control and maritime communications; the leading language of science, technology, computing and commerce; and a major medium of education, publishing and international negotiation.

English is constantly changing as words go in and out of fashion and are introduced to keep up with technology. It has also borrowed much from other English-speaking countries, particularly the US and the Commonwealth countries (see map in the second colour section).

The regions of England covered by the GOs and RDAs

options for unitary local government in areas that have two-tier authorities; these must be restructured into unitary authorities in any region where an assembly is established. The reviews are expected to take a year and the referendums could be held in autumn 2004. Once at least one region has voted for an elected assembly, further legislation will need to be introduced to provide for an assembly to be set up.

The assemblies would represent areas based on the existing administrative boundaries used by the GOs and RDAs. They would have between 25 and 35 members, including a leader and a cabinet of up to six members chosen by, and wholly accountable to, the full assembly. The voting system would be the Additional Member System of proportional representation (see glossary).

Most of each assembly's money would come through a single government grant, with the assembly deciding how it should use this to address regional priorities. An elected regional assembly in the North East, for example, would have a grant of around £350 million and would influence spending of a further £600 million. Additional funds would be raised through the council tax, collected on behalf of the assembly by the local authorities.

Economy

The spring 2003 Labour Force Survey recorded 24.7 million people economically active in England, of whom 23.4 million were in employment. The unemployment rate for England was 5.0 per cent, and varied from 3.8 per cent in the South East and the South West to 7.0 per cent in London.

Economic performance varies considerably between and within the regions. On many indicators London has the best economic performance in England: it is a major economy accounting for 16.5 per cent of UK gross value added (GVA, see Table 2.3, Table 23.12, page 344 and glossary), with 16,000 companies employing 256,000 people in manufacturing; and it is a major tourist destination with tourism providing 225,000 jobs. However, it is also a region divided between extremes of wealth and deprivation, with 20 per cent of London's wards among the 10 per cent most deprived in England. The areas suffering the highest disadvantage qualify for Objective 2 funding from the EU Structural Funds for 2000 to 2006 to help redress this imbalance. Three areas of England – Merseyside, South Yorkshire, and Cornwall and the Isles of Scilly – qualified for Objective 1 EU funding (see page 345).

The North East has the smallest population of the English regions. Over half is rural, including two National Parks and two Areas of Outstanding Natural Beauty (AONBs, see page 263). Economic activity is centred on the estuaries of three rivers, the Tyne, the Wear and the Tees, and was traditionally based on coal, steel and shipbuilding. Manufacturing remains important, but the

Table 2.3 Regional gross value added,[1] 2001, England[2]

	£ billion	£ thousand
	Gross value added	Gross value added per head
North East	27.7	11.0
North West	87.6	13.0
Yorkshire and the Humber	61.9	12.5
East Midlands	55.4	13.3
West Midlands	68.8	13.1
East of England	85.8	15.9
London	140.4	19.5
South East	138.9	17.3
South West	63.6	12.9
England	**730.0**	**14.8**

1 At current basic prices.
2 Excludes compensation of employees and gross operating surplus (which cannot be assigned to regions) and statistical discrepancy.
Source: Office for National Statistics

regional economy has diversified into microelectronics, biotechnology and the automotive industry, and there is a growing service sector.

The North West is home to the Lake District National Park and sections of the Pennine Way, as well as large towns and cities including Blackpool, Liverpool and Manchester. It has the largest production centre for film and television outside London. Traditional economic activities include shipping, textiles and engineering. Other sectors include biotechnology, chemicals, aerospace and information and communications technology.

Yorkshire and the Humber has three National Parks, two AONBs, three sections of Heritage Coast and three Ramsar wetlands sites (see page 269). Tourism supports around 140,000 jobs. The region's traditional industries of coal mining, steel, engineering and textiles have generally declined. This has been partly offset by a growth in financial, legal and telephone-based services; Leeds is England's second financial/business services centre.

Over 90 per cent rural, the East Midlands is the fourth largest English region by area and the second smallest by population. It includes a National Park, the National Forest, an AONB, and Ramsar wetlands around the Wash. Agriculture and food processing are important, while the manufacturing industries in the former coalfield areas are in decline. A key area of growth is the diverse service sector.

Manufacturing accounts for 19 per cent of employment in the West Midlands region. Just over 50 per cent of the population live in large conurbations, such as Birmingham, Coventry and Stoke-on-Trent. Much of the countryside around the conurbations is designated as AONBs.

The East of England region has a large concentration of new and growing businesses covering a wide range of activities including food and drink, biotechnology, pharmaceuticals and the film industry. It has the leading UK Science Parks in and around Cambridge, where there is a concentration of businesses engaged in high-technology manufacturing and computer-aided design. The region has several National Nature Reserves, Community Forests, and an AONB.

Around 40 per cent of the South East region's area is protected and 6,400 square kilometres are

designated AONBs, 33 per cent of the English total. Economic activity is closely linked with London and the region's economy accounted for 16.3 per cent of UK GVA in 2001.

The South West region has the largest area of any English region. It is mainly agricultural and over a third of the area is designated either as a National Park or as an AONB. It has 60 per cent of England's Heritage Coast. The region's economy is varied. Alongside the traditional areas of agriculture and fishing, food and drink, and tourism, there has been a growth in the financial and business services sectors, multimedia and electronics.

Further reading

Regional Trends (annual publication). Office for National Statistics. The Stationery Office.

Social Trends (annual publication). Office for National Statistics. The Stationery Office.

Economic Trends (monthly publication). Office for National Statistics. The Stationery Office.

Your Region, Your Choice: Revitalising the English Regions. Cm 5511. The Stationery Office, 2002.

Websites

Department of Trade and Industry
www.dti.gov.uk

Greater London Authority
www.london.gov.uk

Local Government Association
www.lga.gov.uk

Office of the Deputy Prime Minister
www.odpm.gov.uk

Office for National Statistics
www.statistics.gov.uk

United Kingdom Parliament
www.parliament.uk

www.

3 Wales

Population

Wales (*Cymru* in Welsh) had a population of just over 2.9 million in 2002, 4.9 per cent of the population of the United Kingdom. About two-thirds lived in the southern valleys and the lower-lying coastal areas. Cardiff, the capital, grew in the 19th century as a coal exporting port. The two other large ports of Swansea and Newport also depended for their prosperity on the surrounding mining and metal production during the Industrial Revolution. They are still among the most densely populated areas today.

The population grew by around 100,000 between 1991 and 2002 with the local authority area of Ceredigion having the greatest population growth (nearly 17 per cent, including a large student population). Merthyr Tydfil had the greatest population fall, losing 6 per cent of its population (see Table 3.1). The highest population density was in Cardiff, with over 2,200 people per sq km. The lowest was in Powys, with 25 people per sq km.

Representation at Westminster and in Europe

Wales returns 40 Members of Parliament (MPs) to the House of Commons at Westminster (see Table 3.2). All MPs for Welsh constituencies and up to five others who may be added from time to time are members of the House of Commons Welsh Grand Committee. Its role is to consider Bills referred to it at second reading stage, questions tabled for oral answer, ministerial statements, and other matters relating exclusively to Wales.

Following devolution, the UK Government retains responsibility in Wales for certain matters, including foreign affairs, defence and overall

Table 3.1 Population and population change by local authority, June 2002, Wales

	Population (thousands)	Change in population 1991–2002 (%)
Blaenau Gwent	69	−4.6
Bridgend (Pen-y-bont ar Ogwr)[1]	129	−0.5
Caerphilly (Caerffili)	170	−0.2
Cardiff (Caerdydd)	309	3.9
Carmarthenshire (Sir Gaerfyrddin)	176	3.4
Ceredigion (Sir Ceredigion)	77	16.8
Conwy	110	2.4
Denbighshire (Sir Ddinbych)	94	5.4
Flintshire (Sir y Fflint)	149	5.1
Gwynedd	117	1.9
Isle of Anglesey (Sir Ynys Mon)	68	−2.0
Merthyr Tydfil (Merthyr Tudful)	56	−6.3
Monmouthshire (Sir Fynwy)	85	5.8
Neath Port Talbot (Castell-nedd Port Talbot)	135	−3.1
Newport (Casnewydd)	139	2.5
Pembrokeshire (Sir Benfro)	114	1.5
Powys	127	6.5
Rhondda, Cynon, Taff (Rhondda, Cynon, Taf)	231	−1.7
Swansea (Abertawe)	224	−2.7
Torfaen (Tor-faen)	91	−0.1
Vale of Glamorgan (Bro Morgannwg)	120	1.7
Wrexham (Wrecsam)	129	4.1
Wales (Cymru)	**2,919**	**1.6**

1 Welsh-language local authority names are given in parenthesis if there are differences between the English and Welsh names.
Sources: Office for National Statistics and National Assembly for Wales

Table 3.2 Electoral representation, May 2003, Wales

	National Assembly (AMs)			UK Parliament (MPs)	European Parliament (MEPs)
	Constituency seats	Regional seats	Total seats		
Labour	30	0	30	34	2
Plaid Cymru – the Party of Wales	5	7	12	4	2
Conservative	1	10	11	0	1
Liberal Democrats	3	3	6	2	0
Independent	1	0	1	0	0
Total seats	**40**	**20**	**60**	**40**	**5**

Source: UK Parliament

economic policy (for more details see appendix A, page 476).

Once the devolved administrations were fully functioning, the Government considered that there was no longer a need for full-time Cabinet ministers and free-standing departments to conduct the remaining Welsh and Scottish business within the UK Parliament and government. The Wales Office was therefore moved to a new Department for Constitutional Affairs in June 2003. From that date, Welsh interests have been represented in the UK Cabinet and the House of Commons by the Leader of the House of Commons, who combines this role with that of Secretary of State for Wales, supported by staff in the Department for Constitutional Affairs.

The Secretary of State for Wales remains the Cabinet Minister responsible for ensuring that the devolution settlement continues to operate in the best interests of Wales. The Secretary of State also brings forward primary legislation, deals with constitutional issues, bids for the Assembly's budget and liaises with the Assembly. Wales Office ministers sit on 24 Cabinet Committees and four Joint Ministerial Committees, representing Welsh interests at a detailed level. They also liaise regularly with members of the Assembly Cabinet.

The Welsh Budget is voted for by the UK Parliament. The Assembly's budget for 2003/04 is £11.2 billion.

Wales elects five Members of the European Parliament (MEPs) in Brussels (see Table 3.2). Wales forms a single constituency and voting is by proportional representation. The Welsh Assembly Government EU Office in Brussels looks after Welsh interests in the European Union.

National Assembly for Wales and Welsh Assembly Government

Proposals to devolve certain powers and responsibilities to a National Assembly were narrowly endorsed by the Welsh people in 1997; of those who voted 50.3 per cent were in favour. The *Government of Wales Act 1998* laid down the necessary statutory framework to establish the National Assembly for Wales, which held its first elections in May 1999 and began functioning as a devolved administration two months later. The Assembly sits for a four-year term and elections were held for the second term in May 2003.

The National Assembly for Wales has powers to make secondary legislation (see page 42) to meet distinctive Welsh needs on issues that have been devolved (see appendix A page 486). Primary legislation on Welsh affairs continues to be made in the UK Parliament at Westminster (see page 40).

In February 2002 the National Assembly voted to make clear the difference in the roles of the ministers and the Assembly as a whole. The Welsh Assembly Government develops and implements policy. It is accountable to the National Assembly and is primarily located in Cathays Park, Cardiff. The National Assembly debates and approves legislation and holds the Assembly Government to account. Its debating chamber and members are located at Cardiff Bay.

The Assembly comprises 60 members (AMs): 40 from local constituencies (with the same

2003 elections

The second elections for the National Assembly were held in May 2003. The Labour Party again secured the highest share of the vote. It also won the highest number of seats, gaining an extra two to hold half of all the Assembly seats. As a result, it decided to abandon the coalition with the Liberal Democrats that had been in place since 2000.

Plaid Cymru – the Party of Wales was the second largest party winning 12 seats, but its share of the vote fell and it lost five seats compared with 1999. The Conservative Party's share of the vote increased and it gained two seats, bringing its total to 11. The Liberal Democrats' share of the vote rose slightly but the number of seats held remained the same at six. One Independent candidate was elected, representing the Wrexham constituency.

The turnout across regions and constituencies overall was 38 per cent, down 8 percentage points compared with the 1999 elections. Turnout was generally highest in Mid and West Wales, and lowest in South Wales.

Of the 60 Assembly members, 46 were re-elected and 14 were new. It is believed to be the first legislative body in the world where there are an equal number of male and female members.

boundaries as those for Welsh seats in the House of Commons) and 20 regional members. It is elected by the Additional Member System (AMS) of proportional representation. Electors have two votes: one for a constituency AM under the traditional first-past-the-post system, and one to elect four AMs for each of the five electoral regions. These regional seats are allocated so that the total representation from each geographical area, including the Member elected under first-past-the-post, corresponds with the share of votes cast for each political party in the region.

The First Minister heads the Assembly and is supported by a Cabinet of eight ministers in charge of: finance, local government and public services; government business; social justice and regeneration; health and social services; economic development and transport; education and lifelong learning; environment, planning and the countryside; and culture, the Welsh language and sport. The Assembly is also responsible for over 50 public bodies.

Local government

The 22 Welsh unitary (single-tier) authorities (see map on page 17) have collective responsibility for spending around a third of the National Assembly's budget. The Assembly sets the policy framework and makes the secondary legislation within which local government operates. The Assembly also has a responsibility to ensure that local decision-making reflects the requirements of the law and, where appropriate, priorities fixed by the Assembly. Whole council elections are held every fourth year, with the next due in 2004.

In 2001/02 local government was broadly financed by government grants (58 per cent), a share of non-domestic rates (12 per cent), council tax (10 per cent), rents and charges (14 per cent), and borrowing. The unitary authorities employ 158,000 people, around 12 per cent of the people in employment in Wales. The budget for local government for 2003/04 was £3.2 billion.

Local authorities are responsible for schools (broadly 31 per cent of resources); housing

Distinctive facts about Wales

Welsh literature has a long tradition and Welsh language literature is one of the oldest in Europe. Music is also important to the Welsh people and Wales is well-known for its choral singing. Special festivals (eisteddfodau), encourage literature and music. The media in Wales include Welsh and English language newspapers, local radio stations and the television broadcaster, Sianel Pedwar Cymru (S4C, see chapter 17).

The Millennium Stadium in Cardiff has a seating capacity of 72,500 and a roof that can be fully opened and closed within 20 minutes, making it an all-weather venue for a variety of sporting events, opera, concerts, shows and exhibitions. Among the many sporting activities in Wales, there is particular interest in rugby union, which has come to be regarded as the Welsh national game.

About 25 per cent of the land in Wales is designated as a National Park or Area of Outstanding Natural Beauty. The three National Parks are Snowdonia, the Brecon Beacons and the Pembrokeshire Coast. In addition, Wales has over 1,000 Sites of Special Scientific Interest and many nature conservation sites (see chapter 19).

Unitary authorities in Wales

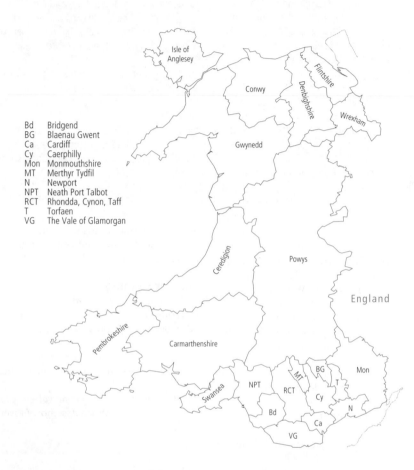

Bd   Bridgend
BG   Blaenau Gwent
Ca   Cardiff
Cy   Caerphilly
Mon   Monmouthshire
MT   Merthyr Tydfil
N   Newport
NPT   Neath Port Talbot
RCT   Rhondda, Cynon, Taff
T   Torfaen
VG   The Vale of Glamorgan

(20 per cent); social services (14 per cent); police (8 per cent); and transport (5 per cent). The remaining resources are used on waste management; the fire services; libraries and archives, museums and art galleries; consumer protection; environmental health; planning and economic development; leisure and parks; and environmental services.

As required by the *Government of Wales Act*, the Assembly has set up a Partnership Council to advise it on the exercise of any of its functions and to make representations on matters affecting, or of concern to, local government. It comprises

locally elected representatives – including those from the unitary authorities, National Parks, police and fire authorities, and community councils – and selected Members of the Assembly. The Council also assists the Assembly to prepare guidance and advice to local councils.

Communities and community councils

Welsh unitary authorities are subdivided into areas called 'communities'. There are around 1,000 communities, about 750 of which have community councils with similar powers and functions to parish councils in England (see page 9).

The Welsh language

Welsh is a Celtic language closely related to Cornish and Breton. The language as spoken today is descended directly from Early Welsh which emerged as a distinct tongue around the sixth century. The National Assembly and the UK Government are committed to treating the Welsh and English languages on an equal basis.

The National Assembly encourages Welsh-medium education in schools. Since September 2000, Welsh has been taught – as a first or second language – to all pupils between the ages of five and 16, and other subjects are also taught in Welsh to primary and secondary schoolchildren in about 500 schools (see chapter 10).

The 2001 Census revealed that 72 per cent of residents in Wales aged three and over had no knowledge of Welsh, while 16 per cent could speak, read and write the language. The remainder could understand Welsh and in some cases speak or read it.

The regional pattern of being able to speak Welsh showed a broadly east–west split. At least half the population were able to speak Welsh in Gwynedd, the Isle of Anglesey, Ceredigion and Carmarthenshire, all on the western side of the country. Monmouthshire, Blaenau Gwent and Newport in the south east had the lowest proportion of the population speaking Welsh.

Economy

The Welsh economy, which traditionally relied on coal and steel, experienced major changes during the 20th century. In recent years, Wales has attracted a more varied range of manufacturing industries, with a significant number of investments by overseas companies including many at the forefront of technology. Although there has been a decline in the steel industry over recent years, it remains important to the Welsh economy, with crude steel production in Wales (at around 4.7 million tonnes in 2001) accounting for 35 per cent of UK steel output.

Gross value added (GVA, see glossary and Table 23.12 page 344) per head was £11,400 in 2001. There were 1.4 million people economically active in Wales, of whom 1.3 million were in employment in spring 2003. Unemployment, at 4.4 per cent, was below the UK rate of 5.0 per cent. Over half of people in employment worked in the service industries and one-fifth were employed by manufacturing industries.

West Wales and the Valleys have qualified for Objective 1 status EU funding from 2000 to 2006. This funding is designed to promote growth in regions that have less than 75 per cent of average EU per capita gross domestic product (see page 345).

The Welsh Development Agency (WDA, see page 345) was set up in 1976 to enhance the local economy by responding to the needs of business in Wales, and to attract investment. It is accountable to the Welsh Assembly Government.

Further reading

Wales Office Departmental Report 2003: The Government's Expenditure Plans 2003–04 to 2005–06. The Stationery Office, 2003.

Iaith Pawb – A National Action Plan for a bilingual Wales. Welsh Assembly Government, 2003.

Creative Future: Cymru Greadigol – A Culture Strategy for Wales. Welsh Assembly Government, 2002.

Websites

National Assembly for Wales and Welsh Assembly Government
www.wales.gov.uk

Wales Office
www.walesoffice.gov.uk

Wales Tourist Board
www.visitwales.com

WWW.

4 Scotland

Population

In mid-2002 the estimated population of Scotland was 5.1 million, 8.5 per cent of the population of the United Kingdom. There has been a 0.6 per cent decline over the past 11 years. West Lothian had the largest proportional increase, at 10.3 per cent, while Eilean Siar had the largest decrease, falling by 10.7 per cent (see Table 4.1).

The population density in Scotland is the lowest in the United Kingdom, averaging 65 people per square kilometre in 2002. This figure masks a wide difference between Scotland's area of highest population density, Glasgow City at 3,290 people per square kilometre, and the lowest in the Highland council area at 8 people per square kilometre.

Three-quarters of the population live in the central lowlands where two of Scotland's largest cities are situated: the capital, Edinburgh (population 448,000) in the east and Glasgow (population 577,000) in the west.

Representation at Westminster and in Europe

Scottish constituencies are represented by 72 of the 659 seats in the House of Commons (see page 35) at Westminster. However, the 1997 White Paper *Scotland's Parliament*, which set out the UK Government's proposals for the Scottish Parliament, acknowledged the need to reduce Scotland's representation at Westminster following devolution. The *Scotland Act 1998*, which established the Scottish Parliament and Executive (see page 20) provided for this by removing the statutory minimum of 71 Scottish seats at Westminster, and requiring the Boundary

Table 4.1 Population and population change by council area, June 2002, Scotland

	Population (thousands)	Change in population 1991–2002 (%)
Aberdeen City	209	−2.3
Aberdeenshire	227	5.3
Angus	108	−0.2
Argyll & Bute	91	−2.7
Clackmannanshire	48	−0.4
Dumfries & Galloway	147	0.1
Dundee City	144	−7.3
East Ayrshire	120	−3.5
East Dunbartonshire	107	−2.6
East Lothian	91	7.5
East Renfrewshire	90	4.5
Edinburgh, City of	448	2.7
Eilean Siar[1]	26	−10.7
Falkirk	146	2.1
Fife	351	1.0
Glasgow City	577	−8.2
Highland	208	2.1
Inverclyde	84	−8.5
Midlothian	81	1.2
Moray	87	3.3
North Ayrshire	136	−1.7
North Lanarkshire	321	−1.7
Orkney Islands	19	−1.6
Perth & Kinross	135	6.1
Renfrewshire	172	−2.1
Scottish Borders, The	107	3.4
Shetland Islands	22	−2.6
South Ayrshire	112	−1.3
South Lanarkshire	302	−0.1
Stirling	86	6.5
West Dunbartonshire	93	−4.5
West Lothian	160	10.3
Scotland	**5,055**	**−0.6**

1 Formerly Western Isles.
Source: Office for National Statistics and General Register Office for Scotland

Commission for Scotland to determine the level of Scottish representation by applying the same electoral quota as in England. The Commission published its provisional recommendations for new Westminster constituency boundaries in February 2002, recommending that there should be 59 Scottish seats. Public inquiries and consultations are taking place and the Commission is due to make its final report by December 2006.

Following devolution, responsibility for a number of issues remains with the UK Parliament and Government as 'reserved matters' under the *Scotland Act 1998*, including foreign affairs, defence and overall economic policy (for a more detailed list see appendix A page 476).

Until June 2003, the Secretary of State for Scotland represented Scotland's interests in the UK Government, and was supported by a free-standing department, the Scotland Office. However, now that the devolved administrations are well established, the UK Government considers that there is no longer a need for full-time Cabinet ministers and free-standing departments to conduct the remaining Scottish and Welsh business within the UK Parliament and Government. Since June 2003, Scottish interests have been represented in the UK Cabinet and the House of Commons by the Secretary of State for Transport, who combines this role with that of Secretary of State for Scotland. The Scotland Office retains its separate identity but as part of the new Department for Constitutional Affairs (DCA). A Parliamentary Under Secretary of State with responsibility for Scotland operates from the

DCA, as does the Advocate General for Scotland, one of the UK law officers. These three ministers are questioned regularly in the House of Commons by Members of Parliament (MPs) at Scottish Questions.

The House of Commons Scottish Grand Committee comprises all MPs from Scottish constituencies and may be convened anywhere in Scotland as well as at Westminster. Its business includes questions tabled for oral answer, ministerial statements, and debates that are referred to it, including those on statutory instruments and matters relating to Scotland. The Scottish Affairs Select Committee (for information on select committees see page 38) is appointed by the House of Commons to examine the expenditure, administration and policy of the Scotland Office, including relations with the Scottish Parliament.

Scotland elects eight of the UK's 87 members (MEPs) to the European Parliament, using the d'Hondt system of proportional representation (see glossary). There is an office in Brussels specifically to promote Scotland's interests within the European Union.

The Scottish Parliament and Scottish Executive

The first Scottish Parliament for some 300 years was elected in 1999. This followed a referendum in 1997, in which 74 per cent of those who voted

Table 4.2 Electoral Representation in Scotland, May 2003

	Scottish Parliament			UK Parliament	European Parliament
	Constituency seats (MSPs)	Additional seats (MSPs)	Total seats (MSPs)	MPs	MEPs
Scottish Labour	46	4	50	55	3
Scottish National Party	9	18	27	5	2
Scottish Conservative and Unionist Party	3	15	18	1	2
Scottish Liberal Democrats	13	4	17	10	1
Scottish Greens	0	7	7	0	0
Scottish Socialist Party	0	6	6	0	0
Scottish Senior Citizens Unity Party	0	1	1	0	0
Independents	2	1	3	0	0
Speaker of the House of Commons	.	.	.	1	.
Total seats	**73**	**56**	**129**	**72**	**8**

Source: Scottish Parliament

The new Parliament building

The new Parliament building

The Scottish Parliament is currently based at the General Assembly Hall on the Mound in Edinburgh. A new Parliament building is due to be completed in autumn 2003 at Holyrood, at the lower end of the city's Royal Mile, where the previous Scottish Parliament met in Parliament House from 1640 to 1707. Once in Holyrood, MSPs will work in a high-tech environment, using swipe cards and pin numbers to vote electronically from their seats.

In June 2003 the First Minister ordered an independent inquiry into the cost and lifespan of the building, which is some two-and-a-half years behind schedule and £335 million over budget.

endorsed the UK Government's proposals to establish a Scottish Parliament and Executive to administer Scottish affairs. On a second question – whether to give the new Parliament limited tax-varying powers – 64 per cent were in favour. Legislation was subsequently introduced in December 1997 and the following November the *Scotland Act 1998* passed into law. Parliamentary elections were held in May 1999, and the Parliament and Executive took up their full powers on 1 July 1999.

Anything the *Scotland Act 1998* does not reserve to the UK Parliament is devolved to the Scottish Parliament and the Scottish Executive. This includes education, training, most health issues and most aspects of home affairs. A more detailed list of devolved powers can be found in appendix A, page 487. In all devolved areas the Scottish Parliament can amend or repeal existing Acts of the UK Parliament and pass new legislation of its own.

Unlike the Westminster Parliament, the Scottish Parliament does not have a second chamber to scrutinise legislation that comes before it. Detailed consideration of Bills is carried out in committees, which take evidence from a variety of outside sources, including interest groups, individuals and experts.

The Scottish Parliament's 129 members (MSPs) are elected for a fixed four-year term. The 73 single-member constituency seats are elected under the first-past-the-post system and each of the eight Scottish Parliament regions returns a further seven MSPs using the Additional Member System (see glossary), a type of proportional

representation that is designed to ensure that the share of seats each party receives in the Parliament will reflect as closely as possible its level of support among voters.

The Scottish Executive is Scotland's devolved government and is accountable to the Scottish Parliament. The Executive is led by a First Minister, an MSP who is nominated by the Parliament. The First Minister appoints the other Scottish ministers. As the Scottish Labour Party does not have an overall majority in the Scottish Parliament they have formed a coalition with the Scottish Liberal Democrats who have three seats in the Cabinet, including that of Deputy First Minister. The Executive has ten departments (see appendix A).

Finance

The Scottish Executive's budget for 2003/04 is £22.8 billion, rising to almost £26 billion in 2005/06. The majority of the funding for the Scottish Parliament comes from the UK

2003 elections

The second elections to the Scottish Parliament were held in May 2003. The average turnout across regions and constituencies was 49 per cent, compared with 59 per cent in the 1999 elections. The Scottish Labour Party and the Scottish National Party both lost seats, while gains were made by the Scottish Green Party and the Scottish Socialist Party, which increased their number of MSPs from one each, to seven and six respectively.

The Scottish Labour Party is again the largest single party in the Scottish Parliament (see Table 4.2), with 50 MSPs, compared with 56 MSPs in the previous Parliament. It has 46 of the 73 constituency seats, compared with 53 in the last Parliament, including nearly all those in central Scotland. The Scottish National Party remains the second largest party, with 27 MSPs, compared with 35 MSPs elected in the previous Parliament. Two-thirds of its seats come from the 'top up' proportional representation system, as do 15 of the Scottish Conservative and Unionist Party's 18 seats, making the latter the third largest party in the Parliament. The number of Scottish Liberal Democrats' seats remained the same, gaining an extra constituency seat but losing a regional one. The Scottish Senior Citizens Party won its first parliamentary seat, and the number of independent MSPs rose to three.

Unitary council areas in Scotland

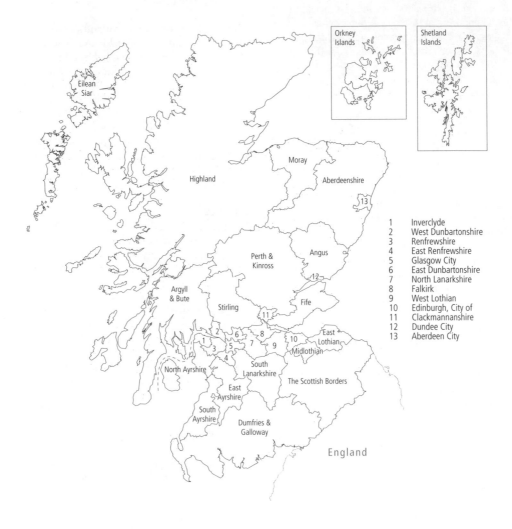

1   Inverclyde
2   West Dunbartonshire
3   Renfrewshire
4   East Renfrewshire
5   Glasgow City
6   East Dunbartonshire
7   North Lanarkshire
8   Falkirk
9   West Lothian
10 Edinburgh, City of
11 Clackmannanshire
12 Dundee City
13 Aberdeen City

Parliament's block grant. Other sources of revenue include non-domestic rate income (business rates). The Scottish Parliament is solely responsible for the allocation of the total Scottish budget. The Scottish Parliament has the power to increase or decrease the basic rate of income tax in Scotland – currently 22 pence in the pound – by a maximum of 3 pence. A person is liable to pay income tax if he or she is a UK resident for tax purposes and either spends 50 per cent or more of the tax year in Scotland or has his or her only or principal home there. The 1999/2003 Parliament did not exercise its right to vary income tax.

Local government

Scotland's 32 unitary (single-tier) councils are responsible for the full range of local government services, including education, social work, police and fire services, roads, public transport, local planning, urban development, housing, libraries, leisure and recreation. They can either provide these services themselves, or buy them in from other authorities or the private sector.

Although local authorities are independent and manage their own day-to-day business, the First

Minister has powers to oversee their work in areas such as finance, town and country planning, transport and housing.

Six of the eight police and fire brigades cover the area of more than one local authority and are administered by joint boards appointed by the authorities in their areas. These boards appoint their own Chief Constables and Firemasters who are responsible for day-to-day operations.

There is more information on local government in the United Kingdom in chapter 6.

Community councils

Scotland also has around 1,200 community councils. They are similar to parishes in England (see page 9) and as such are non-political, broadly-based organisations through which communities can speak and act on issues they have identified locally. Although they have no statutory powers, they do have a right to be consulted on local planning issues.

Community planning is a key theme in the *Local Government in Scotland Act 2003*, which provides a framework for local authorities, other public and private bodies, the voluntary sector and the local community to improve service delivery and link national and local priorities.

Gaelic language

Scottish Gaelic, a Celtic language related to Irish, was introduced into Scotland in about AD 500. According to the 2001 Census 58,650 people aged three or over (1.2 per cent of the population) spoke Gaelic. This compares with 65,980 Gaelic speakers in 1991 (1.3 per cent of the population). Gaelic speakers mostly live in the Eilean Siar Council Area, where 60 per cent of the population speak Gaelic.

The Scottish Executive provided over £13.0 million to support Gaelic in 2002/03; of this, £8.5 million was spent on broadcasting, through programmes commissioned by the Gaelic Broadcasting Committee (GBC). The GBC itself provided a further £2 million. A new Gaelic Media Service is expected to replace the GBC in April 2004, once the Communication Bill on Gaelic Broadcasting is enacted. The new service will be able to operate a dedicated Gaelic broadcasting channel on a digital platform.

Economy

Compared with 2001, output in the Scottish service sector grew by 4 per cent in 2002, while there was a 10 per cent drop in the production sector and a 4 per cent drop in construction. This contrast between growth in services and decline in production was more pronounced than in the rest of the United Kingdom. Growth in the service sector and developments in high-technology industries, particularly electronics, have taken the place of the traditional Scottish industries of coal mining, steel production and shipbuilding. The biotechnology industry has achieved international renown with the world's first cloned mammal (see page 376), and with work in signal transduction that has made a significant contribution to the treatment of cancer.

Gross value added (GVA, see glossary and Table 23.12, page 344) per head in 2001 was £13,700. The spring 2003 Labour Force Survey recorded that there were 2.5 million people economically active in Scotland, of whom 2.4 million were in employment. Unemployment, at 5.6 per cent, was above the UK rate of 5.0 per cent. The service industries provided 44 per cent of jobs and manufacturing industries 14 per cent. The number of people who worked in manufacturing was highest in small towns (15 per cent) and lowest in rural areas (11 per cent). The percentage whose main job was in the banking, finance and insurance sector was highest in urban areas (16 per cent) and lowest in rural areas (11 per cent). There was little difference between areas for other sectors, such as public administration, education and health.

Scotland is the sixth largest equity management centre in Europe and 15th in the world. Ten of Scotland's top 20 companies are in the financial services sector, including Scotland's largest company by capital value. Around 70 per cent of the UK financial services market outside London are in Scotland.

Offshore oil and gas production has made a significant contribution to the UK economy since the late 1960s. Many of the 117 UK offshore oilfields are to the east of the Shetland and Orkney Islands or off the east coast of the mainland. Scotland has four oil terminals, three gas terminals and two refineries.

In the remote rural areas, nearly one in four people in employment work from home, double the proportion in Scotland as a whole. Rural areas are under-represented in all the key growth areas in the Scottish economy: banking and finance, high technology manufacturing, information communication and technology (ICT) services, and research and development.

Forests cover 17 per cent of Scotland's land area and Scotland accounts for 47 per cent of total woodland in the United Kingdom (see page 408). Scottish sawmills account for 39 per cent of UK sawn wood production.

Some 210,000 people work in tourism-related industries in Scotland, around 9 per cent of the workforce. Tourists spend about £4 billion a year in Scotland; 18 per cent of this is spent by visitors from outside the United Kingdom.

Food and drink is also a growing sector with over 1,200 companies across a variety of food products. Whisky production continues to be important to Scotland; in 2002, 942,000 bottles were exported (see page 417).

Scottish Enterprise and Highlands and Islands Enterprise (see page 344) manage domestic support for industry and commerce, while Scottish Development International, a joint operation between the Scottish Executive and Scottish Enterprise, encourages inward investment. In 2001/02, 59 inward investment projects were recorded, which were expected to lead to investment of £271 million and the creation or safeguarding of nearly 6,400 jobs.

Further reading

The Scottish Budget: Annual Expenditure Report of the Scottish Executive. Scottish Executive, 2003.

Scotland Office Departmental Report 2003: The Government's Expenditure Plans 2003–04 to 2004–05. The Stationery Office, 2003.

A few distinctive facts about Scotland
Education in Scotland has a different structure to that of other parts of the United Kingdom, particularly in the school curriculum and the system of public examinations (see chapter 10).

The Scottish legal system (see chapter 14) differs in many respects from the rest of the United Kingdom. During the 16th century, certain aspects of medieval church law and much of the Roman, or civil, law as developed by the jurists of Holland and France were brought together to form the basis of Scots law. The 1707 Treaty of Union allowed Scotland to keep Scots law, its own courts and its legal profession. The prosecution, prison and police services are also separate.

Scotland has several major collections of the fine and applied arts, such as the National Gallery of Scotland and the Scottish National Gallery of Modern Art in Edinburgh, and the Burrell Collection in Glasgow.

Websites

Scottish Executive
www.scotland.gov.uk

The Scottish Parliament
www.scottish.parliament.uk

Scotland Office
www.scottishsecretary.gov.uk

Convention of Scottish Local Authorities
www.cosla.gov.uk

Scottish Development International
www.lis.org.uk

Scottish Tourist Board
www.visitscotland.com

WWW.

5 Northern Ireland

Population

Northern Ireland's population in mid-2002 was 1.7 million, 2.9 per cent of the population of the United Kingdom. Just over 39 per cent live in the area covered by the Eastern Health and Social Services Board, at the centre of which is the capital, Belfast. The population increased by 5.6 per cent between 1991 and 2002. Population density in 2002 was highest in the district council area of Belfast (at 2,500 people per square kilometre) and lowest in Moyle (at only 33 people per square kilometre). Around 36 per cent of the population was aged under 25 in 2002, a higher proportion than in other parts of the United Kingdom.

In the 2001 Census, 40 per cent of the Northern Ireland population said that their religion was Catholic; 21 per cent Presbyterian; 15 per cent Church of Ireland; 3 per cent Methodist; 6 per cent belonged to other Christian traditions; and 0.3 per cent of the population belonged to other (non-Christian) traditions. The remainder either had no religion, or did not state their religion.

Representation at Westminster and in Europe

For UK Parliament general elections, Northern Ireland is divided into 18 single-seat constituencies and Members of Parliament (MPs) are elected by the 'first-past-the-post' electoral system. The four Sinn Féin MPs have not taken their seats in the Commons. However, since December 2001 they have had access to facilities at Westminster.

The Secretary of State for Northern Ireland is a member of the UK Cabinet whose main function is to ensure that the devolution settlement works satisfactorily. The Secretary of State is head of the

Table 5.1 Population and population change by Board[1] and district council, June 2002, Northern Ireland

	Population (thousands)	Change in population 1991–2002 (%)
Eastern	666	2.0
Ards	74	13.5
Belfast	274	−6.4
Castlereagh	66	7.9
Down	65	10.6
Lisburn	109	8.3
North Down	77	5.0
Northern	430	7.5
Antrim	49	7.1
Ballymena	59	4.0
Ballymoney	27	13.4
Carrickfergus	38	14.9
Coleraine	56	6.9
Cookstown	33	6.0
Larne	31	4.5
Magherafelt	40	11.1
Moyle	16	9.4
Newtonabbey	80	5.4
Southern	316	8.7
Armagh	55	5.2
Banbridge	42	26.1
Craigavon	82	8.0
Dungannon	48	6.1
Newry and Mourne	89	5.9
Western	285	7.9
Derry	106	8.8
Fermanagh	58	6.4
Limavady	33	12.2
Omagh	49	6.5
Strabane	38	6.2
Northern Ireland	**1,697**	**5.6**

1 Health and Social Services Board areas.
Source: Office for National Statistics and Northern Ireland Statistics and Research Agency

Table 5.2 Electoral representation, Northern Ireland

	House of Commons June 2001 General Elections	European Parliament MEPs
Democratic Unionist	5	1
Sinn Féin[1]	4	0
Ulster Unionist	3	1
Independent Unionist	3	0
Social Democratic and Labour	3	1
Total	**18**	**3**

1 The Sinn Féin members have not taken their seats in the House of Commons.
Source: UK Parliament

Northern Ireland Office (NIO) and has permanent responsibility for matters not devolved to the Northern Ireland Assembly, including constitutional and security issues as they relate to Northern Ireland (see appendix A, page 476 for a more detailed list). When the Northern Ireland Assembly is suspended, the Secretary of State also assumes responsibility for the direction of the Northern Ireland departments (see appendix A, page 489).

The Westminster Parliament has established a Northern Ireland Grand Committee to consider Bills, statutory instruments and matters relating exclusively to Northern Ireland. It also provides for oral questions to NIO Ministers and ministerial statements. It includes all sitting Northern Ireland MPs and up to 25 others as nominated by the committee of selection.

There is also a Northern Ireland Affairs Select Committee, which examines the expenditure, policy and administration of the Northern Ireland Office. This Committee has the power to send for people, papers and records, and has investigated areas such as drug abuse, aggregates taxation, employment, electricity prices, education, BSE and the security forces in Northern Ireland.

Northern Ireland forms a single, multi-seat constituency to elect three of the 87 UK representatives to the European Parliament (MEPs). As with local and Assembly elections, the single transferable vote form of proportional representation is used. The next European parliamentary elections are planned for May 2004.

Northern Ireland Assembly and Executive

When in session, the Northern Ireland Assembly meets in Parliament Buildings at Stormont, Belfast. The Assembly was the prime source of authority for devolved responsibility to run most domestic affairs and had full legislative and executive authority until it was suspended on 14 October 2002. It was dissolved on 28 April 2003 in preparation for the elections due in May, but these were subsequently postponed (see box).

The Northern Ireland Assembly has ten statutory committees and six standing committees.[1] Membership of committees is in broad proportion to party strength, in order to ensure that the opportunity of committee places is available to all Members. Each statutory committee has a scrutiny, policy development and consultation role in relation to its department, and a role in the initiation of legislation. The Committee of the Centre, a standing committee, fulfils a similar role with respect to the Office of the First Minister and Deputy First Minister.

Elections to the Northern Ireland Assembly use the single transferable vote system of proportional representation. The 18 constituencies are the same as those for the UK Parliament, but each returns six MLAs (Members of the Legislative Assembly), giving the Assembly a total of 108 members.

One of the first actions of a new Assembly is to appoint Ministers for each of the ten Northern

Suspension of the devolved administration
The Northern Ireland Assembly and the Executive were suspended with effect from midnight on 14 October 2002, in order to stabilise the political situation in Northern Ireland. The UK Government considered that it was not for the time being possible to hold together an inclusive power-sharing Executive, since the confidence within the community necessary to underpin it had broken down.

As a result of the state of political dialogue in Northern Ireland the *Northern Ireland Assembly (Elections and Periods of Suspension) Act 2003* was passed, which had the effect of further postponing the Assembly elections from 29 May 2003 to an unspecified date, intended to be in autumn 2003.

1 For an explanation of standing committees, see page 40.

Physical features

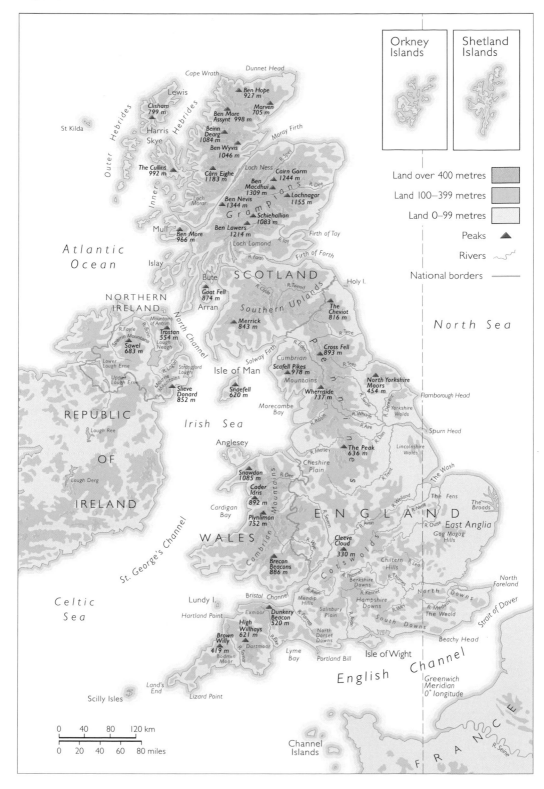

Orkney Islands

Shetland Islands

Land over 400 metres
Land 100–399 metres
Land 0–99 metres
Peaks ▲
Rivers
National borders

Dunnet Head
Cape Wrath
Ben Hope 927 m
Morven 705 m
Lewis
Clisham 799 m
Ben More Assynt 998 m
St Kilda
Harris
Beinn Dearg 1084 m
Skye
Ben Wyvis 1046 m
Moray Firth
R. Spey
The Cuillins 992 m
Càrn Eighe 1183 m
Loch Ness
Cairn Gorm 1244 m
Ben Macdhui 1309 m
R. Dee
Lochnagar 1155 m
Loch Morar
Ben Nevis 1344 m
Grampions
Schiehallion 1083 m
Mull
Ben More 966 m
Ben Lawers 1214 m
Firth of Tay
Atlantic Ocean
Outer Hebrides
Inner Hebrides
Islay
Loch Lomond
R. Tay
Firth of Forth
SCOTLAND
R. Forth
Holy I.
Bute
R. Clyde
R. Tweed
Goat Fell 874 m
NORTHERN IRELAND
Arran
Southern Uplands
The Cheviot 816 m
North Sea
Mountains of Antrim
R. Foyle
R. Bann
Trostan 554 m
Merrick 843 m
R. Tyne
Sperrin Mountains
Lough Neagh
Sawel 683 m
North Channel
Pennines
Lower Lough Erne
R. Lagan
Strangford Lough
Solway Firth
R. Eden
Cross Fell 893 m
Upper Lough Erne
Mourne Mountains
Slieve Donard 852 m
Isle of Man
Cumbrian
R. Tees
Scafell Pikes 978 m
Mountains
North Yorkshire Moors 454 m
REPUBLIC
Snaefell 620 m
Whernside 737 m
Flamborough Head
Morecambe Bay
R. Ribble
R. Wharfe
Yorkshire Wolds
R. Swale
R. Derwent
OF
Lough Ree
Irish Sea
R. Aire
Spurn Head
R. Ribble
R. Don
Anglesey
The Peak 636 m
Lincolnshire Wolds
IRELAND
Cheshire Plain
Lough Derg
Snowdon 1085 m
R. Dee
R. Trent
The Wash
Cardigan Bay
Cader Idris 892 m
R. Mersey
The Fens
The Broads
Plynlimon 752 m
R. Severn
R. Welland
R. Nene
WALES
ENGLAND
East Anglia
R. Ouse
Gog Magog Hills
St. George's Channel
Cambrian Mountains
Brecon Beacons 886 m
Cleeve Cloud 330 m
R. Avon
Celtic Sea
Lundy I.
Bristol Channel
R. Wye
Cotswolds
Chiltern Hills
R. Lea
North Foreland
Hartland Point
Exmoor
Dunkery Beacon 520 m
R. Parrett
Mendip Hills
Berkshire Downs
R. Thames
North Downs
Dover
High Willhays 621 m
Salisbury Plain
R. Kennet
Hampshire Downs
R. Wey
R. Medway
The Weald
Strait of Dover
Brown Willy 419 m
R. Exe
North Dorset Downs
R. Avon
South Downs
Dartmoor
R. Tamar
Lyme Bay
Portland Bill
Isle of Wight
Beachy Head
Scilly Isles
Land's End
Lizard Point
English Channel
Greenwich Meridian 0° longitude
Channel Islands
FRANCE
R. Seine

0   40   80   120 km
0   20   40   60   80 miles

Motorways and major roads

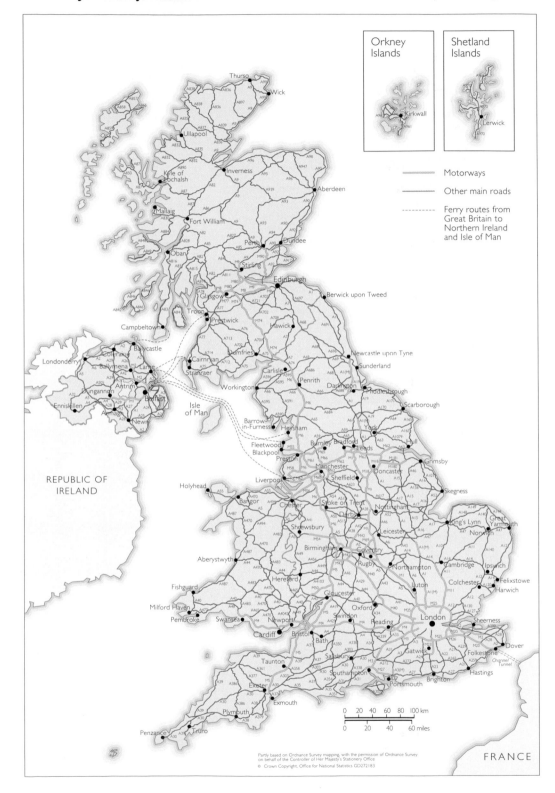

Passenger railway network

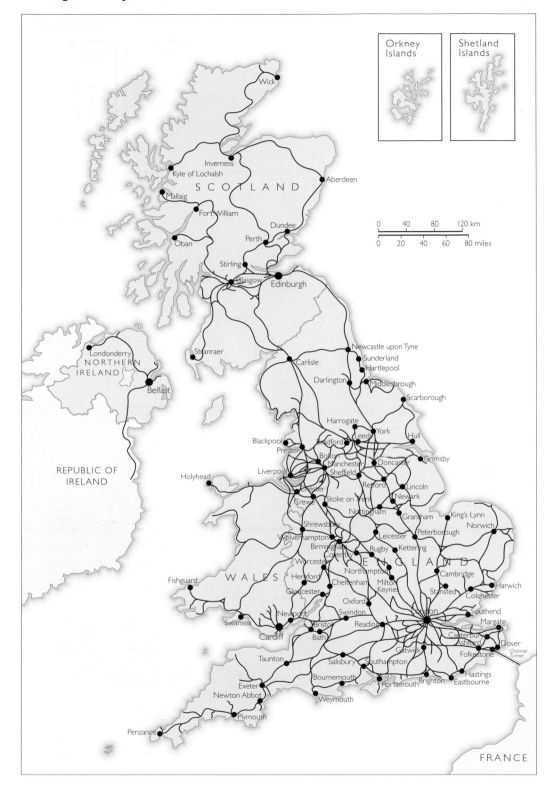

Major conservation and recreation areas

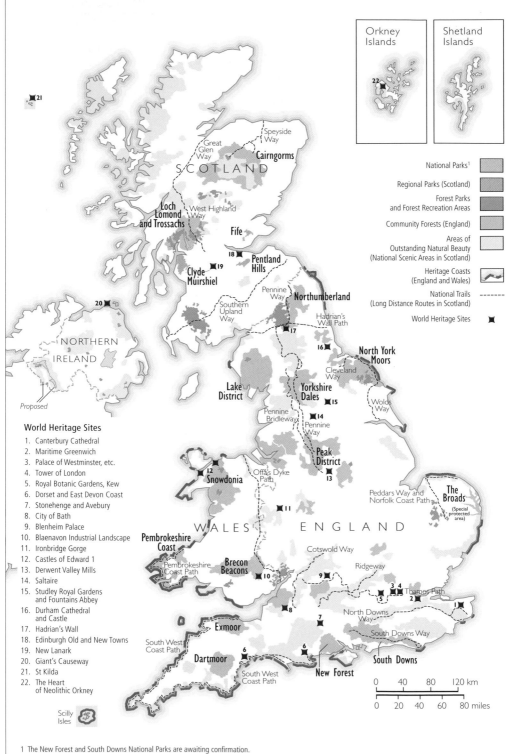

Orkney Islands

Shetland Islands

National Parks[1]

Regional Parks (Scotland)

Forest Parks and Forest Recreation Areas

Community Forests (England)

Areas of Outstanding Natural Beauty (National Scenic Areas in Scotland)

Heritage Coasts (England and Wales)

National Trails (Long Distance Routes in Scotland)

World Heritage Sites

World Heritage Sites

1. Canterbury Cathedral
2. Maritime Greenwich
3. Palace of Westminster, etc.
4. Tower of London
5. Royal Botanic Gardens, Kew
6. Dorset and East Devon Coast
7. Stonehenge and Avebury
8. City of Bath
9. Blenheim Palace
10. Blaenavon Industrial Landscape
11. Ironbridge Gorge
12. Castles of Edward 1
13. Derwent Valley Mills
14. Saltaire
15. Studley Royal Gardens and Fountains Abbey
16. Durham Cathedral and Castle
17. Hadrian's Wall
18. Edinburgh Old and New Towns
19. New Lanark
20. Giant's Causeway
21. St Kilda
22. The Heart of Neolithic Orkney

SCOTLAND

Great Glen Way

Speyside Way

Cairngorms

Loch Lomond and Trossachs

West Highland Way

Fife

Clyde Muirshiel

Pentland Hills

Pennine Way

Northumberland

Hadrian's Wall Path

Southern Upland Way

NORTHERN IRELAND

Proposed

North York Moors

Cleveland Way

Lake District

Yorkshire Dales

Wolds Way

Pennine Bridleway

Pennine Way

Peak District

Offa's Dyke Path

Snowdonia

Peddars Way and Norfolk Coast Path

The Broads
(Special protected area)

WALES

ENGLAND

Pembrokeshire Coast

Pembrokeshire Coast Path

Brecon Beacons

Cotswold Way

Ridgeway

Exmoor

South West Coast Path

Dartmoor

South West Coast Path

New Forest

North Downs Way

South Downs Way

South Downs

Scilly Isles

0   40   80   120 km

0   20   40   60   80 miles

1 The New Forest and South Downs National Parks are awaiting confirmation.
These and the Cairngorms Park incorporate Areas of Outstanding Natural Beauty and National Scenic Areas.

Countdown to devolution

Northern Ireland was governed by direct rule from Westminster between 1972 and 1999 (see page 7) but this was never intended to be permanent. Over the years, successive UK and Republic of Ireland Governments have worked closely together to try to bring lasting peace to Northern Ireland, recognising the need for new political arrangements acceptable to both sides of the community. The key events leading up to the establishment of the Northern Ireland Assembly were:

- **1985**: an Anglo-Irish Agreement provided a new basis for relations between the United Kingdom and the Republic of Ireland, creating an Intergovernmental Conference (see page 28).

- **1993**: the Downing Street Declaration set out the UK and Republic of Ireland Governments' views on how a future settlement might be achieved and restated that any constitutional change would require the consent of a majority of people in Northern Ireland.

- **1997**: The UK Government confirmed its intention of making the talks process as inclusive as possible and maintained that any agreement reached would need the broad support of the parties representing each of the main communities.

- **1998 (April)**: multi-party talks held in Belfast concluded with the Belfast (Good Friday) Agreement. Legislation was passed at Westminster authorising a referendum on the settlement in Northern Ireland and permitting elections to a new Northern Ireland Assembly. The Republic of Ireland Parliament also considered the Agreement and passed legislation authorising a concurrent referendum in the Republic of Ireland.

- **1998 (May)**: referendums were held in both parts of Ireland, and the Agreement received a clear endorsement. Northern Ireland voted 71 per cent in favour and 29 per cent against, while in the Republic of Ireland the result was 94 per cent and 6 per cent respectively.

- **1998 (June)**: a new Northern Ireland Assembly of 108 members was elected.

- **1999**: power was devolved to the Assembly and its Executive Committee of Ministers under the *Northern Ireland Act 1998*. At the same time a number of institutions set up to assist intergovernmental dialogue became fully functional (see below and page 28).

Ireland departments (see appendix A, page 489); this is done using the d'Hondt system (see glossary). It must also elect a First Minister and a Deputy First Minister on a cross-community basis. These 12 Ministers form the administration's Executive, which meets regularly to prioritise Executive business and recommend a common position on issues where necessary.

Programme of government

A programme of government is decided on each year within an agreed budget. This programme is subject to approval by the Assembly on a cross-community basis, following scrutiny in Assembly Committees. While the Assembly is suspended, the Northern Ireland departments work directly to the Secretary of State for Northern Ireland.

Civic Forum

When the Assembly is not suspended, a 60-member Civic Forum represents the business, trade union, voluntary and other sectors of the Northern Ireland community. It acts as a consultative mechanism on social, economic and cultural issues.

North/South Ministerial Council

The North/South Ministerial Council was established in December 1999 following the Belfast (Good Friday) Agreement. It seeks to build on the co-operation that already exists between Northern Ireland and the Republic of Ireland on issues of mutual interest. Its purpose is to bring together those with executive responsibilities to:
- develop consultation, co-operation and action within the island;
- direct the work of the North/South Implementation Bodies that were set up under the Belfast Agreement to deal with waterways, food safety, trade and business development, special European Union programmes, marine matters and language; and
- oversee cross-border co-operation in agriculture, education, health, environment, transport and tourism.

The North/South Ministerial Council is unable to meet during suspension. In devolution it meets in plenary format twice a year, with Northern Ireland representation led by the First Minister and Deputy First Minister. Sectoral meetings, with each side represented by appropriate Ministers, are held on a more frequent basis. The Council has a joint secretariat and is jointly funded.

The British–Irish Council

The British–Irish Council was set up under the Belfast (Good Friday) Agreement in 1998 to 'promote the harmonious and mutually beneficial development of the totality of relationships among the people of its member administrations'. It has representatives from the UK and Republic of Ireland Governments, the devolved institutions in Northern Ireland, Scotland and Wales, as well as from Jersey, Guernsey and the Isle of Man.

The Council meets at summit level twice a year. Northern Ireland interests are represented by the First Minister and the Deputy First Minister. It also meets in sectoral format on a regular basis with each side represented by the appropriate Minister. Since the suspension of devolution NIO Ministers have represented Northern Ireland interests.

The British–Irish Intergovernmental Conference

The British–Irish Intergovernmental Conference was set up in 1998 to promote bilateral co-operation on matters of mutual interest between the two governments. It covers many areas including:
- asylum and immigration issues;
- EU and international issues;
- social security and methods of fraud detection;
- education;
- policy on misuse of drugs;
- the combating of international crime; and
- fiscal issues.

It meets as required at summit level, the Prime Minister, Taoiseach (Republic of Ireland Prime Minister) and other Ministers attending as appropriate.

Security and justice

The Government's security policy seeks to secure lasting peace based on the Belfast (Good Friday)

Agreement, in which the rights and identities of all traditions in Northern Ireland are respected and safeguarded. The Government also remains committed to ensuring that the security forces in Northern Ireland have available the powers they need to counter the terrorist threat. In *Responding to a Changing Security Situation: The Government's Approach*, a security strategy report updated in March 2002, the Government confirmed its aim to return to normal security arrangements in Northern Ireland as soon as possible. It reported that troop levels in Northern Ireland (fewer than 13,500) were at their lowest since 1970. Routine military patrolling was also down by 50 per cent since the Belfast (Good Friday) Agreement.

In the 2002 Spending Review the Government's plans provide for an additional £140 million expenditure in 2005/06 compared with 2002/03, so that the Northern Ireland Office can continue to:
- implement fully its Belfast (Good Friday) Agreement pledges;
- build a modern and efficient police service in Northern Ireland;
- make key reforms in the justice system; and
- provide proper funding for initiatives such as the Northern Ireland Human Rights Commission (see page 29), the Bloody Sunday Inquiry,[2] and support for the victims of the troubles.

Reform of policing

The police take primary responsibility for the prevention and investigation of all crime in Northern Ireland, including terrorism. If necessary, the police can call on the Armed Forces for support.

The *Police Service (Northern Ireland) Acts 2000* and *2003* contained measures to set up a new and more accountable police service and to redress the religious imbalance in the police service between Protestants and Catholics. The first group of recruits trained specifically for the new police service graduated in April 2002. The Government aims to increase Catholic representation in the police service to 30 per cent by 2011. In 2003 just under 13 per cent of regular officers in the police service were Catholic.

---

2 On 30 January 1972, 13 civilians were killed during a civil rights march in Londonderry. The day became known as 'Bloody Sunday'. In 1998 the weight of new evidence led to a new inquiry being set up.

Reform of criminal justice

The Criminal Justice Review, published in March 2000, was the most far-reaching survey of criminal justice in Northern Ireland for 30 years (see page 208). An updated Criminal Justice Implementation Plan was published in June 2003, setting out progress so far and containing detailed plans and timescales for the continuing implementation process.

Human rights and equality

A commitment to protect human rights and promote equality was central to the Belfast (Good Friday) Agreement. The subsequent *Northern Ireland Act 1998* placed a statutory duty of equality on all public authorities and established the following bodies:

The Northern Ireland Human Rights Commission – to advise the Government on human rights issues, particularly on the need for any legislation. In May 2003, after extensive consultation, the Commission published its second Strategic Plan, covering the period 2003–06. The Plan identifies four goals:

- delivering a Bill of Rights for Northern Ireland;
- identifying and addressing human rights violations;
- promoting awareness and understanding of human rights; and
- increasing the effectiveness of the Commission.

The Equality Commission for Northern Ireland – to be responsible for fair employment, equal opportunities, racial equality, disability issues and enforcing the statutory duty of equality on public authorities.

The Parades Commission – to help implement the *Public Processions (Northern Ireland) Act 1998*, which regulates public processions in Northern Ireland. The majority of parades each year are organised by the Protestant/Unionist community and take place during the six months from around Easter to the end of September.

The Victims Commission – whose 1998 report *We Will Remember Them* led the Government to appoint a Minister for Victims and establish a Victims Liaison Unit in the Northern Ireland Office. Since then, the Government has committed more than £18 million to support victims of inter-community unrest in Northern Ireland.

Local government

Northern Ireland is divided into 26 local government districts (see map on page 30), each forming a single-tier (unitary) district council. They are responsible for environmental health; refuse collection; leisure and recreation facilities; tourist amenities; building control and cemeteries. This is a narrower range of functions than local authorities elsewhere in the United Kingdom. However, the district councils nominate locally elected representatives to sit as members of the various statutory bodies dealing with other issues of local interest, for example, education, libraries and healthcare. They also have a consultative role in matters such as planning, roads and housing; and offer leadership and support in local economic development.

Finance

Unlike the other parts of the United Kingdom, local authorities in Northern Ireland are not financed through a council tax. Instead they raise revenue to help fund the services they provide by levying a domestic rate on homes and a business rate on commercial property. Additional finance comes from the general grant and reserves.

The Local Government (Miscellaneous Provisions) Order was introduced in December 2002.[3] The main effect of the Order will be to change the distribution of the resources element of general grant, with the aim of making district council funding more equitable. The new formula for distributing resources measures the wealth of a council against its estimated needs; councils whose needs exceed their wealth will be entitled to a share of the grant. The Order also extends existing powers for district councils to promote economic development in their areas and to engage in community safety activity through Community Safety Partnerships.

In 2003/04 net revenue expenditure by local authorities in Northern Ireland was estimated at £338 million: £283 million financed from district rates; £50 million by general grant and £5 million from reserves.

---

3 This Order had passed through several stages in the Northern Ireland Assembly before the Assembly was suspended in October 2002. The legislation was subsequently approved by the UK Parliament using the Order in Council procedure.

District councils in Northern Ireland

Cf   Carrickfergus
Cr   Castlereagh
ND North Down
Nta Newtownabbey

Economy

Since 1997 the Northern Ireland economy has grown at around 2 per cent a year and economic growth was again forecast at 2 per cent for 2002. Gross value added (see glossary and Table 23.12, page 344) per head in 2001 was £11,300, below the rest of the United Kingdom, except the North East region of England. According to the spring 2003 Labour Force Survey, there were 786,000 people economically active in Northern Ireland, of whom 745,000 were in employment. Unemployment, at 5.3 per cent, was just above the UK rate of 5.0 per cent. Around 32 per cent of jobs are in the public sector, compared with 19 per cent of jobs in the United Kingdom overall.

Between 1997 and 2002 Northern Ireland manufacturing output increased by 11 per cent, although it contracted during 2001 as the global economy slowed. Engineering and allied industries grew by 29 per cent during this period.

Engineering accounts for over half of all manufacturing exports. Output in the leather, textiles and textile products sector continued to fall in 2002, while other manufacturing sectors either grew slightly or remained stable. Output in the electricity, gas and water, and mining and quarrying sectors also decreased during 2002.

Provisional results from the Northern Ireland Annual Business Inquiry for 2001, published in April 2003, showed that the value of business income, after payment for goods and services, was worth some £13 billion. This represents an increase of nearly 15 per cent on the previous year.

The Economic Development Forum (EDF) provides a formal mechanism through which a wide range of organisations can advise Northern Ireland ministers on issues relating to the development and future competitiveness of the economy. Membership of the forum comprises central government, local government and the major social partners. The EDF's first publication *Working Together for a Stronger Economy* was launched in June 2002 and sets out seven key strategic priorities to be addressed if the Northern Ireland economy is to be significantly strengthened by the year 2010.

Think/Create/Innovate: The Regional Innovation Strategy for Northern Ireland was published in June 2003. It identifies a series of actions to build on Northern Ireland's innovation and research and development capabilities, while addressing its weaknesses. The areas highlighted for growth include biotechnology, nanotechnology, communications engineering and polymer processing.

Economic assistance

Through the EU Structural Funds allocation 2000–06 (see page 345) Northern Ireland receives over €1 billion (around £704 million) of assistance. This support is provided through the Building Sustainable Prosperity and Community Initiatives Programmes – INTERREG, EQUAL LEADER and URBAN. In addition, continuation of funding from the EU Programme for Peace and Reconciliation in Northern Ireland and the Border Region of Ireland 2000–04 (PEACE II) provides €566 million (around £400 million) to support the continued efforts to create a peaceful and stable society and to promote reconciliation.

Discussion on further EU funding beyond 2006 is under way, although it is acknowledged that post-2006 support will focus on the accession countries in Eastern Europe (see page 63).

Further reading

Northern Ireland Office Departmental Report 2003: The Government's Expenditure Plans 2003–04 to 2004–05. Cm 5929. The Stationery Office, 2003.

Some distinctive facts about Northern Ireland

- The 2001 Census found that 167,490 people in Northern Ireland had some knowledge of the Irish language.

- Northern Ireland has some excellent facilities for the arts. The Waterfront Hall in Belfast is an entertainment venue and convention centre and home to the Ulster Concert Orchestra, while the Odyssey Centre on the east bank of the River Lagan includes a science centre, IMAX film theatre, indoor arena, entertainment pavilion and piazzas.

- A fifth of the total area in Northern Ireland is designated as an Area of Outstanding Natural Beauty and just under a sixth is Green Belt land (see chapter 19).

Websites

Northern Ireland Assembly
www.niassembly.gov.uk

Northern Ireland Executive
www.northernireland.gov.uk

Northern Ireland Office
www.nio.gov.uk

Northern Ireland Tourist Board
www.discovernorthernireland.com

WWW.

6 Government

The United Kingdom is a parliamentary democracy, based on universal suffrage. It is also a constitutional monarchy in which ministers of the Crown govern in the name of the Sovereign, who is both Head of State and Head of the Government. There is no single document that forms the UK constitution; instead, the relationship between the State and the people relies on statute law, common law and conventions.[1]

The UK Parliament (the legislature) makes primary legislation, although it has devolved a range of issues to the Scottish Parliament, the National Assembly for Wales and, when it is sitting, the Northern Ireland Assembly (see chapters 3 to 5). Under the constitution, Parliament is supreme and it continues to have the authority over government and law-making in the United Kingdom as a whole (see page 34). The *executive* comprises the Government (members of the Cabinet and other ministers responsible for policies); government departments and agencies; local authorities; public corporations; independent regulatory bodies; and certain other organisations subject to ministerial control. The Government derives its authority and membership from Parliament and can only stay in office if it is able to command a majority in the House of Commons. The *judiciary* (see chapter 14) determines common law and interprets legislation.

In her role as Monarch, The Queen is head of the executive and plays an integral part in the legislature. She heads the judiciary and is both the commander-in-chief of all the Armed Forces of

---

1 Conventions are rules and practices which are not legally enforceable but which are regarded as indispensable to the working of government.

Constitutional changes
In June 2003 the Government announced a series of constitutional changes designed to put the relationship between the executive, legislature and judiciary on a modern footing and to separate the powers of the legislature and the judiciary. As a result, it proposes to abolish the office of Lord Chancellor (see page 38) after parliamentary approval of legislation, and to institute new arrangements for judicial appointments (see page 201) and for the role of the Speaker in the House of Lords, which is currently performed by the Lord Chancellor. A new Supreme Court is planned to replace the Law Lords as the highest court in the land. A Department for Constitutional Affairs (DCA, see page 47) has been set up, and the Scotland Office and the Wales Office (see page 20 and page 15 respectively) now form part of the DCA.

the Crown and 'supreme governor' of the established Church of England. In practice, the Monarch acts on the advice of her ministers.

Parliamentary electoral system

For electoral purposes the United Kingdom is divided into 659 constituencies, each of which returns one member to the House of Commons. Constituencies vary in size and area; the average electorate is around 68,000. There are four permanent Parliamentary Boundary Commissions – one each for England, Wales, Scotland and Northern Ireland – that review constituency size to ensure that constituencies have broadly similar numbers of electors. When the latest series of reviews for 2003 to 2007 has been completed, the four Commissions will be absorbed into the Electoral Commission (see page 33).

Table 6.1 General Election results by party, June 2001, UK

	MPs elected	% share of UK vote
Labour	412[1]	40.7
Conservative	166[2]	31.7
Liberal Democrats	52	18.3
Scottish National	5	1.8
Plaid Cymru – The Party of Wales	4	0.7
Ulster Unionist	6[3]	0.8
Democratic Unionist	5	0.7
Social Democratic and Labour	3	0.6
Sinn Féin[4]	4	0.7
Speaker	1	0.1
Other[5]	1	0.1

1 One Labour MP has subsequently changed parties and now sits as a Liberal Democrat. In September 2003 the Liberal Democrats gained the Labour-held seat of Brent East in a by-election following the death of the MP.
2 One Conservative MP now sits as an Independent Conservative.
3 Three Ulster Unionist MPs have resigned the party whip and are now classed as independent unionists.
4 The Sinn Féin Members have not taken their seats.
5 The constituency of Wyre Forest was won by the independent Kidderminster Hospital and Health Concern candidate.
Source: House of Commons

Voters

British citizens, and citizens of other Commonwealth countries and the Republic of Ireland resident in the United Kingdom, may vote in parliamentary elections provided that they are aged 18 or over; included in the register of electors for the constituency; and not subject to any legal incapacity to vote.

People not entitled to vote include members of the House of Lords, foreign nationals resident in the United Kingdom (other than Commonwealth citizens or citizens of the Republic of Ireland), some patients detained under mental health legislation, sentenced prisoners and people convicted within the previous five years of corrupt or illegal election practices. Members of the Armed Forces, Crown servants and staff of the British Council employed overseas (together with their wives or husbands if accompanying them) may be registered at an address in the constituency where they would live if not serving abroad. British citizens living abroad may apply to register as electors for a period of up to 15 years after they have left the United Kingdom.

Voting procedures

Voting is not compulsory in the United Kingdom and the simple majority system is used for Westminster elections; proportional representation is used in the elections to the Scottish Parliament, National Assembly for Wales and the Northern Ireland Assembly (see chapters 3 to 5). Each elector may cast one vote and usually does so in person at a polling station. Candidates are elected if they have more votes than any of the other candidates (although not necessarily an absolute majority over all other candidates). As in other European Union countries, participation in voting at General Elections has declined, and the turnout in the 2001 General Election was 59 per cent, the lowest since the First World War.

The Government has taken a number of measures designed to increase the number of people who vote in elections, including the introduction of postal voting on demand and a rolling electoral register, updated monthly, to enable voters to register at any time of the year. New voting procedures are being tested at local elections (see page 52).

Candidates

British citizens, and resident citizens of other Commonwealth countries and the Republic of Ireland, may be elected as Members of Parliament (MPs) provided that they are aged 21 or over and are not disqualified. Disqualified people include undischarged bankrupts; members of the House of Lords; and holders of certain offices listed in the *House of Commons Disqualification Act 1975*.

Each candidate's nomination must be proposed and seconded by two electors registered in the constituency and signed by eight others. Candidates do not have to be backed by a political party. A candidate must also deposit £500, which is returned if he or she receives 5 per cent or more of the votes cast.

The maximum sum a candidate may spend on a General Election campaign is £5,483 plus 4.6 pence for each elector in a borough constituency, or 6.2 pence for each elector in a county constituency. A higher limit of £100,000 has been set for by-elections because they are often seen as tests of national opinion in the period between General Elections. All election expenses, apart from the candidate's personal expenses, are subject to these statutory rules. A candidate is also entitled to send one election communication to each voter free of postal charges.

Electoral Commission

The Electoral Commission is an independent body set up under the *Political Parties, Elections*

and Referendums Act 2000 (see also page 49).
It aims to ensure public confidence and
participation in the democratic process in the
United Kingdom by modernising the electoral
process, promoting public awareness of electoral
matters and regulating political parties. It has
a statutory obligation to maintain a series of
registers, including the register of political parties,
the register of donations to political parties and
the register of campaign expenditure by political
parties (see page 49).

Proposals to modernise electoral law

In June 2003 the Electoral Commission made a
series of recommendations aimed at making it
easier and more convenient to vote, while
safeguarding the integrity of the system. These
include:

- the introduction of a UK-wide electronic register,
  compiled locally, which would enable people to
  vote at any polling station;
- individual registration, rather than registration by
  households, to enhance security;
- standardised polling hours, from 7.00 am to
  10.00 pm, to avoid confusion and maximise
  opportunities to vote;
- greater consistency in the nomination process
  for different elections and the removal of barriers
  to candidacy, such as the need for a candidate
  to put down a deposit;
- more robust security arrangements for absent
  voting, such as new offences concerning the
  abuse of postal voting; and
- measures promoting equal access to elections,
  such as providing statutory forms in a variety of
  languages and formats.

These proposals are being considered by the
Department for Constitutional Affairs.

Parliament

Origins

Medieval kings had to meet all royal expenses,
private and public, out of their own income. If
extra resources were needed for an emergency,
such as going to war, the Sovereign would seek
help from his barons in the Great Council – a
gathering of leading men which met several times
a year. During the 13th century several English
kings found their own private revenue, together
with aid from the barons, insufficient to meet the
expenses of government. They therefore called not
only their land-owning barons to the Great
Council but also representatives of counties, cities
and towns, mainly to get them to agree to
additional taxation. In this way the Great Council
came to include those who were summoned *by
name* (who, broadly speaking, were later to form
the House of Lords) and those who were
representatives of communities – the Commons.
These two groups, together with the Sovereign,
became known as 'Parliament' – a term meaning a
meeting for *parley* or discussion.

Originally the King's legislation needed only the
agreement of his councillors, but, starting with the
right of individuals to present petitions, the
Commons was eventually allowed to appeal to the
Crown on behalf of groups of people.

During the 15th century they won the right to
take part in the process of giving their requests –
or 'Bills' – the form of law. In 1707 the English
and Scottish Parliaments passed laws creating a
single Parliament for Great Britain with ultimate
authority over England, Wales and Scotland.

Powers

There are three parts of Parliament – the elected
House of Commons, the appointed House of
Lords and the Sovereign. They meet together only
on occasions of symbolic significance such as the
State Opening of Parliament, when the Commons
is summoned by the Sovereign to the House of
Lords. The agreement of all three is normally
needed to pass laws, but that of the Sovereign is
given as a matter of course.

Parliament at Westminster can legislate for the
United Kingdom as a whole and has powers to
legislate for any parts of it separately. However, by
convention it will not normally legislate on
devolved matters in Scotland or Northern Ireland
without the agreement of the Scottish Parliament
or, when it is sitting, the Northern Ireland
Assembly. Under the Acts of Parliament which set
up these administrations, the Westminster
Parliament still has UK-wide responsibility in a
number of areas, including defence, foreign affairs,
economic and monetary policy, social security,
employment, and equal opportunities.

As there are no legal restraints imposed by a
written constitution, Parliament may legislate as it
pleases, as long as the United Kingdom meets its
obligations as a member of the European Union

(see page 60). It can make or change law, and overturn established conventions or turn them into law. It can even legislate to prolong its own life beyond the normal period without consulting the electorate.

In practice, however, Parliament does not assert itself in this way. Its members work within the common law and normally act according to precedent. The House of Commons is directly responsible to the electorate, and, during the 20th century, the House of Lords increasingly recognised the supremacy of the elected chamber.

Functions

The main functions of Parliament are:

- to pass laws;
- to provide (by voting for taxation) the means of carrying on the work of government;
- to scrutinise government policy and administration, including proposals for expenditure; and
- to debate the major issues of the day.

In performing these, Parliament helps to bring the relevant facts and issues to the attention of the electorate. By custom, Parliament is also informed before important international treaties and agreements are ratified. The making of treaties is, however, a royal prerogative carried out on the advice of the Government and does not need parliamentary approval.

Meetings

A Parliament has a maximum duration of five years, but not all Parliaments serve their full term. The maximum life has been prolonged by legislation only in rare circumstances, such as the two World Wars of the last century. The Sovereign dissolves Parliament and calls for a General Election on the advice of the Prime Minister.

The life of a Westminster Parliament is divided into sessions. Each usually lasts for one year – normally beginning and ending in October or November – although a session may be longer if there has been an election. There are 'adjournments' (when the House does not sit) at night, at weekends, at Christmas, Easter and the late Spring Bank Holiday. From 2003, as part of the new working hours for Parliament (see box on page 36), the traditional long summer break from late July to October has been modified, so that both Houses now rise earlier in July, but return for a period of two weeks in September before a

further break which coincides with the political party conferences.

At the start of each session the Sovereign's speech to Parliament outlines the Government's policies and proposed legislative programme. Each session is ended by the Sovereign dismissing it – called 'prorogation'. Parliament then 'stands prorogued' for a few days until the new session begins. Prorogation brings to an end nearly all parliamentary business.

House of Commons

The House of Commons consists of 659 elected MPs. In September 2003 there were 119 women MPs, and 12 MPs who had declared that they were of minority ethnic origin. Of the 659 seats, 529 represent constituencies in England, 40 in Wales, 72 in Scotland, and 18 in Northern Ireland.

After a Parliament has been dissolved, and a General Election has been held, the Sovereign summons a new Parliament. When an MP dies, resigns[2] or is made a member of the House of Lords, a by-election takes place.

Members are paid an annual salary of £56,358 (from April 2003) and provided with up to £74,985 for staff salaries and £18,799 for incidental expenses involved in running an office (excluding certain IT equipment which is provided centrally). For ministers' salaries see page 47. All MPs are entitled to travel allowances and to free stationery, inland telephone calls and postage from Parliament, and there are various other allowances, such as a supplementary allowance payable to MPs for Inner London and certain other seats to reflect the higher cost of living in the capital.

Officers of the House of Commons

The chief officer of the House of Commons is the Speaker (see page 38), an MP elected by other MPs to preside over the House. Other officers include the Chairman of Ways and Means and two deputy chairmen, who are also MPs and may act as Deputy Speakers. They are elected by the House as nominees of the Government, but may come from the Opposition as well as the Government party. The House of Commons Commission, a

---

2 By tradition, an MP who wishes to resign from the House can do so only by applying for office as Crown Steward or Bailiff of the Chiltern Hundreds, or Steward of the Manor of Northstead. These positions disqualify the holder from membership of the House of Commons.

Modernisation of the House of Commons

Various changes have been made to modernise the working practices and procedures of the House of Commons in recent years, including:

- new working hours for Parliament,[3] with earlier sitting days on Tuesdays, Wednesdays and Thursdays and fewer Friday sessions. These will apply for an experimental period until the end of the current Parliament. The new hours are designed to make it easier for MPs with families and those with provincial constituencies;
- the introduction of September sittings of the House of Commons;
- the announcement of the parliamentary calendar a year in advance, so that MPs can plan the time they spend in their constituencies;
- the introduction of a new debating chamber – Westminster Hall;
- a new system for nominating MPs to select committees (see page 38);
- more opportunities to call ministers to account and to debate reports by select committees;
- consultation with Opposition parties on the shape of the legislative programme;
- an extension of the examination of European legislation by Parliament; and
- new arrangements to allow Bills to be carried over from one session to the next.

statutory body chaired by the Speaker, is responsible for the administration of the House.

Permanent officers (who are not MPs) include the Clerk of the House of Commons – the principal adviser to the Speaker on the House's privileges and procedures. The Clerk's other responsibilities relate to the conduct of the business of the House and its committees. The Clerk is also accounting officer for the House. The Serjeant at Arms, who waits upon the Speaker, carries out certain orders of the House. He is also the official housekeeper of the Commons' part of the Palace of Westminster and is responsible for security.

House of Lords

Composition

The House of Lords consists of:

- hereditary peers;

Table 6.2 Composition of the House of Lords at July 2003

	Hereditary	Life	Bishops	Total
Conservative	50	161	.	211
Labour	4	183	.	187
Liberal Democrat	5	60	.	65
Crossbench[1]	33	147	.	180
Archbishops and bishops	.	.	24	24
Other[2]	.	7		7
Total members[3]	**92**	**558**	**24**	**674**

1 Includes Law Lords.
2 Comprises 1 Green, 1 Independent Conservative, 1 Independent Labour, 1 Independent Socialist and 3 non-affiliated members.
3 Excludes 13 peers on leave of absence. Two bishops have retired and their successors in the House of Lords have not yet taken their seats.
Source: House of Lords

- life peers created to help carry out the judicial duties of the House (up to 12 Lords of Appeal in Ordinary or 'Law Lords' and a number of other Lords of Appeal);[4]
- all other life peers; and
- the Archbishops of Canterbury and York, the Bishops of London, Durham and Winchester, and the 21 next most senior bishops of the Church of England.

The Government wants the House of Lords to be more representative of UK society. Under the *House of Lords Act 1999*, the number of hereditary peers was reduced from over 750 to 92. Another innovation was the appointment of non-political peers chosen from public nominees. In April 2001, 15 non-political life peers were selected from 3,166 applications.

The number of peers eligible to sit at 1 July 2003 is shown in Table 6.2, which also shows the representation of the main political parties. Crossbenchers, many of whom have specialist knowledge and expertise, do not vote with a political party. There were 113 women peers in July 2003.

Members of the House of Lords receive no salary for their parliamentary work, but they can claim for expenses incurred in attending the House (for

---

3 In the Commons the sitting hours since January 2003 have been Mondays 2.30 pm to 10.30 pm, Tuesdays and Wednesdays 11.30 am to 7.30 pm, Thursdays 11.30 am to 6.00 pm and Fridays (on certain days) 9.30 am to 3.00 pm.

4 The House of Lords is currently the final court of appeal for civil cases in the United Kingdom and for criminal cases in England, Wales and Northern Ireland, but in June 2003 the Government announced its intention to create a new Supreme Court.

Further reform of the Lords

A White Paper, *The House of Lords – Completing the Reform*, was published in November 2001. A Joint Committee of the House of Commons and the House of Lords was set up in May 2002 to take the reform forward and it drew up a range of options. A series of votes was held in February 2003 on options, ranging from a wholly elected House of Lords to a wholly appointed House. The House of Commons voted against all the options proposed; the House of Lords also rejected the options for change, although it did vote in favour of an all-appointed House. In June 2003 the Government announced the constitutional changes outlined on page 32. The House of Lords subsequently appointed a select committee to consider establishing a Speakership independent of the executive, and in July 2003 the Government published a consultation paper on its proposal to replace the Law Lords with a Supreme Court.

In September 2003 the Government issued a consultation paper containing its proposals on the next stage of House of Lords reform. It is proposing to introduce a Bill which would:

- remove the remaining hereditary peers;
- establish a statutory independent Appointments Commission, which would determine the number and timing of appointments to be made to the House,[5] select independent Members and oversee party nominations (including vetting them on grounds of propriety);
- bring provisions on the disqualification of Members on the grounds of conviction for an offence into line with those in the House of Commons; and
- give life peers the option of renouncing their peerages.

which there are maximum daily rates) and for certain travelling expenses. Attendance in the House averages about 350 to 450 members a day.

Officers of the House of Lords

The Speaker in the Lords has limited powers compared with those of the Speaker of the House of Commons (see page 38) as the Lords themselves control the proceedings under the guidance of the Leader of the House, who leads the governing party in the House and is a member of the Cabinet.

As Clerk of the House of Lords, the Clerk of the Parliaments is responsible for the records of proceedings of the House of Lords and for the text of Acts of the UK Parliament. He is the accounting officer for the House, and is in charge of its administrative staff, known as the Parliament Office. The Gentleman Usher of the Black Rod, usually known simply as 'Black Rod', is responsible for security, accommodation and services in the House of Lords' part of the Palace of Westminster.

Parliamentary privilege

To ensure that Parliament can carry out its duties without hindrance, certain rights and immunities apply collectively to each House and its staff, and individually to each Member. These include freedom of speech; first call on the attendance of Members, which means that Members are free from arrest in civil actions and excused from serving on juries, or being forced to attend court as witnesses; and the right of access to the Crown, which is a collective privilege of the House. Further privileges include the rights of the House to control its own proceedings (so that it is able, for instance, to keep out 'strangers'[6] if it wishes); to decide upon legal disqualifications for membership and to declare a seat vacant on such grounds; and to punish for breach of its privileges and for contempt. Parliament has the right to punish anybody, inside or outside the House, who commits a breach of privilege – that is, offends against the rights of the House.

Parliamentary procedure

Parliamentary procedure is largely based on precedent and is set down by each House in a code of practice known as its 'Standing Orders'. The debating system is similar in both Houses. Every subject starts off as a proposal or 'motion' by a member. After debate, in which each member (except the person putting forward the motion) may speak only once, the motion may be withdrawn: if it is not, the Speaker or Chairman 'puts the question' whether to agree to the motion or not. The question may be decided without voting, or by a simple majority vote. The main difference between the two Houses is that in the House of Lords the Lord Chancellor, or the deputising Chairman, does not control procedure; instead such matters are decided by the general feeling of the House, which is sometimes interpreted by its Leader or a Government Whip.

---

5 Except for the archbishops and bishops, and up to five direct appointments as ministers per Parliament for the Prime Minister.

6 All those who are not members or officials of either House.

Lord Chancellor

The office of Lord Chancellor is older than any other in the United Kingdom except the Crown. In precedence the Lord Chancellor is the second subject outside the Royal Family, after the Archbishop of Canterbury. Early Lord Chancellors were clerics, but from 1672 all holders of the office have been lords. Famous figures to have held the post include St Thomas à Becket, Cardinal Wolsey and Sir Thomas More.

The Lord Chancellor participates in all three branches of government: as head of the judiciary; as a Cabinet minister, with ministerial responsibility for much of the administration of justice; and as Speaker of the House of Lords. As Speaker, the Lord Chancellor has traditionally presided over debates in the House of Lords from his seat on the woolsack.[7] The legislation that is planned to abolish the post will have the effect of separating these roles.

In the Commons the Speaker has full authority to enforce the rules of the House and must uphold procedure and protect minority rights. The Speaker may or may not allow a motion to end discussion so that a matter may be put to the vote, and has powers to stop irrelevant and repetitious contributions in debate. In cases of serious disorder the Speaker can adjourn or suspend the sitting. The Speaker may order MPs who have broken the rules of behaviour of the House to leave the Chamber, or may suspend them for a number of days.

The Speaker supervises voting in the Commons and announces the final result. If there is a tie, the Speaker gives a casting vote (usually to keep the situation as it is), without expressing an opinion on the merits of the question. Voting procedure in the House of Lords is broadly similar, except the Lord Chancellor can vote, but does not have a casting vote.

Public access to parliamentary proceedings

Proceedings of both Houses are normally public and are broadcast on television and radio, either live or, more usually, in recorded or edited form. Complete coverage is available on cable and satellite television and broadcasting of

parliamentary debates on the Internet began in January 2002.

Select committees

Select committees are appointed for a particular task, generally one of inquiry, investigation and scrutiny. They report their conclusions and recommendations to the House as a whole; in many cases they invite a response from the Government, which is also reported to the House. A select committee may be appointed for a Parliament, or for a session, or for as long as it takes to complete its task. Each committee is constituted on a basis that is in approximate proportion to party strength in the House.

In their examination of government policies, expenditure and administration, select committees may question ministers, civil servants, interested bodies and individuals. Through hearings and published reports, they bring before Parliament and the public an extensive amount of fact and informed opinion on many issues, and build up considerable expertise in their subjects of inquiry.

Fifteen committees have been set up by the House of Commons to examine aspects of public policy, expenditure and administration across the main government departments and their associated public bodies. The Foreign Affairs Select Committee, for example, 'shadows' the work of the Foreign & Commonwealth Office. There are also a number of other regular Commons select committees, including the Public Accounts Committee and 'domestic' select committees covering the internal workings of Parliament.

Both Houses have a select committee to keep them informed of EU developments, and to enable them to scrutinise and debate EU policies and proposals, while three Commons standing committees debate specific European legislative proposals.

In the House of Lords there are four major select committees – working in the same manner as House of Commons committees – on the European Communities, Science and Technology, Economic Affairs and the Constitution. There are also select committees on aspects of public and private legislation, and on the internal workings of the House, while ad hoc committees are appointed to examine issues outside the remit of the main committees. Most of the Lords' judicial work is conducted in the Appeal and Appellate Committee.

---

7 The woolsack is a seat in the form of a large cushion stuffed with wool, a tradition dating from the medieval period, when wool was the chief source of the country's wealth. Today the wool comes from several Commonwealth countries, to symbolise unity.

Examination of government policy

In addition to the scrutiny by select committees, both Houses offer a number of other opportunities for the Opposition and the Government's own backbenchers to examine policy. In the House of Commons, these include:

- *Question Time:* for 55 minutes on Monday, Tuesday, Wednesday and Thursday when the House is sitting, ministers answer MPs' questions. Prime Minister's Question Time takes place for half an hour every Wednesday. Parliamentary Questions are one means of finding out about the Government's intentions. They are also a way of raising complaints brought to MPs' notice by constituents. MPs may also put questions to ministers for written answer; the questions and answers are published in *Hansard*. There were nearly 80,000 oral or written questions in the 2001–02 session.
- *Adjournment debates:* MPs use motions for the adjournment of the House to raise constituency cases or matters of public concern. There is a half-hour adjournment period at the end of the business of the day, and opportunities for private Members adjournment debates in Westminster Hall on Tuesdays and Wednesdays.
- *Emergency debates:* an MP wishing to discuss a 'specific and important matter that should have urgent consideration' may, at the end of Question Time, ask for an adjournment of the House. On the very few occasions when this action is successful, the matter is debated for three hours in what is known as an emergency debate, usually on the following day.
- *Early day motions (EDMs):* backbench MPs may express their views on particular issues in this way. A number of EDMs are tabled each sitting day; they are very rarely debated but can be useful in measuring the amount of support for the topic by the number of MPs who add their signatures to the EDM.
- *Opposition days:* on 20 days in each session (sometimes divided into half-days) opposition parties choose the business to be discussed. Of these days, 17 are allocated to the Leader of the Opposition and three to the second largest opposition party.
- *Expenditure debates:* the details of proposed government expenditure are debated on three days in each session.
- *Procedural opportunities:* criticism of the Government may also occur during the

debate on the Queen's Speech at the beginning of each session, on motions of censure for which the Government provides time, and in debates on the Government's legislative and other proposals.

- *Motions of no confidence:* as a final act of parliamentary control, the House of Commons may force the Government to resign by passing a resolution of 'no confidence'. The Government must also resign if the House rejects a proposal which the Government considers so vital to its policy that it has declared it a 'matter of confidence' or if the House refuses to vote the money required for the public service.

Control of finances

The UK Parliament (and in particular the House of Commons) has the responsibility of overseeing revenue generation and public expenditure. It has to be sure that the sums granted on each area of spending are used only for the purposes intended. No payment out of the central government's public funds can be made, and no taxation or loans authorised, except by Act of Parliament. However, limited interim payments can be made from the Contingencies Fund.

Hansard

Hansard, the Official Report of each day's proceedings, celebrated its 200th anniversary in 2003. In previous centuries, publication of things said in the House of Commons was punishable as a breach of the privileges of the House. The reports are known as *Hansard* after the name of the family of printers and publishers who published parliamentary papers in the 19th century. *Hansard* is an edited verbatim report of proceedings providing a clear and independent record of all proceedings in which MPs' and Members of the Lords' words are reported, in accordance with terms of reference drawn up by a select committee in 1907 and reproduced in *Erskine May*, the authoritative source on parliamentary procedure. In both Houses of Parliament *Hansard* is published the following morning, both in hardcopy form and on the website (*www.hansard-westminster.co.uk*). As well as reporting on the proceedings on the floor of both Houses, each daily report includes the answers to Parliamentary Questions put down for a written reply.

The Finance Act is the most important piece of annual legislation. It authorises the raising of revenue and is based on the Chancellor of the Exchequer's Budget statement (see page 341). Scrutiny of public expenditure is carried out by House of Commons select committees.

The law-making process in the UK Parliament

Statute law consists of Acts of Parliament (primary legislation) and delegated or secondary legislation (see page 42) made by ministers under powers given to them by an Act. While the *interpretation* of the law is refined constantly in the courts (see chapter 14), *changes* to statute law can only be made by Parliament. Since devolution, the Scottish Parliament and, when it is sitting, the Northern Ireland Assembly can also make primary legislation on devolved matters – see pages 20 and 26. Draft laws take the form of parliamentary Bills.

Public Bills

Bills that change the general law and make up the major part of the parliamentary legislative process are called Public Bills. They can be introduced into either House, by a government minister or any MP or peer. Most Public Bills that become Acts of Parliament are introduced by a government minister and are known as 'Government Bills'. A Government Bill is generally accompanied by Explanatory Notes, which are designed to provide background information on the Bill and what it is seeking to achieve.

The main Bills forming the Government's legislative programme are announced in the Queen's Speech at the State Opening of Parliament, which usually takes place in November or shortly after a General Election. The Bills themselves are introduced into one or other of the Houses over the following weeks.

Before a Government Bill is drafted, there may be consultation with professional bodies, voluntary organisations and others with an interest, including pressure groups looking to promote specific causes. 'White Papers', which are government statements of policy, often contain proposals for changes in the law. These may be debated in Parliament before a Bill is introduced. As part of the process of modernising

parliamentary procedures (see page 36), more Bills are published in draft for pre-legislative scrutiny and most are considered in joint committees (with membership drawn from both Houses) before beginning their passage through Parliament. The aim is to allow an input from backbenchers and other interested parties at an early stage, helping to save time and reducing the number of amendments made during the legislative process. The Government may also publish consultation papers, sometimes called 'Green Papers', setting out proposals which are still taking shape and inviting comments from the public.

Other Bills

Bills introduced by other MPs or peers are known as 'Private Members' Bills. Early in each session backbench members of the Commons ballot for the chance to introduce a Bill on one of the Fridays when such Bills have precedence over government business, and the first 20 Members whose names are drawn win this privilege. There are also other opportunities for MPs to present a Bill, while peers may introduce Private Members' Bills in the House of Lords at any time. However, these Bills rarely become law – eight were enacted in the 2001–02 session.

Private Bills are promoted by people or organisations outside Parliament (often local authorities) to give them special legal powers. They go through a similar process to Public Bills, but most of the work is done in committee, where procedures follow a semi-judicial pattern.

Passage of Government Bills

Public Bills must normally be passed by both Houses (see Figure 6.3 on page 41). Bills relating mainly to taxation or expenditure are almost always introduced in the Commons.

Committees of the Whole House

Either House may vote to turn itself into a 'Committee of the Whole House' in order to consider Bills in detail after their second reading. This allows unrestricted discussion: the general rule that an MP or peer may speak only once on each motion does not apply in committee.

Standing committees

House of Commons standing committees debate and consider Public Bills at the committee stage. The committee examines a Bill clause by clause, and may amend it before reporting back to the

Figure 6.3 How legislation is made in the UK

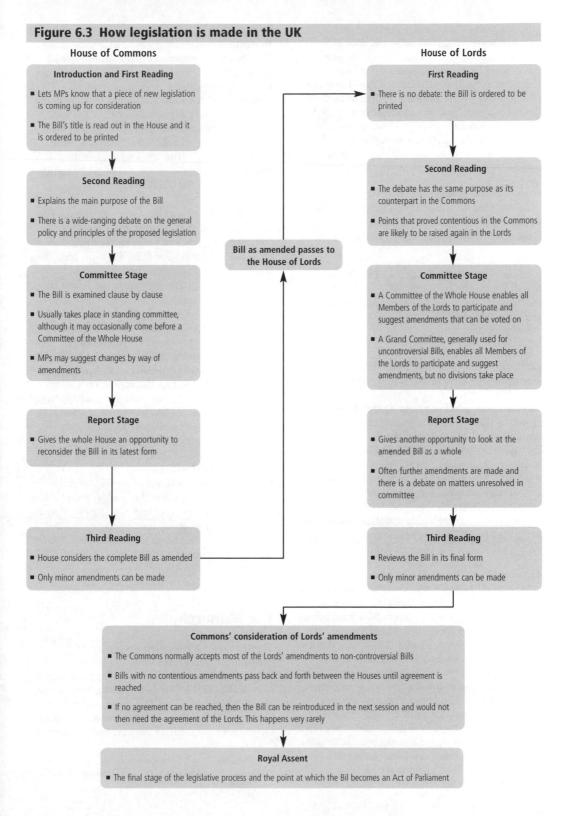

House of Commons

Introduction and First Reading
- Lets MPs know that a piece of new legislation is coming up for consideration
- The Bill's title is read out in the House and it is ordered to be printed

Second Reading
- Explains the main purpose of the Bill
- There is a wide-ranging debate on the general policy and principles of the proposed legislation

Committee Stage
- The Bill is examined clause by clause
- Usually takes place in standing committee, although it may occasionally come before a Committee of the Whole House
- MPs may suggest changes by way of amendments

Report Stage
- Gives the whole House an opportunity to reconsider the Bill in its latest form

Third Reading
- House considers the complete Bill as amended
- Only minor amendments can be made

Bill as amended passes to the House of Lords

House of Lords

First Reading
- There is no debate: the Bill is ordered to be printed

Second Reading
- The debate has the same purpose as its counterpart in the Commons
- Points that proved contentious in the Commons are likely to be raised again in the Lords

Committee Stage
- A Committee of the Whole House enables all Members of the Lords to participate and suggest amendments that can be voted on
- A Grand Committee, generally used for uncontroversial Bills, enables all Members of the Lords to participate and suggest amendments, but no divisions take place

Report Stage
- Gives another opportunity to look at the amended Bill as a whole
- Often further amendments are made and there is a debate on matters unresolved in committee

Third Reading
- Reviews the Bill in its final form
- Only minor amendments can be made

Commons' consideration of Lords' amendments
- The Commons normally accepts most of the Lords' amendments to non-controversial Bills
- Bills with no contentious amendments pass back and forth between the Houses until agreement is reached
- If no agreement can be reached, then the Bill can be reintroduced in the next session and would not then need the agreement of the Lords. This happens very rarely

Royal Assent
- The final stage of the legislative process and the point at which the Bill becomes an Act of Parliament

House. Ordinary standing committees do not have names but are designated by letters, such as Standing Committee A. Each committee generally has around 18 members, with a party balance reflecting as far as possible that in the House as a whole, but larger or more contentious Bills may have more members, up to a maximum of 50. In the Lords, various sorts of committees on Bills may be used (such as Grand Committees and select committees, see page 38) instead of, or as well as, a Committee of the Whole House.

In the Commons the House may vote to limit the time available for considering a Bill. This is done by passing a 'timetable' motion proposed by the Government, commonly known as a 'guillotine'.

When a Bill has passed through all its parliamentary stages, it is sent to The Queen for Royal Assent, after which it becomes an Act of Parliament. The Royal Assent has not been refused since 1707. In the 2001–02 session 47 Public Bills were enacted.

Limitations on the power of the Lords

The main legislative function of the House of Lords is to act as a revising chamber, complementing but not rivalling the elected House of Commons. As a result, there are some limitations on its powers. Under the provisions of the *Parliament Acts* of *1911* and *1949*, the powers of the Lords in relation to 'money Bills' are very restricted. Bills authorising taxation or national expenditure are passed without amendment as a formality. A Bill dealing only with taxation or expenditure must become law within a month of being sent to the Lords, whether or not the Lords agree to it, unless the Commons direct otherwise.

The *Parliament Acts* also make it possible for a Bill to be passed by the Commons without the consent of the Lords in certain, though rare, circumstances. The Lords do not usually prevent Bills from being enacted that the Commons are keen to pass, although they will often amend and return them for further consideration. If no agreement is reached between the two Houses on a non-financial Commons Bill, the Lords can delay the Bill for a period that, in practice, amounts to around a year. Following this, the Bill may be presented to The Queen for Royal Assent, provided the Commons has passed it in the current session and previous session. There is one important exception: any Bill to lengthen the life of a Parliament needs the full assent of both Houses.

Secondary legislation

To reduce unnecessary pressure on parliamentary time, primary legislation often gives ministers or other authorities the power to make detailed rules and regulations under an Act by means of secondary or 'delegated' legislation (usually in the form of 'statutory instruments' or 'SIs'). About 3,000 SIs are issued each year. Such powers are normally delegated only to authorities directly accountable to Parliament or to the devolved legislatures, to minimise the risk of undermining the authority of the UK Parliament.

Acts which allow for delegated legislation usually give Parliament the opportunity to agree ('affirmative procedure') or disagree ('negative procedure') with any resulting SIs, while some also require that organisations affected must be consulted before rules and orders can be made.

A joint committee of both Houses reports on the technical propriety of these SIs. To save time on the floor of the House, the Commons uses standing committees to debate the merits of instruments (unless they are simply laid before the House or subject to negative resolution); actual decisions are taken by the House as a whole. In the Lords, debates on SIs take place on the floor of the House. In contrast to primary legislation, the Lords have the power of veto on SIs.

Joint committees

Joint committees, with a membership drawn from both Houses, are appointed in each session to deal with Consolidation Bills[8] and SIs. The two Houses may also agree to set up joint select committees on other subjects, such as the Joint Committee on the Reform of the House of Lords (see page 37) and on Human Rights.

The Monarchy

The Monarchy is the oldest institution of government. The Queen's title in the United Kingdom is 'Elizabeth the Second, by the Grace of God of the United Kingdom of Great Britain and Northern Ireland and of Her other Realms and Territories Queen, Head of the Commonwealth, Defender of the Faith'. In the Channel Islands and

---

8 A Consolidation Bill brings together several existing Acts into one, with the aim of simplifying the statutes.

Figure 6.4 Principal members of the Royal Family from the reign of Queen Victoria to July 2003

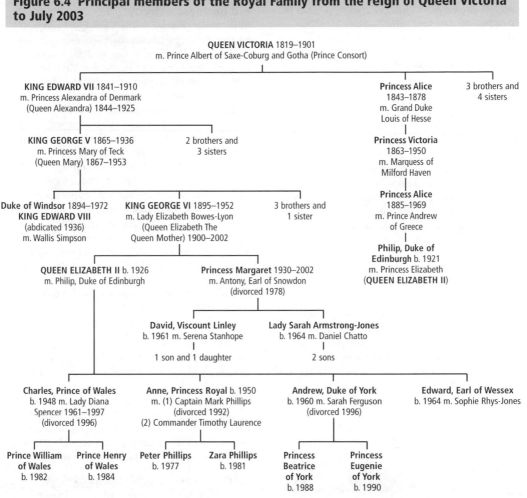

the Isle of Man, Her Majesty is represented by a Lieutenant-Governor.

In addition to being the Sovereign of the United Kingdom, The Queen is Head of State of 15 other realms[9] and Head of the Commonwealth (see page 64). In each country where she is Head of State, Her Majesty is represented by a Governor-General, appointed by her on the advice of the ministers of the country concerned and

independent of the UK Government. In the Overseas Territories (see page 69) The Queen is usually represented by a Governor who is a member of the Diplomatic Service (see page 51) responsible to the UK Government for the administration of the country in which they serve.

Succession

The title to the Crown derives partly from statute and partly from common law rules of descent. Despite interruptions in the direct line of succession, inheritance has always been how the Monarchy has passed down the generations, with sons of the Sovereign coming before daughters in

9 Antigua and Barbuda; Australia; the Bahamas; Barbados; Belize; Canada; Grenada; Jamaica; New Zealand; Papua New Guinea; St Kitts and Nevis; St Lucia; St Vincent and the Grenadines; Solomon Islands; and Tuvalu.

succeeding to the throne. When a daughter does succeed, she becomes Queen Regnant, and has the same powers as a King. The 'consort' of a King takes her husband's rank and style, becoming Queen. No special rank or privileges are given to the husband of a Queen Regnant.

Under the Act of Settlement of 1700, only Protestant descendants of Princess Sophia, the Electress of Hanover (a granddaughter of James I of England and VI of Scotland), are eligible to succeed. The first eight members of the Royal Family in order of succession to the Throne are: The Prince of Wales, Prince William of Wales, Prince Henry of Wales, The Duke of York, Princess Beatrice of York, Princess Eugenie of York, The Earl of Wessex, and the Princess Royal. The order of succession to the throne can be altered only by common consent of the countries of the Commonwealth of which the Monarch is Sovereign.

The Sovereign succeeds to the throne as soon as his or her predecessor dies: there is no interval without a ruler. He or she is at once proclaimed at an Accession Council, to which all members of the Privy Council (see page 45) are called. Members of the House of Lords, the Lord Mayor, Aldermen and other leading citizens of the City of London are also invited.

The Coronation

The Coronation follows the accession. The ceremony has remained essentially the same for over 1,000 years, although details have changed to match the customs of the time. It takes place at Westminster Abbey in London in the presence of representatives of both Houses of Parliament and all the major public organisations in the United Kingdom. The Prime Ministers and leading members of the Commonwealth nations and representatives of other countries also attend.

The 50th anniversary of the Coronation of Queen Elizabeth II was celebrated on 2 June 2003. The central feature was a service at Westminster Abbey, which was attended by The Queen, other senior members of the Royal Family and over 2,000 guests, including more than 200 people who had attended the 1953 ceremony and 34 people who were born on the day of the Coronation.

Royal income, expenditure and business activity

Public funds (known as the 'Civil List') and government departments together meet the costs of The Queen's official duties. In 2000 a Royal Trustees' Report recommended that Civil List payments should remain at the 1991 level of £7.9 million a year for a further ten years from 2001. About 70 per cent of The Queen's Civil List provision is needed to meet the cost of staff. Under the Civil List, the Duke of Edinburgh receives an annual parliamentary allowance of £359,000 to enable him to carry out his public duties. Parliamentary annuities paid to other members of the Royal Family to carry out royal duties are reimbursed by The Queen. In return for the Civil List and other financial support, The Queen surrenders the income from the Crown Estate (£170.8 million in 2002/03) and other hereditary revenues to the nation. The Prince of Wales does not receive a parliamentary allowance since he is entitled to the annual net revenues of the Duchy of Cornwall.

In June 2002 an annual report of Civil List expenditure was published for the first time as part of the Royal Household's commitment to openness and accountability in its use of public money. According to the latest report, issued in June 2003, The Queen's total expenditure as Head of State in 2002/03 was £36.2 million, of which £16.6 million was spent on the upkeep of the royal palaces, £4.2 million on royal travel, and £526,000 on communications and information services.

The Queen's private expenditure as Sovereign comes from the Privy Purse, which is financed mainly from the revenues of the Duchy of Lancaster;[10] her expenditure as a private individual is met from her own personal resources. Since 1993 The Queen has paid income tax on all personal and Privy Purse income. She also pays tax on any realised capital gains on private investments and on assets in the Privy Purse. The Prince of Wales also pays tax on the income from the Duchy of Cornwall so far as it is used for private purposes.

There are guidelines setting out how members of the Royal Family can pursue careers. These are subject to regular review.

---

10 The Duchy of Lancaster is a landed estate that has been held in trust for the Sovereign since 1399. It is kept quite apart from his or her other possessions and is separately administered by the Chancellor of the Duchy of Lancaster.

The Monarch's role in government

As a result of a long process of change during which the Monarchy's absolute power has been gradually reduced, custom now dictates that The Queen usually follows ministerial advice. Within this framework she performs a range of important duties, such as summoning and dissolving Parliament; and giving Royal Assent to legislation passed by the UK or Scottish Parliament or by the Northern Ireland Assembly. She formally appoints important office holders, including the Prime Minister and other government ministers (see below), judges, officers in the armed forces, governors, diplomats, bishops and some other senior clergy of the Church of England. The Queen also confers peerages, knighthoods and other honours.[11] In international affairs, as Head of State, she has the power to declare war and make peace, to recognise foreign states and conclude treaties.

The Queen holds Privy Council meetings, gives audiences to her ministers and officials in the United Kingdom and overseas, receives accounts of Cabinet decisions, reads dispatches and signs State papers. She is consulted on many aspects of national life, and must show complete impartiality.

The Privy Council

The Privy Council was formerly the chief source of executive power in the State, but as the system of Cabinet government developed in the 18th century, the Cabinet took on much of its role. Today the Privy Council is the main way in which ministers advise The Queen on the approval of Orders in Council (such as those granting Royal Charters or enacting subordinate legislation) or on the issue of royal proclamations (such as the summoning or dissolving of Parliament).

In August 2003 there were 516 Privy Counsellors, whose appointments are for life. The Privy Council consists of all members of the Cabinet, other senior politicians, judges and individuals from the Commonwealth; only members of the Government participate in its policy work. The Prime Minister recommends membership of the Privy Council to the Sovereign.

Privy Council Office

The secretariat of the Privy Council is the Privy Council Office. This is headed at ministerial level by the Lord President of the Council, a post that is usually combined with another senior post, currently that of Leader of the House of Lords. Much of the work of the Privy Council Office is concerned with the affairs of around 400 institutions, charities and companies incorporated by Royal Charter, together with responsibilities in connection with higher education and with some statutory regulatory bodies for the professions.

Committees of the Privy Council

Privy Council committees (of which the Cabinet is technically one), are normally made up of ministers with the relevant policy interest, such as those dealing with legislation from the Channel Islands and the Isle of Man.

The Judicial Committee, whose members have held high judicial office, is the final court of appeal from courts in UK Overseas Territories, those Commonwealth countries that have retained this method of appeal after independence, and the Channel Islands and the Isle of Man. The Committee also considers devolution issues concerning the powers and functions of the executive and legislative authorities in Scotland, Wales and Northern Ireland, and deals with appeals from medical and veterinary disciplinary bodies and certain ecclesiastical appeals.

Her Majesty's Government

The Government consists of ministers responsible for the conduct of national affairs. After a General Election, The Queen appoints the leader of the party that won the most seats in the House of Commons as Prime Minister. She appoints all other ministers on the Prime Minister's recommendation. About 100 members of the governing party receive ministerial appointments, including up to 20 who are appointed to the Cabinet (see page 48). Most ministers are Members of the Commons; the remainder sit in the Lords.

The composition of governments can vary both in the number of ministers and in the titles of some offices. New ministerial offices may be created, others may be abolished, and functions may be transferred from one minister to another.

---

11 Although most honours are conferred by The Queen on the advice of the Prime Minister, a few are granted by her personally – the Order of the Garter, the Order of the Thistle, the Order of Merit and the Royal Victorian Order.

Prime Minister

The Prime Minister is also, by tradition, First Lord of the Treasury and Minister for the Civil Service. The Prime Minister's unique position of authority comes from majority support in the House of Commons and from the power to appoint and dismiss ministers. By modern convention, the Prime Minister always sits in the Commons.

The Prime Minister presides over the Cabinet (see page 48), is responsible for allocating functions among ministers and has regular meetings with The Queen to inform her of the general business of the Government. The Prime Minister represents the United Kingdom at major international events, such as the annual meeting of the Group of Eight leading industrialised countries (see page 64).

The Prime Minister's other responsibilities include recommending a number of appointments to The Queen. These include: Church of England archbishops, bishops, certain deans and some 200 other clergy in Crown 'livings'; senior judges, such as the Lord Chief Justice; members of the Privy Council; and Lords Lieutenant. The Prime Minister also recommends certain civil appointments, including the Poet Laureate, some university posts, and appointments to several public boards and institutions and various royal and statutory commissions.

The Prime Minister's Office, No 10 (so called after the Prime Minister's official residence at 10 Downing Street) supports him in his role as head of government. It works with the Cabinet Office to provide central direction for the development, implementation and presentation of government policy. No 10 is staffed by a mixture of civil servants and special advisers (see page 50) and is headed by a chief of staff. There are a number of units within No 10, including:

- the Policy Directorate, which provides advice to the Prime Minister on domestic and economic policy issues;
- the Parliamentary Section, which handles all parliamentary affairs for the Prime Minister;
- the European and Foreign Policy Advisers' Office;
- the Events and Visits Office, which manages all visits between the Prime Minister and overseas Heads of Government;
- the Strategic Communications Unit (which devises and coordinates the Prime Minister's communications strategy), the Press Office

and the Corporate Communications Division, responsible for all forms of communications directly to and from the public, including the No 10 website (*www.pm.gov.uk*); and
- the Honours and Appointments Section.

Following the General Election in June 2001, several new units were set up within the Cabinet Office to assist the Prime Minister. These include:
- the Prime Minister's Delivery Unit. This was established to monitor progress and strengthen the Government's capacity to deliver its key priorities;
- the Strategy Unit, which carries out strategic reviews and policy analysis; and
- the Office of Public Services Reform, which is working with departments on ensuring the needs of customers are taken into account and that the principles of public service reform (see page 56) are incorporated into policy making and service delivery.

Deputy Prime Minister

The Deputy Prime Minister is First Secretary of State, deputising for the Prime Minister in his responsibilities in the United Kingdom and abroad and chairing a number of Cabinet committees and sub-committees. In 2002 the Office of the Deputy Prime Minister (ODPM) was separated from the Cabinet Office (see page 48) and established as a central government department in its own right. Its responsibilities now include regional policy; local government (including finance); planning; housing and homelessness; urban policy; and the Fire Service.

The ODPM works with other departments to reduce social exclusion and to promote neighbourhood renewal and regional prosperity through, respectively, the Social Exclusion Unit, the Neighbourhood Renewal Unit and the Regional Coordination Unit (including the Government Offices for the Regions, see page 10). A Sustainable Communities Delivery Unit has been set up to help implement the Sustainable Communities Action Plan (see page 290).

Departmental ministers

Ministers in charge of government departments are usually in the Cabinet; they are known as 'Secretary of State' or may have a traditional title, as in the case of the Chancellor of the Exchequer.

Non-departmental ministers

The holders of various traditional offices, namely the President of the Council, the Chancellor of the Duchy of Lancaster, the Lord Privy Seal, the Paymaster General and, from time to time, Ministers without Portfolio, may have few or no departmental duties. They are therefore available to carry out any duties the Prime Minister may wish to give them. In the present administration, for example, the Chancellor of the Duchy of Lancaster is the Minister of State in the Cabinet Office.

Lord Chancellor and law officers

The post of Lord Chancellor (see page 38) will be formally abolished when the major constitutional changes announced in June 2003 are implemented. The Attorney General, assisted by the Solicitor General, is the chief legal adviser to the Government. The Attorney General has overall responsibility for the Treasury Solicitor's Department, superintends the Director of Public Prosecutions as head of the Crown Prosecution Service, the Director of the Serious Fraud Office and the Director of Public Prosecutions in Northern Ireland. The Lord Advocate and the Solicitor General for Scotland are the principal ministerial advisers to the Scottish Executive on legal matters (see page 204).

Other ministers

Ministers of state are middle-ranking ministers. They normally have specific responsibilities, and are sometimes given titles which reflect these functions, for example, 'Minister for Lifelong Learning, Further and Higher Education'.

The most junior ministers are parliamentary under-secretaries of state (or, where the senior minister is not a secretary of state, simply parliamentary secretaries). They may be given responsibility under the departmental minister for specific aspects of the department's work.

Ministerial salaries

The salaries of ministers in the House of Commons (from April 2003) start at £84,483 a year for a parliamentary under-secretary, rising to £93,413 for a minister of state and to £127,791 for a Cabinet minister (inclusive of the parliamentary salary, see page 35). The Prime Minister receives an annual salary of £175,414. The Leader of the Opposition in the Commons receives a salary of £121,840 (inclusive of his parliamentary salary).

Department for Constitutional Affairs

As part of a series of major constitutional changes (see page 32), the Department for Constitutional Affairs (DCA) (*www.dca.gov.uk*) was set up in June 2003 under the Lord Chancellor, who has also taken on the new title of Secretary of State for Constitutional Affairs. It has taken over most of the functions previously exercised by the Lord Chancellor's Department. In addition, while they each retain their own Secretary of State, the Scotland Office and the Wales Office are now located within the DCA as the Government considers that there is no longer a need for separate freestanding departments for Scotland and Wales following devolution.

Ministerial salaries in the House of Lords (as at April 2003) range from £65,936 for a parliamentary under-secretary to £75,706 for a minister of state and to £96,960 for a Cabinet minister.

Three Opposition whips in the Commons and the Opposition Leader and Chief Whip in the Lords also receive additional salaries.

Ministerial responsibility

Ministerial responsibility refers both to the collective responsibility for government policy and actions which ministers share, and to ministers' individual responsibility for the work of their own departments.

Collective responsibility means that all ministers unanimously support government policy once it has been settled. The policy of departmental ministers must agree with the policy of the Government as a whole. Once the Government has decided its policy on a particular matter, each minister is expected to support it or resign. On rare occasions, ministers are allowed free votes in Parliament on important issues of principle or conscience.

Ministers are individually accountable for the work of their departments and agencies, and have a duty to Parliament to answer for their policies, decisions and actions.

Departmental ministers normally decide all matters within their responsibility. However, many issues cut across departmental boundaries and need the agreement of more than one minister.

The full Cabinet or a Cabinet committee considers proposals where the issue raises major policy concerns, is likely to lead to significant public comment or criticism, or where the departmental ministers concerned have been unable to agree.

On taking up office ministers resign directorships in private and public companies, and must ensure that there is no conflict between their public duties and private interests. Detailed guidance on handling ministers' financial interests is set out in the Ministerial Code.

The Cabinet

The Prime Minister may appoint up to 20 ministers to sit in the Cabinet; these may include both departmental and non-departmental ministers. The Cabinet balances ministers' individual duties with their collective responsibility as members of the Government and takes the final decisions on all government policy.

Cabinet meetings

The Cabinet meets in private and its business is confidential, although after 30 years Cabinet papers usually become available for inspection in the National Archives at Kew, Surrey. Normally the Cabinet meets weekly when Parliament is sitting, and less often when it is not.

Cabinet committees take some of the pressure off the full Cabinet by settling issues among smaller groups of people, or at least by clarifying the issues and defining points of disagreement. Cabinet committees include those dealing with defence and overseas policy, economic policy, home and social affairs, the environment, and local government. The membership and terms of reference of all ministerial Cabinet committees are published. Where appropriate, the Secretary of the Cabinet and other senior Cabinet Office officials attend meetings.

The Cabinet Office

The Cabinet Office supports the Government in delivering its priorities, including providing high-quality public services and coordinating matters of national security. The department has five key objectives:

- to support the Prime Minister in leading the Government;
- to support the Government in transacting its business;
- to help deliver key public service priorities;

- to lead the reform programme for public services; and
- to coordinate security, intelligence and civil contingencies matters.

The Cabinet Secretary is a senior civil servant who reports directly to the Prime Minister and is also the Head of the Home Civil Service.

The party political system

The party system, which has existed in one form or another since the 18th century, depends upon there being organised political groups, each of which presents its policies to the electorate for approval. In practice, most candidates in elections, and almost all winning candidates, belong to one of the main parties. A system of voluntary registration for political parties in the United Kingdom was introduced in 1998.

The origins of the Conservative Party go back to the 18th century, while the Labour Party emerged in the last decade of the 19th century. The Liberal Democrats were formed in 1988 when the Liberal Party, which also traced its origins to the 18th century, merged with the Social Democratic Party, formed in 1981. Other parties include two nationalist parties: Plaid Cymru – The Party of Wales (founded in 1925) and the Scottish National Party (founded in 1934). Northern Ireland has a number of parties. They include the Ulster Unionists, formed in the early part of the 20th century; the Democratic Unionists, founded in 1971 by a group which broke away from the Ulster Unionists; the Social Democratic and Labour Party, founded in 1970; and Sinn Féin, which is the political wing of the IRA.

Since 1945 the traditional two-party system of government in the UK Parliament has been maintained, with power being held by either the Conservative Party or the Labour Party, each having won eight General Elections. However, the 52 seats won by the Liberal Democrats in the 2001 General Election (see Table 6.1 on page 33) represented the highest number of seats won by a third party since before the Second World War.

The party which wins most seats (although not necessarily the most votes) at a General Election, or which has the support of a majority of members in the House of Commons, usually becomes the Government. By tradition, the Sovereign invites the leader of that party to form a government. The largest minority party becomes the official Opposition, with its own leader and 'shadow cabinet'.

The party system in Parliament

Leaders of the Government and Opposition sit opposite one another on the front benches in the debating chamber of the House of Commons, with their supporters ('the backbenchers') sitting behind them. Benches to the right of the Speaker are used by the Government and its supporters; those to the left are occupied by the Opposition and members of the other parties. There are similar seating arrangements for the parties in the House of Lords, but many peers do not wish to be associated with any political party, and therefore choose to sit on the 'crossbenches'.

The effectiveness of the party system in Parliament relies to a large extent on the relationship between the Government and the Opposition parties. Depending on the relative strengths of the parties in the House of Commons, the Opposition may try to overthrow the Government by defeating it on a 'matter of confidence' vote. In general, however, the Opposition aims to contribute to the formulation of policy and legislation by constructive criticism; to oppose government proposals with which it disagrees; to table amendments to Government Bills; and to put forward its own policies in order to improve its chances of winning the next General Election.

The Government Chief Whips in the Commons and the Lords, in consultation with their Opposition counterparts, arrange the scheduling of government business; they do so under the direction of the Prime Minister and the Leaders of the two Houses. Collectively, the Chief Whips and Leaders of the political parties or groups are often referred to as 'the usual channels' when the question of finding time for a particular item of business is being discussed.

The Chief Whips and their assistants, who are usually chosen by the party leaders, manage their parliamentary parties. Their duties include keeping members informed of forthcoming parliamentary business, maintaining the party's voting strength by ensuring members attend important debates, and passing on to the party leadership the opinions of backbench members.

The term 'whip' also applies to the weekly circular sent out by each Chief Whip to all their MPs or peers notifying them of parliamentary business. The degree of importance is indicated by the number of times that the debate or division is underlined. Items underlined once are routine and attendance is optional. Those underlined twice are more important and attendance is required unless – in the Commons – a 'pair' (a member of the Opposition who also intends to be absent from the division) has been arranged. Items underlined three times are highly important, attendance is required, and pairing is not normally allowed. 'Three-line whips' are imposed on important occasions, such as second readings of significant Bills and motions of no confidence.

Financial controls over parties

The *Political Parties, Elections and Referendums Act 2000* contained provisions to make party funding more open, by restricting the sources of political donations, controlling spending on elections and regulating the finances of organisations campaigning at referendums. Among the provisions of the Act, political parties may only accept donations of over £200 from 'permissible donors' – individuals on the UK electoral register and organisations (such as companies, trade unions and political parties) that are registered and do business in the United Kingdom. All donations of over £5,000 to a political party's central organisation must be reported to the Electoral Commission (see page 33) on a quarterly basis, and on a weekly basis during a General Election campaign. Similar controls on donations apply to other organisations and individuals campaigning at elections and referendums.

In addition, donations of over £1,000 to constituency associations or to individual MPs, members of the devolved administrations and members of local authorities must be reported to the Electoral Commission. There is a cap on campaign spending by political parties during General Elections; a party must not spend more than £30,000 for each constituency contested. Third parties campaigning at elections (such as trade unions) are also subject to expenditure limits set at 5 per cent of the maximum for political parties. There are separate rules for expenditure on referendum campaigns.

Government departments

The main role of government departments and their agencies (see page 51) is to implement government policy and advise ministers. They are staffed by politically impartial civil servants and generally receive their funding from Parliament. They often work alongside local authorities, non-departmental public bodies, and other government-sponsored organisations. The structure and functions of departments are sometimes reorganised if there are major changes in government policy.

Most departments are headed by secretaries of state, supported by ministers. However, some are non-ministerial departments headed by a permanent office holder and secretaries of state with other duties are accountable for them to Parliament. For example, the Secretary of State for Education and Skills accounts to Parliament for the work of the Office for Standards in Education (Ofsted). Ofsted is headed by HM Chief Inspector of Schools in England, who is largely independent of the Secretary of State.

The functions and geographic remit of the main government departments and agencies are set out in appendix A, pages 476–91.

Non-departmental public bodies

A non-departmental public body (NDPB, sometimes known as a 'quango') is a national or regional public body, working independently of ministers to whom it is accountable. There are two main types of NDPB:

- *Executive NDPBs* are those with executive, administrative, commercial or regulatory functions. They carry out set functions within a government framework but the degree of operational independence varies. Examples include the Audit Commission, the Disability Rights Commission and English Partnerships.
- *Advisory NDPBs* are those set up by ministers to advise them and their departments on particular matters. Examples include the Committee on Standards in Public Life and the Scientific Advisory Committee on Nutrition. Some Royal Commissions are also classified as advisory NDPBs.

Over 800 NDPBs are sponsored by the Government. A list is issued annually in the Cabinet Office publication *Public Bodies*, which is also available electronically via the Cabinet Office website.

The Civil Service

The constitutional and practical role of the Civil Service in England, Scotland and Wales is to help the Government of the United Kingdom, the Scottish Executive and the National Assembly for Wales formulate their policies, carry out decisions and administer public services for which they are responsible. A separate Northern Ireland Civil Service serves the local administration (see page 51).

Civil servants are servants of the Crown; in effect this means the Government of the United Kingdom and the devolved administrations. Ministers of the Crown, who are in turn answerable to the appropriate Parliament or Assembly, generally exercise executive powers. The Civil Service as such has no separate constitutional personality or responsibility. The duty of the individual civil servant is first and foremost to the minister in charge of the department in which he or she is serving. A change of minister, for whatever reason, does not involve a change of staff.

With the exception of the Prime Minister, Cabinet ministers in the UK Government may each appoint up to two special advisers. The Prime Minister may also authorise the appointment of one or two special advisers by ministers who regularly attend Cabinet. The Prime Minister approves all appointments and they are paid for from public funds. In September 2003 there were 75 special advisers in post. Their appointments end when the Government's term of office finishes, or when the appointing minister leaves the Government or moves to another appointment.

Civil servants

The number of permanent civil servants (on a full-time equivalent basis), including those in the Diplomatic Service (see page 51), fell from 751,000 in 1976 to 499,600 in October 2002. However, in the year to October 2002 the number of permanent staff rose by 4.1 per cent. In October 2002 there were around 4,150 staff at Senior Civil Service Level (on a headcount basis). Part-time working has increased over recent years, with 15.4 per cent of all civil servants working part time in October 2002, compared with 14.4 per cent in October 2001.

In April 2002 about half of all civil servants (full-time equivalent) provided services direct to the public. These included paying benefits and pensions, running employment services, staffing prisons, issuing driving licences, and providing services to industry and agriculture. The rest were divided between central administrative and policy duties; support services; and services that were largely financially self-supporting. Some 80 per cent of civil servants (full-time equivalent) worked outside London.

Equality and diversity

The Civil Service aims to create a culture in which the different skills, experience and expertise that individuals bring are valued and used. It follows the Government's equal opportunities policy, which states that there must be no unfair discrimination on the basis of age, disability, gender, marital status, sexual orientation, race, colour, nationality, ethnic or national origin or (in Northern Ireland) community background. In October 2002, on a headcount basis, some 52.0 per cent of civil servants were female; minority ethnic representation was 7.9 per cent; and about 3.6 per cent of staff employed were known to have a disability.

One of the Cabinet Office's targets is to ensure that the Civil Service becomes more open and diverse. In particular, there are targets by 2004/05 for 35 per cent of the Senior Civil Service (SCS) to be women, 25 per cent of the top 600 posts to be filled by women, 3.2 per cent of the SCS to be from minority ethnic backgrounds and 3 per cent of the SCS to be disabled people. In October 2002, around 25.8 per cent of the SCS were women, 23.1 per cent of those in the top management posts were women (including four at Permanent Secretary level), 2.8 per cent of the SCS were from minority ethnic backgrounds and 1.7 per cent were disabled.

Civil Service Commissioners

The Civil Service Commissioners, who are independent of government, are responsible for ensuring that recruitment to the Civil Service is made on merit on the basis of fair and open competition. The Commissioners produce a recruitment code, audit the recruitment policies and practices of departments and agencies to ensure that they comply, and approve appointments through external recruitment to the most senior levels of the Civil Service. They also hear appeals under the Civil Service Code, which sets out the constitutional framework within which all civil servants work and the values they are expected to uphold.

Central management

As Minister for the Civil Service, the Prime Minister is responsible for central coordination and management of the Civil Service. He is supported by the Head of the Home Civil Service (whose function is combined with that of the Cabinet Secretary – see page 48), who is responsible for leading the programme of Civil Service reform and for the most senior appointments in the Civil Service. The Cabinet Office oversees the central framework for management of the Civil Service. Day-to-day responsibility for a wide range of terms and conditions has been delegated to departments and agencies, and to the devolved administrations in Scotland and Wales.

Executive agencies

In October 2002 there were 87 executive agencies in Great Britain, employing 270,200 staff (full-time equivalents), 54 per cent of civil servants. Executive agencies were introduced to deliver government services more efficiently and effectively within available resources. They are part of the Civil Service but, under the terms of individual framework documents and subject to overall budgets agreed with their parent department and/or the Treasury, they have delegated authority to employ their own staff and organise service provision in ways best suited to meet customer needs. Agencies are headed by chief executives who are personally responsible for day-to-day operations. They are normally directly accountable to the responsible minister, who in turn is accountable to Parliament.

The Diplomatic Service

The Diplomatic Service, a separate service of some 3,550 people, provides staff for the Foreign & Commonwealth Office (FCO, see page 71) in London and at UK diplomatic missions abroad. Terms and conditions of service are comparable, but take into account the special demands of the Diplomatic Service, particularly the requirement to serve abroad. UK civil servants, members of the armed forces and individuals from the private sector may also serve in the FCO and at overseas posts on loan or attachment.

Northern Ireland

The Northern Ireland Civil Service (NICS) is modelled on its counterpart in Great Britain, and has its own Civil Service Commission. Its present role is to support the Northern Ireland Executive in the administration of public services for which it has responsibility. During the suspension of devolution (see page 26), the NICS reports to the Secretary of State for Northern Ireland. There were about 26,000 permanent non-industrial civil servants in the NICS at 31 March 2003. There is a degree of mobility between the NICS and the Civil Service in the rest of the United Kingdom.

Local government

Elections

Local authorities in Great Britain consist of over 22,000 elected councillors. The procedure for local government voting is broadly similar to that for elections to the UK Parliament, except that proportional representation is used in Northern Ireland.[12] Eligibility rules for voters are also similar to those for UK parliamentary elections, except that citizens of other Member States of the EU may vote. To stand for election, candidates must either be registered as an elector or have some other close connection within the electoral area of their candidature, such as their principal place of employment.

Whole council elections are held every four years in all county councils in England, borough councils in London, and about two-thirds of non-metropolitan district councils. In all other district councils (including the metropolitan districts) one-third of the councillors are elected in each of the three years when county council elections are not held. However, a few non-metropolitan district councils now hold biennial elections with half of the councillors elected every two years. Whole council elections are every fourth year in Scotland, Wales and Northern Ireland, although the council elections due in 2003 in Wales were postponed in order to avoid a clash with the elections for the National Assembly (see page 15).

Electronic and postal voting

In the May 2003 local elections, 61 local authorities in England carried out electoral pilots, involving 6.4 million electors, in the biggest test so far of new voting procedures. Voting was conducted electronically in 17 areas, via a range of channels, including interactive digital television, touch-tone telephone, mobile phone text messaging and the Internet. About 21 per cent of voters in e-voting pilot areas chose to use the new methods to cast

> ### Local election results in 2003
> In May 2003 local elections were held in 340 district-level local authorities in England and Scotland, with some elections (including all those in Scotland) being for the whole council and others for one-third of the council. The Conservative Party made substantial net gains in seats and now has more councillors in Great Britain than any other party for the first time since 1991. It made a net gain of 31 councils, while the Labour Party made a net loss of 28 councils and the Liberal Democrats a net gain of five.

their vote and, in general, the e-pilots worked well, with no reported security problems.

All-postal elections were held in 35 local authorities. Turnout in these areas averaged around half the electorate, compared with one-third across England as a whole.

In September 2003 the Government welcomed the recommendations made by the Electoral Commission in its evaluation of the trials, and announced its intention:

- to consult on making all-postal ballots the normal method of voting at local elections in England and Wales;
- to promote further e-voting pilots on a larger scale; and
- to adopt several other electoral innovations for local elections, including barcodes and new types of security marks on ballot papers, and electronic counting.

Local authorities in Scotland can apply to Scottish ministers for approval to run similar pilots at local by-elections. Three all-postal ballots were piloted at by-elections in 2002, and all worked well and showed an increased turnout.

Powers

Local authorities work within the powers laid down under various Acts of Parliament. Their functions are far-reaching. Some are mandatory, which means that the authority must do what is required by law, while others are discretionary, allowing an authority to provide services if it wishes. In certain cases, ministers have powers to secure uniformity in standards in order to safeguard public health or to protect the rights of individual citizens. Where local authorities exceed their statutory powers, they are regarded as acting outside the law and can be challenged in court.

---

12 In Scotland it is proposed to introduce proportional representation in time for the next local government elections in 2007.

The main link between local authorities and central government in England is the Office of the Deputy Prime Minister (ODPM). However, other departments, such as the Department for Education and Skills, the Department for Work and Pensions, the Department of Health, the Department for Environment, Food and Rural Affairs, and the Home Office, are also concerned with various local government functions.

In Scotland, Wales and Northern Ireland local authorities now deal mainly with the devolved Parliament and Assemblies (see chapters 3 to 5).

Provision of local services

The duty of Best Value requires local authorities to deliver services by the most economic, efficient and effective means available to meet the requirements of local communities; and to make arrangements to secure continuous improvements. Best Value Performance Indicators (BVPIs) were introduced in 2000/01 to provide a rounded view of local authority delivery across key local services. BVPIs cover five dimensions of performance and are a key component of the performance management framework for local authorities in England, the Comprehensive Performance Assessment (CPA).

The Audit Commission announced the results of the first round of the CPA for all single-tier and county councils in England in December 2002 and found that half of these councils were rated as excellent or good. The 22 councils rated as excellent have been given greater freedom than other councils to decide how to spend money from central government (other than that destined for schools). They will also benefit from a reduction in the number of plans they have to produce for scrutiny by central government and will have a three-year holiday from most inspection activity. CPA for district councils is being introduced over an 18-month period from June 2003 and the Audit Commission aims to have assessed all district councils by the end of 2004.

Local Public Service Agreements (PSAs) are voluntary agreements negotiated between individual local authorities and the Government. The Government commits to a specific amount of reward grant to a local authority if it achieves a performance target that is more demanding than would otherwise have been expected of it. Of the 150 local authorities in England eligible for a local

> ### Local Government Act 2003
> The *Local Government Act 2003* contains a number of provisions designed to give greater freedom and flexibility to local authorities in England and Wales. These include:
> - allowing local authorities to fund local improvements by borrowing money without government consent, provided they can afford to take on the debt;
> - giving local authorities new powers to trade and charge for non-statutory services;
> - introducing Business Improvement Districts to enhance town centres and other areas; and
> - rewarding local authorities that promote business development in their areas by allowing them to keep a proportion of their local business rates.

PSA, 147 have indicated that they want one. By July 2003, 94 agreements had been concluded and a further 48 were in negotiation.

Employees

About 2.7 million people are employed by local authorities in the United Kingdom. These include school teachers, the police, firefighters, and other non-manual and manual workers. Education is the largest service, with about 1.4 million jobs. Over 40 per cent of local government employees work part time. Councils are individually responsible, within certain legislative requirements, for deciding the structure of their workforces.

Internal organisation

Some districts have the ceremonial title of borough, or city, both granted by royal authority. Traditionally, their councillors choose a mayor (a provost in Scotland) to act as presiding officer and perform ceremonial duties. In the City of London and certain other large cities, he or she is known as the Lord Mayor. In Scotland the presiding officer of the council of the four longest established cities – Aberdeen, Dundee, Edinburgh and Glasgow – is called the Lord Provost.

The *Local Government Act 2000* required local authorities in England and Wales to implement new decision-taking structures, including the option of a directly elected mayor. In most authorities the arrangements are based on one of three executive frameworks: a mayor and cabinet;

Fire Service dispute

The Fire Service was affected by a long-running industrial dispute, which began in May 2002 when the Fire Brigades Union (FBU) put forward a claim for a substantial pay increase. The dispute ended in June 2003 when the FBU voted to accept a pay increase linked to changes in working practices.

In June 2003, the Government published a White Paper *Our Fire and Rescue Service*. This included proposals to:

- rename the Fire Service as the Fire and Rescue Service;
- place a greater emphasis on fire prevention; and
- change the way in which the Service is managed, including setting up a new structure for strategic direction, a new regional framework, and devolving responsibility for fire policy in Wales to the National Assembly for Wales.

council manager. Within these options local authorities have considerable flexibility to work under a constitution that reflects local circumstances. By mid-2003, 386 local authorities had introduced new constitutions, with the majority opting for a style of executive where the leader of the cabinet is chosen by other councillors. By August 2003, 30 referendums had been held on mayors, leaders and cabinets, and 11 had voted in favour of a directly elected mayor.

Councillors are paid a basic allowance but may be entitled to additional allowances and expenses for attending meetings or taking on special responsibilities.

Decision-making and scrutiny

All new decision-making structures are required to incorporate rigorous arrangements for review and scrutiny of councils' policies and the decisions they make. Some decisions, such as the acceptance of policies and the budget, are reserved for the full council, but most of those relating to the implementation of policy are for the executive. The executive is also responsible for preparing the policies and budget to propose to the council.

The public (including the press) is admitted to meetings of the executive when key decisions are being discussed. They also have access to agendas,

reports and minutes of meetings and certain background papers. In addition, local authorities must publish a forward plan setting out the decisions that will be taken over the coming months. Local authorities may exclude the public from meetings and withhold papers only in limited circumstances.

Local authority finance

Local government expenditure accounts for about 25 per cent of public spending in the United Kingdom. In 2002/03 expenditure by local authorities in the United Kingdom was about £105.7 billion: nearly £96.5 billion on current expenditure and £9.3 billion on capital expenditure. Education accounted for 33 per cent of local authority expenditure (see Table 6.5).

Local authorities in Great Britain raise revenue through the council tax (see chapter 24); in England this meets about 26 per cent of their revenue expenditure. Their spending is, however, financed primarily by grants from central government or the devolved administrations and by the redistribution of revenue within each country from their national non-domestic rate, a property tax levied on businesses and other non-domestic properties. Capital expenditure is financed primarily by borrowing within limits set by central government and from capital receipts from the disposal of land and buildings.

District councils in Northern Ireland continue to raise revenue through the levying of a domestic rate and a business rate.

Table 6.5 Local authority current and capital expenditure 2002/03,[1] UK

	£ billion
Education	35.1
Health and personal social services	15.1
Social security	12.7
Law, order and protective services	12.5
Transport	6.3
Culture, media and sport	3.0
Housing	1.7
Other environmental services	9.8
Accounting adjustments	6.9
Miscellaneous other	2.6
Total	**105.7**

1 Estimated expenditure based on local authority budget plans.
Source: *Public Expenditure Statistical Analyses 2003*

Financial safeguards

Local councils' annual accounts must be audited by independent auditors appointed by the Audit Commission in England and Wales, or in Scotland by the Accounts Commission for Scotland. In Northern Ireland the chief local government auditor carries out this role. Local electors have a right to inspect the accounts to be audited.

Standards and accountability

A number of safeguards are in place to ensure the probity of individuals in carrying out their public duties.

Committee on Standards in Public Life

The Committee on Standards in Public Life, set up in 1994, is an independent body reporting to the Prime Minister and has responsibility for examining concerns about the standards of conduct of all holders of public office, including arrangements relating to financial and commercial activities, and making recommendations for changes to ensure the highest standards of propriety in public life.

Its reports have resulted in a number of changes, including a new regulatory regime for political party funding in the United Kingdom, overseen by the independent Electoral Commission (see page 33); new rules governing the conduct and discipline of MPs; the introduction of new Codes of Conduct for government ministers and special advisers; mandatory registration of all peers' relevant financial interests and a short Code of Conduct for members of the House of Lords; and changes in the ethical framework for local government.

Its ninth report, *Defining the boundaries within the Executive*, published in April 2003, made a number of recommendations designed to clarify the roles of ministers, civil servants and special advisers. In its response published in September 2003, the Government accepted the majority of the Committee's recommendations. Among the measures it is taking:

- an independent adviser will be appointed to provide ministers and Permanent Secretaries with an additional source of professional advice on the handling of complex financial issues;

- a draft Bill will be published for consultation after the Public Administration Select Committee has issued its proposals for a Civil Service Act; and
- a new section will be added to the Code of Conduct for Special Advisers to clarify relationships between special advisers and permanent civil servants.

Parliamentary Commissioner for Standards

The post of Parliamentary Commissioner for Standards was created in 1995, following recommendations of the Committee on Standards in Public Life. The Commissioner, who is independent of government, can advise MPs on matters of standards, and hold initial investigations into complaints about alleged breaches of the rules by Members. The Commissioner reports to the House of Commons Select Committee on Standards and Privileges.

Financial interests of MPs and Members of the House of Lords

The House of Commons has a public register of MPs' financial (and some non-financial) interests. Members with a financial interest must declare it when speaking in the House or in Committee and must indicate it when giving notice of a question or motion. They must also disclose any relevant financial interest in other proceedings of the House and in dealings with other Members, ministers or civil servants. The House of Lords has its own register on similar lines to that for MPs, based on a Code of Conduct that came into force in 2002.

Commissioner for Public Appointments

The Commissioner for Public Appointments is independent of government and is responsible for regulating, monitoring and reporting on ministerial appointments to a range of public bodies: non-departmental public bodies (NDPBs, see page 50), public corporations, nationalised industries, National Health Service bodies and the appointment of utility regulators. Departments are required to follow the Commissioner's Code of Practice. This covers the seven principles to be applied to these appointments – ministerial responsibility, merit, independent scrutiny, equal opportunities, probity, openness and transparency, and proportionality.

Complaints

Parliamentary Commissioner for Administration

The Parliamentary Commissioner for Administration – more usually known as the Parliamentary Ombudsman – investigates complaints from members of the public (that have been referred by MPs) alleging that they have been unfairly treated through maladministration. The Ombudsman is independent of government and reports to a select committee of the House of Commons. The Ombudsman's area of authority covers maladministration by government departments and certain other public bodies, but excludes complaints about government policy, the content of legislation and certain other matters.

In making investigations, the Ombudsman has access to all departmental papers, and has powers to call people to give evidence. Once an investigation is complete, a report of the findings is sent to the MP who referred the complaint with a copy for the complainant. When a complaint is upheld, the Ombudsman normally recommends that the department or other body makes some kind of redress (which might be financial in appropriate cases). There is no appeal against the Ombudsman's decision. The Ombudsman received 1,973 new complaints in 2002/03, 8 per cent fewer than in 2001/02.

Separate arrangements apply for complaints about the devolved administrations and devolved public bodies. In Wales complaints can be made directly to the Welsh Administration Ombudsman and in Scotland to the Scottish Public Services Ombudsman. The latter post is a new office set up in October 2002, replacing separate Scottish parliamentary, health service, local government and housing association ombudsmen.

Local government complaints system

Complaints of maladministration by local authorities or by certain local bodies are investigated by independent Commissions for Local Administration, often known as 'the Local Ombudsman service'. A report is issued on each complaint fully investigated and, if injustice is found, the Local Ombudsman normally proposes a solution. There are Local Government Ombudsmen in England and Wales; in Northern Ireland there is a Commissioner for Complaints. In Scotland responsibility now rests with the Scottish Public Services Ombudsman.

Modernising government

The Government has set out four principles of public service reform, which support its delivery and reform programme:

- high national standards, within a framework of clear accountability, designed to ensure that citizens have the right to high-quality services wherever they live;
- devolving decision-making, so that local leaders have responsibility and accountability for delivery;
- greater flexibility in the delivery of public services; and
- more choice for the customers of public services, including greater choice of service provider.

The Government has taken a number of measures to modernise and improve public services. Public Service Agreements (PSAs) have been set up, both at a national and local level. PSAs set out publicly each government department's plans to deliver results in return for the investment being made and include the department's aims, objectives and performance targets. They are an integral part of the Government's spending plans (see page 354). The Charter Mark scheme, which aims to help public service organisations become more focused on the needs of users, is being remodelled to support the Government's strategy.

The reform programme is being taken forward by a number of units within the Cabinet Office, including the Prime Minister's Delivery Unit and the Office of Public Services Reform. In addition, a new Reform Strategy Group is working with government departments to redesign services around the needs of customers.

Freedom of information

The *Freedom of Information Act 2000* provides for a statutory right of access to recorded information held across the public sector. The Act is due to enter force in 2005 and will affect over 100,000 organisations, including Parliament, government departments, local authorities, schools and health authorities.

The main features of the Act are:

- a right of wide general access to information, subject to clearly defined exemptions and conditions;
- a requirement to consider discretionary disclosure in the public interest even when an exemption applies;

- a duty to publish information; and
- powers of enforcement through an independent Information Commissioner and an Information Tribunal.

The Information Commissioner is also responsible for promoting the rules for the processing of personal information set out in the *Data Protection Act 1998*.

National Statistics

National Statistics, the United Kingdom's independent national statistical service, was set up in June 2000. It aims to provide an accurate, up-to-date, comprehensive and meaningful picture of the UK economy and society to support the formulation and monitoring of economic and social policies by government at all levels. In line with the Government's commitment to greater openness and accessibility of publicly held information, all its online data are available free of charge.

The UK in the European Union

As a Member State of the European Union (EU), the United Kingdom is bound by European Community (EC) legislation and wider policies based on a series of treaties since the 1950s (see chapter 7). Almost all UK government departments are involved in EU-wide business, and European legislation is an increasingly important element of government.

The Community enacts legislation that is binding on the national governments of the Member States or, in certain circumstances, on individuals and companies within those states. UK government ministers take part in the discussions and decision-making, and all the Member States take the final decision collectively.

The Office of the UK Permanent Representative to the EU (UKREP), based in Brussels, conducts most of the negotiations on behalf of the UK Government. Following UK devolution, the devolved administrations are consulted when the UK Government line on EU issues is developed.

Council of the European Union

This is the main decision-making body. Member States are represented by the ministers appropriate to the subject under discussion. When, for instance, health matters are being discussed, the United Kingdom's Secretary of State for Health attends with his or her European counterparts. Ministers from the devolved administrations can also attend these meetings and, at the appropriate UK minister's request, devolved administration ministers can represent the United Kingdom. The Presidency of the Council changes at six-monthly intervals and rotates in turn among the Member States of the EU.

In some cases Council decisions must be unanimous; in others they are taken by qualified majority voting (a qualified majority is the number of votes required for a decision to be adopted) with votes weighted according to a country's population – currently ten each for France, Germany, Italy and the United Kingdom; eight for Spain; five each for Belgium, Greece, The Netherlands and Portugal; four each for Austria and Sweden; three each for Denmark, Finland and the Republic of Ireland; and two for Luxembourg. The threshold for the qualified majority is currently set at 62 votes out of 87. This system will be adapted to include the ten new Member States that are joining in May 2004. A new voting system, agreed in the Treaty of Nice (see page 60), will come into effect on 1 November 2004. Negotiations on further changes to the voting system began in October 2003 (see page 63).

European Council

This usually meets at least three times a year and comprises the Heads of State or Government (accompanied by their foreign ministers), the President of the European Commission and one other Commissioner. The Council defines general political guidelines.

European Commission

This is the executive body. It implements the Council's decisions, initiates legislation and ensures that Member States put it into effect. Each of the Commissioners, who are drawn from Member States, is responsible for a specific policy area, for example, education, transport or agriculture. The Commissioners are independent of their countries and serve the EU as a whole.

European Parliament

This plays an increasing role in the legislative process. There are 626 directly elected members (MEPs), including 87 from the United Kingdom (see Table 6.6). The Parliament is consulted about major decisions and has shared power with the Council of the European Union over the EC budget. In areas of legislation, its role varies between *consultation*, where it can influence but does not have the final say in the content of legislation; *co-operation and assent* procedures, where its influence is greater; and *co-decision*, where a proposal requires the agreement of both the Council and the European Parliament. The Parliament meets in full session in Strasbourg for about one week every month. Its committee work normally takes place in Brussels.

Table 6.6 European Parliament elections, June 1999

United Kingdom	Number of MEPs
Conservative	36
Labour	29
Liberal Democrats	10
UK Independence Party	3
Green	2
Plaid Cymru – The Party of Wales	2
Scottish National Party	2
Democratic Unionist Party	1
Ulster Unionist Party	1
Social Democratic and Labour Party	1
Total	**87**

Source: House of Commons

Elections to the European Parliament take place every five years, under a proportional representation system.[13] For the next election in June 2004 most Member States have to make · reductions in the number of MEPs to accommodate representatives from the ten states due to join the EU in 2004 (see page 63). The *European Parliament (Representation) Act 2003* makes provision for the number of UK MEPs to be reduced, and in the 2004 election the United Kingdom is expected to elect 78 MEPs. The Act also enables the people of Gibraltar to vote in European parliamentary elections as part of a UK constituency.

EC legislation

Some EC legislation is issued jointly by the Council of the European Union and the European Parliament, some by the Council and some by the Commission under delegated powers. It consists of Regulations, Directives and Decisions:

- *Regulations* are directly applicable in all Member States, and have the force of law without the need for implementing further measures;
- *Directives* are equally binding as to the result to be achieved but allow each Member State to choose the form and method of implementation; and
- *Decisions*, like Regulations, do not normally need national implementing legislation. They are binding on those to whom they are addressed.

Other EU institutions

Each Member State provides one of the judges to serve in the European Court of Justice, the final authority on all aspects of Community law. Member States must apply its rulings, and fines can be imposed on those failing to do so. The Court is assisted by a Court of First Instance, which handles certain cases brought by individuals and companies. The United Kingdom is also represented on the Court of Auditors, which examines Community revenue and expenditure, to see that it is legally received and spent.

13 The d'Hondt system of proportional representation (see glossary) is used for England, Scotland and Wales, under which an elector may cast his or her vote for a party list of candidates. England is divided into nine regions while Scotland and Wales each constitute one region. These 11 regions each return between four and 11 MEPs, depending on the size of the electorate of each region. Northern Ireland, which also constitutes one region, continues to use the single transferable vote system to return its three MEPs.

The United Kingdom is represented on the
Committee of the Regions by elected members
from devolved administrations and local
authorities. The Committee was set up by the
Maastricht Treaty as a representative forum giving
local and regional authorities a voice in the EU.

EU constitution

The Convention on the Future of Europe,
established by the European Council in December
2001, has drawn up a draft constitution for an
enlarged EU. This draft constitution was
considered by the EU Heads of Government at a
meeting of the European Council at Thessaloniki
(Greece) in June 2003, and was judged to be a
good basis for starting the intergovernmental
conference, which opened in October 2003 (see
page 63).

Further reading

Cabinet Office Departmental Report 2003.
Cm 5926. The Stationery Office, 2003.

Civil Service Statistics. Cabinet Office, annual.

*Office of the Deputy Prime Minister Annual Report
2003.* Cm 5906. The Stationery Office, 2003.

Websites

The UK Monarchy
www.royal.gov.uk

Cabinet Office
www.cabinetoffice.gov.uk

Central government
www.ukonline.gov.uk

Department for Constitutional Affairs
www.dca.gov.uk

Electoral Commission
www.electoralcommission.org.uk

National Assembly for Wales
www.wales.gov.uk

National Statistics
www.statistics.gov.uk

Northern Ireland Executive
www.northernireland.gov.uk

Office of the Deputy Prime Minister
www.odpm.gov.uk

Prime Minister's Office
www.pmo.gov.uk

Scottish Executive
www.scotland.gov.uk

United Kingdom Parliament
www.parliament.uk

WWW.

7 International relations

The United Kingdom has global foreign policy interests. It is a member of the European Union (EU), the Group of Eight (G8), the North Atlantic Treaty Organisation (NATO), the Organisation for Security and Co-operation in Europe (OSCE), the Council of Europe, and the United Nations (UN). It has a close relationship with the United States and with a large number of countries through the Commonwealth.

European Union

The United Kingdom joined the EU in 1973. The EU promotes coordinated social and economic progress among its Member States, and common foreign and security positions. The EU's principal institutions and its legislative processes are described on pages 57–59.

Treaties
A series of treaties govern the structure and operation of the EU. Any amendments to the treaties must be agreed unanimously and must then be ratified by each Member State according to its own constitutional procedures. In the United Kingdom, Parliament must scrutinise and where necessary provide legislative powers to implement new EU treaties before they can be ratified.

Treaties of Rome
The 1957 Treaties of Rome established the European Community. They aimed to create a common internal, or single, market (see page 61), encompassing the elimination of customs duties between Member States, free movement of goods, people, services and capital, and the removal of distortions in competition within this market. The *1986 Single European Act*, which incorporated measures to complete the single market, reaffirmed these aims. Under the Treaties of Rome

the European Commission speaks on behalf of the United Kingdom and the other Member States in international trade negotiations.

Maastricht Treaty
The 1992 Maastricht Treaty amended the Treaties of Rome and made new commitments that encompassed moves towards economic and monetary union (see page 61). It established the European Union, which comprises the European Community as well as intergovernmental arrangements for a Common Foreign and Security Policy (CFSP, see page 62) and for increased co-operation on justice and home affairs policy issues (see page 62). It also enshrined the principle of subsidiarity, under which action in areas where the Community and Member States share competence should be taken at European level only if objectives cannot be achieved by Member States acting alone and can be better achieved by the Community. In addition, the Treaty introduced the concept of EU citizenship as a supplement to national citizenship.

Amsterdam Treaty
The Amsterdam Treaty, in force since 1999, provides for: further protection and extension of citizens' rights; integration of the 'social chapter' (previously a separate protocol to the Maastricht Treaty) into the treaty framework following its adoption by the United Kingdom; new mechanisms to improve the operation of the CFSP; an increase in the number of areas subject to co-decision between the Council of Ministers and the European Parliament; and simplification of the co-decision procedure.

The Treaty of Nice
The Treaty of Nice was signed in February 2001 and entered into force on 1 February 2003 following ratification by all EU Member States. It introduces changes to the EU's institutional

machinery in preparation for enlargement (see page 63). From 2005, the number of votes in the Council of the European Union attributed to each Member State will change to take account of prospective new members, the total rising from 87 votes held by the current 15 Member States to up to 345 votes held by 27 Member States. France, Germany, Italy and the United Kingdom will each have 29 votes. Assuming 27 Member States, the total required for a qualified majority (see page 62) will increase from 62 to 255, and for a blocking minority from 26 to 91.

Qualified majority voting will extend to 35 more areas, including trade in some services, aspects of asylum and immigration policy, and regulation of the European Court of Justice. From 2005, the European Commission will comprise one member from each country, up to 27. However, the recommendations of the European Convention, if adopted, could supersede some of the Treaty of Nice provisions (see page 63).

The Treaty of Accession
The Treaty of Accession, signed by 25 heads of state in Athens on 16 April 2003, provides for the accession to the EU of ten new members on 1 May 2004, subject to treaty ratification by all the signatory states (see page 63). All candidate countries except Cyprus have held referendums on EU membership and have voted 'yes'. Under the Treaty, nationals of the ten new Member States will enjoy the right to move freely within the EU from 1 May 2004 for all purposes except for work. The Treaty allows for the imposition of transitional work restrictions on nationals of the new Member States, except Cyprus and Malta, until 30 April 2011. The UK Government announced in December 2002 that it would waive its right to impose work restrictions on nationals of the eight states affected by transitional measures, subject to certain safeguards. The UK Government may re-impose restrictions on some or all of the eight states, and may refuse nationals of one or more of the eight the right to work in the United Kingdom, in the event of an unexpected threat to a region or occupational sector of the UK labour market.

Policies
The Community budget and broader EU policies are described below. Policies affecting more specific UK sectors – for example, the Common Agricultural Policy – are covered in the appropriate chapters.

European Community budget
The Community's revenue consists of levies on agricultural imports from non-member countries, customs duties, a proportion of value added tax (VAT) receipts, and contributions from Member States based on gross national product (GNP). Increasingly, more revenue is being raised from contributions linked to GNP and less from VAT receipts and customs payments. The United Kingdom continues to receive an annual budget rebate, which has been in place since 1984 and is guaranteed until at least 2006. The United Kingdom receives the rebate because it is contributing more to the EU financially than it is getting back, largely because of the relatively small size of its farming industry.

Single market
The single European market, providing for the free movement of people, goods, services and capital within the EU, came into effect in 1993 (see also page 371). Its benefits include the removal of customs barriers, the liberalisation of capital movements, the opening of public procurement markets and the mutual recognition of professional qualifications. Under the European Economic Area (EEA) Agreement, which came into force in 1994, most of the EU single market measures also apply to Iceland, Liechtenstein and Norway.

Economic and monetary union
The Maastricht Treaty (see page 60) provided for the establishment of a European economic and monetary union in stages, culminating in the establishment on 1 January 1999 of a single currency, the euro, by the participating EU Member States. Three EU Member States – Denmark, Sweden and the United Kingdom – are not participating in the final stage of the economic and monetary union, and remain outside the euro area. The UK Government has set out five economic tests that must be met before any decision to join can be made (see page 340).

Conversion rates between the national currencies of the 12 participating Member States and the euro were legally fixed on 1 January 1999.[1] The euro is now the legal currency in the euro area and the European Central Bank assumed responsibility for formulating monetary policy for these countries. Euro notes and coins were introduced

---

1 The rate for Greece became fixed when it joined the euro on 1 January 2001.

throughout the euro area on 1 January 2002, and by 1 March 2002 national banknotes and coins in the euro area ceased to be legal tender.

Regional and infrastructure development

There are significant economic and social imbalances in the EU and these will increase with enlargement. Four Structural Funds promoting economic advancement in underdeveloped regions and supporting the conversion of areas facing structural difficulties aim to address such imbalances (see also page 345).

- The European Regional Development Fund finances infrastructure projects and schemes to promote development and diversification of industry.
- The European Social Fund supports human resource and equal opportunities schemes, and training measures for the unemployed and young people.
- The Guidance Section of the European Agricultural Guidance and Guarantee Fund supports agricultural restructuring and some rural development activities.
- The Financial Instrument for Fisheries Guidance promotes the modernisation of the fishing industry.

The United Kingdom will receive €15.5 billion (over £10 billion) from the Structural Funds in 2000–06. A Cohesion Fund, set up under the Maastricht Treaty, is designed to reduce disparities between EU members' economies. Greece, the Republic of Ireland, Portugal, and Spain, the four Member States whose GNP was less than 90 per cent of the EU average, received such funding in 2003.

In the run up to enlargement, the EU has prepared tailor-made financial programmes for the period 2000–06 to help the candidate countries prepare for membership. These include the Instrument for Structural Policies for Pre-accession (ISPA), which finances environment and transport projects with a budget of €7.28 billion, and the Special Accession Programme for Agriculture and Rural Development (Sapard), which supports agricultural development with a €3.64 billion budget. They join the existing Phare programme (the main channel for EU financial and technical co-operation with Eastern and Central Europe), with a €10.92 billion budget, which aims to strengthen the administrative and institutional capacity of accession countries and to finance investment projects. These account for 30

per cent and 70 per cent of Phare's budget respectively. After accession, the Structural Funds and the Cohesion Fund will replace such assistance. The European Council meeting in Brussels in October 2002 set aside an additional €23 billion for structural spending in the new Member States for the period 2004–06.

Common Foreign and Security Policy

The intergovernmental CFSP, introduced under the Maastricht Treaty, provides for unanimous agreement among Member States on common policies and/or joint action on a wide range of international issues, in the belief that Member States carry more weight when able to speak with one voice on international affairs than any single Member State alone. The Amsterdam Treaty (see page 60) preserves the principle of unanimity in all policy decisions but states that those decisions concerning common strategies, which are themselves unanimously agreed, will be by qualified majority voting. A Member State may prevent a vote being taken by qualified majority voting for 'important and stated reasons of national policy'. In addition, qualified majority voting does not apply to decisions having military or defence implications. A Member State may abstain and stand aside from an EU decision/action that does not affect its interests.

In 1998, the United Kingdom and France launched an initiative at St Malo to strengthen the EU's capacity to respond to crises, on the premise that the Union could only play a coherent and effective political role if underpinned by a credible military capability. By May 2003 the EU had operational capability across the full range of tasks (see page 81), albeit limited and constrained by recognised shortfalls. Efforts are under way to ensure the level of capability intended is fully met.

Justice and home affairs

The Maastricht Treaty established intergovernmental arrangements for increased co-operation among EU states on justice and home affairs issues. These issues include visa, asylum, immigration and other policies related to free movement of people; and police, customs and judicial co-operation in criminal matters, including co-operation through EUROPOL (see page 78). This is a growing aspect of EU work and includes both Community-based and intergovernmental areas of co-operation. A protocol annexed to the Amsterdam Treaty recognises the right the United Kingdom to exercise its own frontier controls.

Enlargement

A key policy objective of the EU is to enlarge the Union to include those European nations that share its democratic values and aims, and that are functioning market economies, able to compete in the EU and to take on the obligations of membership. In 1998, it launched an accession process with the applicant states and began formal negotiations with Cyprus, the Czech Republic, Estonia, Hungary, Poland, and Slovenia. In 1999, the EU agreed to invite six other countries – Bulgaria, Latvia, Lithuania, Malta, Romania and Slovakia – to open accession negotiations (launched in February 2000) and also confirmed Turkey's candidacy for membership.

In 1999, the European Council agreed the EU's budgetary arrangements for the period 2000–06. These included financial provision for the new Member States to join the Union in that period.

In December 2002, following a decade of extensive reforms and, more recently, detailed negotiations, the Copenhagen European Council agreed that Cyprus, the Czech Republic, Estonia, Hungary, Latvia, Lithuania, Malta, Poland, Slovakia and Slovenia could join the EU on 1 May 2004. The 15 existing EU Member States and ten new Member States signed the Treaty of Accession in Athens on 16 April 2003 (see page 61); subject to ratification by all existing Member States and at least one new Member State, this comes into force on 1 May 2004 for all those that have ratified it. The ten new Member States will participate in the June 2004 elections to the European Parliament.

At Copenhagen, the European Council also agreed on the shared objective of accepting Bulgaria and Romania as EU members in 2007, subject to further progress in complying with membership criteria. Accession negotiations with Turkey may be opened following the European Council meeting in December 2004, providing the Council decides that Turkey has fulfilled the Copenhagen political criteria relating to democracy.

In February 2002, the Convention on the Future of Europe began a year-long fundamental examination of the EU's institutions to consider how to make an expanded EU more democratic, effective and transparent. It was chaired by former French President Valéry Giscard d'Estaing and was made up of representatives of EU Member States and Parliaments, the European Commission, the European Parliament and the 13 countries hoping to join the EU.

The Convention drew up proposals for an EU constitution and recommended the powers that national governments should retain and those that they should hand over to Brussels. It also proposed the establishment of an EU president, an elected European Commission president, an elected EU foreign minister, a legally binding charter of rights, a common foreign policy, a legal 'personality' for the EU and greater co-operation on social security, justice and home affairs. The draft proposed a simpler voting system in which decisions would pass if supported by at least half of all Member States, representing at least 60 per cent of the EU's population.

At a summit in Greece in June 2003, EU leaders described the Convention's draft as a 'good basis' for negotiations, although Poland, Spain and the United Kingdom voiced concerns over issues such as voting rights and national vetoes. An intergovernmental conference began negotiating the draft in October 2003, with a view to producing a final treaty by May 2004.

Other international organisations

United Nations

The United Kingdom is a founder member of the UN and one of the five permanent members of the Security Council, along with China, France, Russia and the US. It supports the purposes and principles of the UN Charter, including the maintenance of international peace and security, the development of friendly relations among nations, the achievement of international co-operation on economic, social, cultural and humanitarian issues, and the protection of human rights and fundamental freedoms.

The United Kingdom is the fifth largest contributor both to the UN regular budget – paying about £42 million in 2002 – and to UN peacekeeping budgets, and is one of the largest voluntary contributors to UN funds, programmes and specialised agencies. In 2001, the total UK contribution to the UN exceeded £425 million. The UK Government advocates modernising the UN to enhance its effectiveness, including reforming the Security Council's composition, and welcomed the Secretary-General's report on reform *Strengthening of the United Nations: an agenda for further change*, published in September 2002. The UK Government is committed to reinforcing the UN's role in preventing and resolving conflicts around the world (see also page 75).

Commonwealth

The Commonwealth has 54 members[2] including the United Kingdom (see map in the second colour section). It is a voluntary association of independent states, nearly all of which were once British territories. It promotes international peace and order, democracy, the rule of law, good governance, freedom of expression and human rights, as well as economic and social development. The Secretary-General has a role in conflict prevention and resolution and the organisation provides election observer missions and democracy advisory services. Comprising around 28 per cent of the world's countries, it represents a combined population of 1.7 billion people.

The Queen is Head of the Commonwealth and is Head of State of the United Kingdom and 15 other member countries (see page 42). The Commonwealth Secretariat, based in London, is the main intergovernmental agency of the Commonwealth. It helps host governments to organise Commonwealth Heads of Government Meetings (CHOGM – these take place in a different Commonwealth country every two years), ministerial meetings and other conferences. It administers assistance programmes agreed at these meetings, including the Commonwealth Fund for Technical Co-operation, which provides expertise, advisory services and training to developing countries in the Commonwealth. The theme of the next CHOGM, due to take place in December 2003 in Abuja, Nigeria, will be 'Democracy and Development: Partnerships for Peace and Prosperity'.

North Atlantic Treaty Organisation

Membership of NATO is central to UK defence policy (see chapter 8). Each of the 19 Member

States – Belgium, Canada, the Czech Republic, Denmark, France, Germany, Greece, Hungary, Iceland, Italy, Luxembourg, The Netherlands, Norway, Poland, Portugal, Spain, Turkey, the United Kingdom and the US – has a permanent representative at NATO headquarters in Brussels.

The main decision-making body is the North Atlantic Council. It meets at least twice a year at foreign minister level, and once a week at permanent representative level. Defence ministers also meet at least twice a year.

In March 2003, the 19 NATO Member States signed Accession Protocols inviting seven countries – Bulgaria, Estonia, Latvia, Lithuania, Romania, Slovakia and Slovenia – to join the alliance. These will officially accede to NATO at the summit in Istanbul in May 2004, subject to ratification of the Protocols by all current members.

Group of Eight

The United Kingdom is one of the Group of Eight (G8) leading industrialised countries. The other members are Canada, France, Germany, Italy, Japan, Russia (included as a full member from 1998, although the other countries continue to function as the G7 for some discussions) and the US.

The G8 is an informal group with no secretariat. Its presidency rotates each year among the members, the key meeting being the annual summit of Heads of Government. Originally formed in 1975 (as the G7) to discuss economic issues, the G8 agenda now includes a wide range of foreign affairs and international issues such as terrorism, nuclear safety, the environment, UN reform and development assistance. Heads of State or Government agree a communiqué issued at the end of summits.

The French Government hosted the G8 summit in Evian-les-Bains in June 2003. The summit participants agreed to coordinate their economic policies to support the global economic recovery, and reaffirmed existing commitments on trade, debt and aid. They supported the establishment of a Counter-Terrorism Action Group to combat terrorism worldwide and agreed to the reconstruction of a fully sovereign, stable and democratic Iraq. They also expressed concern over continued violence in Zimbabwe, and called on the country's government to respect the right of peaceful demonstration. The US is to host the next G8 summit in 2004.

---

2 Pakistan and Zimbabwe are suspended from the councils of the Commonwealth. Pakistan was suspended in October 1999 following a military coup. Zimbabwe was suspended for a year in March 2002 following international criticism of the conduct of its presidential elections. The Commonwealth subsequently extended Zimbabwe's suspension until December 2003, when Commonwealth Heads of Government are due to meet. Both cases will be reviewed at that time.

Organisation for Security and Co-operation in Europe

The United Kingdom is a member of the OSCE, a regional security organisation with 55 participating states from Europe, Central Asia and North America. All decisions are taken by consensus. The OSCE is based in Vienna, where the United Kingdom has a permanent delegation. The main areas of work are:

- early warning and prevention of potential conflicts through field missions and diplomacy and the work of the OSCE High Commissioner on National Minorities;
- observing elections and providing advice on human rights, democracy and law, and the media;
- post-conflict rehabilitation, including civil society development; and
- promoting security through arms control and military confidence-building.

The United Kingdom contributed around £19 million in 2002/03 towards the OSCE's general expenses.

Council of Europe

The United Kingdom is a founding member of the Council of Europe, which is open to any European state accepting parliamentary democracy, the rule of law and fundamental human rights. There are 45 full Member States; Serbia and Montenegro joined the organisation in April 2003. One of the Council's main achievements is the European Convention on Human Rights (see page 72).

The United Kingdom is one of the major financial contributors to the Council of Europe: the Foreign & Commonwealth Office (FCO) pays 13 per cent of the Council of Europe's general expenses, around £17 million in 2003/04.

Other international bodies

The United Kingdom is a member of many other international bodies. These include the International Monetary Fund (IMF), which regulates the international financial system and provides credit to member countries facing balance-of-payments difficulties; the World Bank, which provides loans to finance economic and social projects in developing countries; the Organisation for Economic Co-operation and Development (OECD), which promotes economic growth, support for less developed countries and worldwide trade expansion; and the World Trade Organisation (WTO, see page 371). Other organisations to which the United Kingdom belongs or extends support include the regional development banks in Africa, the Caribbean, Latin America and Asia, and the European Bank for Reconstruction and Development.

Regional relations

North America

The UK Government regards close transatlantic links between the United Kingdom, the US and Canada as essential to the guarantee of security and prosperity in both Europe and North America.

The United Kingdom and the US co-operate closely on nuclear, defence and intelligence issues. As founding members of NATO, both states are deeply involved in Western defence arrangements and, as permanent members of the UN Security Council, work closely together on major international issues. In addition, they have important economic links. The United Kingdom and the US are each other's biggest source of inward investment, and the US is the largest single UK trading destination.

The United Kingdom maintains strong political and economic links with Canada, which like the United Kingdom is a member of the Commonwealth, as well as NATO and other key international organisations. The United Kingdom is the second largest investor in Canada, and Canada is the second largest investor in the United Kingdom.

Middle East

Iraq

The United Kingdom condemned Iraq's invasion of Kuwait in 1990 and was a member of the coalition of forces that expelled Iraqi troops from Kuwait in 1991. UN sanctions against Iraq remained in force (although with substantial humanitarian exemptions) because Iraq failed to comply with Security Council resolutions, particularly those relating to the elimination of weapons of mass destruction. Sanctions were revised in May 2002 to allow Iraq to import civilian goods and were lifted in May 2003 (see below).

Iraq stopped co-operating with the UN Special Commission to Oversee the Destruction of Iraq's weapons of mass destruction (Unscom) in October 1998. The following year, UN Security Council Resolution 1284 created the UN Monitoring, Verification and Inspection Commission (Unmovic) to replace Unscom. Iraq rejected this resolution.

UN weapons inspectors returned to Iraq in November 2002, supported by a UN resolution that threatened serious consequences if the country were in material breach of its terms. In February 2003, the US informed the UN that inspections were failing to bring about disarmament and in March the US issued an ultimatum to Iraq. On 20 March 2003, American missiles hit targets in Baghdad, marking the start of the US-led campaign supported by a coalition of 30 countries (see page 80).

The coalition declared that the military objectives of the conflict had been achieved on 14 April 2003. On 22 May, the UN Security Council approved a resolution supporting the US-led administration in Iraq, lifting economic sanctions against the country and encouraging the Iraqi people to form a representative government. An inaugural meeting of the Iraqi Governing Council – the key element in the Iraqi interim administration – took place on 13 July 2003.

Arab-Israeli peace process

The UK Government fully supports the US initiative to give renewed momentum to the peace process. In April 2003 the Quartet (US, EU, UN and Russia) presented their 'roadmap' for a permanent two-state solution by 2005. Phase One stipulates an end to Palestinian violence; Palestinian political reform; a freeze on Israeli settlement expansion and withdrawal from Palestinian areas occupied from 28 September 2000. Phase Two involves the creation of a provisional Palestinian state and the holding of an international conference. Phase Three calls for a second international conference; a permanent status agreement on borders and the end of conflict. The UK Government continues to press for an end to the violence and for a resumption of political engagement: it believes there can be no military solution to the conflict. A lasting solution must protect Israel's security, provide a just settlement for the Palestinians and a comprehensive resolution of the dispute, including the Syrian and Lebanese tracks.

Central and Eastern Europe, and Central Asia

Economic assistance

The United Kingdom and other Western countries continue to help the former Soviet bloc states to manage economic problems following the fall of Communism, and assist in promoting the development of market economies. The IMF supports stabilisation programmes and the World Bank helps to finance structural reform in nearly every country in the region. This process is bolstered by European Bank for Reconstruction and Development investments and the EBRD's role in attracting additional private investment.

The EU's Phare scheme primarily aids Central European countries in the process of reform and development of their infrastructure. Countries of the former Soviet Union (excluding Estonia, Latvia and Lithuania) and Mongolia receive help through a parallel programme (Tacis), which concentrates on democratisation, financial services, transport, energy (including nuclear safety) and the reform of public administration. The Community Assistance for Reconstruction, Development and Stabilisation (CARDS) programme focuses on countries in the Western Balkans.

Association and co-operation agreements

The EU has strengthened relations with Bulgaria, the Czech Republic, Estonia, Hungary, Latvia, Lithuania, Poland, Romania, Slovakia and Slovenia through the conclusion of Europe (Association) Agreements. The agreements have provided an institutional framework supporting the process of integration, ahead of the accession of these countries to the EU (see page 63).

EU Partnership and Co-operation Agreements are in force with Armenia, Azerbaijan, Belarus, Georgia, Kazakhstan, Kyrgyzstan, Moldova, Russia, Turkmenistan, Ukraine and Uzbekistan. Trade and Co-operation Agreements with Albania and Macedonia are also in force. The purpose of these agreements is to reduce trade barriers, promote wide-ranging co-operation and increase political dialogue.

Stabilisation and Association Agreements (SAA) also offer the prospect of ultimate EU membership and closer links to states in south-eastern Europe, provided that these countries meet the EU's conditions on democracy, electoral and media freedoms, economic reform and respect for human rights and the rule of law. The EU signed its first SAA, with Macedonia, in April 2001. It concluded an SAA with Croatia in October 2001, and opened negotiations with Albania in January 2003. The EU is carrying out a feasibility study for an SAA in Bosnia and Herzegovina and is expected to launch a feasibility study in the Union of Serbia and Montenegro during 2003.

Mediterranean

The United Kingdom and other EU Member States have developed closer links with 12 Mediterranean partners (Algeria, Cyprus, Egypt, Israel, Jordan, Lebanon, Malta, Morocco, the Palestinian Authority, Syria, Tunisia and Turkey) on the basis of the Barcelona Declaration of 1995, which aims to promote peace and prosperity in the region. Libya has been invited to join up to the Declaration but had not done so by mid-2003. The EU also has Euro-Mediterranean Association Agreements covering political dialogue, free trade and co-operation in a number of areas with Algeria, Egypt, Israel, Jordan, Lebanon, Morocco, the Palestinian Authority and Tunisia. Cyprus, Malta and Turkey have long-standing Association Agreements with the EU. Cyprus and Malta, together with the 15 existing and eight other prospective EU Member States, signed the Accession Treaty in Athens on 16 April 2003 (see page 61).

Africa

The UK Government is working to promote peace, security, prosperity and democracy in Africa and has declared African development a policy priority. It supports efforts to prevent or end African conflicts; promote trade, reduce debt and encourage sustainable development. The United Kingdom supports African governments, organisations and individuals committed to the principles of democracy, accountability, human rights, and the rule of law. It delivers its efforts to reduce conflict in sub-Saharan Africa through the UK Conflict Prevention Pool for Africa, which involves the Department for International Development, the FCO and the Ministry of Defence.

The UK Government has welcomed the New Partnership for Africa's Development (NEPAD), an African-led strategy for sustainable growth and development that was endorsed by the Organisation of African Unity in July 2001. In

support of NEPAD, the G8 countries (see page 64) adopted an assistance action plan at their summit in Canada in June 2002, and their personal representatives for Africa reported on progress at the G8 summit in France in June 2003. The United Kingdom is to increase bilateral aid to Africa to £1 billion a year by 2005/06, in order to help build the new partnership.

With the EU and the Commonwealth, the United Kingdom has continued to protest at the violation of human rights in Zimbabwe, and has called for inter-party dialogue leading to free and fair elections. The UK Government has continued with its programme of humanitarian assistance in response to the serious food shortage in Zimbabwe. The United Kingdom is the largest bilateral aid donor after the US (£117 million since 2001).

Since the abolition of apartheid and the election of the first African National Congress government in 1994, South Africa's relations with the United Kingdom have broadened into areas ranging from development assistance to military co-operation and from sporting links to scientific partnerships. The United Kingdom is South Africa's largest single trading partner and largest foreign investor. The EU and South Africa signed a trade, development and co-operation agreement in 1999, providing for the creation of a free trade area and for further substantial development assistance from the EU. In 2003, the UK Government welcomed South Africa's contribution to resolving conflicts in Burundi and the Democratic Republic of the Congo, and its efforts to deal with the problems of Zimbabwe.

In July 2003, the United Kingdom agreed to contribute troops to a UN-mandated, interim mission to stabilise the town of Bunia in the north-east of the Democratic Republic of the Congo, pending deployment of further UN reinforcements. UK military personnel also participated in the UN peacekeeping missions in the Congo and Sierra Leone in 2003.

Asia-Pacific region

The United Kingdom has well-established relations with Australia, China, Japan, the Republic of Korea, New Zealand and many South East Asian nations, and has defence links with some countries in the region. In 1997, the United Kingdom returned Hong Kong to Chinese sovereignty under the provisions of the 1984

Sino-British Joint Declaration. It continues to have responsibilities towards Hong Kong and the 3.6 million British passport holders living there. The territory is also the second largest UK export market in Asia.

The United Kingdom is a member, with Australia, Malaysia, New Zealand and Singapore, of the Five Power Defence Arrangements, which were set up in 1971. UK commercial activity has developed through increased trade and investment, and through the establishment of business councils, joint commissions or industrial co-operation agreements. The United Kingdom is also taking advantage of increased opportunities for English language teaching, co-operation in science and technology, and educational exchanges.

The Asia–Europe Meeting (ASEM) process was inaugurated in 1996. ASEM's aim is to foster closer economic and political ties between EU countries and Brunei, China, Indonesia, Japan, the Republic of Korea, Malaysia, the Philippines, Singapore, Thailand and Vietnam. The fourth ASEM took place in Copenhagen, Denmark, in September 2002.

The United Kingdom is a member of the South Pacific Commission, which provides technical advice and assistance to its Pacific Island members, with which the United Kingdom has long-standing and Commonwealth ties.

Afghanistan
The United Kingdom made a major contribution to the defeat of the Taliban regime by a US-led coalition that began military action in October 2001. The Taliban had close links with the Al Qaida terrorist network, responsible for the attacks on the US on 11 September 2001.

By December 2001, the Taliban regime had collapsed and the UN brought together representatives of the various Afghan ethnic groups for talks in Bonn, Germany. The Bonn Agreement set out a roadmap towards stable, democratic and fully representative government in Afghanistan.The Afghan Interim Authority was established on 22 December 2001, with a six-month mandate to run the country until an emergency *Loya Jirga* (Grand Council) of representatives from across Afghanistan could be held to elect a President. To support the new government, the United Kingdom was the initial leader of a UN-mandated 5,000-strong

International Security Assistance Force (ISAF) which helped to stabilise Kabul.

The emergency *Loya Jirga* met in Kabul in June 2002 to elect the President of the country, and approve a transitional administration. This will govern until 2004 and its tasks include drafting a new constitution, coordinating international development assistance, overseeing the formation of a national army, reforming the public sector and preparing for elections at the end of its term.

The UK Government is committed to the reconstruction of Afghanistan and has pledged £322 million over five years. It has spent £170 million since September 2001 on humanitarian and reconstruction needs. The United Kingdom leads international assistance on counter-narcotics work. In July 2003, it deployed a joint military-civilian Provincial Reconstruction Team (PRT) to Mazar-e-Sharif in northern Afghanistan. The aim of the PRT is to help with the reform and reconstruction of security arrangements and to extend the authority of the central government, leading to improved security in the regions.

Latin America and the Caribbean
Important British links with Latin America date from the early 19th century. The rise of democracy and increasingly free market economies have enabled the United Kingdom to strengthen its contemporary ties with the region, and it is now one of the largest investors after the US.

The first UK/Caribbean Forum, held in 1998 in Nassau, Bahamas, marked the beginning of a new longer-term process of co-operation between the United Kingdom and the countries of the region. The Forum is now a biennial event, hosted alternately by the United Kingdom and a Caribbean country. The fourth meeting will take place in the United Kingdom in 2004.

The EU plays an increasingly important role in the United Kingdom's relationship with Latin America and the Caribbean. The first summit of EU, Latin American and Caribbean Heads of State and Government took place in 1999 and a second meeting was held in May 2002, when the EU and Chile signed a trade agreement (the EU's only other such agreement in Latin America is with Mexico).

Overseas Territories

UK Overseas Territories (OTs) have a combined population of around 197,000. The territories are listed on page 70. Most have considerable self-government and their own legislatures. Governors appointed by The Queen are responsible for external affairs, internal security, defence and international financial services. Most domestic matters are delegated to locally elected governments and legislatures. The British Indian Ocean Territory, the British Antarctic Territory, and South Georgia and the South Sandwich Islands have non-resident Commissioners, rather than Governors. None of the Territories has expressed a desire for independence from the United Kingdom.

The United Kingdom aims to provide the OTs with security and political stability, ensure efficient and honest government, and support their economic and social advancement. The Overseas Territories Economic Diversification Fund was established in 2001 to help them to develop a sustainable economic future. The FCO's Good Governance Fund for the OTs allocated over £3 million in 2002/03 to activities focused on good governance, law enforcement and human rights. Offshore financial service industries are of major importance in several of the Territories. The UK Government's policy is to ensure that these meet international standards of regulation and that effective steps are taken to combat financial crime and regulatory abuse.

New citizenship provisions under the *British Overseas Territories Act 2002* took effect on 21 May 2002. From that date, all existing OT citizens (with the exception of those deriving their citizenship from a connection with the British Sovereign Base Areas of Cyprus) automatically became British citizens, with the right of abode in the United Kingdom.[3] By the end of 2002, some 7,042 British Overseas Territories citizens had applied for British citizen passports. A continuing constitutional review process, designed to bring the Territory constitutions up to date to reflect a more modern relationship between the United Kingdom and OT Governments, is also in progress.

An OT Consultative Council, comprising UK ministers and the Chief Minister or equivalent from each Territory meets annually.

Falkland Islands

The Falkland Islands are the subject of a territorial claim by Argentina. The UK Government does not accept the Argentine claim and is committed to defending the Islanders' right to live under a government of their own choosing. This right of self-determination is enshrined in the United Nations Charter and is embodied in the 1985 Falkland Islands Constitution. The United Kingdom and Argentina nevertheless maintain good bilateral relations and co-operate on practical issues of common interest affecting the South Atlantic, such as conservation of fish stocks and surveying of the continental shelf. A review of the Falkland Islands Constitution is under way

Gibraltar

British-Dutch forces captured Gibraltar in 1704 and Spain ceded the island to Britain in perpetuity under the 1713 Treaty of Utrecht. However, Spain has long sought its return. In July 2001, the 'Brussels Process' (talks between the United Kingdom and Spain on a range of Gibraltar-related issues, including sovereignty) was re-launched. In July 2002, the UK Government indicated that although a number of issues remained to be resolved, the United Kingdom and Spain had reached a broad measure of agreement on the principles that should underpin a lasting settlement:

- that the United Kingdom and Spain should share sovereignty over Gibraltar;
- that there should be more internal self-government;
- the retention of UK traditions, customs and way of life;
- the retention of the right to UK nationality for Gibraltarians, who should also gain the right to Spanish nationality;
- the retention of Gibraltar's own institutions; and
- that Gibraltar could, if it chose, participate fully in the EU single market and other EU arrangements.

The UK Government reiterated that the people of Gibraltar would have the final say in a UK-organised referendum. The Government of Gibraltar organised a referendum on the question of joint sovereignty with Spain on

---

3 Many British Overseas Territories' citizens from Gibraltar and the Falkland Islands already possessed British citizenship under previous legislation applying to those Territories.

The Overseas Territories at a glance

Anguilla (capital: The Valley)
Area: 90 square kilometres
Population: 12,000
Economy: tourism, financial services, fishing
History: British territory since 1650.

Bermuda (capital: Hamilton)
Area: 53 square kilometres
Population: 62,000
Economy: reinsurance, tourism
History: first British settlers in 1609–12. Government passed
to the Crown in 1684
UN World Heritage Site: town of St George and related
fortifications (from 2000).

British Antarctic Territory
Area: 1.7 million square kilometres
Population: no indigenous population. The United Kingdom
has two permanent British Antarctic Survey stations, staffed
by 40 people in winter and 200 in summer. Scientists from
other Antarctic Treaty nations have bases in the Territory
History: the British claim dates back to 1908. By October
2002, 45 states, including the United Kingdom, had become
Members of the Antarctic Treaty System, which provides a
framework for the peaceful use of the Antarctic.

British Indian Ocean Territory (capital: Diego Garcia)
Area: 54,400 square kilometres of ocean, including the
Chagos Archipelago land area
Population: military. No indigenous inhabitants
Economy: territory used for defence purposes by the United
Kingdom and the United States
History: ceded to Britain by France under the 1814 Treaty of
Paris.

British Virgin Islands (capital: Road Town)
Area: 153 square kilometres
Population: 21,000
Economy: tourism, international financial services
History: discovered in 1493 by Columbus and annexed by
Britain in 1672.

Cayman Islands (capital: George Town)
Area: 260 square kilometres
Population: 42,000
Economy: tourism, offshore finance
History: the 1670 Treaty of Madrid recognised Britain's claim.

Falkland Islands (capital: Stanley)
Area: 12,173 square kilometres
Permanent population: 3,000, plus military garrison.
Economy: fishery, tourism, agriculture
History: first known landing in 1690 by British naval captain,
John Strong. Under British administration since 1833, except
for brief Argentine occupation in 1982.

Gibraltar
Area: 6.5 square kilometres
Population: 27,000
Economy: tourism, banking and finance
History: ceded to Britain in 1713 under the Treaty of Utrecht.

Montserrat (capital: Plymouth, although destroyed by
volcanic activity which has rendered the south of the island
an exclusion zone)
Area: 102 square kilometres
Population: 4,500
Economy: construction, tourism
History: colonised by English and Irish settlers in 1632.

Pitcairn, Ducie, Henderson and Oeno (capital: Adamstown)
Area: 4.5 square kilometres
Population: 43
Economy: fishing, agriculture and postage stamp sales
History: occupied by mutineers from the British ship *Bounty*
in 1790; annexed as a British colony in 1838
UN World Heritage Site: Henderson Island (from 1988).

St Helena (capital: Jamestown)
Area: 122 square kilometres
Population: 5,000
Economy: fishing, agriculture and tourism.
History: taken over in 1658 by the British East India
Company.

Ascension Island (Dependency of St Helena)
Area: 90 square kilometres
Population: 1,000
Economy: communications and military base
History: the British garrison dates from Napoleon's exile on
St Helena after 1815.

Tristan da Cunha (Dependency of St Helena)
Area: 98 square kilometres
Population: 300
Economy: fishing
History: occupied by a British garrison in 1816
UN World Heritage Site: Gough Island Wildlife Reserve (from
1995).

South Georgia and the South Sandwich Islands
Area: Some 170 kilometres long, varying in width from
2 to 40 kilometres
Population: no indigenous population. British Antarctic
Survey stations at King Edward Point and Bird Island
History: first landing by Captain Cook in 1775.

Turks and Caicos Islands (capital: Cockburn Town)
Area: 430 square kilometres
Population: 20,000
Economy: tourism, property development, real estate,
international finance and fishing
History: Europeans from Bermuda first occupied the islands
around 1678, then planters from southern states of America
settled after the American War of Independence in the late
18th century.

7 November 2002. Of those participating, almost 99 per cent voted against the principle. The UK Government noted the result and stressed that the principle of Gibraltarian consent, as set out in Gibraltar's 1969 Constitution, remained central to its approach. The UK Government continues to believe that dialogue with both Spain and Gibraltar is the best way to secure a permanent settlement to the dispute.

The UK Parliament passed the *European Parliament (Representation) Act* in May 2003. This Act will allow the people of Gibraltar to vote in elections to the European Parliament, starting in the European Parliamentary elections in 2004. To introduce this change, some associated legislation needs to be passed in Gibraltar. The Electoral Commission will advise on which constituency in England or Wales Gibraltar should join, in consultation with many parties, including the people of Gibraltar.

Gibraltar has an elected House of Assembly. Responsibility for a range of 'defined domestic matters' is devolved to elected local ministers. The Territory is within the EU, as part of the United Kingdom Member State, although it is outside the common customs system and does not participate in the Common Agricultural or Fisheries Policies or the EU's value added tax arrangements. The people of Gibraltar have been declared UK nationals for EU purposes.

Administration of foreign policy

Foreign & Commonwealth Office
The FCO is in charge of foreign policy. Its head is the Secretary of State for Foreign and Commonwealth Affairs, who is responsible for the work of the department and for the Diplomatic Service (see page 51). The FCO maintains diplomatic, consular and commercial relations with about 190 countries, and the United Kingdom has 233 diplomatic posts worldwide. As well as around 2,000 UK-based FCO diplomats, UK diplomatic missions employ 9,860 locally engaged staff. Staff overseas deal with political, commercial and economic work, entry clearance to the UK and consular work, aid administration, information and other activities such as culture, science and technology.

The FCO's only executive agency, Wilton Park in Steyning, West Sussex, organises conferences in the United Kingdom that are attended by politicians, business people, academics and other professionals from all over the world. It holds some 50 conferences a year and contributes to the analysis and discussion of key international policy challenges and issues.

An important function of the FCO is to promote understanding of UK foreign policies and to project an up-to-date image of the United Kingdom worldwide, beyond the sphere of government-to-government diplomacy. A new, £5 million Public Diplomacy Programme Fund will support two or three major campaigns each year, and will also allow diplomatic posts overseas to bid for funds to achieve specific policy objectives.

Key elements of FCO-funded public diplomacy work include:
- the FCO website and the new *www.i-uk.com* portal site, launched in October 2002 in conjunction with the British Council, Visit Britain (see page 473), Trade Partners UK and Invest UK (see page 373), to provide information on the United Kingdom to an overseas audience;
- scholarship schemes for overseas students (see page 126) and programmes for influential foreign visitors;
- the BBC World Service (see page 243);
- the British Council (see page 72);
- British Satellite News, used extensively by overseas radio and television broadcasters to supplement their news coverage. BSN has a bilingual website (*www.bsn.org.uk*);
- the London Correspondents' Unit, which is the FCO's specialist link with foreign correspondents based in London;
- the London Press Service, which supplies material for publication overseas.

A new advisory committee designed to improve the cohesion, effectiveness and impact of government efforts to promote the United Kingdom overseas was established in 2002. The Public Diplomacy Strategy Board, which subsumes the work of the Britain Abroad Task Force, has agreed a national public diplomacy strategy to support key UK overseas interests and objectives. The Board meets four times a year, and includes top management from other government departments, non-governmental organisations (NGOs) and the private sector, with a shared interest in how the United Kingdom is perceived overseas.

British Council

The British Council is the principal UK agency for educational and cultural relations overseas. Operating in 109 countries, its work includes teaching English, promoting UK education and training, running information centres, supporting good governance and human rights, and encouraging appreciation of UK science, arts, literature and design.

It is financed partly by a grant from the FCO and partly by income from revenue-earning activities such as English language teaching and the administration of examinations. Some of the programmes organised by the Council as part of the UK aid programme receive funding from the Department for International Development (see page 73).

In 2001/02, the Council dealt with 1.8 million enquiries, welcomed 6.6 million visitors to its libraries and information centres, and issued 6.7 million books and videos to 300,000 British Council library members. It also administered 840,000 professional and academic examinations.

In the same period, the British Council attracted an audience of 7 million people worldwide to its arts events, and many more through radio and television coverage. It also went on tour to 50 countries with the science exhibition *Innovation UK*, seen by half a million visitors.

Educational exchanges
The British Council recruits teachers for work overseas, organises short overseas visits by UK experts, encourages cultural exchange visits, and organises academic interchange between UK universities and colleges and those in other countries. In 2001–02 the Council arranged 40,000 vocational training weeks for UK students and trainers in 29 European countries, and helped over 16,000 young people to participate in exchange projects.

Human rights

The UK Government has stated its commitment to work for improvements in human rights standards around the world and, in September 2003, published its sixth *Annual Report on Human Rights* describing the activities and initiatives pursued from July 2002 to July 2003. The Human

Rights Project Fund, launched in 1998, provides direct financial assistance for grass-roots human rights projects around the world.

International conventions

United Nations
Universal respect for human rights is an obligation under the UN Charter. Expressions of concern about human rights do not, therefore, constitute interference in the internal affairs of another state.

The UK Government supports the Universal Declaration of Human Rights, which the UN General Assembly adopted in 1948. Since this is not a legally binding document, the General Assembly in 1966 adopted two international covenants on human rights, imposing legal obligations on those states ratifying or acceding to them. The covenants came into force in 1976, the United Kingdom ratifying both in the same year. One covenant deals with economic, social and cultural rights and the other with civil and political rights. Other international instruments that the United Kingdom accedes to include those on:
- the elimination of racial discrimination;
- the elimination of all forms of discrimination against women;
- the rights of the child;
- the elimination of torture and other cruel, inhuman or degrading treatment or punishment;
- the prevention of genocide;
- the abolition of slavery; and
- the status of refugees.

Council of Europe
The UK is also bound by the Council of Europe's Convention for the Protection of Human Rights and Fundamental Freedoms (ECHR), which covers areas such as:
- the right to life, liberty and a fair trial;
- the right to marry and have a family;
- freedom of thought, conscience and religion;
- freedom of expression, including freedom of the press;
- freedom of peaceful assembly and association;
- the right to have a sentence reviewed by a higher tribunal; and
- the prohibition of torture and inhuman or degrading treatment.

The rights and obligations of the ECHR were enshrined in UK law upon the implementation of the *Human Rights Act 1998* in 2000 (see page 189).

International Criminal Court

The United Kingdom has supported the establishment of an International Criminal Court to try cases of genocide, crimes against humanity and war crimes. The Government signed the Court's Statute in 1998 and ratification took place in October 2001. Over 60 other states have ratified the Statute (although not the US, which does not recognise its jurisdiction), enabling the Court to come into existence on 1 July 2002. The Court is based in The Hague in The Netherlands and its powers are not retrospective.

In March 2003, 18 judges took their oath and elected a president and vice-president of the Court. Elections were later held for the chief prosecutor and the registrar of the Court, and all principal officers of the Court were in place by 1 July 2003.

Development co-operation

UK development aid policy is focused on its commitment to internationally agreed development targets – Millennium Development Goals – such as halving the proportion of people living in extreme poverty and providing universal access to primary education and improved healthcare by 2015. The UK Government believes that globalisation – involving, for example, increased flows of goods, services, capital and trade – offers poor countries opportunities to access knowledge and technology, new trade and investment, if they can be brought into the global economy.

In January 2003, the Government launched an International Finance Facility (IFF) to meet the Millennium Development Goals. Its founding principle is long-term but conditional funding, guaranteed to the poorest countries by the richest ones. The IFF proposal is aimed at doubling levels of aid for the world's poorest countries, from just over $50 billion a year to $100 billion per year in the years to 2015.

In 2002/03 total Department for International Development (DFID) expenditure was £3.3 billion (see Figures 7.1, 7.2 and 7.3): £1.8 billion on bilateral aid and £1.4 billion on multilateral aid.

DFID's projected budget is £3.7 billion during 2003/04. Further increases announced in 2002 will

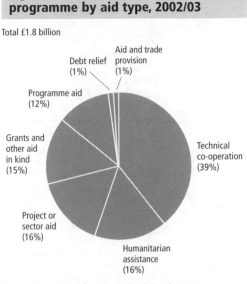

Figure 7.1 DFID bilateral aid programme by aid type, 2002/03

Total £1.8 billion

- Debt relief (1%)
- Aid and trade provision (1%)
- Programme aid (12%)
- Grants and other aid in kind (15%)
- Technical co-operation (39%)
- Project or sector aid (16%)
- Humanitarian assistance (16%)

Source: Department for International Development

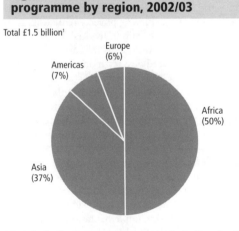

Figure 7.2 DFID bilateral aid programme by region, 2002/03

Total £1.5 billion[1]

- Europe (6%)
- Americas (7%)
- Africa (50%)
- Asia (37%)

1 Excludes funding for global projects and for the Pacific region. The Pacific region accounts for less than 1 per cent of funding.
Source: Department for International Development

take it to £4.6 billion by 2005/06. This figure includes, for the first time, a £1 billion annual bilateral programme for Africa.

Official Development Assistance (ODA) is set to rise from 0.26 per cent of gross national income in 1997 to 0.33 per cent by 2003/04 and to 0.40 per cent by 2005/06, reflecting the Government's commitment to progress towards the UN target of 0.7 per cent.

Figure 7.3 DFID multilateral aid programme by recipient agency, 2002/03

Total £1.4 billion

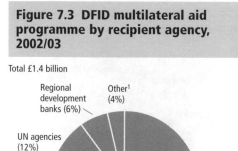

1 Includes Global Environmental Assistance (2%), International Monetary Fund (1%) and other agencies.
Source: Department for International Development

Poverty reduction

The UK Government considers that growth, equity and security are the three central requirements for achieving poverty reduction. It is shifting its assistance from individual projects to direct support to governments that are implementing agreed poverty reduction strategies and better financial management. The *International Development Act 2002* outlaws the use of UK aid for any other purpose than poverty reduction. DFID is committed to spending 90 per cent of its aid budget in the poorest countries.

Debt relief

The heavy burden of servicing debt reduces the ability of the poorest countries to tackle poverty effectively. The Government is pressing for continued progress on implementation of the revised 1999 Heavily Indebted Poor Countries (HIPC) debt initiative, which is designed to deliver broader and faster relief to countries committed to poverty reduction. The United Kingdom goes further than required under the HIPC initiative and is writing off 100 per cent of debt from HIPC countries once they qualify for relief.

Good governance and human rights

The quality of governance has a major impact on economic growth and the effectiveness of services. The UK Government is focusing on issues such as:
- democratic accountability (bringing poor people into the democratic process);

- fundamental freedoms (including rights to education, health and an adequate livelihood);
- combating child labour;
- tackling corruption and money laundering;
- better revenue and public finance management;
- access to basic services; and
- personal safety and security in the community, with access to justice.

Women's empowerment

Eliminating gender discrimination and supporting measures to improve women's equality are crucial to reducing poverty and upholding human rights. A priority in UK assistance is the promotion of equal access to education for all girls and boys.

Health

Three of the eight Millennium Development Goals involve health: reduction of child mortality; improvement in maternal health; and the fight against diseases (including HIV, tuberculosis (TB) and malaria). The impact of these major diseases on the poor is an important obstacle to social and economic development. Since 1997, the United Kingdom has committed over £1.5 billion to support the development of health systems in partner countries.

The United Kingdom was a high-profile advocate for the Global Fund for AIDS, TB and Malaria (GFATM) to increase access to effective treatments against these diseases. Launched in January 2002, the Fund has attracted US$ 4.7 billion in pledges over eight years from 40 countries.

Education

Education is a fundamental right and the key to economic and social development. Worldwide an estimated 115 million children of primary school age do not go to school, while one in five adults is illiterate. UK resources are focused on basic and primary education. The United Kingdom is working with other governments to develop well-integrated and sustainable education systems and to help provide high-quality primary education. Reading, writing and numeracy skills are an integral part of many aid programmes. They give access to information, for example on health, and the market economy and are a vital link to greater opportunities for improving people's livelihoods and their human rights.

The environment

Maintaining and improving the environment are crucial to the elimination of poverty. The Government's priority is to promote better environmental management, reverse environmental degradation and reduce poor people's vulnerability to the effects of global environmental trends (particularly climate change).

Conflict and natural disasters

Conflict and natural disasters are major barriers to poverty reduction. Many of the 40 poorest countries are either in the midst of armed conflict or have recently emerged from such conflict. UK objectives are to reduce the tensions that lead to conflict, limit the means of waging warfare, and provide the early timely and effective humanitarian assistance and support needed for long-term reconstruction and development.

The United Kingdom targets its humanitarian assistance upon those in greatest need and seeks to improve the quality and speed of the response to a disaster; promote effective recovery and early transition from emergency assistance to rehabilitation and reconstruction; and help countries to reduce their vulnerability to natural, environmental and industrial disasters. The United Kingdom also upholds its commitment to strengthening the response of the multilateral institutions to humanitarian relief and crisis management.

During 2002/03, the United Kingdom played a pivotal role in helping to re-establish stability in Sierra Leone, and supported efforts to promote peace in Angola, the Democratic Republic of the Congo and Sudan. By 31 July 2003, the United Kingdom had committed £185 million to humanitarian and reconstruction efforts in Iraq. It had also responded to a number of humanitarian crises around the world, including food shortages in Ethiopia and southern Africa. In October 2002, it set up a Southern African Humanitarian Crisis Unit in Johannesburg to work more effectively with the regional offices of the UN, Red Cross, NGOs and donors in South Africa.

Peacekeeping and security

The UN is the principal body responsible for the maintenance of international peace and security. On 30 April 2003, there were 36,987 military personnel and civilian police from 97 countries serving in 14 peacekeeping operations around the world. The United Kingdom provides civilian police, military observers and troops for a range of UN missions and NATO deployments.

Cyprus

The United Kingdom has a contingent of about 390 troops in the UN Force in Cyprus, established in 1964 to help prevent the recurrence of fighting between Greek and Turkish Cypriots. Since the hostilities of 1974, when Turkish forces occupied the northern part of the island, the Force has been responsible for monitoring the ceasefire and for control of a buffer zone between the two communities.

Bosnia and Herzegovina

The UK Government supports the consolidation of a peaceful, multi-ethnic and democratic Bosnia and Herzegovina, and is helping to implement the 1995 Dayton/Paris Peace Agreement. The Stabilisation Force (SFOR) comprises troops from NATO nations and other contributing countries. The United Kingdom supplies around 1,400 troops to SFOR. SFOR ensures compliance with the military requirements of the Dayton Agreement and supports the organisations responsible for Dayton's civil aspects, including the Office of the High Representative, the EU Police Mission, the UN High Commissioner for Refugees, and the OSCE.

The United Kingdom helps to fund the International Criminal Tribunal in The Hague, established to bring to trial those indicted for war crimes in the former Yugoslavia, and provides staff, information and forensic science expertise. UK forces have been at the forefront of SFOR's efforts to detain war crimes suspects.

Kosovo

A UN interim civilian administration (UNMIK) continues to govern Kosovo. It was established in the war-ravaged province of the Federal Republic of Yugoslavia in 1999 by a UN Security Council resolution. The United Kingdom provides 123 civilian police, along with specialist officers, local government administrators and judicial experts to UNMIK, which is helping to establish self-government in the province. The United Kingdom maintains its commitment to the Kosovo Force (KFOR), contributing around 1,400 personnel to KFOR operations.

Arms control

The United Kingdom has a clear national interest in preventing proliferation of weapons of mass destruction and promoting international control, given the global reach of modern weapons. The terrorist attacks in the US on 11 September 2001 highlighted the need to prevent terrorists from obtaining such weapons.

Weapons of mass destruction

Nuclear weapons
The main instrument for controlling nuclear weapons is the Treaty on the Non-Proliferation of Nuclear Weapons (NPT), which entered into force in 1970 and to which the UK Government remains committed. The United Kingdom helped to secure its indefinite extension in 1995. In 2002 and 2003, the United Kingdom was an active contributor to the Preparatory Committees for the 2005 NPT Review Conference.

The United Kingdom participated in negotiations on the Comprehensive Test Ban Treaty (CTBT), which it signed in 1996 and ratified in 1998. The CTBT, with its permanent verification system, will come into force upon ratification by the remaining 13 of 44 named states. The UK Government is also pressing for the negotiation of a treaty banning the future production of fissile material for use in nuclear weapons.

The United Kingdom welcomed the Treaty of Moscow (Strategic Offensive Reductions Treaty) between Russia and the USA. This came into force in 2003 and will reduce these countries' respective strategic nuclear warheads by two-thirds by 2012.

While large nuclear arsenals and the risks of proliferation continue to exist, the Government believes that the minimum nuclear deterrent (see page 84) will remain a necessary element of UK security.

Biological weapons
The 1972 Biological and Toxic Weapons Convention (BTWC) provides for a worldwide ban on such weapons, but there are no effective compliance mechanisms. The United Kingdom continues to look for ways of strengthening the Convention.

The BTWC 5th Review Conference in November 2002 unanimously agreed a programme of work

for the next three years that will include national implementation of the Convention, sharing best practice on disease surveillance, and developing a code of conduct for scientists. The UK Government strongly supports this programme of follow-up work.

Chemical weapons
The 1993 Chemical Weapons Convention, which came into force in 1997, provides for a worldwide ban on these weapons. The Organisation for the Prohibition of Chemical Weapons (OPCW), which is responsible for verification, held its first review conference in May 2003. This set out key work areas for the OPCW over the next few years and provided a foundation for further work to strengthen the implementation of the Convention, in particular seeking universal adherence to the Convention and improving the effectiveness of verification.

Conventional armed forces
The UK Government continues to work with its NATO partners and other European countries to develop and improve agreements on enhancing stability in Europe, in the light of the changed security environment. The main agreements reached are:

- the Conventional Armed Forces in Europe (CFE) Treaty (originally signed in 1990 and adapted at an OSCE summit in 1999), which limits the numbers of heavy weapons in the NATO and former Warsaw Pact countries, and includes a verification regime. The CFE Treaty is widely regarded as a linchpin of European security;
- the Vienna Document, developed under the auspices of the OSCE, which is a politically binding agreement concerning the promotion of stability and openness in military matters in Europe. Revised in 1999, it contains confidence and security-building measures, and verification arrangements; and
- the 1992 Open Skies Treaty, which provides for overflight and photographing of the entire territory of the 27 participating states to monitor their military capabilities and activities. The Treaty entered into force on 1 January 2002.

The UN Register of Conventional Arms, which came into effect in 1992, is intended to allow greater transparency in international transfers of conventional arms and to help identify excessive arms build-up in any one country or region.

Countries are requested on a voluntary basis to report imports and exports of seven categories of major conventional weapons that have been assessed as having the greatest potential to be destabilising. Participation in the Register has grown since its inception; by the end of July 2003, 165 Member States had participated at least once, while almost all the major producers, exporters and importers of conventional arms were reporting regularly to the Register.

Landmines

The United Kingdom signed the Ottawa Convention banning the use, production, trade, transfer and stockpiling of anti-personnel landmines in 1997, and destroyed its stockpile after the Convention entered into force in 1999.

The United Kingdom has a programme to support humanitarian demining activities. This aims to help affected countries develop the capacity to clear landmines and to improve the coordination of international demining resources.

Export controls

The United Kingdom is a founding member of all the international export control regimes that govern the export of conventional arms, technology associated with weapons of mass destruction, missiles and 'dual-use' items.

In 1997, the UK Government issued new criteria for assessing licence applications for arms exports, one of which prohibits the granting of licences where there is a clearly identifiable risk that weapons might be used for internal repression or international aggression. At the same time, it banned the export of certain items that evidence clearly showed were used for torture or other abuses. It is committed to preventing British companies from manufacturing, selling or procuring such equipment, and is seeking a global ban.

In 1998, EU Member States agreed on a Code of Conduct on Arms Exports, setting common standards to which all EU members would adhere. In 2003 the United Kingdom also supported an EU common position on trafficking and brokering.

Export Control Act

Under the *Export Control Act 2002*, a licence will be required for arms trafficking and brokering activities in military equipment, which take place wholly or partly in the United Kingdom. Full extraterritorial controls will be introduced on UK

persons whose activities facilitate the supply of military equipment to embargoed destinations, and the export of torture equipment or long-range missiles to any destination. The Act also introduces new controls on the transfer abroad of military technology by electronic means, and the transfer of technology, by any means which is or may be intended for use in connection with a weapons of mass destruction programme. New controls will also be introduced on the electronic transfer abroad of military technology, where the physical export of the same goods is already controlled.

International terrorism

Countering international terrorism is a key foreign policy objective. The UK Government regards acts of terrorism as unacceptable in all circumstances and opposes concessions to any terrorist demands. It works bilaterally with other like-minded governments, and multilaterally through the UN, EU, G8 and other international and regional organisations, to promote effective and sustained action against terrorist groups and to foster closer international coordination of the fight against terrorism. The United Kingdom played a leading role in securing UN Security Council Resolution 1373 in the immediate aftermath of the 11 September attacks. Under UK chairmanship of the UN Counter-Terrorism Committee between October 2001 and April 2003, 188 states made initial reports to the Committee.

The UK Government has stepped up assistance to countries that lack the means to tackle terrorism, and is committed to challenging the political, social and economic conditions that terrorists exploit. It has allocated £24 million for counter-terrorism work over the next three years through the FCO's Global Opportunities Fund. The United Kingdom has ratified all 12 UN terrorism conventions, the most recent – the International Convention for the Suppression of Financing of Terrorism – in February 2001, upon the entry into force of the *Terrorism Act 2000*.

International crime

The United Kingdom supports international efforts to combat illegal drugs, working with producer and transit countries, especially those where drug production and trafficking represent a direct threat to the United Kingdom.

Over 70 drug liaison officers are stationed in UK missions in key countries, in co-operation with the host governments. The United Kingdom is working with its EU partners to help Latin American, Caribbean and Central Asian states stem the transit of drugs across their territories. The UK Government contributed £10 million to anti-drugs assistance overseas in 2002/03. The United Kingdom is one of the biggest contributors to the UN Office on Drugs and Crime.

The EU is spending £6.9 million on Europe-wide anti-drugs action, plus £0.69 million to help each of the EU applicant countries of Central and Eastern Europe (see page 63). EU governments are considering measures to strike at drug traffickers, including tough common minimum jail sentences, travel bans and the confiscation of drug traffickers' passports.

The United Kingdom also supports international efforts to counter financial crime, for example through its membership of the Financial Action Task Force against money laundering, and by backing regional anti-money laundering groups.

Together with its EU partners, the United Kingdom is confronting serious and organised international crime, for example via the European Police Office (EUROPOL), which supports investigations and operations conducted by national law enforcement agencies. EU Member States also belong to the International Criminal Police Organisation (Interpol). The National Criminal Intelligence Service UK (see page 193) provides liaison with Interpol.

The United Kingdom participated in negotiations for the UN Convention Against Transnational Crime as well as three protocols covering the smuggling of migrants, trafficking in human beings and illegal firearms. The Convention was signed by 120 states, including the United Kingdom, in 2000.

Further reading

Foreign & Commonwealth Office Departmental Report 2003. Cm 5913. The Stationery Office, 2003.

Department for International Development Departmental Report 2003: The Government's Expenditure Plans 2001–02 to 2005–06. Cm 5914. The Stationery Office, 2003.

Annual Report on Human Rights 2003. Foreign & Commonwealth Office, 2003.

Websites

Foreign & Commonwealth Office
www.fco.gov.uk

Department for International Development
www.dfid.gov.uk

Ministry of Defence
www.mod.uk

British Council
www.britcoun.org

Commonwealth
www.thecommonwealth.org

Council of Europe
www.coe.int

European Union (Europa)
www.europa.eu.int

Organisation for Security and Co-operation in Europe
www.osce.org

United Nations
www.un.org

www.

8 Defence

Overview

The primary objectives of UK defence policy are to guarantee the security and defence of the United Kingdom and its Overseas Territories (see page 69), including defence against terrorism, and to support the Government's foreign policy objectives, particularly in promoting international peace and security. The Ministry of Defence (MoD) is responsible for implementing defence policy and is also the headquarters of UK military services.

The 1998 Strategic Defence Review (SDR, see page 85) remains the foundation of the Government's defence policy. It concluded that while there was no direct military threat to the United Kingdom or its Overseas Territories following the end of the Cold War, there were new threats, including organised crime, the proliferation of nuclear, chemical and biological weapons, and the break-up of the old communist states, with attendant ethnic and religious conflict. A White Paper, published in autumn 2003, provides an updated statement of defence policy, and sets out plans for ensuring that UK Armed Forces remain among the most effective and flexible in the world.

An update to the SDR, *The Strategic Defence Review: A New Chapter*, was issued in July 2002. This was the MoD's part of the Government's comprehensive examination of its strategies, preparedness and contingency planning in response to the terrorist attacks on the USA in September 2001. It highlighted the need to ensure that the right forces, concepts and capabilities were in place to deal with the new threats posed by international terrorism. It also focused on enhancing the Armed Forces' ability to support civil authorities in home security, and established 14 regionally based Civil Contingency Reaction Forces (using Volunteer Reserve personnel and based around Territorial Army infantry battalions).

The United Kingdom plays a full part in contributing to international peace and security through the North Atlantic Treaty Organisation (NATO) and the European Union (EU, see page 60), and through other international organisations such as the United Nations (UN, see page 63) and the Organisation for Security and Co-operation in Europe (OSCE, see page 65).

The Government is involved in the development of European military capabilities to strengthen Europe's contribution to NATO, and to allow the EU to conduct crisis management operations where NATO is not engaged (see page 81). The Armed Forces also contribute to the peacetime security of the United Kingdom and its Overseas Territories, and assist in humanitarian and peacetime operations worldwide.

North Atlantic Treaty Organisation

The defence of the United Kingdom and its economic and wider interests is linked to the security of the Euro-Atlantic area. NATO is the primary means of guaranteeing that security. The NATO Alliance embodies the unique defence and security partnership between North America and Europe and membership of NATO is one of the cornerstones of UK defence policy. The United Kingdom is a founder member and most of its forces are assigned to the organisation. The Alliance is open to new applicants willing and able to assume the obligations and responsibilities of membership. Seven countries (Bulgaria, Estonia,

Iraq war 2003

UK forces played a pivotal role in the assault on Iraq by a US-led coalition. The war began on 20 March 2003 with a missile attack against Baghdad. In the following days, US and UK ground troops entered Iraq from the south, with US forces moving into central Baghdad on 9 April. US commanders announced that the military objectives of the conflict had been achieved on 14 April and the UK Government set out a three-point programme to rehabilitate Iraq. On 22 May the UN Security Council overwhelmingly approved a resolution lifting economic sanctions against Iraq and giving US and UK forces interim control of the country.

The UK contribution to the Iraq campaign included:
- a naval task force of 17 ships, including the aircraft carrier HMS *Ark Royal*, the helicopter carrier HMS *Ocean*, two submarines and mine counter-measure vessels;
- an amphibious force numbering 4,000 personnel;
- a significant Royal Fleet Auxiliary deployment that supported both land and maritime operations and the delivery of humanitarian aid;
- a land force of around 26,000 personnel, including the 1st and 7th Armoured Brigades, the 16th Air Assault Brigade and the 102nd Logistics Brigade; and
- an air component numbering around 100 fixed-wing aircraft and 27 support helicopters, backed by some 8,000 personnel.

Latvia, Lithuania, Romania, Slovakia and Slovenia) were invited to join the 19 members of the Alliance at the NATO Summit in Prague in November 2002. They are expected to accede by the next summit, which will be held in Istanbul in May 2004.

The Alliance's current security tasks are as follows:
- to provide a firm basis for stability and security in the European and Atlantic areas;
- to serve as a transatlantic forum for discussions on any issues that affect Allied interests;
- to deter and defend against any threat of aggression directed towards any NATO member state wherever that threat may arise – an attack on one member is treated as an attack on all;
- to contribute to effective conflict prevention and crisis management; and
- to promote partnership, co-operation and dialogue with other countries in the Euro-Atlantic area, including Russia.

NATO was created in 1949 in response to the ideological, political and military threat from communism and the former USSR. It has adapted to changes in the security environment in Europe, which have involved a fundamental transformation in the Alliance's relationship with Russia after 11 September 2001. A summit meeting in Rome in May 2002 established the NATO-Russia Council (NRC) to replace the NATO Russia Permanent Joint Council. The NRC provides NATO allies and Russia with a mechanism for consultation, consensus-building, co-operation and joint action on a wide range of security issues of common interest, including terrorism, crisis management and non-proliferation. Work has been progressing well on a range of issues, with NATO and Russia working as equal partners.

NATO has been reassessing its defence policy in the aftermath of the 2001 terrorist attacks in the United States. NATO foreign ministers agreed at Prague in November 2002 that Alliance forces could be used wherever they were needed to counter the new threats of terrorism and weapons of mass destruction. Subsequent decisions were that NATO should take the lead role on the International Security Assistance Force (ISAF) in Afghanistan, and offer assistance to Poland in its operation in Iraq.

Heads of State and Government of NATO member countries also adopted a package of measures at Prague that will strengthen the Alliance's preparedness and ability to manage the full spectrum of security challenges, including terrorism and the spread of weapons of mass destruction. The transformation of NATO will involve:
- a new command structure and headquarters designed to meet the challenges of the new security climate;
- a rapid response force – NATO Response Force; and
- the development of new capabilities to fill critical combat shortfalls.

The administration of NATO will also be reformed in order to strengthen the management of staff and resources and to improve coordination on key issues such as project and programme development.

The first steps of this reform began in August 2003, when NATO's international staff were reorganised into six main divisions: defence investment; defence policy and planning; executive management; operations; political affairs and security policy; and public diplomacy.

At Prague, NATO leaders endorsed a comprehensive review of the Euro-Atlantic Partnership Council (EAPC) Partnership for Peace, giving NATO a practical strategy for engaging with the contrasting groups of countries within the EAPC, taking account of the individual needs of countries in the different regions and NATO's new relationship with Russia. NATO also agreed on a programme to upgrade the political and practical dimensions of the NATO Mediterranean Dialogue. NATO is committed to developing its relationship with Ukraine, through the NATO-Ukraine Commission. At the Prague Summit, NATO and Ukraine launched an action plan to develop closer political and practical co-operation.

European security and defence policy (ESDP)

Parallel to reforms inside NATO, and in response to operations such as Bosnia and Kosovo (see page 83), the EU countries initiated a programme aimed at improving their ability to implement their common foreign and security policy objectives in circumstances where NATO as a whole did not wish to become involved.

At their summit meeting in St Malo in 1998 the UK Prime Minister and the French President proposed that the EU should have the capacity for military action to respond to international crises. In particular, it should be able to take on humanitarian and rescue tasks, peacekeeping, and the tasks of combat forces in crisis management. These proposals were adopted at the Cologne European Council in June 1999. The Helsinki Declaration in 1999 set out the framework for European defence arrangements that were firmly rooted in NATO but that also allowed Europe to take a greater share of the security burden, with a focus on strengthening the EU's military capabilities. By December 2003 the EU intends to be able to deploy 60,000 troops with air and naval support, within 60 days, and sustain them for a year. The UK contribution to an individual operation could involve 12,500 ground troops, 18 warships and 72 combat aircraft. The ESDP is not

a standing army – rather a pool of national armies, under sovereign, national command, that can be called upon when needed to carry out EU peacekeeping, humanitarian and rescue tasks.

EU–NATO

As agreed at NATO's Washington Summit in 1999 and the Nice European Council in December 2002, the EU will act only where NATO as a whole is not engaged. In December 2002 the EU and NATO signed a joint agreement ensuring that the EU could call on key NATO facilities in order to run its own military operations. Following this agreement and the decision taken by NATO in March 2003 to cease Operation Harmony in Macedonia, the EU launched its first military peace-support operation drawing on NATO capabilities – Operation Concordia – to help build peace and security in the country. In June 2003 the EU launched its first ESDP Operation without recourse to NATO – Operation Artemis – in the Democratic Republic of the Congo.

While the ESDP provides an invaluable tool for the EU in support of its broader common and foreign security policy objectives, NATO remains responsible for the collective defence of its members and will retain a major role in crisis management.

UK security

The UK and its Overseas Territories

The Armed Forces are responsible for safeguarding UK territory, airspace and territorial waters. They also operate around the world to protect UK interests and are responsible for the defence of the Overseas Territories – support for whom includes a regular naval presence in the Caribbean (see page 83). In addition, they assist the civil authorities in both the United Kingdom and the Overseas Territories.

Maritime defence

The Royal Navy is responsible for the strategic nuclear deterrent that is deployed at sea continuously (see page 84). The ships of the Navy and Royal Fleet Auxiliary aim to patrol, police and defend UK territorial waters and to protect UK rights and interests (including offshore oil and gas reserves) in the surrounding seas and around the world. The maintenance of a 24-hour, year-round presence in waters around the British Isles, in conjunction with the RAF's maritime patrol aircraft, upholds security of the seas and reassures merchant and other types of shipping. Threats to British-flagged ships overseas, particularly in view of the continuing global terrorist threat, also remain a national responsibility. A worldwide expeditionary capability is maintained around aircraft carriers that operate RAF Joint Force Harriers.

Land defence

The Army aims to have the capability to defend the United Kingdom and its Overseas Territories through the deployment of either the whole or appropriate elements of its available forces. In addition the Army is committed to such tasks as offering military aid to peace support and humanitarian operations, responding to regional conflicts outside the NATO area and contributing forces to counter a strategic attack on NATO. It works closely with the other services and is geared towards rapid reaction and mobility, pre-empting a crisis rather than waiting for one to happen. It usually acts with its allies but it can act alone if required.

Air defence

A system of layered defences maintains the air defence of the United Kingdom and the surrounding seas. The Air Surveillance and Control System (ASACS), supplemented by the NATO Airborne Early Warning Force (to which the RAF contributes six aircraft), provides continuous radar cover. The RAF contributes four squadrons of Tornado F3 air defence aircraft, supported by tanker aircraft, and in wartime, an additional F3 squadron. Royal Navy air defence destroyers may be linked to the ASACS, providing radar and electronic warfare coverage, and surface-to-air missiles. Ground-launched Rapier missiles defend the main RAF bases. Naval aircraft also contribute to UK air defence.

Overseas garrisons

The United Kingdom maintains garrisons or detachments in Ascension Island, Belize, Brunei, the Sovereign Base Areas of Cyprus, Diego Garcia, the Falkland Islands and Gibraltar. Gibraltar contains support, logistics, communications and training facilities in the western Mediterranean, while Cyprus provides base facilities in the eastern Mediterranean. The garrison on the Falkland Islands demonstrates the Government's commitment to upholding the Islanders' right to determine their own future (see page 69). The garrison in Brunei is maintained at the request of the Brunei Government. In addition, a jungle warfare-training unit is maintained in Belize.

Northern Ireland

The Armed Forces support the police in Northern Ireland in maintaining law and order and countering terrorism. The number of units deployed at any one time depends on the prevailing security situation. The Royal Navy patrols territorial waters around Northern Ireland and its inland waterways to deter and intercept the movement of terrorist weapons. The Royal Marines provide troops to meet Royal Navy and Army commitments, while the RAF provides elements of the RAF Regiment and Chinook and Puma helicopters. Around 13,500 military personnel were based in Northern Ireland at the beginning of 2003; the lowest number since 1970.

Other tasks

Other activities include the provision of military aid to the civil authorities, such as:

- support during the outbreak of foot-and-mouth disease in 2001 and providing emergency cover during the firemen's strike of 2003;
- assisting the police in response to terrorist threats and helping in the fight against drugs;
- assistance in dealing with terrorist devices and bombs left over from both world wars;
- fishery protection duties;
- military search and rescue; and
- other support to the civil community, for example during floods.

The UK in NATO

Maritime forces

Most Royal Navy ships are committed to NATO, making permanent contributions to its standing naval forces in the Atlantic and the Mediterranean, providing a High-Readiness Force Maritime Headquarters and contributing to NATO Reaction Forces. The United Kingdom also contributes to NATO's maritime augmentation forces, which are held at the lowest state of readiness and, in peacetime, comprise ships mainly in routine refit or maintenance.

The main components of the fleet available to NATO are:

- three Invincible class aircraft carriers operating Joint Force Harrier aircraft and Sea King or Merlin anti-submarine helicopters;
- 31 destroyers and frigates and 22 mine counter-measure vessels;
- 12 nuclear-powered attack submarines for long-range, stealth operations and precision land attack with Tomahawk missiles; and
- amphibious forces, including a commando brigade of the Royal Marines, and specialist shipping. These provide a self-contained expeditionary capability.

Land forces

The key land component of NATO's Rapid Reaction Forces is the multinational HQ of the Allied Command Europe Rapid Reaction Corps (ARRC) and its supporting forces. Capable of deploying at short notice up to four NATO divisions, the HQ ARRC is currently commanded by a British general. The United Kingdom provides two of the ten divisions available to the Corps – a division of three armoured brigades stationed in Germany and a division of three mechanised brigades based in the United Kingdom. Up to 55,000 UK troops may be assigned to HQ ARRC for operations. An air-mobile brigade, assigned to one of the Corps' multinational divisions, is also based in the United Kingdom.

Air forces

The RAF contributes to NATO's Immediate and Rapid Reaction Forces and its main defence forces, allocating around 100 aircraft and 40 helicopters. Tornado F3, Harrier and Jaguar aircraft, and Rapier surface-to-air missiles form part of the Supreme Allied Commander Europe's Immediate Reaction Force, while Harrier, Jaguar and Tornado GR4 aircraft provide offensive support and tactical reconnaissance for the Rapid Reaction Forces. Chinook and Puma helicopters, forming part of the Joint Helicopter Command, supply troop airlift facilities for the ARRC or other deployed land forces. The RAF provides Nimrod maritime patrol aircraft and search and rescue helicopters. In addition, the RAF is the main European provider of air-to-air refuelling and strategic airlift, and contributes to the NATO airborne early warning and control component.

Wider security interests

UK forces working within NATO, assisting the United Nations, operating in coalition with allies or acting alone may undertake military tasks to promote wider UK security interests. Since the attacks in the US on 11 September 2001, UK Armed Forces have taken a prominent role in the fight against terrorism. The United Kingdom, for example, contributed considerable forces in the Iraq war in the early part of 2003 (see page 80).

UK military personnel participating in UN-commanded operations are helping to maintain the peace in the Democratic Republic of the Congo, Cyprus, East Timor, Georgia and Sierra Leone. Over 2,500 troops are with NATO on UN-mandated operations in Bosnia-Herzegovina and Kosovo. In July 2003 the United Kingdom agreed to contribute about 85 troops to a UN-mandated, EU-led, interim mission to stabilise the town of Bunia in the north-east of the Democratic Republic of the Congo pending the deployment of further UN reinforcements. The Ministry of Defence supplies experienced, specialist personnel to the UN's humanitarian mine action programmes in Bosnia-Herzegovina and Kosovo, and to UN policing programmes in Kosovo. A large proportion of the newly formed Joint Rapid Reaction Force could be made available for future UN peacekeeping operations, although any decision to deploy it rests with the United Kingdom.

The number of operations against traffickers in illicit drugs has increased in recent years. In the Caribbean, a Royal Navy destroyer or frigate works closely with the US, the Overseas Territories in the area and the regional authorities to combat such trafficking. For example, in an operation carried out in June 2003, HMS *Iron Duke*, in conjunction with HM Customs and Excise, intercepted a vessel found to be carrying cocaine with a value of £250 million and thought to be destined for sale in Europe.

UK forces in recent years have also participated in international evacuation or humanitarian relief operations in Angola, the Caribbean and Central America, the Democratic Republic of the Congo, East Timor, Eritrea, Mozambique, Rwanda, Sierra Leone and Somalia.

In recognition of the changed post-Cold War strategic environment, the Strategic Defence Review concluded that the MoD and the Armed Forces should be a force for good in the world, and help prevent and contain crises. A new defence mission, 'defence diplomacy', was created to give greater priority, impetus and coherence to

UK intelligence and security services

The United Kingdom has three intelligence and security services: the Secret Intelligence Service (SIS), the Security Service and the Government Communications Headquarters (GCHQ). The SIS and GCHQ are responsible to the Foreign and Commonwealth Secretary, while the Security Service is responsible to the Home Secretary. The planned budget for these agencies in 2003/04 is £1,088 million. The main role of the SIS is the generation of secret intelligence on issues related to UK vital interests in the fields of security, defence, and foreign and economic policies. The Security Service (also known as MI5) is responsible for the protection of the United Kingdom against threats to national security, primarily from terrorism and espionage. GCHQ carries out signals intelligence, supporting national security, military operations and law enforcement, and also helps to secure government communications and key systems supporting UK national infrastructure. The MoD has its own defence intelligence staff, which provides intelligence analyses, assessments, advice and strategic warnings to the MoD, the Armed Forces and the Government.

various activities designed to prevent conflicts and promote peacetime diplomacy.

Three specific military tasks contribute to the defence diplomacy mission:
- arms control, non-proliferation, and confidence and security building measures;
- outreach activities designed to contribute to security and stability in Central and Eastern Europe, particularly in Russia but also extending to the Trans-Caucasus and Central Asia, through bilateral assistance and co-operation programmes; and
- military assistance programmes with overseas forces and defence communities not covered by outreach.

Nuclear forces

The United Kingdom, along with other members of NATO, has radically reduced its reliance on nuclear weapons, although it retains four Trident submarines as the ultimate guarantee of national security. It continues to support mutual, balanced and verifiable reductions in the number of nuclear weapons worldwide (see page 76). The Government

will allow the inclusion of UK nuclear weapons in multilateral negotiations when it is satisfied that sufficient progress has been made to do so without endangering UK security interests.

After examining UK deterrence requirements, the Government concluded that the country needed fewer than 200 operationally available nuclear warheads – a reduction of one-third. The United Kingdom maintains one Trident submarine on patrol throughout the year. It carries a load of up to 48 warheads, compared with the previous maximum of 96. The submarine's missiles are not targeted and it is normally on several days' 'notice to fire'. Trident submarines on patrol also carry out a variety of secondary tasks without compromising their security. These include hydrographic data collection, equipment trials and exercises with other vessels.

The Trident Strategic Weapon System has three component parts:
- four Vanguard-class ballistic missile submarines – HMS *Vanguard*, *Vigilant*, *Victorious* and *Vengeance*. The four submarines enable the United Kingdom to maintain a continuous deterrent patrol at sea over the life of the Trident force. Continuous patrol ensures that at no time can a potential attacker detect a gap in UK defences;
- 58 Trident D-5 long-range ballistic missiles carried and launched by the Vanguard-class submarines; and
- a stockpile of UK-designed and built nuclear warheads with which to arm the D-5 missiles.

Defence equipment

Modern equipment is an essential part of the UK force restructuring programme, as it helps to increase the flexibility and mobility of the Armed Forces.

Improvements in the Royal Navy equipment programme include the introduction of:
- the Astute-class attack submarines;
- two new aircraft carriers, which will deploy the new, jointly operated RN/RAF F35 Joint Combat Aircraft;
- the Type 45 destroyer, which will deploy an anti-air missile system developed with France and Italy;
- two new landing platform dock (LPD) ships, *Albion* and *Bulwark*. These will operate with

new, high-speed landing craft to enable the swift insertion or withdrawal of vehicles, troops, refugees or evacuees with the minimum of risk. HMS *Albion* entered service in April 2003 and HMS *Bulwark* will enter service in 2004;

- updates to the Swiftsure and Trafalgar submarines which will enable them to launch Tomahawk Land Attack Missiles; and
- six new roll-on/roll-off ferries, providing significantly enhanced maritime transport capability.

The Army front line is being strengthened through the introduction of:
- the Bowman communications system;
- Apache attack helicopters equipped with new anti-tank missiles; and
- improved Rapier and new Starstreak air defence missiles.

Improvements within the RAF include:
- the upgrading of the Tornado GR1 fleet to GR4 standard (now completed);
- the introduction of the Eurofighter Typhoon combat aircraft;
- the introduction of new Nimrod maritime patrol and attack aircraft;
- the introduction of EH101 and Chinook support helicopters;
- the replacement of the Joint Force Harrier force with the F35 Joint Combat Aircraft operating from the new aircraft carriers and from land;
- the introduction of the C-17, C-130J, and A400M transport aircraft and new air-to-air refuelling aircraft to replace VC10 and Tristar aircraft; and
- the introduction of significant new weapons systems, including the Storm Shadow Stand-Off Missile; the ASRAAM and Meteor air-to-air missiles; and a new precision-guided bomb.

Strategic Defence Review implementation

The Strategic Defence Review (SDR), published in 1998, was a foreign-policy-led reassessment of UK security interests and defence needs in the post-Cold War world. It proposed a radical modernisation programme of the UK Armed Forces to provide more capable, more flexible and better-equipped forces. Implementation began in

1998 and will continue until well into the next decade, although work had been completed on nearly three-quarters of the measures by the summer of 2003. The MoD Spending Review 2002 settlement will allow the United Kingdom to press ahead with the implementation of the SDR.

The SDR has led to the establishment of a Joint Rapid Reaction Force which includes elements from all the armed services. This has operated successfully in Afghanistan, the Balkans, East Timor, Iraq and Sierra Leone. Other SDR measures include the Smart Acquisition initiative (see page 87).

Progress on other elements of the SDR in 2002/03 included:
- completing work to upgrade the medical facilities aboard the two re-supply vessels, RFA *Fort George* and RFA *Fort Victoria*, and to refit the hospital ship, RFA *Argus*. The upgraded facilities aboard RFA *Argus* were used in operations in Iraq;
- selecting contractors for two new aircraft carriers. The aircraft that will fly from the new carriers – the short take-off and vertical landing (STOVL) version of the new Joint Strike Fighter – are on track for delivery with the first of the carriers in 2012; and
- progress on defence diplomacy – many measures to expand the MoD's outreach programme are complete, with increases in the number of Defence Attachés in Central and Eastern Europe and Central Asia.

The Armed Forces

Commissioned ranks
Commissions, either by promotion from the ranks or by direct entry based on educational and other qualifications, are granted for the short, medium and long term. All three services have school, college and university sponsorship schemes.

Commissioned ranks receive initial training, depending on their Service, at the Britannia Royal Naval College, Dartmouth; the Commando Training Centre, Lympstone, Devon (for the Royal Marines); the Royal Military Academy, Sandhurst; or the Royal Air Force College, Cranwell. Specialist training follows and may include degree courses at service establishments or universities. The Joint Services Command and Staff College at Shrivenham (Wiltshire) provides courses of higher training for officers, designed to emphasise the joint approach to tactical and operational levels of conflict.

Non-commissioned ranks

Engagements for non-commissioned ranks vary widely in length and terms of service. Subject to a minimum period, entrants may leave at any time if they give 18 months' notice (12 months for certain engagements). Discharge may also be granted on compassionate or medical grounds.

After basic training, non-commissioned personnel receive supplementary specialist training throughout their careers. Study for educational qualifications is encouraged, and Service trade and technical training leads to nationally recognised qualifications. New vocational training and educational initiatives have been launched to improve recruitment and retention. The Army Foundation College offers a 42-week course combining military training with the opportunity to acquire national qualifications. The course aims to attract high-quality recruits who will go on to fill senior posts in front-line roles.

Reserve forces

The United Kingdom relies heavily on the contribution made by reserves. Their main role is to support UK regular forces by serving both at home and overseas, but they also play a crucial role in responding to natural disasters within the United Kingdom, such as flooding or the foot-and-mouth disease outbreak that occurred in 2001. Over 6,000 reservists were called up for the war in Iraq, and reserves are also serving in peacekeeping and humanitarian operations in Bosnia, Kosovo and Sierra Leone. They are fully integrated with UK regular forces and are able to operate with high levels of skill in situations that can be very demanding.

There are two types of reserves:
- regular reserves, who are former members of the regular Armed Forces liable for service in an emergency; and
- volunteer reserves, who are recruited directly from the civilian community. They may join the Royal Naval Reserve, the Royal Marines Reserve, the Territorial Army or the Reserve Air Forces (which comprise the Royal Auxiliary Air Force and the Royal Air Force Reserve).

To support the regular forces, the reserves – both individuals and formed units – need to be fully

Table 8.1 Strength of service and civilian personnel, 2003, UK

	Numbers
Royal Navy	42,490
Army	116,420
Royal Air Force	53,520
Regular reserves	212,600
Volunteer reserves	44,900
Civilians	102,500
of whom UK-based	88,700
Employed locally	13,800

Source: Defence Analytical Services Agency

integrated with regular formations and readily available for service, where necessary through selective compulsory call-out, in situations short of a direct threat to the United Kingdom. Reserves are also liable for service in peace support operations. Training for this role takes place at the Reserve Training Mobilisation Centre at Chilwell near Nottingham. Under the SDR, Royal Navy and RAF volunteer reserve numbers will increase and, while the strength of the Territorial Army has fallen from around 57,000 in 1998 to around 41,000 in 2003, it is more closely integrated with the regular Army, with greater emphasis on combat support.

Administration

Defence management

The MoD is both a Department of State and the highest-level military headquarters. The Secretary of State for Defence is the cabinet minister charged with making defence policy and providing the means by which it is conducted. The Secretary of State is also the Chairman of the Defence Council and of its three Boards: the Admiralty Board, the Army Board and the Air Force Board. Although ultimately responsible for all aspects of defence, the Secretary of State is supported by three subordinate ministers: Minister of State for the Armed Forces, the Parliamentary Under-Secretary of State and Minister for Defence Procurement, and the Parliamentary Under-Secretary of State and Minister for Veterans.

The Chief of the Defence Staff (CDS) and the Permanent Secretary advise the Secretary of State. The CDS is the head of the Armed Forces and the principal military adviser to the Secretary of State and the Government. The Permanent Secretary is the Government's principal civilian adviser on defence and has primary responsibility for policy, finance and administration of the department. Defence agencies such as the Defence Procurement Agency undertake a large proportion of the MoD's support activities.

The defence budget

The defence budget for 2002/03 was £31.4 billion, rising to £33.0 billion in 2003/04, £33.8 billion in 2004/05, and £34.7 billion in 2005/06. This growth in defence spending, the largest sustained real increase for some 20 years, aims to provide the necessary investment in the Armed Forces' capabilities and structures to deal with extra priorities outlined in *The Strategic Defence Review: A New Chapter,* including the war against terrorism.

Defence procurement

The largest element of the defence budget is expenditure on equipment and spares. The Defence Procurement Agency buys weaponry and other equipment for the Armed Forces and spends around £6 billion a year. A further £4.6 billion goes on supporting equipment in service through repairs, and on the purchase of spares and other stores by the Defence Logistics Organisation. The Smart Procurement Initiative was a key element of the 1998 Strategic Defence Review.

The Review has sustained and broadened its aim of providing better, cheaper equipment more quickly and, as a result, has been renamed Smart Acquisition. Smart Acquisition applies not only to the procurement of new equipment but to its support in service, and to stores and supplies. The principles of Smart Acquisition are currently being extended to the non-equipment areas of the MoD, such as the infrastructure and services of the defence estate.

International procurement collaboration

The United Kingdom is a member of NATO's Conference of National Armaments Directors, which promotes equipment collaboration between NATO nations. It is also a founder member of OCCAR, an armament co-operation organisation formed with France, Germany and Italy for managing joint procurement activities. Current collaborative programmes in which the United Kingdom participates include:

- development of the Eurofighter Typhoon (with Germany, Italy and Spain);
- a maritime anti-air missile system (with France and Italy);
- a 'beyond visual' anti-air missile system (with France, Germany, Italy, Spain and Sweden);
- the EH101 helicopter (with Italy); and
- the large transport Airbus A400M aircraft (with Belgium, France, Germany, Italy, Spain and Turkey).

Further reading

The Strategic Defence Review: A New Chapter. Cm 5566. Ministry of Defence. The Stationery Office, 2002.

Defence Policy 2001. Ministry of Defence. The Stationery Office, 2001.

Expenditure Plans. Cm 5412. Ministry of Defence. July 2002

The Government's Expenditure Plans 2002–2003 to 2004–2005 and Main Estimates 2002–2003. Ministry of Defence. The Stationery Office, 2003.

Websites

UK Army
www.army.mod.uk

MI5
www.mi5.gov.uk

Ministry of Defence
www.mod.uk

NATO
www.nato.int

Royal Air Force
www.raf.mod.uk

Royal Navy
www.royalnavy.mod.uk

WWW.

9 The social framework

The population of the United Kingdom has grown and changed significantly over the last half-century. Increased life expectancy and lower fertility rates have led to an ageing population, while immigration has led to ethnic diversity. Living arrangements and relationship patterns have changed; more people are living alone, cohabitation before marriage is increasingly common and there has been a rise in births outside marriage. Many more women now participate in the labour market, although they still earn less than men and are under-represented in senior management. The standard of living has risen, but some people and communities are still affected by poverty and social exclusion.

Population

The population of the United Kingdom was estimated to be 59.2 million in mid-2002, an increase of 0.3 per cent on the previous year. Projections based on the 2001 mid-year estimates suggest that the population will continue to increase, reaching 63 million people by 2025 and peaking at almost 64 million in 2040 before beginning a gradual decline.

Age and gender
The United Kingdom has an ageing population. Between 1971 and 2002 there was an 18 per cent decrease in the number of children aged under 16. In contrast there was a 27 per cent increase in the number of people aged 65 and over. The number of people aged 85 or over more than doubled. Projections suggest that this ageing trend will continue and that the number of people aged 65 and over will exceed the number aged under 16 by 2014 (Figure 9.1).

Lower fertility rates and lower mortality rates have both contributed to the ageing trend. In 2002 projected life expectancy at birth in the United Kingdom was 76 years for males and 80 years for

Figure 9.1 Dependent population: by age, UK

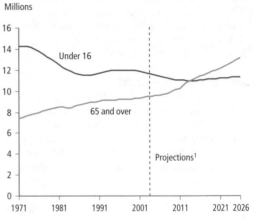

Millions

1 2001-based projections.
Source: Office for National Statistics; Government Actuary's Department; General Register Office for Scotland; Northern Ireland Statistics and Research Agency

females. This represents an increase, over the last 30 years, of around 7 years for men and 5 years for women. The average age of the population is projected to rise from 39 years in 2002 to 42 in 2026.

An ageing population is characteristic of countries across the EU. Seventeen per cent of the total EU population was aged 65 and over in 2001 compared with 12 per cent in 1970. This age group accounted for 16 per cent in the United Kingdom in 2001, compared with 18 per cent in Italy and Greece, and 11 per cent in the Republic of Ireland.

More boys than girls are born each year, but there are more women overall – 30.3 million females compared with 28.9 million males in 2002, with women beginning to outnumber men from the age of 22. From age 90 women outnumber men by more than three to one.

Births and deaths

There were 668,800 live births in the United Kingdom in 2002, a live birth rate of 11.3 per 1,000 population. There has been a gradual reduction in the number of births since 1990, when the figure was approximately 800,000, but projections suggest that the number will remain relatively constant at around 670,000 over the next 40 years.

Some 608,000 deaths were registered in the United Kingdom in 2002, a crude rate of 10.2 per 1,000 population. The number of deaths each year has remained relatively constant over the last century, in spite of population growth. However, as the ageing of the population continues, deaths are projected to increase, and are expected to exceed births from 2029.

A rising standard of living and developments in medical technology and practice have contributed to large declines in mortality rates over the last hundred years. Death rates are higher for males than females in all age groups, explaining some of the gender imbalance among the older population.

Households and families

The number of households in Great Britain increased by 32 per cent between 1971 and 2003. Household growth has outpaced population growth (which was only 6 per cent between 1971 and 2002) because of the trend towards smaller households. By spring 2003, 29 per cent of households consisted of just one person, compared with 18 per cent in 1971.

In Great Britain the proportion of households that consisted of a couple with dependent children fell from 35 per cent in 1971 to 22 per cent in spring 2003. Lone parents with dependent children increased from 3 per cent of households in 1971 to 6 per cent in 2003.

Marriage, cohabitation and divorce

Patterns of marriage and cohabitation have changed over the last 30 years. Although the majority of men and women still marry at some stage of their lives, the proportion of the population who are married at any one time has fallen. In 1971, 71 per cent of men and 65 per cent of women aged 16 and over in England and Wales were married; by 2001 this had fallen to 55 per

Figure 9.2 Households: by type of household and family, 2003,[1] UK

Total: 25.1 Million

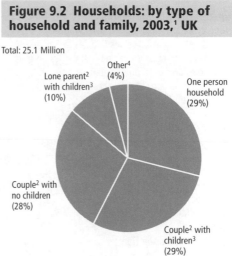

- Other[4] (4%)
- Lone parent[2] with children[3] (10%)
- One person household (29%)
- Couple[2] with no children (28%)
- Couple[2] with children[3] (29%)

1 These estimates are not seasonally adjusted and have not been adjusted to take account of the 2001 Census.
2 Other individuals who were not family members may also be included.
3 Includes non-dependent children.
4 Households consisting of two or more unrelated adults, and households with more than one family.
Source: Labour Force Survey, Office for National Statistics

cent of men and 52 per cent of women (Table 9.3). Over the same period the proportion of the population who were single or divorced increased.

While the proportion of the population who are married has decreased, the proportion cohabiting has risen. Results from the General Household Survey suggest that around 12 per cent of 16- to 59-year-olds in Great Britain were cohabiting in 2001/02. Cohabitation before marriage has become increasingly common, although 13 per cent of people aged 16 to 59 reported at least one cohabiting union that had not led to marriage.

Table 9.3 Marital status of the population,[1] 2001, England and Wales

		Percentages
	Men	Women
Single	33.9	26.7
Married	55.1	51.5
Widowed	3.7	12.7
Divorced	7.3	9.1
All	**100**	**100**

1 Adults aged 16 and over.
Source: Office for National Statistics

Figure 9.4 Marriages and divorces, UK

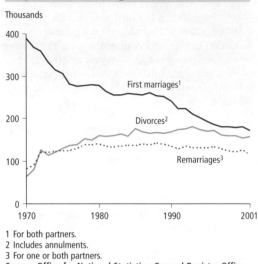

Thousands

1 For both partners.
2 Includes annulments.
3 For one or both partners.
Source: Office for National Statistics; General Register Office for Scotland; Northern Ireland Statistics and Research Agency

In 2001 there were 286,000 marriages in the United Kingdom. Of these, 172,000 were first marriages for both partners, less than half the number in 1970, when the number of first marriages was at a post-war peak. First marriages accounted for 83 per cent of all marriages in 1970 but only 60 per cent in 2001.

Around 157,000 divorces were granted in the United Kingdom in 2001, a slight increase on the number granted in 2000 and the first rise since 1996 (Figure 9.4). Divorces reached a peak of 180,000 in 1993, before dropping gradually until 2000. The median length of marriage for couples divorcing in England and Wales in 2001 was 10.9 years. There has been little change in this duration since data first became available in 1963, when it was just under 11.5 years.

The marriage rate in the United Kingdom was close to the EU average in 2001 (Table 9.5). Divorce rates are affected by religious, social, cultural and legal differences between Member States. Countries in northern and western Europe typically have higher divorce rates, while the rates are lower in the Republic of Ireland and southern Europe.

Family formation

There were 763,000 conceptions in England and Wales in 2001, a fall of 13 per cent from 1970,

when the number peaked at 877,000. More than three-quarters of conceptions in 2001 led to a maternity (a live or still birth). This proportion has fallen steadily from 91 per cent in 1970. Conceptions to teenage women (aged under 20) are more likely to lead to an abortion –

Table 9.5 Marriage and divorce rates, 2001, EU comparison

| | Rates per 1,000 population | |
	Marriages	Divorces
Denmark	6.8	2.7
Portugal	5.7	1.8
Greece	5.5	1.1
Spain	5.1	0.9
Irish Republic	5.0	0.7
Netherlands	5.0	2.3
France	4.9	1.9
United Kingdom	4.8	2.6
Finland	4.8	2.6
Germany	4.7	2.4
Italy	4.5	0.7
Luxembourg	4.5	2.3
Austria	4.2	2.5
Belgium	4.1	2.8
Sweden	4.0	2.4
EU average	4.8	1.9

Souce: Eurostat

The Commonwealth

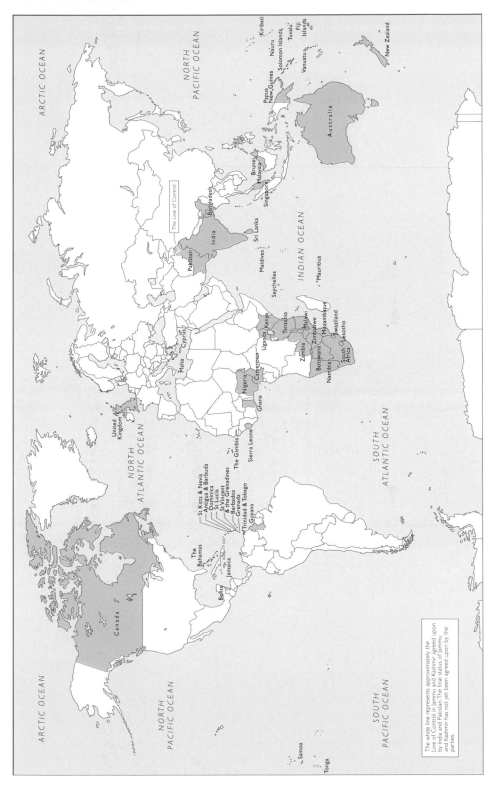

ARCTIC OCEAN

NORTH PACIFIC OCEAN

Kiribati

Tuvalu

Nauru

Fiji Islands

Solomon Islands

Vanuatu

New Zealand

Papua New Guinea

Australia

Brunei

Malaysia

Singapore

The Line of Control

Bangladesh

India

Sri Lanka

Pakistan

Maldives

Seychelles

INDIAN OCEAN

Mauritius

Cyprus

Malta

Uganda

Kenya

Tanzania

Malawi

Mozambique

Swaziland

Lesotho

Cameroon

Zambia

Zimbabwe

Botswana

Namibia

South Africa

Nigeria

Ghana

Sierra Leone

The Gambia

United Kingdom

NORTH ATLANTIC OCEAN

SOUTH ATLANTIC OCEAN

St Kitts & Nevis

Antigua & Barbuda

Dominica

St Lucia

St Vincent & the Grenadines

Barbados

Grenada

Trinidad & Tobago

Guyana

The Bahamas

Jamaica

Belize

Canada

ARCTIC OCEAN

NORTH PACIFIC OCEAN

SOUTH PACIFIC OCEAN

Samoa

Tonga

The white line represents approximately the Line of Control in Jammu and Kashmir agreed upon by India and Pakistan. The final status of Jammu and Kashmir has not yet been agreed upon by the parties.

The European Union

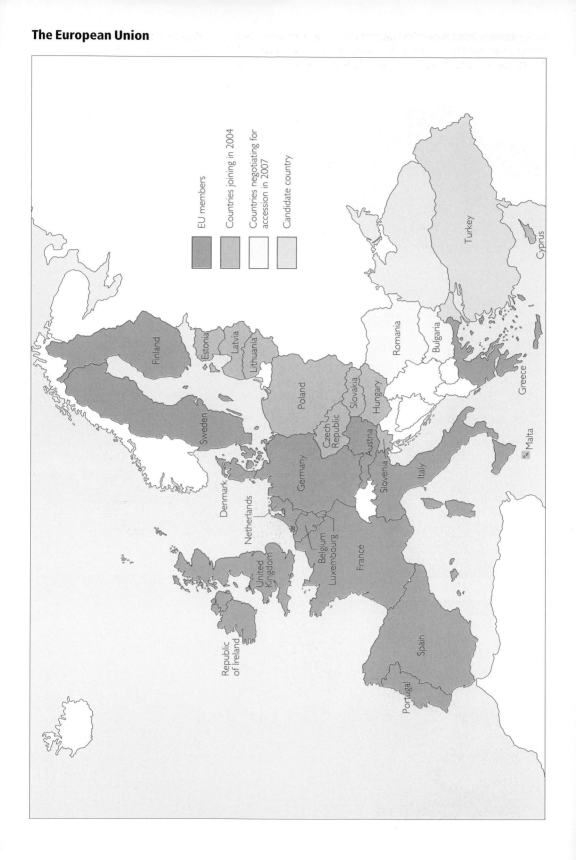

Legend:
- EU members
- Countries joining in 2004
- Countries negotiating for accession in 2007
- Candidate country

Finland
Estonia
Latvia
Lithuania
Sweden
Poland
Slovakia
Hungary
Czech Republic
Denmark
Germany
Austria
Slovenia
Netherlands
Belgium
Luxembourg
France
Italy
United Kingdom
Republic of Ireland
Spain
Portugal
Romania
Bulgaria
Turkey
Greece
Cyprus
Malta

26 September 2002 the British Empire & Commonwealth Museum opens in the Brunel building at Bristol's Temple Meads Station, pictured *(top left)* after it was built in the 1840s. Five months after the Museum opened, it won a Museum & Heritage Award for Excellence.

Centre left: The Islands of the Empire gallery in the Museum covers UK expansion into the Pacific and Australia, and the impact this had on the inhabitants.

Below: The Rise of Victoria's Empire: this gallery shows how surveying, policing and law were introduced, as well as systems of standardised time, weights and currencies.

4 November 2002 the Essex Wildlife Trust breaches a 3.5-kilometre sea wall to convert 84 hectares of arable farmland at Abbotts Hall Farm on the Blackwater estuary into saltmarsh and grassland. This is part of a project to help restore UK coastal wetlands and provide a cost-effective and sustainable sea defence.

16 November 2002 a five-month exhibition bringing together over 380 outstanding works from Mexico's Aztec past opens at the Royal Academy, London. It attracted more than 465,000 visitors.

Terracotta 'eagle man', probably representing the sunrise *c. 1440–69*. The eagle warriors were one of the two top ranking Aztec military orders.

Lifesize terracotta figure of Mictlantecuhtli, god of the dead and ruler of the underworld *c. 1480*. Hanging from the god's stomach is a huge liver, the organ inhabited by the spirit that since ancient times has been associated with death.

Xilonen, goddess of maize *c. 1500*. Her headdress is capped with precious quetzal feathers, signifying the value and importance of her protection.

c. 1500. Dogs were valued for their loyalty and their watchfulness, helping to protect homes and crops.

Divorce law in the UK

In order to apply for a divorce in the United Kingdom it is necessary to meet certain residential requirements and, in England or Wales, to have been married for at least a year (two years in Northern Ireland). There is no minimum requirement in Scotland although residential requirements must still be met. The sole ground for divorce is the irretrievable breakdown of the marriage. To prove this, one of the following facts must be established:

- adultery;
- unreasonable behaviour (such as mental or physical cruelty);
- desertion;
- two years' separation (if both parties consent to divorce); or
- five years' separation.

The length of time it takes to be granted a divorce depends on whether children or property are involved, and on whether the divorce is contested. In a straightforward case in England, Wales and Northern

Ireland, it might take up to six months for the court to grant a 'decree nisi'. Application for the 'decree absolute' – the final stage – can be made six weeks later. In Scotland, where there is a simplified procedure for the more straightforward cases, the court may issue an 'extract decree of divorce' after about eight weeks.

The court will not grant a divorce until it has looked at arrangements for the children. Both parents continue to have 'parental responsibility' but the court will, if necessary, make a residence order determining who the child should live with. If the parents cannot agree the terms on which the non-resident parent has contact with the child, the court will also make a contact order. It may also, if necessary, transfer rights in the family home.

The division of property and financial support for either party or for the children can be arranged through the court, through the Child Support Agency (see page 151) or by voluntary agreement.

40 per cent of conceptions to women in this age group were terminated by a legal abortion in 2001, compared with 15 per cent of conceptions to women aged 30 to 34.

The fertility rate in the United Kingdom in 2001 was 54.5 live births per 1,000 women of childbearing age, a fall of 40 per cent since 1961. Since the 1970s fertility rates have been below the level needed for the long-term natural replacement of the population. This is partly because there has been a trend towards later childbearing and a tendency for people to have smaller families. In England and Wales women giving birth are now three years older than those in the early 1970s – in 2002 the mean age of women at childbirth was 29.3 years, compared with 26.2 in 1971. There has also been a growth in the number of women remaining childless. In England and Wales 9 per cent of women born in 1945 were still childless at the age of 45; this increased to 15 per cent of those born in 1955. It is expected that the trend will continue.

Fertility rates have also declined across the rest of Europe. In 2001 the average total fertility rate for the EU was 1.46 children per woman (Table 9.6) and no EU Member State had a total fertility rate above the level needed for the long-term

replacement of the population (2.1 children per woman). The UK rate was 1.63 in 2001.

Most children are born to married couples, but an increasing proportion of births occur outside marriage – 41 per cent in England and Wales in 2002, compared with 8 per cent in 1971. Most of this growth is accounted for by the increase in births to cohabiting couples. Seventy-seven per cent of jointly registered births by unmarried parents were by parents living at the same address.

Countries above the European average (29 per cent) for the proportion of births outside marriage are mainly located in northern Europe – for example, 55 per cent of all births in Sweden in 2001 occurred outside marriage compared with 10 per cent of births in Italy.

Migration

Population movements occur both within the United Kingdom and internationally. During the second half of the 20th century there was an internal movement of people from the coal, shipbuilding and steel industry areas in the north of England, Scotland and Wales to the south of England and the Midlands where the light

Table 9.6 Total fertility rate, 2001, EU comparison

	Total fertility rate
Irish Republic	1.98
France	1.89
Denmark	1.75
Finland	1.73
Netherlands	1.71
Luxembourg	1.65
Sweden	1.65
Belgium	1.64
United Kingdom	1.63
Portugal	1.46
Germany	1.35
Austria	1.33
Greece	1.25
Italy	1.25
Spain	1.24
EU average	1.46

Source: Eurostat

industries and service industries are based. Over the same period there was immigration from Commonwealth countries, followed more recently by an increase in the number of people seeking asylum in the United Kingdom.

Internal migration

In 2002, it is estimated that Wales gained 14,000 people from migration within the United Kingdom, Scotland gained 5,000 people, and Northern Ireland experienced a small net gain of around 300 people. England experienced a net loss of almost 18,000 people. At a regional level, the greatest net loss due to internal migration occurred in London, where 108,000 more people moved from the capital to other regions of the country than moved into London. Over a third of people leaving London for elsewhere in the UK moved into the South East region and a quarter into the East of England. The South West had the highest net gain of all the regions in England due to internal migration (35,000 people).

Young adults are the most mobile age group. Many people in their twenties leave their home area to study or seek employment. In 2002 London experienced the largest net increase of people aged 16 to 24 due to migration within the United Kingdom (10,000 people) but experienced

a net loss in all other age groups, especially those associated with young families: the under-15s and people aged 25 to 44. The West Midlands experienced the biggest net loss of 16- to 24-year-olds, of over 4,000.

International migration

Although the United Kingdom experienced a net loss of people due to migration during the 1970s and early 1980s, the position has since reversed and net migration into the UK is now a factor in population growth. It is estimated that 172,000 more people migrated to, rather than from, the United Kingdom in 2001, an increase of more than a quarter on the 2000 level.

Immigration law

Immigration into the United Kingdom is largely governed by the *Immigration Act 1971*. Rules made under this Act set out the requirements to be met by those who are subject to immigration control and seek entry to, or leave to remain in, the United Kingdom. The 1971 Act has been amended by subsequent legislation, including the *Immigration and Asylum Act 1999* and the *Nationality, Immigration and Asylum Act 2002*. Among other things, the latter introduced new offences, such as people trafficking for the purposes of prostitution, and powers of entry to business premises to search for offenders.

Nationals of the European Economic Area (EEA) – EU Member States and Norway, Iceland and Liechtenstein – are not subject to substantive immigration control. They may work in the United Kingdom without restriction and, provided they are working or able to support themselves financially, have the right to reside in the United Kingdom.

Visas

Under the Immigration Rules, nationals of certain countries must obtain a visa before they can visit the United Kingdom. Other nationals, subject to immigration control, require entry clearance when coming to work or settle. Visas and other entry clearances are normally obtained from the nearest UK diplomatic post in a person's home country. In 2001 there were around 2 million applications for entry clearance, with around 1.7 million being successful.

Settlement in the UK

In 2002, nearly 116,000 people were granted permanent settlement in the United Kingdom,

New visa requirements

The Home Office and the Foreign & Commonwealth Office keep visa policies under review to ensure they are responsive to changing circumstances. In April 2002 the Home Office lifted the requirement for holders of Macao Special Administrative Region Passports to obtain a visa before visiting the UK, and in November nationals of the Maldives, Mauritius and Papua New Guinea were also given visa free access for visits.

New visa requirements were introduced for Zimbabwean nationals in November 2002 and for Jamaican nationals in January 2003, in both cases because relatively large numbers of people had been refused entry to the United Kingdom or had failed to return home once granted temporary admission to the country. In June 2003, a further 16 countries were added to the list. These new regulations are intended to reduce delays at immigration control for people arriving from these countries.

8 per cent more than in 2001 (Table 9.7). Forty per cent of these grants were to Asian nationals, and a further 34 per cent to African nationals.

Managed migration

The Government believes that managed migration can help overcome recruitment difficulties, bring innovation and capital into the country and counteract the effects of the ageing of the population. It has taken steps to encourage people with skills and expertise to work in the United Kingdom, by overhauling the work permit system and by introducing special schemes for certain categories of migrant, including entrepreneurs, temporary workers in hotels and catering, and overseas nurses, doctors and dentists who

graduate in this country and wish to switch to work permit employment.

It has also introduced a Highly Skilled Migrant Programme, piloted in 2002 but now extended indefinitely. Under this programme, skilled individuals who are not EEA nationals can apply to come to the United Kingdom to seek work or self-employment opportunities. Applications are assessed on a points-based system in the following areas:

- educational qualifications;
- work experience;
- past earnings;
- achievement in a chosen field; and
- a special category for overseas doctors wishing to be self-employed GPs.

Successful applicants are granted leave to enter the UK for one year, following which further leave may be granted depending on the individual's employment status. There were 1,195 successful applicants under the programme in 2002.

Asylum

The United Kingdom has a tradition of giving asylum to those in need of protection, and is a signatory to the 1951 United Nations Convention and its 1967 Protocol relating to the Status of Refugees. These provide that lawful residents, who have been granted refugee status, should enjoy treatment at least as favourable as that accorded to the indigenous population.

Trends

In the late 1980s applications to the United Kingdom for asylum (based on the principal applicant) started to rise sharply from around 4,000 a year during 1985 to 1988, to almost 12,000 in 1989. The number of applications received has

Table 9.7 Grants of settlement: by region of origin, UK

							Thousands
	Asia	Africa	Americas	Europe[1]	Oceania	Other[2]	All regions
1981	30.0	4.1	6.3	6.6	4.5	7.5	59.1
1991	25.2	9.6	7.2	5.6	2.4	3.9	53.9
1996	27.9	13.0	8.5	7.5	3.5	1.4	61.7
2001	43.3	31.4	11.9	13.8	5.4	0.9	106.8
2002	46.5	39.1	11.7	11.7	6.3	0.6	115.9

1 Includes European Economic Area (EEA) countries – EEA nationals are not obliged to seek settlement and the figures relate only to those who choose to do so.
2 Mainly British overseas citizens and those whose nationality was unknown.
Source: Home Office

continued to increase and reached a record 84,130 in 2002, an 18 per cent increase on the 2001 level. In the first six months of 2003 applications for asylum averaged around 4,430 a month. This was 33 per cent lower than in the same period a year earlier. Reforms to the asylum system and measures to secure the Channel Tunnel and move UK border controls to France may have contributed to this overall decline.

The main nationalities applying for asylum in the United Kingdom in 2002 were:
- Iraqi (14,570 applicants);
- Zimbabwean (7,655 applicants);
- Afghan (7,205 applicants);
- Somali (6,540 applicants); and
- Chinese (3,675 applicants).

Around 83,540 asylum decisions were made in 2002; a 31 per cent fall on the number in 2001. Ten per cent of these decisions were grants of asylum, compared with 9 per cent in 2001. A further 24 per cent of decisions in 2002 were grants of exceptional leave to remain and 66 per cent were refusals. Many failed asylum seekers appeal against refusal; of the 64,405 appeals determined by adjudicators in 2002, 13,875 (22 per cent) were successful.

In 2002 the United Kingdom received more asylum applications than any other EU country – 24 per cent of total applications to EU countries, compared with 17 per cent for Germany. However, when the relative size of each country is taken into account, the United Kingdom ranked eighth, with 1.7 asylum seekers per 1,000 population. Austria had the highest rate at 4.9, while Portugal had the lowest (less than 0.1 per 1,000 population).

Recent reforms
The *Nationality, Immigration and Asylum Act, 2002*, includes provisions relating to:
- the creation of a system of accommodation centres to house and provide services for asylum seekers and their dependants;
- simplified arrangements for detention, temporary release and removal of asylum seekers; and
- new rules for immigration and asylum appeals, intended to shorten the process.

Further changes have been announced in 2003. For example:
- the list of safe countries from which asylum applications are presumed unfounded has

been extended, with the addition of seven more countries;
- the policy of granting exceptional leave to remain has been replaced by a more restricted category of humanitarian protection, for those who are in need of protection but who do not qualify as refugees under the 1951 Convention;
- support for living costs and help with housing will no longer be available to those who do not claim asylum when they arrive at a port, or as soon as possible thereafter; and
- to prevent people claiming asylum in the United Kingdom when they have refugee status elsewhere, people holding refugee travel documents will require a visa before travelling to the United Kingdom.

In May 2003 the Government announced it would be bringing in further legislation to allow for a single appeal route against an asylum decision, and for steps to counter fraudulent claims by people who deliberately destroy their documents. It also intends to tackle abuse of the Legal Services Fund.

Support for asylum seekers
Since April 2000 the National Asylum Support Service (NASS) has been responsible for the provision of support for those asylum seekers who are destitute. Support is provided until their claim is finally decided (when those granted refugee status or humanitarian protection are entitled to claim public funds). The support is in the form of cash benefits; a single adult aged 25 or over receives approximately £38 a week. Accommodation may also be provided, on a 'no choice' basis at one of a number of centres throughout the United Kingdom. Children of compulsory school age in families seeking asylum are entitled to attend school, and asylum seekers and their dependants are eligible to receive free healthcare.

Legal advice is available from immigration law advisers and firms of solicitors contracted to provide immigration services under the Community Legal Services Fund (formerly the Legal Aid scheme). They provide advice on the initial claim and on any appeal.

Citizenship

Under the *British Nationality Act 1981*, there are several forms of British nationality:

- British citizenship generally applies to those with a close connection with the UK, the Channel Islands or the Isle of Man;
- UK Overseas Territories citizenship applies to people with a close connection with one of the Overseas Territories (see page 69);
- British National (Overseas) Status, which could be acquired by people who, before July 1997, were connected with Hong Kong; and
- for those connected with a former British colony, Ireland (before 1949), or former British India, or a territory that was formerly under British protection, there are categories such as British Overseas citizenship, British subject, and British protected person.

Under the *British Overseas Territories Act 2002*, British overseas territories citizens became British citizens automatically on 21 May 2002 if, immediately before that date, they were connected with a 'qualifying territory' (a British Overseas Territory other than the Sovereign Base Areas in Cyprus).

British citizens have the right to live permanently in the United Kingdom and are free to leave and re-enter the country at any time. British citizenship is acquired automatically at birth by a child born in the UK or a 'qualifying territory' (if born on or after 21 May 2002) if his or her mother (or father, if the child is legitimate) is:

- a British citizen; or
- settled in the UK; or
- settled in that 'qualifying territory' (if appropriate).

British citizenship may also be acquired by registration or naturalisation, and in some circumstances by children who have been adopted. Among those entitled to apply for registration are British nationals, children born in the UK who did not automatically acquire British citizenship at birth, and stateless people. Naturalisation is at the Home Secretary's discretion and there are a number of residential and other requirements. Details can be found on the website of the Immigration and Nationality Directorate of the Home Office (*www.ind.homeoffice.gov.uk*).

In 2002, 120,145 people were granted British Citizenship in the United Kingdom (33 per cent more than in 2001) and 9,385 were refused. Residence in the United Kingdom continued to be the most frequent basis on which people were granted British citizenship, amounting to 48 per

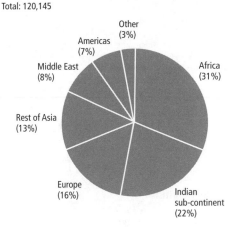

Figure 9.8 Grants of British citizenship in the UK, by previous nationality, 2002

Total: 120,145

- Other (3%)
- Americas (7%)
- Middle East (8%)
- Rest of Asia (13%)
- Africa (31%)
- Europe (16%)
- Indian sub-continent (22%)

Source: Home Office

cent of grants in 2002, while marriage to a British citizen accounted for 29 per cent.

The *Nationality, Immigration and Asylum Act 2002* includes provision for a citizenship ceremony, including a citizenship pledge, and a requirement that naturalisation applicants demonstrate knowledge about life in the United Kingdom. A consultation document on ceremonies was published in July 2003. This envisages that the first citizenship ceremonies will take place in January 2004, with most successful applicants being required to participate in ceremonies from April 2004. An independent advisory group on Life in the United Kingdom reported on the implementation of the 'knowledge about life in the United Kingdom' requirement in September 2003. It proposed a short practical course and an assessment in both language and citizenship.

Ethnicity and identity

For centuries people from overseas have settled in the United Kingdom, either to escape political or religious persecution or in search of better economic opportunities. Irish people have a long history of migration to this country and many Jewish refugees arrived towards the end of the 19th century and in the 1930s. Substantial immigration from the Caribbean and the Indian subcontinent dates principally from the 1950s and 1960s, when the Government encouraged

Table 9.9 Population by ethnic group,[1] April 2001, UK

	Total population		Minority ethnic population
	Thousands	%	%
White	54,154	92.1	n/a
Mixed	677	1.2	14.6
Asian or Asian British			
Indian	1,053	1.8	22.7
Pakistani	747	1.3	16.1
Bangladeshi	283	0.5	6.1
Other Asian	248	0.4	5.3
Black or Black British			
Black Caribbean	566	1.0	12.2
Black African	485	0.8	10.5
Black Other	98	0.2	2.1
Chinese	247	0.4	5.3
Other	231	0.4	5.0
All minority ethnic population	4,635	7.9	100
All population	**58,789**	**100**	.

1 Different versions of the ethnic group question were asked in England and Wales, and in Scotland and Northern Ireland, to reflect local differences in the requirement for information. However, results are comparable across the UK as a whole.
Source: Census, Office for National Statistics

immigration from these areas to tackle labour shortages. Many people of south Asian descent also entered the United Kingdom from Kenya, Malawi and Uganda in the 1960s and 1970s. Recent trends in asylum applications have also added to the cultural and religious diversity of the UK population (see page 93).

In the 2001 Census, 4.6 million people (8 per cent of the UK population) described themselves as belonging to a minority ethnic group. These groups have a younger age profile than the White population, reflecting past immigration and fertility patterns. In Great Britain a further 691,000 people identified themselves as White Irish.

People from minority ethnic groups were more likely to live in England than in the rest of the United Kingdom. They made up 9 per cent of the population of England in 2001 compared with

2 per cent of the populations of both Scotland and Wales and 1 per cent of the population of Northern Ireland. Nearly half (45 per cent) of the total minority ethnic population lived in London, where they comprised 29 per cent of all residents. However, the extent to which individual minority ethnic groups were concentrated in London varied considerably; for example, 78 per cent of Black Africans lived in London compared with just 19 per cent of Pakistanis.

Equal opportunities

Race equality

People from some minority ethnic groups are more likely to experience poverty and social exclusion. Table 9.10 shows the percentage of people who were living in low income households in 2001/02, categorised on the basis of the ethnic origin of the household reference person (HRP – see glossary). A higher percentage of individuals were living in a low income household when the HRP belonged to a minority ethnic group – particularly when the HRP was of Pakistani/Bangladeshi descent.

There are, however, considerable variations between minority ethnic groups and also some instances where a minority ethnic group does better than White groups. For example:

- school pupils of Indian origin are more likely than White pupils or those from other minority ethnic groups to achieve five or more GCSE grades A* to C. Sixty per cent of 16-year-old pupils of Indian origin achieved these

Table 9.10 Individuals in low income[1] households, by ethnic group,[2] 2001/02, Great Britain

	Before housing costs	After housing costs
	Percentages	
White	16	20
Black Caribbean	24	35
Black non-Caribbean	29	45
Indian	21	27
Pakistani/Bangladeshi	55	63
Other ethnic groups	27	38

1 See glossary.
2 Ethnic origin of the household reference person.
Source: Households Below Average Income Series, Department for Work and Pensions

grades in England and Wales in 2002, compared with 52 per cent of White pupils and 36 per cent of those from the Black groups.

- Households headed by someone of Indian descent are more likely to own their own homes: in England, 81 per cent were owner-occupiers over the period 1999–2002, compared with 71 per cent of White households, 33 per cent of Bangladeshi households and 27 per cent of Black African households.
- People of Chinese and Indian origin have relatively low unemployment rates, 6 per cent of Chinese people of working age and 7 per cent of Indian people were unemployed in the United Kingdom in 2001–02, a similar proportion to that of the White group (5 per cent). On the other hand, people of Bangladeshi descent had the highest unemployment rate (21 per cent).

Race relations policy and legislation

The Home Office has overall responsibility for policy and legislation on racial equality. In Great Britain the *Race Relations Act 1976* makes it unlawful for anybody to discriminate on grounds of race, colour, nationality (including citizenship), or ethnic or national origins (referred to as 'racial grounds'). The Act applies to employment, training, education and the provision of goods and services. Legislation along similar lines was introduced in Northern Ireland in 1977.

The *Race Relations (Amendment) Act 2000* extended the scope of the 1976 Act to cover the way public authorities carry out all their functions. Public authorities listed under the Act have a statutory general duty to work to eliminate unlawful racial discrimination and promote equal opportunities and good relations between people from different racial groups. Certain listed public bodies also have specific duties to fulfil. These include producing and publishing a race equality scheme to explain how they will meet these general duties, and monitoring the ethnic origin of staff and applicants for jobs, promotion and training. The Commission for Racial Equality (CRE) has published a statutory code of practice to provide guidance to public bodies on how to meet these duties.

The *Crime and Disorder Act 1998* created racially aggravated versions of a number of existing offences in England and Wales, including assault, criminal damage and harassment. These racially aggravated offences carry a higher maximum penalty. Other provisions in criminal law prohibit incitement to racial hatred and the publication or dissemination of material that is likely to incite racial hatred.

The *Race Relations Act 1976 (Amendment) Regulations 2003* (which came into force in July 2003) are designed to ensure that the United Kingdom meets the standards of legal protection from racial discrimination and harassment required by the EC Race Directive.

Commission for Racial Equality

The CRE was set up under the *Race Relations Act 1976*, in order to tackle racial discrimination and promote equal opportunities and good race relations in Great Britain. The CRE has the power to investigate companies and organisations if it has sufficient evidence that unlawful racial discrimination has taken place, and it can issue non-discrimination notices, requiring them to change their polices and practice. The CRE also provides legal advice to people who think they have been discriminated against; in 2002 around 1,300 people made formal applications for assistance. In 2002/03 the CRE supported the work of 91 racial equality councils in Great Britain. These are voluntary bodies, jointly funded by the CRE and local authorities to promote good race relations locally.

In Northern Ireland equivalent responsibilities rest with the Equality Commission for Northern Ireland, whose remit also covers other types of unlawful discrimination (see page 98).

Gender

The economic and domestic lives of women have changed considerably over time, and women have taken an increasing role in the labour market. In 1971, 55 per cent of women of working age in the United Kingdom were in employment, compared with 91 per cent of men. By spring 2003, in Great Britain, the rate for women had increased to 70 per cent while the rate for men had declined to 79 per cent. The likelihood of women being in employment, however, varies according to whether they have dependent children. Employment rates are lowest for those women with a child under the age of five (52 per cent in spring 2003 – see also page 127).

The gap between men and women's pay widened between 2001 and 2002, returning to its April

Draft Gender Recognition Bill

In July 2003 the Government published a draft Gender Recognition Bill for pre-legislative scrutiny by the Joint Committee on Human Rights. The Bill would establish a Gender Recognition Panel with the power to decide applications by transsexual people seeking legal recognition in their acquired gender. People would have the right, from the date of recognition, to marry in their acquired gender and to be given a new birth certificate.

Before issuing a gender recognition certificate, the panel would have to be satisfied that the applicant has been diagnosed as having the medical condition gender dysphoria; has lived in the acquired gender throughout the preceding two years, and intends to continue to live in the acquired gender. There would be a fast track procedure for transsexual people who have lived in their acquired gender for at least six years.

2000 level. At £383, the average gross weekly earnings of women who worked full time in April 2002 were £130 less than those for men, although the gap had been narrowing in recent years. These gender differences are largely due to differences in working hours and occupation. Women are more likely than men to work part time and to be in administrative and secretarial occupations (see page 130). Women are under-represented in senior management positions. For example, in 2002, only 7 per cent of directors in the FTSE 100 firms were women, and only one company had a female chief executive officer.

Equal opportunities policy and legislation

The *Sex Discrimination Act 1975*, which applies in Great Britain, makes it unlawful to discriminate between men and women in employment, education, training and the provision of housing, goods, facilities and services. Discrimination in employment against married people and discriminatory job recruitment advertisements are also unlawful. Under the *Equal Pay Act 1970*, women and men are entitled to equal pay when doing work that is the same or broadly similar, work that is rated as equivalent, or work that is of equal value. Parallel legislation on sex discrimination and equal pay applies in Northern Ireland.

There are two Ministers for Women, supported by the Women and Equality Unit (WEU) based in the Department of Trade and Industry. They are responsible for a range of gender equality issues in Government (including issues of sexual orientation) and are sponsors of the Equal Opportunities Commission. The Equality Unit in the Scottish Executive and the Gender Policy Unit in the Northern Ireland Executive are also responsible for work in this area.

Equal Opportunities Commission

The EOC was established under the *Sex Discrimination Act 1975*. It is an independent statutory body, which has the powers to:

- work towards the elimination of discrimination on the grounds of sex or marital status;
- promote equality of opportunity between women and men;
- review, and propose amendments to, the *Sex Discrimination Act* and the *Equal Pay Act*; and
- provide legal advice and assistance to individuals who have been discriminated against.

Northern Ireland has its own Equality Commission responsible for tackling discrimination and promoting gender equality. Since 1999 the remit of this Commission has also included race, religious and political beliefs, marital status, and disability.

Changes to the equality laws

In October 2002 the Government published proposals for merging the Equal Opportunities Commission, the Commission for Racial Equality and the Disability Rights Commission (see page 99) to form a single equality body in Great Britain, responsible for the promotion of equality in relation to sex, race, disability, sexual orientation, religion and age. The Government will be responding to the public consultation, which ended in February 2003.

New regulations on equality will come into force in December 2003: the Employment Equality (Sexual Orientation) Regulations 2003 and the Employment Equality (Religion and Belief) Regulations 2003. These regulations will outlaw discrimination in employment and vocational training, and help to meet the Government's implementation of the European Employment Directive. Separate regulations are being introduced in Northern Ireland.

Disability

In the 2001 Census, 10.9 million people in the United Kingdom described themselves as having a long-term illness, health problem or disability which limited their daily activities or work they could do. Disabled people are at greater risk of poverty and social exclusion and have lower employment rates overall than their non-disabled counterparts. They are more reliant on state benefits as a source of income and more likely to live in low income households. According to the spring 2003 Labour Force Survey, 49 per cent of the approximately 7 million disabled people of working age in the United Kingdom were in employment, compared with 81 per cent of non-disabled people. People with learning difficulties and mental health problems were the least likely to be in employment.

The unemployment rate for disabled people was nearly twice as high as for non-disabled people (8.2 per cent and 4.5 per cent respectively). The likelihood of being long-term unemployed (12 months or longer) was also higher, at 33 per cent of unemployed disabled people compared with 20 per cent of non-disabled people.

European Year of Disabled People
The European Commission has made 2003 the European Year of Disabled People. In addition to the 800,000 euros given to the United Kingdom by the European Commission, the UK Government has contributed £2 million to support the Year. This funding is being used to set up projects across the United Kingdom to promote the rights and participation of disabled people. The Department for Work and Pensions is co-ordinating the UK programme of activities. There are also plans to publish a draft Disability Bill, including changes to the *Disability Discrimination Act* affecting the public sector, transport and premises, and the widening of the definition of disability.

Disability rights policy and legislation
The *Disability Discrimination Act 1995* gives disabled people in the United Kingdom rights in the areas of employment, access to goods, facilities and services, buying or renting land or property and (from October 2002) education. In addition the Act allows the Government to set minimum standards so that disabled people can use public transport easily. The definition of disabled under the Act requires a mental or physical impairment

that has an adverse effect on someone's ability to carry out normal day-to-day activities. The adverse effect must be substantial and long term.

The rights of access afforded to disabled people under the Act place a duty on businesses to adjust the way they provide services to the public, changing their policies, practices and procedures where reasonable. From 2004 they will have to take steps to remove, alter or provide means of avoiding physical features that make it impossible or unreasonably difficult for disabled people to use their services. A Code of Practice on the rights of access that disabled people must be afforded was issued by the Disability Rights Commission in 2002; this Code also provides practical guidance and information for employers.

There is a Minister for Disabled People, supported by the Disability Unit in the Department for Work and Pensions. The Unit provides advice and policy information relating to disability in the United Kingdom.

Disability Rights Commission
The DRC, established under the *Disability Rights Commission Act 1999*, is an independent body, funded by the Government, that works towards eliminating discrimination and promoting equal opportunities for disabled people in Great Britain. It also promotes good practice with employers and service providers and advises the Government on the working of the disability legislation. In 2001/02 the DRC received over 80,000 calls to its helpline and provided legal representation and support in 60 cases.

Low-income households

Although there have been substantial long-term improvements in the standard of living, there remain concerns about the relative deprivation of some people and communities. The distribution of income and wealth is uneven. For example:

- the average original[1] income of the top 20 per cent of UK households in the UK in 2001/02 (£62,900) was around 18 times greater than for those in the bottom 20 per cent (£3,500). Benefits and, to a lesser extent, taxes reduce this inequality so that the ratio for final income is four to one;

---

1 Original income is income before any state intervention in the form of taxes and benefits.

- in 2001/02, 17 per cent of the population of Great Britain lived in households with a low income (see glossary), before housing costs are taken into account, although this has fallen since the peak of 21 per cent in 1992. Lone parent families, pensioners and children are more likely to live in a low-income household than people of working age who do not have children; and
- the wealthiest 10 per cent of the population of the UK owned 54 per cent of marketable wealth in 2000, or 72 per cent of marketable wealth excluding the value of dwellings.

The population within the United Kingdom differs in age structure, labour market conditions and other social characteristics, which in turn results in varying proportions of people living on low incomes. The income distribution in Inner London is heavily polarised: in 2001/02 there were more individuals in both the top and bottom quintiles than any other region (both before and after housing costs). Individuals living in Wales, the North East, and Yorkshire and the Humber were most likely to live in low-income households, while people living in the South East, the East region and, before housing costs, Outer London, were least likely to have low incomes. However, this masks what can be large differences between areas within each region.

Fifteen per cent of the population of the EU were living in low-income households in 1999, but there were considerable differences between the Member States. For example, 9 per cent of the population of Sweden were at risk of poverty, compared with 21 per cent each of the populations of Greece and Portugal. The United Kingdom and Spain ranked joint third worst behind Greece and Portugal, with 19 per cent of their populations living in low-income households in that year.

Social exclusion

Social exclusion is a term for individuals or areas suffering from a combination of linked problems, such as unemployment, poor skills, low incomes, unfair discrimination, poor housing, high crime, bad health and family breakdown.

The Social Exclusion Unit (SEU), based in the Office of the Deputy Prime Minister, was set up in 1997 to reduce social exclusion in England. The Unit liaises with the Welsh, Scottish and Northern Ireland administrations, which have their own

strategies for tackling social exclusion. Current and future projects include:
- raising the educational attainment of children in care;
- employment and enterprise in deprived areas; and
- mental health and social exclusion.

Previously published reports have led to new policies to tackle, for example, truancy, rough sleeping, teenage pregnancy and neighbourhood renewal.

Neighbourhood Statistics
Neighbourhood Statistics (*www.neighbourhood. statistics.gov.uk*) was created in 2001 as part of the National Strategy for Neighbourhood Renewal (see page 304). It is a joint initiative involving central government departments, the devolved administrations, local government and the wider public services, for the benefit of all these bodies and for the community more generally. Data from the 2001 Census provides the core of this information resource, expanded with other data held across the public sector.

Social participation

There are over 500,000 voluntary and community groups across the United Kingdom, ranging from national and international bodies to small local groups. Many of these groups are involved in activities that improve the quality of life in the local community, working in areas as diverse as social welfare, education, sport, heritage, the environment and the arts.

Thirty-two per cent of adults in Great Britain interviewed in the 2001 ONS Omnibus Survey had volunteered at least once in the past 12 months. More than half of those who had volunteered had done some form of voluntary activity in the previous four weeks. Voluntary activity increased with age; 64 per cent of adults aged 70 or over had volunteered in the last four weeks, compared with 46 per cent of adults aged 16 to 29. Women volunteered more often than men and were more likely to raise or collect money and give practical help, while men were more likely to give non-professional advice and serve on committees.

The Active Community Unit at the Home Office aims to promote and develop the voluntary and community sector and encourage people to become actively involved in their communities. Following the 2002 Spending Review by HM Treasury, the Unit has been given £188 million over the next three years to support the community and voluntary sector.

The Youth Service is a partnership between local government and voluntary organisations concerned with the informal personal and social education of young people aged 11 to 25 (5 to 25 in Northern Ireland). Local authorities manage their own youth centres and clubs and provide most of the public support for local and regional organisations. In England there is also a nationwide support service for 13- to 19-year-olds (Connexions, see page 112).

Charities

The Charity Commission for England and Wales is the statutory organisation responsible for the regulation of charities. To become a registered charity in England and Wales an organisation must have purposes that are exclusively philanthropic, such as:

- the relief of financial hardship;
- the advancement of education;
- the advancement of religion; or
- other charitable purposes for the benefit of the community, such as the promotion of urban and rural regeneration or the relief of unemployment.

In 2002/03, approximately 7,400 applications were received for registration from organisations, of which 5,038 were accepted and placed on the Public Register of Charities. There were approximately 187,300 registered charities in England and Wales at the end of March 2003.

Some charitable organisations are not required to register with the Commission – for example some churches and schools. Charities elsewhere in the United Kingdom are not required to register with a government organisation, but do need to seek recognition of their charitable status with the Inland Revenue for tax purposes.

The Charity Commission does not make grants, but advises trustees about administrative matters and has a statutory responsibility to ensure that charities make effective use of their resources. It has the power to investigate and supervise charities, including measures to protect both charities and donors from fraudulent fund-raisers. One of the Commission's duties is to investigate allegations of fraud or dishonesty; over 300 investigations were carried out in 2002/03.

Funding

At the end of March 2003, the total annual income of all registered charities in England and Wales was estimated at over £30 billion. Approximately 6 per cent of registered charities receive nearly 90 per cent of the total annual income recorded, while around two-thirds have an income of £10,000 or less a year and account for less than 1 per cent of the annual total.

Table 9.11 Income and expenditure of the top fund-raising charities,[1] 2000/01, UK

£ million

	Voluntary income	Total income	Total expenditure
Cancer Research UK	239	263	239
Oxfam	122	189	159
The National Trust	118	201	202
Royal National Lifeboat Institution	107	121	96
British Heart Foundation	104	114	117
Salvation Army	88	99	81
NSPCC	74	91	83
British Red Cross	71	158	164
Macmillian Cancer Relief	63	69	64
RSPCA	60	69	78

1 Ranked by voluntary income.
Source: Charities Aid Foundation

Voluntary organisations may receive income from several sources, including:

- central and local government grants;
- contributions from individuals, businesses and trusts;
- earnings from commercial activities and investments; and
- fees from central and local government for services provided on a contractual basis.

Since its introduction in 1994 the National Lottery (see page 257) has given charities and voluntary organisations substantial funding for projects across a range of activities. Another valuable source of revenue for charities is through tax relief and tax exemptions. When an individual makes a donation under the Gift Aid scheme the charity can claim back the basic rate of tax, increasing the value of the donation by 28 per cent based on current tax rates. Under the Payroll Giving Scheme, employees and those drawing a company pension can make tax-free donations from their earnings. Higher rate taxpayers receive relief at 40 per cent. In 2002/03, over 500,000 PAYE employees gave in this manner, giving £86 million. In addition, gifts of land and property, and gifts of quoted stocks and shares can be offset against income.

The Charities Aid Foundation (CAF) is a registered charity that works to increase resources for the voluntary sector in the United Kingdom and overseas. As well as providing services that are both charitable and financial, CAF undertakes a comprehensive programme of research and is a leading source of information on the voluntary sector.

Further reading

Asylum Statistics, United Kingdom. Home Office.

Birth Statistics. Office for National Statistics. (Available only on the ONS website.)

Control of Immigration: Statistics, United Kingdom. Home Office.

Family Spending. Office for National Statistics. The Stationery Office.

Health Statistics Quarterly. Office for National Statistics. The Stationery Office.

Households Below Average Income. Department for Work and Pensions.

Individual Incomes of Men and Women. (Available only via the Women and Equality Unit website.)

International Migration. Office for National Statistics. The Stationery Office.

Key Population and Vital Statistics. Office for National Statistics. The Stationery Office.

Living in Britain: Results from the General Household Survey. Office for National Statistics. The Stationery Office.

Marriage, Divorce and Adoption Statistics. Office for National Statistics. (Available only via the ONS website.)

Patterns and Trends in International Migration in Western Europe. Eurostat.

Persons Granted British Citizenship, United Kingdom. Home Office.

Population Trends (quarterly publication). Office for National Statistics. The Stationery Office.

Recent demographic developments in Europe. Council of Europe.

European Social Statistics – demography. Eurostat.

Social Focus in Brief – Ethnicity. Office for National Statistics, 2003. (Available only via the ONS website.)

Social Trends (annual publication). Office for National Statistics. The Stationery Office.

United Kingdom National Accounts, The Blue Book. Office for National Statistics. The Stationery Office.

Websites

Charities Aid Foundation
www.cafonline.org

Charity Commission
www.charitycommission.gov.uk

Commission for Racial Equality
www.cre.gov.uk

Department for Constitutional Affairs
www.dca.gov.uk

Department for Work and Pensions
www.dwp.gov.uk

Disability Rights Commission
www.drc.org.uk

Equality Commission for Northern Ireland
www.equalityni.org

Equal Opportunities Commission
www.eoc.org.uk

Government Actuary's Department
www.gad.gov.uk

Home Office
www.homeoffice.gov.uk

National Youth Agency
www.nya.org.uk

Office for National Statistics
www.statistics.gov.uk

Social Exclusion Unit
www.socialexclusionunit.gov.uk

Women and Equality Unit
www.womenandequalityunit.gov.uk

WWW.

10 Education and training

Parents are required by law to ensure that their children receive full-time education between the ages of five and 16 in Great Britain and between four and 16 in Northern Ireland. About three-quarters of young people in the United Kingdom choose to stay in full-time education after this age, either in school or further education colleges. About a third of all young people enter universities or other institutions of higher education. Increasing emphasis is being placed on lifelong learning as a way of creating skills and improving employment prospects in a changing labour market.

Pre-school children

Pre-school education is continuing to expand in order to ensure that all children begin primary school with key skills such as listening, concentration and learning to work with others, and a basic foundation in literacy and numeracy. The proportion of three- and four-year-olds enrolled in schools in the United Kingdom rose from 26 per cent in 1972/73 to 64 per cent in 2002/03 (see Figure 10.1). In 2002/03, 38 per cent were enrolled in other settings offering early education such as playgroups in the private and voluntary sectors, either instead of, or in addition to, their school place.

Since 1998 in England, the Government has guaranteed a free, part-time early education place for all children after their fourth birthday if their parents want one. Free places can be in the state, private or voluntary sectors, as long as the providers agree to work to curricular goals. By January 2003, 88 per cent of three-year-olds also had a free place, and all children of that age will be guaranteed one by April 2004.

The devolved administrations are also expanding provision for three-year-olds. Since April 2002 local authorities in Scotland had a duty to secure a pre-school education place for all three- and four-year-old children, whose parents want one.

Childcare

There is a need for good quality, affordable and accessible childcare to help support parents into employment and training as well as to provide development and social opportunities for children. To meet this need, childcare strategies have been implemented across the United Kingdom. In England, most childcare is privately run, and paid for by parents; low and middle income families can receive help with the costs of their childcare through the tax credit system.

Throughout the United Kingdom the Sure Start programme (see page 152) brings together a wide range of initiatives (including early education and

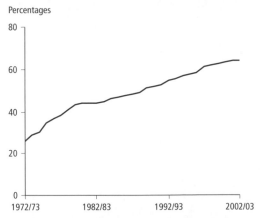

Figure 10.1 Children under five[1] in schools as a percentage of all children aged three and four, UK

Percentages

1 Pupils aged three and four at 31 December each year. The figure for 2002/03 includes 2001/02 data for Wales, Scotland and Northern Ireland.
Source: Department for Education and Skills; National Assembly for Wales; Scottish Executive; Northern Ireland Department of Education

childcare) to improve the health and well-being of families and children.

Schools

About 94 per cent of pupils in the United Kingdom receive free education paid for from public funds, while 6 per cent attend independent fee-paying schools.

State schools

In England and Wales state schools are classified into three broad categories. Community schools are mainly schools that were traditionally owned and funded by Local Education Authorities (LEAs). Foundation schools include many of the former grant-maintained schools. Voluntary schools are divided into controlled and aided, of which many are connected to a particular religious faith. LEAs are responsible for employing staff and for admission arrangements in community and voluntary-controlled schools. The governing body performs this role in foundation and voluntary-aided schools.

In Scotland all state schools are directly managed by local authorities. However, there are also eight grant-aided schools, seven of which are special educational needs schools. In Northern Ireland all schools must be open to all religions. In practice, however, most Protestant children attend one of the 636 controlled schools, managed by education and library boards, while most Catholic children attend one of the 542 voluntary-maintained schools. There are, in addition, 54 voluntary grammar schools (which tend to be Catholic or non-denominational in character). The 47 integrated schools aim to educate Catholic and Protestant children together; these schools may be either controlled or grant-maintained. The Government has a statutory duty to encourage integrated education as a way of breaking down sectarian barriers. Publicly financed schools can apply to become integrated, following a majority vote by parents.

Primary schools

In England and Wales, local education authorities must provide all children with a school place no later than the start of the term after their fifth birthday. Primary schools consist mainly of infant schools for children aged five to seven, junior schools for those aged seven to 11, and combined junior and infant schools for both age groups. First schools in some parts of England cater for ages five to nine or ten as the first stage of a three-tier system: first, middle and secondary. Middle schools cover various age ranges between eight and 14 and usually lead on to comprehensive upper schools.

Excellence and Enjoyment – a strategy for primary schools, published in May 2003, incorporates the national literacy and numeracy strategies and provides for English primary schools to set their own child-based targets at Key Stage 2 (see page 109).

In Scotland, education authorities must also provide all children with a school place no later

Table 10.2 Number of schools by type, 2002/03,[1] UK

Type of school	England	Wales	Scotland	Northern Ireland	United Kingdom
State nursery	475	40	2,586	96	3,197
State primary	17,861	1,624	2,258	920	22,663
State secondary	3,436	227	386	235	4,284
of which specialist schools	992	.	.	.	992
Non-maintained schools	2,180	56	122	25	2,383
of which City Technology Colleges	15	.	.	.	15
Special schools[2]	1,160	44	230	48	1,482
Pupil referral units	360	28	.	.	388
All schools	**25,472**	**2,019**	**5,582**	**1,324**	**34,397**

1 Includes 2001/02 data for Wales, Northern Ireland, and non-maintained and special schools in Scotland. Nursery schools data for Scotland relate to 2000/01.
2 Catering for children with special educational needs (see page 106). The great majority of special schools are publicly maintained.
Source: Department for Education and Skills; National Assembly for Wales; Scottish Executive; Northern Ireland Department of Education

than the start of the term after their fifth birthday. Public primary schools normally lead to the transfer to secondary school at the age of 12.

In Northern Ireland, primary schools cater for children aged four to 11. Some children are educated in the fee-charging preparatory departments of grammar schools.

Secondary schools

In 2002/03 around 88 per cent of the 3.3 million state secondary pupils in England, and in 2001/02 all 212,000 pupils in Wales, attended comprehensive schools. These largely take pupils without reference to ability or aptitude, providing a wide range of secondary education for all or most of the children in a district. All 305,000 Scottish state pupils attend non-selective schools.

Secondary education in Northern Ireland is organised largely on selective lines, with grammar schools admitting pupils on the basis of '11-plus' Transfer Tests in English, mathematics and science. In 2002/03 63,100 pupils attended grammar schools (41 per cent of secondary pupils), of whom 9,800 were being educated in integrated schools. Following public consultation on the proposals in the Burns Report published in October 2001, the Minister with responsibility for education established a working group to bring forward advice and recommendations on options for future alternative arrangements for post-primary education, including the development of alternative transfer arrangements with a view to withdrawing the current tests as soon as practicable. The group was due to report by the end of October 2003.

Special educational needs

A child has special educational needs (SEN) if he or she has significantly greater difficulty in learning than other children of the same age, or a disability which makes it difficult to use normal educational facilities. Approximately 1.8 million pupils with SEN were identified in the United Kingdom in 2001/02. Each one has the right to receive a broad and balanced education and state schools must publish information for parents about their SEN policy.

If an education authority or board believes that it should determine the education for a child with SEN, it must draw up a formal statement of the child's special needs and the action it intends to

Table 10.3 Number of pupils by school type, 2002/03,[1] UK

Type of school	Thousands
State nursery[2]	148
State primary	5,184
State secondary	3,992
Non-maintained schools	643
Special schools[3]	112
Pupil referral units	12
All schools	**10,092**

1 Figures based on head counts. Includes 2001/02 data for Wales, Northern Ireland, and in Scotland, non-maintained and special schools. Nursery schools data for Scotland, relate to 2000/01.
2 Nursery classes within primary schools are included in primary schools except for Scotland, where they are included in nursery schools.
3 Includes maintained and non-maintained sectors.
Source: Department for Education and Skills; National Assembly for Wales; Scottish Executive; Northern Ireland Department of Education

take to meet them. Just over 290,000 children with SEN have these statements (called Record of Needs in Scotland). Parents have a right of appeal if they disagree with decisions about their child. Over 60 per cent of SEN pupils with statements are educated in mainstream schools while most of the others are educated in special schools.

In England, a new SEN Code of Practice came into force in January 2002. It includes rights and duties introduced by the *Special Educational Needs and Disability Act 2001* and associated regulations. An SEN Code of Practice for Wales came into effect in April 2002. Careers Wales is charged with conducting annual reviews for those pupils who have a statement of special educational needs. In Scotland a Bill on Additional Support for Learning Education will be introduced to Parliament in 2003/04 and in Northern Ireland legislation similar to the 2001 Act was due to be introduced in 2003 following consultation.

Independent schools

Independent schools are not funded by the state and obtain most of their finances from fees paid by parents. Some of the larger independent boarding schools are known as 'public schools'. Independent schools providing full-time education for five or more pupils of compulsory school age are required to register with the appropriate government department and are subject to inspection.

Communication Aids Project (CAP)

CAP provides specialised communication equipment such as laptop computers and voice output services, to pupils in England experiencing significant difficulties in communicating. The project, which has helped 1,650 children since it started in April 2002, was recently extended to March 2006 with a further £10 million of funding from the Department for Education and Skills (DfES).

The Cybrarian project

The DfES is also developing the Cybrarian project to support adult learners with disabilities who wish to use the Internet. Cybrarian will contain navigation, knowledge management, personalisation and diagnostic tools with technical and user support appropriate for each user.

The Independent Schools Council (ISC) represents the seven independent schools' associations in the United Kingdom and has overall responsibility for the Independent Schools Inspectorate (ISI). In England and Wales the ISI inspects schools in the ISC every six years, using criteria approved by Ofsted and Estyn (see page 124) and the Government. Independent schools have to pass an inspection to qualify for membership of an association within ISC. All other independent schools are inspected by the relevant national inspectorates.

In England, the Independent/State School Partnership (ISSP) Scheme, set up in 1997, aims to encourage the sharing of experience and good practice between the two sectors. Some of the projects that receive funding focus on sport or are aimed at gifted and talented pupils.

Raising standards

School performance tables were introduced across the United Kingdom in 1993 to enable parents to compare school exam performance and identify failing schools. In both Northern Ireland and Wales the tables have since been abolished in favour of results published by individual schools. Scotland includes attainment as one of a range of measures used to monitor progress towards the five national priorities in education (see page 109).

Specialist schools

The Government wishes to increase the number of specialist schools in the belief that this will raise standards and promote diversity in secondary education. Although they focus on a chosen specialism, specialist schools must still meet the full national curriculum requirements (see page 110). Any maintained secondary school in England can apply to be designated as a specialist school in one of the following subject areas: technology, languages, humanities, music, sports, arts, science, engineering, business and enterprise, or mathematics and computing. Schools can also combine two specialisms. The number of specialist schools reached 1,448 in September 2003, covering almost 50 per cent of pupils in maintained secondary schools. The Government has set a target to increase this to 2,000 schools by 2006.

City Technology Colleges

There are 14 City Technology Colleges situated in urban areas across England. They are state-funded independent schools run by private sponsors, operating outside the normal local government framework. They provide free education for 11- to 18-year-olds in inner city areas, with a curriculum focusing on science and technology.

Academies

Academies are publicly funded independent schools in England. They may be set up to replace existing schools that have been facing challenging circumstances, or as part of a wider school reorganisation, or where there is an unmet demand for school places. Sponsors from the private and voluntary sectors, church and other faith groups help to set up and run these schools. They provide free education to secondary age pupils of all abilities, including provision for children with SEN. Academies aim to offer a broad and balanced curriculum, including a specialism.

The *Education Act 2002* has allowed the City Academy model to expand into rural areas, and provides for all-age, primary and sixth form Academies. It also enables City Technology Colleges to become Academies. The Government aims to establish at least 53 Academies by 2007.

Other initiatives

Excellence in Cities (EiC) tackles educational problems facing children in English cities. Local partnerships implement the EiC programme and focus on the needs and aspirations of individual pupils and their parents. The programme includes about 1,000 secondary schools and one-third of all secondary age pupils, and some 1,000 primary schools.

The Beacon Schools initiative is intended to raise standards by sharing and spreading good practice. The initiative is supporting schools in the most under-achieving areas. By September 2003 there were 1,064 Beacon Schools in England of which 422 were in EiC areas. In April 2003 the leading-edge partnership programme was launched with 103 partnerships. Its aim is to identify, extend and disseminate innovation and excellence in secondary education. The Government intends to establish 300 such partnerships by 2006.

Education Action Zones have been formed in deprived areas in order to help raise educational standards. Zones are built around groups of about 15 to 25 schools. An action forum runs each zone. In 2003 there were 1,348 schools with 493,565 pupils participating in 72 zones.

ICT in Schools Programme
The ICT in Schools Programme, building on the earlier National Grid for Learning Programme (NGfL), is the Government's key initiative for improving ICT provision in English schools. The new programme aims to establish a wide range of digital resources for teaching and learning by the end of 2006, and equip teachers to be more effective users of ICT in the classroom.

By May 2003, the computer-to-pupil ratio in England was 1:8 in primary schools and 1:5 in secondary schools. Over 96 per cent of eligible teachers in England had registered for ICT teacher training through the New Opportunities Fund, and over 99 per cent of schools had signed up for the training.

International comparisons
In 2001, the International Association for the Evaluation of Educational Achievement coordinated an assessment of the reading abilities of over 140,000 ten-year-old pupils in 35 countries. Pupils in both England and Scotland were ranked above the international average score of 500, with English pupils ranked third of the countries taking part. The study also found that homes in England had more children's books than any other country in the survey. Table 10.4 shows the mean achievement score for the EU and G8 countries that took part.

Curriculum
All state schools in the United Kingdom must provide religious education, but parents have the right to withdraw their children from these classes. In Northern Ireland the main churches

Truancy
Unauthorised absences in English primary and secondary schools accounted for 0.72 per cent of half-days in 2002, the equivalent of 7.5 million days missed annually. During the second national truancy sweep – which took place over a week in December 2002 – police and educational welfare officers across the country apprehended 7,341 young people who did not have a valid reason to be out of school. Of these, over half were accompanied by an adult.

Reducing truancy is one of the goals of the £342 million Behaviour Improvement Programme (BIP), which runs from 2002 to 2006. It has been part of the EiC initiative since April 2003 and is targeted at maintaining positive behaviour and attendance. Measures being introduced include more frequent truancy sweeps, improved multi-agency support for pupils at risk of developing the emotional, social and behavioural problems that can lead to truancy, electronic registration systems that confirm the attendance of each pupil in every class and alternatives to exclusion.

About 7,500 parents of truants were prosecuted in 2002. Measures in the Anti Social Behaviour Bill would make it possible to introduce fixed penalty notices and parenting contracts for parents of truants. The Government is committed to reducing truancy by 10 per cent between 2002 and 2004.

have approved a core syllabus for religious education, which must be taught in all grant-aided schools.

All state secondary schools in the United Kingdom are required to provide sex education for all pupils, including education about HIV/AIDS and other sexually transmitted diseases.

England, Wales and Northern Ireland
Children follow the National Curriculum in England and Wales and the Northern Ireland Curriculum in Northern Ireland. The curricula contain programmes of study for age groups split into key stages (see Table 10.5). These stages outline what pupils are entitled to be taught and set out expected standards of performance. The programmes of study represent a statutory minimum – schools have flexibility to add other elements, to choose how they teach the content of the curriculum, and to focus more or less time on particular aspects. There are four key stages

Table 10.4 Mean score for reading achievement[1], 2001

Country	Reading achievement score
Sweden	561
Netherlands	554
England	553
Canada	544
United States	542
Italy	541
Germany	539
Scotland	528
Russian Federation	528
France	525
Greece	524
International average	
(35 countries)	**500**

1 All pupils had four years' formal schooling prior to test except in England and Scotland with five years and in Russia where some had three years.
Source: Progress in International Reading Literacy Study (PIRLS) 2001; National Foundation for Educational Research

covering the ages of compulsory schooling. Key Stages 1 and 2 are studied in primary schools, and Stages 3 and 4 in secondary schools.

Subjects such as drama and dance, although part of the curriculum, can also be taken as optional separate subjects. It is intended that over time every primary school child should have the opportunity to learn to play a musical instrument and explore one of a range of sports. Pilot schemes are being run in 12 areas and Ofsted will report on the implications for wider roll-out by January 2004.

Scotland

There is no statutory national curriculum in Scotland. There are five national priorities in education set out under the following headings:
- achievement and attainment;
- framework for learning;
- inclusion and equality;
- values and citizenship; and
- learning for life.

The content and management of the curriculum are the responsibility of educational authorities and individual headteachers. National guidelines for pupils aged five to 14 set out the ground to be covered and the way pupils' learning should be assessed and reported.

Table 10.5 Organisation of compulsory school years

	Pupil ages	Year group	Attainment expected in final year of the group[1]
England and Wales			
Key Stage 1	5–7	1–2	Level 2
Key Stage 2	7–11	3–6	Level 4
Key Stage 3	11–14	7–9	Level 5/6
Key Stage 4	14–16	10–11	GCSE
Northern Ireland			
Key Stage 1	4/5–8	1–4	Level 2
Key Stage 2	8–11	5–7	Level 3/4
Key Stage 3	11–14	8–10	Level 5/6
Key Stage 4	14–16	11–12	GCSE
Scotland			
(Curriculum	5–7	P1–P3	Level A
following	7–8	P3–P4	Level B
national	8–10	P4–P6	Level C
guidelines from	10–11	P6–P7	Level D
ages 5 to 14)	11–13	P7–S2	Level E
NQ[2]	14–15	S3–S4	Standard Grade

1 For more details see pages 110–111.
2 Standard Grades are now part of the National Qualifications (NQ) framework in Scotland. They are broadly equivalent to GCSEs.

Table 10.6 Compulsory subjects at Key Stages

	England	Wales[1]	Northern Ireland[2]
All Key Stages			
English	•	•	•
Welsh/Irish		•	•
Mathematics	•	•	•
Science	•	•	•
Physical education	•	•	•
Design and technology	•		•
ICT[3]	•		
Cross-curricula themes			•
Key Stages 1 to 3			
History	•	•	•
Geography	•	•	•
Art and design	•	•	•
Music	•	•	•
Technology			•
Key Stages 3 and 4			
Citizenship	•		
Modern foreign language	•	•	•
Cross-curricula themes[4]			•
Humanities			•

1 In Wales, art and design is art; technology includes design and ICT. A language is optional at Key Stage 4.
2 Irish is taken in Irish-speaking schools. Science includes technology at Key Stages 1 and 2. Design and technology is taken at Key Stages 3 and 4 only.
3 Information and communications technology.
4 Cross-curricula themes include cultural heritage, education for mutual understanding, health education and ICT at Key Stages 1 to 4, and economic awareness and careers education at Key Stages 3 and 4. At Key Stage 4 pupils must choose a humanities subject.

There are curriculum guidelines for languages, mathematics, ICT, environmental studies, expressive arts, religious and moral education, health education, and personal and social development. Pupils can study a modern European language during the last two years of primary education.

There are 58 units in primary schools where education takes place through the Gaelic language. There are some other schools where Gaelic can be learned as a second language.

Attainment

The attainment of pupils in core subjects at ages seven, 11 and 14 has been steadily improving at each key stage since 1996, with tests and teacher assessments showing a similar pattern. However,

Language teaching in primary schools

The National Languages Strategy for England was launched in December 2002, one aim of which is to ensure that by the end of the decade every pupil from age seven to 11 will have the opportunity to study at least one of the working languages of the European Union. Language Pathfinder projects are being funded in 19 LEAs to support the introduction of languages in primary schools.

In Wales, a pilot scheme to give children the opportunity to learn a modern foreign language began in September 2003. The scheme, involving 96 primary schools, is part of the Welsh Assembly Government's *Languages Count* strategy and is due to run until July 2006.

The Scottish Executive was funding more than 20 language projects in 2002/03, including a 'partial immersion project' in an Aberdeen primary school, where the expressive arts component of the curriculum is taught to primary 1 pupils in French. As pupils progress through the school, the amount of the curriculum delivered in French will gradually be increased to 80 per cent.

the percentage of pupils achieving the expected levels in each subject tends to fall off between Key Stages 1 and 3. Girls consistently outperform boys in English and Welsh, whereas results for maths and science are broadly similar. Table 10.7 shows the results of teacher assessments in England – unlike tests, these are carried out in all three subjects at each stage.

Scotland

The percentage of pupils attaining target levels increased between 1999/2000 and 2001/02 for most local authorities, across all subjects. As in England and Wales, the proportions of pupils achieving the expected level were lower in the older age groups (see Table 10.8).

Qualifications

Examinations in England, Wales and Northern Ireland, are typically taken at the following ages:
- age 16 – General Certificate of Secondary Education (GCSE, graded A* to G).
- age 17 – General Certificate of Education Advanced Subsidiary (AS level, graded A to E) which is equivalent to 50 per cent of an A level.
- age 18 – General Certificate of Education Advanced (A level, graded A to E).

Table 10.7 Pupils reaching expected standards according to teacher assessments, 2002, England

Percentages

	English	Mathematics	Science
Key Stage 1[1]			
Boys	81	87	88
Girls	89	90	91
Key Stage 2[2]			
Boys	67	74	82
Girls	78	75	83
Key Stage 3[3]			
Boys	59	69	66
Girls	75	72	69

1 Percentage of pupils achieving level 2 or above.
2 Percentage of pupils achieving level 4 or above.
3 Percentage of pupils achieving level 5 or above.
Source: Department for Education and Skills

How pupils in the UK are assessed
England and Wales
Pupils are assessed formally at the ages of seven, 11 and 14 by their teachers and/or by national tests in the core subjects of English, mathematics and science. In some schools in Wales, Welsh is also assessed. At age 14, pupils are also assessed in other subjects. In Wales there is no statutory national testing at age seven, and the Welsh Minister for Education is considering alternatives to formal testing at 11 and 14.

Northern Ireland
Pupils are formally assessed at the age of 14 in English, mathematics and science. The requirements are broadly similar to those in England and Wales. Assessment takes the form of teacher assessment and tasks or tests.

Scotland
Progression is measured by attainment of six levels, based on the expectation of the performance of the majority of pupils at certain ages between five and 14 (see Table 10.5). Pupils are assessed by their teachers and by tests in reading, writing and mathematics which are selected and administered from a national catalogue. Tests can take place at any time during the school year and at any age.

Table 10.8 Pupils attaining target levels in each subject, 2001/02, Scotland

Percentages

	P3	P6	S2
Mathematics	95	79	54
Reading	87	85	59
Writing	85	73	50

Source: Scottish Executive

In Scotland, the National Qualifications (NQ) framework covers Standard Grade (usually taken at age 16 and graded 1 to 7); and Access, Intermediate 1 and 2, Higher and Advanced Higher qualifications (usually taken at ages 17 and 18 and graded A to C – except for Access qualifications, which have no external assessment component).

Specifications and assessment procedures must comply with national guidelines and be accredited by the Qualifications and Curriculum Authority (QCA) in England, by its Welsh counterpart, Qualifications, Curriculum and Assessment Authority for Wales/Awdurdod Cymwysterau, Cwricwlwm ac Asesu Cymru (ACCAC), or the Northern Ireland Council for Curriculum, Examinations and Assessment (CCEA). These independent government agencies are responsible for ensuring that the curriculum and qualifications are of high quality, coherent and flexible. NQs in Scotland are managed by the Scottish Qualifications Authority (SQA).

In 2001/02, 53 per cent of pupils in the United Kingdom gained five or more GCSE grades A* to C or equivalent, compared with 45 per cent in 1995/96.

In England new GCSEs in vocational subjects were introduced in September 2002. These are designed to replace the General National Vocational Qualification (GNVQ) Part One. Northern Ireland also introduced vocational GCSEs at this time. They are available in eight subjects: applied art and design; applied business; engineering; health and social care; applied ICT; leisure and tourism; manufacturing; and applied science. In Scotland the General Scottish Vocational Qualification (GSVQ) is the equivalent.

In 2001/02, 38 per cent of young people in schools and further education in the United Kingdom achieved two or more GCE A levels or equivalent, with female pupils obtaining better results than males (see Figure 10.10). A generation or so ago, in 1965/66, 9 per cent of female and 13 per cent of male school leavers achieved this level.

The Welsh Baccalaureate

The Welsh Baccalaureate Pilot Project is a six year project to develop and test a new qualification, initially for 16- to 18-year-olds, which will incorporate existing qualifications together with a common core curriculum. The components of the core curriculum will be: key skills, Wales, Europe and the world (including a language module), work-related education and personal and social education. Eighteen centres, including schools and further education institutions, are involved in the first phase of the pilot, which began in September 2003.

Careers

All young people in full-time education are entitled to career information, advice and guidance.

In England, Connexions is an integrated information, advice and guidance service for 13- to 19-year-olds, which aims to help young people make a smooth transition to adulthood and working life. It offers confidential support on any subject the young person chooses, including educational and career options. There are 47 local Connexions Partnerships and a network of personal advisers based in a variety of settings, including schools and colleges. There is also a confidential telephone helpline and an interactive online advice service (*www.connexions-direct.com*).

Careers Wales works with schools and colleges to deliver information, advice and guidance to all age groups. It facilitates work experience placements for students in schools and further education colleges and provides additional help to those most at risk of failing to realise their potential. Careers Wales operates advice helplines and can be contacted online on *www.careerswales.com*.

In Northern Ireland careers education is a cross-curricular theme in secondary schools. Work experience for young people is fostered through the Northern Ireland Business Education Partnership, which supports a network of local partnerships and five area partnerships aligned to the five education and library boards.

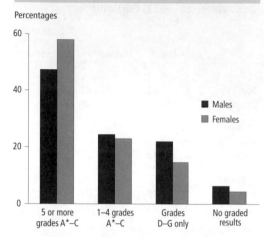

Figure 10.9 Pupils obtaining GCSE or equivalent qualifications,[1] 2001/02, UK

1 Percentage of pupils aged 15 at the start of the academic year, or in year S4 in Scotland, who obtained the grade shown. See text for explanation of Scottish qualifications.
Source: Department for Education and Skills; National Assembly for Wales; Scottish Executive; Northern Ireland Department of Education

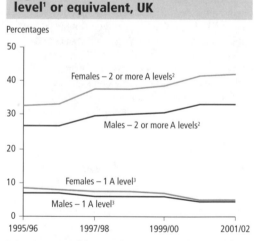

Figure 10.10 Achievement at GCE A level[1] or equivalent, UK

1 As a percentage of those aged 18 (17 in Scotland). Two AS levels count as one A level pass.
2 Or three or more highers.
3 Or one or two highers. Includes those with 1.5 A levels.
Source: Department for Education and Skills; National Assembly for Wales; Scottish Executive; Northern Ireland Department of Education

Careers Scotland offers a careers advisory service to all ages and, like Careers Wales, has a particular focus on supporting vulnerable young people.

Young people and adults

14- to 19-year-olds
In January 2003, following consultation on the Green Paper *14–19: Extending opportunities, raising standards*, the Government announced proposals for education and training for 14- to 19-year-olds in England. These include:

- courses that are better tailored to students' needs and aptitudes, including a range of academic, vocational, technical and mixed options;
- a reduction in the National Curriculum at Key Stage 4 to make space for this wider choice;
- more GCSE courses that provide vocational and applied options alongside academic options;
- young people to be entitled to study literacy, numeracy and computer skills to level 2, until they are 19 years old; and
- schools and the Connexions service (see page 112) to help young people plan ahead for the whole 14 to 19 phase from the end of Key Stage 3, using Individual Learning Plans.

A working group on 14–19 reform (*www.14-19reforms.gov.uk*) has been established to consider changes in the longer term.

Further education
After compulsory education is finished, young people can choose to stay on at school, attend college or take part in work-based learning. About three-quarters of 16-year-olds continue in full-time education in school sixth forms, sixth form colleges or further education colleges, compared with under half twenty years ago. The further education sector delivers a broad range of learning, including:

- academic and vocational learning for 16- to 19-year-olds;
- vocational education and training for adults seeking employment;
- workforce development for employers;
- second chance general education for adults; and
- learning for leisure and personal development.

Student support
Young people aged 16 to 19 in further education in England are entitled to free learning and do not have to pay tuition or other fees. Further Education Learner Support Funds (£67 million in 2003/04) are available to help students aged 16 to 19 who are, or whose families are, on a low income or in particular financial difficulty. Funding is available for course-related costs, including transport, childcare, residential and hardship funding.

Adults on government-funded courses are expected to make a financial contribution towards the cost of their tuition fees unless they are on a low income or studying basic skills. Learner Support Funds for those aged 19 and over include Access Funds, which can help towards the cost of books, equipment, transport and tuition fees (£55 million in 2002/2003), Childcare Support Funds (£40 million for 2003/204) and Residential Bursaries (£2 million in 2003/2004).

The National Council for Education & Training in Wales (ELWa) and the Scottish Further Education Funding Council provide similar help for eligible students in further education. In 2002/03 the Welsh Assembly Government introduced Assembly Learning Grants, for which further education students are eligible (depending upon age, income and course of study).

Table 10.11 Students[1] in further and higher education, by type of course and sex, UK

		Thousands
	Males	Females
2000/01		
Further education[2]		
Full-time	543	543
Part-time	1,528	2,376
All further education	2,071	2,918
2001/02		
Higher education[3]		
Undergraduate		
Full-time	519	620
Part-time	257	380
Postgraduate		
Full-time	86	86
Part-time	140	151
All higher education	**1,003**	**1,238**

1 Home and overseas students.
2 Excludes adult education centres.
3 Includes Open University.
Source: Department for Education and Skills; National Assembly for Wales; Scottish Executive; Northern Ireland Department of Education

Centres of Vocational Excellence (CoVEs)
CoVEs aim to meet employers' skills needs by providing vocational skills training across a range of occupations, such as catering, computing and construction. The Learning and Skills Council (see page 119) aims to develop a network of at least 400 CoVEs in England by the end of March 2006. CoVEs are mainly based in further education colleges, but the programme has been extended to develop centres with work-based learning providers. By autumn 2003 there were 250 CoVEs, over 200 of which were within colleges.

In Northern Ireland the Executive provides funding and support through the Further Education Funding Formula. Funding is also provided to colleges and students through a number of special budgets, which are designed to widen access, increase participation, address skills shortages and enhance the role of the sector in supporting economic development.

Higher education
Around 30 per cent of young people in England and Wales, 45 per cent in Scotland and 44 per cent in Northern Ireland take degree and other advanced courses in universities and other colleges. An increasing number of mature students also study for these qualifications.

Universities and higher education colleges
There are 89 university institutions in the United Kingdom, including the Open University. This figure does not include the constituent colleges of the universities of London and Wales, both of which have a federal structure. UK universities enjoy academic freedom, appoint their own staff, admit students and award their own degrees. The universities of Oxford and Cambridge date from the 13th century and the Scottish universities of St Andrews, Glasgow and Aberdeen from the 15th century.

In addition, there are 63 higher education colleges. Some are very specialised, such as art and design, teacher education and agriculture colleges, while others are multi-disciplinary. Some award their own degrees and qualifications, while in others these are validated by a university or national body. Applications for full-time first degrees and Higher National Diploma courses are usually made through the Universities and Colleges Admission Service (UCAS). In 2002 nearly 370,000 applicants were accepted into higher education through UCAS. Around 29,000 students were accepted as deferred entrants for places after the following academic year – nearly double the figure for 1994 and accounting for nearly 8 per cent of accepted applications.

Students at university in England, Wales and Northern Ireland usually spend three years of study, leading to a bachelor's degree, such as a Bachelor of Arts (BA) or Bachelor of Science (BSc). There are some four-year courses, especially for those studying languages, and medical and veterinary courses normally require five or six years. A full-time first degree in Scotland (where students usually start a year earlier) generally takes four years for Honours and three years for the broad-based Ordinary degree.

In 2002 some 267,000 students gained a first degree in the United Kingdom compared with around 159,000 students in 1992 and 102,000 in 1982. Fifty-six per cent of first degree graduates in 2002 were women, and 11 per cent gained their award through part-time and other modes of study.

Some students go on to do postgraduate studies. These usually lead to a masters degree, such as a Master of Arts (MA) or Master of Science (MSc), or to a doctorate (PhD). A masters degree usually lasts one year full-time or two years part-time. A PhD usually lasts three years full-time or six years part-time. The Government also launched the 'New Route PhD' in 2001 in response to the changes in knowledge and skills demanded of PhD graduates. It lasts four years and combines a research project with a programme of formal coursework and professional skills development.

Applications for postgraduate study are made directly to the university.

The Open University
Founded in 1969 and since copied in other parts of the world, the Open University (OU) is a non-residential university offering over 375 degree and other courses for adult students who wish to study in their own time. Students do not need any formal academic qualifications to register for most courses and admission is normally on a 'first come, first served' basis. Teaching is through a combination of printed texts, correspondence tuition, television broadcasts, audio/video cassettes and, for some courses, short residential schools. Some 160,000 of its 218,000 students study online from home and many OU learning

Provision for disabled students

In England and Northern Ireland, the National Disability Team (*www.natdisteam.ac.uk*) has a contract to help improve provision for disabled students in higher education. It is providing support between 2003 and 2005 for 55 projects funded by the Higher Education Funding Council for England and the Department for Employment and Learning in Northern Ireland, aimed at improving provision in small and/or specialist institutions. The team is also developing and disseminating resources relating to the learning and teaching of disabled students.

In 2003 around 9,000 students who had declared a disability or additional requirement were studying with the Open University – this is believed to be the largest number in any higher education institution in the United Kingdom or the EU. Tapes, transcripts, comb-bound materials and special format examination papers are the commonest additional services provided but increasingly students are receiving electronic versions of course material. A range of specialist equipment such as talking scientific calculators, personal radio aids and subtitle recorders/decoders are also available. Students with severe disabilities receive a free professional assessment of their needs for specialist IT hardware and software (such as voice-recognition software and computers with synthetic speech output) and in most cases the university will pay for the equipment if the student is not eligible for relevant government grants.

resources are delivered on interactive CD-ROM or computer software. There is a network of local tutorial centres for contact with part-time tutors and fellow students.

Other distance learning

With the growth of the Internet, some UK universities and colleges now offer study through distance learning. This usually means learning at home or work, with no need to visit the learning centre. Courses are available at many levels, including degree and postgraduate qualifications. The Department for Education and Skills (DfES) offers advice on which institutions are recognised as having degree awarding powers and recommends that a check is made before applying for an online course.

UK eUniversities Worldwide (UKeU) is a public-private initiative. The venture will aim to provide an e-learning platform to deliver high-quality higher education from established UK universities

and colleges, principally via the Internet. The first pilot courses became available in spring 2003.

Widening access

The Government's aim is that by 2010, 50 per cent of those aged 18 to 30 will have participated in higher education by the time they are 30.

The AimHigher programme in England aims to get more young people from disadvantaged backgrounds to apply for and get into higher education by improving links between schools, colleges and universities. In September 2003, 40 new areas joined the 91 existing areas funded until 2006. Some aspects of the AimHigher programme have also been adopted in Wales.

Finance

In 2002/03 LEAs and central government spent £6.3 billion on higher education in the United Kingdom. Government finance is distributed to higher education institutions by Higher Education Funding Councils in England, Wales and Scotland, and in Northern Ireland by the Department for Employment and Learning. The private University of Buckingham does not receive public funds.

Institutions also charge tuition fees, which are partly funded by students. From 2006, universities in England will be entitled to set variable fees for individual courses, up to a cap of £3,000, which will rise in line with inflation. Any rise above the current level of £1,125 will be subject to an access agreement in partnership with the Office for Fair Access (OFFA, see box on page 116). In addition, institutions provide paid training, research or consultancy for commercial firms, and many establishments have endowments or receive grants from foundations and benefactors.

Student finance

Eligible full-time students in England and Wales receive help towards their tuition fees, and loans and grants towards living costs.

The amount they can expect to contribute towards tuition fees depends on their own and their family's income. Students from families with low incomes do not pay anything. In 2003/04 the maximum contribution was £1,125 per year. From 2006 students will not be required to make a contribution until after they have finished studying.

Low interest student loans provide help with living costs. The maximum loan available in 2003/04 for eligible full-time students living away from home

White Paper on higher education

The Future of Higher Education, published in January 2003, contains proposals aimed at widening access to universities and helping them remain competitive in the world economy. The strategy principally covers higher education in England, but some proposals will also affect higher education in other parts of the United Kingdom.

Measures announced in the White Paper and in April 2003 include:
- increased spending on research, to be concentrated in leading departments and in larger units, including collaborations;
- the creation of a new UK-wide Arts and Humanities Research Council;
- a permanent third stream of funding to encourage work with employers, including the funding of Knowledge Exchanges;
- additional funding to reward excellence in teaching;
- an increase in the provision of foundation degrees (work-related degrees, which can lead to full university honours degrees);
- the introduction of variable fees of up to £3,000 per annum, payment of which will be deferred until after graduation;
- the re-introduction of grants of up to £1,000 to help the most disadvantaged students; and raising the earnings threshold at which students pay back fees and student loans from £10,000 to £15,000 from April 2005;
- the creation of an Office for Fair Access (OFFA), which will monitor new Access Agreements, drawn up by those institutions wishing to increase fees above the current level of £1,125; and
- financial incentives for universities to build up their own endowments and other revenue.

was £4,000 (£4,930 for those in London). Loans are repaid on the basis of income after the student has completed his or her course, and only when he or she starts earning over £10,000 a year (increasing to £15,000 in April 2005).

Help is also available for eligible part-time students. Those on low incomes can obtain help towards the cost of tuition fees and also a one-off loan payment of £500 per academic year to help with course costs. From September 2004, a new package of help for part-time students will be available, which includes the replacement of the £500 loan with a grant of £250.

Additional non-repayable help is targeted at certain students, particularly those with disabilities, dependants, or those entering higher education from low-income families. Students who get into financial difficulties may also be eligible for help from their institution.

From 2004/05, Higher Education Grants of £1,000 will be available to students with student and family income of £15,200 or less. A partial grant will be available where the income is between £15,201 and £21,185.

Student support in Scotland

Student loans and supplementary grants are also the main source of help with living costs in Scotland. Students from low-income families are entitled to have up to £2,000 of their annual loan entitlement replaced by a non-repayable bursary. Most graduates who have started courses since 2001/02 are required to make a one-off payment of £2,000 to the Graduate Endowment when they complete their course and start earning over £10,000 a year (mature students, lone parents and students with a disability are exempt). Since 2000/01 tuition fees have not been payable by eligible full-time Scottish-domiciled students or EU students studying in Scotland.

In Northern Ireland support for higher education students generally operates on a similar basis to England and Wales. However, from September 2003 means-tested bursaries of up to £2,000 became available to low-income families.

Postgraduate support

Most postgraduates have to pay a significant contribution towards tuition fees. In 2003/04 the assumed fee for a one-year masters programme in England was £2,940, although this varies with the programme of study and the institution. Some postgraduates receive an award from a public body, some support themselves through a mixture of public and private finance, and others receive funding through scholarships and bursaries. Most public funding is provided by Research Councils (see chapter 26) that operate throughout the United Kingdom, the Students Awards Agency for Scotland and the Department for Employment and Learning in Northern Ireland. Employers may offer support by paying all or part of the tuition fees and/or costs such as examination fees and books, and by allowing paid leave for study.

Adult education

Education for adults provided by LEAs is carried out in a wide range of locations, including LEAs' own premises, local community centres, libraries, museums, schools and both adult and further education colleges. Overall, about half of LEAs provide adult and community learning through direct delivery; the other half are through contracts with other providers, predominately voluntary sector organisations, community learning centres and colleges. The duty to secure such education rests with the Learning and Skills Council in England and the National Council for Education and Training for Wales (ELWa, see page 119). Adult education in Scotland is a statutory duty of education authorities and is generally known as community learning and development. In Northern Ireland it is provided by the further education sector, supplemented by the work of a range of non-statutory providers. General adult education courses include languages, physical education/sport/ fitness and practical craft skills, such as embroidery or woodwork. Adult education courses may lead to a formal qualification, but many do not.

The National Institute of Adult Continuing Education and the Basic Skills Agency jointly manage the Adult and Community Learning Fund on behalf of the DfES. The Fund supports innovative learning opportunities and aims to encourage people who have been reluctant to participate in learning and who may be disadvantaged as a result.

The Workers' Educational Association (WEA) (*www.wea.org.uk*) is the largest UK voluntary provider of adult education. Founded in 1903, it runs over 10,000 courses each year through local and regional centres, providing learning for more than 110,000 adults. The WEA is a national charity and is supported by the Government through funding from the Learning and Skills Council in England, and in Scotland by the Scottish Executive and local authorities.

Literacy and numeracy

The Adult Basic Skills Strategy Unit, based in the DfES, is responsible for the implementation of *Skills for Life*, the national strategy for improving adult literacy and numeracy in England. Around 7 million adults in England have literacy levels below level 1 (equivalent to GCSE grades D–G) or what is expected of 11-year-olds, and even more have a problem with numeracy. Launched in

21st century skills

In July 2003, the Government published its strategy for skills, *21st Century Skills: Realising Our Potential.* The strategy aims to help individuals acquire and develop skills that will keep them employed and help them to lead rewarding lives and make a greater contribution to their communities. Closely associated with the skills strategy is a target to reduce the number of adults in the UK workforce who lack NVQ2 or equivalent qualifications by at least 40 per cent by 2010. Any adult in the labour force without a full level 2 qualification will have access to free learning in order to gain their first qualification at this level. A new Skills Alliance will also be created, linking up the work of the key government departments involved with economic and skills issues – the DfES, the DTI, the DWP and HM Treasury.

March 2001, *Skills for Life* caters for the literacy, language (English for Speakers of Other Languages – ESOL) and numeracy needs of all post-16 learners, including those with learning difficulties or disabilities, from pre-entry level up to and including level 2 (equivalent to GCSE grades A*–C). All basic skills provision is free to the learner no matter where or how it is delivered. The National Basic Skills Strategy for Wales was also launched in March 2001 and seeks to tackle basic skills deficiencies in all age groups. It is implemented by the Basic Skills Agency.

In Scotland, a new development centre was established in January 2003 to implement the recommendations of the Adult Literacy and Numeracy in Scotland 2001 report. The centre, Learning Connections, is part of Communities Scotland. In Northern Ireland a framework and consultation paper on Adult Literacy was launched in July 2002.

Work-related training

Several programmes are available to help increase and enhance work-related skills. These are offered as part of the learning pathways available to 16- to 19-year-olds and can also be part of an existing employee's training. The Government has several initiatives to help people train for work and achieve occupationally specific qualifications such as NVQs (see page 118).These include the New Deal (see page 135), Modern Apprenticeships and work-based learning for adults – open to those aged 25 and over who have been unemployed for six months or longer.

Vocational qualifications

National Vocational Qualifications (NVQs) and the equivalent Scottish Vocational Qualifications (SVQs) are occupationally specific qualifications, based on competences, which are assessed in the workplace. They cover sectors such as business, engineering and health and social care. The qualifications are derived from national standards developed by employer-led bodies and approved across the United Kingdom by the Qualifications and Curriculum Authority.

NVQs or SVQs are awarded at five levels. Vocational GCSEs and Vocational A levels are an alternative to GCSEs and GCE A levels in England, Wales and Northern Ireland (see also page 110) and are offered at levels 2 and 3 (respectively) of the National Qualifications Framework (NQF). There are also a range of awarding body 'own brand' qualifications which encompass level 1 to level 4 of the NQF and include Business and Technology Council (BTEC) National Diplomas and Higher National Diplomas or City and Guilds qualifications. NQs in Scotland include vocational subjects alongside traditional academic ones.

Vocational and academic comparability

Vocational and academic qualifications are broadly comparable at the following levels:

- an NVQ or SVQ level 5 is comparable to a higher degree;
- an NVQ or SVQ level 4 is comparable to a first degree, BTEC Higher National qualifications, an RSA Higher Diploma, a nursing qualification or other higher education;
- an NVQ or SVQ level 3 is comparable to two GCE A levels or NQF accredited vocational-related qualifications, including an RSA Advanced Diploma, City and Guilds Level 3 Progression Awards and BTEC National Diplomas; and
- an NVQ or SVQ level 2 is comparable to five GCSEs at grades A* to C, an RSA Diploma, a City and Guilds level 2 or a BTEC First Diploma.

Modern Apprenticeships (MAs)

MAs provide structured learning programmes for young people that combine work-based training with off-the-job learning and Foundation Modern

Apprenticeships offer training to NVQ level 2 and Advanced Modern Apprenticeships to level 3. The quality of MAs is being improved through technical certificates that develop knowledge and understanding, and through an Apprenticeship diploma or equivalent. More than 80 sectors of business and industry already offer MAs, ranging from accountancy to sport. Each industry has its own guidance on entry requirements. The Government is committed to ensuring that 28 per cent of 16- to 21-year-olds in England will have entered apprenticeship by 2004.

Wales

The Welsh Assembly Government, in collaboration with ELWa (see below) has integrated work-based learning programmes for adults and young people into a single *All Age* programme. Within the All Age provisions, the Skillbuild route is targeted at those young people who are most at risk in the labour market and aims to develop social skills, literacy, numeracy, ICT and other skills. The Modern and Foundation Modern Apprenticeship routes are now open to all and the Modern Skills Diploma for Adults, which was introduced in April 2001, provides high-level (level 3 and above) skills training. All the programmes are open to those in employment. Other initiatives in Wales include the development of the Credit and Qualifications Framework (CQFW), the second phase of Individual Learning Accounts (ILA Wales) to help people plan and pay towards the cost of learning, and the Learning Worker Project pilot for those in employment without a level 3 qualification.

Scotland

In Scotland all young people aged 16 and 17 are entitled to training under the government-funded Skillseekers scheme. The emphasis is on training leading to a recognised qualification, up to SVQ level 3, and provided via an individual training plan with employer involvement. Around 78 per cent of Skillseekers are in paid employment, with the remainder on work placements and in receipt of a training allowance. The Scottish Credit and Qualifications Framework (SCQF) brings all mainstream academic and vocational Scottish qualifications into a single unified framework. All qualifications within the framework are credit rated and levelled to show equivalencies between qualifications to make the education and training system easier for learners and employers.

Northern Ireland

In Northern Ireland the Jobskills Programme is available to all 16- to 17-year-olds. It provides training to NVQ level 2 with progress routes to NVQ level 3 through Modern Apprenticeship arrangements.

Learning providers

Learning and Skills Council

In England, the Learning and Skills Council (LSC) is the planning and funding body for all post-16 education and training outside the university sector. With a budget of £8 billion for 2003/04, its objectives include maximising the achievement and participation of young people in education and training, increasing demand for learning by adults, improving the level of basic skills in the workplace, increasing employer engagement and improving the quality of provision.

Wales

The National Council for Education and Training for Wales (ELWa) (*www.elwa.ac.uk*) has a similar remit to the LSC. It is responsible for post-16 education and training, with the exception of higher education. There are 21 local voluntary partnerships (Community Consortia for Education and Training) linking LEAs, schools, colleges, voluntary organisations, private training providers, employers and trade unions. Higher education remains the responsibility of the Higher Education Funding Council for Wales (HEFCW).

Scotland

A network of Local Enterprise Companies is responsible for the delivery of the Scottish Executive's national training programmes. They run under contract to two non-departmental public bodies: Scottish Enterprise and Highlands and Islands Enterprise.

Northern Ireland

The Department for Employment and Learning (DEL) of the Northern Ireland Executive is responsible for higher and further education, employment, skill development and lifelong learning. The department's Learning and Skills Advisory Board was formed in January 2002 to advise on the business development of education, training and employment services.

Sector Skills Councils

In April 2002 the Sector Skills Development Agency was given responsibility for setting up a new Sector Skills Council (SSC) network, to replace National Training Organisations. It is expected that the new network will largely be in place by April 2004. SSCs are independent UK-wide organisations developed by groups of employers in industry and business sectors. They bring together employers, trade unions and professional bodies, working with government to develop the skills needed by UK businesses.

New Technology Institutes

In May 2002 the locations of 18 New Technology Institutes (NTIs) in England were announced. The NTIs are formed through partnerships between higher education institutions, further education colleges, and private sector partners, and provide training in advanced technology skills both to businesses and students. Partnerships for all 18 NTIs have been established and all should be fully operational by 2004/05.

Ufi/learndirect

Ufi/learndirect was set up to stimulate demand for learning and to make it more accessible through the use of ICT. The learndirect network currently numbers more than 2,030 centres across England, Wales and Northern Ireland. Between them they deliver around 650 courses, 75 per cent of which are offered online, covering a range of topics including IT skills, business skills and the basics of reading, writing and numbers. There is a telephone helpline and a website (*www.learndirect.co.uk*) offering information and advice on over 600,000 learning opportunities in the United Kingdom to people aged 16 and over. In Scotland a similar but distinct organisation (Scottish Ufi) (*www.learndirectscotland.com*) operates over 400 learning centres.

Financial support

Career development loans are designed to help people pay for vocational education or learning in Great Britain. Loans of between £300 and £8,000 are provided through major banks. Interest payments during training and for one month after are funded by the Government, before repayment by the student begins. The loans help to pay for courses lasting up to two years and, if relevant, for up to one year's practical work experience where it forms part of the course. Around 17,000 loans were taken out in 2002/03, totalling over £74 million. Over 184,000 loans have been taken out since the scheme began in 1988.

Teaching and other staff

In 2002/03 the average UK pupil to teacher ratios for state nursery, primary and secondary schools were 24.8, 22.1 and 16.4 respectively. In the younger age groups the work of qualified teachers is more likely to be supplemented by teaching assistants (see below).

Figure 10.12 shows trends in teacher numbers in maintained schools. Since 1997/98 the decline in the overall number of teachers has been reversed. However, the number of male teachers in the United Kingdom has continued to fall.

England and Wales
New teachers in state primary and secondary schools must be graduates and hold Qualified Teacher Status (QTS). In independent schools it is strongly recommended that new teachers obtain QTS. It can be achieved in a number of ways, including a one-year Postgraduate Certificate in Education (PGCE) course or a three- or four-year Bachelor of Education degree.

Graduate and Registered Teacher Programmes offer the opportunity for trainees to earn a salary while following a teacher training programme in a school. These schemes, available only in England, along with the Overseas Trained Teacher Programme, are particularly suitable for overseas-trained teachers who do not hold QTS, mature career changers, school support staff and people who have had previous teaching experience.

All teachers working in state schools must be registered with the General Teaching Council for England or for Wales. These are teachers' professional bodies which, among other things, have the power to strike a teacher from the register on grounds of professional misconduct or incompetence.

Scotland
All teachers in education authority schools must be registered with the General Teaching Council for Scotland. The Council gives advice to the Scottish Executive on teacher supply and the professional suitability of teacher training courses. It is also responsible for disciplinary procedures under which a teacher guilty of professional misconduct may be removed temporarily or permanently from the register.

Teacher qualification procedures are similar to those in England and Wales, including the Bachelor of Education degree and the PGCE. There is also a combined degree, sometimes known as a concurrent degree. All pre-service courses are validated by a higher education institution accredited by the Council and approved by the Scottish Executive. The Education Inspectorate has powers to inspect teacher education and training.

Northern Ireland
All entrants to teaching in grant-aided schools are graduates and hold an approved teaching qualification. Initial teacher training is integrated with induction and early in-service training, the latter covering a period of three years. The General Teaching Council in Northern Ireland has similar duties to those in England and Wales. As with the rest of the United Kingdom, the main teacher training courses are the Bachelor of Education degree and the PGCE. The education and library boards have a statutory duty to provide curricular support services and in-service training.

Teaching assistants
The term teaching assistant refers to those whose primary role is either to assist the teacher in the classroom, or to provide support for individual pupils. There are no nationally set qualifications for this role, although some local authorities have

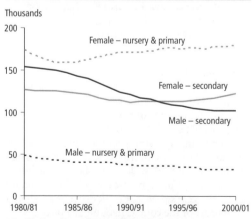

Figure 10.12 Full-time teachers,[1] by gender, UK

Thousands

Female – nursery & primary

Female – secondary

Male – secondary

Male – nursery & primary

1980/81 1985/86 1990/91 1995/96 2000/01

1 Qualified teachers only. As at 31 March of each year.
Source: Department for Education and Skills; National Assembly for Wales; Scottish Executive; Northern Ireland Department of Education

Raising Standards and Tackling Workload: a National Agreement

In January 2003, Government in England and Wales, employers and trade unions agreed to work towards a reform of the roles and responsibilities of school staff. The timetable for reform is as follows:

From September 2003:
- teachers will no longer be required to undertake administrative and clerical tasks on a routine basis;
- improvements will be made to teachers' and headteachers' work/life balance; and
- all teachers (including the head) will have a reasonable allocation of time in support of their leadership and management responsibilities.

From September 2004:
- the number of hours that a teacher can be required to cover for absent colleagues will be limited to 38 hours a year.

From September 2005:
- all teachers will be given guaranteed time within the school day for planning preparation and assessment. This should be a minimum of 10 per cent of their teaching time; and
- headteachers will have dedicated time to lead their schools.

The agreement also covered details of the new role for teaching assistants (see page 120).

their own requirements. National Occupational Standards for teaching assistants have been published and NVQs (levels 2 and 3) based on the standards are being developed. There were over 122,000 teaching assistants in England in January 2003, an increase of 16,000 since 2002. The role of teaching assistants is set to be expanded with new Higher Level Teaching Assistants and changes in the working pattern for teachers proposed in the Raising Standards and Tackling Workload national agreement (see box).

Headteachers

In England the National College for School Leadership (NCSL) provides a range of programmes for the development of school leaders at all levels. The three national headship training programmes are: the National Professional Qualification for Headship (NPQH) for aspiring headteachers; the Headship Induction Programme (HIP) – formerly the Leadership and Management Programme for New Headteachers; and the Leadership Programme for Serving Headteachers. From April 2004 it will be mandatory for all first-time heads to hold the NPQH or to be working towards it.

Wales and Northern Ireland have their own versions of the NPQH, adapted to suit their respective school systems. The Scottish Executive announced in December 2001 its intention to make the Scottish Standard for Headship mandatory in Scotland from August 2005. At present, the only route to gaining the Standard is through the Scottish Qualification for Headship.

Teacher recruitment and retention

The purpose of the Teacher Training Agency (TTA) is to raise standards in schools in England and in Wales by attracting able and committed people to teaching and by improving the quality of teacher training. Government measures to tackle teacher recruitment and retention issues in England include:
- a 10 per cent increase in the number of teacher training places available, including at least 6,000 places on the Graduate Teacher Programme for those over the age of 24 by 2005/06, compared with 3,400 in 2002/03;
- a 30 per cent increase between 2002/03 and 2005/06 in funding for the TTA's recruitment activities; and
- an increase (from 1,500 to 2,000) in the number of flexible training places for people wanting to train while still working.

Government measures in England and Wales include:
- a £6,000 bursary paid to PGCE students;
- a £4,000 'golden hello' for those who train in and then go on to teach in subjects in which there are shortages of teachers. These subjects are English (including drama), mathematics, modern languages, design and technology, information and communications technology, science and, in Wales, Welsh; and
- the Repayment of Teachers' Loans scheme (RTL), under which the student loans of newly qualified teachers in these shortage subjects is paid back by the Government for as long as they continue to teach.

In order to increase the numbers of students working towards PGCE(FE) in Wales, the Welsh

Assembly has extended the £6,000 PGCE(FE) Teacher Training Bursary pilot for a further year to include the academic year 2003/04.

Allied professions

A range of other professions are involved in education and training. Examples are given below.

Childcare

There are a range of relevant qualifications for those working in childcare. For example, in nursery work, trainees under supervision work towards a level 2 qualification on the National Qualifications Framework in Early Years Education, Childcare and Playwork. On the job progression can then be made to a managerial or supervisory position by working towards a level 3 qualification.

Careers advisers

In England and Wales fully qualified advisers are required to hold a relevant qualification at NVQ or SVQ level 4 or equivalent. In England career guidance is delivered by Connexions Personal Advisers who must also be qualified to NVQ level 4 or equivalent and complete a number of specific Connexions training programmes.

Further and higher education

There were 56,000 full-time further education (FE) lecturers and 78,000 full-time higher education lecturers in the United Kingdom in 2000/01. With the exception of Wales and Northern Ireland, professional teaching qualifications are not essential in this sector, although prospects tend to be better for those who have them. In Wales the Further Education Teachers' Qualifications Regulations 2002, which came into force on 1 July 2002, require new FE teachers to hold or work towards a Stage 3 FE teaching qualification. The Welsh Assembly Government will also be making regulations under the provisions of the *Education Act 2002*, to ensure new Principals of Further Education Institutions in Wales gain or hold a Principalship qualification. In Scotland lecturers on full-time permanent contracts are encouraged to obtain a qualification, and the Scottish Further Education Funding Council provides funding to cover the cost of training. In Northern Ireland a Postgraduate Certificate in Further and Higher Education is required if an approved teaching qualification is not already held.

Administration and management

State schools in England and Wales are maintained by local education authorities (LEAs). With a few exceptions, this is also the position in Scotland. In Northern Ireland five education and library boards fund all controlled and maintained schools and the Department of Education funds voluntary grammar and grant-maintained integrated schools. FE colleges in the United Kingdom are legally independent institutions with independent governing bodies that include nominations from the local community and businesses. Universities and higher education colleges are legally independent corporate institutions with individual governing bodies.

A number of central government departments are responsible for education policy:
- the DfES in England;
- the Welsh Assembly Government Training and Education Department;
- the Scottish Executive Education Department (primary and secondary education) and the Scottish Executive Enterprise, Transport and Lifelong Learning Department; and

Ministers for children

In June 2003 the Government announced the creation of a new Minister for Children within the DfES. The new Ministerial post is responsible for: the Sure Start Unit; the Children and Young People's Unit; the Connexions Service National Unit; the Department's pastoral support for school-age children; children's social care; the Teenage Pregnancy Unit; the Family Policy Unit and family law. The post was created partly in response to the Laming report into the death of eight-year-old Victoria Climbié (see page 154), which proposed a more integrated system of support for children.

In Wales, the Assembly Government has a Minister with special responsibility for Children and Young People.

Within the Scottish Executive, there has been a Minister for Education and Young People since November 2001, responsible for key policy areas relating to children and young people, including childcare, pre-school and school education, Sure Start, child protection and support services.

Great Britons

24 November 2002
Left: Sir Winston Churchill is voted the Greatest Briton by the UK public in a BBC poll . . .

6 February 2003
Bottom left: Professor Stephen Hawking wins the most votes in the Great Disabled Britons poll, run by the BBC's new *Ouch!* website. The website is designed to reflect life as a disabled person . . . and

14 August 2003
Bottom right: Sir Isaac Newton (painted by John Vanderbank in 1725) is voted the Greatest Briton by an international audience in a BBC World poll.

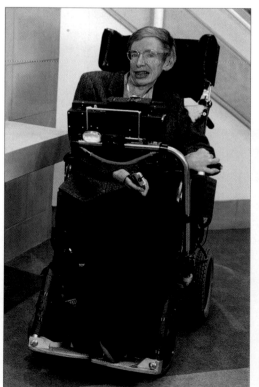

4 December 2002 the National Maritime Museum Cornwall opens in Falmouth, featuring interactive displays about boats and the relationship between human beings and the sea.

29 December 2002 Brighton's West Pier, a derelict Grade I listed building awaiting renovation, breaks in half and slips into the sea during heavy storms.

January 2003 70th anniversary of the London Underground map. Harry Beck's design classic, the simplified 'diagram' of the London Underground, was produced as a pocket map with 750,000 copies printed in January 1933. Stocks ran out within a month. The simple schematic style has been used as a template for maps of transport systems in places as far away as New York, St Petersburg and Sydney.

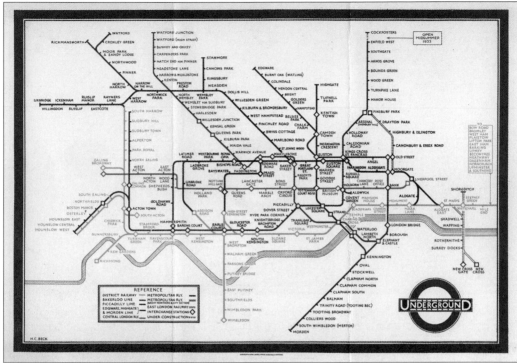

Below: The world's first passenger underground railway opened 140 years ago, on 10 January 1863. As it developed, maps of the system tried to follow the geography of the streets above and became increasingly complicated.

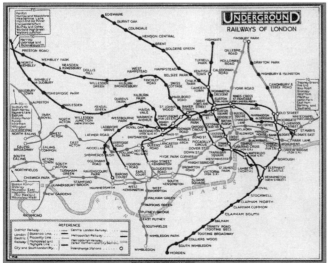

Above: Harry Beck continued to work for London Transport until 1960. He was in his late twenties when he designed the map.

7 January 2003 English Heritage announces repair grants for more than 20 cathedrals including Salisbury, which is the tallest medieval building in the United Kingdom.

8 January 2003 Central London gets its heaviest snowfall since February 1991.

2002 Spending Review

Under the 2002 Spending Review a record increase in education spending is envisaged in the United Kingdom with spending forecast to rise to 5.6 per cent of GDP by 2005/06 from 5.0 per cent in 2001/02. For example, in England the Review set out that:

- spending will rise by an average of 6 per cent a year in real terms, to £57.8 billion in 2005/06;
- payments directly to schools will be at least £165,000 for a typical secondary school, and £50,000 for a primary school: increases of £50,000 and £10,000 respectively; and
- from September 2004, Education Maintenance Allowances of up to £30 a week will be available to 16- to 19-year-olds, depending on parental income, with additional bonuses for attendance and achievement.

Further investment will be made in childcare and early years learning, further education, improving the basic skills of adults, and expanding Modern Apprenticeships and work-related qualifications.

- the Department of Education and the Department for Employment and Learning in Northern Ireland.

The education service in Great Britain is financed in the same way as other local government services (see page 54), with education authorities funding schools largely on the basis of pupil numbers. Specific central government grants are made to LEAs in Great Britain in order to improve school performance in literacy, numeracy and ICT. The Government allocates resources directly to schools for them to use as they wish. In Northern Ireland the costs of education and library boards are met directly by the Northern Ireland Executive.

School management

England and Wales

All state schools work in partnership with LEAs. They receive their recurrent funding, via the LEAs' school funding formulae, as budget shares. A school is free to spend its budget share as it sees fit provided it does so 'for the purposes of the school'. Schools are run by governing bodies, comprising parents, school staff, LEA and local community representation.

The *Education Act 2002* established a 'Power to Innovate' which enabled the Education and Skills Secretary to exempt schools, Education Action Zones and LEAs from educational legislation for a limited period. The power lifts regulatory requirements so they can trial a specific innovative project, initially for up to three years, that has the potential to raise standards of education.

LEAs and school governing bodies responsible for pupil admissions are expected to take part in local discussions with headteachers, churches and others, in order to coordinate admission arrangements, taking account of statutory codes of practice. Any disagreements on school organisation or admissions in England are referred to an independent adjudicator; those regarding religious or denominational admission criteria are referred to the Secretary of State for Education and Skills. In Wales the Assembly Government decides all cases of disagreement.

Admission authorities are not allowed to introduce selection by ability, unless it is for sixth form admission or is designed to ensure that pupils of all abilities are admitted and that no one level of ability is over- or under-represented. Where existing partial selection by ability is challenged, the Adjudicator (in Wales the Assembly Government) decides whether it should continue.

In England there are 164 designated grammar schools which select pupils on ability. Local parents are allowed to petition for a ballot and (if sufficient numbers locally wish it) to vote on whether to keep these selective admission arrangements.

Building schools for the future

In March 2003, an extra £3.2 billion was allocated through Government spending and private finance initiatives to modernise school buildings until 2006. Four LEAs will pilot the 'Building Schools for the Future' approach, which will test new procurement and delivery methods. As part of this programme, eleven design teams have been invited to create 21st century school designs. They include:

- London Eye designers Marks Barfield;
- Gateshead Millennium Bridge architects, Wilkinson Eyre;
- award-winning school designers Fielden and Clegg; and
- Will Alsop, designer of the award-winning Peckham Library.

Scotland

Nearly all Scottish schools are education authority schools financed by the authorities and central government. The headteacher is responsible for decision-making on at least 80 per cent of school-level expenditure.

In May 2002, 84 per cent of eligible education authority schools had a school board consisting of elected parents and teachers and members co-opted from the local community. In addition to promoting contact between parents, school and community, they are involved in procedures to appoint senior staff and to determine the community use of school premises. They may also take on further executive functions by delegation from their education authority.

The eight grant-aided schools are all run by boards of managers that receive government grants.

Northern Ireland

Boards of governors are responsible for the management of individual schools and include elected parents and teachers among their members. Virtually all schools have delegated budgets under which school governors determine spending priorities.

Rights of parents

England and Wales

Parents have a statutory right to information about schools and to express a preference for a school for their child. There is an appeal system if their choice is not met. Parents must be given a copy of the annual report from the school governors, which includes summaries of the school's results in National Curriculum assessment tests, public examinations, vocational qualifications (if applicable) and rates of pupil absence.

Parents must be given a written annual report on their child's achievements in all subjects, including results of tests and examinations. Arrangements must also be made for the discussion of reports with teachers.

Parents are also entitled to see or be provided with a copy of their child's pupil record within 15 school days of making a written request. Unless there is a court order preventing it, all parents have a right to participate in decisions about their child's education.

Home/school agreements set out the responsibilities of schools, pupils and parents and are a statutory requirement for all maintained schools.

Scotland

Parents have a statutory right to express their choice of school and the education authority must meet this request except in certain circumstances set out in law. There is an appeal system if their choice is not met. Information is published on budgeted school running costs, examination results, pupil attendance and absence, 5–14 attainment targets and results, and the destinations of school leavers. Schools are required to provide parents with information about their children's attainment in each subject, pupil attainment targets and teachers' comments on their progress.

Northern Ireland

The system of reporting to parents is broadly similar to that in England and Wales, except that no annual performance tables on a school-by-school basis are published.

Educational standards

England and Wales

The Office for Standards in Education (Ofsted) in England and the Office of Her Majesty's Chief Inspector in Wales (Estyn) aim to improve the quality and standards of education through independent inspection and advice.

Schools are inspected at least once in six years, but more often where weaknesses have been identified in an earlier inspection. All schools must produce an action plan to address the key issues raised in the inspection report. A school failing to provide an acceptable standard of education is deemed to need Special Measures and remains subject to regular monitoring visits by inspectors.

The *Education Act 2002* allows for earlier and wider intervention in weak and failing schools. The Act introduced new powers to replace a governing body with an interim executive board if the governing body is part of the problem. LEAs will also be expected to invite external partners to help turn round weak and failing schools. These partners could be successful schools, other LEAs, other educational establishments, voluntary, faith or private bodies.

Ofsted is also responsible for inspecting all 16 to 19 education and training in sixth form and further education colleges (which it carries out with the Adult Learning Inspectorate) and for the regulation of all early years childcare providers.

The Adult Learning Inspectorate performs the same function as Ofsted for post-19 provision in colleges and for work-based learning, adult and community learning and Ufi/learndirect. In Wales, Estyn already has responsibility for these areas as well as adult education, work-based training and provision of careers guidance.

Scotland

Her Majesty's Inspectorate of Education began operating as an executive agency of the Scottish Executive in 2001. It inspects, reviews and reports on state and independent schools, further education colleges and the education functions of local authorities. Reports are published and are usually followed up within two years.

Northern Ireland

The Education and Training Inspectorate monitors, inspects and reports on standards of education and training provided by schools, colleges and other grant-aided organisations, and provides information and policy advice to the Department of Education, the Department of Culture, Arts and Leisure, and the Department for Employment and Learning.

International links

Large numbers of people from other countries come to the United Kingdom to study, and many British people work and train overseas. The British Council (see chapter 7) encourages links between educational institutions in the United Kingdom and developing countries.

The Commonwealth Education Fund

This Fund was launched in 2002 to highlight the need for universal primary education in the Commonwealth and to raise children's awareness of development issues. Actionaid, Oxfam and Save the Children administer the Fund. The Government announced a grant of £10 million to the fund over the years to December 2005, and will match contributions by businesses and others. An estimated 75 million children in the Commonwealth do not complete a basic education.

European Union schemes

The *Socrates* education programme supports partnerships between schools, colleges and universities, language learning, mobility opportunities for educational staff, pupils and students, and a range of multinational projects. Programmes available through Socrates include:

- The *Comenius* programme focuses on the first phase of education, from pre-school and primary to secondary and further education, aiming to enhance the quality of teaching, promote language learning and encourage movement around Europe through school partnerships, projects for the training of education staff and school education networks.
- The *Erasmus* programme provides grants enabling university students from across Europe to study part of their course in another European country for between three and 12 months. On average about 9,000 UK students take part each year. Since it began in 1987 more than 1 million students have participated in Erasmus, of whom about 120,000 were from the United Kingdom.
- The *Grundtvig* programme is aimed at lifelong learning and supports a wide range of activities designed to promote innovation and the improved availability, accessibility and quality of educational provision for adults through European co-operation.

The *Leonardo da Vinci* vocational training programme supports co-operation in vocational training across Europe through multinational pilot projects, work placements and trainer exchanges, and research projects.

Overseas students and teachers in the UK

In 2000/01 there were 88,200 overseas students in further education institutions in the United Kingdom, and 231,645 in higher education in 2001/02. Most pay fees covering the full costs of their courses. Nationals of other EU states generally pay the lower level of fees applicable to UK home students.

In order to teach in maintained schools in England and Wales, it is generally necessary to hold QTS (see page 120). Regulations do not allow for the automatic recognition of teaching qualifications gained abroad unless the teacher is a national of the EEA (see page 61) or Switzerland.

Other nationals can be appointed under certain circumstances as temporary teachers (who may then gain QTS through a school-based training programme), or, in England only, through the Overseas Trained Teachers programme.

Government scholarship schemes
The Government makes provision for foreign students to study in the United Kingdom through its Chevening Programme and other scholarship schemes. In 2002 about 4,000 overseas students received awards from scholarship schemes funded in part by the Foreign & Commonwealth Office (FCO), and other government departments. In addition to the Chevening Programme, these are the Commonwealth Scholarships and Fellowships Plan, Department for International Development Shared Scholarships, Marshall Scholarships, and North Atlantic Fellowships. The FCO is increasing the number of scholarships jointly funded with UK or foreign commercial firms, and with academic and other institutions.

Other schemes
The Overseas Research Students Award Scheme, funded by the higher education funding councils, provides help for overseas full-time postgraduate students with outstanding research potential. In addition, most British universities and colleges offer bursaries and scholarships for which graduates of any nationality are eligible. Other public and private scholarships are available to students from overseas and to British students who want to study in other countries.

The Teachers' International Development Programme aims to provide teachers with opportunities for international study visits or exchanges which will enable them to experience good practice, develop international educational links with other schools, carry out research and share information with a network of other participants. Around 6,000 teachers have participated in the programme since its launch in May 2000.

Further reading
Choice and Excellence – A Vision for Post 14 Education. Department for Education and Skills, 2002.

Education and Training Statistics for the United Kingdom. Department for Education and Skills. Annual.

Education for the 21st Century – Post Primary Review. Department of Education, Northern Ireland, 2001.

Excellence and Enjoyment – a strategy for primary schools. Department for Education and Skills, 2003.

Languages for all, languages for life. Department for Education and Skills, 2002.

The Future of Higher Education. White Paper. Cm 5735. Department for Education and Skills, 2003.

The Government's Expenditure Plans 2003–04 to 2004–05. Cm 5902. Department for Education and Skills and Office for Standards in Education. The Stationery Office, 2002.

The Learning Country – A Comprehensive Education and Lifelong Learning Programme to 2010 in Wales. National Assembly for Wales, 2001.

14–19: Extending opportunities, raising standards. Green Paper. Department for Education and Skills, 2002.

21st Century Skills: Realising Our Potential. White Paper. Cm 5810. Department for Education and skills, 2003.

Websites

Department for Education and Skills
www.dfes.gov.uk

Scottish Executive
www.scotland.gov.uk

Welsh Assembly Government
www.learning.wales.gov.uk

Department of Education (NI)
www.deni.gov.uk

Department for Employment and Learning (NI)
www.delni.gov.uk

WWW.

11 The labour market

The number of people employed in the UK labour market was 27.9 million in spring 2003. Both full-time and part-time employment have risen over the last decade. The increase has been predominantly in the service sector, in which over three-quarters of employees now work. At the same time unemployment has fallen considerably since the last peak at the end of 1992. In 2001 it reached its lowest level since the introduction of the International Labour Organisation (ILO) measure of unemployment in 1984. Unemployment in spring 2003 was down slightly on spring 2002.

Patterns of employment

The Labour Force Survey (LFS) carried out by the Office for National Statistics shows that, on a seasonally adjusted basis, 29.4 million people aged 16 and over were economically active in the United Kingdom in spring (March to May) 2003. This figure comprised 27.9 million in employment[1] and 1.5 million unemployed (see Table 11.1). The 27.9 million people aged 16 and over in employment represented an increase of 254,000 on the previous year and comprised 15.1 million men and 12.9 million women. The employment rate (the proportion of people in employment) among those of working age (men aged 16 to 64 and women aged 16 to 59) was 74.7 per cent, close to the previous high achieved in 1990. The economic activity rate was 78.7 per cent for people of working age. Among this age group, some 7.7 million people were economically inactive (see box).

One of the main long-term trends in the labour market is the increased participation of women in employment. In spring 2003, nearly 70 per cent of

1 There are two main measures of employment: the number of people in employment and the number of jobs; they differ because a person can have more than one job.

Table 11.1 Employment, spring 2003, UK

Thousands, seasonally adjusted

	Men	Women	Total
All aged 16 and over	22,448	24,169	46,618
Total economically active	15,947	13,440	29,387
of whom:			
In employment	15,055	12,858	27,913
Unemployed	892	582	1,474
Economic activity rate (%)[1]	*84.1*	*73.0*	*78.7*
Employment rate (%)[1]	*79.3*	*69.8*	*74.7*
Unemployment rate (%)	*5.6*	*4.3*	*5.0*

1 For men aged 16 to 64 and women aged 16 to 59.
Source: Labour Force Survey, Office for National Statistics

Economic activity
The labour market can be divided into two groups: the economically active and inactive. The economically active are defined as those who are either in employment (employee, self-employed, unpaid family worker or on a government-supported training programme) or unemployed and actively seeking work. The economically inactive are people who are not in work, but who do not satisfy all the criteria for unemployment, such as those in retirement and those not actively seeking work.

Unemployment
The unemployment figure is based on LFS estimates of the number of people without a job who are seeking work. It refers to the number available to start work within two weeks who have either looked for work in the previous four weeks or are waiting to start a job they have already obtained. It is based on internationally agreed definitions and is the official measure of UK unemployment.

working age women were in employment, compared with 47 per cent in 1959 (the year for which estimates are first available). Among many reasons for their greater involvement is that more women delay having children until their thirties and are then more likely to return to work afterwards, making use of a range of childcare options. Other reasons include the increasing levels of educational attainment among women and changing social attitudes to women working. The difference in the employment rates between men and women is narrowing, from 47 percentage points in 1959 to 9 percentage points in 2002.

Within the United Kingdom employment rates vary. In spring 2003 many inner city areas and former industrial areas had the lowest rates – for example, 58 per cent in Manchester and Middlesbrough. Conversely, some of the highest employment rates were in Scotland and central and southern England. The highest rates in Great Britain were in Flintshire (Wales), Bracknell Forest (England) and Argyll and Bute (Scotland), all over 85 per cent. Within Northern Ireland, Newtownabbey had the highest employment rate (83 per cent).

In March 2000, the Lisbon European Council agreed an aim to achieve an overall EU employment rate as close as possible to 70 per cent by 2010. In 2002, the overall employment rate in the EU was 64 per cent and the United Kingdom was one of only four out of the 15 Member States with employment rates above the 2010 overall target. The United Kingdom has also met the 2010 target of an employment rate for women of more than 60 per cent (Table 11.2).

Young people

The economic activity of young people is closely linked to their participation in full-time education (FTE). Of those 16- to 17-year-olds not in FTE in spring 2003, 78 per cent were economically active, including 22 per cent who were unemployed. For those in FTE, 46 per cent were economically active. Youth unemployment increased slightly between spring 2002 and 2003 with 402,000 people aged 18 to 24 unemployed in spring 2003. The number of young people unemployed for more than a year increased by 6,000 over the same period, a rise of 13 per cent.

Older workers

There were 6.2 million people aged between 50 and state pension age in employment in spring 2003,

Table 11.2 Employment rates, 2002, EU[1]

Percentages

	Males	Females
Netherlands	83	66
Denmark	80	73
United Kingdom	78	65
Portugal	76	61
Luxembourg	76	52
Sweden	76	73
Austria	75	61
Irish Republic	75	55
Spain	73	44
Germany	72	59
Greece	72	43
Finland	71	67
France	70	56
Italy	69	42
Belgium	68	51

1 People aged 15–64, except for the United Kingdom where data refer to people aged 16–64.
Source: Labour Force Surveys, Eurostat

representing 22 per cent of all people in employment. Their employment rate increased by 2 percentage points on the previous year to 70 per cent. The economic inactivity rate among men aged 50 to 64 increased from 23 per cent in 1984 to peak at 29 per cent in 1995 and has since declined to 25 per cent in spring 2003. The rate for women aged 50 to 59 declined from 41 per cent to 31 per cent between 1984 and 2003. Over 90 per cent of people above retirement age were economically inactive in spring 2003, but 934,000 were in employment, and almost 600,000 of these were women.

In spring 2003, 15 per cent of the unemployed were over 50, of whom 36 per cent had been unemployed for more than 12 months. The Government will be bringing forward legislation to outlaw age discrimination in employment and training by 2006 (see page 138). Its Age Positive website (www.agepositive.gov.uk) aims to promote the Code of Practice on Age Diversity in Employment. The code highlights the business benefits of an age-diverse workforce and sets the standard for non-ageist approaches to recruitment, selection, training, promotion, redundancy and retirement. The website includes good practice guides with case studies illustrating how organisations have tackled some of the issues.

Disabled people

In spring 2003 there were about 7 million people of working age with long-term disabilities in the United Kingdom, of whom just under half were in employment. The LFS uses the *Disability Discrimination Act* definition which includes both work limiting and non-work limiting disabled people. The unemployment rate among disabled people was higher than for those not disabled (8.2 per cent compared with 4.5 per cent). Among the economically inactive, those with disabilities were more likely to want a job than those without disabilities.

In January 2003 the Government set up the Disability Employment Advisory Committee (*www.deac.org.uk*) to consider and advise on how disabled people can be supported to find and keep work. The Government will also begin piloting a series of measures from October 2003, aimed at enhancing the employment prospects of new recipients of incapacity-related benefits by providing greater support earlier on in their claims.

Minority ethnic groups

There are marked differences between the economic activity rates of different ethnic groups. Men and women from the White group are more likely to be economically active than their counterparts from minority ethnic groups.

In 2001/02 economic activity rates were 85 per cent for White men and 74 per cent for White women. Black Caribbean women had rates almost as high as White women, at 72 per cent. People of Bangladeshi origin had the lowest economic activity rates among both men (69 per cent) and women (22 per cent).

In 2001/02 people from minority ethnic groups had higher unemployment rates than White people. This was the case for both men and women. Bangladeshi men had the highest unemployment rate at 20 per cent – four times that for White men. The unemployment rate among Indian men was only slightly higher than that for White men, 7 per cent compared with 5 per cent. For all the other minority ethnic groups, unemployment rates were between two and three times higher than those for White men. This pattern was the same across different age groups.

For men from all ethnic groups, unemployment was much higher among young people aged under 25 than for older people. Over 40 per cent of young Bangladeshi men were unemployed. Young Black African, Pakistani, and Black Caribbean men and those belonging to the Mixed group also had very high unemployment rates – ranging from 25 per cent and 31 per cent. The comparable unemployment rate for young White men was 12 per cent.

The picture for women was similar to that for men. Bangladeshi women had the highest unemployment rate, at 24 per cent, six times greater than that of White women (4 per cent). Seven per cent of Indian women were unemployed. Women in all other ethnic groups had rates between 9 per cent and 16 per cent. Rates for young women under the age of 25 years were considerably higher than for older women and this was true for all ethnic groups.

In March 2003 the Government published *Ethnic Minorities and the Labour Market*. This outlined a strategy for targeted action to meet the needs of different groups, for example by involving the parents of schoolchildren, providing access to more flexible employment programmes or business advice, and raising awareness among particular employers. The strategy focuses on improving the employability of minority ethnic groups; improving their connection with work; promoting equal opportunities; and delivering change through reform of government structures.

Households with no one in work

The number of workless households (among households where at least one adult was of working age) was 3.0 million in spring 2003, a decrease of 90,000 since spring 2002 and 194,000 fewer than five years earlier. This represented a rate of worklessness of 15.9 per cent in spring 2003, compared with 17.5 per cent in 1998.

Economic inactivity

In spring 2003, there were 7.7 million economically inactive people of working age in the United Kingdom, of whom 2.1 million wanted a job but were not seeking work or were not available to start. Sickness and disability were the main reasons for economic inactivity among men. Looking after the family or home was the most common reason for inactivity among women – 41 per cent of women who wanted a job gave this as their main reason for inactivity in 2003. Government policy is aimed at helping those who are currently inactive to make the transition

Table 11.3 Employment status of the workforce[1], UK

Thousands

	1999	2000	2001	2002	2003
Employees	23,528	23,955	24,192	24,339	24,430
Self-employed	3,125	3,065	3,074	3,124	3,309
Unpaid family workers	100	108	96	95	85
Government-supported training and employment programmes	155	140	146	102	88
Total in employment	**26,907**	**27,267**	**27,508**	**27,659**	**27,913**
of whom:					
Full-time workers	20,137	20,387	20,565	20,650	20,692
Part-time workers	6,770	6,880	6,943	7,009	7,221
Temporary workers	1,673	1,685	1,684	1,546	1,489
Workers with a second job	1,255	1,164	1,158	1,124	1,125

1 Spring figures, seasonally adjusted.
Source: Labour Force Survey, Office for National Statistics

towards activity, primarily through the New Deal programme (see page 135) and the introduction of Jobcentre Plus (see page 136).

Working patterns

For the past decade, about three-quarters of those in employment have been permanent full-time workers; the figure in spring 2003 was 74 per cent. However, significant numbers of people have alternative employment patterns, such as part-time working and second or temporary jobs.

Part-time work

There were over 7 million people in part-time work in the United Kingdom in spring 2003 (Table 11.3), of whom 79 per cent were women. Over the past decade the number of people working part time has increased by over 1 million, but as a proportion of all those in employment it has remained at around 25 per cent. People work part time for a variety of reasons. In spring 2003 nearly 74 per cent did not want a full-time job while 8 per cent were working part time because they could not find full-time work, a proportion which has steadily decreased over the past decade.

Secondary and temporary work

Just over 1.1 million people had a second job in spring 2003, a similar number as the previous year (Table 11.3). About 1.5 million people (about 6 per cent of all employees) were engaged in temporary jobs in spring 2003, 4 per cent fewer

than the number in spring 2002. Temporary employment is lower in the United Kingdom than in most other EU countries. Around a quarter of temporary employees in spring 2003 worked in a temporary job because they could not find a permanent one. The *Employment Act 2002* gives fixed-term employees the right to equal treatment on pay, pensions, holidays, sick pay and training.

Self-employment

In spring 2003, 3.3 million people (nearly three-quarters of whom were men) were self-employed in the United Kingdom (Table 11.3). This represented 12 per cent of those in employment, a small increase since spring 2002. Agriculture, fishing and construction had the highest proportions of self-employed people, while relatively few of those engaged in manufacturing and public administration were self-employed.

Occupations and industries

There has been a long-term growth in managerial and professional occupations and a decline in skilled trades, elementary[2] occupations and process, plant and machine operatives.

The patterns of occupations followed by men and women are quite different (Table 11.4). Nearly a

---

2 Occupations involving mainly routine tasks which do not require formal qualifications, but usually have a period of formal on-the-job training.

Table 11.4 Employment by sex[1] and occupation, spring 2003[2], UK

	Percentages	
	Males	Females
Managers and senior officials	18	10
Professional occupations	13	11
Associate professional and technical	13	14
Administrative and secretarial	5	23
Skilled trades	20	2
Personal service	2	14
Sales and customer service	4	12
Process, plant and machine operatives	12	3
Elementary occupations	12	12
All employees[3] (million)	15.0	12.8

1 Males aged 16 to 64, females aged 16 to 59.
2 Not seasonally adjusted.
3 Includes a few people who did not state their occupation.
  Percentages are based on totals which exclude this group.
Source: Labour Force Survey, Office for National Statistics

quarter of women employees are in administrative and secretarial work, while men are most likely to be employed in skilled trades or as managers and senior officials. These occupations are among the least likely to be followed by women. Conversely women are more likely than men to be employed in the personal services and in sales and customer services. Only the professional and associated occupations, and elementary occupations, are followed by similar proportions of men and women.

Employment by sector

One of the major long-term trends in employment in the United Kingdom has been the large increase in employment in service industries (see Table 11.5). Between March 1983 and March 2003 the jobs in service industries increased from 16.6 million to 23.3 million, a rise of 40 per cent, compared with a rise in the total number of jobs of 18 per cent. Growth in finance and business services was particularly strong, up by 87 per cent in this period, although there was a fall in the year to March 2002.

In recent years most other sectors have experienced falling levels of employment, particularly the traditional manufacturing industries, such as steel, shipbuilding and textiles. Between 1983 and 2003 the total number of manufacturing jobs declined by 31 per cent, while jobs in agriculture and fishing declined by 35 per cent. The biggest long-term decline, however, has been in energy and water with a reduction of 66 per cent between 1983 and 2003, reflecting, among other things, a large fall in jobs in the coal industry.

Pay and conditions

Earnings

According to the New Earnings Survey, average gross weekly earnings for full-time adult employees (whose pay was not affected by

Table 11.5 Workforce jobs by industry, March 2003,[1] UK

	Workforce jobs (thousands)	Per cent of workforce jobs	Percentage change 1983–2003
Agriculture and fishing	415	1.4	−34.6
Energy and water	209	0.7	−65.5
Manufacturing	3,781	12.8	−31.4
Construction	1,935	6.5	10.9
Services	23,262	78.6	39.8
of which:			
Distribution, hotels and restaurants	6,863	23.2	28.1
Transport and communication	1,809	6.1	13.7
Finance and business services	5,712	19.3	86.9
Public administration, education and health	7,094	24.0	29.0
Other services	1,785	6.0	57.7
All jobs	**29,602**	**100**	17.8

1 Seasonally adjusted.
Source: Office for National Statistics

absence) were £465 in Great Britain (an increase of 4.6 per cent since April 2001). In Northern Ireland the figure was £390. In 2002, London had the highest average earnings within the United Kingdom (£624 per week) and the North East had the lowest (£400 per week, see Table 11.6).

Table 11.6 Average gross weekly pay,[1] 2002, Great Britain

	£
Great Britain	**464.7**
England	471.7
North East	399.3
North West	426.8
Yorkshire and the Humber	409.9
East Midlands	413.0
West Midlands	427.3
East	459.6
London	624.1
South East	496.7
South West	421.7
Wales	399.7
Scotland	427.0

1 Full-time employees on adult rates, whose pay was unaffected by absence.
Source: New Earnings Survey 2002, Office for National Statistics

In Great Britain average hourly pay for full-time male adult employees whose pay was not affected by absence was £12.59 in April 2002, compared with £10.22 for female employees. Average hourly earnings excluding overtime for women were 81.1 per cent of those for men, a slight widening of the pay gap from 81.5 per cent in 2001. This was largely the result of differences at the top end of the earnings distribution, though the pay gap has steadily narrowed since 1987 (see page 97). For full-time employees in Northern Ireland the hourly rate for men was £10.26 compared with £9.16 for women.

General managers of large companies and organisations were the highest paid occupation, receiving just over ten times the average gross weekly pay of those working as retail cash desk and check-out operators (Table 11.7).

National minimum wage

The statutory national minimum wage (NMW) took effect from 1 April 1999. Minimum wage rates, from 1 October 2003, are:

- £4.50 an hour for those aged 22 or above; and

Table 11.7 Highest and lowest paid occupations,[1] April 2002, Great Britain

Average gross weekly pay (£)

Highest paid	
General managers of large companies and organisations	2,079
Treasurers and company financial managers	1,235
Medical practitioners	1,160
Management consultants, business analysts	933
Underwriters, claims assessors, brokers, investment analysts	924
Lowest paid	
Petrol pump forecourt attendants	212
Waiters, waitresses	211
Kitchen porters, hands	210
Launderers, dry cleaners, pressers	207
Retail cash desk and check-out operators	205

1 Full-time employees on adult rates, whose pay was unaffected by absence. Certain occupations have been excluded due to the small size of the sample.
Source: New Earnings Survey 2002, Office for National Statistics

- £3.80 an hour for workers aged 18 to 21, and for those aged 22 or over receiving accredited training in the first six months of a new job with a new employer.

Almost all workers who are 18 or over are covered by the NMW, including casual workers, agency workers, part-time workers, overseas workers and workers in small businesses. Workers to whom NMW is not payable include the majority of the self-employed, people under 18 years of age, prisoners, some voluntary workers, members of the armed forces and unrelated people living in their employer's home who are treated as part of the family (for example, au pairs). Apprentices and those engaged as Modern Apprentices (see page 118) or under similar schemes are excluded for the first year of their employment or until they are 19. The Low Pay Commission (which recommends the level of NMW) will be reviewing the case for introducing a minimum wage for 16- to 17-year-olds.

The NMW is enforced through a combination of measures. For example:
- employers are required to keep NMW records;
- Inland Revenue Compliance Officers investigate all complaints about non-payment of the NMW. They visit employers thought to

be likely to pay below the minimum wage and take enforcement action where necessary; and

- individuals can take action through an employment tribunal or civil court.

The Department of Trade and Industry (DTI) and the Inland Revenue publicise employer obligations and employee rights, principally through direct advertising, the DTI employment rights website (*www.tiger.gov.uk*) and the NMW helpline.

Fringe benefits
Fringe benefits offered by some employers include schemes to encourage financial participation by employees in their companies, pension schemes, medical insurance, subsidised meals, company cars and childcare schemes.

Many companies have adopted employee share schemes, where employees acquire shares or options to buy shares from their employer. An all-employee share ownership plan, called Share Incentive Plan (SIP), was introduced in 2000, allowing employees to buy shares from their pre-tax and National Insurance contribution salary and to receive free shares, with tax incentives for longer-term shareholding.

Hours of work
The most common hours worked by both men and women were between 31 and 45 hours, but

one in three men and one in ten women worked over 45 hours a week in spring 2003. Women were more likely than men to be working less than 30 hours a week (Figure 11.8).

Hours worked tend to be longest in agriculture, energy and water, and transport and communications, and shortest in public administration, education and health. The differences between industries also reflect the mix of part-time and full-time workers, as well as any difference in the standard working week. Self-employed people work, on average, longer hours than full-time employees.

Regulations implementing two European Directives on working time and on young workers (in relation to rest and health assessments for adolescents) are in force in the United Kingdom. They apply to full-time, part-time and temporary workers and provide for:

- a maximum working week of 48 hours (on average), although individual workers can choose to work longer;
- a minimum of four weeks' annual paid leave;
- minimum daily, weekly and in-work rest periods;
- a limit for night workers of an average eight hours' work in a 24-hour period; and
- a right for night workers to receive free health assessments.

There are specific provisions for adolescent workers in respect of the entitlement to rest and health assessments. Specific working time and night work limits for 16- and 17-year-olds came into force in April 2003.

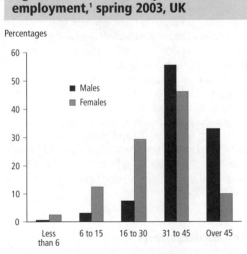

Figure 11.8 Usual weekly hours of employment,[1] spring 2003, UK

Percentages

Males
Females

Less than 6 / 6 to 15 / 16 to 30 / 31 to 45 / Over 45

1 Includes employees, self-employed, unpaid family workers and those on government-supported training schemes.
Source: Labour Force Survey, Office for National Statistics

Workforce skills

The demand for different types of skills varies across the United Kingdom and this is reflected in the structure of the organisations responsible for managing skills, described in chapter 10.

The Government published a Skills Strategy and Delivery plan for England in July 2003 (see also page 117), which:

- sets out how it aims to close the productivity gap with competitors through a highly skilled, productive workforce;
- provides a framework and delivery plan for meeting the economy's skill needs, involving

Work–Life balance

The DTI's Work–Life balance campaign aims to convince employers of the economic benefits of work–life balance, such as improvements in the quality of people's work, efficiency savings and increased profits. Much of the *Employment Act 2002* addresses issues associated with work–life balance, such as the provision of flexible working arrangements (see page 151). Provisional results from the DTI's Work–Life Balance 2003 Survey showed that more than nine out of ten employers agree that people will work best when they can strike a healthy balance between work and the rest of their lives and that just over 80 per cent of employers said they have some work–life balance practices in place.

all government departments, the Learning and Skills Council, Sector Skills Councils, Regional Development Agencies and other agencies; and

- published for the first time a statement of the roles of employers, individuals and the Government in skills development, including the state's role in providing institutional qualifications and quality frameworks.

The Skills in England Survey 2002 highlighted how strong employment growth has increased the demand for skills. Sectoral and other structural changes have changed the pattern of employment in favour of high-level non-manual occupations and at the expense of traditional manual jobs. The average level of formal qualifications held has also risen. These broad patterns are common across all regions but there are significant regional differences. Skills requirements within occupations are also increasing with higher qualifications, greater generic skills needs and longer training times needed.

The Learning and Training at Work survey for the DfES found that in 2002 IT was the most common course offered by employers (Figure 11.9). Overall, 90 per cent of employers had provided some job-related training to their employees in the previous 12 months.

The Scottish Executive's strategy for lifelong learning, *Life Through Learning; Learning Through Life*, was published in February 2003. It sets out the Executive's five goals to achieve the best possible match between the learning opportunities open to people and the skills necessary to strengthen Scotland's economy.

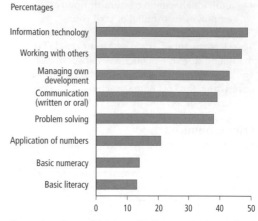

Figure 11.9 Employers offering learning opportunities, 2002, England

Percentages

Source: Learning and Training at Work Survey, IFF Research Ltd for the Department for Education and Skills

Futureskills Scotland carried out the Skills in Scotland 2002 survey. The findings illustrated that skills shortages, although uncommon, were concentrated in particular sectors – hotels and restaurants, health and social work, other business activities, mechanical engineering, construction, and retailing.

Investors in People

Investors in People (IiP) is the National Standard that sets a level of good practice for improving an organisation's performance through its people. It is designed to improve business performance by linking the training and development of employees to the organisation's business objectives. Reported benefits include increased productivity, higher profits, lower rates of absenteeism and improved morale. Investors in People UK, which is responsible for the promotion, quality assurance and development of the Standard, has carried out an extensive review to simplify the Standard and make it more accessible, especially for small firms. As at March 2003 almost 7 million employees worked in IiP recognised organisations, covering just over a quarter of the UK workforce.

Unemployment

There was a steadily downward trend in the unemployment rate from 1993 to spring 2001

Figure 11.10 Unemployment¹ in the UK

Millions

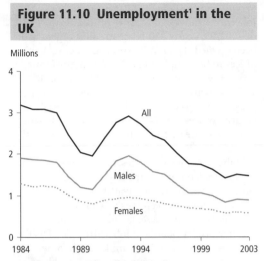

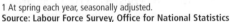

1 At spring each year, seasonally adjusted.
Source: Labour Force Survey, Office for National Statistics

(Figure 11.10). During 2002 there was a slight increase, before the rate started to fall again towards the end of the year. The unemployment rate in spring 2003 was 5.0 per cent, down 0.2 percentage points from spring 2002. The new rate represents about 1.5 million unemployed people (see Table 11.1) and compares with the EU average of 8.1 per cent and a rate of 6.2 per cent in the United States. Within the United Kingdom, unemployment rates in spring 2003 were 5.0 per cent in England, 4.4 per cent in Wales, 5.6 per cent in Scotland, and 5.3 per cent in Northern Ireland. In England, London and the North East had the highest unemployment rates, at 7.0 per cent and 6.4 per cent. The lowest unemployment rates were in the South East and South West at 3.8 per cent. In addition, there were significant variations in unemployment rates within regions.

In recent years there has been a substantial fall in long-term unemployment. In spring 2003 some 315,000 people aged 16 and over had been unemployed for a year or more, of whom 154,000 had been out of work for two years or more. These figures represent falls of 5 per cent and 13 per cent respectively since spring 2002.

In June 2003, 952,000 people were claiming unemployment-related benefits, representing 3.1 per cent of the total UK workforce. Around two-thirds of claimants had been claiming benefits for less than six months.

Redundancies

Redundancy levels in the United Kingdom have remained roughly constant since the statistical series began in 1995. In spring 2003, the redundancy rate was 6.4 per 1,000 employees. Redundancy rates were highest in manufacturing and construction, and lowest in the public administration, education and health sectors.

Labour market policy

The Government's strategy for ensuring employment opportunity for all was set out in its Green Paper, *Towards Full Employment in a Modern Society*, published in 2001. It is based on:

- helping people to move from welfare to work, through extending the series of New Deal programmes (see page 137);
- easing the transition to work by removing barriers to working and ensuring that people are financially secure when moving from welfare to work;
- making paid work more attractive, through promoting incentives to work and reforming the tax and benefits system (see chapters 24 and 12); and
- securing progression in work through lifelong learning, to ensure that people are well trained and able to adapt to changing economic circumstances.

New Deal

The Government's welfare-to-work policy is delivered throughout the United Kingdom primarily through 'New Deal' programmes, targeted at specific groups (see page 137). In 2003/04 the provision for expenditure on New Deals includes £340 million for young people, £255 million for the 25 plus programme, £82 million for lone parents and £27 million for disabled people.

Recruitment and job finding

There are a variety of ways in which people look for work in the United Kingdom. According to the LFS, in winter 2001/02, more than half of all employees found out about the vacancy for their current job either by hearing about it from someone who worked there or by replying to an advertisement. In June 2003 there were an estimated 601,000 vacancies in the United Kingdom, down 3.1 per cent on June 2002.

Welfare-to-work

The Department for Work and Pensions (DWP) operates a number of programmes aimed at helping people into work, including:

- *Employment Zones* – aiming to provide new ways of helping unemployed people into work, these have been piloted as an alternative to the New Deal 25 plus client group in 15 areas where there are high concentrations of unemployment. From October 2003 this approach was extended to 18- to 24-year-olds who would otherwise be returning to the New Deal for a second time and to lone parents in existing Employment Zone areas;

- *Action Teams for Jobs* – operating in 63 areas in Great Britain, these aim to remove the barriers to employment faced by jobless people and, by working with employers, to move them into suitable vacancies. The teams look at innovative ways of achieving their aim, and lessons learned are incorporated in the main Jobcentre Plus services;

- *Step Up* – a programme aimed at providing guaranteed jobs for up to 50 weeks in areas of high unemployment, for those who have not been successful on the New Deal;

- *Progress2work* – a £40 million programme helping drug misusers find employment. Progress2work Link Up, which began in October 2002, is piloting the same approach with a wider group, including offenders, alcohol misusers and the homeless;

- *Adviser Discretion Fund (ADF)* – which gives Jobcentre Districts flexibility to address the specific barriers to work affecting their communities; and

- *Ambition Programmes* – industry-specific training and recruitment programmes in sectors such as IT, retailing, energy, construction and the public sector.

Jobcentre Plus

In Great Britain the Jobcentre Plus network (*www.jobcentreplus.gov.uk*) provides help in finding jobs and pays benefits to people of working age. It has responsibility for running local offices formerly managed by the Employment Service and the Benefits Agency, including Jobcentres and social security offices. By the end of 2002/03, nearly 250 Jobcentre Plus offices had been opened. The DWP expects the network of offices to be completed by 2006. Until this time, services will continue to be provided in local social security offices and Jobcentres. A similar programme to combine Jobcentre and social security offices is under way in Northern Ireland. The new offices are known as 'Jobs and Benefits'.

All Jobcentre Plus vacancies are now available on the Internet, on one of the largest job banks in the world. Vacancies are also available through electronic touch-screen kiosks, known as 'Jobpoints', which are replacing traditional vacancy display boards in Jobcentres. The DWP is planning to install Jobpoint kiosks in other locations, such as supermarkets, prisons, libraries and community centres. Employers with a vacancy can use the Employer Direct service, which provides a single national telephone number for employers to have their vacancies advertised on the Internet and on all Jobpoint terminals.

Jobability.com

The website *www.jobability.com* was set up in March 2002 in response to the Disability Rights Commission's *Actions Speak Louder Than Words* campaign. It advertises vacancies and provides jobsearch advice for disabled people. Recruiters who use the site agree to interview any person who matches the job specification, and can look at the CVs posted on the website by jobseekers. There are over 3,500 jobs advertised on the site a month and an average of 12,000 jobseekers a month looking for jobs.

Advisory services

Most customers who make a claim for a working age benefit have to take part in a meeting with a personal adviser, for example to discuss help to find work or support such as training or childcare. If the individual is claiming benefits other than Jobseeker's Allowance (JSA, see page 158), it is his or her decision whether or not to look for work.

Jobcentre Plus advisers see all jobseekers when a claim is made for JSA to assess their eligibility and to provide advice about jobs, training and self-employment opportunities. To receive the allowance, each unemployed person has to complete a Jobseeker's Agreement, which sets out his or her availability for work, the types of job

New Deal for:	Main features
Young people (NDYP)	■ Aimed at 18- to 24-year-olds who have been unemployed and claiming Jobseeker's Allowance (JSA) for six months.
	■ Begins with a period of advice and guidance, called 'the gateway'.
	■ After the gateway a young person enters an intensive programme of activity, including subsidised employment, self-employment, training or placement with a voluntary organisation.
	■ All options include an element of education and training.
	■ After the options there is a period of follow-through for all participants still on the programme. This lasts for 4 to 6 months and comprises regular interviews with personal advisers.
25 plus	■ A compulsory programme for people aged 25 and over who have been claiming JSA for 18 months or more (or 18 months out of the previous 21 months). Personal advisers have discretion over early admittance for certain groups, such as disabled people, homeless people, ex-offenders, recovering addicts and refugees.
	■ A gateway period of up to 4 months, with weekly interviews and jobsearch support from a personal adviser.
	■ An intensive period of 13 weeks, for those aged 25 to 49, where individuals choose a mix of subsidised activities based on their needs, including employment, work-focused training, work placements and self-employment support.
	■ A follow-through period of 6 weeks which can be extended to a maximum of 13 weeks.
50 plus	■ A voluntary programme for those aged over 50 who have been claiming work-related benefits for 6 months or more.
	■ Offers personal advice, jobsearch help and financial support via the Working Tax Credit.
	■ An in-work training grant of up to £1,500 over two years.
	■ Advice on starting up a business.
Lone parents	■ Compulsory meeting with a personal adviser to discuss work issues and give advice on in-work benefits.
	■ Participation in the scheme is voluntary, after the initial interview.
	■ Participation in a work trial (if appropriate).
	■ Help with the costs of approved training or education courses.
	■ Help with costs incurred while training, such as travel expenses and registered childcare costs.
	■ Outreach service for those living in isolated communities, and those who do not generally come into contact with government agencies.
Disabled people	■ Delivered by a range of organisations called Job Brokers, whose job is to help disabled people locate and move into work.
	■ Job Brokers offer advice on jobsearch and training, and offer support when the jobseeker starts work.
	■ Disabled people are eligible for inclusion in all New Deal activities without a qualifying period.
Partners	■ Designed for the partners of people claiming a range of work- and sickness-related benefits, with the aim of reducing the number of workless households.
	■ Offers help with jobsearch activities, training opportunities, and a short course to refresh or boost existing skills before starting a job, or help and support with setting up a new business.

Workability
The Workability project, run by the charity Leonard Cheshire, provides disabled adults with computer equipment in their own homes, training them in new skills and providing them with help in the jobsearch process. As well as free equipment, Workability participants are given free computer software. Training is provided through colleges offering certificated training. The project is open to unemployed disabled people aged between 19 and 50, who have been hindered in their search for work.

that are being looked for, and the steps that, if taken, offer the best chance of securing work.

Employment agencies
There are many private employment agencies, including several large firms with significant branch networks. The law governing the conduct of employment agencies is less restrictive in the United Kingdom than in many other EU countries, but agencies must comply with legislation which establishes a framework of minimum standards designed to protect agency users, both workers and employers.

The Recruitment and Employment Confederation is the association representing the private recruitment and staffing industry in the United Kingdom. It has a membership of over 6,000 recruitment agencies and over 8,000 recruitment consultants. All members must abide by a code of good recruitment practice.

Industrial relations

Individual employment rights
Employment protection legislation provides a number of safeguards for employees. For example, most employees have a right to a written statement setting out details of the main conditions, including pay, hours of work and holidays.

Employees with at least two years of continuous employment with their employer are entitled to lump sum redundancy payments if their jobs cease to exist and their employers cannot offer suitable alternative work.[3]

---

3 The statutory redundancy payment is calculated according to a formula based on a person's age, the number of years of continuous service up to a maximum of 20 years and his or her weekly pay up to the current maximum of £250 per week. However, many employers pay more than the statutory amount.

Minimum periods of notice are laid down for both employers and employees. Most employees who believe they have been unfairly dismissed have the right to complain to an employment tribunal (see below), subject to the general qualifying period of one year's continuous service. If the complaint is upheld, the tribunal may make an order for re-employment or award compensation.

Legislation prohibits discrimination, in employment, training and related matters, on grounds of sex or marital status, disability, race, nationality (including citizenship) or ethnic or national origin (see page 96). The disability discrimination legislation applies to employers with 15 or more employees. In Northern Ireland discrimination in employment, training and related matters on grounds of religious belief or political opinion is also unlawful. Regulations coming into force in December 2003 will implement parts of the European Employment Directive, by extending protection against discrimination in employment and training to cover sexual orientation and religion. The Government issued a consultation paper in July 2003 outlining proposals that would implement that part of the Directive relating to age discrimination.

The purpose of the *Equal Pay Act 1970* is to eliminate pay discrimination between women and men, when doing work that is the same or broadly similar, work which is rated as equivalent, or work which is of equal value.

The Disability Rights Commission, the Equal Opportunities Commission and the Commission for Racial Equality have powers to investigate cases of discrimination at work in Great Britain. The Equality Commission in Northern Ireland has similar powers.

All pregnant employees have the right to statutory maternity leave with their non-wage contractual benefits maintained, and to protection against detriment and dismissal because of pregnancy. Statutory maternity, paternity and adoption pay are described in chapter 12 (page 151).

Employment tribunals
Employment tribunals in Great Britain have jurisdiction over complaints covering a range of employment rights, including unfair dismissal,

Employment Act 2002

In addition to new provisions on paternity, maternity, adoption, and flexible working for parents of young children, this Act included a number of provisions relating to employment tribunals and the resolution of disputes in the workplace:

- reforms of the employment tribunals system, including provision for cost recovery for management time in vexatious cases;
- requirements on employers to provide statutory grievance procedures at the workplace to help resolve disputes;
- requirements on employees, in most cases, to begin these procedures before taking a complaint to a tribunal;
- changes to the way tribunals calculate awards, to take into account whether the procedures have been used; and
- rights to time off for trade union learning representatives.

These provisions apply in Great Britain.

redundancy pay, equal pay, and sex and race discrimination. New tribunal regulations, including provisions designed to deter cases with weak claims and defences, took effect in 2001 and the reforms brought about by the *Employment Act 2002* (see box) will come into force in October 2004. Tribunals received over 98,000 applications in 2002/03. Northern Ireland has a separate tribunal system.

In March 2003 the Government announced plans to bring the top ten non-devolved tribunals (including the employment tribunals) into its new, unified Tribunals Service. Full policy proposals are expected to be published in a White Paper by the Department for Constitutional Affairs in late 2003.

Labour disputes

In the past 20 years there has been a general decline in working days lost through labour disputes. In the year to February 2003 there were 146 stoppages of work arising from labour disputes in the United Kingdom, and 1.3 million working days were lost as a result, up from 0.6 million in the year to February 2002. During this period 38 per cent of working days lost were in the public administration and defence sector, with the next highest sector being education, at 29 per

cent. Stoppages over wage rates and earnings accounted for 84 per cent per cent of days lost.

Trade unions and employers' organisations

Trade unions

Trade unions have members in nearly all occupations. As well as negotiating pay and other terms and conditions of employment with employers, they provide benefits and services, such as educational facilities, financial services, legal advice and aid in work-related cases. In 2001/02 there were 7.8 million trade union members in the United Kingdom according to the Certification Office.[4] According to the LFS the proportion of employees who were union members was 29 per cent in autumn 2002 (compared with 32 per cent in 1995), and the proportion among all those in employment was 27 per cent (29 per cent in 1995).

Trade union membership is more prevalent among older employees, those with long service and those in the public sector. By occupation, membership is highest among professionals, nearly half of whom were trade union members in 2002. The long-term decline in membership has been particularly noticeable where membership has traditionally been high – among male employees, manual workers and those in production industries. Public administration has the highest density of union members, around 60 per cent of all employees. Sectors with relatively few union members include agriculture, forestry and fishing; hotels and restaurants; and wholesale and retail trades.

The largest union in the United Kingdom is the public service union UNISON, which has around 1.3 million members. Other unions with membership over 500,000 are:
- Amicus – formed by the merger in 2002 of the Amalgamated Engineering and Electrical Union and the Manufacturing, Science and Finance union;
- the Transport and General Workers Union; and
- the GMB – a general union with members in a wide range of industries.

---

4 There are two main sources of information on trade union membership: the Labour Force Survey and data provided by trade unions to the Certification Office. Differences in coverage can result in slightly different estimates.

At the end of March 2003 there were 196 trade unions on the list maintained by the Certification Officer, who, among other duties, is responsible for certifying the independence of trade unions. Entry on the list is voluntary but to be eligible a trade union must show that it consists wholly or mainly of workers and that its principal purposes include the regulation of relations between workers and employers or between workers and employers' associations. A further 20 unions were known to the Certification Officer.

Trades Union Congress

The national body of the trade union movement in England and Wales is the Trades Union Congress (TUC), founded in 1868. In January 2003 its affiliated membership comprised 69 trade unions, which together represented some 6.7 million people.

There are six TUC regional councils for England and a Wales Trades Union Council. The TUC annual Congress meets in September to discuss matters of concern to trade unionists. A General Council represents the TUC between annual meetings.

In Scotland there is a separate national body, the Scottish Trades Union Congress, to which UK unions usually affiliate their Scottish branches. Nearly all trade unions in Northern Ireland are represented by the Northern Ireland Committee of the Irish Congress of Trade Unions (ICTU). Most trade unionists in Northern Ireland are members of unions affiliated to the ICTU, while the majority also belong to unions based in Great Britain, which are affiliated to the TUC.

The TUC participates in international trade union activity, through its affiliation to the International Confederation of Free Trade Unions and the European Trade Union Confederation. It also nominates the British workers' delegation to the annual International Labour Conference.

Trade union and industrial relations law

Among the legal requirements governing trade unions are:

- All individuals have the right not to be dismissed or refused employment (or the services of an employment agency) because of membership or non-membership of a trade union.
- Where a union is recognised by an employer for collective bargaining purposes, union

officials are entitled to paid time off for undertaking certain trade union duties and training. The employer is also obliged to disclose information to the union for collective bargaining purposes.

- A trade union must elect every member of its governing body, its general secretary and its president. Elections must be held at least every five years and be carried out by a secret postal ballot under independent scrutiny.
- If a trade union wishes to set up a political fund, its members must first agree in a secret ballot a resolution adopting those political objectives as an aim of the union. The union must also ballot its members every ten years to maintain the fund. Union members have a statutory right to opt out of contributing to the fund.
- For a union to have the benefit of statutory immunity when organising industrial action, the action must be wholly or mainly due to a trade dispute between workers and their own employer. Industrial action must not involve workers who have no dispute with their own employer (so-called secondary action) or involve unlawful forms of picketing. Before calling for industrial action, a trade union must obtain the support of its members in a secret postal ballot.

Employers' organisations

Many employers in the United Kingdom are members of employers' organisations, some of which are wholly concerned with labour matters, while others are also trade associations concerned with commercial matters in general. Employers' organisations are usually established on an industry basis rather than a product basis, for example, the Engineering Employers' Federation. A few are purely local in character or deal with a sector of an industry or, for example, with small businesses; most are national and are concerned with the whole of an industry. At the end of March 2003, there were 91 employers' associations on the list maintained by the Certification Officer and a further 91 were known to the Certification Officer.

Most national organisations belong to the CBI (Confederation of British Industry, see page 351), which represents around 200,000 businesses.

ACAS

The Advisory, Conciliation and Arbitration Service (ACAS, *www.acas.org.uk*) is an independent statutory body with a general duty of promoting the improvement of industrial relations. ACAS aims to operate through the voluntary co-operation of employers, employees and, where appropriate, their representatives. Its main functions are collective conciliation; provision of arbitration and mediation; advisory mediation services for preventing disputes and improving industrial relations through the joint involvement of employers and employees; and the provision of a public enquiry service. ACAS also conciliates in disputes on individual employment rights, and in 2001 introduced a new voluntary arbitration system for resolving unfair dismissal claims.

ACAS online training

In March 2003 ACAS launched an online learning package to help organisations with practical discipline and grievance procedures. This is a response to the new statutory responsibilities outlined in the *Employment Act 2002* (see page 139).

In Northern Ireland the Labour Relations Agency, an independent statutory body, provides services similar to those provided by ACAS in Great Britain.

Health and safety at work

There has been a long-term decline in injuries to employees in the United Kingdom, partly reflecting a change in industrial structure away from the traditional heavy industries, which tend to have higher risks. In Great Britain in 2002/03 there were 226 deaths of employees and the self-employed from injuries at work, which represented a fatal injury rate of almost one per 100,000 workers. In Northern Ireland in 2001/02 there were nine fatal accidents in the workplace.

Falls from a height, being struck by a moving vehicle and being struck by a moving/flying object continue to be the three most common kinds of accident, accounting for 22 per cent, 17 per cent and 14 per cent of fatal injuries respectively.

The principal legislation in this area in Great Britain is the *Health and Safety at Work, etc. Act 1974*. It imposes general duties on everyone concerned with work activities, including employers, the self-employed, employees, and manufacturers and suppliers of materials for use

at work. Associated Acts and Regulations deal with particular hazards and types of work. Employers with five or more staff must prepare a written statement of their health and safety policy and bring it to the attention of their staff. The regulatory regime for health and safety at work in Northern Ireland broadly mirrors that of England, Scotland and Wales. The principal legislation is contained in the Health and Safety at Work (Northern Ireland) Order 1978 as amended by the Health and Safety at Work (Amendment) (Northern Ireland) Order 1998.

The DWP has lead responsibility for the sponsorship of the Health and Safety Commission and Health and Safety Executive. Other government departments have specific health and safety responsibilities, for example, the DTI for civil nuclear matters and the Department for Transport for rail passenger safety. The Health and Safety Executive for Northern Ireland has primary responsibility for enforcing legislation there.

Health and Safety Commission

The Health and Safety Commission (HSC) has responsibility for developing policy on health and safety at work in Great Britain, including proposals for new or revised regulations and approved codes of practice. Recent work has concentrated on a simpler and more effective system of regulation.

The HSC has advisory committees covering subjects such as toxic substances, genetic modification and the safety of nuclear installations. There are also several industry advisory committees, each covering a specific sector of industry.

Health and Safety Executive

The Health and Safety Executive (HSE) is the primary instrument for carrying out the HSC's

European Week for Safety and Health at Work

The European Week for Safety and Health at Work is a campaign that takes place every October to highlight safety issues on different themes each year. The theme for 2003 is hazardous substances – chemicals used in the workplace, dusts and fumes which cause occupational asthma, asbestos and the need for COSHH (Control of Substances Hazardous to Health) assessments.

policies and has day-to-day responsibility for enforcing health and safety law.

In premises such as offices, shops, warehouses, restaurants and hotels, legislation is enforced by inspectors appointed by local authorities, working under guidance from the HSE.

The HSE's Technology Division provides technical advice on industrial health and safety matters. The Health and Safety Laboratory (HSL), an agency of the HSE, aims to ensure that risks to health and safety from work activities are properly controlled. This involves HSL in two main areas: operational support through incident investigations and studies of workplace situations; and longer-term work on analysis and resolution of occupational health and safety problems.

Further reading
Labour Market Trends. Office for National Statistics. Monthly.

Labour Market Bulletin. Northern Ireland Department for Employment and Learning. Annual.

Towards Full Employment in a Modern Society. Department for Education and Employment, HM Treasury and the Department of Social Security. Cm 5084. The Stationery Office, 2001.

Equality and Diversity: Age Matters. Department of Trade and Industry, 2003.

Annual reports
Advisory, Conciliation and Arbitration Service. ACAS.

Certification Officer. Certification Office for Trade Unions and Employers' Associations.

Health and Safety Commission. HSC.

Websites

Department for Education and Skills
www.dfes.gov.uk

Department for Employment and Learning (Northern Ireland)
www.delni.gov.uk

Department of Trade and Industry
www.dti.gov.uk

Department for Work and Pensions
www.dwp.gov.uk

Health and Safety Executive
www.hse.gov.uk

Learning and Skills Council
www.lsc.gov.uk

Office for National Statistics
www.statistics.gov.uk

The Scottish Executive
www.scotland.gov.uk

Trades Union Congress
www.tuc.org.uk

WWW.

12 Social protection

Social protection refers to support provided to those who are in need or at risk by central government, local authorities, private bodies, voluntary organisations and individuals. Help may be provided to children and families; older people and survivors (such as widows); those who are sick, physically disabled or sensorily impaired; people with learning disabilities or mental health problems; and low earners and the unemployed. The Government principally provides social protection through the social security system and health and personal social services. Services relating specifically to health are included in chapter 13.

The social security system is designed to secure a basic standard of living for people in financial need. It provides income during periods of inability to earn (including periods of sickness and unemployment), pensions for retired people, financial help for low-income families and assistance with costs arising from disablement. The provision of these benefits is administered by the Department for Work and Pensions (DWP) in Great Britain (principally through the Jobcentre Plus network and the Pension Service) and the Social Security Agency of the Department for Social Development in Northern Ireland. The Inland Revenue administers tax credits (see page 146).

Personal social services refers to the assessment for and provision of practical help and support for older people, disabled people, vulnerable children and young people, those with mental health problems or learning disabilities, and their families and carers. These services may be residential, day care, short-break or 'domiciliary' (provided for people needing support to live in their own homes). In certain circumstances, direct cash payments may be made to enable individuals to obtain relevant services for themselves.

In Great Britain, these personal social services are provided or commissioned by certain local authorities and by the voluntary and not-for-profit sectors. The social services departments of local authorities are responsible for ensuring the direct provision or commissioning of services and for ensuring that people receive a high-quality service, regardless of the provider. In Northern Ireland services are provided by Health and Social Services (HSS) Trusts.

Central government is responsible for establishing national policies, securing resources, issuing guidance and overseeing standards. The Commission for Social Care Inspection, which is due to become fully operational after April 2004, will inspect all aspects of personal social services in England (see page 146).

Various voluntary and charitable organisations also offer care, assistance and support to vulnerable members of society. Examples include Help the Aged, which campaigns, researches and develops practical solutions to problems that affect older people; Barnardo's, which helps children to deal with problems like abuse, homelessness and poverty, and to tackle the challenges of disability; and the Royal National Institute for the Blind (RNIB), which campaigns, funds research and offers practical support and advice to anyone with a sight problem. Citizens Advice (see page 473) offer free, confidential, impartial and independent advice on many social issues including benefits, housing, debt, legal matters, employment and immigration.

Expenditure

Average UK social protection expenditure per head was £3,683 in 2000, similar to the EU average

Figure 12.1 Expenditure[1] on social protection in the EU, 2000

£ thousand per head

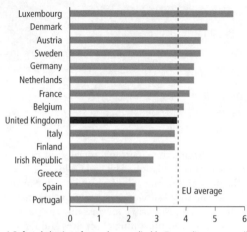

1 Before deduction of tax, where applicable. Tax credits are generally excluded. Figures are Purchasing Power Parities per inhabitant.
Source: Eurostat

Figure 12.3 Local authority personal social services expenditure,[1] 2001/02, England

Total: £13.6 billion

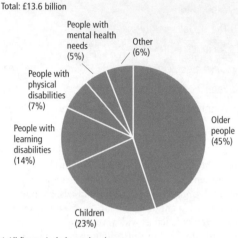

1 All figures include overhead costs.
Source: Department of Health

(see Figure 12.1). These figures include central and local government expenditure on social security and personal social services, sick pay paid by employers, payments made from occupational and personal pension schemes, and administration costs, but they exclude most tax credits. They are expressed in Purchasing Power Parities (which take account of the general level of prices within each

country) in order to allow direct comparisons. As well as different levels of expenditure in the countries of the EU, the figures reflect differences in demographic structures, unemployment rates and other social, institutional and economic factors.

Social security is the largest single area of UK government spending, constituting £115 billion in 2002/03 – 27.5 per cent of total managed expenditure. Figure 12.2 shows how social security benefits expenditure (excluding tax credits) is distributed among different kinds of recipients within Great Britain. The majority of this expenditure is for older people (£57 billion).

In 2001/02 gross expenditure on personal social services by local authorities was £13.6 billion in England. Expenditure on older people accounted for 45 per cent of the total and expenditure on children accounted for 23 per cent (see Figure 12.3). In Scotland expenditure on social work services was £1.8 billion. Local authorities in Wales spent £747 million.

Figure 12.2 Expenditure on social security benefits,[1] 2002/03, Great Britain

Total expenditure: £110 billion

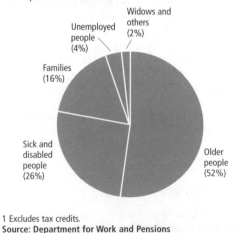

1 Excludes tax credits.
Source: Department for Work and Pensions

The social security system

Benefits

Benefits can be grouped into four types:

- *contributory*, paid to people who have made the required contributions to the *National Insurance Fund* (see page 145);

Selected key benefits and tax credits (from April 2003)

The basic *State Retirement Pension* is a taxable weekly benefit payable, if the contribution conditions have been met, to women from the age of 60 and men from the age of 65 (from 2020, the state pension age for both men and women will be 65). The full basic pension is £77.45 for a single person and £123.80 for a married couple – lower rates apply for those who have not paid full contributions. It is not possible for people in work to choose to contract out of the basic scheme. There is an additional state pension scheme (see page 148), although many people contract out of this and belong instead to occupational schemes (run by employers), or personal pension plans (see page 148).

Child Benefit is a tax-free, universal, non-contributory payment of £16.05 a week for the eldest qualifying child and £10.75 for each other child. It is not affected by income or savings and is payable for children up to the age of 16, and for those under 19 who continue in full-time, non-advanced education.

Income Support is payable to certain people aged 16 or over who are not required to be available for work, and whose savings are below £8,000 (£16,000 for people in residential care or a nursing home). Those eligible include lone parents, carers, and long-term sick and disabled people. Income Support is based on circumstances, including age and whether the claimant is single, a lone parent or has a partner. The rates at April 2003 were £32.90 for a person aged 16–17, £43.25 for someone aged 18–24 and £54.65 a week for people aged 25 or over. Couples aged 18 or over receive £85.75. There are additional allowances for dependent children and premium payments for those with extra expenses, for example, people with disabled children.

Pension Credit replaced *Minimum Income Guarantee* in October 2003. It guarantees everyone aged 60 or over a weekly income of at least £102.10 a week for a single person or £155.80 for a couple. For pensioners aged 65 and over some existing income and savings are not taken into account, to avoid penalising people who have saved in the past.

Working Tax Credit (WTC) is administered by the Inland Revenue. It is for people on low incomes who usually work at least 16 hours a week and are:

- aged 16 or over and responsible for at least one child; or
- aged 16 or over and disabled; or
- aged 25 or over and usually work at least 30 hours a week.

In addition to the basic credit, there are additional elements for single parents and couples, disabled people, childcare costs, and people aged 50 or more who are returning to work after a period on benefit.

Child Tax Credit (CTC) is a payment to support families with children. It is for people who are aged 16 and over and responsible for at least one child or young person who lives with them. As with WTC, it is administered by the Inland Revenue. The amount of CTC paid depends on income and number of children. There are additional amounts for children aged under one and for those with disabilities.

- *means-tested*, available to people whose income and savings are below certain levels;
- benefits which are neither means-tested nor contributory, mainly paid to offset extra costs, for example of disability, or paid universally, for example Child Benefit; and
- payments made by employers to employees who are sick, expecting a baby or adopting a child (these payments are based on earnings and the terms and conditions of employment).

Most benefits are increased annually in line with percentage increases in retail prices. The main benefits (payable weekly) are described above and on page 157.

From April 2003 the Government began paying benefits, state pensions and war pensions directly into an account at a bank, building society or Post Office (see universal banking services, page 454). This method of payment, called Direct Payment, will be phased in over two years.

National Insurance contributions (NICs)

With the exception of a small National Health Service (NHS) allocation, all NICs are paid into the National Insurance Fund. All contributory benefits and their administrative costs are paid out of the Fund.

Entitlement to many benefits, for example the State Retirement Pension, Incapacity Benefit and contributory Jobseeker's Allowance, is dependent upon the payment of NICs or the award of credits. Employees and the self-employed aged under 65, and employers, are all liable to pay contributions once an individual's earnings exceed a certain amount. Where an employer operates a final salary pension scheme (see page 148), the employee and his or her employer pay a reduced rate of contribution to offset the cost of the contribution to the pension. The current NIC rates are set out on the Inland Revenue website (*www.inlandrevenue.gov.uk/rates*). Self-employed people pay lower NICs than employees but receive fewer benefits; in particular, they do not receive the State Second Pension (see page 148).

Tax credits

Administered by the Inland Revenue, tax credits have been introduced with the aim of improving the way the Government supports families with children and working people on low incomes, including disabled workers. The main tax credits are the Working Tax Credit and Child Tax Credit (see page 145).

Social care providers

Providers of care range from families, friends and volunteers to large statutory, voluntary and private sector organisations. In England and Wales, the *Care Standards Act 2000*, and in Scotland the *Regulation of Care (Scotland) Act 2001*, established independent bodies to inspect and regulate social care services. Their remit includes a wide range of care services such as care homes and children's homes, as well as private hospitals and clinics. The National Care Standards Commission (NCSC), the Scottish Commission for the Regulation of Care (SCRC) and the Care Standards Inspectorate for Wales (CSIW) all took over their regulatory powers in April 2002.

In March 2003 legislation was introduced into Parliament to establish two new independent inspectorates: the Commission for Healthcare Audit and Inspection (see page 184) and the Commission for Social Care Inspection (CSCI). The CSCI, which will operate in England from April 2004, will be a single comprehensive inspectorate for social care, bringing together the work currently undertaken by the Social Services Inspectorate (SSI), the SSI/Audit Commission joint review team and the social care functions of the NCSC. It will:

- carry out inspections of all public, private, and voluntary social care organisations, including local social services authorities;
- register services that meet national minimum standards;

- publish an annual report to Parliament on national progress on social care and an analysis of where resources have been spent; and
- validate all published performance assessment statistics on social care.

The CSIW and SCRC will continue to regulate care standards in Wales and Scotland respectively. In Wales, social services authorities are inspected by a separate body, the Social Services Inspectorate for Wales.

Informal carers

Much of the care given to people with long-term physical or mental ill-health, a disability or problems relating to old age is provided by family members, friends and neighbours. The 2001 Census found that one in ten people in the United Kingdom (5.9 million people) were providing unpaid care (looking after, giving help or support) to family members, friends, neighbours or others. The majority of these carers (68 per cent) were providing unpaid care for up to 19 hours a week, but around 21 per cent (1.3 million people) were providing unpaid care for 50 or more hours a week.

Carers can receive financial help from the Government. From October 2002 the upper age limit of 65 was removed from the *Invalid Care Allowance* and in April 2003 it was renamed *Carer's Allowance*. This is now paid to full-time carers who are aged 16 or over and who are spending at least 35 hours a week looking after someone who is getting Attendance Allowance, Disability Living Allowance (at the middle or highest rate for personal care) or Constant Attendance Allowance.

The rate of Carer's Allowance in April 2003 was £42.45 a week. For every complete tax year it is received, this is counted as a contribution to the State Second Pension (see page 148).

Carer's Allowance is not paid to full-time students or if the carer is earning above £75 a week (after allowable expenses). Carers entitled to Carer's Allowance and on low income may be able to qualify for the carer premium paid with income-related benefits such as Income Support. The carer premium is currently £24.80 a week.

The *Carers and Disabled Children Act 2000* provides carers in England and Wales with the right to have their need for services assessed by the local authority, and for the local authority to provide services direct to carers. The Act also extended the power of local authorities to offer direct payments to carers. Local authorities can help young carers using powers in the *Children Act 1989*, which allow them to provide services to other family members – such as helping a disabled parent fulfil his or her parenting role – where that is the best way to help the child.

The *Community Care and Health (Scotland) Act 2002* (see page 150) entitles carers to have their ability to provide care assessed independently of the needs of the person receiving care. The Act also provides carers in Scotland with the right to have their views taken into account when any assessment of needs is carried out.

Local authorities

Local authority social services departments provide a wide range of support and services to children and their families, older people and those with learning disabilities, physical disabilities or mental health needs. This includes the assessment of needs, the provision of help, such as meals on wheels and home help, and the running of day centres and residential homes. Efforts are made in the provision of services to promote independence and choice, and to help disabled people live as independently as possible. A new framework for delivering housing support services, the Supporting People Programme, began in England and Wales in 2003 (see page 290).

The *Care Standards Act 2000* established separate bodies in England and Wales to regulate the social care workforce. The General Social Care Council in England and the Care Council for Wales both became operational in October 2001. They have responsibility for promoting high standards of conduct and training for social care workers by agreeing and issuing statutory codes of practice, setting up a register of social care workers, dealing with matters of conduct, and regulating and supporting social work education and training. The Scottish equivalent, the Scottish Social Services Council, was set up by the *Regulation of Care (Scotland) Act 2001* and became operational in 2001.

Social services star ratings

In 2002 the Social Services Inspectorate began publishing star ratings for local councils with social services responsibilities in England. Each council's performance across all social services was rated on a scale of zero to three stars. In November of that year 11 councils (7 per cent) achieved a three-star rating, 52 (35 per cent) were awarded two stars and 75 (50 per cent) got a one-star rating. Twelve councils (8 per cent) received no stars.

Residential and nursing homes

Care homes provide a range of facilities for people who cannot manage at home, and some are registered to provide nursing care. Most care homes are run by the independent sector. The cost of care and accommodation is funded in a number of ways: by the NHS where the person's primary need is for healthcare, by local authority social services, or by the individual following a means test. The elements covered by the means test vary in England, Scotland and Wales (see page 150).

Table 12.4 Residents (non-staff) in communal medical and care establishments,[1] April 2001, Great Britain

Thousands

	Under state pension age[2]	Over state pension age[2]	Total
NHS			
Psychiatric hospital/home	9	5	14
Other hospital home	14	10	24
Local authority			
Children's home	2	–	3
Nursing home	–	2	2
Residential care home	5	36	42
Other home	1	1	1
Housing association			
Home or hostel	4	7	10
Other			
Nursing home	11	136	147
Residential care home	34	150	183
Children's home	2	–	2
Psychiatric hospital/home	3	4	7
Other hospital home	–	–	–
Other medical and care home	3	5	8

1 Any person, who had been living, or intended to live, in the establishment for six months or more, excluding the owner, staff or their relatives.
2 State pension age is 60 for women and 65 for men.
Source: Census 2001, Office for National Statistics and General Register Office for Scotland

Under the *Care Standards Act 2000*, national minimum standards for care homes for younger adults (aged 18–65) and for care homes for older people came into force in England in April 2002. The standards cover areas such as choice of home, health and personal care, daily life and social activities, complaints and protection, environment, staffing, management and administration. Broadly similar standards apply in Wales and Scotland.

Older people

People over retirement age represent the fastest growing section of the community (see chapter 9). Over 50 per cent of social security benefit expenditure in Great Britain is on older people (see Figure 12.2).

Pensions

In 2001/02 the State Retirement Pension was received by around 11 million people (including those living overseas) and accounted for nearly £42 billion of social security benefit expenditure. In the same year, according to the Family Resources Survey, 57 per cent of employees and 42 per cent of the self-employed were contributing to either an occupational or a personal pension scheme or both (see below).

State pensions

The basic State Retirement Pension (see also page 145) is based on NICs and payable when people reach state pension age, unless they choose to defer. In 2003 the charge deducted from pensions and benefits if pensioners were in hospital for more than six weeks was abolished. They can now receive their full state pension while in hospital, for up to 52 weeks.

It is possible to build up an additional state pension based on NICs and earnings. Until recently this was known as the *State Earnings-Related Pension Scheme* (*SERPS*), but in April 2002 the *State Second Pension* was introduced to reform SERPS. Any SERPS entitlement that has already been built up is protected, both for those who have already retired and for those who have not yet reached pensionable age.

The State Second Pension provides an additional pension for low and moderate earners, and for certain carers and people with a long-term illness or disability who have not been able to make contributions.

Occupational pensions

An occupational pension scheme is an arrangement employers make to provide pensions for their employees when they retire. These schemes may also provide a tax-free lump sum on retirement, and benefits for the dependants of an employee if he or she dies. It is common for both employer and employee to contribute, based on a percentage of the employee's earnings. All employers with five or more employees are required to provide their employees with access to a stakeholder pension scheme (see below) if they do not provide access to an occupational scheme or to a personal pension with an employer contribution of at least 3 per cent.

There are two main types of occupational pension scheme:

- *final salary* (sometimes known as *defined benefit*) schemes, which offer a predetermined level of pension benefit, expressed as a fixed proportion of the employee's final salary for every complete year as a scheme member. The scheme gives the member the option to convert part of the pension to a tax-free lump sum or may specifically provide a separate tax-free lump sum; and

- *money purchase* schemes, in which the contributions of the employer and the employee are invested. The size of the fund depends on the amount of these contributions and the performance of the investment. When an employee retires or leaves the scheme, he or she can receive a proportion of the fund as a tax-free lump sum, while the remainder must be used to purchase an annuity. An annuity is an arrangement by which a life assurance company pays a regular income, usually for life, in return for a lump-sum premium.

Personal pensions

Personal pensions provide another way of making regular savings for retirement. Financial services companies, such as insurance companies, banks, investment companies and building societies, offer these plans and employers may make contributions in addition to those of employees. The money in the fund is invested to provide a pension when the owner retires.

Stakeholder pensions are a form of personal pension introduced by the Government in April 2001 to provide a pension option for people who do not have access to a good occupational or personal pension. Regulations provide that transfers can be made without charge from one stakeholder pension to another arrangement (including a different stakeholder) and for people to vary the amount that they contribute to the scheme. The annual administration charge must not exceed 1 per cent of fund value.

Regulation

The Occupational Pensions Regulatory Authority (Opra) is the regulator of pension arrangements offered by employers and the registrar for occupational and personal pension schemes in the United Kingdom. It ensures that pension schemes comply with the *Pensions Act 1995* and the Pensions (Northern Ireland) Order 1995, which aimed to make pensions more secure. Opra's Pension Schemes Registry maintains a register of all UK tax-approved occupational and personal pension schemes with two or more members, and offers a service for tracing pension schemes (*www.opra.gov.uk/registry/regmenu.shtml*) when people have lost touch. The Government has announced that it will introduce a new regulator in 2005.

The Pensions Ombudsman deals with complaints of maladministration against occupational and personal pension schemes and adjudicates on disputes. The Office of the Pensions Advisory Service (OPAS) gives help and advice to people who have problems with their pensions.

Pension reform

As people are living longer, the pension industry is required to support a greater number of pensioners for longer periods. This increased pressure on pension funds has been amplified in recent years by falling share prices because pension funds rely on financial stock market returns to pay policyholders. As a result, many employers have closed their final salary schemes to new employees, increased employee contributions or, in a very few cases, wound up existing schemes.

A survey of 255 companies undertaken by the National Association of Pension Funds in April/May 2003 found that only 19 per cent offered final salary schemes to new employees and that 40 per cent of the companies operating a final salary scheme had closed them to new members in the previous 12 months.

In December 2002, after an independent review by Alan Pickering, the Government published a Green Paper on pension reform, including

proposals to increase choice, simplify the pensions tax framework, protect consumers and encourage older workers to remain in employment.

In June 2003, following a consultation exercise, the Government published *Simplicity, security and choice: Working and saving for retirement – action on occupational pensions*, which set out a number of steps it will be taking to protect members of pension schemes. These include:

- the introduction of a Pension Protection Fund for defined benefit pension schemes in the United Kingdom, which will protect pension rights accrued when a company ceases to operate;
- revising the priority order which applies on wind-up to ensure that assets are fairly distributed reflecting the length of service of the employees;
- ensuring that where a solvent company chooses to wind up a pension scheme it meets its pension promise in full; and
- the introduction of a new pension regulator with a legal framework that will enable it to tackle the areas of greatest risk and to concentrate on removing fraud and bad practice.

The action plan also outlines measures to simplify and encourage greater flexibility in pension provision. The rate at which firms have to increase pension payments each year in line with inflation will be reduced from a maximum of 5 per cent to 2.5 per cent.

Other financial support

In addition to the *State Retirement Pension* (see page 148), people aged 60 or over are eligible for other benefits.

Most people aged 60 and over are entitled to a *Winter Fuel Payment*, generally £200 for each eligible household, to provide help towards the cost of winter fuel bills. From winter 2003/04 an extra £100 will be paid to households that include someone aged 80 and over.

Free NHS prescriptions and eye tests are provided to those aged 60 or over. People receiving Pension Credit can also get free NHS dental treatment, wigs and fabric supports, vouchers towards the cost of glasses or contact lenses, and refunds of necessary travel costs to hospitals for NHS treatment (including check-ups). Pensioners aged 75 and over can claim a free television licence.

Table 12.5 Pensioners[1] in receipt of selected social security benefits, 2001/02, Great Britain

Percentages

	Working Families Tax Credit or Income Support	Housing Benefit	Council Tax Benefit	State Retirement Pension	Incapacity or Disablement Benefits[2]	Child Benefit	Any benefit/ tax credit
Pensioner couple	6	10	17	98	25	1	100
Single pensioner							
Male	15	25	31	98	20	–	99
Female	24	27	38	96	19	–	99

1 Single person or couple living as married and any dependent children, where the head of household is over state pension age (60 for females and 65 for males).
2 Incapacity Benefit, Disability Living Allowance (Care and Mobility components), Severe Disablement Allowance, Industrial Injuries Disability Benefit, War Disablement Pension, Attendance Allowance and Disabled Person's Tax Credit.
Source: *Family Resources Survey 2001–2002*, Department for Work and Pensions

Across the United Kingdom older people are entitled to free travel or concessionary fares on public transport (see page 313).

Care services for older people
Some £6.2 billion was spent by English local authorities on older people in 2001/02, 45 per cent of their total spending on personal social services (see Figure 12.3).

Wherever possible, services are designed to help older people live at home. These services may include advice and help given by social workers, domestic help, the provision of meals in the home, sitters-in, night attendants and laundry services, as well as direct payments, day centres, lunch clubs and recreational facilities.

In England nearly 684,000 people (almost 9 per cent of all people aged 65 or over) were being helped to live at home by local authorities at the end of September 2002. During a survey week in September 2002 an estimated 2.98 million hours of home care services were either provided or purchased by local authorities in England for nearly 367,000 households. Gross expenditure by local authorities on day and home care provision for older people amounted to £1.8 billion in 2001/02.

At the time of the 2001 Census nearly 324,000 people over retirement age were living in residential care or nursing homes in Great Britain (see Table 12.4). Residents who need regular and frequent care from a registered nurse are care for in homes that are registered to provide nursing care. In England, residents' care and accommodation is funded by the NHS where the person's primary need is for healthcare, by social services or by the individual following a means test.

The Welsh Assembly Government has also implemented a policy to ensure that the services of a registered nurse are free of charge in all care settings. Funding has been set at a level of £100 a week per individual self-funder who is assessed as needing nursing care. In Scotland, the *Community Care and Health (Scotland) Act 2002* provides for free personal care and free nursing care (in care homes that provide nursing). The Act allows people to make top-up payments if they wish to enter more expensive accommodation than that which the local authority would normally pay for (they may also defer these payments until their home is sold after death). The Act also expands access to direct payments for non-residential service users, giving people the ability to purchase their own services.

Families and children
Financial support
The Child Tax Credit and the Working Tax Credit (see page 145) were introduced in April 2003. These tax credits bring together the support for children previously provided through the Working

Families' and Disabled Person's Tax Credits, the Children's Tax Credit, Income Support and Jobseeker's Allowance.

In April 2003 maternity leave was extended. All pregnant employees now have the right to 26 weeks' ordinary maternity leave and most can take a further 26 weeks' additional maternity leave. *Statutory Maternity Pay* is paid directly from the employer for a maximum of 26 weeks to women who have been working for the same employer for 26 weeks and who earn on average at least £77 a week. It is paid at a rate equal to 90 per cent of their average weekly earnings for the first six weeks and a standard rate of £100 a week for the remaining 20 weeks, or at the 90 per cent rate if average earnings are less than £100.

Women who are not eligible for Statutory Maternity Pay because, for example, they are self-employed or have recently changed jobs or left their job, may qualify for a weekly *Maternity Allowance*, which is paid for up to 26 weeks at a standard rate of £100, or a rate equal to 90 per cent of their average weekly earnings if this is less than £100.

From April 2003 fathers have a new right to two weeks' paternity leave within eight weeks of the child's birth. *Statutory Paternity Pay* is paid at the same standard rate as Statutory Maternity Pay – £100 per week (or 90 per cent of average weekly earnings if this is less).

Also from April 2003, employees who adopt a child have a right to take adoption leave and receive *Statutory Adoption Pay*, on a similar basis to maternity leave and pay. Where a couple adopt jointly, they can choose which one of them will take adoption leave and pay. The other may take paternity leave and pay.

Subject to certain qualifying requirements, both mothers and fathers are entitled to 13 weeks' unpaid parental leave until the child's fifth birthday. Parents of disabled children can take 18 weeks up to the child's 18th birthday.

New legislation came into effect in April 2003 giving parents of children aged under six and parents of disabled children aged under 18 the right to request flexible working patterns. Employers have a duty to consider these requests seriously and may only refuse on business grounds.

Child Trust Fund

A Child Trust Fund was announced in the 2003 Budget. The Fund will provide every child born after September 2002 with an initial endowment at birth of £250 (or £500 for the poorest families). Parents, family members and friends will be able to make additional contributions, up to an annual limit of £1,000. Children will be able to access their accounts when they reach the age of 18.

Families affected by unemployment or on low incomes may be able to get a *Sure Start Maternity Grant* of up to £500 to help with the cost of buying things for the new baby.

In the 2003 Budget a number of reviews were announced of: financial support for 16- to 19-year-olds; child poverty; and delivering better childcare. In addition, a new income tax exemption for foster carers was announced, along with new measures to help lone parents and partners of benefit claimants find work.

Child Support Agency

The function of the Child Support Agency (*www.csa.gov.uk*) is to ensure that parents who live apart meet their financial responsibilities to their children. Where both parents and the qualifying child live within the United Kingdom it:

- assesses claims for child support maintenance;
- traces and contacts non-resident parents;
- helps conclude paternity disputes when a man denies he is a child's father; and
- collects and passes on maintenance payments to the parent who is caring for the child, taking action to make the non-resident parent pay if necessary.

In March 2003 the way that child support payments are calculated was changed for new applicants (people who applied before this date will transfer to the new arrangements later).

For non-resident parents whose net income is £200 per week or more, the new rates are 15 per cent for one child, 20 per cent for two children and 25 per cent for three or more children. Those with a net income of less than £200 per week pay reduced rates. Non-resident parents with income of less than £100 (or who are on specified benefits) pay a flat rate of £5 per week.

The calculation also takes account of children in the non-resident parent's current family, including step-children but does not take account of the income of the parent who is caring for the child, the income of either parent's current partner, housing costs or travel to work costs.

Other support for families and children

Local authorities in England and Wales and Health and Social Services Trusts in Northern Ireland are required to safeguard and promote the welfare of any children in need and, so far as is consistent with that, to promote the upbringing of children by their parents, by providing a range of services to meet their assessed needs. The services which may be provided include advice, guidance, counselling, help in the home and family centres. Help can be provided to the immediate family of the child or to any other member of the family, if it is done with a view to safeguarding and promoting the child's welfare. Local authorities can provide these services directly or arrange them through another agency such as a voluntary organisation. They are also required to publicise the help available to families in need.

Local authorities also help people fleeing domestic violence, often working with specialist voluntary organisations that provide refuges where women and children receive short-term accommodation and support, pending a more permanent solution.

In June 2003 the Government announced the creation of a new Minister for Children in England. The post brings together, at a national level, responsibilities for a broad range of policies and programmes to meet the needs of children and young people (see page 122).

In September 2003 the Government set out proposals for a Children's Commissioner in England. In Wales, a Children's Commissioner was appointed in 2001, the first in the United Kingdom. Scotland and Northern Ireland are about to appoint commissioners.

Sure Start

The Government's Sure Start initiative brings together a number of programmes for children and families – from pregnant mothers to children up to age 14 (or 16 for those with special needs). Sure Start aims to provide universal, free part-time early education for three- and four-year-olds, and more extensive childcare and family support services, with greater assistance where there is greater need.

Every Child Matters – Green Paper on children
(www.dfes.gov.ukleverychildmatters)

In September 2003 the Government published a Green Paper, *Every Child Matters*, proposing measures to protect children from neglect and harm, promote their wellbeing and support all children to develop their full potential. The proposals include:

- establishing integrated teams of health and education professionals, social workers and Connexions advisers based in and around schools and children's centres;
- removing legal, technical and cultural barriers to information sharing so that there can be effective communication between everyone with a responsibility for children;
- establishing a clear framework of accountability at a national and local level with the appointment of a Children's Director in every local authority responsible for bringing all children's services together as Children's Trusts;
- new duties on police, health staff and others to safeguard children and require them to come together into Local Safeguarding Children Boards;
- children's services to be judged on joint working through an integrated inspection framework overseen by Ofsted;
- a national campaign to recruit more foster parents and a workforce reform package to make working with children an attractive career, and improve the skills and effectiveness of the children's workforce; and
- the appointment of an independent Children's Commissioner to champion children's views.

The policies and proposals contained in The Green Paper apply to England only, except where they relate to non-devolved responsibilities, such as Home Office services, where they also apply to Wales.

Every Child Matters was published alongside *Keeping Children Safe*, a detailed response to the recommendations made in Victoria Climbié inquiry report (see page 154) and in the Joint Chief Inspectors' report Safeguarding Children. Keeping Children Safe includes details of the responses to each one of the recommendations in both reports.

In England a Sure Start Unit was set up in December 2002 to work with local authorities and their communities. The Unit reports to both the

Department for Education and Skills and the DWP. The first 32 of a new network of children's centres were established in disadvantaged areas in June 2003 to offer a wide range of early years and family services to their communities, and build on Sure Start local programmes and other initiatives.

In Wales, Cymorth – the Children and Youth Support Fund – provides support with the aim of improving the life chances of children and young people from disadvantaged families. Through Sure Start Scotland, all 32 local authorities are funded to work in partnership with health services and voluntary organisations to identify local need and deliver services to vulnerable families with very young children. The Scottish Executive is also working towards an Integrated Strategy for the Early Years covering young children (from pre-birth to five) and their families.

Day care
Day care facilities are provided for young children by childminders, playgroups, crèches, and out of school clubs, run privately by voluntary organisations or, in some cases, by local authorities.

The Office for Standards in Education (Ofsted) (see page 124) has responsibility for the regulation of day care provision for children in England. Its Early Years Directorate registers and inspects provision for children up to the age of eight. Inspectors assess the suitability of premises, staff, and the welfare and development of the children on the basis of National Standards which set minimum levels of quality for day care.

In Scotland, local authority responsibility for regulation of day care providers for children transferred to the new Scottish Commission for the Regulation of Care (the 'Care Commission') in April 2002. New national care standards for early education and childcare up to the age of 16 have been published, and HM Inspectorate of Education and the Care Commission are developing an inspection regime to be used in conjunction with these standards and other key documents.

In Wales, local authority responsibility for the regulation of childminding and day care for children under eight transferred to the National Assembly for Wales in April 2002. Regulations and new national minimum standards have been published. The CSIW (see page 146) is responsible for ensuring that childminders and providers of

day care for young people are suitable and that they comply with the regulations and standards.

Local HSS Trusts in Northern Ireland are responsible for the regulation of day care providers, covering provision for children up to the age of 12.

Child protection
Child protection is the joint concern of a number of different agencies and professions. Local authority-led area child protection committees determine how the different agencies should co-operate to help protect children from abuse and neglect in their area.

In England and Wales a child may be brought before a family proceedings court if he or she is suffering, or is likely to suffer, significant harm. The court can commit children to the care of the local authority under a care order or a supervision order. Certain pre-conditions have to be satisfied to justify such an order. These are that significant harm, or likelihood of harm, is attributable to a lack of reasonable parental care or because the child is beyond parental control. However, an order is made only if the court is also satisfied that this will positively contribute to the child's wellbeing and be in his or her best interests. All courts have to treat the welfare of children as the paramount consideration when reaching any decision about their upbringing. There is a general principle that, wherever possible, children should remain at home with their families.

In Scotland, children who have committed offences or are in need of care and protection may be brought before a Children's Hearing, which can impose a supervision requirement on a child. In some cases, the supervision requirement will have a condition attached to it that the child must live away from home where the Hearing believes the child will receive the right help or supervision – either with foster parents, in a children's home or at a special residence. Supervision requirements are reviewed at least once a year until ended by a Children's Hearing.

Local authority social services departments help children who are in need, including those considered to be at risk of significant harm, and each department holds a register of children considered to be at risk. There were around 29,000 children on child protection registers in England, Wales and Northern Ireland at 31 March 2002.

Victoria Climbié and Kennedy McFarlane

Eight year old Victoria Climbié died of hypothermia in London in February 2000. Her great-aunt, to whom her parents had entrusted her care, and her great-aunt's boyfriend, were convicted of her murder in 2001. After their conviction, an independent public inquiry was set up to investigate the circumstances surrounding her death and the role that social workers, housing staff, health workers and the police played in failing to prevent it.

The report of the inquiry was published in January 2003 and included 108 recommendations to overhaul children's services in England.

The Government's main response to the inquiry, *Keeping Children Safe*, was published in September, alongside the Green Paper *Every Child Matters* (see page 152).

In Scotland a Child Protection Review was announced in March 2001, following the Hammond Report into the death of three-year-old Kennedy McFarlane who was murdered by her mother's boyfriend. The review report, *It's everyone's job to make sure I'm alright*, was published in November 2002. In response to the findings of the report, the Scottish Executive announced a five-point plan. The actions to be taken were:

- a three-year reform programme for child protection services;
- a team of experts to oversee reform and tackle poor performance locally;
- a tough new system of inspection to ensure that reform is delivered;
- a Children's Charter setting out the support that every child has the right to expect; and
- increased investment in helplines, including £500,000 to allow Childline to open a new call centre and increase by up to 60 per cent the number of children it is able to help.

Fostering and children's homes

When a child is made the subject of a care order, the local authority has legal responsibility for the child. Although it consults with the child's parents about where the child should live, the local authority makes the final decision. Children can also be accommodated by a local authority through a voluntary agreement with their parents. In the year ended 31 March 2002 there were some 39,200 children in foster care and 6,800 in children's homes in England (see Table 12.6). In Wales there were just under 4,000 children being looked after by local authorities, the majority of whom were in foster homes.

Local authorities and HSS Trusts in Northern Ireland must also provide accommodation for children who have no parent or guardian, who have been abandoned, or whose parents are unable to provide for them. They have a duty to ensure that the welfare of children being looked after away from home is properly safeguarded. This includes protecting their health, providing for their education and ensuring contact with their families. They are as far as possible expected to work in partnership with the parents of children who are in their care.

The *Children Leaving Care Act 2000* introduced duties on local authorities in England and Wales to assess and meet the needs of young people leaving care, as well as a requirement that each care leaver should have a written plan (called a Pathway Plan) and the support of a personal adviser. Local authorities must keep in touch with care leavers and ensure they have access to suitable accommodation.

Younger children are placed wherever possible with foster carers, sometimes as a short-term measure (for example when parents are temporarily unable to look after their child because of illness in the family) or, if necessary, for longer periods. Children's homes can be run by local authorities, or by private or voluntary organisations.

Under the *Care Standards Act 2000*, all children's homes as well as fostering services are required to register with the NCSC (see page 146) or its equivalent bodies in Scotland and Wales. The Commission is responsible for inspecting all children's homes to assess the quality of care provided.

Adoption

There were 5,459 adoption orders in England and Wales in 2002. An adoption order gives parental responsibility for a child to the adoptive parent(s) and must be obtained by relatives and step-parents seeking to adopt, as well as by non-relatives who have been approved by an adoption agency. Under the *Adoption Act 1976*, adoption orders can be granted to applicants by the High Court, county courts and magistrates' courts.

10–20 January 2003 calling Houston, Texas: 26 Scottish students attend winter camp at the Lyndon B Johnson Space Center. They had all studied distance learning courses developed by NASA, and were selected by the Scottish Space School Foundation.

7 February 2003 the famous towers at Wembley Stadium are demolished. Work on the new stadium should be completed in 2006.

7 February 2003 some 70,000 fridges from all over south-east England wait to be recycled in a worked-out chalk pit at Greystone Quarry in East Sussex. A mobile fridge demanufacturing unit cleared the backlog by the summer.

LUKE MACGREGOR

11 February 2003 armed troops and police patrol London's Heathrow Airport as a precautionary measure against a suspected terrorist threat.

REUTERS / PETER MACDIARMID

12 February 2003 Everton's Wayne Rooney, at 17 years 111 days, is the youngest footballer to play for England.

14 February 2003 Dolly, the first cloned mammal, dies. The decision to put down the six-year-old sheep was taken at the Roslin Institute, Edinburgh after tests revealed she had a progressive lung disease. She had also been suffering from arthritis. Her body is on display in the Royal Museum in Edinburgh.

27 February 2003 *Bottom:*
Dr Rowan Williams raps three times with his staff on the West Door of Canterbury Cathedral, to gain entry for his enthronement as Archbishop. He is the first Welsh Archbishop of Canterbury for at least 1,000 years.

Right: St Augustine (died AD 604) landed on the Isle of Thanet in AD 597. The foundation stone for Canterbury Cathedral was laid five years later and Augustine became the first Archbishop of Canterbury. Dr Williams is the 104th Archbishop.

Table 12.6 Children looked after by local authorities,[1] England, March 2002

	Number
Foster placements	39,200
Children's homes and hostels[2]	6,800
With parents	6,700
Placed for adoption	3,600
Living independently or in residential employment	1,100
Residential schools	1,100
Other	1,100
Total	**59,700**

1 Excludes children looked after under an agreed series of short-term placements.
2 Includes local authority, voluntary sector and private children's homes and secure units.
Source: Department of Health

From April 2003, people who adopt a child may be eligible for new rights to time off work and Statutory Adoption Pay (see page 151).

In August 2001 the National Adoption Standards for England were published. These standards are intended to ensure that children, prospective adopters, adoptive parents and birth families receive a consistent and high-quality adoption service no matter where they live. From April 2003, the NCSC assumed responsibility for the registration and inspection of voluntary adoption agencies and the inspection of local authority adoption services in England. The CSIW has similar responsibilities in Wales. Adoption standards for Scotland were published in March 2002 and are due to come into force in 2003. Draft standards and guidance for Wales were issued in 2001 and standards for Northern Ireland will be issued at a later date.

The Adoption Register for England and Wales holds information on children waiting to be adopted and approved adoptive families waiting to adopt. The aim is to tackle delays in finding suitable adoptive families where a local family cannot be found, or the child needs to move away from the area.

People with a sickness or disability

At the time of the 2001 Census 10.9 million people, or 18.5 per cent of the UK population, reported a

Adoption and Children Act

The *Adoption and Children Act 2002* will modernise the legal framework for domestic and inter-country adoption. The aim is to improve the adoption service and promote greater use of adoption. Among its provisions are measures to:

- align adoption law with the *Children Act 1989* to make the child's welfare the paramount consideration in all decisions to do with adoption;
- introduce a new duty on local authorities to provide an adoption support service and a right for people affected by adoption to request and receive an assessment of their needs for such a service;
- allow unmarried couples to adopt together – at present only married couples and single people are legally allowed to adopt children;
- reduce delays by providing a legal basis for the Adoption Register to suggest matches between children and approved adopters and through measures requiring the courts to draw up timetables for adoption;
- provide for a more consistent approach to the way in which people can gain access to information held in adoption agency records, so that adopted adults and their adult birth relatives may apply for information that could be disclosed if consent is given; and
- improve the legal controls on inter-country adoption, and the legal controls on arranging adoptions and advertising children for adoption.

The majority of provisions in the Act relate to England and Wales only, but some provisions also extend to Scotland and/or Northern Ireland.

long-term illness, health problem or disability which limited their daily activities or work. Over the past decade there has been increasing emphasis on the provision of support services that enable disabled people to live independently in the community whenever possible. The year 2003 was officially designated the European Year of Disabled People by the European Commission. In the United Kingdom, 171 projects totalling £2.3 million have been funded by the Government and the Commission.

The Disability Rights Commission (DRC) aims to eliminate discrimination against disabled people, promote equal opportunities, encourage good practice and advise the Government on the operation of the *Disability Discrimination Act 1995*

Hi-Notes – after-school music clubs for Deaf young people
This project is one of the events funded for the European Year of Disabled People. Running from 29 April 2003 to 31 March 2004 in Newsome (Huddersfield) and Batley in Yorkshire, these weekly after-school music clubs aim to give Deaf people the opportunity to participate in and enjoy music and give performances of their work. The project, which is administered by the charity Music and the Deaf, includes Deaf people in an activity from which they are normally excluded and provides stimulating after-school activities.

(see page 99). The Equality Commission (see page 98) has a similar role in Northern Ireland.

The Department of Health publication *A Practical Guide for Disabled People or Carers* provides information about services from government departments and agencies, the NHS and local government and voluntary organisations. It is available on-line at *www.doh.gov.uk/disabledguide*. The Disability Unit in the DWP (see page 99) runs a website to help disabled people learn more about their rights and the relevant legislation for disabled people in the United Kingdom (*www.disability.gov.uk*).

In England, disabled children are a priority area in the Government's 'Quality Protects' programme to transform children's social services. Some £60 million has been earmarked for services for disabled children and their families between 2001/02 and 2003/04.

A Green Paper, *Pathways to Work*, was published in November 2002. It outlined a series of proposals to help people with an illness or disability to find work. Key proposals include:
- early support from personal advisers, including work-focused interviews and action plans;
- specialist programmes, including new rehabilitation services provided jointly by Jobcentre Plus and the NHS; and
- greater financial incentives to work, including a *Return to Work Credit* of £40 a week for 52 weeks for those finding a job that pays less than £15,000 per year.

In May 2003 the Government, in association with the charities Scope and the Royal National Institute for Deaf People (RNID), published three linked guidance documents for professionals who work with very young disabled children. The guidelines aim to create stronger partnerships between parents and service providers in the areas of education, health and social services, and ensure that children receive effective support.

A range of concessions on public transport are available for people with disabilities (see page 313).

Care services for people with physical disabilities

Local authority social services departments and HSS Trusts in Northern Ireland help with social rehabilitation and adjustment to disability. They are required to identify the number of disabled people in their area and to provide and publicise services. These may include advice on personal and social problems arising from disability, as well as occupational, educational, social and recreational facilities, either at day centres or elsewhere.

Other services provided may include minor adaptations to homes such as ramps for wheelchairs, or bath rails (with housing authorities providing assistance for major adaptations such as stairlifts and ground-floor toilets), the delivery of cooked meals, support with personal care at home and direct payments with which disabled people can purchase support to meet their assessed need. Local authorities and voluntary organisations may provide severely disabled people with residential accommodation, either on a permanent basis or temporarily in order to relieve their existing carers. Special housing may be available for those able to look after themselves.

Services for people with learning disabilities

The Government's policies for improving services for people with learning disabilities, their families and carers in England are set out in *Valuing People: A New Strategy for Learning Disability for the 21st Century*, published in 2001. Learning Disability Partnership Boards have been set up in local council areas in England to take forward the Valuing People programme at local level. A team of regionally based workers was set up in 2002 to provide support to Partnership Boards and share good practice.

Social services departments and HSS Trusts in Northern Ireland can provide or arrange short-term care, support for families in their own

Main benefits available to sick and disabled people (at April 2003)

Employers are responsible for paying *Statutory Sick Pay* to employees up to a maximum of 28 weeks. There is a single rate (£64.35 a week) for all qualifying employees, provided their average gross weekly earnings are at least £77.

Incapacity Benefit is paid to people of working age who become sick or disabled and stop working or looking for work as a result. Entitlement begins when entitlement to Statutory Sick Pay ends or, for those who do not qualify for Statutory Sick Pay, from the fourth day of sickness. Payments, which depend on age and the length of illness, range from £54.40 to £72.15 a week.

Severe Disablement Allowance is a tax-free benefit for people who have not been able to work for at least 28 weeks because of illness or disability but who cannot get Incapacity Benefit because they have not paid enough NICs. The benefit is £43.60 a week, plus additions of up to £15.15 depending on the person's age when he or she became incapable of work. Additions for adult dependants and for children may also be paid. In April 2001 this Allowance was abolished for new claims. From that date, people aged 16 to 20, or 16 to 25 if they were in education or training at least three months immediately before age 20, can instead claim Incapacity Benefit without having to satisfy the contribution conditions.

Disability Living Allowance is a non-contributory tax-free benefit to help severely disabled people aged under 65 with extra costs incurred as a result of disability. Entitlement is measured in terms of personal care and/or mobility needs. There are two components: a care component which has three weekly rates – £56.25, £37.65 and £14.90 – and a mobility component with two weekly rates, of £39.30 and £14.90. It is payable to those aged three or over who have severe difficulty walking, or aged five or over who need help getting around.

Attendance Allowance (AA) is paid to people who need help to look after themselves. It is paid if a person becomes ill or disabled on or after his or her 65th birthday and needs help for at least six months. There are different rates depending on whether the claimant needs care during the day, during the night, or both, and on the extent of the disability. However, AA is not affected by savings or income under normal circumstances. AA ranges from £37.65 to £56.25 a week depending on circumstances.

Industrial Injuries Disablement Benefit is a benefit for people who have been disabled by an accident at work or through a prescribed disease caused by a particular type of employment. The rate is between £14.07 and £114.80 a week depending on the level of disablement and age.

People with disabilities may also be eligible for Working Tax Credit (WTC) (which replaced Disabled Person's Tax Credit in April 2003) (see page 145) and cold weather payments (see page 149). People injured as part of activity in the armed forces may be entitled to War Disablement Pension (see page 159).

---

homes, residential accommodation and support for various types of activity outside the home. People with learning disabilities may also be able to receive direct payments from local authorities to let them buy for themselves the support that will meet their assessed needs. The aim is to ensure that, as far as possible, people with learning disabilities can lead full lives in the community. The NHS provides specialist services when the ordinary primary care services cannot meet healthcare needs.

People with a mental health problem

Government policy aims to ensure that people with mental health problems should have access to all the services they need as locally as possible. Under the Care Programme Approach in England, each service user should receive an assessment leading to the formulation of an agreed care plan.

A care coordinator is appointed to keep in contact with the service user, and review his or her care plan regularly in the light of the individual's changing needs. The separate Welsh Mental Health Strategy employs many of the same principles in delivering services in Wales.

In Scotland, each NHS board works with its local authority care partners, with users of mental health services and with their carers in order to develop joint strategies and provide local and comprehensive mental health services. These plans are expected to conform with the Framework for Mental Health Services and to comply with standards set by the Clinical Standards Board for Scotland. Northern Ireland has an integrated health and social services structure allowing a multi-disciplinary approach to care management.

Arrangements made by social services authorities for providing care in the community include direct payments, home help, day centres, social centres and residential care. Social workers are increasingly being integrated with mental health staff in community mental health teams under single management. These teams include assertive outreach, crisis resolution, home treatment and early intervention teams. Assertive outreach is a way of managing the care of severely mentally ill people in the community by visiting service users at home and liaising with other services such as the GP or social services. Help is usually provided to find housing, secure an adequate income, and sustain basic daily living – shopping, cooking and washing. Social workers help patients and their families with problems caused by mental illness. In certain circumstances they can apply for a person with a mental disorder to be compulsorily admitted to and detained in hospital. There are safeguards for patients to ensure that the law is used appropriately.

Unemployed people

Jobseeker's Allowance (JSA) is a benefit for unemployed people seeking work. Claimants must be capable of, available for, and actively seeking work. They must normally be at least 18 years of age and under pension age. JSA can be either contribution-based or income-based:

- *Contribution-based JSA* is available to those who have paid enough NICs. They are entitled to a personal JSA for up to six months (£53.95 a week for a person aged 25 or over), regardless of any savings or partner's income.
- *Income-based JSA*: those on a low income are entitled to an income-based JSA, payable for as long as the jobseeker requires support and continues to satisfy the qualifying conditions. The amount a claimant receives comprises an age-related personal allowance (£53.95 a week for a single person aged 25 or over), plus other allowances. Some allowances are determined by circumstances on a basis similar to Income Support (see page 145).

Recipients of JSA and people aged under 60 who receive Income Support can benefit from a *Back to Work Bonus*. The aim of this scheme is to encourage people to keep in touch with the labour market by undertaking small amounts of work while claiming benefit. It allows people to accrue a tax-free lump sum of between £5 and £1,000 if

working part-time while in receipt of Income Support or JSA. There are a number of other financial benefits for unemployed people to help them back into employment, including various *New Deals* (see chapter 11).

People on low incomes

People on low incomes can claim *Income Support* (see page 145) or, for those over 60, Pension Credit (which replaced Minimum Income Guarantee in October 2003). In 2001/02 there were nearly 4 million people receiving Income Support in Great Britain. Other benefits for which unemployed people and those on low incomes may be eligible include exemption from NHS charges, vouchers towards the cost of spectacles, publicly funded legal help and free school meals for their children. People on low incomes, pensioners, widows, widowers and long-term sick people on Incapacity Benefit may be eligible for extra help to meet the cost of VAT (value added tax) on their fuel bills.

Housing Benefit is an income-related, tax-free benefit which helps people on low incomes meet the cost of rented accommodation. The amount paid depends on personal circumstances, income, savings, rent and whether other people are sharing the home. It also normally depends on the general level of rents for properties with the same number of rooms in the locality. Most single people under 25 years old who are not lone parents and who are renting privately have their Housing Benefit limited to the average cost of a single non-self-contained room (that is, with shared use of kitchen and toilet facilities) in the locality.

Council Tax Benefit helps people to meet their council tax payments (the tax set by local councils to help pay for services, see page 364). The scheme offers help to those claiming Income Support and income-based JSA and others with low incomes. In Northern Ireland, where council tax was not introduced, Housing Benefit helps with the cost of rent and/or rates.

The *Social Fund* provides payments, in the form of loans or grants, to people on low incomes to help with expenses which are difficult to meet out of regular income. These payments can be:

- *budgeting loans* for intermittent expenses;
- *community care grants* to help, for example, people resettle into the community from care, or to remain in the community, to ease

exceptional pressure on families, to set up home as part of a planned resettlement programme or to meet certain travel expenses; and
- *crisis loans* to help people in an emergency or as a result of a disaster where there is serious risk to health or safety.

Budgeting loans and community care grants are available only to people who are receiving social security benefits and some tax credits.

Widows and widowers

Bereavement Payment is a one-off payment to widows under the age of 60, and widowers under the age of 65 – or those over 60/65 whose spouses were not entitled to a basic State Retirement Pension when they died. It is payable provided their spouses paid a minimum number of NICs.

Widowed Parent's Allowance is a regular payment for widows or widowers bringing up children. It is based on the late spouse's NICs and continues while the children are still dependent. *Bereavement Allowance* is a regular payment, also based on the late spouse's NICs, which is payable for 52 weeks to widows and widowers aged 45 and over who are not bringing up children.

A number of charities and voluntary organisations advise and support people who have been bereaved. In 2001 a consortium of some of the leading bodies published a set of national standards for bereavement care (*www.bereavement.org.uk/standards/index.asp*).

War pensioners

In April 2002 the War Pensions Agency was renamed the Veterans Agency (VA). It is part of the Ministry of Defence (MoD) and provides advice and help with new and ongoing claims for war disablement pensions and war widows'/widowers' pensions. In addition, the Agency is the single point of contact within the MoD for providing information and advice on issues of concern to veterans and their families.

The War Pensioners' Welfare Service (WPWS), through working closely with ex-Service organisations and other statutory and voluntary organisations, provides a comprehensive advice and support service for all war pensioners and war widows/widowers living in the United Kingdom and the Republic of Ireland.

There are approximately 260,000 beneficiaries of *War Disablement* and *Widows' Pensions*, of whom 22,000 live outside the United Kingdom. The majority are Second World War veterans, but there are also small numbers of First World War veterans, ex-National Servicemen and those disabled in recent conflicts, such as Northern Ireland, the Falklands, Bosnia and the Gulf War. War Disablement Pension is payable to ex-members of the armed forces as a result of disability due to Service. It can also be claimed by, among others, civilians, merchant seamen and members of the Polish forces under British command, although special conditions apply in these cases. War Widows'/Widowers' Pension is payable to widows/widowers of ex-members of the armed forces where death is due to or hastened by Service.

Asylum seekers

Asylum seekers receive limited cash benefits and may qualify for other services (see page 94).

Arrangements with other countries

As part of the European Union's efforts to promote the free movement of labour, regulations provide for equality of treatment and the protection of benefit rights for people who move between Member States. The regulations also cover retired pensioners and other beneficiaries who have been employed, or self-employed, as well as dependants. Benefits covered include Child Benefit and those for sickness, maternity, unemployment, retirement, invalidity, accidents at work and occupational diseases.

The United Kingdom has reciprocal social security agreements with a number of other countries which also provide cover for some national insurance benefits and family benefits.

Further reading
Department for Work and Pensions Departmental Report: The Government's Expenditure Plans 2003–04 to 2005–06. Cm 5921. The Stationery Office, 2003.

Department of Health Departmental Report 2003. The Government's Expenditure Plans. Cm 5904. The Stationery Office, 2003.

Websites

Child Support Agency
www.csa.gov.uk

Citizens Advice
www.adviceguide.org.uk

Department for Social Development, Northern Ireland
www.dsdni.gov.uk

Department for Work and Pensions
www.dwp.gov.uk

Department for Work and Pensions disability website
www.disability.gov.uk

Department of Health
www.doh.gov.uk

Department of Health, Social Services and Public Safety (Northern Ireland)
www.dhsspsni.gov.uk

Inland Revenue
www.inlandrevenue.gov.uk

National Assembly for Wales
www.wales.gov.uk

National Care Standards Commission
www.carestandards.org.uk

Occupational Pensions Regulatory Authority
www.opra.gov.uk

Pension Guide
www.pensionguide.gov.uk

Pensions Ombudsman
www.pensions-ombudsman.org.uk

Pension Service
www.thepensionservice.gov.uk

Scottish Commission for the Regulation of Care
www.carecommission.com

Scottish Executive
www.scotland.gov.uk

Social Security Agency (Northern Ireland)
www.ssani.gov.uk

Veterans Agency
www.veteransagency.mod.uk

www.

13 Health

The state of public health

The 2001 Census included a new question on general health: 69 per cent of the UK population reported 'good health', 22 per cent 'fairly good' health, while the remaining 9 per cent reported that their health was 'not good'.

Life expectancy

Over the past century major social and economic trends such as improvements in nutrition and housing, advances in medicine and technology, and the development of health services that are freely available to all, have led to significant improvements in the nation's health. The substantial increase in life expectancy provides one of the best indicators of this. In 1901 boys born in the United Kingdom could expect to live to around 45 years of age and girls to around 49. By 2001 life expectancy at birth had increased to over 75 and 80 years respectively (see Figure 13.1). Within the United Kingdom, in the period 1999 to 2001, life expectancy at birth was highest in England at 76 years for males and 80 years for females, and lowest in Scotland at 73 for males and 79 for females.

Declines in infant mortality have contributed greatly to these improvements. In 1921, 84.0 children per 1,000 live births in the United Kingdom died before the age of one; by 2001 the rate was 5.5. Within the United Kingdom in 2001, England had the lowest infant mortality rate at 5.4 infants per 1,000 live births and Northern Ireland the highest at 6.1.

Cancer

About a third of people in the United Kingdom will be diagnosed with cancer during their lifetime and about a quarter will die from the disease. As average life expectancy has risen, the population at risk of cancer has grown, with two-thirds of cases

Figure 13.1 Life expectancy[1] at birth, UK

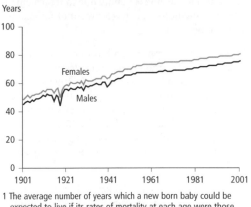

Years

1 The average number of years which a new born baby could be expected to live if its rates of mortality at each age were those experienced in the year of its birth.
Source: Government Actuary's Department

occurring in those aged over 65. There are over 200 different types of cancer but the four major types – breast, lung, colorectal and prostate – account for over half of all cases diagnosed.

Cancers are now the most common cause of death among females aged 15 to 74 years, and the second most common in males in this age group, after circulatory disease. Age-standardised[1] death rates (for those aged 15 to 74 years) from cancer among males in the United Kingdom peaked at around 2,700 per million in the late 1960s. By 2001 the rate had fallen to just under 1,900 per million. For females, cancer death rates peaked much earlier at a rate of 2,100 per million in 1926. By 2001 the rate had fallen to its lowest recorded level of 1,500 per million.

---

1 Age-standardised death rates enable comparisons to be made over time (and between males and females), which are independent of changes in the age structure of the population.

While lung cancer remains the most common cause of cancer death among males, since the mid-1970s it has shown by far the greatest decline in death rates from any form of cancer, falling from a peak of 110 per 100,000 in 1974 to 59 per 100,000 in 2001. This reduction is closely linked to the decline in male smokers (see page 164). In contrast, the lung cancer death rate among females has risen since the 1970s, but in 2001 was still just half that of males.

Breast cancer is the most common cause of cancer death among all females. The death rate from this form of cancer rose from 38 per 100,000 in 1971 to 42 per 100,000 in 1986. Since 1990 the rate has steadily declined and in 2001 it was 31 per 100,000. The decline is mainly due to treatment advances including the development of tamoxifan and chemotherapy.

Prostate cancer is the second most common cause of cancer death among males: the death rate peaked at around 30 per 100,000 in 1992 and then declined to around 27 deaths per 100,000 between 1997 and 2001. In the ten years to 2001 death rates from colorectal cancer declined by 20 per cent among males and 29 per cent among females. This is the third most common cause of cancer death for both sexes.

Cancer patient survival is a key indicator of the effectiveness of cancer control in the population. Effective treatments for some cancers, such as chemotherapy for childhood leukaemia, have led to dramatically improved survival during the last 20 years. There is, however, considerable variation in the survival rates from the most common forms of cancer in the United Kingdom.

Survival rates from lung cancer are low compared with the other most common cancers. For patients diagnosed with lung cancer in England during 1993 to 1995, the one-year survival rate (the proportion of patients surviving at least one year) was 21 per cent. The five-year survival rate based on the same period of diagnosis was 6 per cent. In contrast, the five-year survival rate for colon cancer was 44 per cent in males and 43 per cent in females. Survival rates for cancer where screening is available were even higher. The five-year survival rate for prostate cancer was 60 per cent, and 76 per cent for breast cancer in females.

Circulatory disease
The United Kingdom has one of the highest premature death rates from circulatory disease

Figure 13.2 Mortality[1] from circulatory diseases, UK[2]

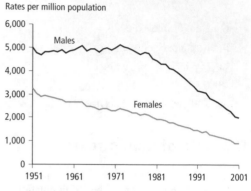

Rates per million population

1 People aged 15 to 74. Data have been age standardised using the European standard population.
2 Data for UK except 2000, which are for England and Wales only.
Source: Office for National Statistics

(which includes heart disease and strokes) in Europe. A number of risk factors have been identified, including drinking alcohol, smoking, obesity and lack of regular exercise.

The female age-standardised death rate (for those aged 15 to 74 years) from circulatory disease has declined consistently from the early 1950s (see Figure 13.2). Among males, the rate only began to decline in the early 1970s but has since fallen by 61 per cent, from 5,100 per million in 1972 to 2,000 per million in 2001.

Asthma
Asthma is a disease of the lungs in which the airways are unusually sensitive to a wide range of

Table 13.3 New cases[1] of asthma, 1996 and 2001, England and Wales

Rates per 100,000 population

	Males	Females
Aged 1–4		
1996	152	112
2001	75	56
All ages		
1996	41	46
2001	26	29

1 Mean weekly incidence. A diagnosis for the first time or a previously diagnosed asthmatic person having a new attack.
Source: The Royal College of General Practitioners

stimuli, including inhaled irritants and allergens. In England and Wales in 2001, incidence rates of new diagnoses of asthma were higher in males than females up to the age of 14 and then higher in females in all age groups from 15 to 74 years. In recent years there has been a decline in the number of new cases diagnosed in both sexes, especially in the 1–4 age group, when new cases are most likely to occur (see Table 13.3).

Diabetes

In 1998 there were an estimated 1.2 million people in England and Wales with a diagnosis of diabetes. If not properly managed, it can result in a range of long-term complications, such as heart disease, stroke, kidney disease, blindness and foot problems that can lead to amputation.

Between 1994 and 1998, the overall age-standardised prevalence of diagnosed diabetes in England and Wales increased by 18 per cent among males, from 18.9 to 22.3 per 1,000, and by 20 per cent among females, from 13.7 to 16.4 per 1,000. Diabetes is more common among older people. The age-specific rates in 1998 in England and Wales peaked in the 75 to 84 year age group at 87 per 1,000 males and 66 per 1,000 females.

A National Service Framework for diabetes was introduced in January 2003 (see box on page 183). The Scottish Diabetes Framework was published in April 2002 (see page 183).

Infectious diseases

Although diseases such as measles, tuberculosis (TB) and whooping cough became far less common during the last century, their occurrence still fluctuates. Figure 13.4 shows an epidemic of measles in 1994 before it resumed its underlying trend in 1995. The incidence of TB increased by nearly a fifth between 1991 and 2002 and is now more common than either measles or whooping cough. The rise has been particularly noticeable in London, where nearly 40 per cent of cases now occur.

Immunisation

Current government targets are for 95 per cent of children to be immunised by the age of two against diphtheria, tetanus, polio, whooping cough, Haemophilus influenzae b (Hib), meningitis C and measles, mumps and rubella. In the light of public concerns about the safety of the combined measles, mumps and rubella (MMR) vaccine, coverage against these diseases in 2001/02 fell to 85 per cent, the lowest level since 1990.

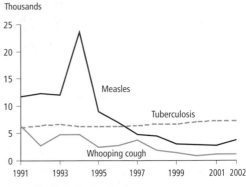

Figure 13.4 Notifications of selected infectious diseases, UK

Thousands

Source: Health Protection Agency

In 1999 the United Kingdom was the first country in the world to introduce immunisation against Group C meningococcal disease, which had been progressively rising throughout the 1990s. Between 1998 and 2001 there was a decline of over 90 per cent in the number of cases and deaths.

Flu vaccination

A national flu vaccination campaign ran in England from October to December 2002. The campaign was aimed at older people, who are the most vulnerable to the disease, and included television and press advertising. During winter 2002–03, 5.5 million people aged 65 and over were immunised. This was over 350,000 more than in the previous year and represented an uptake of 69 per cent. The Government's target was 70 per cent.

Sexually transmitted diseases

The prevalence of sexually transmitted diseases has been increasing in recent years, especially among young people. In 2002 genital chlamydia was the most common sexually transmitted infection diagnosed in genito-urinary medicine clinics in England, Wales and Northern Ireland, with almost 85,700 cases. This was 14 per cent more than in 2001 and was more than double the 34,200 cases diagnosed in 1996.

The number of Human Immunodeficiency Virus (HIV) diagnoses in the United Kingdom since 1996 has also risen each year. The Communicable Disease Surveillance Centre (CDSC) reported that

55,550 cases had been diagnosed by March 2003. Of the 5,340 people diagnosed during 2002, over half contracted the virus through heterosexual sex, which was nearly double the proportion ten years earlier. Almost 80 per cent of these heterosexually acquired infections were estimated to have occurred abroad, with over 2,000 attributed to infection in Africa.

Mental health

In 2002/03 there were around 2 million attendances at National Health Service (NHS) outpatient facilities for psychiatric specialities in England, 276,000 of which were new attendances. A total of 49 million items of mental health drugs were dispensed in the community during 2002, with a net ingredient cost of £584 million. The number of prescription items for anti-depressant drugs more than doubled in the ten years to 2002, from 10 million to 26 million.

A survey carried out by the ONS in 2000 found that one in six people aged 16 to 74 living in private households in Great Britain had a neurotic disorder, such as depression, anxiety or a phobia. Nineteen per cent of women were affected, compared with 14 per cent of men. While a third of all those responding to the survey were unemployed or economically inactive, nearly three-quarters of those reporting a neurotic disorder were in these groups.

Substance misuse

Alcohol

The consumption of alcohol in excessive amounts can lead to an increased likelihood of problems such as high blood pressure, cancer and cirrhosis of the liver. The current Department of Health advice is that consumption of between three and four units[2] a day for men and two to three units a day for women should not lead to significant health risks. In 2001/02, 39 per cent of men and 22 per cent of women in Great Britain exceeded the recommended amount of alcohol on their heaviest drinking day in the week prior to being interviewed.

The annual number of alcohol-related deaths in England and Wales has been rising for many years.

Between 1979 and 2000 the number more than doubled, from 2,506 to 5,543. Of the deaths in 2000, 85 per cent were due to chronic liver disease and cirrhosis, with the remaining 15 per cent due to other alcohol-related causes. In 2000 the age-standardised rate for alcohol-related deaths among men was 13 per 100,000 population, almost twice the rate among women (7 per 100,000). Services to combat alcohol misuse are described on page 181.

Smoking

More cancer deaths in the United Kingdom can be attributed to smoking tobacco than to any other single risk factor. In 1974, 51 per cent of men and 41 per cent of women in Great Britain reported that they were regular cigarette smokers. By 2001/02 these proportions had fallen to 28 per cent of men and 26 per cent of women. Measures to encourage a further reduction are described on page 182.

The prevalence of cigarette smoking varies markedly by socio-economic group. In 2001/02, while only 21 per cent of men and 18 per cent of women in the managerial and professional group smoked, 35 per cent and 31 per cent respectively did so among the routine and manual group.

Drugs

Results from the 2001/02 British Crime Survey indicate that 15 per cent of men and 9 per cent of women aged 16 to 59 in England and Wales had taken an illicit drug in the previous year. Young people are more likely than older people to use drugs. The most commonly used drug in 2001/02 among those aged 16 to 24 was cannabis (see Table 13.5). Ecstasy was the most commonly used Class A drug (see glossary). Since 1996 there has been an increase in the use of cocaine among young people, especially among young men. In contrast the use of amphetamines has declined.

In 2001 there were almost 2,900 deaths due to drug-related poisoning in England and Wales, a slight fall from 2000. Heroin and/or morphine were involved in 889 of these deaths; more than any other drug. The number of deaths involving cocaine and ecstasy both increased to their highest recorded levels. In contrast, deaths from paracetamol overdose fell to their lowest recorded level. This decrease may be due to legislation in 1998, which limited the maximum amount of paracetamol allowed in a pack. Other measures to

---

2 A unit of alcohol is 8 grams by weight or 10 millilitres (ml) by volume of pure alcohol. This is the amount contained in half a pint of ordinary strength beer or lager, a single measure of pub spirits (25 ml), one glass of ordinary wine or a small pub measure of sherry or other fortified wine.

Table 13.5 Prevalence of drug misuse by young adults,[1] 2001/02, England and Wales

	Percentages	
	Males	Females
Cannabis	33	21
Amphetamines	7	3
Ecstasy	9	4
Magic mushrooms and LSD	3	1
Cocaine	7	2
All Class A drugs	12	5
Any drug	35	24

1 Those who had used drugs in the previous year as a percentage of the total population of 16- to 24- year-olds.
Source: British Crime Survey, Home Office

prevent the misuse of drugs are described on page 182.

Diet and nutrition

There have been marked changes in the British diet since the early 1970s. One aspect has been a long-term rise in the consumption of poultry, while that of red meat (such as beef) has fallen. In addition, the use of convenience food – both frozen and ready meals, and snacks – has increased.

Between 1993 and 2001 the proportion of men aged 16 and over in England who were classified as obese rose from 13 to 21 per cent. Among women the proportion rose from 16 to 23 per cent.

The Department of Health recommends that a healthy diet should include at least five portions of fresh fruit or vegetables (excluding potatoes) a day (see box). In 2001 the National Diet and Nutrition Survey found that only 13 per cent of men and 15 per cent of women in Great Britain were eating according to these guidelines. Average daily consumption among people aged 19 to 64 years was below 3 portions for both men and women.

In February 2003, *Food and Well Being, the Nutrition Action Plan for Wales* was launched. The plan focuses on eradicating food poverty by improving access to healthy and affordable food. The plan is being implemented by the Food Standards Agency Wales in partnership with the Welsh Assembly Government.

The National Health Service

The National Health Service (NHS) was created in 1948 to provide healthcare for the UK resident

Five a day logo introduced

To promote consumer awareness of the health benefits of eating fruit and vegetables, a '5 a day' logo was introduced by the Department of Health in March 2003. The logo appears in supermarkets and on food packaging and is used on fresh, chilled, frozen, canned and dried fruit and vegetables that do not have any added sugar, salt or fat. To guide consumers, a portion indicator appears on products stating how many portions of fruit and vegetables are in a typical serving.

population, based on need, not the ability to pay. It is made up of a wide range of health professionals, support workers and organisations. The service is funded by the taxpayer and is accountable to Parliament. All taxpayers, employers and employees contribute to the cost, so that members of the community who do not require healthcare help to pay for those who do. Most forms of treatment are provided free, but others such as prescription drugs, eye tests and dentistry may incur a charge.

In England the NHS is managed by the Department of Health, which is responsible for developing and implementing policies and for the regulation and inspection of health services. The devolved administrations have similar responsibilities in other parts of the United Kingdom.

NHS Direct

NHS Direct, a nurse-led telephone helpline, was launched in England in 1998. It aims to provide fast and convenient access to health information and advice, helping people to care for themselves and their families, and directing them to the most appropriate level of care when they need professional help. During 2001/02 NHS Direct handled around 5 million calls. Wales has a similar service, NHS Direct Wales, which offers advice in both English and Welsh. In Scotland, NHS 24 was launched in 2002.

NHS Direct Online (*www.nhsdirect.nhs.uk*), an Internet extension of the telephone-based services, receives around 230,000 visitors a month. The website features an electronic version of the NHS Direct self-help guide, an encyclopedia of over 450 health topics and an interactive enquiry service for health information.

Health Action Zones

Health Action Zones (HAZs) were originally established in deprived areas of England, but have since been extended to other parts of the country. There are 26 HAZs; each is a partnership between the health service, local councils, voluntary groups and local businesses. Participants co-operate to tackle inequalities and deliver better services and healthcare, focusing on areas such as programmes to stop smoking, mental health, coronary heart disease and cancer, and the health of ethnic minorities. Responsibility for the further development of HAZ initiatives has been devolved to Primary Care Trusts (PCTs, see page 167).

Four HAZs have been established in Northern Ireland and an initiative to encourage local healthcare partnerships has been launched in Scotland.

Electronic initiatives

The NHS is making increasing use of new technology in patient care and is undertaking a major information technology (IT) development programme. This is focusing on improving the IT infrastructure and developing electronic national services for prescriptions, patient records and booking appointments.

NHSnet is a range of voice and data services used by the NHS, covering radio, telephone and computer-based communications. In 2002/03, £45 million was invested to upgrade NHSnet and provide broadband Internet access to general practitioners (GPs) and hospitals. By April 2004 all clinicians and support staff should have broadband Internet access. A national NHS directory service will also be available with access to all staff.

In the longer term, it is intended that NHSnet will support electronic booking systems and replace paper-based health records with electronic versions. By the end of 2006 the Government intends that every patient in England will be able to access his or her own electronic record, containing a summary of key personal and health data. NHSnet will also give doctors secure access to patients' records in an emergency when they are away from home. An equivalent scheme, HPSSnet, has been set up by Northern Ireland Health and Personal Social Services (HPSS).

NHS Plus

NHS Plus was established in 2001 as a national network providing occupational health services to the private sector in England, in particular focusing on small and medium-size businesses. Services provided by NHS Plus include workplace risk assessment, health surveillance, medical advice on sickness absence and retirement, stress counselling and drug and alcohol screening. Over 50 per cent of NHS Trusts had signed up to provide this service by August 2003, and NHS Plus turnover grew by around 17 per cent in each of the preceding two financial years.

The NHS in England

In March 2003 the Government published the Health and Social Care (Community Health and Standards) Bill. This sets out government proposals for the next stage in its programme of NHS reform and investment. The key aims of the Bill are to:

- decentralise control of the NHS and establish NHS Foundation Trusts (see page 168), which would assume direct control of local hospitals from the Secretary of State for Health;
- increase the involvement of local communities in the running of NHS Trusts by allowing NHS hospital boards of governors to be elected from and by local communities rather than appointed by central government; and
- ensure greater accountability for spending on health and social care through the establishment of two new commissions – the Commission for Healthcare Audit and Inspection and the Commission for Social Care Inspection (see page 146).

The Government's key objectives and targets against which progress will be measured are set out in the 2003–06 priorities and planning framework – *Improvement, expansion and reform: the next three years*. The framework aims to encourage planning at a local level and more diversity in service provision.

From 2003 PCTs and relevant Care Trusts (see page 167) will be responsible for creating local plans which address the needs of their communities and incorporate the national priorities. These plans will be brought together by Strategic Health Authorities (see page 167) into a Local Delivery Plan for their area. As part of this process local health services now receive three-year budgets, instead of annual allocations.

Among the targets for service standards set in the framework are:

- guaranteed access to a primary care professional within 24 hours and to a primary care doctor within 48 hours, from 2004;
- maximum waiting time in hospital accident and emergency departments to be reduced to four hours from arrival to admission, transfer or discharge, by the end of 2004; and
- the maximum wait for an outpatient appointment to be reduced to three months and the maximum wait for inpatient treatment to six months, by the end of 2005.

Strategic Health Authorities

A new structure for health administration came into effect in England in 2002 (see Figure 13.6). The *NHS Reform and Health Care Professions Act 2002* provided for 28 Strategic Health Authorities (SHAs), with typical populations of between 1.5 and 2.4 million. They are responsible for creating, in consultation with stakeholders, a framework for local health services, and for building capacity, supporting performance improvement and managing the performance of PCTs and of NHS Trusts in their areas.

Figure 13.6 NHS structure in England

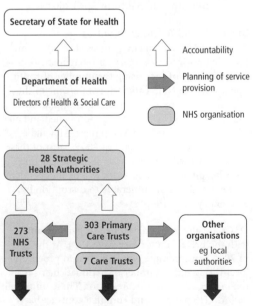

Provision of all health and care services to the local population

Source: Department of Health

Primary Care Trusts

Responsibility for deciding which health services the local population needs and for ensuring the provision of these services lies with the 303 local PCTs across England. PCTs are groups of between 50 and 100 GP practices and healthcare professionals.

Appropriate provision of all other services, including hospitals, dentists, mental health services, Walk-in Centres, NHS Direct (see page 165), patient transport (including accident and emergency), population screening, pharmacies and opticians, is also the responsibility of PCTs, together with developing health improvement programmes and seeing that local NHS organisations work effectively with local authorities and social services. By 2004, 75 per cent of NHS spending will be directly controlled by doctors and nurses in the local PCTs.

Care Trusts

Care Trusts are NHS bodies that work in both health and social care and can be established where NHS organisations and local authorities agree to work together. A Care Trust is usually set up where it is felt that closer integration between health and social care is needed or would be beneficial at a local level. Seven Care Trusts had been established by August 2003.

NHS Trusts

NHS Trusts are the organisations responsible for running most NHS hospitals. Although the statutory functions of the Trusts were not changed following the NHS reorganisation, they are now overseen by the SHAs.

Walk-in Centres

NHS Walk-in Centres are a network of nurse-led centres where no appointment is necessary. They offer quick access to a range of services, including healthcare advice and information, and treatment for minor ailments and injuries. They are intended to complement GP surgeries and help reduce pressure on GPs. By the end of 2002, 42 NHS Walk-in Centres had opened in England.

Health education

Established as a special health authority in 2000, the Health Development Agency works to improve the health of people and communities in England, and in particular to reduce health inequalities. In partnership with others, it gathers evidence of best

In a typical week in England:

- more than 800,000 people are treated in NHS hospital outpatient clinics;
- 600,000 visit an NHS dentist for a check-up;
- over 10,000 babies are delivered by the NHS;
- NHS ambulances make over 60,000 emergency journeys;
- pharmacists dispense approximately 12 million items in the community on NHS prescriptions; and
- NHS surgeons perform around 1,400 hip operations, 1,050 heart operations and 1,500 hernia operations.

practice, advises on standards and develops the skills of all those working to improve health.

Since April 2002 the Department of Health has been responsible for the development and delivery of public health campaigns, including those on childhood immunisation, drugs, alcohol and sexual health. Events promoted during 2003 included:

- No Smoking Day (12 March);
- Parkinson's Awareness Week (4–13 April);
- National Men's Health Week (9–15 June) (see page 178);
- Sexual Health Week (4–10 August); and
- Breast Cancer Awareness Month (October).

Commission for Patient and Public Involvement in Health

The Commission for Patient and Public Involvement in Health (CPPIH) was established in January 2003. The Commission is a national body responsible for promoting public involvement in the decision making process for local NHS services. It will provide a structure for this by setting up a Patient and Public Involvement (PPI) Forum in each Primary Care and NHS Trust in England. The first PPI forums will come into existence in December 2003 following the abolition of Community Health Councils, which had previously represented NHS patients. The PPI forums will comprise 15 to 20 lay members supported by staff appointed by the Commission from not-for-profit organisations with knowledge of the local community.

NHS Foundation Trusts

The Health and Social Care (Community Health and Standards) Bill (see page 166) includes proposals for the creation of NHS Foundation Trusts. If the proposals are enacted, these trusts would be established as Public Benefit Corporations, and would have direct control and ownership of local hospitals. They would operate on a not-for-profit basis and earn money through agreements with PCTs to provide care and treatment according to a national tariff. Contracts between PCTs and NHS Foundation Trusts would set out the expected level of activity and the associated cost.

The NHS Foundation Trusts would be free to borrow money for investment from the public and private sectors and to retain operating surpluses to invest in new services. They would also be able to recruit and employ their own staff and offer extra rewards for improvements in productivity. The trusts would operate under terms of authorisation issued by an independent regulator and be monitored by the Commission for Healthcare Audit and Inspection (CHAI) (see page 184), who would be charged with ensuring that they maintain NHS standards and values.

Hospitals attaining a three-star rating in the Department of Health's annual performance tables would be able to apply for foundation trust status. Suitability to become an NHS Foundation Trust would also depend on an evaluation of financial performance and management. Subject to legislation, the first NHS Foundation Trusts will become fully operational from April 2004.

Diagnosis and Treatment Centres

Diagnosis and Treatment Centres (DTCs) – which provide pre-booked surgery and diagnostic tests – are a new way of increasing the number of routine operations the NHS can perform in some of the specialities where waiting times are longest. By May 2003, 15 NHS-run DTCs had opened and a further 31 were under development. All will be fully operational by the end of 2005. Most of these units are, or will be, on the same site as existing NHS hospitals, but their work will be independent of them and so not vulnerable to disruption by emergency pressures.

DTCs are also being developed in partnership with the private sector (see page 187). At the end of 2002 a programme was launched to procure 11 local DTCs and a number of national chains from the independent healthcare sector. These units will be for NHS patients and run on a contract basis with local PCTs. The new independent healthcare sector DTCs are expected to begin operating during 2004.

NHS Choice

In 2002, two pilot schemes were launched offering patients who had waited more than six months for an operation the opportunity to have it performed earlier at a different hospital. The Heart Choice project was launched nationally in July and the London Patient Choice Project, which offers operations to cataract patients, in October. By February 2003 nearly half of qualifying heart patients had opted for earlier treatment elsewhere as had 70 per cent of cataract patients under the London Patient Choice Project. By July 2003 the choice scheme had been extended to cover a wider range of treatments for patients in the south of England, Trent, Greater Manchester and West Yorkshire. It is intended that by summer 2004 all patients who have been waiting six months for any form of elective surgery should be able to choose at least one alternative public or private hospital for treatment.

The NHS in Wales

In Wales, the operation of the NHS is the responsibility of the Welsh Assembly Government, whose ten-year health programme – *Improving Health in Wales – A Plan for the NHS with its Partners* – was published in 2001. Effective partnership working is an important theme of the Welsh Plan.

At a national level, a Health and Well-being Partnership Council was established, chaired by the Health and Social Services Minister. The council brings together key personnel from the NHS, local government, the voluntary and independent sectors, staff and professional groups, and patients' representatives in order to ensure the direction and leadership of the agenda for health and well-being. The council is supported by a network of similar partnerships at a local level.

The Assembly Government has the power to make changes to the structure of the NHS in Wales through secondary or 'delegated' legislation and specific Welsh clauses were introduced in the *NHS Reform and Health Care Professions Act 2002*. The Act provided for the creation of 22 Local Health Boards (LHBs), which replaced the existing five Health Authorities in Wales on 1 April 2003. The LHBs report to three new regional offices within the NHS Wales Department of the National Assembly. The new structure resulted in changes at two levels:

- at a local level, health groups were developed into the new LHBs and their role

strengthened. They also took on new responsibilities for commissioning and delivering healthcare in their localities; and
- at a national level, both LHBs and NHS Trusts became fully accountable to the Assembly Government for the services they provide and commission.

The Act also placed a duty on each LHB and local authority in Wales to formulate and implement a 'health and well-being' strategy for the population in their area. This will include agreeing joint investment priorities and co-operation with other organisations such as NHS Trusts, Community Health Councils, voluntary bodies and local businesses. In autumn 2002 the Welsh Assembly Government issued a consultation document *Well Being in Wales*. This set out the direction and national context under which the strategy will be developed and implemented.

Since devolution, the Welsh Assembly Government decides its own spending priorities, including the budget for the NHS in Wales. The planned health budget for 2003/04 is £3.9 billion, an increase of £1 billion on 1999/2000. Much of this additional investment is being directed towards tackling the priorities outlined in *Improving Health in Wales*: coronary heart disease; cancer services; mental health services; intensive care; primary and community care; children's services; and local priorities set out in Health Improvement Programmes. Other measures will address waiting lists and waiting times, pressures on admissions, human resource development for the NHS workforce, and the establishment of a new Inequalities in Health Fund.

In April 2003 Health Commission Wales was established as an independent agency under the Welsh Assembly Government. The agency has responsibility for planning and commissioning specialised health services, including cancer and cardiac services and the Welsh Blood Service (see page 180). Funding allocated to Health Commission Wales in 2003/04 was £345 million.

The NHS in Scotland

The Scottish Executive's health policy focuses on prevention and health improvement. Its Health Department is responsible both for the executive leadership of NHSScotland and for the development and implementation of health and community care policy.

In March 2003 the Scottish Executive Health Department published *Improving Health in Scotland – The Challenge*. This builds on earlier publications and outlines a plan to improve Scotland's health in the following priority areas:

- early years – stressing the importance of infant and child health to later life;
- teenagers – encouraging young people to make healthy lifestyle choices, with all schools involved in a health promotion programme by 2007;
- the workplace – engaging employers in improving health at work; and
- communities – active health improvement programmes introduced through Community Planning Partnerships, which will bring together the NHS, local authorities and the voluntary sector at a local level.

To achieve these aims, the Executive's core spending on health is planned to rise from £6.2 billion in 2002/03 to £6.7 billion in 2003/04 – this represents approximately a third of the devolved Scottish budget. In addition, a new way of sharing NHS funds across Scotland is in place to address relative healthcare needs, including those caused by deprivation and by geographical remoteness.

Scotland has 15 unified NHS Boards, each of which is responsible for all NHS services in its area. The Boards are required to show how they are involving the public, and how this has affected the provision of services. Local Health Councils also provide a voice for the local population in each area.

The 15 NHS Boards and 32 local authorities work together to strengthen the localised focus of health provision, and every local authority has a seat on its principal NHS Board. Acute services and primary care continue to be delivered through NHS Trusts, and the Island Boards remain as integrated structures with no separate Trusts.

Other NHS bodies, such as the Scottish Ambulance Service, NHS Health Scotland and NHS Quality Improvement Scotland (see page 184), provide services on a national basis. The Scottish Executive is committed to developing a more patient-centred health service, and published its plans in 2001 in *Patient Focus, Public Involvement*. This has led to all Scottish NHS Boards developing public involvement frameworks that are monitored through the Executive's Performance Assessment Framework.

In February 2003 the Scottish Executive published the White Paper *Partnership for Care*. This sets out a package of proposed reforms that include:

- development of a wider range of services (diagnosis, treatment and rehabilitation) delivered in local communities;
- establishment of Community Health Partnerships that will be more accountable to local communities and more integrated with social work services;
- abolition of NHS Trusts, with NHS Boards being required to devolve greater authority to frontline services;
- guaranteed waiting times for treatment, initially for certain heart surgery, but to be extended to other services with national waiting time targets;
- independent monitoring of services by NHS Quality Improvement Scotland;
- establishment of a new Scottish Health Council to ensure that NHS Boards fulfil their new duties; and
- increased involvement of, and accountability to, patients through the introduction of an integrated care record, a new statement of patient's rights and responsibilities and a new complaints procedure.

Under the *Fair for All* initiative, the NHS in Scotland is committed to ensuring that services and employment policies are sensitive to the needs of different ethnic groups as well as disadvantaged and excluded groups.

The Scottish Health Plan includes the same clinical priorities as the NHS Plan for England: coronary heart disease (CHD); cancer; and poor mental health. In July 2001 the Executive published a comprehensive plan *Cancer in Scotland: Action for Change*. An extra £60 million has been targeted for improving cancer care. Annual investment plans are published by the regional cancer advisory groups in partnership with local NHS Boards and Trusts and the Scottish Cancer Group.

In October 2002 the Scottish CHD/Stroke Reference Group published a *CHD and Stroke Strategy for Scotland*. The Minister for Health and Community Care announced funding of over £40 million over three years to help implement it. Priorities are the creation of Managed Clinical Networks for cardiac services and stroke in each NHS Board area, and the development of national databases for CHD and stroke.

After smoking, poor diet is the most significant contributor to poor health in Scotland, being linked to high levels of cancer and heart disease. By 2005 the Executive has set targets to:

- double the average intake of fruit and vegetables to more than 400g per day;
- reduce the average intake of food energy from total fat to no more than 35 per cent; and
- reduce the average intake of food energy from saturated fatty acids to no more than 11 per cent.

To raise the profile of healthy eating among the general public, the Scottish Executive launched a healthy eating campaign, *Healthy Living*, in January 2003. The campaign is delivered through a range of television, radio and press advertising, while a telephone helpline and dedicated website provide the public with further information and advice.

NHS 24 was launched in Scotland in 2002. This is a nurse-led telephone advice service similar to NHS Direct in England (see page 165). The first call centre covered the Grampian region. The service will be fully operational across Scotland by the end of 2004. There are also plans to introduce an NHS 24 online service.

The NHS in Northern Ireland

The Department of Health, Social Services and Public Safety (DHSSPS) is responsible for the development and implementation of health and community care policy in Northern Ireland. In March 2002 it published a public health strategy, *Investing for Health*. This focuses on the key objectives of preventing ill health and reducing health inequalities among different groups in the population. In order to meet these objectives, the strategy recognises the importance of working alongside other departments with responsibilities for housing, the environment and education. By 2010 it aims to:

- increase life expectancy by at least three years for men and two years for women;
- halve the gap in average life expectancy between those living in the fifth most deprived wards and the population as a whole; and
- reduce by a fifth the gap in the proportion of people with a long-standing illness in the lowest and the highest socio-economic groups.

Northern Ireland's four health and social services boards are responsible for identifying the healthcare needs of people in their area, securing hospital and community health services, providing primary care services, and administering contracts. The boards have a major role to play in the implementation of *Investing for Health*. They are responsible for establishing an 'Investing for Health Partnership', reflecting the main public, voluntary and community interests in their area. They are also responsible for producing Health and Well-being Investment Plans.

The Health Promotion Agency plays a key role in identifying needs and in developing and implementing programmes designed to promote health and prevent ill health. It coordinates regional health promotion activities throughout Northern Ireland, undertakes public education campaigns, evaluates and disseminates research findings, provides training and works with other health agencies, personal social services and other bodies in helping to implement the Government's public health policies.

One of the wider impacts of the Belfast (Good Friday) Agreement in 1998 (see page 27) was the setting up of bodies for cross-border co-operation between Northern Ireland and the Republic of Ireland. Co-operation on health matters was identified as an area suitable for consideration by the North/South Ministerial Council. Joint Working Groups have been set up in five areas: accident and emergency services; emergency planning; high technology equipment; cancer research; and health promotion. These groups are looking in detail at where co-operation can yield the greatest benefit for people in both Northern Ireland and the Republic of Ireland. Joint ventures have included the production of an all-Ireland cancer incidence report, a folic acid advertising campaign, promotion of physical fitness, and training and research initiatives.

The Food Safety Promotion Board is involved in supporting North/South scientific co-operation, and promoting links between institutions working in the field of food safety, such as laboratories, food safety enforcement agencies and research bodies.

Finance

The NHS is financed mainly through general taxation, along with an element of National Insurance contributions (see chapter 12) paid by the employed, their employers and the self-employed. In 2002/03 an estimated 81 per cent of the NHS was financed through general taxation, with 11 per cent from National Insurance contributions and 8 per cent from charges and other receipts.

In the April 2002 Budget, the Chancellor of the Exchequer announced increases in National Insurance contributions from April 2003 to provide extra funding for the NHS. Spending on the NHS will increase from £68.1 billion in 2002/03 to £109.4 billion in 2007/08. This will result in the proportion of UK gross domestic product spent on health services increasing from 7.8 per cent to 9.4 per cent over this five-year period. Government spending plans for the three financial years from 2003/04 are set out in Table 13.7.

Table 13.7 Government expenditure plans[1] for the NHS, UK

| | | £ billion |
| | | of which |
	Total expenditure	capital investment
2003/04	74.9	3.5
2004/05	82.2	4.1
2005/06	90.5	5.3

1 As announced by the Chancellor of the Exchequer in the April 2002 Budget.
Source: HM Treasury

Some NHS funding is raised from other, non-government, sources. For example, some hospitals increase revenue by taking private patients, who pay the full cost of their accommodation and treatment. Hospitals can also use private finance for NHS capital projects, under the Private Finance Initiative (PFI), which aims to promote commercial partnership between the public and private sectors (see page 187). This involves new NHS facilities being designed, built, maintained and owned by the private sector, which then leases them back to the NHS. The NHS retains control of key planning and clinical decisions.

Charges
Around 617 million prescription items, worth around £6.8 billion, were dispensed in the community in England in 2002. The proportion of items provided free of charge was 82 per cent. The following groups are exempt from prescription charges:

- people aged 60 and over;
- children under 16 and full-time students under 19;
- women who are pregnant or have given birth in the previous 12 months;
- people with certain medical conditions; and
- people who receive (or whose partners receive) certain social security benefits (see chapter 12), or who otherwise qualify on low income grounds.

Hospital building programme
Nearly a third of hospitals pre-date the formation of the NHS in 1948. The largest building programme in the history of the NHS is currently in progress. Since May 1997, 30 major hospital schemes have opened, 23 of which were funded under PFI. A further seven are under construction, six of them under PFI.

There are charges for most types of NHS dental treatment, including examinations. However, the following people are entitled to free treatment: women who begin a course of treatment while pregnant or within 12 months of having a baby; children under 18; full-time students under 19; and adults who are on low incomes or receiving the same benefits or tax credits as for free prescriptions.

Free NHS sight tests are available for people aged 60 and over, children under 16, full-time students under 19, adults on low incomes or receiving the same benefits or tax credits as for free prescriptions, and people who have, or are at particular risk of, eye disease. Around 10.5 million sight tests were paid for by health authorities in England and Wales in the year to 31 March 2002.

Fraud prevention
The NHS Counter Fraud Service was established in 1998 and incorporated into the NHS Counter Fraud and Security Management Service (CFSMS) in April 2003. As a result of the work of the CFSMS there has been a financial benefit to the NHS totalling £295 million.

NHS workforce
The NHS is one of the largest employers in the world. In 2001 there were the equivalent of over one million full-time direct care employees in NHS hospital and community health services in Great Britain (see Table 13.8).

Table 13.8 NHS workforce, hospital and community health service staff,[1] 2001, Great Britain

	Thousands
Direct care staff	687
of which	
Medical and dental	76
Nursing, midwifery and health visitors	440
Other non-medical	171
Management and support staff	319
General medical practitioners	38
General dental practitioners	22
All staff	1,066

1 Figures on a full-time equivalent basis.
Source: Department of Health; National Assembly for Wales; NHSScotland

Doctors and dentists

Only people on the medical or dentists' registers may practise as doctors or dentists in the NHS. University medical and dental schools are responsible for undergraduate teaching, and the NHS provides hospital and community facilities for training.

Full registration as a doctor requires five or six years' training in a medical school, in a hospital and in the community, with a further year's hospital experience. The regulating body for the medical profession in the United Kingdom is the General Medical Council (GMC), and the main professional association is the British Medical Association (BMA). As a result of high-profile cases, such as that of Harold Shipman (see box), clinical governance has become an increasing concern.

In June 2003, GPs voted to accept a new General Medical Services contract negotiated between the employer's body – the NHS Confederation – and the General Practitioners Committee of the BMA. The new contract will result in the following changes:
- a contract between each GP practice and their PCT, as opposed to a contract with each individual GP. This is aimed at giving practices greater freedom to decide how to provide their services to best meet local needs;
- new proposals enabling practices to transfer some services, including out of hours care, to their PCT;

- a quality and outcomes framework to reward GPs on the basis of the quality of patient care rather than simply the number of patients they treat;
- a recruitment and retention package to tackle GP shortages;
- measures to provide patients with improved access to a wider range of services;
- new career opportunities for practice staff, including nurses and practice managers; and
- a major modernisation of GP premises and their information and technology systems.

GP practices will also benefit from the additional NHS funding announced by the Government in April 2002 (see page 172). UK spending on primary care will rise by 33 per cent between 2003/04 and 2005/06, to a total of £8 billion.

For a dentist, five years' training at a dental school and satisfactory completion of one year's mandatory vocational training are required before becoming eligible to work as a principal or associate in the General Dental Services of the NHS. All general dental practitioners are paid by a combination of capitation fees for children registered with the practice, continuing care payments for adults registered, and a prescribed scale of fees for individual treatments. The regulating body for the dental profession in the

Harold Shipman

In January 2000 a Manchester GP, Harold Shipman, was convicted of murdering 15 elderly patients. A public inquiry into the case was established by Parliament in January 2001, with a remit to consider the full extent of Shipman's unlawful activities, review the investigations into his case and the monitoring of primary care, and recommend steps to protect patients in the future.

The work of the inquiry is divided into two phases. Phase 1, published in July 2002, concluded that in addition to the 15 patients of whose murder Shipman was convicted, he killed at least 200 others between 1975 and 1998. Phase 2, which concerns the systems in operation during Shipman's medical career together with proposals for change, began in May 2002. Reports in July 2003 covered aspects of the police investigation, death certification and the investigation of deaths by coroners. The final report is due for publication in 2004.

United Kingdom is the General Dental Council, and the main professional association is the British Dental Association.

Nurses, midwives and health visitors

The majority of nursing students undertake the pre-registration Diploma in Higher Education programme, which emphasises health promotion as well as care of the sick and enables students upon qualification to work either in hospitals or in the community. The programme lasts three years (full-time) and consists of periods of university study combined with practical experience in hospital and in the community.

Midwifery education programmes for registered general/adult nurses take 18 months, while the direct entry programme lasts three years (full-time). Health visitors and district nurses are registered adult nurses who have a further specialist qualification and care for clients in the community.

The Nursing and Midwifery Council (NMC) is responsible for regulating and registering nurses, midwives and health visitors throughout the United Kingdom. In April 2002 it formally replaced the United Kingdom Central Council for Nursing, Midwifery and Health Visiting. It also took over some of the functions of the English National Board, which was also abolished at this time.

Nurse consultants

In 2000 the first nurse consultant posts were introduced. The NHS Plan committed the Government to establishing 1,000 such posts by 2004, and by April 2003 over 860 posts had been approved. The positions combine specialist practice with leadership, consultancy, education and research responsibilities.

Modern matrons

In April 2001 the first 'modern matron' posts were created. Each matron is in overall charge of a group of hospital wards, helping to ensure high standards of care. They set and monitor standards for cleaning and catering, and have authority to take action where these are not met. Over 2,000 appointments had been made by April 2003.

In the same month, a £2 million fund was established for matrons in charge of Accident and Emergency departments. Each matron will receive a one-off £10,000 budget to use to improve aspects of the environment such as cleaning, decor and children's play areas.

Funding for training places

In March 2003 the Government announced increased funding to provide more than 8,000 extra training places for nurses, midwives, therapists and healthcare scientists between 2003 and 2006. These places are in addition to the existing annual intakes of new students. The extra funding will provide opportunities for the development of staff who do not hold professional qualifications and for the continuing professional development of qualified staff.

Pharmacists

Only people on the register of pharmaceutical chemists may practise as pharmacists. Registration requires four years' training in a school of pharmacy, followed by one year's practical experience in a community or hospital pharmacy approved for training by one of the regulatory bodies for the profession – the Royal Pharmaceutical Society of Great Britain and the Pharmaceutical Society of Northern Ireland.

Community pharmacists are paid professional fees for dispensing NHS prescriptions. From 2003 supplementary prescribing was introduced with the aim of speeding access to medicines for patients with conditions such as asthma, diabetes, coronary heart disease and high blood pressure. This allows suitably trained pharmacists and nurses to issue repeat prescriptions to patients, avoiding the need for them to revisit their doctors. The target is to have 1,000 pharmacists and 10,000 nurses trained as supplementary prescribers by the end of 2004.

Opticians

The General Optical Council regulates the professions of optometrists (ophthalmic opticians) and dispensing opticians in the United Kingdom. Only registered optometrists may test sight. Their training takes four years (five years in Scotland), including a year of practical experience under supervision. Dispensing opticians take a two-year full-time course with a year's practical experience, or follow a three-year part-time day-release or distance learning course while employed with a registered optician.

Other health professions

The Health Professions Council (HPC) was established in 2002 as a UK-wide regulatory body responsible for setting and monitoring the standards of professional training, performance and conduct of 12 healthcare professions: arts therapists, chiropodists, clinical scientists, dieticians, medical laboratory technicians (biomedical scientists), occupational therapists, orthoptists, paramedics, physiotherapists, prosthetists and orthotists, radiographers, and speech and language therapists. The HPC replaced the Council for Professions Supplementary to Medicine and its 12 professional boards.

Council for the Regulation of Health Care Professionals

In April 2003 the Council for the Regulation of Health Care Professionals (CRHCP) was established to oversee the individual regulators of healthcare professions in the United Kingdom. The Council will not be involved in the direct regulation of the professions, but will be responsible for ensuring consistency in the work of the regulators where necessary, and help Parliament to hold the regulators more effectively to account. The creation of the council meets a commitment set out in the 2000 NHS Plan and was also one of the recommendations made in the 2001 report of the public inquiry into children's heart surgery at the Bristol Royal Infirmary.

Recruitment

The NHS Plan published in 2000 set targets for 7,500 more consultants, 2,000 more GPs, 20,000 extra nurses and 6,500 more therapists and other health professionals to be working in the NHS in England by 2004. The 'Return to Practice' initiative, which seeks to attract former staff back to the NHS, has been running since February 1999. Under this initiative, nearly 13,900 nurses, midwives and health visitors had returned to work in the NHS by March 2003.

Affordable childcare and accommodation have both been prioritised in order to retain and recruit NHS staff. The target for 2004 was 150 on-site nurseries with 7,500 subsidised childcare places. By July 2003, 120 nursery schemes had opened or were being created, to provide 5,200 places. In September 2001 the Starter Home Initiative was launched (see page 293). This scheme provides key public workers with equity loans and shared

NHS Professionals

NHS Professionals was established in 2000 as the NHS in-house staff agency, with the role of matching healthcare staff seeking temporary work with the NHS Trusts that needed them. By the end of 2003 it is to be established as a Special Health Authority and will take on an additional role in respect of temporary staffing agencies. This will involve managing agency framework contracts, and setting standards and the policy framework for NHS temporary staffing.

ownership arrangements. By 2004 it is expected that around 5,000 NHS staff will have benefited from the scheme.

The NHS is also recruiting from abroad, and in 2000 set a target of recruiting 1,000 doctors and 2,000 nurses by March 2005, focusing on countries where there are surpluses of suitably qualified staff. To increase capacity and reduce waiting times, the Government has also introduced an overseas clinical teams initiative whereby surgeons and their existing teams of suitably qualified medical specialists are being employed by the NHS. The priority areas for overseas teams are the new Diagnosis and Treatment Centres (see page 168).

Services for children, women, men and older people

Children

Important activities in promoting the health of children include:

- prevention of childhood accidents;
- immunisation and vaccination (see page 163);
- screening and health surveillance; and
- health education on diet and exercise.

Babies and pre-school children

A comprehensive programme of health surveillance for pre-school children is run by community health services and GPs. They receive an annual payment for every child registered on the programme (in Scotland this is carried out by the Community Paediatric Service, which may be based in a primary care or acute services trust).

Health visitors have a central role in health promotion and in identifying the healthcare needs of under-fives and helping to ensure access to services. They visit new-born babies at home between 10 and 14 days after birth. Later checks usually take place at:

- six to eight weeks (with a physical examination by a health visitor, GP or clinic doctor);
- six to nine months (including hearing and sight assessments);
- 18 months to two years; and
- pre-school, at three- to four-and-a-half years.

NHS numbers allocated at birth

From October 2002 responsibility for issuing NHS numbers to babies born in England and Wales was transferred from the Registrar of Births and Deaths to NHS Trusts. Under the new system, NHS numbers are issued electronically by maternity units as near to the time of birth as possible. Community health departments then receive an electronic birth notification containing the baby's NHS number. The new system is intended to reduce the possibility of medical notes for any treatment before registration going astray. Parents have up to six weeks to register a birth with their local register office.

School health services

Children attending state schools have access to the school health service, as well as usually being registered with a GP and a dentist. In addition to providing health advice to children and young people, the service assists teachers with pupils who have medical needs.

School nurses check hearing, sight, speech and weight, and administer vaccinations, including Bacillus of Calmette and Guerin (BCG), diphtheria, tetanus, and polio boosters. They are also involved in health education, counselling and sex education.

Child guidance and child psychiatric services provide help and advice to families and children with psychological or emotional problems. In recent years efforts have been made to improve co-operation between community-based child health services and local authority education and social services for children. This is particularly important in the prevention of child abuse and for the health and welfare of children in care.

Following successful pilots in England in 2000 and 2001, the National School Fruit Scheme is being expanded region by region. By the end of 2002 over 500,000 children aged four to six were receiving free fruit each school day. By 2004 the scheme will be available across the whole of England.

In Scotland, nutritional standards for school meals were set with the publication of *Hungry for Success* in February 2003. The Scottish Executive also announced that free fruit would be made available three times a week to all primary 1 and 2 children. In addition a breakfast services fund of £300,000 has been made available to local authorities to support existing services and establish new ones.

Children's National Service Framework

In 2001 the Secretary of State for Health announced the development of a new Children's National Service Framework (NSF) in England. This will be aimed at developing new national standards across the NHS and social services and is due to be published in 2004.

The first part of the NSF, the Standard for Hospital Services, was launched in April 2003 and set new national standards to deliver more child-friendly services in hospitals, including dedicated children's units in accident and emergency departments. The new standards cover the design and delivery of hospital services for children and the safety and quality of care, and will help to ensure children are cared for in hospital settings which adequately reflect the needs of their own age-group. The standards mean NHS hospitals should consider introducing:

- separate facilities for young children from those provided for adolescents;
- designated play areas for young children and privacy for adolescents;
- education support, so children do not fall behind in their schooling;
- regular security reviews to ensure access to children's wards is limited;
- play specialists who help children cope with the distress of being in hospital; and
- surveys of children and their parents to help inform inspections undertaken by CHAI (see page 184).

Women

Women have particular health needs related to certain forms of cancer and pregnancy.

Screening

Screening programmes are in operation for breast and cervical cancers. Under the UK breast cancer screening programme, every woman aged between 50 and 64 is invited for mammography (breast X-ray) every three years by computerised call-up and recall systems. In addition, all women over the age of 64 can refer themselves for screening. The automatic recall system is to be extended to women aged 65 to 70 by 2004 in England. In Scotland, the extension to women aged 65 to 70 began on a phased basis in spring 2003 and will be implemented over a three-year round of screening. In England, 1.3 million women of all ages were screened, and 8,545 cases of cancer were diagnosed, in 2001/02. In Scotland, 128,000 women were screened, with 884 cases of cancer diagnosed. In Northern Ireland, 35,948 women were screened for breast cancer in 2001/02.

National policy for cervical screening is that women should be screened every three to five years (three-and-a-half to five-and-a-half years in Scotland) to detect indications of the developmental stage which may proceed to cancer. The programme invites women aged 20 to 64 (20 to 60 in Scotland) for screening. However, since many women are not invited immediately when they reach their 20th birthday, the age group 25 to 64 is used to give a more accurate estimate of coverage of the target population. By the end of March 2002, 82 per cent of women aged 25 to 64 had been screened at least once in the previous five years in England, 87 per cent in Scotland, 80 per cent in Wales and 72 per cent in Northern Ireland.

Maternity

A woman is entitled to care throughout pregnancy, birth and the postnatal period. Care may be provided by a midwife, a community-based GP, a hospital-based obstetrician, or a combination of these. Special preventive services are provided under the NHS to safeguard the health of pregnant women and mothers with young children. Services include free dental treatment, health education, and vaccination and immunisation of children against certain infectious diseases (see page 163).

There is a welfare food scheme for mothers on low incomes, providing formula feed and vitamins free of charge. Proposals to reform the scheme and rename it *Healthy Start* were published in October 2002. The main proposals were:

- to broaden the nutritional range of foods beyond milk and infant formula;

- to provide a fixed value food voucher allowing greater access to a wider range of foods; and

- to provide professional healthcare advice to scheme members, covering nutrition and breast feeding.

The changes necessary to introduce the new scheme will be brought in through the Health and Social Care (Community Health and Standards) Bill (see page 166). The *Healthy Start* scheme is expected to be launched in 2004.

In England, two guides are given to first-time mothers free of charge. *The Pregnancy Book* is a complete guide to a healthy pregnancy, labour and giving birth, as well as life with a new baby. *Birth to Five* is a guide to the early stages of development, nutrition, weaning and common childhood ailments. The Scottish equivalent is *Ready, Steady, Baby!* produced by the Health Education Board for Scotland. New mothers also receive a Personal Child Health Record for their child. This helps parents to keep a record of immunisations, tests, birth details and health checks.

In 2001 the Scottish Executive published the national *Framework for Maternity Services in Scotland*. This sets out the basis against which each NHS Trust and NHS Board should judge its own service provision, and covers key aspects of maternity care, the organisation of maternity services, and women's and parents' information needs.

In England, the Children's NSF (see page 176) will include standards for maternity services, with an extra £100 million invested between 2001/02 and 2002/03 to fund capital improvements to modernise the facilities in maternity units. The Government is also committed to providing an extra 2,000 midwives by 2005, compared with 2000 levels.

Teenage pregnancy

The Social Exclusion Unit's report on teenage pregnancy in England, published in 1999, set out a national strategy to halve the rate of under-18 conceptions by 2010, with an interim reduction of 15 per cent by 2004. It also aims to increase the participation of teenage parents in education and work in order to reduce their risk of social exclusion. To aid delivery of these aims, every local authority area has a ten-year local teenage pregnancy strategy and a detailed three-year action plan. Between 2000 and 2001 the conception rate for women aged under 18 in England declined from 43.9 to 42.3 per 1,000 women aged 15 to 17 years.

Abortion

Under the *Abortion Act 1967*, as amended, the three categories to which no time limit applies are:

- prevention of grave permanent injury to the physical or mental health of the woman;
- where there is a substantial risk of serious foetal handicap; or
- where continuing the pregnancy would involve a risk to the life of the pregnant woman greater than if the pregnancy were terminated.

A time limit of 24 weeks applies to the largest category of abortion – risk to the physical or mental health of the pregnant woman – and also to abortion because of a similar risk to any existing children of her family. The Act does not apply in Northern Ireland.

Between 2001 and 2002 the number of legal abortions performed on women resident in England and Wales rose by 0.5 per cent to 176,400. The overall age-standardised rate rose from 17.0 to 17.1 abortions per 1,000 women aged between 15 and 44. In Scotland, the number fell by 4.6 per cent to 11,473, with the overall age-standardised rate falling from 11.9 to 11.4 per 1,000 women aged between 15 and 44.

Men

The lower life expectancy of men (see page 161) is the most significant indication of the health inequalities that exist between the sexes. Two possible reasons for this are that men tend to have less healthy lifestyles in terms of diet, smoking and higher alcohol and drug intake, and they are involved in more accidents. They also risk later diagnosis and treatment because, according to some experts, they do not consult a doctor as quickly as women when a problem arises. To address these issues, Health Action Zones (see page 166) and Healthy Living Centres are developing programmes to improve men's health.

In recent years government and other health campaigns have aimed to raise awareness and improve treatments for male-specific cancers. In England the NHS Cancer Plan set out the Government's intention to introduce prostate

National Suicide Prevention Strategy

In 1999 the Government set a target to reduce the death rate from suicide in England by a fifth by 2010, from an age-standardised rate of 9.1 per 100,000 in 1996. Research has shown that the main risk factors associated with suicide are: being male; living alone; unemployment; alcohol or drug misuse; and mental illness. To support the achievement of the target, the National Suicide Prevention Strategy was launched by the Department of Health in September 2002. Young men are a key target of the strategy, as suicide is the most common cause of death among men aged under 35. The strategy's six goals are to:
- reduce risk factors among the most high risk groups;
- promote mental well-being in the wider population;
- make the means of committing suicide less available and less lethal;
- improve the reporting of suicidal behaviour in the media;
- promote research on suicide and suicide prevention; and
- improve the monitoring of progress towards meeting the target set for 2010.

cancer screening as soon as screening and treatment techniques are sufficiently developed. In the meantime, a prostate cancer risk management programme has been launched in both England and Scotland. One element of this is a project for prostate specific antigen (PSA) testing. Extra government funding for research has also been allocated. In 2003/04 funding for the NHS Prostate Cancer Programme was £4.2 million, a twentyfold increase since 1999.

Everyman Campaign

The Institute of Cancer Research's *Everyman Campaign* seeks to raise awareness and funding for male cancers. In November 2000 it opened the first dedicated male cancer research centre in the United Kingdom. The construction of the centre was funded by donations from the public, as well as companies, trusts and foundations. Research is being carried out into many different aspects of male cancers, including gene isolation, dietary factors, hereditary risks and the development of more effective treatments.

Older people

Poor health, including mobility difficulties, affects a higher proportion of older people than any other group. As more people are living longer (see page 161) there is a need for the NHS to provide services that focus on the needs of older people.

In 2001 the Government published the National Service Framework (NSF) for Older People. This set out national standards for the care of older people across health and social services (see page 183) in England. The standards apply whether an older person is being cared for at home, in a residential setting or in a hospital.

The NSF focuses on conditions which are particularly significant for older people and which have not been covered in other NSFs (see page 183). Two of the aims for 2004 are that:

- every general hospital which provides care for stroke victims should have plans to introduce a specialised stroke service; and
- every general practice should be using protocols agreed with local specialist health and social care services to diagnose, treat and care for patients with depression and dementia.

In March 2003 an NSF progress report was published. It showed that since 2001 there had been a 13 per cent increase in the number of people over the age of 65 receiving heart bypass operations and a 16 per cent increase in the number of older people receiving cataract and knee replacement operations.

In Scotland, *Adding Life to Years*, the report of the Chief Medical Officer's Expert Group on the Healthcare of Older People, was published in January 2002. The first annual report on its implementation was published in September 2003.

Hospital and specialist services

District general hospitals offer a broad spectrum of clinical specialities, supported by a range of other services such as anaesthetics, pathology and radiology. Almost all have facilities for the admission of emergency patients, either through accident and emergency departments or as direct referrals from GPs. Treatments are provided for inpatients, day cases, outpatients and patients who attend wards for treatment such as dialysis.

Digital hearing aids

Some 1.8 million people use hearing aids in England, including 18,000 children. In April 2003 the Government announced a £94 million programme to modernise hearing aid services. By 2005 digital hearing aids will be available in every hearing aid service across England. These aids first became available on the NHS in April 2000, and by April 2003 almost a third of NHS audiology departments were providing them. In Scotland, the Executive has made additional funding available to health boards towards the cost of providing digital hearing aids and in February 2003 announced an investment of £8 million in the modernisation of hearing aid services.

Some hospitals also provide specialist services covering more than one region or district, for example for heart and liver transplants and rare eye and bone cancers. There are also specialist hospitals, such as the Great Ormond Street Hospital for Children, Moorfields Eye Hospital, and the National Hospital for Neurology and Neurosurgery, all in London. These hospitals combine specialist treatment facilities with the training of medical and other students, and international research.

Organ transplants

United Kingdom Transplant (a special health authority of the NHS) provides a 24-hour support service to all transplant units in the United Kingdom and the Republic of Ireland for the matching and allocation of organs for transplant. In many cases transplants are multi-organ.

In the United Kingdom, 1,721 kidney transplants were performed during 2002, and at the end of that year there were 6,462 patients waiting for this operation. At the end of 2002 there were five designated adult cardio-thoracic transplant centres and one paediatric transplant centre in England, and one adult centre in Scotland. During the year, 158 heart, 112 lung, and 16 heart/lung transplants were performed. There are six designated adult and three paediatric liver transplant units in England and one adult unit in Scotland. In 2002, 712 liver transplants were performed.

People who are willing to donate their organs after death may carry a donor card. The NHS Organ Donor Register contained around 10 million

South Asian organ donor campaign

Due to a high rate of diabetes (see page 163) and high blood pressure, people of Asian origin in the United Kingdom are three times as likely to develop conditions that lead to kidney failure. In February 2003, 841 Asian people in the United Kingdom were awaiting an organ transplant. As transplants are much more likely to succeed if donor and recipient are from the same ethnic group, the Department of Health launched a campaign to encourage more Asian people to become organ donors. As well as placing adverts in minority ethnic media, the campaign was supported by community health forums. Leaflets in minority ethnic languages were mailed to all GPs in the United Kingdom.

Epilepsy Action Plan

In February 2003 the Epilepsy Action Plan was launched to help improve services for people with epilepsy and their families and carers. The plan covers a wide range of strategies and policies, including:

- investment of £1.2 million between 2003 and 2005 on a project to improve quality and access in neurology services;
- providing the National Society for Epilepsy with a £288,600 grant spread over three years from 2003 to 2006 to improve support and information for sufferers and their families;
- medicines management programmes to raise awareness among health professionals; and
- the development of more GPs and nurses with a special interest in neurology.

names at December 2002. The Government aims to have 16 million people registered by 2010.

Blood services

Blood services are run by the National Blood Service in England and north Wales, the Welsh Blood Service, the Scottish National Blood Transfusion Service and the Northern Ireland Blood Transfusion Service. The United Kingdom is self-sufficient in blood components.

Over 3 million donations are made each year by voluntary unpaid donors in the United Kingdom. These are turned into many different life-saving components and products for patients. Red cells, platelets and other components with a limited 'life' are prepared at blood centres, while the production of plasma products is undertaken at the Bio Products Laboratory in Elstree (Hertfordshire) and the Protein Fractionation Centre in Edinburgh.

Each of the four national blood services coordinates programmes for donor recruitment, retention and education, and donor sessions are organised regionally, in towns and workplaces. Donors are aged between 17 and 70. Blood centres are responsible for blood collection, screening, processing and supplying hospital blood banks. They also provide laboratory, clinical, research, teaching and specialist advisory services and facilities. These blood centres are subject to nationally coordinated quality audit programmes, through the Medicines and Healthcare Products Regulatory Agency (see page 185).

Ambulance and patient transport services

NHS emergency ambulances are available free to the public through the 999 telephone system for medical emergencies and accidents, as well as for doctors' urgent calls. Rapid response services, in which paramedics use cars and motorcycles to reach emergency cases, have been introduced in a number of areas, particularly major cities with areas of high traffic density. Helicopter ambulances, provided through local charities and part funded by the NHS, serve many parts of the United Kingdom. In England, between 2001/02 and 2002/03 the number of emergency calls to the NHS rose by 7 per cent to 5.0 million and the number of emergency patient journeys grew by 3 per cent to 3.2 million.

Non-emergency patient transport services are free to NHS patients considered by their doctor, dentist or midwife to be medically unfit to travel by other means. In many areas the ambulance service organises volunteer drivers to provide a hospital car service for non-urgent patients. Patients on low incomes may be eligible for reimbursement of costs of travelling to hospital.

Hospices

Hospice (or palliative) care is a special type of care for people whose illness may no longer be curable, enabling them to achieve the best possible quality of life during the final stages. The first hospices in the United Kingdom were opened in 1967 and were provided on a voluntary basis. Most care continues to be provided by the voluntary sector,

Additional funding for palliative care services

In December 2002 the Government announced a £50 million a year budget for palliative care services between 2003/04 and 2005/06. The funding will be allocated by a joint NHS and voluntary sector National Partnership Group. The group will assess investment plans from local cancer networks and plans that are approved will receive allocations from the budget.

Developments likely to stem from the new funding include:

- increased support to patients and their carers at home;
- increased numbers of nurse specialists in hospital and community teams to provide advice and support to patients, their carers and healthcare professionals; and
- an increase in the number of specialist hospice beds for those patients and families with complex needs.

but is also increasingly provided within NHS palliative care units, and by hospitals and community palliative care teams. The care may be provided in a variety of settings: at home (with support from specially trained staff), in a hospice or palliative care unit, in hospital or at a hospice day centre.

Palliative care focuses on controlling pain and other distressing symptoms, and on providing psychological support to patients, their families and friends, both during the illness and into bereavement. Palliative care services mostly help people with cancer, although patients with other life-threatening illnesses, such as AIDS, motor neurone disease and heart failure, are also cared for. Currently 22 specialist hospice inpatient units provide respite care for children from birth to 16 years of age. Palliative care networks for children are being established across England to coordinate how and where services are provided. In Scotland there is currently one children's hospice. A second is being built and will be operational by April 2004.

The National Council for Hospices and Specialist Palliative Care Services brings together voluntary and health service providers in England, Wales and Northern Ireland, in order to provide a coordinated view of the service. Its Scottish

counterpart is the Scottish Partnership for Palliative Care.

Sexual health

The Government's public health strategy includes the provision of sexual health services. Free contraceptive advice and treatment are available from GPs and family planning clinics, which also offer tailored services for young people. Clinics are able to provide condoms and other contraceptives free of charge and since 2001, emergency or 'morning after' pills have been available from pharmacists without a prescription.

The Department of Health has developed a national sexual health and HIV strategy to bring together current initiatives in these areas, including work on chlamydia, the incidence of which has been increasing (see page 163). The first phase of a national screening programme for chlamydia was launched in August 2002 with the announcement of ten sites across England where screening will take place. A further ten sites will be open by the end of 2003. The first ten sites were targeted at women aged 16 to 24, as this group is at greatest risk of infection. However, testing will also be offered to men presenting with symptoms, and greater uptake of testing among men will be promoted.

The Scottish Executive is also developing plans for a sexual health strategy. The Welsh Assembly Government's *Strategic Framework for Promoting Sexual Health*, launched in 2000, is now being implemented. Local sexual health strategies are in place, and a two-year HIV prevention campaign targeted at homosexual men has been commissioned.

Alcohol

Part of the funds allocated for health promotion in England is for promoting the Government's sensible drinking guidelines, and equivalent bodies are similarly funded in other parts of the United Kingdom. 'Drinkline' provides confidential telephone advice about alcohol problems and services in England and Wales. Treatment and rehabilitation within the NHS includes inpatient and outpatient services in general and psychiatric hospitals and some specialised alcohol treatment units. The Government is developing a National Alcohol Harm Reduction Strategy for England that it aims to implement by 2004.

There is also close co-operation between statutory and voluntary organisations. In England, Alcohol

Concern and other voluntary organisations play a prominent role in improving services for problem drinkers and their families, increasing public awareness of alcohol misuse, and improving training for professional and voluntary workers. The Scottish Council on Alcohol has a similar function in Scotland.

In January 2002 the Scottish Executive published a *Plan for Action on Alcohol Misuse*. The two key priorities of the Plan are to reduce binge drinking by adults and reduce harmful drinking by children and young people. Licensing law is also being reviewed to look at the effects of licensing on health and public order.

In Northern Ireland, a Regional Drug Strategy Coordinator was appointed in 2001 to take forward the Drug Strategy and the Strategy for Reducing Alcohol Related Harm.

Tobacco
Cigarette advertising on UK television has been banned since 1965. In February 2003 the first of a number of far wider restrictions came into effect under the *Tobacco Advertising and Promotions Act 2002*. Provisions in the Act will lead to a ban on most forms of tobacco advertising, promotion and sponsorship in the United Kingdom. The timetable is as follows:

- a ban on advertising of tobacco products in magazines, newspapers, billboards and the Internet from February 2003;
- a ban on promotions such as gift coupons and direct mail from May 2003;
- a ban on domestic sponsorship of cultural and sporting events;
- restrictions on point of sale advertising in shops, and on vending machines and websites by the end of 2003;
- phasing out of indirect tobacco advertising by the end of 2004; and
- a ban on international sponsorships such as Formula One (in line with an agreed EU directive) from July 2005.

Since April 2001 nicotine replacement therapy (NRT) has been available on prescription from GPs. NRT can provide the body with nicotine in decreasing doses until the craving can be coped with. This complements bupropion, which was made available on NHS prescription on its launch in 2000. Both of these treatments were endorsed by the National Institute for Clinical Excellence (see page 183) in April 2002.

To encourage more smokers to quit, NHS smoking cessation services are now available across England. The services offer information, counselling and motivational help to smokers who want to stop. The Government target for 2001/02 was for 50,000 smokers to have quit by the four-week follow-up stage. Results show that of the 227,300 smokers who set a quit date in 2001/02, 119,800 reported that they had successfully quit at the four-week stage.

Health warnings
From January 2003 larger and more stark health warnings have been carried on all tobacco products sold in the United Kingdom. They were introduced as part of an EU Directive under which warnings should cover 30 per cent of the front and 40 per cent of the back of packets. General warnings such as 'smoking kills' or 'smoking seriously harms you and others around you' are printed on the front of the packet. The back carries one of fourteen more specific warnings, which will be rotated at regular intervals.

Drugs
The misuse of drugs, such as heroin, cocaine and amphetamines, is a serious social and health problem (see page 164). The Government launched its ten-year anti-drugs strategy *Tackling Drugs to Build a Better Britain* in 1998. This acknowledged the link between drug misuse and social conditions and problems; signalled a change in spending priorities in order to stop the problem happening, rather than reacting to it when it does; and introduced targets for reducing drug misuse based on evidence and experience.

In 2002 an updated version of the strategy was published building on the progress and lessons learned since 1998. This focused on the most dangerous drugs and the communities and individuals most affected by them. It aims to discourage young people from using drugs in the first place and to provide support to parents and family members who are concerned about drugs. Key objectives and targets include:

- the launch of an awareness campaign in spring 2003 highlighting the risks of Class A drugs and encouraging young people and their parents to seek further advice and help;
- an increase in the penalties for dealing Class C drugs to match the penalties for Class B drugs;

- expanding the provision and improving the quality of drug education so that by March 2004 all primary and secondary schools have drug education policies; and
- expanding prevention programmes so that by March 2004 all young offenders, pupils attending Pupil Referral Units and children looked after by Social Services Departments participate.

Within the overall UK strategy, there are separate detailed strategies for Wales, Scotland and Northern Ireland. The Welsh Assembly's anti-drugs strategy was published in May 2000 in *Tackling Substance Misuse in Wales: a Partnership Approach*. Scotland's drugs strategy is set out in *Tackling Drugs in Scotland – Action in Partnership*, published in 1999, and in the Scottish Executive's *Drug Action Plan*, published in May 2000. The strategy for Northern Ireland is set out in *Drug Strategy for Northern Ireland*, published in 1999.

A feature of the UK drug strategy is the close link between the agreed national policy and the programmes delivered at a local level by Drug Action Teams (DATs).[3] In England there are currently around 150 DATs, composed of all those involved in drugs issues at a local level (for example PCTs, the social and probation services, and the police). They agree a local strategy that applies the national policy to the particular conditions in their area, and report annually to the Home Office on the progress achieved.

Medical standards

Standards of care

NHS Charters
The NHS Charter for England – *Your Guide to the NHS* – provides information on how patients can access appropriate services to meet their healthcare needs, sets out a series of standards for each stage in the patient's care, and lists improvements patients can expect in the future. In Wales, the Health and Social Care Charter is backed up with local charters at local health board level. A revised Charter for NHSScotland is planned.

---

3 These comprise DATs in England and Scotland, Drug and Alcohol Action Teams (DAATs) in Wales, and Drug and Alcohol Coordination Teams (DCTs) in Northern Ireland. The arrangements in Scotland are mixed, including DATs, DAATs, and some teams that also have responsibility for smokers.

Ten-year plan for diabetes services
The NSF for diabetes was introduced in England in January 2003. It aims to help people manage their own condition and to prevent them from developing the common complications of the disease. Key targets include:
- by 2006, every person with diabetes or at risk of developing it will be offered regular check-ups and appropriate treatment to ensure that any complications are identified as soon as possible; and
- by 2007, every PCT will provide eye screening services for all people with diabetes.

In addition, in February 2003 the Government announced the launch of nine screening pilots in inner city areas. The pilots will increase the identification of people at risk of Type 2 diabetes through screening of their blood sugar levels.

National Service Frameworks
The first National Service Frameworks (NSFs) were introduced in England in 1998, in order to set national standards and reduce variations in service within the NHS. Since 1998 NSFs for cancer, paediatric intensive care, mental health, coronary heart disease, older people (see page 179) and diabetes (see box below) have been launched. An NSF for children's services (see page 176) is being developed, and NSFs for renal services and long-term conditions (with a focus on neurological conditions) will follow.

In Scotland, NHS Quality Improvement Scotland (see page 184) has developed clinical standards across a range of conditions, including breast, lung, colorectal and ovarian cancers, secondary prevention in coronary heart disease, stroke, diabetes, schizophrenia and renal services. Peer reviews by teams including patient representatives are carried out against these standards.

National Institute for Clinical Excellence
The National Institute for Clinical Excellence (NICE) was established in 1999 to develop national standards for best practice in clinical care within the NHS in England and Wales. This includes drawing up guidelines based on clinical and cost effectiveness and ensuring that they apply to all parts of the NHS. The Institute's membership is drawn from the health professions, the NHS, academics, health economists and patients. It appraises new drugs and technologies,

and produces clinical guidelines. By March 2003 NICE had produced guidance on 86 drugs, 18 surgical procedures and 92 devices.

In March 2003 treatments referred to NICE for appraisal in its next work programme included those for hormonal treatments for early breast cancer, dual chamber pacing for coronary heart disease, parent training programmes for the treatment of prevention of child conduct disorder and new treatments for diabetic foot ulcers.

NHS Quality Improvement Scotland is responsible for developing and running a national system of quality assurance in healthcare for the NHS in Scotland, and provides a single source of national advice on the most clinically and cost-effective health technologies, playing a similar role to NICE in England and Wales.

Complaints

Under the current NHS complaints system, complaints should be resolved speedily at local level, but if the complainant remains dissatisfied with the local response he or she can request an independent review. Where such an investigation takes place, a report setting out suggestions and recommendations is produced. Complainants who remain dissatisfied, or whose request for a panel investigation is turned down, can refer their complaint to the Health Service Commissioner (see below).

In 2000/01, 95,944 written complaints were made about hospital and community health services in England, and 44,442 complaints were made about family health services (including general medical and dental services). In Scotland in 2000/01 there were 8,106 written complaints about hospital and community health services and 2,677 about family health services.

Health Service Commissioners

England and Wales each have Health Service Commissioners. They are responsible for investigating complaints about health service bodies that have not been dealt with to the satisfaction of the member of the public concerned. The English and Welsh posts are at present held by one person (with a staff of about 250), who is also Parliamentary Commissioner for Administration (the Ombudsman, see page 56). The Health Service Commissioner reports annually to Parliament and to the Welsh Assembly Government. In Scotland, complaints about the health service can be directed to the Scottish

Public Services Ombudsman, who is also the parliamentary and housing commissioner, and reports to the Scottish Parliament. In Northern Ireland, complaints about health and social services bodies are investigated by the Commissioner for Complaints.

Health Service Commissioners can investigate complaints that a person has suffered hardship or injustice as a result of a failure in a service provided by a health service body (including action by health professionals arising from the exercise of clinical judgement); complaints of a failure to provide a service to which the patient was entitled; or maladministration by an NHS body.

Inspection and regulation

The *NHS Reform and Health Care Professions Act 2002* introduced changes to the way in which health and social services will be regulated. Further legislation included in the Health and Social Care (Community Health and Standards) Bill would introduce two new independent inspectorates: the Commission for Healthcare Audit and Inspection and the Commission for Social Care Inspection (CSCI, see page 146).

Commission for Healthcare Audit and Inspection

CHAI was established in shadow form in 2003 and, subject to primary legislation, will be fully operational from April 2004. It will bring together the regulation of the public and private health sectors in England and Wales. Separate arrangements will continue in Scotland. CHAI will investigate the performance of all NHS organisations and private hospitals in England and Wales and bring the financial monitoring work of the Audit Commission within the NHS, the work of the Commission for Health Improvement and the private healthcare role of the National Care Standards Commission (see page 187). Following assessments, CHAI will publish star ratings for all NHS organisations and be able to recommend special measures where there are persistent problems. It will also publish an annual report to Parliament on national progress on healthcare and how resources have been used.

Safety

Health Protection Agency

The Health Protection Agency (HPA) was established in April 2003 with a remit covering biological, chemical and radiological hazards, infectious disease control and health emergency planning. It combines the public health functions that were previously the responsibility of bodies such as the Public Health Laboratory Service, the Microbiological Research Authority, the National Focus for Chemical Incidents and the National Poisons Information Service.

Medicines and medical equipment

The Medicines and Healthcare products Regulatory Agency (MHRA) was established in April 2003 through the merger of the Medicines Control Agency and the Medical Devices Agency. The MHRA is responsible for the regulation of both medicines and healthcare products in the United Kingdom and for safeguarding the interests of patients and users by ensuring that medicines, equipment and other products meet appropriate standards of safety, quality and performance, and that they comply with relevant EC Directives.

Only medicines that have been granted a marketing authorisation issued by the European Agency for the Evaluation of Medicinal Products or the MHRA may be supplied to the public. Marketing authorisations are issued following scientific assessment on the basis of safety, quality and effectiveness.

In March 2003 the Government published new guidance on the design of medicine labels and packaging, aimed at reducing medication error. *The Best Practice Guidance Document* sets out the factors that should be considered when designing medicine labels, including layout, size of text and colours used. A total of 15 different pieces of information are legally required to appear on a medicine label, but the guidance advises that five of these (the name of the medicine, strength, route of administration, dose and warnings) should be grouped together for ease of use.

Food safety

Under the *Food Safety Act 1990*, it is illegal to sell or supply food that is unfit for human consumption or falsely or misleadingly labelled. The Act covers a broad range of commercial activities related to food production, the sources from which it is derived, such as crops and animals, and articles that come into contact with food. There are also more detailed regulations, which apply to all types of food and drink and their ingredients. Local authorities are responsible

for enforcing food law in two main areas: trading standards officers deal with the labelling of food, its composition and most cases of chemical contamination; and environmental health officers deal with hygiene, cases of microbiological contamination of foods, and food which is found to be unfit for human consumption.

The Food Standards Agency (FSA), which began operating in 2000, is responsible for all aspects of food safety and standards in the United Kingdom and represents the Government on food safety and standards issues in the European Union. The FSA has national offices in Scotland, Wales and Northern Ireland. The Agency's key aims are to:

- reduce food-borne illness by 20 per cent between 2000 and 2006 by improving food safety throughout the food chain;
- help people to eat more healthily;
- promote honest and informative labelling to help consumers;
- promote best practice within the food industry; and
- improve the enforcement of food law.

Research

The Medical Research Council (MRC, see also chapter 26) supports medical research in the United Kingdom by providing funding for research programmes and infrastructure, and by investing in training and employment, both in universities and its own research centres. The MRC receives an annual grant from the Office of Science and Technology (part of the Department of Trade and Industry). In 2002/03 the MRC received £374 million and realised a further £78 million from external sources, such as joint-funding initiatives and commercial activities.

The MRC advises the Government on matters relating to medical research, and co-operates with health departments throughout the United Kingdom, the NHS and other government departments concerned with biomedical and health service research. It also works closely with other research councils, medical research charities, industry and consumers, to identify and respond to current and future health needs.

Human fertilisation and embryology

The world's first 'test-tube baby' was born in the United Kingdom in 1978, a result of the technique of *in vitro* fertilisation. The social, ethical and legal implications were examined by a committee of inquiry and led eventually to the passage of the *Human Fertilisation and Embryology Act 1990*. The Human Fertilisation and Embryology Authority (HFEA) licenses and inspects centres providing certain infertility treatments, undertaking human embryo research or storing gametes or embryos. It also maintains a code of practice giving guidance to licensed centres and reports annually to Parliament.

A small percentage of embryos are currently tested before implant to make sure they are free from serious genetic diseases. In April 2003 the Court of Appeal upheld an HFEA decision to permit the screening of embryos which have been tested in this way, for the purpose of identifying ones with tissue matching that of a seriously ill older brother or sister. At birth, tissue-compatible stem cells from the baby's umbilical cord may then be used to save the life of the sibling.

Information for donor-conceived children

Over 18,000 people have been born in the United Kingdom as a result of treatment with donated sperm, eggs or embryos since the *Human Fertilisation and Embryology Act 1990* required the HFEA to maintain a register of such births. In January 2003 the Government announced that, subject to parliamentary approval, new rules would be introduced meaning that those children conceived by donation since 1990 could, when they reach the age of 18, request non-identifying information about their donor from the HFEA. This information could include a physical description, occupation and interests, although not the donor's actual identity or any information that might identify them.

Health arrangements with other countries

The member states of the European Economic Area (EEA, see page 92) have special health arrangements under which EEA nationals resident in a member state are entitled to receive emergency treatment, either free or at a reduced cost, during visits to other EEA countries. These arrangements also apply in Switzerland. Treatment is provided, in most cases, on production of a valid Form E111, which people in the United Kingdom normally obtain from a post office before travelling. There are also arrangements for

people who go to another EEA country specifically for medical care, or who require continuing treatment for a pre-existing condition.

Unless falling into an exempted category (for instance those persons engaging in employment, taking up permanent residence or seeking asylum in the United Kingdom), visitors to the United Kingdom are generally expected to pay for all non-emergency treatment. The United Kingdom also has a number of separate bilateral agreements with some other countries, such as Australia and New Zealand.

Following European Court of Justice rulings in July 2001, NHS patients in the United Kingdom are entitled to receive hospital care in other countries in the EEA. This has provided an additional option to NHS bodies seeking to increase the number of patients being treated and so reduce their waiting times. In order to address the clinical, legal and quality issues in sending patients abroad for treatment, an overseas treatment pilot was launched in January 2002. During the pilot 190 patients from three sites in south-east England were referred to hospitals in France and Germany. An evaluation of this pilot, commissioned by the Department of Health, was published in August 2002.

By April 2003 some 500 patients had received treatment in hospitals in Belgium, France and Germany. The Department of Health is seeking to identify further overseas hospitals in which NHS patients can receive treatment, and has established two NHS overseas commissioners responsible for identifying suitable capacity. The Department has also issued guidance to assist NHS bodies wishing to refer patients to other countries in the EEA. The majority of overseas referrals are expected to be for orthopaedic procedures, in particular for major joint replacements.

Health provision outside the NHS

Private healthcare

As an alternative to the NHS, people can pay for their own health and social care, for example by joining a private healthcare organisation or simply paying for private treatment when the need arises. In addition, there is the option of private medical insurance, which, depending on the premium paid, will cover people's healthcare in times of need. In 2001, 6.7 million people in the United Kingdom were covered by private medical insurance, more than three times the number in 1971 (2.1 million). The overall cost of claims to private medical insurers rose by 6.4 per cent between 2000 and 2001 to £2.1 billion.

The National Care Standards Commission (NCSC) is an independent public body set up under the *Care Standards Act 2000* to regulate social care (see chapter 12) and private and voluntary healthcare services in England, in institutions such as care homes, children's homes, boarding schools, private hospitals and private clinics. From April 2002 the NCSC assumed responsibility for the registration and inspection of these services from local authority and health authority inspection units. It carries out regular inspections and has the power to ensure that standards meet national minima. The private healthcare role of the NCSC will become the responsibility of CHAI (see page 184) from April 2004. In Wales, these functions are performed by the Care Standards Inspectorate for Wales, a division within the Welsh Assembly Government, and in Scotland by the Scottish Commission for the Regulation of Care, a non-departmental public body established under the *Regulation of Care (Scotland) Act 2001*.

Partnerships

Government policy aims to increase diversity and plurality in the provision of NHS services, especially for elective surgery. In 2000 the Department of Health signed an agreement with the independent healthcare sector (which comprises the private and voluntary sectors), covering care, workforce planning and service planning. It involves the NHS using the independent sector's spare capacity; transfer of patients between the two sectors; exchange of information; and joint working on preventive and rehabilitation services.

In December 2002 the Government published a prospectus, *Growing Capacity: independent sector diagnosis and treatment centres*. This marked the launch of a procurement process for a series of independent sector Diagnosis and Treatment Centres projects with expressions of interest being invited from both UK and overseas independent healthcare providers (see page 168).

Private dental care

The UK market for private dentistry has expanded rapidly in recent years, growing by almost 50 per cent in real terms between 1997 and 2001, to a value of over £1 billion. Around 7 million people in the United Kingdom regularly receive private dental treatment. In March 2003 the Office of Fair Trading (OFT, see page 473) published a report on these services. Key findings included:

- consumers often lack basic information about prices, quality of service and what treatments are available on the NHS. This makes it harder for them to make informed choices;
- standards promoted in professional guidance published by the General Dental Council (see page 174) are not routinely monitored and enforced and compliance in some areas is low;
- unlike the NHS, there is no universal complaints system (see page 184) and procedures for dealing with complaints and securing redress for customers are often inadequate; and
- regulatory restrictions on the supply of dentistry services limit consumer choice, competition, business freedom and the potential to develop and deliver better services.

Complementary and alternative medicine

There has been an increasing interest in, and use of, complementary and alternative medicine (CAM) in recent years. An Office for National Statistics survey published in April 2001 found that one in ten people in the United Kingdom had used a complementary therapy in the last year. There has also been an increase in the number of practitioners providing CAM treatments. A 2000 survey commissioned by the Department of Health indicated that there were around 50,000 in the United Kingdom and that almost 10,000 conventional healthcare professionals were practising CAM services of some kind.

Access to CAM therapies can be given to patients through the NHS. This will usually be where there is good evidence of effectiveness, where practitioners are regulated to an acceptable standard, and where the GP considers that a therapy could be beneficial to the individual patient.

Two CAM professions (osteopaths and chiropractors) are regulated by law. The Government has also made a commitment to bring acupuncturists and herbal medicine practitioners into statutory regulation. The reports of two working groups established to make recommendations on the statutory regulation of these two therapies were published in 2003.

Further reading

Delivering the NHS Plan: Next steps on investment, next steps on reform. Cm 5503. The Stationery Office, 2002.

Securing our Future Health: Taking a Long-Term View. The Stationery Office, 2002.

Department of Health Departmental Report 2003. The Government's Expenditure Plans. Cm 5904. The Stationery Office, 2003.

Improving Health in Wales – A Plan for the NHS with its Partners. Welsh Assembly Government, 2001.

Our National Health: A plan for action, a plan for change. Scottish Executive Health Department, 2000.

Improving Health in Scotland – The Challenge. Scottish Executive Health Department, 2003.

Investing for Health. Department of Health, Social Services and Public Safety, Northern Ireland, 2000.

Statistical publications

Health Statistics Quarterly. Office for National Statistics. The Stationery Office.

Health and Personal Social Services Statistics for England. Department of Health. The Stationery Office.

Scottish Health Statistics. Information and Statistics Division, NHSScotland.

Health Statistics Wales. National Assembly for Wales.

On the State of the Public Health. The Annual Report of the Chief Medical Officer of the Department of Health. The Stationery Office.

Health in Scotland. The Annual Report of the Chief Medical Officer on the State of Scotland's Health. Scottish Executive.

Welsh Health: Annual Report of the Chief Medical Officer. National Assembly for Wales.

Websites

Department of Health
www.doh.gov.uk

Welsh Assembly Government
www.wales.gov.uk

Scottish Executive Health Department
www.scotland.gov.uk

NHSScotland, Information and Statistics Division
www.show.scot.nhs.uk/isd

Department of Health, Social Services and Public Safety, Northern Ireland
www.dhsspsni.gov.uk

Health Protection Agency
www.hpa.org.uk

Human Fertilisation and Embryology Authority
www.hfea.gov.uk

National Care Standards Commission
www.carestandards.org.uk

NHS Direct
www.nhsdirect.nhs.uk

WWW.

14 Crime and justice

The legal framework

The United Kingdom has three legal systems (operating in England and Wales, Scotland and Northern Ireland) and three systems of criminal justice. In each system there is emphasis on the independence of both prosecuting authorities and the judiciary, but unlike many countries, there is no single criminal or penal code that sets out the principles on which the justice system operates.

The standard of proof required in criminal cases is that of 'beyond reasonable doubt', whereas in civil law – which is primarily concerned with regulating disputes between individuals or organisations – a case only has to be proved on the balance of probabilities. In both criminal and civil cases, the courts make their decisions on an adversarial rather than an inquisitorial basis.

In all three legal systems many areas of law have developed over the centuries through the decisions of the courts. Consistency is achieved because the decisions of higher courts are binding on those lower down the hierarchy. The House of Lords[1] is the ultimate appeal court in the United Kingdom, except for Scottish criminal cases.

Statutes passed by the Westminster or Scottish Parliaments are the ultimate source of law, but there is also a legal duty to comply with European Community (EC) law. Courts in the United Kingdom are obliged to apply the latter in cases where the two conflict. A statute may confer power on a minister, local authority or other executive body to make delegated legislation (see page 40).

EC law, which applies in the United Kingdom as a member of the European Union (see page 58), is derived from the EC treaties, from the Community legislation adopted under them, and from the decisions of the European Court of Justice. That court has the highest authority, under the Treaties of Rome, to decide points of EC law. Where a point arises before a British court, it may refer the point of law to the European Court for it to decide. Sometimes a court is obliged to make a reference to the European Court.

The European Convention on Human Rights was incorporated into UK law under the *Human Rights Act 1998*. This covers, among other things, the right to a fair trial, to freedom of thought and expression, and to respect for family and private life. All public authorities, including the courts, must act compatibly with these rights. The rights in the Convention do not take precedence over an Act of Parliament. Where they conflict, the higher courts may make a declaration of incompatibility and Parliament then decides what action to take.

---

1 In June 2003 the Government announced a series of constitutional changes (see page 33), which will include a new Supreme Court to take over the judicial functions of the House of Lords.

Crime

Crime measured by surveys

It has been estimated from the British Crime Survey (see box) that 12.3 million crimes were committed against adults living in private households in the 12 months before interview in 2002/03, a 2 per cent decrease on the previous year. The risk of being a victim of crime during this period was estimated at around 27 per cent, one-third lower than the risk in 1995 (40 per cent).

The most recent surveys in Scotland (covering crime in 1999) and Northern Ireland (covering crime in 2000–01) both estimated that the risk of being a victim was 20 per cent. In both cases, crime had fallen since the previous survey.

Recorded crime

In England and Wales the term 'recorded crime' refers to notifiable offences recorded by the police according to rules set down by the Home Office. Recorded crime includes a wide range of offences from homicide to minor theft and criminal damage, but does not include most of the 'summary' offences (such as motoring offences) that are dealt with by magistrates. In Scotland the term 'crimes' is similarly used for the more serious criminal acts (roughly equivalent to indictable and 'triable-either-way' offences – see page 194) and

How crime is measured

There are two main measures of the extent of crime in the United Kingdom: surveys of the public, such as the British Crime Survey (BCS – covering England and Wales), and the recording of crimes by the police.

Surveys of the public give a better measure of many types of crime because they include offences that are not reported to the police. They also give a more reliable picture of trends because they are not affected by changes in levels of reporting to the police, or by variations in police recording practice.

The BCS is based on interviews with around 33,000 adults in England and Wales and asks people about their experience of crime in the 12 months before interview. The sample does not include children (under 16) or people living in institutions. Murder, fraud, sexual offences and victimless crimes such as illegal drug use are not covered. There are similar crime surveys in Scotland and Northern Ireland.

Crime data collected by the police are a by-product of the administrative procedure of completing a record for crimes that they investigate. They provide an important indicator of police workload, and can be used to analyse local patterns of offending.

Before 2002, police forces in England and Wales did not necessarily record that a crime had taken place if there was no evidence to support the claim of the victim. In April 2002, every force adopted a new National Crime Recording Standard (NCRS), which aims to take a more victim-oriented approach and provide greater consistency between forces.

The combined effect of the NCRS and other changes to the counting rules since 1998 has been to inflate the number of crimes in police statistics. Recent statistics give a more complete picture, but they need to be adjusted for the effect of the NCRS before they can be compared with earlier years.

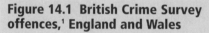

Figure 14.1 British Crime Survey offences,[1] England and Wales

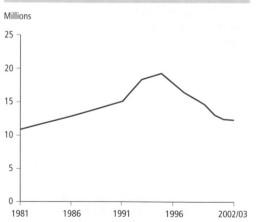

Millions

1 Data refer to survey years, 1981,1983,1987,1991,1993, 1995, 1997, 1999, 2000, 2001/02 & 2002/03. Until 2000, respondents were asked to recall their experience of crime in the previous calendar year. From 2001/02, when the BCS became a continuous survey, the recall period was changed to the 12 months prior to interview.

Source: British Crime Survey, Home Office

less serious crimes are termed 'offences'. In Northern Ireland the definitions used are broadly comparable with those in England and Wales.

There are differences in legal systems and recording practices between the different parts of the United Kingdom. However, Table 14.2 suggests that the crime rate is higher in England and Wales, and that a higher proportion of crime is detected (cleared up in Scotland, see glossary).

Table 14.2 Recorded crime, 2002/03

	England & Wales	Scotland[1]	Northern Ireland
Notifiable offences ('000s)	5,899	427	142
Detection rate[2] (percentages)	24	46	23
Offences per 1,000 population	113	84	84

1 Figures for Scotland refer to 2002.
2 Detections are referred to as clear-ups in Scotland.
Source: Home Office, Scottish Executive, Police Service of Northern Ireland

In 2002/03, in England and Wales, around 55 per cent of offences recorded by the police involved forms of theft or burglary, while 16 per cent involved violence (Figure 14.3).

Offenders

In 2001, 467,000 people were cautioned for, or found guilty of, an indictable offence in England and Wales. Table 14.4, which gives offending rates per 10,000 population, shows that 16- to-24 year-old men and women are over 12 times as likely to be cautioned or convicted as their counterparts aged 35 and over. The overall rate for males aged ten and over was 167 per 10,000, compared with a rate of 37 for females.

Measures to reduce crime

A wide range of measures are being taken to try to reduce the overall level of crime. For example,

Figure 14.3 Recorded crime in England and Wales: by offence category, 2002/03

Total: 5.9 million

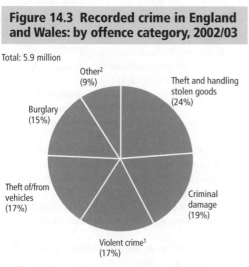

Other[2] (9%)
Theft and handling stolen goods (24%)
Burglary (15%)
Theft of/from vehicles (17%)
Criminal damage (19%)
Violent crime[1] (17%)

1 Robbery, violence against the person and sex offences.
2 Including fraud, forgery and drugs offences.
Source: Home Office

Table 14.4 Offenders found guilty of, or cautioned for, indictable offences, 2001, England and Wales

Rate per 10,000 population

Age	Males	Females
10–15	218	86
16–24	584	121
25–34	246	55
35 and over	46	10
All aged 10 and over	167	37

Source: Home Office

there are 376 Crime and Disorder Reduction Partnerships (CDRPs) in England and Wales bringing together the police, fire authorities, Primary Care Trusts, health authorities (in Wales), local authorities and other relevant organisations, in order to develop local strategies. The partnerships are supported by ten Home Office Regional Teams.

The Building Safer Communities Fund is a three-year programme for CDRPs, running from 2003/04, which combines a number of former initiatives into a single funding stream. It is being used to support initiatives such as:
- tackling drug-related crime and strengthening communities against drugs;
- tackling repeat victimisation through anti-burglary projects;
- measures to reduce anti-social behaviour through pub watch schemes; and
- work with young people at risk of truancy and offending.

Street crime, defined as robbery, snatch theft, carjacking and gun-related crime, is concentrated in a relatively small number of mainly urban areas. The Street Crime Initiative was launched in ten police force areas of England in March 2002, in response to sharp rises in robbery. A wide range of agencies work in partnership, including the police, Crown Prosecution Service, courts, youth services and government departments. Latest figures show that recorded robbery fell by 14 per cent in 2002/03 (adjusted for the NCRS, see page 190) in England and Wales.

Within the Scottish Executive Justice Department, the Crime Prevention Unit has responsibility for developing crime prevention, community safety and domestic abuse policy on behalf of Scottish Executive ministers. All 32 local councils in Scotland have formed community safety partnerships and multi-agency domestic abuse partnerships. The Community Safety Unit within the Criminal Justice Directorate of the Northern Ireland Office is helping to establish 26 local community safety partnerships. The partnerships are developing local action plans, based on an audit of crime and disorder issues.

Drug misuse

The UK-wide drugs strategy, introduced to coordinate the fight against illegal drugs, has four main aims:

- helping young people resist drug misuse;
- protecting communities from drug-related anti-social and criminal behaviour;
- enabling people to overcome drug problems through treatment; and
- reducing the supply of illegal drugs on the streets.

The Government Office Drug Teams deliver the Government's drug strategies at a regional level. The teams have been established in each of the nine government regions in England. They support the work of around 150 Drug Action Teams (see page 183) which deliver the strategy at a local level.

In April 2003 the Government launched the Criminal Justice Interventions Programme, with an emphasis on ensuring that drug misusers receive treatment throughout the various stages of the criminal justice system and that they are re-integrated into society. The programme is initially concentrating on areas with high levels of theft-related crime, but is expected to expand.

The *Crime and Disorder Act 1998* introduced drug treatment and testing orders, targeted at persistent offenders (aged 16 and over) who show a willingness to co-operate with treatment and are before the court for an offence that is sufficiently serious to attract a community sentence as penalty. The orders also contain mandatory testing and court review requirements through which offenders' progress can be monitored. The orders were introduced in England and Wales in October 2000 and are being introduced on a phased basis in Scotland.

Under the *Criminal Justice and Court Services Act 2000*, drug testing of some types of offender is being piloted in nine areas in England and Wales

until March 2004. The Act provides for the taking of samples from people in police detention, and at other points in the criminal justice system, to test for the presence of specified class A drugs.

Scotland has its own drugs strategy within the UK framework and has also introduced national standards for drugs services. In an effort to reduce the availability of drugs in Scotland and to target organised drug crime, the Scottish Drug Enforcement Agency was launched in 2000. Northern Ireland also has its own drugs strategy, set within the UK framework. Tackling the criminal gangs involved in drugs is one of the strategic priorities for the Northern Ireland Organised Crime Taskforce in 2003.

Firearms

The Criminal Justice Bill (see page 197), currently before Parliament, provides for a mandatory minimum sentence of five years in England and Wales for the possession or distribution of firearms prohibited under the *Firearms Act 1982*. This would include handguns and automatic weapons. A National Forensic Firearms Intelligence Database would help track the provenance of guns and ammunition used in crimes. The age at which a young person can acquire and use an air weapon would be raised from 14 to 17. A new offence of possessing an imitation firearm or an air weapon in a public place without reasonable excuse is being introduced as part of the Anti-Social Behaviour Bill.

Terrorism

Permanent measures to counter terrorism on a UK-wide basis are contained in two recent Acts: the *Terrorism Act 2000* and the *Anti-Terrorism, Crime and Security Act 2001*. Provisions in these Acts – which extend the definition of terrorism to cover ideological and religious motivation – include:

- an offence of inciting terrorist acts abroad from within the United Kingdom;
- powers to seize suspected terrorist cash at borders;
- a judicial authority to consider applications for extensions of detention of terrorist suspects;
- specific offences relating to training for terrorist activities;
- offences relating to weapons of mass destruction;

- better security at airports and nuclear sites; and
- an extension of police powers to detain and question those suspected of terrorist offences.

Other developments since the attacks in the United States in September 2001 include the creation of a dedicated crisis coordination centre through the Civil Contingencies Secretariat, and the establishment of a joint contact group between senior officials in the United Kingdom and the United States. The work of this group will include:
- closer working on the development of biometrics technology, such as iris and facial recognition;
- pooling of knowledge and resources;
- enhanced protection for borders through visa and passenger intelligence sharing; and
- strategies to prevent and deal with attacks on electronic communications.

National crime agencies
Details of most criminal justice agencies can be found in the sections devoted to England and Wales, Scotland and Northern Ireland (see right and pages 204 and 208). However, three agencies have a wider jurisdiction and are mentioned here.

The *British Transport Police* (BTP) is the national police force for the railways throughout Great Britain. It is the only national force that is routinely involved in day-to-day public policing, dealing with some 81,400 crimes and 40,000 minor offences in 2002/03. The BTP also deals with major incidents on the railways, protects the railways from vandalism and supports victims of accidents. Other activities include combating terrorism and policing travelling football supporters. A police authority for the BTP will be set up in 2004 to regulate and monitor its activity.

The *National Criminal Intelligence Service* (NCIS) is responsible for collecting and analysing criminal intelligence for use by police forces and other law enforcement agencies in the United Kingdom. NCIS coordinates the activities of the Security Services in support of the law enforcement agencies against organised crime, and liaises with the International Criminal Police Organisation (Interpol), an independent agency that facilitates international police co-operation. NCIS also provides the channel for communication between the United Kingdom and EUROPOL (see page 78).

The *Serious Fraud Office* prosecutes cases of serious or complex fraud in England, Wales and Northern Ireland, with teams of lawyers, accountants, police officers and other specialists conducting investigations. The Office has wide powers that go beyond those normally available to the police and prosecuting authorities.

England and Wales

Policing
Police powers and procedures are defined by legislation and accompanying codes of practice. Evidence obtained in breach of the codes may be ruled inadmissible in court. The codes must be available in all police stations.

Stop and search
Police officers can stop and search people and vehicles if they reasonably suspect that they will find stolen goods, offensive weapons or implements that could be used for burglary and other offences. The officer must record the grounds for the search and the person searched is entitled to a copy of the officer's report. Some 740,700 stop and searches were carried out by the police in England and Wales in 2001/02. New guidance providing stricter regulation of stop and search has recently been introduced, supported by a new set of training packages.

Arrest
The police may arrest a suspect on a warrant issued by a court, but can also do so without a warrant for arrestable offences (those for which the sentence is fixed by law or for which the term of imprisonment is five years or more).

Detention and questioning
Suspects must be cautioned before the police can ask any questions about an offence. For arrestable offences, a suspect can be detained in police custody without charge for up to 24 hours. Someone suspected of a serious arrestable offence can be held for up to 96 hours, but not beyond 36 hours unless a warrant is obtained from a magistrates' court.

Charging
Once there is sufficient evidence, the police have to decide whether a detained person should be charged with an offence. If the police institute criminal proceedings against a suspect, the Crown Prosecution Service (see page 194) then takes control of the case.

For minor offences, the police may decide to caution an offender rather than prosecute. A caution is not the same as a conviction, and will only be given if the person admits the offence. Under the *Crime and Disorder Act 1998*, cautioning for young offenders has been replaced with the police final warning scheme. This provides for 10- to 17- year-olds to be given a reprimand for most first offences and a final warning for a second offence. Those given final warnings are referred to the local Youth Offending Team (see page 202).

If the police decide to charge someone, that person may be released on bail to attend a magistrates' court. If not granted police bail, the defendant must be brought before a magistrates' court (or, if under 18, a youth court) as soon as possible. There is a general right to bail, but magistrates may withhold it. If bail is refused, an accused person has the right to apply again, subject to some limitations, to the Crown Court or to a High Court judge. In certain circumstances, the prosecution may appeal to a Crown Court judge against the granting of bail by magistrates.

Complaints

Members of the public can make complaints against the police if they feel that they have been treated unfairly or improperly. In England and Wales the investigation of the more serious cases is supervised by the Police Complaints Authority (PCA). From April 2004, a new system will be introduced under the *Police Reform Act 2002*. An Independent Police Complaints Commission (IPCC) will replace the PCA. It will have its own investigators with powers to monitor and inspect the handling of complaints by police forces, consider appeals, and investigate serious misconduct whether or not a complaint has been made.

Community relations

Stricter regulation of stop and search powers (see above) is one of a number of measures that have been taken to improve relations between the police and the communities they serve. Racial discrimination by the police was made unlawful in the *Race Relations Act 2000*, and the police were given a duty to promote race equality.

In 1999 the Government set employment targets for the recruitment, retention and progression of minority ethnic police officers in England and

Community policing

- Neighbourhood and street wardens work with the police and local authorities to help build community confidence and tackle anti-social behaviour. Wardens patrol communities to provide information and reassurance, report problems such as graffiti and abandoned cars, and check on vulnerable people (for example victims of crime).
- Community support officers operate under the control of the local chief constable. They can be given limited police powers to deal with low-level disorder and anti-social behaviour – for example issuing penalty notices for cycling on the pavement, littering and dog fouling; dealing with abandoned vehicles; and confiscating alcohol from young people.

Wales. The targets are intended to ensure that by 2009 forces will reflect their local population and milestones have been set for the intervening years. At the end of March 2002, 2.6 per cent of police officers in England and Wales were from a minority ethnic group, compared with a target for 2002 of 3.0 per cent. On the other hand, civilian support staff from those belonging to a minority ethnic group reached 5.3 per cent, compared with a target of 5.0 per cent.

The prosecution process

The Crown Prosecution Service (CPS) (see page 201) is responsible for prosecuting people in England and Wales who have been charged by the police with a criminal offence.

When deciding on whether to go ahead with a case, Crown Prosecutors must first be satisfied that there is enough evidence to provide a realistic prospect of conviction against each defendant on each charge. They must then decide whether it is in the public interest to proceed. A prosecution will usually take place unless there are public interest factors against it clearly outweighing those in favour.

Court procedures

There are two types of criminal offence. *Summary offences* are the least serious and may be tried only in a magistrates' court. *Indictable offences* are subdivided into 'indictable-only' (such as murder, manslaughter or robbery), which must be tried on indictment[2] at the Crown Court by judge and jury, and *'either-way'*, which may be tried either summarily or on indictment. The flow of cases through the criminal justice system is shown in Figure 14.5.

Magistrates may impose a fine of up to £5,000 and/or a maximum sentence of six months' imprisonment, but can send the offender to the Crown Court if they feel their sentencing powers are not sufficient. These arrangements will change if the Criminal Justice Bill is enacted (see page 197).

Youth courts are specialist magistrates' courts, which sit separately from those dealing with adults. They handle all but the most serious charges against people aged at least ten (the age of criminal responsibility) and under 18.

Trial
The law presumes an accused person is innocent until proved guilty beyond reasonable doubt by the prosecution. Accused people have a right at all stages to stay silent; however, when questioned, failure to mention facts which they later rely upon in their defence may not be helpful to their case. If the defendant pleads guilty, the judge will simply decide upon the appropriate sentence.

Criminal trials normally take place in open court (that is, members of the public and press are allowed to hear the proceedings) unless there are specific reasons why this would not be appropriate. If a not guilty plea is entered, the prosecution and defence form opposing sides in an 'adversarial' system. They call and examine witnesses and present opposing versions of the case. Strict rules of evidence govern how this may be done. Written statements by witnesses are allowed with the consent of the other party or in limited circumstances at the discretion of the court. Otherwise evidence is taken from witnesses testifying orally on oath.

The Courts Bill, currently before Parliament, includes provisions for a Criminal Procedure Rule Committee. Working to a programme agreed by ministers, the Committee will make rules for all criminal courts in England and Wales, including magistrates' courts, the Crown Court and the Court of Appeal, Criminal Division. The aim is to modernise and streamline the criminal trial process. It is expected that the Committee will be established in 2004.

Publicly funded legal services
Advice and assistance are available without reference to an individual's means to anyone who is arrested and held in custody at a police station, or other premises, or who appears before a court.

Where a defendant is charged with a criminal offence, he or she may apply for a representation order, which entitles him or her to the services of a solicitor and/or barrister, depending on the type of case. There is no means test to decide eligibility for representation. The court must be satisfied that it is in the interests of justice that publicly funded representation should be granted. At the end of the case, the trial judge in the Crown Court has power to order the defendant to pay back some or all of the costs of his or her defence.

In criminal proceedings the Legal Services Commission (see page 204), through the Criminal Defence Service, makes arrangements for duty solicitors to assist unrepresented defendants in the magistrates' courts. Advocacy assistance is also available in some other specified circumstances. During 2002/03 over 1.5 million acts of assistance, were granted by the Criminal Defence Service at a total net cost of around £526 million. Criminal legal aid work in the Crown Court and higher courts amounted to a further £569 million.

Eight Public Defender Service (PDS) offices are being piloted. The PDS directly employs criminal solicitors and offers a complete service from the police station, through the magistrates' court and on to the Crown Court as appropriate. Clients may choose whether to be represented by PDS or duty solicitors.

The jury
In jury trials in England and Wales the judge decides questions of law, sums up the case to the jury, and discharges or sentences the accused. The jury is responsible for deciding questions of fact. The jury's verdict may be 'guilty' or 'not guilty' and the latter would result in an acquittal. Juries may, subject to certain conditions, reach a verdict by a majority of at least 10–2.

If an accused person is acquitted, there is no right of appeal from the prosecution, and the accused cannot be tried again for that same offence.

---

2 An indictment is a written accusation against a person, charging him or her with serious crime triable by jury.

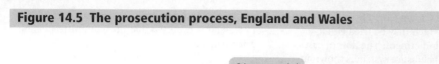

Figure 14.5 The prosecution process, England and Wales

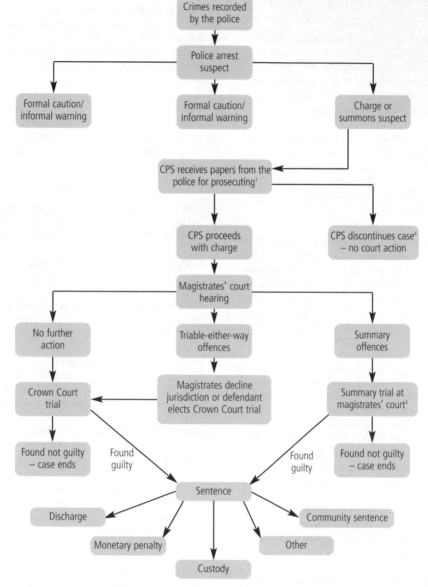

1 Although the majority of prosecutions are handled by the Crown Prosecution Service, other organisations can also bring prosecutions.
2 A case will be under continued review, and may be discontinued at any stage before the hearing at the magistrates' court or the prosecution may offer no evidence. In addition, the charge may be altered up to the final decision of the court.
3 Magistrates may currently commit to the Crown Court for sentence, but this will change if the Criminal Justice Bill is enacted (see page 197).
Source: A Guide to the Criminal Justice System in England and Wales, Home Office, 2000.

However, an acquittal may be set aside and a retrial ordered if there is proof that a juror has been interfered with or intimidated.

A jury is independent of the judiciary and any attempt to interfere with its members is a criminal offence. People aged between 18 and 70 whose names appear on the electoral register are liable to be chosen at random for jury service. People in certain occupations, such as police officers, lawyers and doctors, are exempted from serving.

Sentencing and appeals

The court sentences the offender after considering all the relevant information it has on the case, which may include a pre-sentence or any other specialist report, and a mitigating plea by the defence. A fine is the most common punishment, and most offenders are fined for summary offences. A court may also make compensation orders, which require the offender to pay compensation for personal injury, loss or damage resulting from an offence; or impose a conditional discharge, where the offender, if he or she offends again, may be sentenced for both the original offence and for the new one.

In 2001, 323,000 people were sentenced for indictable offences in England and Wales. Table 14.6 shows how the form of sentence varied according to the type of offence committed. A majority of those convicted of drug or motoring offences were fined or discharged, while a majority of those convicted of robbery, sexual offences or burglary were given immediate custodial sentences. Overall, nearly one in three offenders were given community sentences.

Community sentences

A range of community sentences are used in cases where a fine or custodial sentence would not be appropriate. A court community rehabilitation order requires offenders to maintain regular contact with their probation officer. The aim is to secure the rehabilitation of the offender, protect the public and prevent re-offending. The order can last from six months to three years; an offender who fails to comply without good reason with any of the requirements can be brought before the court again. A community punishment order involves unpaid work within the community.

Young offenders

A range of powers have been introduced which aim to ensure that the sentences imposed by the courts make young offenders face up to the consequences of their actions. Those aged 16 and 17 may also be subject to most of the adult community sentences. Non-custodial penalties for young offenders include:

- fines and compensation orders;
- referral orders, which require the young person to meet with a youth offender panel led by members of the local community and to agree a programme to repair the harm done and prevent further offending. These orders account for 30 per cent of all sentences passed on 10- to 17-year-olds;
- reparation orders, which require young offenders to make specific reparation either to their victims or to the wider community;
- curfew orders with electronic monitoring, which keep young offenders off the street at times when they are more likely to offend;
- action plan orders – a three month community sentence with an emphasis on education and parental involvement;
- attendance centre orders, where young offenders are required to attend a centre for two or three hours on alternate Saturdays for specific activities; and
- supervision orders, where young offenders must comply with specific requirements, such as education and training, and reparation.

Criminal Justice Bill

This Bill seeks to establish a new framework for sentencing in England and Wales. Its provisions will, if enacted:

- extend the sentencing powers of magistrates from 6 to 12 months;
- require magistrates to sentence all those they have found guilty, rather than committing some to be sentenced in the Crown Court;
- allow defendants to ask for trial by judge alone in the Crown Court;
- allow trial by judge alone in serious and complex fraud trials, and in some other complex and lengthy trials, or where the jury is at risk of intimidation;
- allow witnesses to refer in court to their previous and original statements and change the laws on reported evidence ('hearsay'); and
- introduce an exception to the double jeopardy rule (which prevents defendants from being tried twice for the same offence) in serious cases, where there is compelling new evidence.

These penalties may be complemented by orders made in the civil courts. A parenting order requires parents or guardians to attend counselling or a guidance programme for up to three months, while a child safety order places children under ten under the supervision of a social worker or Youth Offending Team (see page 202).

The main custodial penalty for offenders aged 12 to 17 is the detention and training order, introduced in April 2000. Half of the order is spent in custody and the other half under supervision in the community. The order may last for a minimum of four months to a maximum of two years. Early release with electronic monitoring is available for those serving eight months or more under the order.

Custodial sentences

One in four of those convicted of an indictable offence in 2001 in England and Wales was given a custodial sentence (Table 14.6). Life imprisonment is the mandatory sentence for murder, and is also available for certain other serious offences.

Prison accommodation ranges from open prisons to high-security establishments. Sentenced prisoners are classified into different risk-level groups for security purposes. Women prisoners are held in separate prisons or in separate accommodation in mixed prisons. Remand prisoners (those currently awaiting trial) enjoy wider rights and privileges than convicted prisoners.

There have been recent increases in the prison population, which in April 2003 numbered over 72,000. Measures taken to alleviate potential overcrowding in prisons include greater use of community (non-custodial) sentences for minor offenders; expanding the capacity of prisons and making effective use of statutory arrangements governing the early release of prisoners. Those serving shorter terms (less than four years) may be automatically released at specific points in their sentences, while those detained for longer require Parole Board approval or the consent of a government minister.

Appeals

A person convicted by a magistrates' court may appeal to the Crown Court or the High Court, on points of law, and for his or her trial to be re-heard. Appeals from the Crown Court go to the Court of Appeal (Criminal Division). A further appeal can be made to the House of Lords on points of law of public importance, if permission is given. A prosecutor cannot appeal against an acquittal, but there is a system for reviewing rulings of law and sentences that appear too lenient.

During 2002, a total of 7,718 applications for leave to appeal were received, of which 1,914 were against conviction in the Crown Court and 5,804 against the sentence imposed.

Table 14.6 Offenders sentenced for indictable offences, 2001 England and Wales

				Percentages			
				Fully			
			Community	suspended	Immediate		All sentenced
	Discharge	Fine	sentence	sentence	custody	Other	(thousands)
Theft and handling stolen goods	21	20	35	–	21	2	126.4
Drug offences	18	44	18	1	19	1	45.7
Violence against the person	12	11	41	1	32	3	35.4
Burglary	4	2	40	–	51	2	24.7
Fraud and forgery	17	16	42	2	21	2	18.2
Criminal damage	22	17	41	–	11	8	10.5
Motoring offences	5	46	23	1	24	1	7.9
Robbery	1	–	27	–	70	2	6.8
Sexual offences	4	3	27	2	62	2	3.8
Other offences	10	43	18	1	17	10	43.8
All indictable offences	16	24	32	1	25	3	323.2

Source: Home Office

The Criminal Cases Review Commission, which is independent of both government and the courts, reviews alleged miscarriages of justice. Referral of a case to this body depends on some new argument or evidence coming to light, not previously raised at the trial or on appeal.

Criminal justice agencies

The criminal justice system in England and Wales is made up of personnel working in a number of different agencies, reporting to the Home Office, the Department for Constitutional Affairs and the Attorney General's Office, as illustrated in Figure 14.7.

The police service

There are 43 police forces organised on a local basis in England and Wales. The Metropolitan Police Service and the City of London force are responsible for policing London.

Police forces are maintained in England and Wales by local police authorities. In the 41 police areas outside London they normally have 17 members – nine locally elected councillors, three magistrates and five independent members. The authorities set local policing objectives in consultation with the chief constables and local community, while the Government sets priorities for the police as a whole.

Each force is headed by a chief constable (in London the Commissioner of the City of London Police and the Commissioner of the Metropolitan Police), appointed by their police authorities with government approval. Independent inspectors of constabulary report on the efficiency and effectiveness of police forces. Police numbers are shown in Table 14.8 on a full time equivalent basis.

Specialist crime bodies

The role of the *National Crime Squad* is to prevent and detect organised and serious crime across police force and national boundaries in England and Wales and to support provincial forces in their investigation of serious crime.

The *Forensic Science Service* is an executive agency of the Home Office that provides scientific support to police forces through its six regional laboratories. It also operates the national DNA database in England and Wales, which is used to match DNA profiles taken from suspects to profiles from samples left at scenes of crime.

Police reform

The *Police Reform Act 2002* introduced measures to modernise and standardise the work of police forces, and to make them more accountable. These include:

- publication of the first annual National Policing Plan in November 2002, setting out the Government's strategic priorities for policing over a three year period;
- granting the Home Secretary powers to direct a police authority to produce, in conjunction with the relevant chief officer, an action plan to address poor performance that has been highlighted by HM Inspectorate of Constabulary;
- the extension of constabulary powers to police support staff (community support officers, detention officers, escort officers and investigative officers) in order to free up police officers for front-line duties (see page 194); and
- new arrangements for the investigation of complaints against the police (see page 194).

The courts

A *magistrates' court* usually comprises three representatives of the local community who do not have professional legal qualifications, known as lay magistrates or justices of the peace (JPs). They sit with a court clerk who advises them on law and procedure. In some areas a paid professional District Judge (Magistrates' Courts) sits alone instead of the JPs. District Judges (Magistrates' Courts) – who were formerly known as stipendiary magistrates – are becoming more common, although most cases are still dealt with by lay magistrates.

Table 14.7 Police officer strength in England and Wales at 31 March 2003

	Numbers
ACPO rank[1]	210
Chief Superintendent	493
Superintendent	860
Chief Inspector	1,760
Inspector	6,435
Sergeant	19,114
Constable	105,578
All ranks	134,450

1 Chief constable and deputy or assistant chief constable.
Source: Home Office

Figure 14.8 Structure of the criminal justice system, England and Wales

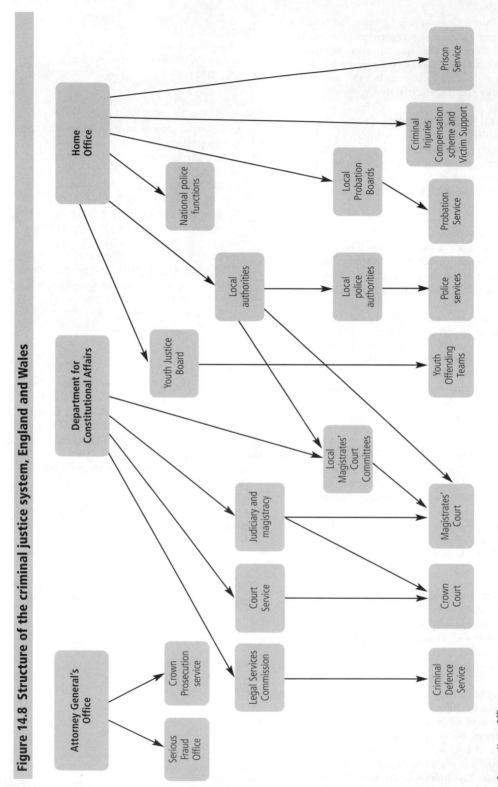

Source: Home Office

As part of the continuing reform of the criminal justice system, the Courts Bill includes proposals to establish local courts boards. A new executive agency would manage the courts system in England and Wales, taking over from the Court Service and Magistrates' Court Committees.

The *Crown Court* sits at about 90 venues in England and Wales, in six regional areas called circuits, and is presided over by High Court judges, circuit judges and part-time recorders. Not all Crown Courts handle cases of the same level of seriousness. Judges sat for 89,029 days in the Crown Court in 2002: the bulk of this time was spent by circuit judges (74 per cent) and recorders (20 per cent).

A coroner (usually a senior lawyer or doctor) must hold an inquest if a person died a violent or unnatural death, or died suddenly while in prison or in other specified circumstances. He or she may also need to hold an inquest if the cause of death remains unknown following a post-mortem examination. The *coroner's court* establishes how, when and where the death occurred. A coroner may sit alone or, in certain circumstances, with a jury.

The judiciary

Judges are appointed from the ranks of practising barristers and solicitors. They have independence of office and can be removed only in rare and limited circumstances involving misconduct or incapacity. They are not subject to ministerial control or direction. Judges are currently advised by legally qualified clerks of court.

Arrangements for the appointment of judges are currently overseen by the Lord Chancellor, who recommends the more senior appointments to The Queen. The Government announced in June 2003 that it would be bringing forward legislation to abolish the office of Lord Chancellor as part of a series of constitutional changes designed to put the relationship between the executive, legislature and judiciary on a modern footing and to separate the powers of the legislature and the judiciary (see page 32). In July 2003 it issued a consultation paper in which it proposed to establish an independent Judicial Appointments Commission to recommend candidates to the Secretary of State for Constitutional Affairs (who would continue to recommend the more senior appointments to The Queen). The Government is proposing that the new Commission would have an equal balance of judicial representatives, legally qualified members and lay members.

The *Lord Chief Justice* of England and Wales is second in rank to the Lord Chancellor in the judicial hierarchy. He has some responsibilities for the organisation and work of the criminal courts, including issuing practice directions to the courts and members of the legal professions on criminal law and court procedures.

The *Home Secretary* has overall responsibility for criminal law, the police service, the prison system, the probation service, and for advising the Crown on the exercise of the royal prerogative of mercy.

The *Attorney General* and the *Solicitor General* are the Government's main legal advisers, providing advice on a range of legal matters, including proposed legislation. They may also represent the Crown in difficult or publicly important domestic and international cases.

A wide range of statutory and non-statutory bodies advise the Government. These include the police inspectorates, the Magistrates' Courts Service, the Audit Commission, the Criminal Justice Consultative Committee, law reform bodies such as the Law Commission and ad hoc Royal Commissions and departmental committees. The Youth Justice Board for England and Wales monitors the operation of the youth justice system, advises the Home Secretary on its operation, sets national standards, and promotes good practice.

Prosecution authorities

The Crown Prosecution Service (CPS – see also page 194) is headed by the *Director of Public Prosecutions (DPP)*, who reports to the Attorney General. Although the CPS works closely with the police, it is a governmental body independent of them. Its role is to:

- advise the police on possible prosecutions;
- review prosecutions started by the police to ensure that the right defendants are prosecuted on the correct charges before the appropriate court;
- prepare cases for court;
- prosecute cases at magistrates' courts; and
- instruct counsel to prosecute cases in the Crown Court and higher courts.[3]

---

3 A number of CPS lawyers are qualified to appear in some cases in the Crown Court and other higher courts.

Other prosecuting authorities include the Serious Fraud Office (see page 193), which also answers to the Attorney General; and bodies such as the Inland Revenue, Customs and Excise Commissioners, local authorities and trading standards departments, all of which prosecute cases in their own discrete areas of work. Individual citizens may bring private prosecutions for most crimes, but some need the consent of the Attorney General and these cases may be taken over by the DPP.

An Independent Inspectorate (HM Crown Prosecution Service Inspectorate) reports on the performance of the Crown Prosecution Service and the Prosecution Group of HM Customs and Excise.

The legal profession
Although people are free to conduct their own cases if they so wish, barristers and solicitors, or other authorised litigators, generally represent the interests of parties to a dispute. Barristers practise as individuals, but join a group of other barristers in Chambers. Solicitors usually operate in partnership with other solicitors, but some are self-employed. Large firms of solicitors employ not only qualified staff, but also legal executives and support staff.

The Bar Council is the professional body representing barristers and the Law Society of England and Wales represents solicitors. The professions are self-regulating, with the professional bodies exercising disciplinary control over their members.

The Legal Services Ombudsman for England and Wales oversees the way in which the relevant professional bodies handle complaints about barristers, solicitors and other legal practitioners.

The Probation Service
In 2001 a unified National Probation Service for England and Wales was formed, led by a National Director who reports directly to the Home Secretary. The service is based in 42 areas, each of which has the same boundaries as a police force and Crown Prosecution Service area. The service supervises offenders in the community under direct court orders and on release on licence from custody. It also prepares reports for the courts to assist them in deciding on the most appropriate sentence.

HM Inspectorate of Probation has both an inspection and an advisory role, and also monitors any work that the Probation Service carries out in conjunction with the voluntary and private sectors.

Youth Offending Teams
The 155 Youth Offending Teams in England and Wales bring together relevant agencies, including police, probation, social services, education and health. They are responsible for delivering local youth justice services, such as community-based intervention programmes – supervising young offenders who are subject to non-custodial orders and those on the community phase of the detention and training order. The teams also work with young people at risk of offending.

The Prison Service
The Prison Service in England and Wales is an executive agency of the Home Office. There are currently 138 prison establishments (nine of which are run by private contractors).

Every prison establishment in England and Wales has an Independent Monitoring Board (formerly a Board of Visitors) comprising volunteers drawn from the local community and appointed by the Home Secretary. They monitor complaints by prisoners and the concerns of staff, and report as necessary to ministers.

An independent prisons inspectorate for England and Wales reports on the treatment of prisoners and prison conditions, and submits annual reports to Parliament. Each prison establishment is visited about once every three years.

Prisoners who fail to get satisfaction from the Prison Service's internal request and complaints system may complain to the independent Prisons Ombudsman.

Civil justice
Jurisdiction in civil matters in England and Wales is administered mainly by the county courts and the High Court, the latter handling the more substantial and complex cases. County courts also handle family proceedings, such as divorce, domestic violence and matters affecting children. Most civil disputes do not go to court, or do not reach trial. Many are dealt with through statutory

or voluntary complaints mechanisms, or through mediation and negotiation. Arbitration is common in commercial and building disputes. Ombudsmen have the power to determine complaints in the public sector and, on a voluntary basis, in some private sector activities (for example, banking, insurance and pensions).

Successful actions taken in the civil courts can result in damages being awarded to the individual pursuing the claim. The amount awarded in each case varies according to the circumstances.

The total number of claims issued in county courts in England and Wales rose from 2.3 million in 1988 to 3.7 million in 1991, but have since declined (see Figure 14.9). The majority of claims dealt with concern the recovery and collection of debt. The next most common types of claim relate to recovery of land and personal injury. Magistrates' courts have limited civil jurisdiction: in family matters (when they sit as a Family Proceedings Court) and in miscellaneous civil orders.

A large number of tribunals exist to determine disputes. Most deal with cases that involve the rights of private citizens against decisions of the State in areas such as social security, income tax and mental health. Some tribunals deal with other disputes, such as employment. In all, there are some 80 tribunals in England and Wales which together deal with over 1 million cases a year.

A new unified tribunals service was announced in 2003 as part of a wider government strategy of modernisation that has included reforms in the civil and criminal justice systems. The new service will have at its core the top ten non-devolved tribunals, covering areas such as employment, immigration, tax and pensions.

Courts

The High Court is divided into three Divisions:
- The *Queen's Bench Division* deals with disputes relating to contracts, general commercial matters (in a specialist Commercial Court), and breaches of duty – known as 'liability in tort' – covering claims of negligence, nuisance or defamation.
- The *Chancery Division* deals with disputes relating to land, wills, companies and insolvency.
- The *Family Division* deals with matrimonial matters, including divorce, and the welfare of children.

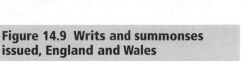

Figure 14.9 Writs and summonses issued, England and Wales

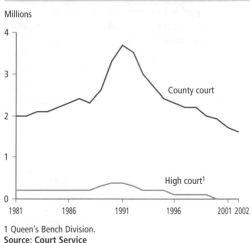

Millions

1 Queen's Bench Division.
Source: Court Service

Appeals in most civil cases were reformed by the *Access to Justice Act 1999*. The general principle is that appeal 'lies' to the next level of judge in the court hierarchy. A county court appeal lies from a district judge to a circuit judge and from a circuit judge to a High Court judge. In the High Court appeal lies from a master or district judge of the High Court to a High Court judge and from a High Court judge to the Court of Appeal.

As in criminal cases, appeals from magistrates' courts in civil matters go to the High Court, on matters of law, or to the Crown Court, if the case is to be re-heard. A further appeal on points of law of public importance would go to the House of Lords.

Proceeding with a claim

There is currently a system of three tracks to which disputed claims are assigned by a judge according to the value and complexity of the case. These are the:
- small claims track, for cases worth less than £5,000, at an informal hearing by a district judge;
- fast track, for cases from £5,000 to £15,000, with a fixed timetable from allocation to trial; and
- multi-track, for cases worth over £15,000 or of unusual complexity, which are supervised by a judge and given timetables tailored to each case.

Publicly funded legal help

The Legal Services Commission administers the Community Legal Service (CLS). The CLS Fund provides legal help and representation to qualifying applicants, depending on their personal financial circumstances and the merits of their case. It supports eligible people in cases of divorce and other family issues, and also in non-family cases including welfare benefits, debt, housing and property, immigration and nationality, clinical negligence, and actions against the police.

Recipients may be asked to make a contribution, depending on their personal financial circumstances and the outcome of the case. During 2002/03 there were 1.0 million acts of assistance under the CLS and the total net expenditure was £813 million. In recent years there has been a switch in emphasis to encourage early resolution of disputes without recourse to protracted and expensive legal action.

In addition to providing legal help and representation in civil matters, CLS activities extend to providing access to legal advice for the wider community. CLS Partnerships bring together organisations offering legal and advice services into local networks in England and Wales. These include solicitors' firms, Citizens Advice (see page 473), law centres, local authority services and other independent advice centres.

Scotland

The Scottish Executive Justice Department, under the Minister for Justice, is responsible for civil and criminal law and justice, criminal justice social work services, police, prisons, courts administration, legal aid, and liaison with the legal profession in Scotland.

The Department also has responsibility for all matters of the law of Scotland and its operation as it relates to international law and relations with other legal systems, including those of other parts of the United Kingdom. The Scottish Court Service, an executive agency of the Scottish Executive Justice Department, deals with the work of the Supreme Courts and the sheriff courts.

The Lord Advocate and the Solicitor General for Scotland provide the Scottish Executive with advice on legal matters and represent its interests in the courts. Since devolution, the Advocate General for Scotland has provided advice on Scots law to the UK Government.

The role of the Scottish Parliament is to make laws on matters devolved to it (see chapter 4 and Appendix A). In these areas, it is able to amend or repeal existing Acts of the United Kingdom Parliament and to pass new legislation for Scotland of its own. It can also consider and pass private legislation, promoted by individuals or bodies (for example, local authorities).

Policing

Scotland has eight territorial police forces. Other police forces that operate in Scotland include the British Transport Police and the Ministry of Defence police. Police authorities and joint police boards in Scotland are composed entirely of elected councillors.

The police have a general duty to uphold and enforce the law and maintain the peace in Scotland. They are provided with powers through both common law and statutory law to carry out this duty, including powers of arrest and detention.

Distinguishing features of the Scottish legal system

- The Scottish Parliament has legislative competence over most aspects of the law and the legal system in civil and criminal matters, including the prosecution system, the courts administration and certain judicial appointments.
- The Lord Advocate is responsible for the investigation of crime through the Crown Office, and for prosecutions in the High Court, sheriff court and district court.
- Unlike in England, there is no general right of prosecution. The prosecution is undertaken by the Lord Advocate in the interests of the public as a whole, and not on behalf of the police and other agencies such as Customs and Excise or individual citizens.
- The police report details of alleged crimes to the procurator fiscal, who has discretion whether or not to prosecute. Procurators fiscal are also responsible for the investigation of all sudden and suspicious deaths, as there are no coroners in Scotland.
- Scottish juries contain 15 people and reach a verdict by simple majority.

As in England and Wales, the police have responsibility for a number of more specialist tasks, including criminal investigation, traffic management and community liaison. The relevant police authority or joint board determines the budget and the resources available to each force.

The police in Scotland can arrest someone without a warrant, under wide common law powers, if suspects are seen or reported as committing a crime or are a danger to themselves or others. Someone suspected of an imprisonable offence may be held for police questioning without being arrested, but for no more than six hours without being charged. If arrested, suspects must be charged and cautioned. The case is then referred to the procurator fiscal.

HM Inspectorate of Constabulary for Scotland considers representations from complainants dissatisfied with the way the police have handled their complaints. A consultation paper with proposals for strengthening the independence of the police complaints system in Scotland was published in July 2001. More detailed proposals are expected in autumn 2003.

The Scottish Drug Enforcement Agency provides specialist support to Scottish Police forces in the prevention and detection of drug trafficking and other serious and organised crime. Police forensic science services are currently provided by four regional laboratories, based with the Tayside, Strathclyde, Lothian & Borders and Grampian police.

Criminal justice

Prisons

The Scottish Prison Service is an executive agency. In 2002/03 there were 16 prison establishments (15 public and one privately-run), and an average daily prison population of around 6,500.

There are statutory arrangements governing the early release of prisoners. Offenders serving terms of less than four years may be automatically released at specific points in their sentences. Those detained for longer require Parole Board approval. Ministers are statutorily obliged to give effect to the Parole Board's directions.

Legal aid

The Scottish Legal Aid Board manages legal aid in Scotland. Its main tasks are to grant or refuse applications for legal aid; to pay solicitors or advocates for the legal work that they do; and to advise Scottish ministers on legal aid matters. Where legal aid is granted to the accused in criminal proceedings, he or she is not required to pay any contribution towards expenses.

Scots law

The legal principles, rules and concepts of Scots law can be traced from diverse sources, including Roman law, canon law and the influences of other European systems. The main sources are judge-made law, certain legal treatises having 'institutional' authority, legislation, and EC law. The first two sources are sometimes referred to as the common law of Scotland. Legislation, as in the rest of the United Kingdom, consists of statutes (Acts of the UK or Scottish Parliament) or subordinate legislation authorised by the UK or Scottish Parliament.

Many statutory offences are, however, shared with England and Wales through UK-wide legislation (for example road traffic law) and laws relating to issues such as environmental pollution.

Advocates (broadly speaking the Scottish equivalent of barristers) have audience in the Supreme Courts. Solicitor-Advocates who are accredited specifically for civil or criminal business also have audience in the Supreme Courts. Solicitors in Scotland (numbering 8,926 in October 2002) have audience in the sheriff and district courts (see page 206) and in the other courts and tribunals. They practise largely in partnerships throughout the country.

The professional body for advocates is the Faculty of Advocates. For solicitors the regulator is the Law Society of Scotland. The Scottish Legal Services Ombudsman oversees the way in which these bodies handle complaints.

Prosecution

The Crown Office and Procurator Fiscal Service provide Scotland's independent public prosecution and deaths investigation service. The Department is headed by the Lord Advocate, assisted by the Solicitor-General for Scotland (who are the Scottish Law Officers and members of the Scottish Executive). The Crown Agent, a senior civil servant, is responsible for running the Department.

Procurators fiscal and Crown Office officials prepare prosecutions in the High Court which are conducted by the Lord Advocate and the Solicitor General for Scotland; they in turn delegate the bulk of their work to advocates depute, collectively known as Crown Counsel, of whom there are 18.

The police report gives details of alleged crimes to the local procurator fiscal who has discretion whether or not to prosecute. He or she may receive instructions from the Crown Counsel on behalf of the Lord Advocate.

The office of coroner does not exist in Scotland. Instead the local procurator fiscal inquires into sudden or suspicious deaths. When appropriate, a fatal accident inquiry may be held before the sheriff; this is mandatory in cases of death resulting from industrial accidents and deaths in custody. The inquiry has two purposes: to establish the causes of death; and to make recommendations as to how in future the causes and circumstances which led to individual deaths could be avoided.

Criminal courts

There are three criminal courts in Scotland: the High Court of Justiciary, the sheriff court and the district court. Cases are heard under one of two types of criminal procedure.

In *solemn procedure* in both the High Court of Justiciary and the sheriff court, an accused person's trial takes place before a judge sitting with a jury of 15 people selected at random from the general public. The judge decides questions of law and the jury decides questions of fact and may reach a decision by a simple majority. The jury may decide to find the accused 'guilty', 'not guilty' or 'not proven'; the last two are acquittals and have the effect that the accused cannot be tried again for the same offence.

In *summary procedure* in sheriff and district courts, the judge sits without a jury and decides questions of both fact and law.

Pre-trial hearings (called 'diets') in summary and solemn cases are intended to establish the state of readiness of both the defence and the prosecution.

The *High Court of Justiciary* is the supreme criminal court in Scotland, sitting in Edinburgh, Glasgow and on circuit in other towns. It tries the most serious crimes and has exclusive jurisdiction in cases involving murder, treason and rape.

The 49 *sheriff courts* deal mainly with less serious offences committed within their area of jurisdiction. These courts are organised in six sheriffdoms; at the head of each is a sheriff principal. There are over 100 permanent sheriffs, most of whom are appointed to particular courts. The sheriff has jurisdiction in both summary and solemn criminal cases. Under summary procedure, the sheriff may impose prison sentences of up to three months (in some cases six months) or a fine of £5,000. Under solemn procedure, the sheriff may impose imprisonment for up to three years and unlimited financial penalties.

District courts, which deal with minor offences, are the administrative responsibility of the local authority. The longest prison sentence that can be imposed is generally 60 days and the maximum fine is £2,500. The bench of a district court will usually be made up of one or more justices of the peace. A local authority may also appoint a stipendiary magistrate, who must be a professional lawyer of at least five years' standing, and who has the same summary criminal jurisdiction and powers as a sheriff. At present, only Glasgow has stipendiary magistrates sitting in the district court. A government review of the operation of the district courts is due to be completed by the end of 2003.

Over 139,000 people were proceeded against in Scottish criminal courts in 2001; 4 per cent were dealt with under solemn procedure, 63 per cent in sheriff summary courts, 29 per cent in district courts and 4 per cent by stipendiary magistrates.

Sentencing

In Scotland a court must obtain a social enquiry report before imposing a custodial sentence if the accused is aged under 21 or has not previously served a custodial sentence. A report is also required before making a probation or community service order, or in cases involving people already subject to supervision.

Non-custodial sentences available to the courts include fines, probation orders, community service orders, restriction of liberty orders (monitored by electronic tagging), drug treatment and testing orders, and supervised attendance orders (which provide an alternative to imprisonment for non-payment of fines, and incorporate aspects of work and training).

Some 120,000 people were sentenced in the sheriff courts and district courts in 2001[4] – over a third (44,000) in connection with motoring offences. Of the total, 64 per cent received a monetary penalty, 11 per cent a community sentence, 14 per cent a custodial sentence, and 11 per cent another form of sentence.

Children

Criminal proceedings may be brought against any child aged eight or over, but the instructions of the Lord Advocate are necessary before anyone under 16 years of age is prosecuted. Many of the children under 16 who have committed an offence or are considered to be in need of care and protection may be referred to the Children's Reporter, who decides whether the child should be brought before a Children's Hearing. The hearing, consisting of three people who are not lawyers, determines whether compulsory measures of supervision are required and, if so, the form they should take. In 2001/02 a total of 15,132 children aged under 16 were referred to the Children's Reporter on offence grounds. Young people aged between 16 and 21 who are given custodial sentences are usually placed in young offender institutions.

Probation

In Scotland local authority social work departments supervise offenders on probation, community service and other community disposals – equivalent to community sentences – and ex-prisoners subject to statutory supervision on release from custody.

Appeals

The High Court of Justiciary sits as the Scottish Court of Criminal Appeal. In both solemn and summary procedure, a convicted person may appeal against conviction, or sentence, or both. The Court may dispose of an appeal in a number of ways, including authorising a retrial if it sets aside a conviction. There is no appeal from this court in criminal cases. The Scottish Criminal Cases Review Commission is responsible for considering alleged miscarriages of justice and referring cases meeting the relevant criteria to the Court of Appeal for review. Just under 3,500

---

4 This figure includes those dealt with under summary as well as solemn procedure, and is not therefore comparable with the figures on those sentenced for indictable offences in England and Wales, given on page 191.

appeals were concluded in 2001, equivalent to 3 per cent of the total number of convictions in that year. Of these appeals, 1 per cent resulted in a conviction being quashed and 11 per cent in a reduced sentence.

Civil justice

The bulk of the civil business in Scotland is conducted in the sheriff court which has general jurisdiction and sits throughout the country. An appeal is possible from the sheriff to the sheriff principal and then to the Court of Session. Appeal from the Court of Session is available to the House of Lords.

The *Court of Session* sits in Edinburgh, and may hear cases from the outset or on transfer from sheriff courts and tribunals on appeal. A leading principle of the court is that cases starting there are both prepared for decision, and decided, by judges sitting alone whose decisions are subject to review by several judges.

In addition to its criminal jurisdiction, the *sheriff court* deals with most civil law cases in Scotland. There is, with very few exceptions, no upper limit to the financial level with which the court can deal, and a broad range of remedies can be granted. As in England and Wales, cases may include debts, contracts, reparation, rent restrictions, actions affecting the use of property, leases and tenancies, child protection issues and family actions.

The House of Lords hears relatively few appeals in civil matters from Scotland but, since devolution, the Judicial Committee of the Privy Council (JCPC) has had jurisdiction to consider disputes involving the powers of the devolved administration. When dealing with Scottish cases, the JCPC usually includes at least two Scottish judges.

Where legal aid is granted in civil cases, a contribution may be required.

Civil proceedings

The formal proceedings in the Court of Session are started by serving the defender with a summons or, in sheriff court cases in ordinary actions, an initial writ. A defender who intends to contest the action must inform the court; if he or she fails to do so, the court normally grants a decree in absence in favour of the pursuer. Where a case is contested, both parties must prepare written pleadings, after which a hearing will normally be arranged.

Where actions are raised for sums up to £750 there is a special procedure for small claims which allows those who do not have legal advice to raise the claims themselves in the sheriff court. These are broadly restricted to payment actions. The procedure is intended to be simple and to allow for negotiated settlement at the earliest possible time.

For claims between £750 and £1,500[5] in the sheriff court, a summons incorporates a statement of claim. The procedure is designed to let most actions be settled without the parties having to appear in court. Normally, they, or their representatives, need appear only when an action is defended.

The Scottish Land Court deals with agricultural matters and some environmental issues. The Lands Tribunal for Scotland deals with matters relating to land conditions, right to buy and valuation issues. The Children's Hearing deals with children in need of measures of supervision or care. Tribunals common to the rest of the United Kingdom deal with issues such as unemployment, social security, and asylum and immigration matters (see also page 203).

Northern Ireland

Northern Ireland's legal system is similar to that of England and Wales. Jury trials have the same place in the system, except in the case of offences involving acts of terrorism. In addition, cases go through the same stages in the courts and the legal profession has the same two branches.

People accused of offences specified under terrorism legislation (see page 192) are tried in the Crown Court without a jury. The prosecution must prove guilt beyond reasonable doubt and the defendant has the right to be represented by a lawyer of his or her choice. The judge has to set out in a written statement the reasons for conviction and there is an automatic right of appeal to the Court of Appeal against conviction and/or sentence on points of fact as well as of law.

The probation service in Northern Ireland is administered by the government-funded Probation Board, whose membership is representative of the community.

The Northern Ireland Prison Service is an executive agency of the Northern Ireland Office. There are currently three prison establishments, with an average population (based on monthly counts) in 2002/03 of 1,050. Each prison has a Board of Visitors/Visiting Committee comprising volunteers appointed by the Secretary of State for Northern Ireland. There are no open prisons in Northern Ireland.

An Order in Council is being prepared for Parliament that will allow for the introduction of mandatory drug testing in Northern Ireland prisons towards the end of 2003.

Policing

In November 2001 the Royal Ulster Constabulary became the Police Service of Northern Ireland (PSNI), as part of a series of reforms to the police following the report of the Patten Commission set up under the terms of the Belfast (Good Friday) Agreement (see chapter 5).

The Chief Constable is accountable to a new Policing Board, made up of ten political nominees and nine independent members appointed by the Secretary of State.

District policing partnerships serve as important forums for consultation between the community and the police on policing objectives, priorities and concerns. The Policing Board works with these partnerships in all 26 district council areas. Complaints against the police are investigated by an independent Police Ombudsman.

Administration of the law

A wide-ranging review of the criminal justice system in Northern Ireland was carried out under the terms of the Belfast (Good Friday) Agreement. The report of the Review, published in 2000, made 294 recommendations for change across the criminal justice system. Key recommendations included:

- a focus on promoting human rights within the criminal justice system;
- a new Public Prosecution Service building on the work of the existing Director of Public Prosecutions Office;
- an independent Judicial Appointments Commission;

---

5 These levels are currently under review.

- an independent Criminal Justice Inspectorate
- an independent Northern Ireland Law Commission;
- improvements to youth justice arrangements – including the creation of a Youth Justice Agency; and
- the development of North/South co-operation on criminal justice matters.

The *Justice (Northern Ireland) Act 2002* implemented a number of the Government's decisions on the review. An updated Criminal Justice Implementation Plan was published in June 2003, setting out progress and containing detailed plans and timescales for the continuing implementation process.

The Lord Chancellor is responsible for court administration through the Northern Ireland Court Service, while the Northern Ireland Office, under the Secretary of State, deals with policy and legislation concerning criminal law, the police and the penal system. The Lord Chancellor has general responsibility for legal aid, advice and assistance.

Civil legal aid is administered by the Law Society for Northern Ireland. As in the rest of the United Kingdom, where legal aid is granted for criminal cases it is free.

Superior courts

The Supreme Court of Judicature comprises the Court of Appeal, the High Court and the Crown Court. All matters relating to these courts are under the jurisdiction of the UK Parliament. Judges are appointed by the Crown (but see page 208).

The *Court of Appeal* consists of the Lord Chief Justice (as President) and two Lords Justices of Appeal. The High Court is made up of the Lord Chief Justice and five other judges. The practice and procedure of the Court of Appeal and the High Court are virtually the same as in the corresponding courts in England and Wales. Both courts sit in the Royal Courts of Justice in Belfast.

The Court of Appeal has power to review the civil law decisions of the High Court and the criminal law decisions of the Crown Court, and may in certain cases review the decisions of county courts and magistrates' courts. Subject to certain restrictions, an appeal from a judgement of the Court of Appeal can go to the House of Lords. As in the rest of the United Kingdom, a Criminal

Cases Review Commission, which is independent of both government and the courts, reviews alleged miscarriages of justice.

The *High Court* is divided into a Queen's Bench Division, dealing with most civil law matters; a Chancery Division, dealing with, for instance, trusts and estates, title to land, mortgages and charges, wills and company matters; and a Family Division, dealing principally with such matters as matrimonial cases, adoption, children in care and undisputed wills.

The *Crown Court* deals with all serious criminal cases.

Inferior courts

The inferior courts are the county courts and the magistrates' courts, both of which differ in a number of ways from their counterparts in England and Wales.

County courts are primarily civil law courts. They are presided over by one of 14 county court judges, two of whom – in Belfast and Londonderry/Derry – have the title of recorder. Appeals go from the county courts to the High Court. The county courts also handle appeals from the magistrates' courts in both criminal and civil matters. In civil matters, the county courts decide most actions in which the amount or the value of specific articles claimed is below a certain level. The courts also deal with actions involving title to, or the recovery of, land; equity matters such as trusts and estates; mortgages; and the sale of land and partnerships.

The day-to-day work of dealing summarily with minor local criminal cases is carried out in *magistrates' courts* presided over by a full-time, legally qualified resident magistrate (RM). The magistrates' courts also exercise jurisdiction in certain family law cases and have a very limited jurisdiction in other civil cases.

Further reading

The Lord Chancellor's Departments: Departmental Report 2002–2003. Cm 5910. The Stationery Office, 2003.

Home Office Departmental Report 2003. Cm 5908, The Stationery Office, 2003.

Crime in England and Wales 2002/2003. Home Office, 2003.

A Guide to the Criminal Justice System in England and Wales. Home Office, 2000.

Crime and Criminal Justice in Scotland. Peter Young. The Stationery Office, 1997.

Justice for All. Cm 5563. The Stationery Office, 2002.

Websites

Community Legal Service
www.justask.org.uk

Criminal justice system
www.cjsonline.org

Department for Constitutional Affairs
www.dca.gov.uk

HM Prison Service (England and Wales)
www.hmprisonservice.gov.uk

Home Office
www.homeoffice.gov.uk

Legal Services Commission
www.legalservices.gov.uk

Northern Ireland Executive
www.northernireland.gov.uk

Police services of the UK
www.police.uk

Scottish Executive
www.scotland.gov.uk

Youth Justice Board for England and Wales
www.youth-justice-board.gov.uk

WWW.

15 Religion

Everyone in the United Kingdom has a legal right to freedom of thought, conscience and religion. Religious organisations and groups may conduct their rites and ceremonies, promote their beliefs within the limits of the law, own property, and run schools and a range of other charitable activities. Although predominantly Christian, most world religions are represented in the United Kingdom. In particular there are large Muslim, Hindu, Sikh and Jewish communities.

Religious affiliations in the UK

The 2001 Census was the first to include a religion question in England, Wales and Scotland. In Northern Ireland, where there is a history of sectarian conflict, there has been a religion question since the first Census of Northern Ireland in 1926.

The 2001 Census figures show that 77 per cent of people in England and Wales, 67 per cent in Scotland and 86 per cent in Northern Ireland said they identified with a religion. Some of the variation in these results may be due to the different questions concerning religion which were included in the Census questionnaires in England and Wales, Scotland, and Northern Ireland (see box). Of those people who identified with a religion, 93 per cent in England and Wales and 97 per cent in Scotland said that they belonged to the Christian faith (see page 25 for Northern Ireland data). After Christianity, the most common faiths were Islam, followed by Hinduism, Sikhism, Judaism and Buddhism.

About 15 per cent of the population of England and Wales and 28 per cent of Scotland stated in the 2001 Census that they had no religion, although once again the different questions in the two Censuses may account for some of this variation. Organisations such as the British Humanist Association and the National Secular

Measuring the size of religious communities
A distinction is often drawn between 'community size' – representing a broad identification with a religion or a religious ethic – and 'active membership'. Active membership may be measured in a variety of ways – for example by attendance at places of worship or by membership lists. However, some religions are more highly organised than others, so comparisons based on active membership can be misleading. The religion question asked in the 2001 Census for England and Wales was voluntary and designed to measure identification in a broad sense. It asked 'What is your religion?' (see Table 15.1). Unlike in Scotland and Northern Ireland, there was a single tick box for 'Christian'.

People in Scotland were asked 'What religion, religious denomination or body do you belong to?' with a follow-up question, 'What religion, religious denomination or body were you brought up in?' These two questions were also used in Northern Ireland, but were preceded by a question which asked 'Do you regard yourself as belonging to any particular religion?' The Scottish and Northern Irish forms included tick boxes for the major Christian traditions in those parts of the United Kingdom.

Society represent the views of some of those who do not identify with a religion.

The faith communities

The Christian community in the United Kingdom consists of many denominations. The Anglican and Catholic Churches have the largest congregations. Other Christian denominations form the 'Free Churches' and include Presbyterians, Methodists and Baptists. With the increasing diversity in ethnic background among the UK population there has been a growth in faith communities other than Christian. The

Table 15.1 Belonging to a religion,[1] 2001, England and Wales

Religion	Thousands	Percentages
Christian	37,338	71.7
Muslim	1,547	3.0
Hindu	552	1.1
Sikh	329	0.6
Jewish	260	0.5
Buddhist	144	0.3
Other	151	0.3
All religions	40,322	77.5
No religion	7,709	14.8
Religion not stated	4,011	7.7
All	52,041	100

1 The question was voluntary, with tick box options, and asked 'What is your religion?'.
Source: Census, Office for National Statistics

Church and State

Christianity remains the declared faith of the majority of the UK population and two Churches have special status with regard to the State. In England, since the rejection by Henry VIII of the supremacy of the Pope in 1534, the Anglican *Church of England* has been legally recognised as the official, or 'established', Church. The Monarch is the 'Supreme Governor' of the Church of England and must always be a member of the Church, and promise to uphold it. A similar position was occupied by the Presbyterian *Church of Scotland* until the early 20th century. This continues to be recognised as the national Church in Scotland, but the Monarch holds no constitutional role in its government, although she is represented at the General Assembly (see page 213) through the office of the Lord High Commissioner. Neither of the established Churches are funded by the State. There are no established Churches in Wales or Northern Ireland. In Wales, the Anglican Church is known as the *Church in Wales*.

largest of these is the Muslim community followed by the Hindu, Sikh and Jewish communities.

Anglicans

The Church of England is part of a worldwide Communion of Anglican churches, 38 in all. The four Anglican churches in the United Kingdom are the Church of England, the Church in Wales, the Scottish Episcopal Church, and the Church of Ireland (Northern Ireland). The Church of England has an average weekly church attendance of 1.2 million.

The Church of England is divided into two geographical provinces, each headed by an archbishop: Canterbury, comprising 30 dioceses, including the Diocese in Europe; and York, with 14 dioceses. The dioceses are divided into archdeaconries and deaneries, which are in turn divided into 13,000 parishes, although in practice many parishes are grouped together.

Archbishops, bishops and the deans of some Church of England cathedrals are appointed by The Queen on the advice of the Prime Minister. The Crown Appointments Commission, which includes lay and clergy representatives, plays a key role in the selection of archbishops and diocesan bishops. The Archbishops' Council is the centre of an administrative system dealing with inter-Church relations, inter-faith relations, social questions, recruitment and training for the ministry, and missionary work.

A new Archbishop of Canterbury

Dr Rowan Williams was enthroned as the 104th Archbishop of Canterbury in February 2003. He is the first Welshman to be selected for this position in the Church of England in over 1,000 years. The main roles of the Archbishop include Diocesan Bishop of Canterbury, Primate of All England and leader of the Anglican Communion. He takes the lead in respect of Anglican relationships with other Christian churches in the United Kingdom and abroad, and he also leads in respect of Anglican relationships with other faiths.

The Archbishops of Canterbury and York, the Bishops of Durham, London and Winchester, and the 21 senior diocesan bishops from other dioceses of the Church of England have seats in the House of Lords (see page 36).

The Church Commissioners are responsible for the management of a large part of the Church of England's invested assets. The Crown appoints a Member of Parliament from the governing party to the unpaid post of Second Church Estates Commissioner, to represent the Commissioners in Parliament. The Church Commissioners currently meet some 15 per cent of the Church of England's total running costs, providing support for parish ministry and the pensions of the clergy. Parishes and dioceses meet the remaining costs.

Catholics

The Catholic Church has an average weekly Mass attendance of approximately 1 million in England and Wales, around 200,000 in Scotland and 420,000 in Northern Ireland.

There are eight provinces of the Catholic Church in the United Kingdom – four in England, two in Scotland, one in Wales and one that includes Northern Ireland. The Bishops' Conference is a permanent institution of the Catholic Church whereby the bishops of a country acting together exercise pastoral, legislative and teaching offices as defined by the law of the Church. There is a Bishops' Conference of England and Wales, and a Bishops' Conference of Scotland. The Irish Episcopal Conference covers the whole of Ireland.

There are 22 territorial Catholic dioceses in England and Wales and eight in Scotland. Northern Ireland is covered by seven dioceses, some of which extend into the Republic of Ireland. Each diocesan bishop is appointed by the Pope and governs according to Canon Law and through reference to a Council of Priests, a College of Consultors, a Finance Committee and a Pastoral Council.

Church of Scotland

The Church of Scotland is the largest Protestant church in Scotland with an adult communicant membership in the United Kingdom of approximately 590,000.

The Church has a Presbyterian form of government – that is, government by church courts or councils, composed of ministers, elders, and deacons. The 1,543 congregations are governed locally by courts known as Kirk Sessions. The courts above these are the 'Presbyteries', responsible for a geographical area made up of a number of parishes. The General Assembly, or Supreme Court, meets annually under the chairmanship of an elected moderator, who serves for one year.

Other Christians

The rise of the Puritan movement in the 16th and 17th centuries led to a proliferation of nonconformist churches. The term 'Free Churches' is often used to describe these Protestant churches in the United Kingdom that, unlike the Church of England and the Church of Scotland, are not 'established' Churches. Free Churches include Methodist, Baptist, United Reformed, Salvation Army and a variety of Pentecostal Churches.

The British Methodist Church, the largest of the Free Churches in Great Britain, originated in the 18th century following the evangelical revival under John Wesley. It has approximately 330,000 full members. The present Church is based on the 1932 union of most of the separate Methodist Churches.

Tercentenary of the birth of John Wesley (1703–91)

John Wesley, founder of the Methodist Church, was born on 17 June 1703 in Epworth, Lincolnshire. He attended Charterhouse school in London, graduated from Oxford University and was ordained as a deacon in the Church of England in 1725. Wesley became known as a 'Methodist' because of his methodical and strictly religious lifestyle. On some issues he began to disagree with the Church of England into which he was ordained. In 1739 he preached in the open air for the first time, to a company of miners in Kingswood, Gloucestershire. From the late 1730s until his death in London in March 1791, Wesley travelled thousands of miles promoting and preaching the Methodist movement, often in the open air. In 2003 various conferences and festivals were held in the United Kingdom, as well as a European Methodist Festival in Germany, to commemorate his birth and legacy.

The Baptists first achieved an organised form in the United Kingdom in the 17th century. Today they are mainly organised in associations of churches, most of which belong to the Baptist Union of Great Britain (re-formed in 1812). The union, with 141,000 members, covers England, a significant proportion of the English-speaking Baptist churches in Wales and two Baptist churches in Scotland (both of which belong to the Baptist Union of Scotland). There is also a Baptist Union in Wales comprising both Welsh and English-speaking Baptist churches. The Association of Baptist Churches in Ireland covers all the Baptist churches in Northern Ireland and the Republic of Ireland.

The United Reformed Church, with some 90,000 members in Great Britain, was formed in 1972 from the union of the Congregational Church in England and Wales with the Presbyterian Church in England. In 1982 and 2000 there were further unions with the Reformed Churches of Christ and the Congregational Union of Scotland.

Among the other Free Churches are the Presbyterian Church in Ireland, which has 187,000 members in Northern Ireland; the Presbyterian (or Calvinistic Methodist) Church of Wales, the largest of the Free Churches in Wales with 39,000 members; the Union of Welsh Independents, with 32,000 members; and a number of independent Scottish Presbyterian Churches which are particularly active in the Highlands and Islands.

The Salvation Army was founded in the East End of London in 1865 by William Booth. It has a membership of nearly 50,000 in the United Kingdom and runs over 750 local church and community centres.

The Religious Society of Friends (Quakers), with about 16,500 members, was founded in the middle of the 17th century under the leadership of George Fox. Unitarians and Free Christians, whose origins go back to the Reformation, belong to a similar tradition. There are two branches of the Christian Brethren, founded in the 19th century: the Open Brethren and the Closed or Exclusive Brethren.

People of different cultures coming to settle in the United Kingdom since the Middle Ages have contributed to the diversity of Christian denominations. Christian communities founded by migrants include those of the Orthodox, Lutheran and Reformed Churches of various European countries, the Coptic Orthodox Church, Armenian Church and a number of churches originating in Africa, such as the Cherubim and Seraphim Churches. These tend to be concentrated in the larger cities of the United Kingdom, particularly London. The largest is the Greek Orthodox Church, many of whose members are of Cypriot origin.

Other developments within the Christian tradition have included the rise of Pentecostalism and the charismatic[1] movement. A number of

1 A type of Christianity that emphasises personal religious experience and divinely inspired powers.

Pentecostal bodies were formed in the United Kingdom at the turn of the 20th century. The two main organisations in the United Kingdom today are the Assemblies of God, and the Elim Pentecostal Church.

Since the Second World War immigration from the Caribbean and Africa has led to a significant number of Black Majority Churches, many of which are Pentecostal. These are a growing presence in the United Kingdom and in particular England. The Christian 'house church' movement (or 'new churches') began in the 1970s when some of the charismatics began to establish their own congregations.

Muslims

A Muslim community has existed in the United Kingdom since the 16th century. By the early 19th century Muslim seamen, mainly from Yemen and the Indian subcontinent, had settled in several parts of the country, including Cardiff, South Shields and the London docklands. There was further settlement after the First World War, and again in the 1950s and 1960s as people arrived to meet the shortage of labour following the Second World War.

The 1970s saw the arrival of significant numbers of Muslims of Asian origin from Kenya and Uganda, as well as those arriving directly from the Indian subcontinent. There are well-established Turkish Cypriot and Iranian Muslim communities, and more recently Muslims from Somalia, Iraq, Bosnia and Kosovo have sought refuge in the United Kingdom. In addition, there are smaller numbers of English, West Indian and Chinese Muslims.

Sunni and Shi'a are the two principal traditions within Islam and while both are represented among the Muslim community in the United Kingdom, most UK Muslims belong to the Sunni tradition. Sufism, the spiritually-oriented path of Islam, can be found in both traditions, and members of some of the major Sufi traditions have also developed branches in UK cities. According to the Census there were approximately 1.59 million Muslims in the United Kingdom in 2001.

The Muslim Council of Britain, founded in 1997, represents 400 established national and regional Muslim bodies as well as local mosques, professional associations and other organisations. The Council aims to promote co-operation, consensus and unity on Muslim affairs in the United Kingdom and is a source of information on issues affecting the Muslim community.

Hindus

The Hindu community in the United Kingdom originates largely from India. Most UK Hindus are of Gujarati or Punjabi origin with smaller numbers from Uttar Pradesh, West Bengal and the southern states of India and Sri Lanka. Many have come from countries to which earlier generations of Indians had previously migrated such as Kenya, Malawi, Tanzania, Uganda and Zambia. According to the Census there were approximately 559,000 Hindus in the United Kingdom in 2001.

The main administrative bodies for Hindus are the National Council of Hindu Temples (UK) and the Hindu Council UK. Other national bodies serving the Hindu community include Vishwa Hindu Parishad (UK).

Sikhs

Most of the Sikh community in the United Kingdom originates from the Indian part of the Punjab, although a minority came via East Africa and other former British colonies to which members of their family had migrated. The community in the United Kingdom is believed to be the largest outside the Indian subcontinent. According to the Census there were approximately 336,000 Sikhs in the United Kingdom in 2001. The Network of Sikh Organisations was formed in 1995 to facilitate co-operation between British Sikhs. It provides a forum for organising the celebration of major events in the Sikh calendar, and works with government departments and a number of national organisations to represent Sikh interests at a national level.

Jews

Jews settled in England prior to the Norman Conquest in 1066. They were banished by royal decree in 1290, but re-admitted following the English Civil War (1642–51). Sephardic Jews, who originally came from Spain and Portugal, have been present in the United Kingdom since the mid-17th century. However, the majority of Jews in the United Kingdom today are Ashkenazi, descended from people who emigrated or fled persecution in the Russian Empire between 1881 and 1914, or Nazi persecution in Germany and other European countries from 1933 onwards.

According to the Census there were approximately 267,000 Jews in the United Kingdom in 2001.

The Board of Deputies of British Jews is the officially recognised representative body for the Jewish community. Founded in 1760, the Board's representation is through deputies elected by synagogues, and community organisations. It serves as the voice of the community to both government and the wider non-Jewish community and calls on the Chief Rabbi and the Communal Rabbi of the Spanish and Portuguese Jews' Congregation for religious advice and guidance when needed.

Sixty per cent of those Ashkenazi households who are affiliated to synagogues acknowledge the authority of the Chief Rabbi. The Reform Synagogues of Great Britain, the Union of Liberal and Progressive Synagogues and the Union of Orthodox Hebrew Congregations together account for most of the remaining synagogue-affiliated community membership.

Buddhists

The Buddhist community in the United Kingdom includes people of British, South Asian and South East Asian background. Various strands of Buddhism from the numerous traditions are represented. According to the Census there were approximately 152,000 Buddhists in the United Kingdom in 2001. The Network of Buddhist Organisations links various educational, cultural, charitable and teaching organisations. The Buddhist Society promotes the principles, but does not adhere to any particular school, of Buddhism.

Other traditions

Jainism is an ancient religion brought to the United Kingdom mainly by immigrants from the Gujarat and Rajasthan areas of India. The Zoroastrian religion is mainly represented in the United Kingdom by the Parsi community from India. The founders of the UK community originally settled here in the 19th century. The Bahá'í movement originated in Persia in the 19th century. Rastafarianism, with its roots in the return-to-Africa movement, emerged in the West Indies early in the 20th century and arrived in the United Kingdom with immigration from Jamaica in the 1950s.

Other religious groups in the United Kingdom were originally founded in the United States in the

19th century, including a number deriving from the Christian tradition. Examples include the growing number of Mormons who belong to the Church of Jesus Christ of Latter-day Saints, the Jehovah's Witnesses, the Christadelphians, the Christian Scientists, and the Seventh-day Adventists.

New religious movements

A number of newer religious movements, established since the Second World War and often with overseas origins, are now active in the United Kingdom. Examples include the Church of Scientology, the Transcendental Meditation movement, the Unification Church and various New Age groups.

Places of worship

There are 16,000 Anglican Churches (the earliest dating from the seventh century) and 42 Anglican cathedrals, which serve as focal points of the dioceses. The Church of Scotland and the Church in Wales each have over 1,500 churches.

Cathedral Grants Scheme

Since 1991 English Heritage has provided nearly £38 million through its annual Cathedral Grants Scheme. In January 2003 it announced grants totalling £1.9 million for repairs to over 20 cathedrals in England. These include:

- Salisbury cathedral, which will receive the largest grant (£248,000) towards roof and masonry repairs and the preparation of a conservation plan. Founded in 1220 and built in the early English style, Salisbury is famous for its graceful tower and spire;
- Lincoln cathedral, which will receive £194,000 for the installation of a health and safety system and for work on the Dean's Eye Window (a 13th century wheel window which contains much of the original glass); and
- Southwark cathedral, which will receive £76,000 for the installation of a health and safety system and fire precaution measures. Set in an historic area of London the cathedral has a memorial to Shakespeare, whose Globe Theatre was nearby.

Since 1969, over 1,600 churches in England have become redundant and around £32 million has been raised from their disposal. Redundant churches are increasingly being used for

residential property or as civic, cultural and community centres. The Churches Conservation Trust, funded jointly by the Government and the Church of England, preserves Anglican churches of particular cultural and historical importance that are no longer used as regular places of worship. In 2003, 330 churches were being maintained in this way. A number of outstanding buildings from other denominations and faiths are cared for by the Historic Chapels Trust.

There are over 1,000 mosques and numerous community Muslim centres throughout the United Kingdom. Mosques are not only places of worship; they also offer instruction in the Muslim way of life, and facilities for education and welfare. They range from converted buildings in many towns and suburbs to the Central Mosque in Regent's Park, London, with its associated Islamic Cultural Centre. The main conurbations in London, the Midlands, North West and North East of England, and Scotland, Wales and Northern Ireland also have their own central mosques with a range of community facilities. The East London Mosque has recently launched community schemes concerned with social housing and addressing school truancy.

The first Hindu temple, or mandir, was opened in London in the 1950s and there are now over 140 in the United Kingdom; many are affiliated to the National Council of Hindu Temples (UK). The Swaminarayan Hindu Temple in north London is the largest and was the first purpose-built Hindu temple in Europe.

There are over 200 gurdwaras, or Sikh temples, in the United Kingdom, the majority being in England and Wales. Gurdwaras cater for the

---

The Sri Guru Singh Sabha Gurdwara

In March 2003 the largest gurdwara outside India was opened in Southall, west London. Building work began in May 2000 and was completed at a cost of just under £17 million, all of which was raised by the local Sikh community group Sri Guru Singh Sabha. The building covers 6,000 square metres and provides a first floor prayer hall and a second floor gallery area designed to seat up to 2,000 people, giving a total capacity of 3,000. As well as being a place of worship, the building serves as a community centre providing library and seminar facilities. There is a dining hall capable of serving 20,000 meals at festival weekends.

---

religious, educational, welfare and cultural needs of their community. A 'granthi' is usually employed to take care of the building and to conduct prayers.

Jewish synagogues in the United Kingdom number approximately 300, but there are many additional congregations that do not have their own purpose-built synagogue building.

There are numerous Buddhist centres in the United Kingdom at which meditation or spiritual practice can take place, although religious buildings are not as central to Buddhist life as to that of some other religious traditions.

Religion and society

The influence of Christianity and other religions in the United Kingdom has always extended far beyond the comparatively narrow spheres of organised and private worship. Religious organisations are actively involved in voluntary work and in the provision of schools and other services to the community.

The North West London Eruv
In February 2003 the first community eruv in the United Kingdom was created by the Orthodox Jewish Community in North West London. An eruv is an area within which observant Jews can carry or push objects on the Sabbath (which lasts from sunset on Friday to nightfall on Saturday), without violating a Jewish law that prohibits carrying anything except within the home. The eruv boundary is marked out by poles and in this particular case is 18 kilometres long, enclosing an area of 17 square kilometres.

Religious ceremonies and festivals
Although there are secular alternatives, religious traditions play a major role in commemorating births, marriages, deaths and other important life events.

In 2001 just under 40 per cent of marriages in the United Kingdom were solemnised with a religious ceremony, compared with approximately 60 per cent in 1971. Since 1971 the number of marriages with civil ceremonies has remained fairly steady while the number of marriages with religious ceremonies has declined (see Figure 15.2).

There are, however, wide variations within the United Kingdom. Seventy four per cent of

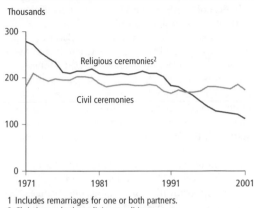

Figure 15.2 Marriages[1] by type of ceremony, UK

Thousands

1 Includes remarriages for one or both partners.
2 Christian and other religious traditions.
Source: Office for National Statistics; General Register Office for Scotland; Northern Ireland Statistics and Research Agency

marriages in Northern Ireland in 2001 involved a religious ceremony, compared with 61 per cent of marriages in Scotland and 36 per cent of marriages in England and Wales.

Two of the most important events in the Christian calendar, Easter and Christmas, are major public holidays in the United Kingdom. Festivals and other events observed by other religions – such as Ramadan and the two Eid festivals (Muslim), Diwali and Janmashtami (Hindu), Vaisakhi (Sikh), the High Holy Days and Passover (Jewish), and the Birthday of the Buddha – are adding to the visible diversity of life in the United Kingdom today.

Religious education
In England and Wales all state schools must provide religious education, each local education authority being responsible for producing a locally agreed syllabus. Syllabuses must reflect Christianity, while taking account of the teachings and practices of the other principal religions represented in the United Kingdom. State schools must provide a daily act of collective worship but parents may withdraw their children from religious education and collective worship.

State supported schools which have a religious character or ethos are often called faith schools. In 2002 there were approximately 7,000 state supported faith schools in England. They were either foundation or voluntary-controlled (entirely funded by the local education authority) or voluntary-aided (funded by the local education authority with contributions to capital expenses by school and parent organisations). In these schools collective worship is in the tenets of the faith of the school. Religious education is in accordance with the locally agreed syllabus, except in voluntary-aided faith schools where it is in the tenets of the faith of the school. Since October 2003 independent schools, including academies and city technology colleges, have been able to apply to be designated as schools with a religious character. This allows them to employ teaching staff with the same religious belief as the school.

In Scotland, education authorities must ensure that schools provide religious education and regular opportunities for religious observance. The law does not specify the form of religious education, but it is recommended that pupils should be provided with a broad-based curriculum, through which they can develop a knowledge and understanding of Christianity and other world religions, and develop their own beliefs, attitudes and moral values and practices. Roman Catholic schools account for nearly all of the 430 state supported faith schools in Scotland.

In Northern Ireland a core syllabus for religious education has been approved by the main churches and this must be taught in all grant-aided schools, though parents may withdraw their children from religious education and collective worship. Integrated education is encouraged and all schools must be open to pupils of all religions, although in practice most Catholic pupils attend Catholic maintained schools or Catholic voluntary grammar schools, and most Protestant children are enrolled at controlled schools or non-denominational voluntary grammar schools. However, the number of inter-denominational schools is gradually increasing. In 2002/03, 15,317 primary and secondary pupils received their education at 'integrated' schools where Protestant and Catholic pupils are taught together.

Welfare

Christian Aid, CAFOD (Catholic Agency for Overseas Development), Muslim Aid, Islamic Relief, Sewa International (a Hindu charity), Khalsa Aid (a Sikh charity) and UK Jewish Aid are among the many UK-based charities that organise appeals and deliver relief aid globally.

Within the United Kingdom the Salvation Army is an important provider of hostel accommodation,

Working with disabled people

Many charities with a religious character work with disabled people. For example, Living PROSPECTS (www.prospects.org.uk) is a Christian-based charity working with people with learning disabilities in the United Kingdom. In 2003 it was supporting about 200 people in a variety of living situations, including residency in one of 25 homes run by the charity. There is a home support scheme to provide short-term help, and there are education classes, recreation facilities and supported employment. Many of these activities are fully integrated with non-disabled people. Another charity with a religious background is Jewish Blind & Disabled (www.jbd.org) which provides sheltered housing for visually impaired and physically disabled people. The charity has six sheltered housing projects in the Greater London area containing over 200 flats, each adapted to the resident's special needs.

and offers other services including work with alcoholics, prison chaplaincy and a family-tracing service. The Quakers have a long tradition of social concern and peacemaking. Trusts with a Quaker history, such as the Cadbury and Rowntree Trusts, support many social initiatives, particularly funding for housing.

The Church Urban Fund, established by the Church of England, is an independent charity that raises money to enable those living in the most disadvantaged urban areas to set up local projects to alleviate the effects of poverty. Although rooted in the Christian faith, the fund does not restrict its grants on the basis of religious belief.

The General Assembly of the Church of Scotland, through its Board of Social Responsibility, is the largest voluntary social work agency in Scotland. The Board runs projects offering care and support to 4,000 people.

Links with government

The Home Office set up a Faith Communities Unit in June 2003. This is responsible for ensuring that policies and services are delivered in ways that are appropriate to faith communities, and that their experience and skills are recognised and utilised.

In England, the Inner Cities Religious Council, based in the Office of the Deputy Prime Minister, provides a forum in which the Government and

3 March 2003 300th anniversary of the death of Robert Hooke (1635–1703), natural philosopher, inventor, biologist, astronomer and architect – he was the architect of Montague House *(also pictured, see 7 June)*, which later became the first home of the British Museum. He coined the word 'cell' to describe the tiniest components of living systems and founded the field of microscopic biology with his published work *Micrographia* – title page showing drawings of Hooke's instruments *(left)*. Drawings of a cranefly showing the head *(below)* and a flea *(bottom left)*.

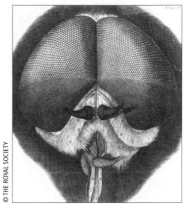

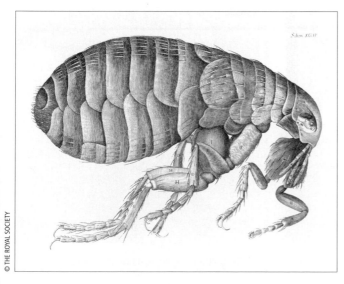

'UT TENSIO, SIC VIS'

The stress applied to any solid is proportional to the strain it produces within the elastic limit for that solid.

Hooke's Law

20 March 2003 British troops begin military action in Iraq as part of an international coalition. Following the fall of Saddam Hussein's regime in April, troops remained in Iraq while a new civilian authority was being set up.

21 March 2003 a Chinook helicopter lifts mortar rounds from the deck of HMS *Ocean*.

3 April 2003 a sniper from the Irish Guards covers Royal Engineers extinguishing a fire at an oil well near Basra.

18 April 2003 A mine awareness campaign for local people: British troops display abandoned Iraqi ordnance to raise awareness of the threat these pose.

17 May 2003 helping to repair the railway line between the port of Umm Qasr and Basra.

24 March 2003 400th anniversary of the death of Queen Elizabeth I (1533–1603). This oil portrait is attributed to John Bettes the Younger *c.1590*, when Elizabeth was in her 50s. It was part of a special exhibition at the National Maritime Museum, Greenwich (Elizabeth's birthplace) that included many personal items and exhibits relating to the mercantile and seafaring nature of her reign.

© NATIONAL MARITIME MUSEUM, LONDON

26 March 2003 the Government grants listed building status to seven communications structures in England. These include the Lighthouse at Dungeness, Kent built in 1959–60 *(bottom right)*, and the Equatorial Group of Telescopes at the old Royal Greenwich Observatory, Herstmonceux, East Sussex, now home of the Observatory Science Centre *(below)*.

COURTESY OF THE OBSERVATORY SCIENCE CENTRE, HERSTMONCEUX

WWW.BRITAINONVIEW.COM / ADY KERRY

30 March 2003 the largest Sikh gurdwara (temple) outside India, the Sri Guru Singh Sabha Gurdwara, opens in Southall, west London. It cost around £17 million, all raised by the local Sikh community, and took three years to build. The stained glass windows are modern interpretations of traditional designs.

faith communities work together on issues relating to urban policy. Chaired by a government minister, the Council includes representatives of the Christian, Hindu, Jewish, Muslim and Sikh faiths. The Churches Regional Network coordinates church involvement in Regional Development Agencies and Regional Assemblies.

Churches in Scotland have created a Scottish Churches Parliamentary Office for formal representation of their interests in the Scottish Parliament. In Wales, the Churches have worked together to appoint a Churches National Assembly Liaison Officer to relate to the National Assembly for Wales.

Legal rights and responsibilities

Article 9 of the European Convention on Human Rights, which was incorporated into the *Human Rights Act 1998*, guarantees everybody in the United Kingdom the right to religious freedom, conscience and religion, subject to the law. In Great Britain religious discrimination is unlawful in the areas of employment and training under an EC Directive to be brought into effect in December 2003.

In England and Wales certain offences motivated by religious hatred are subject to a higher maximum penalty, along the same lines as racially motivated offences (see page 97). Similar provisions apply in Scotland.

In Northern Ireland the 1976 and 1989 *Fair Employment Acts* were updated by the Fair Employment and Treatment (NI) Order 1998, which makes discrimination on grounds of religious belief or political opinion unlawful in employment and training and in the provision of goods, facilities and services.

In addition, under the *Northern Ireland Act 1998*, a public authority, in carrying out its functions relating to Northern Ireland, is obliged to have regard to the need to promote equality of opportunity between persons of different religious beliefs and to have due regard to the desirability of promoting good relations between such people.

Relations between religious traditions

Ecumenical movements

Churches Together in Britain and Ireland is the main coordinating body for the Christian Churches

House purchase by the Muslim community
Sharia law governs how Muslims invest, and under Sharia law, the payment or receipt of interest is forbidden, making conventional mortgages unsuitable for many Muslims. In one approach (the 'murabaha' method), a financier or bank buys the property on the customer's behalf and then sells it to the customer charging an additional lump sum on top of the asking price. In an alternative approach (the 'ijara' method), the bank buys the property, leases it for the term of the finance on a rental, and transfers it to the tenant on payment of the full price. Both approaches mean that the property is bought twice with stamp duty being charged on each transaction.

In April 2003 the Government announced changes to the Finance Bill that will remove the need for duty to be paid twice on Islamic mortgages. The changes are due to come into effect in December 2003.

in the United Kingdom and promotes discussion of faith and doctrinal issues in the Christian community. It also coordinates the work of its 33 member organisations in the areas of social responsibility, international affairs, church life, world mission, racial justice, care of international students and inter-faith relations. Member Churches are also grouped in separate ecumenical bodies, according to country: Churches Together in England, Action of Churches Together in Scotland, Churches Together in Wales (Cytûn), and the Irish Council of Churches.

In Scotland, several Churches have been pursuing unity through the Scottish Churches' Initiative for Union. Among them is the United Reformed Church, itself the outcome of previous unions.

Co-operation between faiths

The Inter Faith Network for the United Kingdom links a wide range of organisations with an interest in inter-faith relations, including the representative bodies of the Bahá'í, Buddhist, Christian, Hindu, Jain, Jewish, Muslim, Sikh and Zoroastrian communities. The Network promotes good relations between faiths in the United Kingdom, and runs a public advice and information service on inter-faith issues. There are many other organisations and local groups in the United Kingdom dealing wholly, or in part, with inter-faith issues. The Council of Christians and Jews works for better understanding among members of these two religions and deals with educational and social issues. The Three Faiths Forum and the Calamus Foundation have as their focus relationships between the Christian, Jewish and Muslim traditions. The Inter-faith Unit of the Islamic Foundation was set up with the specific aim of developing better relations between the Muslim and Christian traditions.

Joint statement on Iraq

Following the start of armed conflict in Iraq in 2003, a joint statement was released by Christian, Jewish and Muslim leaders in the United Kingdom. The six signatories included the Archbishop of Canterbury, the Chief Rabbi, and the Chairman of the Council of Mosques and Imams UK. The statement called for the protocols of the Geneva Convention to be observed on all sides and the rights and needs of civilians innocently affected by the conflict to be protected. The statement also asserted that the conflict was not about or between religions: *'As Christian, Jewish and Muslim religious leaders in this country, we believe that it is vital, amid so much uncertainty and turmoil, to resist any attempt to drive our communities apart.'*

Further reading

UK Christian Handbook 2002/2003, ed. Peter Brierley. Christian Research.

UK Christian Handbook – Religious Trends 2003/ 2004, No. 4, ed. Peter Brierley. Christian Research.

Religions in the UK Directory, 2001–03, ed. Paul Weller, Religious Resource and Research Centre at the University of Derby and The Inter Faith Network for the UK, 2001.

Websites

Department for Education and Skills
www.dfes.gov.uk

The Inter Faith Network for the UK
www.interfaith.org.uk

ODPM/Inner Cities Religious Council
www.urban.odpm.gov.uk/community/faith/index.htm

Office for National Statistics
www.statistics.gov.uk

WWW.

16 Culture

Culture in the United Kingdom is rich and diverse, with a strong tradition of literature, theatre, popular and orchestral music and the performing arts. These, together with collections in UK museums and galleries, act as a magnet for overseas visitors and make a substantial contribution to the economy. According to economic estimates made by the Department for Culture, Media and Sport (DCMS), the creative industries accounted for nearly 8 per cent of UK gross domestic product in 2000, and provided nearly 2 million jobs in December 2001.

Audiences

The percentage of the population who attend various types of cultural event has remained fairly stable since the early 1990s, with the exception of the cinema (see Table 16.1). Admissions to UK cinemas rose from 156 million in 2001 to 176 million in 2002, more than three times the number who attended in 1984, and the highest level since 1971.

Attendance at some of the main museums and galleries in England also rose between 2001/02 and 2002/03, with the Natural History Museum and the Victoria and Albert Museum recording the biggest increases (Table 16.2).

Churches and cathedrals are an important part of UK cultural heritage, attracting many visitors. In 2001, York Minster and Canterbury Cathedral each received over 1 million visitors. Strathclyde Country Park in Scotland, Kew Gardens in

Heritage

Preserving and safeguarding buildings with a special, historical significance is an important task for agencies working within the cultural sector. In 2003 there were 461,000 listed buildings and 32,000 scheduled monuments in the United Kingdom (Table 19.5). A review of heritage protection legislation was announced in November 2002, with the purpose of examining how buildings and monuments could best be preserved for future generations.

In 2003 Liverpool's waterfront and commercial centre was the sole UK nomination for World Heritage Site status. Liverpool was also chosen as European Capital of Culture for 2008 (see page 3).

Table 16.1 Attendance[1] at cultural events, Great Britain

Percentages

	1991/92	1997/98	2001/02	2002/03
Cinema	44	54	57	61
Plays	23	23	24	24
Art galleries/exhibitions	21	22	22	24
Classical music	12	12	12	13
Ballet	6	6	6	7
Opera	6	6	6	7
Contemporary dance	3	4	5	5

1 Percentage of resident population aged 15 and over asked about their attendance 'these days'.
Source: Target Group Index, BMRB International

Table 16.2 Visits to national museums and galleries, 2002/03, England

	Number of visits (million)	Percentage change on 2001/02
Tate Gallery[1]	5.2	−6
National Gallery	4.6	0
British Museum	4.4	−8
National Museum of Science & Industry	3.1	0
Natural History Museum	2.8	31
Victoria and Albert Museum (V&A)	2.4	29
Imperial War Museum	1.9	19
National Portrait Gallery	1.3	−14
National Maritime Museum	1.2	18
National Museums Liverpool	1.1	18
Royal Armouries	0.4	6
Wallace Collection	0.2	0

1 Combined figures for Tate Britain, Tate Modern, Tate Liverpool and Tate St Ives.
Source: Department for Culture, Media and Sport

Table 16.3 Department for Culture, Media and Sport expenditure[1] on selected areas of cultural life

	£ million		
	1991/92	1996/97	2002/03
Museums, galleries and libraries[2]	333	336	494
Historic buildings (England)	n/a	162	155
The arts (England)	212	195	297
Tourism (UK)	44	46	72

1 2002/03 data are estimated outturn.
2 Includes museums and galleries (England), libraries (UK) and museums' library archives (UK).
Source: Department for Culture, Media and Sport

London, the Botanic Gardens in Belfast and the National Botanic Gardens in Carmarthenshire, Wales are also popular destinations for people with an interest in gardening and horticulture. Windsor Castle, the Tower of London and the Roman Baths in Bath are among the top UK heritage attractions.

Expenditure

Government expenditure on the arts is distributed through a number of channels. The DCMS and the devolved administrations of Scotland, Wales and Northern Ireland have overall responsibility for public expenditure in this area. Table 16.3 shows how DCMS expenditure is allocated. Local government, the arts councils (see page 232) and education and library boards in Northern Ireland are also major contributors to arts projects. More details on how finance is distributed are given on pages 232–3.

Highlights of the past year

Among the many cultural highlights of mid-2002 to mid-2003 were:

- in July 2002 a branch of the Imperial War Museum opened in Manchester;
- also in July 2002 *The Massacre of the Innocents* by Rubens was sold for £49.5 million at Sotheby's, breaking the UK record for a single painting;
- phase one of the Darwin Centre, an extension of the Natural History Museum, was completed in September 2002. The Centre provides more accessible storage facilities for museum collections, new laboratories for museum scientists and access behind the scenes for visitors;
- the first major museum in the United Kingdom devoted to Britain's colonial past, the British Empire & Commonwealth Museum, opened in September 2002. It is housed in the old Bristol Temple Meads railway station;
- the continuing success of the Lord of the Rings and Harry Potter films. The second film in each series, *Lord of the Rings: the Two Towers* and *Harry Potter and the Chamber of Secrets* were the first and second highest grossing films in the United Kingdom in 2002;
- in December 2002, a branch of the National Maritime Museum opened in Falmouth, Cornwall, with a collection of around 140 small craft from the past 150 years and including tools and other artefacts;
- an exhibition devoted to the Aztec civilisation, which opened at the Royal Academy in November 2002, bringing together a large number of artefacts not previously seen outside Mexico;
- an exhibition of Art Deco design 1910–39, held at the Victoria and Albert Museum from March to July 2003; and

- in April 2003 the Saatchi Gallery of Modern Art opened in County Hall, London.

Awards

A selection of major award winners is given in Table 16.4 on page 224.

Live performance

Festivals

Hundreds of professional arts festivals take place in the United Kingdom each year. Some, like those in Cardiff and Brighton, last for a month and offer a wide variety of programmes.

The 2003 Edinburgh International Festival featured performances of music, theatre, opera and dance, as well as lectures and discussions. The Edinburgh Festival Fringe (including street events) takes place alongside the main events. In recent years it has proved a training ground for comedians and actors who have progressed to successful careers elsewhere. Other annual Edinburgh events include the International Film Festival, the International Book Festival and the International Jazz and Blues Festival.

The Aldeburgh Festival, founded by Benjamin Britten, focuses on classical music. The Hay Festival, held in Hay-on-Wye, originally focused on literature – the town is renowned for its second-hand bookshops – but has broadened its range in recent years and its programme now includes musical events and contributions from guest speakers. Film festivals include the annual London Film Festival, and newer events such as the Leeds Children's Film Festival and the Brief Encounters short film festival in Bristol.

Glastonbury

One of Europe's biggest outdoor festivals, the Glastonbury Festival, has been running for over 30 years. It includes many forms of youth culture: pop and dance music, fringe theatre, painting, sculpture and textile art. In 2003 about 150,000 people attended to watch over 2,000 performances at some 25 different venues in a greenfield site of 405 hectares.

Drama

The first permanent theatre building to be constructed in London opened in 1576. In 2001, around 11.7 million visits were made to the major commercial and grant-aided theatres in central London. Musicals, thrillers, and comedies provide most of the material for West End productions (see Table 16.5).

The Royal National Theatre on London's South Bank relies in part on public subsidy and sponsorship for support, allowing it to take greater artistic risks and offer cheaper tickets than unsubsidised theatres in London's West End.

According to Arts Council England research, the top ten producing theatres in England are: Royal National Theatre, Royal Shakespeare Company, Manchester Royal Exchange, English Stage Company, Leicester Haymarket, Liverpool Everyman and Playhouse, Northern Stage, Nottingham Playhouse, Sheffield Theatres and Theatre Royal Plymouth.

Clwyd Theatr Cymru in Mold is the national English-speaking theatre company for Wales. The new Welsh language theatre company, Theatr Genedlaethol Cymru, will be established at its temporary base in Llanelli in autumn 2003. The company will begin touring theatres throughout Wales in 2004. There is also a national network of production companies for theatre for young people.

In Scotland the Royal Lyceum Theatre and the King's and Festival Theatres in Edinburgh, and the Citizen's Theatre Glasgow, have full programmes covering a wide range of productions. The Traverse Theatre in Edinburgh is Scotland's main centre for new writing.

Making theatre accessible to all

A number of facilities are available for disabled people in London theatres and elsewhere:

- *audio described performance* for people with visual impairments. Information is received through a discreet headset during the pauses in the performance;
- *sign language interpreted performance* for people who are Deaf and hard of hearing. Trained describers, usually situated to the side of the stage, interpret the script; and
- *captioned performance*, also for people who are Deaf and hard of hearing. Captions of the full or edited script are displayed on an electronic screen usually placed level with the stage at the same time as it is being performed.

Table 16.4 Selected major award winners, 2003,[1] UK

Award	Category	Title of work	Winner
Art			
Turner Prize (2002)		*Artmachine*	Keith Tyson
BP Portrait Award		*Untitled*	Charlotte Harris
Literature			
Whitbread Prizes	Biography & Overall	*Samuel Pepys: The Unequalled Self*	Claire Tomalin
	Children's	*Saffy's Angel*	Hilary McKay
	Poetry	*The Ice Age*	Paul Farley
	First Novel	*The Song of Names*	Norman Lebrecht
	Novel	*Spies*	Michael Frayn
Man Booker Prize (2002)		*Life of Pi*	Yann Martel
Popular music			
Brit Awards	Best Male Artist		Robbie Williams
	Best Female Artist		Ms Dynamite
	Best Group		Coldplay
	Best Newcomer		Will Young
	Outstanding Contribution		Tom Jones
Mercury Music Prize		*Boy In Da Corner*	Dizzee Rascal
Film			
BAFTA Awards	Best Film	*The Pianist*	Roman Polanski
	Best British Film	*The Warrior*	Bertrand Faivre
	Best Actor	*Gangs of New York*	Daniel Day-Lewis
	Best Actress	*The Hours*	Nicole Kidman
TV and video			
BAFTA Awards	Best Drama Series	*Spooks*	
	Best Soap	*Coronation Street*	
	Best Sport	The Commonwealth Games	
	Best Drama Serial	*Shackleton*	
	Best Actor	*The Gathering Storm*	Albert Finney
	Best Actress	*Murder*	Julie Walters
Theatre			
Olivier Awards	Best Actor	*Uncle Vanya*	Simon Russell Beale
	Best Actress	*Vincent in Brixton*	Clare Higgins
	Best New Play	*Vincent in Brixton*	Nicholas Wright
	Best New Comedy	*The Lieutenant of Inishmore*	Martin McDonagh
Radio			
Sony Awards	Best Presenter		Jonathan Ross
	Best Station		BBC Radio 4
Architecture			
Stirling Prize (2002)		Gateshead Millennium Bridge	Wilkinson Eyre Architects

1 Unless otherwise indicated.

Table 16.5 Long-running West End London theatre productions, September 2003

1 *The Mousetrap* 50 years, 10 months
2 *Les Misérables* 18 years, 3 months
3 *The Phantom of the Opera* 17 years, 3 months
4 *Blood Brothers* 15 years, 7 months
5 *The Woman in Black* 14 years, 10 months

Source: Society of West End Theatres

Northern Ireland has six major theatre spaces, including the Opera House and Waterfront Hall in Belfast and the new Millennium Forum in the city of Londonderry/Derry. It also has several independent theatre companies specialising in productions of new work.

Music

Classical music

A wide range of professional orchestras perform regularly throughout the United Kingdom, offering a varied repertoire of classical works from the great composers together with more experimental pieces. Four major symphony orchestras are based in London: the London Symphony Orchestra, the Philharmonia, the London Philharmonic, and the Royal Philharmonic.

In the English regions the Bournemouth Symphony, City of Birmingham Symphony Orchestra, the Hallé Orchestra (based in Manchester) and the Royal Liverpool Philharmonic Orchestra are all well known and highly rated. In Wales the BBC National Orchestra of Wales offers a year-round programme of orchestral and choral music featuring the BBC National Chorus of Wales. The Royal Scottish National Orchestra is based in Glasgow and the Scottish Chamber Orchestra performs throughout Scotland and overseas. The Ulster Orchestra is Northern Ireland's only fully professional orchestra. The BBC has a total of eight orchestras and choruses, including one based in Scotland and the two in Wales.

Three well-established events in the classical musical calendar are the Leeds International Piano Competition for young pianists, the biennial Cardiff Singer of the World Competition and the biennial BBC Young Musicians contest.

Wales Millennium Centre
Construction of the Wales Millennium Centre in Cardiff is currently under way. The centre is scheduled to open in November 2004. Consisting of a main 1,900-seat Lyric theatre, studio theatre and dance theatre together with an additional concourse space for live performances, it will play host to an international showcase of opera, musicals, ballet and dance. When finished, the centre will provide a permanent home for Welsh National Opera, Diversions Dance, and other leading Welsh cultural organisations.

The Promenade Concerts (the 'Proms'), in the Royal Albert Hall in London, are the world's largest music festival. The theme of the 2003 series was Greek Mythology, including performances of Strauss's *Elektra*, Purcell's *Dido & Aeneas* and Tippett's *King Priam*. The centrepiece was a performance of Berlioz's *The Trojans*, marking the bicentenary of the composer's birth. The traditional last night concert was linked to free, simultaneous 'Proms in the Park' in Belfast, Glasgow, Swansea and Hyde Park, London.

English and Welsh choral societies have done much to foster the oratorio tradition at the leading music festivals. English ecclesiastical choral singing is a speciality of the choirs of cathedrals and Oxford and Cambridge University colleges.

Opera

London's Royal Opera House (ROH) at Covent Garden stages over 20 operas a year and attracts performers with international reputations. Glyndebourne Opera (East Sussex), which relies on private patrons for its summer season, is another prestigious venue. The English National Opera at the Coliseum is undergoing major refurbishment.

Popular music

Turnover in the music industry was estimated at over £4 billion in 2000. It employed about 120,000 people. In 2002 over 225 million pop albums and over 52 million pop singles were sold in the UK domestic market, generating a turnover of £1.2 billion.

Sales of albums and singles were down in the year, reflecting competition from other areas of the entertainment sector and the ongoing problem of

Top five singles in 2002

1 Will Young *Anything is possible/Evergreen*

2 Gareth Gates *Unchained Melody*

3 Enrique Iglesias *Hero*

4 Nelly featuring Kelly Rowland *Dilemma*

5 Elvis vs JXL *A Little less Conversation*

Top five artist albums in 2002

1 Robbie Williams *Escapology*

2 Pink *Missundaztood*

3 Enrique Iglesias *Escape*

4 Coldplay *A Rush of Blood to the Head*

5 Blue *One Love*

the illegal copying of recorded music. After peaking at around 90 million in 1997, sales of singles declined by a further 12 per cent in 2001 and 2002, reaching the lowest level since 1992.

UK and US artists continue to dominate the pop charts. Both new artists, such as Will Young and Gareth Gates, as well as long established performers like Elton John, have topped the singles charts. Live music remains popular and many UK groups tour extensively in the United Kingdom and abroad; bands as diverse as Coldplay and the Rolling Stones went on world tours in 2003.

Folk music has always been strong in all parts of the United Kingdom. In Northern Ireland, for example, bands perform in pubs and clubs, playing fiddles and other traditional Celtic instruments. Scottish and Welsh festivals uphold Gaelic and Celtic traditions in music and song.

Dance

Two major ballet companies based in London are the English National Ballet and the Royal Ballet. Other important ballet companies include Birmingham Royal Ballet, Northern Ballet Theatre and Scottish Ballet.

Dance Base, Scotland's new national centre for dance, opened in Edinburgh in 2001. Contemporary dance companies with established reputations are Diversions Dance, Spring Loaded and the Richard Alston Dance Company. Siobhan

Davies and Wayne McGregor are two leading UK choreographers.

Film and broadcast culture

Film

In 2002, cinemas took £755 million at the box office in the United Kingdom, compared with £645 million in 2001. An estimated 51,000 people were employed in the film and video industry. In 2001 film exports were worth £700 million.

In 2002 there was a moderate recovery in production turnover from the 2001 downturn. Nineteen major feature films were produced in the United Kingdom with overseas financing, including *Harry Potter and the Chamber of Secrets*. There were 42 UK-produced films such as *Johnny English*, *Love Actually*, *Wondrous Oblivion*, *Bright Young Things*, *Sylvia*, *This Little Life* and *Young Adam*. In addition, 43 UK co-productions were made abroad, underlining the growth and importance of international partnerships to the UK film industry.

Television

Nearly every UK household owns a television set, and the average person watched around 20 hours of programmes a week in 2000/01.

The kinds of programme produced in the United Kingdom vary enormously. Soaps such as *EastEnders* and *Coronation Street* regularly top the ratings. Individual programmes receiving BAFTA nominations in 2003 as a recognition of particular merit included: one-off drama productions such as *The Gathering Storm*, based on the life of Winston Churchill; topical entertainment shows such as *Have I Got News for You?* and *I'm Alan Partridge*; and the satirical comedy *Bremner, Bird and Fortune*. Documentaries nominated for BAFTA awards included *Feltham Sings*, based on a young offenders institution. *A History of Britain* was nominated for best factual series.

Radio

Every week the BBC broadcasts over 150 hours of classical and other music (both live and recorded) on Radio 3 (see page 242). BBC Radio 1 broadcasts rock and pop, and much of the output of BBC Radio 2 is popular and light music. Among the independent stations, Classic FM offers mainly classical music and Virgin Radio plays rock and pop music. Much of the output of UK local radio stations consists of popular and light music, phone-ins and news.

BBC Radio 4's output is mainly talk-based and includes a wealth of drama, current affairs and documentaries, discussions and full-length plays. Latest estimates indicate that radio programmes reach 90 per cent of the adult population aged 15 and over, with BBC local and national stations taking just over half of the audience share.

More details on the pattern of radio listening, and the range of new digital stations available to listeners, can be found in chapter 17.

Visual arts

Museums and galleries

Over 80 million visits a year are made to the 1,860 registered UK museums and galleries, which include the major national museums, about 1,000 independent museums, and others supported by local authorities, universities, the Armed Services, the National Trust and English Heritage. The number of museums has grown from 800 in 1980.

The Government website *www.24hourmuseum.org.uk* provides a gazetteer of all UK museums and galleries, a magazine, search facilities and educational resources. The site provides live

The British Museum
The British Museum in London celebrated the 250th anniversary of its foundation in 2003. The world's first national public museum was brought about by an Act of Parliament, with the aim of 'gathering objects from all corners of the globe and then organising them in systematic categories, so that points of similarity and difference would emerge and the great scheme of natural law would become clear'.

To commemorate the occasion, the museum staged a series of activities and events throughout the year. These included a family activity day on 7 June (the day the museum came into being in 1753) complete with celebrity storytelling and Viking invaders, a series of special exhibitions and the opening of two new permanent galleries. A new permanent exhibition, *Enlightenment, Uncovering the World in the 18th Century*, will open in the newly restored King's Library in November 2003 and will examine this formative period in the museum's history.

information on over 2,500 institutions. SCRAN (*www.scran.ac.uk*), the Scottish Cultural Resources Access Network, is a history and culture site providing access to images, films, sounds and virtual reality records from museums, galleries, archives and media.

The Designation Scheme was launched in 1997 with the aim of recognising and protecting collections of national and international importance held in England's non-national museums. There are 62 collections held in 52 museums or museum services. The scheme is administered by Resource: the Council for Museums, Archives and Libraries, on behalf of the DCMS.

Designated collections outside London range from Beamish, The North of England Open Air Museum, recreating social history from the 19th and early 20th centuries, to the fine art collections of the Barber Institute in Birmingham. Within London, designated collections include: the Museum of London; the Courtauld Institute Galleries; and London's Transport Museum.

Architecture and design

The Royal Institute of British Architects (RIBA), with about 30,000 members, has been promoting and advancing architecture since receiving its Royal Charter in 1837.

Architecture Week, organised by Arts Council England in partnership with RIBA, is a national celebration of contemporary architecture with events around the country.

The Commission for Architecture and the Built Environment (CABE) is responsible for championing architecture and promoting high standards in the design of buildings and spaces between them. Its new urban unit, CABE Space, was launched in May 2003 and is responsible for encouraging good quality parks and green spaces.

Better use of design by business, the public sector and educational bodies, is supported and encouraged in the United Kingdom by the Design Council. The Council is funded by a grant from the Department of Trade and Industry.

Crafts
'Crafts' in the United Kingdom is an umbrella term covering a huge range of activities, from the

The national museums and galleries of the UK

England

- British Museum (*www.thebritishmuseum.ac.uk*)

- Natural History Museum (*www.nhm.ac.uk*)

- Victoria and Albert Museum (*www.vam.ac.uk*)

- National Museum of Science and Industry (*www.nmsi.ac.uk*) which includes the Science Museum in London, the National Railway Museum in York and the National Museum of Photography, Film and Television, Bradford

- National Gallery (*www.nationalgallery.org.uk*)

- Tate, comprising Tate Britain, Tate Modern and additional collections in Liverpool and St Ives, Cornwall (*www.tate.org.uk*)

- National Portrait Gallery (*www.npg.org.uk*)

- Imperial War Museum (*www.iwm.org.uk*)

- Royal Armouries (*www.armouries.org.uk*)

- National Army Museum (*www.national-army-museum.ac.uk*)

- Royal Air Force Museum (*www.rafmuseum.org.uk*)

- National Maritime Museum, Greenwich and Falmouth, Cornwall (*www.nmm.ac.uk*)

- Wallace Collection (*www.wallacecollection.org*)

- National Museums Liverpool (*www.liverpoolmuseums.org.uk*) a collection of eight museums on Merseyside, including the Walker Art Gallery.

Scotland

- National Museums of Scotland (*www.nms.ac.uk*) – seven museums, including the Royal Museum and the Museum of Scotland

- National Galleries of Scotland (*www.natgalscot.ac.uk*) – five galleries, including the National Gallery of Scotland and the Scottish National Gallery of Modern Art.

Wales

- National Museums and Galleries of Wales (*www.nmgw.ac.uk*) – currently eight museums and galleries including: the National Museum and Gallery, Cardiff; the Museum of Welsh Life at St Fagans; and the Slate Museum at Llanberis. The National Waterfront Museum in Swansea is scheduled to open in 2005.

Northern Ireland

- Museums and Galleries of Northern Ireland (*www.magni.org.uk*) – including the Ulster Museum in Belfast, the Ulster Folk and Transport Museum in County Down, the Armagh County Museum and the Ulster-American Folk Park in County Tyrone.

making of pots and rugs to handmade toys and other personal and household products.

The Crafts Council is the official organisation for crafts in England. Its objectives include raising the profile of crafts in England and abroad, and strengthening and developing the craft economy in support of craftspeople. The Council also organises the annual Chelsea Crafts Fair and other programmes from its London venue, and coordinates British groups at international fairs. Craft Forum Wales supports craft business groups in Wales. Craftworks, an independent company, is the craft development agency for Northern Ireland. The Arts Council of Northern Ireland

funds crafts promotion. In Scotland, the Scottish Arts Council has a Crafts Department, which promotes crafts and helps craftworkers.

The written word

Demand for books remains strong. In 2002 UK publishers issued over 125,390 separate titles (including new and revised editions). The UK book industry exported books worth £1.2 billion in 2002 (see also Table 28.10).

Among the leading trade organisations are the Publishers Association (PA), which has 200 members, and the Booksellers Association, with

Book awards

Gold and Platinum Book Awards were launched in September 2001. By September 2003 Platinum Awards granted to those with sales of 1 million or over, had been awarded to:

Louis de Bernieres *Captain Corelli's Mandolin*

Helen Fielding *Bridget Jones Diary: A Novel*

Helen Fielding *Bridget Jones: Edge of Reason*

Frank McCourt *Angela's Ashes: A Memoir of a Childhood*

Tony Parsons *Man and Boy*

JK Rowling *Harry Potter and the Philosopher's Stone*

JK Rowling *Harry Potter and the Chamber of Secrets*

JK Rowling *Harry Potter and the Prisoner of Azkaban*

JK Rowling *Harry Potter and the Goblet of Fire*

JK Rowling *Harry Potter and the Order of the Phoenix*

Pamela Stephenson *Billy*

David Pelzer *A Child Called It*

about 3,300 members. The PA, through its international division, promotes the export of UK books. The Welsh Books Council promotes the book trade in Wales in both Welsh and English, and the Gaelic Books Council supports the publication of books in Gaelic. The Book Trust encourages reading and the promotion of books through an information service and a children's library.

JK Rowling's *Harry Potter and the Order of the Phoenix*, the fifth in the series, was launched in June 2003. On the first day of its release it sold 1.7 million copies, breaking all records for UK book sales. By June 2003 sales of all *Harry Potter* titles totalled 13 million copies.

Literary and philological societies

Societies to promote literature include the English Association, the Royal Society of Literature and the Welsh Academy (Yr Academi Gymreig). The leading society for studies in the humanities is the British Academy for the Promotion of Historical, Philosophical and Philological Studies (the British Academy).

Other specialist societies are the Early English Text Society, the Bibliographical Society and several devoted to particular authors, such as Jane Austen and Charles Dickens. The Poetry Society sponsors poetry readings and recitals, as does the Scottish Poetry Library. London's South Bank Centre and the British Library run programmes of literary events.

Libraries and archives

Local authorities in Great Britain and education and library boards in Northern Ireland have a duty to provide a free lending and reference library service. There are almost 5,000 public libraries in the United Kingdom. In Great Britain more than 34 million people (58 per cent of the population) are registered members of their local library, and of these around 20 per cent borrow at least once a week. Those who are not registered members can also use many of the local library facilities.

Many libraries have collections of CDs, records, audio- and video-cassettes, DVDs and musical scores for loan to the public, while a number also lend from collections of works of art, which may be originals or reproductions. Most libraries hold documents on local history, and all provide services for children.

About 406 million books and 39 million audio-visual items were borrowed from UK public libraries in 2000/01. The Government is advised on library and archives policy by Resource (see page 232).

The information role is important for all libraries. Nearly all have personal computers with Internet connections for public use. A government initiative under the New Opportunities Fund is providing £50 million for enabling library material to be stored and accessed in digitised form and £20 million for staff training in information and communications technology.

The British Film Institute (*bfi*) maintains the J Paul Getty Conservation Centre, which contains over 275,000 films and 200,000 television programmes, together with extensive collections of stills, posters and designs. The *bfi* National Library houses a large collection of film-related books, periodicals, scripts and other written materials.

The British Library

The British Library (*www.bl.uk*), the national library of the United Kingdom, is custodian of one of the most important research collections in the world (150 million items spanning 3,000 years). It is housed in the largest wholly publicly funded building constructed in the United Kingdom in the 20th century. The total floor space is approximately 100,000 square metres. The basements, the deepest in London, have 340 kilometres of shelving for 15 million books. There are 11 reading areas, three exhibition galleries and a conference centre with a 250-seat auditorium.

The reading rooms in the British Library are open to those who need to see material (for example, manuscripts, newspapers, journals, stamps, maps and CD Roms as well as books) that is not readily available elsewhere and to those whose work or studies require the facilities of the national library. The Library Internet catalogue has details of more than 10 million documents from the past 500 years, including books, journals and reports.

UK publishers are legally obliged to deposit a copy of each new publication in the British Library. The National Libraries of Scotland and of Wales, the Bodleian at Oxford and the Cambridge University Library (and the Library of Trinity College, Dublin) can also claim copies of all new UK publications.

The British Library's Document Supply Centre at Boston Spa is the national centre for inter-library lending within the United Kingdom and between the United Kingdom and other countries.

Manuscripts and other records

In April 2003 the Public Record Office (PRO) and the Historical Manuscripts Commission (HMC) combined to form a new organisation, the National Archives (*www.nationalarchives.gov.uk*). The PRO in Kew houses the records of the superior courts of law of England and Wales and of most government departments, as well as manuscripts of historical documents, such as the *Domesday Book* (1086) and autograph letters and documents of the sovereigns of England. Public

records, with a few exceptions, are available for inspection by everyone 30 years after the end of the year in which they were created.

The HMC gives information and advice about historical papers outside the public records. It also advises private owners, grant-awarding bodies, record offices, local authorities and the Government on the acquisition and maintenance of manuscripts. The Commission maintains the National Register of Archives (the central collecting point for information about British historical manuscripts) and the Manorial Documents Register, both of which are available to researchers.

The National Archives of Scotland in Edinburgh and the Public Record Office of Northern Ireland in Belfast serve a similar purpose.

Education and training

The National Curriculum in England and Wales specifies that all children at school should receive training in the arts, music and literature (see page 108). In Scotland expressive arts are a key component of the pre-school and 5–14 curricular guidelines.

In England Artsmark is a national award scheme run by Arts Council England and supported by the DCMS, the Department for Education and Skills (DfES) and other relevant agencies. An Artsmark is awarded to schools that show a commitment to the full range of the arts – music, dance and art and design.

Other initiatives to encourage cultural excellence in schools include:
- the Music Standards Fund, set up in 1999 and guaranteed to run until 2005/06, which has given just under £60 million a year to protect and expand a range of music services, such as buying musical instruments for schools, providing instrumental tuition and providing extra training for teachers;
- Youth Music, established in 1999 to provide music-making opportunities for children and young people up to the age of 18, concentrating on those who live in areas of social and economic need;
- the Space for Sport and Arts Programme, allocating up to £134 million to enable pupils and the wider community in deprived

areas to participate in art-based and sporting activities by providing new (or modernising existing) facilities in primary schools. The programme will run until 2004; and

- Creative Partnerships, a DCMS-sponsored initiative with additional support from the DfES, aims to give schoolchildren aged five to 18 and their teachers the opportunity to explore their creativity by working with creative professionals. The project was started in 16 local partnership areas in 2002/03 with around 15 to 25 schools in each partnership taking part. An additional £70 million funding for the scheme was announced in June 2003, bringing the total available to £110 million. The additional funding will allow schools from 20 new partnership areas to become involved in the project over the next two years.

For those wishing to pursue a career in the arts, training available at post-16 tends to concentrate on particular specialisms. The DCMS and the DfES allocate £19 million a year in grants for drama and dance students for tuition and maintenance in England and Wales. Over 800 students a year cover their tuition fees in this way, on the same basis as other higher and further education pupils. All training must be at accredited institutions and towards recognised qualifications, with annual evaluation by the DCMS and the DfES to ensure that standards are maintained. Competition to enter the schools of performing arts is keen.

The Royal National Theatre's Education Programme encourages access to drama through youth theatre projects, touring productions, workshops, rehearsed readings, work in schools and a nationwide membership scheme.

Professional training in music is given at universities and conservatoires. Professional training for dancers and choreographers is provided mainly by specialist schools, while all government-funded dance companies provide dance workshops and education activities.

The National Film and Television School is financed jointly by the Government and the film, video and television industries. It offers postgraduate and short-course training for directors, editors, camera operators, animators and other specialists.

Most practical education in art and design is provided in the art colleges and fine and applied art departments of universities and in further education colleges and private art schools. Some of these institutions award degrees at postgraduate level. The Royal College of Art in London is the only wholly postgraduate school of art and design in the world. Art is also taught to degree level at four Scottish art schools.

Administration

The expression of creativity is primarily a personal or group activity, but there is also an official and commercial side to culture. Many artists and performers engaged in cultural activity rely on subsidies and funding from the Government and other patrons of the arts. The Government has a role in protecting the rights of authors through copyright legislation; providing a regulatory framework for cultural activities in areas such as film classification; and encouraging greater public participation in the arts.

Public sector involvement in the arts is expressed in a number of different ways: through the work of the four administrations directly responsible for culture in England, Wales, Scotland and Northern Ireland; through local government support for local initiatives; or through intermediate groups such as the arts councils, which act independently from the Government but are nonetheless publicly funded and take on the role of patrons of the arts.

The policy responsibilities of the DCMS include the arts, public libraries and archives, museums and galleries and the built heritage in England, and UK-wide responsibilities for broadcasting, creative industries, and the National Lottery (see page 233).

Among DCMS objectives for the arts are:

- creating an efficient and competitive market by removing obstacles to growth and unnecessary regulation;
- broadening access to cultural events and to the built environment;
- raising the standards of cultural education and training; and
- ensuring that everyone has the opportunity to achieve excellence in areas of culture and

to develop talent, innovation and good design.

The National Assembly for Wales has responsibility for the arts in Wales and has published a culture strategy, *Creative Future*. The Scottish Executive's National Cultural Strategy provides the basis for the administration of the arts in Scotland, and in Northern Ireland responsibility for the arts rests with the Department of Culture, Arts and Leisure.

Local authorities

Although policy is formulated by the four UK administrations, many initiatives and services are provided at a local level. Local authorities maintain many museums and art galleries, and a network of public libraries. They also provide grant aid for professional and amateur orchestras, theatres, and opera and dance companies.

Arts councils

Arts Council England, the Scottish Arts Council, the Arts Council of Wales and Arts Council of Northern Ireland are independent bodies that distribute government grants and Lottery funding to the visual, performing and community arts and to literature. They give financial assistance and advice not only to the major performing arts organisations, but also to small touring theatre companies, experimental performance groups and literary organisations. The arts councils also commission research into the impact of the arts on society and develop forward strategies.

Arts Council England funds major national arts organisations in England, including the Royal Opera, the Royal Ballet, the Birmingham Royal Ballet, English National Opera, the Royal Shakespeare Company, the Royal National Theatre and the South Bank Centre, and the main touring companies, such as Opera North and English National Ballet.

Resource: the Council for Museums, Archives and Libraries

Resource is the strategic agency working with, and on behalf of, museums, archives and libraries across the United Kingdom, and advising the Government on policy issues. It is currently in the process of establishing regional agencies in each of the nine English regions, which will all be operational by April 2004. It provides funding through these

agencies and their predecessors (which include the Area Museum Councils). It has responsibility for a number of other initiatives, including:

- the portable antiquities scheme, set up to record archaeological objects. Information from the scheme is now available online. Over 30,000 records offer an important research tool for both academics and the public at large;
- schemes for museum registration and designation of collections (see page 227);
- Renaissance in the Regions, a major new government investment programme to tap the potential of England's regional museums; and
- the Acceptance in Lieu Scheme, whereby pre-eminent works of art may be accepted by the Government in settlement of tax and allocated to public galleries.

UK Film Council and *bfi*

The UK Film Council oversees the majority of public funding for film production in the United Kingdom. It is responsible for informing government policy relating to film and works with the industry to develop strategies to support the development of film in the United Kingdom. The organisation has a wide remit, with both cultural and industry objectives to develop a healthy film culture, and to help create a sustainable industry. The Council also funds UK Film Council US (the former British Film Office in Los Angeles), which acts as its information and marketing satellite in the US.

The UK Film Council is the principal funder of the British Film Institute (*bfi*), which promotes audience appreciation of film through cultural and educational initiatives across the United Kingdom. It works with Scottish Screen, the Northern Ireland Film and Television Commission and Sgrîn, the Media Agency for Wales, to develop film culture and industry. The Council also provides funding (£7.5 million a year) to the nine regional screen agencies across England that support the development of film in their regions.

Overall, the UK Film Council was responsible for distributing £150 million of Lottery and government grants to the UK film industry during 2002/03. It channels production funding to support new and innovative film-makers, as well as more mainstream films.

Cinema licensing and film classification

Local licensing conditions differ from area to area, but local authorities have a duty to prohibit children from viewing unsuitable films. In assessing films, authorities normally rely on the judgement of an independent non-statutory body, the British Board of Film Classification (BBFC), to which all items are submitted.

The BBFC is also legally responsible for classifying videos. Films and videos passed by the BBFC are put into one of the following categories:

- U/Uc (universal) – suitable for all. Videos classified Uc are particularly suitable for pre-school children;
- PG (parental guidance) – general viewing, but some scenes may be unsuitable for some children;
- 12/12A (advisory) – in August 2002 certificate 12 was replaced in cinemas by 12A. This allows children under the age of 12 to watch a film in that category, provided they are accompanied by an adult. Parents now have more power to determine what is appropriate for their child and, to help them make an informed decision, each film classified 12A carries consumer information about its contents. There are no plans to change the 12 certificate for video, and no one younger than 12 may be supplied with a video in that category;
- 15 and 18 – no one younger than those ages may see a cinema film or rent or buy a video in those categories;
- Restricted 18 – a category primarily for videos for sale in licensed sex shops to adults only.

It is an offence to admit to a cinema someone who does not meet the age requirement, to supply commercially a video to someone who does not meet the age requirement, or to supply a video that has not been classified. Responsibility for the policy on film and video classification lies with the DCMS.

Authors' copyright and performers' protection

Original literary, dramatic, musical or artistic works (including computer programs and databases), films, sound recordings, cable programmes, broadcasts and the typographical arrangement of published editions are automatically protected by copyright in the United Kingdom if they meet certain legal requirements. The copyright owner has rights against unauthorised reproduction, distribution, public performance, rental, broadcasting and adaptation of his or her work (including putting material on the Internet without permission). In most cases the author is the first owner of the copyright, and the term of copyright in literary, dramatic, musical and artistic works is for the life of the author and for 70 years thereafter. There are similar rules governing copyright on films. Sound recordings and broadcasts are protected for a period of 50 years.

National Lottery

The introduction of the National Lottery in 1994 significantly altered the funding of arts events in the United Kingdom. During the early years of the Lottery, the focus of arts funding was chiefly on major capital projects. Some shift in emphasis occurred from 1998 onwards, with the allocation of funds to smaller, local projects. By June 2003 the arts councils across the United Kingdom had awarded over 27,000 grants worth a total of over £2.1 billion.

In addition, the DCMS has established the National Endowment for Science, Technology and the Arts (NESTA), which uses the income generated by £295 million of Lottery funds to support projects and inventions in the arts and sciences.

Sponsorship

Total UK business investment in the arts in 2001/02 was £111 million, compared with £114 million in 2000/01. Business help for new developments rose from £9 million to £15 million. Sponsorship in kind fell from £18 million in 2001/02 to £14 million in 2002/03.

Arts & Business promotes and encourages partnerships between business and the arts. It has over 350 business members and manages the Arts & Business New Partners Programme on behalf of Arts Council England and the DCMS.

Many arts organisations also benefit from the fund-raising activities and financial support of friends, groups and private individuals. For example, theatre companies have traditionally relied on the support of 'angels', individual sponsors investing often quite small amounts of money to meet the costs of putting on a show, in the prospect of subsequently recouping their investment from box office proceeds.

Further reading

Department for Culture, Media and Sport: Annual Report 2003. Cm 5920. The Stationery Office, 2003.

Websites

Department for Culture, Media and Sport
www.culture.gov.uk

Artsonline
www.artsonline.com

Arts Council England
www.artscouncil.org.uk

Arts Council of Wales
www.artswales.org.uk

Scottish Arts Council
www.scottisharts.org.uk

Arts Council of Northern Ireland
www.artscouncil-ni.org

National Archives
www.nationalarchives.gov.uk

WWW.

17 Communications and the media

Rapid changes have been taking place in the access of UK households to new forms of communication (see Figure 17.1). In particular, ownership of mobile phones, increased from 17 per cent of households in 1996/97 to 65 per cent in 2001/02. Access to the Internet has also grown rapidly and by 2001/02 was approaching the number of households with satellite, digital or cable receivers, at around 40 per cent of households. The development of new technology has allowed Internet access to be gained via means other than the computer, such as the mobile phone.

These changes have not led to a reduction in the use of other forms of communication. Calls from fixed-line telephones have continued to increase, despite the growth in mobile phones, due to the

number of people making dial-up Internet calls. The volume of mail also continues to grow in spite of the competition from phone and email. The postal service has nevertheless seen changes in recent years, with the monopoly once held by Royal Mail ending as the postal service market was opened up for competition in 2003 (see page 237).

With the advent of digital television and radio, alongside the continuing expansion of cable and satellite television, there has been a proliferation of new public service and independent channels. Regulation of broadcast media will become the responsibility of the Office of Communications (Ofcom) in December 2003 (see page 244) but the press will remain self-regulated. Both broadcast and non-broadcast media (including the press) are major vehicles for advertising (see page 248).

Figure 17.1 Households with selected durable goods, UK[1]

Percentages

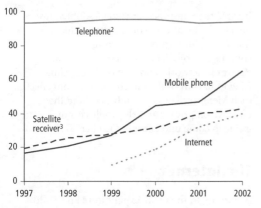

1 Financial year ending on the date shown.
2 Includes both fixed-line and mobile phones.
3 Includes digital and cable receivers.
Source: Family Expenditure Survey and Expenditure and Food Survey, Office for National Statistics

Telecommunications

Turnover of the UK telecommunications services sector grew by 6 per cent in 2002 to £48.3 billion.

Telephone services

Telephone calls from fixed lines were 10 per cent higher in 2002, at 330 billion call minutes, than in 2001 (Table 17.2). This reflected increases in dial-up Internet call volumes during the year, as voice call volumes decreased slightly. Oftel (see page 236) estimated that Internet calls accounted for 49 per cent of fixed call volumes in 2002. The telephone remained one of the most common consumer durable goods in the home and a growing number of customers are installing second lines, often for Internet use. There are 34.9 million fixed lines (including businesses), but there are even more subscribers to mobile phone services (see page 236).

British Telecommunications (BT), which became a private sector company in 1984, remains the biggest fixed-line UK operator, although competitors have increased their share of the market, especially the business market. BT runs one of the world's largest public telecommunications networks, including about 28 million exchange lines. Turnover from continuing businesses in 2002/03 totalled £18.7 billion.

The two main cable operators are ntl and Telewest. By the end of April 2003 cable operators had installed around 5.4 million telephone lines in the United Kingdom.

A variety of new telecommunications services have emerged. For example, many companies offer their customers information services using 0845 and 0800 telephone numbers – over 100 operators supply such services to companies. In September 2001 Oftel gave the go-ahead for the expansion of directory enquiry (DQ) services to be operated by other service providers than BT. The new services operate on 6-digit numbers, all starting with 118. The older DQ numbers (such as 192) went out of use in August 2003.

Table 17.2 Telephone call minutes, 2002, UK

	Call minutes (million)	Percentage change between 2001 and 2002
Fixed-line		
Local calls	72,821	−6
National calls	51,720	−8
International calls	6,894	−13
Calls to mobile phones	14,470	2
Other calls[1]	183,946	27
All calls[2]	329,852	10
Cellular services		
UK calls	50,293	17
Outgoing international calls	741	29
Calls while abroad	1,145	18
All calls	52,179	17

1 Other calls include number translation services, premium-rate calls, directory enquiries, operator calls, the speaking clock, public payphones and calls to Internet Service Providers (ISPs).
2 Figures may include a small amount of double counting, as in some instances calls supplied by an operator to a reseller may be counted by both operator and reseller.
Source: Oftel Market Information

Mobile communications

At the end of 2002 there were some 49.9 million mobile phone users in the United Kingdom, 11 per cent more than a year earlier. The five network suppliers are Orange (part of France Télécom), O$_2$, Vodafone, T-Mobile (a subsidiary of Deutsche Telekom) and 3, which launched its service in the United Kingdom in March 2003. There are also around 50 independent service providers. Vodafone had the largest market share in terms of total retail revenue in 2002 at 34 per cent, Orange had a market share of 27 per cent, O$_2$ had 22 per cent and T-Mobile 18 per cent.

Messaging services such as text messaging (SMS) and picture messaging (MMS) are growing in popularity with 17.3 billion messages being handled by the networks in 2002, a 43 per cent increase on 2001. Text messaging accounted for between 14 and 17 per cent of each of the networks' retail revenue.

Regulation

Oftel (the Office of Telecommunications), a non-ministerial government department headed by the Director General of Telecommunications, is the independent regulatory body for the telecommunications industry. It promotes competition in telecommunications networks and services; carries out regular reviews of markets; and encourages greater broadband and narrowband Internet access. During 2002/03 Oftel started to prepare for the establishment of the new Office of Communications, which will take over its functions in December 2003 (see page 244).

In 2002 the European Parliament adopted five directives which comprise the new regulatory framework for European electronic communications. These directives cover all electronic networks and services in the United Kingdom. Four of the directives came into effect in each Member State on 25 July 2003 and the directive on privacy and electronic communications is due to come into effect in October 2003.

The Internet

According to the ONS Expenditure and Food Survey, in the second quarter of 2003 an estimated 48 per cent of households in the United Kingdom could access the Internet from home, compared with 19 per cent in the first quarter of 1998.

A growing number of homes and businesses are using high-speed broadband connections. According to Oftel, there were over 2.2 million such connections in the United Kingdom by the end of June 2003, nearly three times as many as a year earlier.

The July 2003 ONS Omnibus Survey found that 56 per cent of adults in Great Britain had used the Internet in the three months prior to interview. Table 17.3 shows the most common reasons given for using the Internet. These included using email (83 per cent) and finding information about goods or services (83 per cent). Among those using the Internet for buying or ordering goods, tickets and services for personal use in the 12 months prior to interview, the most popular purchases were for travel, accommodation or holidays (59 per cent), tickets for events (39 per cent), books or magazines (38 per cent) and music or CDs (36 per cent).

In July 2003 computers continued to dominate as the preferred method for accessing the Internet in Great Britain (99 per cent). However, approximately 10 per cent of adults had connected to the Internet using a mobile phone.

Ouch!

Ouch! (*www.bbc.co.uk/ouch*) was launched by the BBC in June 2002 and aims to reflect the life and experiences of disabled people. It provides news, editorial comment and features on issues of particular importance to disabled people. The site includes areas where visitors can email questions and share their experiences or thoughts, as a disabled person, with others. The website is run by the BBC's Interactive Factual Learning department and draws on the skills of disabled people in its writing and content.

Postal services

The Post Office, founded in 1635, pioneered mail services and was the first to issue adhesive postage stamps as proof of advance payment for mail. Under provisions in the *Postal Services Act 2000*, the Post Office ceased to be a statutory authority and its business was transferred to a successor company. In March 2001 the property, rights and liabilities of the Post Office were transferred to Consignia Holdings plc, a company wholly owned by the Crown and nominated for this purpose by order of the Secretary of State for Trade and

Table 17.3 Adults who have accessed the Internet,[1] July 2003, Great Britain

Percentages

Communication	
Using email	83
Using chat rooms or sites	23
Information search and online services	
Finding information about goods or services	83
Finding information about travel and accommodation	72
Finding information related to education	41
Reading or downloading online news	39
Playing or downloading music	26
Downloading other software	26
Listening to web radio	16
Playing or downloading games	13
Purchasing goods, services and banking	
Buying or ordering goods, tickets or services	52
Personal banking and financial services	38
Others	
General browsing or surfing	69
Selling goods or services	7

1 Data are for who that had accessed the Internet in the three months prior to the interview.
Source: Omnibus Survey, Office for National Statistics

Industry. (Consignia Holdings plc was the company described in the *Postal Services Act 2000* as 'the Post Office company'.) In November 2002 Consignia Holdings plc was renamed Royal Mail Holdings plc and the operating subsidiary, Consignia plc, was renamed Royal Mail Group plc. Royal Mail Group serves its UK customers through three main operations – Royal Mail, Parcelforce Worldwide and Post Office Ltd – and employs some 200,000 people.

Competition and regulation

Under the *Postal Services Act 2000*, an independent regulator, the Postal Services Commission (known as Postcomm), was established. It is responsible for licensing postal operators throughout the United Kingdom, including Royal Mail. Every company that delivers letters weighing up to 350 grams and costing less than £1 to post, needs a licence from Postcomm. Royal Mail no longer has a monopoly on postal services; in January 2003 Postcomm opened the market for some business mail services – bulk mail above 4,000 items per mailing from a single user at a single site

Improved access

Royal Mail Group plc has an ongoing programme to implement improved services for disabled people in its post offices. These include:

- improved accessibility for people who are wheelchair users or have mobility difficulties;
- lap trays for people who are unable to access the counter;
- pen grips for people with reduced manual dexterity;
- pension book templates and signature guides to help visually impaired people; and
- induction loops in the majority of directly managed branches to assist hard of hearing customers.

Training has been given to all staff in the Post Office branches owned by the Royal Mail Group in the United Kingdom to audit their premises as part of a programme to improve accessibility. The company has experimented with office layout and equipment, and ideas have been tested by disabled users before they were introduced into post offices. All new measures introduced are intended to comply with the *Disability Discrimination Act* (see page 99).

The Royal Mail under London

In May 2003, the Royal Mail stopped its 75-year-old underground postal system, MailRail. Although the original idea for transporting London's mail underground was envisaged in the 1850s, construction work on the tunnels did not begin until 1914. In 1927 the 'Post Office Underground Railway' began operational service. At its height, the 37 kilometres of track served nine stations, from Paddington to Whitechapel and transported 7 million items a day. In 1987, to mark its 60th anniversary, the service was renamed MailRail. At its closure, only four of the original stations were being used.

in a similar format. This market is estimated to be worth around £1.4 billion a year and represents about 30 per cent of the UK letter market by value. Further competition will be introduced in two stages:

- from 1 April 2005 the bulk mail threshold will be adjusted to open up a total of 60 per cent of the market by value; and
- from 1 April 2007 all restrictions on market entry will be abolished.

By April 2003 Postcomm had awarded long-term licences (valid for a minimum of seven years) to three postal operators in addition to Royal Mail. Nine other companies held interim licences, valid for a minimum of 12 months.

Royal Mail operations

Royal Mail delivers to 27 million addresses in the United Kingdom, handling around 82 million items each working day. The volume of mail has continued to grow despite competition from other forms of communication. Mail is collected from over 113,000 posting boxes, and from Post Office branches and large postal users. The UK postcode system allows mechanised sorting down to part of a street on a delivery round and, in some cases, to an individual address.

Parcelforce Worldwide provides a door-to-door overnight delivery service throughout the United Kingdom, handling 40 million items a year. As well as providing delivery services in the United Kingdom, it offers a range of services to 225 countries and territories across the world.

The UK network of some 17,200 post office branches (of which around 600 are directly run by Post Office Ltd) handles a wide range of transactions, with a total value of £1.2 billion in 2002/03. It acts as an agent for Royal Mail and Parcelforce Worldwide, government departments and local authorities. Post offices also provide banking services, giving customers access to current accounts for seven UK banks and access to basic bank accounts for 17 banks, as well as providing access to National Savings and Investments. Post Office Ltd is also developing its own provision of personal banking services.

About 28 million customers visit a post office each week, with 13 million using them to collect benefit payments. However, the number of people using the post office for this purpose is likely be affected by the Government's programme to pay all benefits directly into bank accounts by 2005. Customers will continue to be able to withdraw their benefit from their account at a post office, if they wish. This new system of benefits payments began in April 2003 and is being phased in over two years by the Department for Work and Pensions. A restructuring programme is expected to reduce the urban network of 9,000 offices to around 6,000.

Television

Around a third of primetime[1] broadcasting on the five main UK terrestrial channels in 2002 was devoted to drama programmes; arts and religious programmes together accounted for less than 2 per cent of broadcasting time. Figure 17.4 shows that the most popular programmes in the United Kingdom are news programmes, with over 9 in 10 people saying they were interested in this genre. Over 8 out of 10 people expressed an interest in factual and drama programmes. Religious programmes had the least appeal.

There are five public service broadcasters in the United Kingdom: the BBC (British Broadcasting Corporation), the ITV network, Channel 4, Channel 5, and S4C (Sianel Pedwar Cymru), which broadcasts Welsh-language programmes. They each have a statutory public service remit, which governs the minimum level of different types of programming they should provide.

Local television services began in 1998 and operate under licence, making use of spare frequencies as and when they are available. There are ten local delivery operators with 15-year licences and five local delivery operators with five-year licences in the United Kingdom.

BBC

The BBC broadcasts 17,000 hours of television each year on its two analogue domestic channels to national and regional audiences. The BBC's two national networks that are financed mainly by a licence fee. BBC One is the channel of broad appeal (documentaries and current affairs, features, drama and light entertainment, sport, religion and children's programmes), while BBC Two aims for more innovation and originality in its programming, catering for specialist audience interests.

Network programmes are made at, or acquired through, Television Centre in London and six bases throughout the United Kingdom (Cardiff in Wales, Glasgow in Scotland, Belfast in Northern Ireland, and Birmingham, Bristol and Manchester in England). Programmes are also commissioned from independent producers – the BBC must ensure that at least 25 per cent of its original programming comes from the independent sector.

1 Between 6.00 pm and 10.30 pm.

Table 17.4 Interest[1] in television programmes: by genre, 2002, UK

Percentages

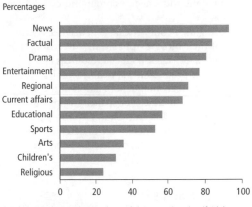

1 People aged 16 and over who said they were 'very' or 'fairly' interested in the programme type.
Source: Independent Television Commission

Education is a central component of the BBC's public service commitment. A range of programmes is broadcast for primary and secondary schools, further education colleges and the Open University (see page 114), while other educational programmes cover numeracy, literacy, language learning, health, work and vocational training. Books, pamphlets, computer software, and audio and video materials supplement the programmes. Details of the digital television channels available from the BBC can be found on page 241.

ITV network

The ITV network's analogue services are broadcast on Channel 3 as ITV1. There are 15 regionally-based independent television companies, which are licensed to supply programmes in the 14 independent television geographical regions.

There are two licences for London, one for weekdays and the other for the weekend. A separate company licensed by the Independent Television Commission (ITC) (see page 244) provides a national breakfast-time service, transmitted on the ITV network. All Channel 3 licences were renewed for a further ten-year period from 1999, 2000 and 2001.

Programmes are broadcast 24 hours a day throughout the country. A shared national and international news service is provided by Independent Television News (ITN).

ITV1 companies are obliged to operate a national programme network. The ITV network centre, which is owned by the companies, independently commissions and schedules programmes.

Operating on a commercial basis, licensees derive most of their income from selling advertising time (see page 248). Their financial resources and programme production vary considerably, depending largely on the population of the areas in which they operate. Newspaper groups can acquire a controlling interest in ITV companies, although measures are in force to deter any undue concentrations of media ownership (see page 247).

Channel 4 and S4C

Channel 4 provides a national 24-hour television service. It is a statutory corporation, licensed and regulated by the ITC, and funded by selling its own advertising time. Its remit is to provide programming that: demonstrates innovation, experiment and creativity in form and content; appeals to the tastes and interests of a culturally diverse society; includes a significant number of educational programmes; and exhibits a distinctive character. Channel 4 does not make its own programmes but commissions them from independent producers and other programme providers, including a number from overseas. Its commercial businesses, including digital channels E4 and FilmFour, are managed via a wholly-owned subsidiary, 4Ventures.

In Wales the fourth analogue channel is allocated to S4C, which is regulated by the Welsh Fourth Channel Authority. Members of the Welsh Authority are appointed by the Government. S4C must ensure that a significant proportion of programming – the majority aired between 6.30 pm and 10.00 pm – is in the Welsh language. At other times it transmits Channel 4 programmes. In 1998 S4C launched a digital service incorporating analogue Welsh programmes and additional material.

Five

The UK's newest analogue terrestrial channel went on air in 1997, its ten-year licence having been awarded by competitive tender to Channel 5 Broadcasting Ltd. Five reaches approximately 84 per cent of the population and is financed by advertising revenue.

Text services

Teletext is a text-based data service, broadcast on Channels 1 to 5 using the spare signal capacity in analogue terrestrial television services. Most television sets in the home are capable of decoding teletext signals, which are displayed as text and simple graphics. Teletext services include regularly updated information on a variety of subjects, including news, sport, travel, weather and entertainment.

The BBC broadcasts its 'Ceefax' teletext service within the BBC One and Two signals. For ITV1, Channel 4, and Channel 5, the teletext service is provided under ten-year broadcasting licences, granted by the ITC (see page 244). All terrestrial channels provide subtitles for people with hearing difficulties on most of their programmes.

Digital terrestrial television (DTT)

A single frequency carrying the signals of several digital services is called a multiplex. The signal can be received by a standard aerial, but has to be converted into sound and vision by using a decoder, either incorporated into the television set or in a separate digital adapter attached to a television.

There are six terrestrial multiplexes capable of supporting services nationwide. One is gifted to, and operated by, the BBC, and the other five are licensed by the ITC.

When DTT was launched in November 1998, there was one multiplex operated by the BBC; one multiplex operated by Digital 3&4, supporting services from ITV, Channel 4 and Teletext; and one multiplex operated by S4C Digital Network (SDN), supporting services from S4C, Channel 5 and other broadcasters.

The remaining three multiplexes were operated from November 1998 to April 2002 by ITV Digital to support pay-TV services. ITV Digital ceased broadcasting in May 2002. In August 2002 the ITC granted the licences for these three multiplexes to new operators – one multiplex to the BBC, and two to Crown Castle International. All DTT services are now free-to-view.

Freeview was launched on 30 October 2002, as an umbrella brand for UK DTT services. It is promoted by DTV Services Ltd, a joint venture between the BBC, Crown Castle International and

BBC Three

The proposals for a new BBC station, BBC Three, were approved by the Department for Culture, Media and Sport (DCMS) in September 2002 and the channel was launched on 9 February 2003 (replacing BBC Choice). It is available free on digital satellite, cable and digital terrestrial television. It is aimed at people in their 20s and 30s offering a variety of programme types including comedy, current affairs, drama, news, science and the arts. The BBC made the following commitments to the programmes broadcast on BBC Three:

- 90 per cent of broadcast hours will be produced in the European Union;
- 80 per cent of programming will be specially commissioned for BBC Three, or repeats of programming specially commissioned for BBC Three;
- 33 per cent of programmes originated and 15 per cent of broadcast hours on BBC Three will be music and arts, education, and news and current affairs;
- at least 25 per cent of new programming will be from the independent sector; and
- no more than 10 per cent of programmes will be acquired from channels other than BBC One, Two and Four.

British Sky Broadcasting (BSkyB, see page 242). Freeview currently offers around 30 TV and radio channels and interactive services. There were an estimated 1.6 million Freeview viewers at the end of March 2003.

Services from the public service broadcasters that are available on analogue terrestrial are also broadcast on Freeview. Other services available on Freeview include:

- four news channels: BBC News 24, ITV News, Sky News and Sky Sports News;
- BBC Parliament (coverage of proceedings in the House of Commons, House of Lords, the Parliament in Scotland and the assemblies in Wales and Northern Ireland);
- BBC Four (in-depth coverage of culture, the arts, science, history, business and current affairs);
- two daytime children's channels, CBBC and, for the under-fives, CBeebies;
- ITV2 (an additional service from the ITV network); and
- S4C2 (an additional service from S4C).

There are also channels such as UK History, several shopping and entertainment channels.

Digital switchover

The Government intends eventually to cease analogue terrestrial television transmission, and to reallocate some of the broadcasting spectrum currently used for analogue television. It believes that switchover could start as early as 2006 and be completed by 2010.

The United Kingdom leads the world in uptake of digital television. Services are available to over 96 per cent of households. By the end of March 2003, around 44 per cent of households (10.8 million) were accessing digital television via DTT, satellite or cable.

Take-up of digital television

In April 2003 the Government released a report jointly prepared by the Independent Television Commission (see page 244) and the BBC. The report, *Progress Towards Digital Switchover*, lists government policy interventions that could be taken to increase take-up of digital television if progress is slow. These include:

- the announcement of a firm switchover date;
- making it compulsory for all new televisions to contain digital decoders;
- a coordinated public information campaign;
- a public commitment to certain high levels of DTT coverage after switchover; and
- growth of a free satellite market as a result of public service channels broadcasting on digital satellite.

Non-terrestrial television

There are two main non-terrestrial television delivery systems (platforms) in the United Kingdom – digital satellite and cable-access television (CATV). These are funded mainly by subscription income. Both platforms offer packages of subscription-only television services, including some premium services such as movie and sports channels and pay-per-view events. Both cable and satellite platforms are required to carry the public service channels at no additional cost to the viewer.

On both platforms, the selection of channels available via subscription is broadly similar, but there are some services that are unique to each platform. Available services include Eurosport,

Cartoon Network, UK Gold (programmes from TV archives), E4 (additional services from Channel 4) and the Discovery Channel (science and nature documentaries).

Foreign language services are also provided, some designed for minority ethnic groups within the United Kingdom, and others aimed primarily at audiences in other countries. Viewers in the United Kingdom can similarly receive a variety of television services from other European countries.

Cable-access television

Cable-access television services are delivered to consumers via underground networks of cables. The signals are decoded using a converter box, which is rented from the cable provider. Cable customers can also access telephone services and, in the case of digital cable, broadband Internet services.

Around 13 million homes in the United Kingdom are passed in the street by a cable network, mostly in urban and suburban areas. The two main cable providers are ntl and Telewest. Both networks are in the process of converting from analogue to digital – at the end of March 2003 there were 2.1 million homes subscribing to digital CATV, and 1.8 million homes subscribing to analogue CATV.

Analogue CATV systems can carry around 65 television services, as well as a range of telecommunications services. Digital CATV can carry around 200 services (TV and radio), and additionally offers the viewer interactive services.

Digital satellite

Also referred to as 'direct to home', satellite television signals are received through a specially designed antenna (or 'dish') mounted on the outside of a building, and are decoded using either a set-top box or an integrated digital television.

Most satellite television in the United Kingdom is provided by BSkyB, which had 6.8 million subscribers by the end of June 2003. Sky Television was launched in 1989 as an analogue-only service, and began simultaneous digital broadcasting in 1998. In October 2001 the analogue signal was switched off, and the renamed Sky Digital became the first digital-only TV platform in the United Kingdom. The platform has been fully interactive since 1999.

Around 200 services (TV and radio) are currently available on the platform. Most of the more popular channels are accessible only by subscription to BSkyB, but there is also a wide variety of free-to-view channels. Customers can choose to buy a BSkyB installation without a subscription, in order to access free-to-view only.

Interactive digital services

Satellite, digital cable and DTT all offer interactive services. The level and complexity of these services depend on the platform and the equipment that the customer has installed.

Interactive services range from electronic programme guides and digital text (an enhanced version of teletext), to home shopping, video-on-demand,[2] home banking, email and Internet access. Interactive television can also involve participating in TV quiz shows, voting in polls, or viewing sports coverage from different camera angles using the remote control.

Radio

Radio's popularity has shown no signs of diminishing, with 91 per cent of the UK adult population listening each week in the first quarter of 2003. News, talk shows and music are the main output of radio stations.

The BBC has five national radio networks, which together transmit all types of music, news, current affairs, drama, education, sport, comedy and a range of features programmes. There are also 39 BBC local radio services covering England and the Channel Islands, and national radio services in Scotland, Wales and Northern Ireland, including Welsh and Gaelic language stations. In spring 2003, BBC radio took a 54 per cent share of the total UK radio audience (Table 17.5).

Around 270 independent local radio (ILR) services also provide music, local news and information, sport, education and consumer advice. The first (and only) national commercial digital radio multiplex started in 1999. This has since been joined by 44 local digital multiplexes providing a wide range of services.

---

2 Video-on-demand enables viewers to dial into a video library, via a cable or telephone network, and call up a programme or film of their choice, which is then transmitted to that household alone.

Table 17.5 Share of radio listening by station, spring 2003, UK

Percentage of listening hours

BBC	
BBC Radio 1	7.9
BBC Radio 2	15.7
BBC Radio 3	1.1
BBC Radio 4	11.8
BBC Radio Five Live	4.7
BBC World Service	0.7
BBC local/regional	11.5
All BBC	53.5
Commercial	
Classic FM	4.6
talkSPORT (Talk radio)	1.7
Virgin radio (AM only)	1.1
All national commercial[1]	7.9
All local commercial	36.6
All commercial	44.5
Other listening[2]	2.0

1 Includes listening to services that only broadcast in digital (less than 1 per cent of the total).
2 Other listening includes any UK station that does not subscribe to RAJAR as well as non-UK and private radio stations.
Source: Radio Authority Joint Audience Research/IPSOS UK

BBC network radio

BBC network radio, broadcasting to the whole of the United Kingdom, transmits nearly 44,000 hours of programmes each year on its five networks:

- Radio 1 is a contemporary music station which also provides news and information, serving a young target audience;
- Radio 2 offers a wide range of popular and specialist music, news, information and entertainment for a mainstream audience;
- Radio 3 covers classical and jazz music, drama, documentaries and discussion;
- Radio 4 offers news and current affairs coverage, complemented by drama, science, the arts, religion, natural history, medicine, finance, comedy and gardening features; it also carries parliamentary coverage and cricket in season on Long Wave, and BBC World Service programmes overnight; and
- Radio Five Live broadcasts news, current affairs and extensive sports coverage.

BBC World Service

In December 2002 the BBC World Service celebrated its 70th anniversary. The service broadcasts in 43 languages (including English) and has an estimated global weekly audience of 150 million listeners. The core programming of news, current affairs, business and sports reports is complemented by cultural programmes, including drama, literature and music.

While maintaining shortwave broadcasts for mass audiences, BBC World Service is making programmes more widely available on FM frequencies and delivering services in major languages through digital broadcasting and on the Internet.

BBC Monitoring, the international non-digital media monitoring arm of BBC World Service, provides transcripts of radio and television broadcasts from 150 countries.

Independent national radio

There are three independent non-digital national radio services, whose licences were awarded by the Radio Authority (see page 244) through competitive tender, and which broadcast 24 hours a day:

- Classic FM, which broadcasts mainly classical music, together with news and information;
- Virgin 1215, which plays rock and pop music (and is supplemented by a separate Virgin station which operates under a local London licence); and
- talkSPORT, a speech-based service.

Independent local radio

Independent local radio (ILR) stations broadcast a wide range of programmes and news of local interest, as well as music and entertainment, traffic reports and advertising. There are also stations serving minority ethnic communities. The Radio Authority awards independent local radio licences in an open competition. The success of local licence applications is in part determined by the extent to which applicants widen choice and meet the needs and interests of the people living in the area, and in part by whether they have the necessary financial resources for the eight-year licence period. Local radio stations do not have guaranteed slots on digital local radio multiplexes.

Digital radio

Commercial national digital radio services cover nearly 85 per cent of households in the United Kingdom. The Radio Authority has awarded one national multiplex licence carrying eight programme services. It has also awarded licences for 44 local digital multiplexes, which will carry about 300 commercial radio services between them.

Current BBC digital radio stations are:
- 1Xtra, broadcasting contemporary black music for a young audience;
- BBC 1–5 and BBC World Service;
- Five Live Sports Extra;
- 6 Music, broadcasting contemporary and classic pop and rock music;
- BBC7, classic and new comedy, drama and children's programmes.
- BBC Asian Network, a station for the Asian communities in the United Kingdom; and

Regulation of broadcast media

Regulation of broadcast media will become the responsibility of the Office of Communications (Ofcom) in December 2003 when it takes over the role of single regulator. Although the BBC will be subject to Ofcom's regulation concerning programme standards and economic regulation, the BBC's Board of Governors will continue to be responsible for managing the corporation's public service remit. Ofcom will assume the responsibilities of the five existing regulators: the Broadcasting Standards Commission (BSC), the Independent Television Commission (ITC), the Office of Telecommunications (Oftel, see page 236), the Radio Authority and the Radiocommunications Agency.

The BSC, a statutory body, monitors standards and fairness on television and radio (on terrestrial and cable and satellite services). It considers complaints received from the public, and adjudicates on claims of unfair treatment in broadcasts and of unwarranted infringement of privacy in programmes or in their preparation.

The ITC is an independent statutory body responsible for licensing and regulating all commercial television services (including BBC commercial services) operating in, or from, the United Kingdom, including those delivered by non-terrestrial platforms. It does not make, broadcast or transmit programmes. The ITC must ensure that a wide range of commercial television services is available throughout the United Kingdom and that they are of a high quality and appeal to a variety of tastes and interests. It must

also ensure fair competition in the provision of these services, and compliance with the rules on media ownership. The ITC regulates the various television services through licence conditions, codes and guidelines. The codes cover programme content, advertising, sponsorship and technical standards. If a licensee does not comply with the conditions of its licence or the codes, the ITC can impose penalties. These range from a formal warning or a requirement to broadcast an apology or correction, to a fine. In extreme circumstances, a company's licence may be shortened or revoked.

The Radio Authority's licensing and regulatory remit covers all independent radio services, including national, local, cable, satellite and restricted services. Its three main tasks are to plan frequencies, appoint licensees with a view to broadening listener choice, and to regulate programming and advertising. It has published codes covering engineering, programmes, news and current affairs, and advertising and sponsorship, to which its licensees must adhere. Satellite radio services must be licensed by the Radio Authority if they are transmitted from the United Kingdom for general reception within the

Communications framework

The *Communications Act 2003* received Royal Assent in July. It will establish a new framework, and a new unified independent regulator (Ofcom). Other provisions include:
- a requirement for Ofcom to establish and maintain a 'Content Board' to ensure that the public's interest in the nature and quality of TV and radio programmes is properly represented within Ofcom's structure;
- making the BBC subject to Ofcom's regulation of standards, while retaining the Board of Governors' role of managing the Corporation's public services and upholding its political and editorial independence;
- granting Ofcom powers concurrent with those of the Office of Fair Trading to promote effective competition in the communications services sector for the benefit of consumers;
- replacing the current system with a new regulatory framework for licensing telecommunications system;
- allowing spectrum trading to secure more efficient use of the available radio frequencies; and
- overhauling rules governing media ownership (see page 247).

country, or if they are transmitted from outside, but are managed editorially from within the United Kingdom.

The Radiocommunications Agency, an executive agency of the Department of Trade and Industry, is responsible for the management of the non-military radio spectrum in the United Kingdom. This involves international representation, commissioning research, and allocating radio spectrum and licensing its use.

The press

On an average weekday it is estimated that around 63 per cent of people aged 15 and over in the United Kingdom read a national newspaper (66 per cent of men and 59 per cent of women in 2002/03). Eighty-five per cent of adults read a regional or local newspaper every week. There are more than 1,300 regional and local newspaper titles and around 100 regional press publishers – ranging from those owning just one title (about half of them) to a few controlling more than 100 each.

The United Kingdom has a long tradition of a free (and often outspoken) press. While newspapers are almost always financially independent of any political party, they can express obvious political leanings in their editorial coverage, which may derive from proprietorial and other non-party political influences.

In addition to sales revenue, newspapers and periodicals earn considerable amounts from advertising. Indeed, the press is the largest advertising medium in the United Kingdom (see page 248). The British press does not receive subsidies from the state.

The national press
The national press consists of ten daily papers and ten Sunday papers. At one time London's Fleet Street area was the centre of the industry, but now all the national papers have moved their editorial and printing facilities to other parts of London or away from the capital altogether. Editions of many papers, such as the *Financial Times*, the *Sun*, *The Guardian* and *The Mirror*, are also printed in other countries.

National newspapers are often described as broadsheet or tabloid papers on the basis of

Talking newspapers
The Talking Newspaper Association of the United Kingdom (TNAUK, *www.tnauk.org.uk*) is a registered charity that records over 200 national newspapers and magazines on audio cassette for visually impaired and disabled people. TNAUK copies and dispatches over 2.5 million audio cassettes a year and reaches over 200,000 visually impaired listeners across the United Kingdom. The charity is run by a team of 30 staff supported by approximately 200 volunteers, and has eight recording studios. It also offers subscribers a choice of other formats including computer disk, email and CD Rom to allow them to access information independently.

differences in format, style and content. Many newspapers have colour pages and most produce extensive supplements as part of the Saturday or Sunday edition, with articles on personal finance, travel, gardening, home improvement, food and wine, fashion and other leisure topics. Increasing competition from other media in the delivery of news, information and entertainment has had an effect on the national press, with a gradual decline in circulation for many titles.

Regional newspapers
Most towns and cities throughout the United Kingdom have their own regional or local newspaper. These range from morning and evening dailies to Sunday papers and others that are published just once a week. They mainly include stories of regional or local interest, but the dailies also cover national and international news, often looked at from a local viewpoint. In addition, they provide a valuable medium for local advertising. Circulation figures for the period July to December 2002 indicate that the regional press sells 13.6 million paid-for newspapers and distributes 25.8 million issues of free titles each week. Over 90 per cent of local and regional titles are now available online.

London has one paid-for evening paper, the *Evening Standard*. Its publisher (Associated Newspapers) also produces a free daily morning newspaper, *Metro*, launched in 1999. There are local weekly papers for every district in Greater London; these are often different local editions of one centrally published paper.

Around 550 free distribution newspapers, mostly weekly and financed by advertising, were published in the United Kingdom in 2002. Top free weekly titles include the *Manchester Metro News*, *Nottingham & Long Eaton Topper* and *Edinburgh Herald & Post*.

There is a broad-based daily and weekly newspaper industry in Scotland covering local, Scottish and UK as well as international issues. The *Daily Record* has the highest circulation and there are also broadsheet newspapers including the *Scotsman* (based in Edinburgh) and the *Herald* (in Glasgow). The press in Wales includes Welsh-language and bilingual papers; Welsh community newspapers receive an annual grant as part of the Government's wider financial support for the Welsh language. Newspapers from the Irish Republic, as well as the British national press, are widely read in Northern Ireland. Regional newspapers in Northern Ireland include the *Belfast Telegraph* and the *Irish Times*.

There are several newspapers and magazines produced by minority ethnic communities in the United Kingdom. Most are published weekly, fortnightly or monthly. A Chinese newspaper, *Sing Tao*, the Urdu *Daily Jang* and the Arabic *Al-Arab*, however, are dailies. Afro-Caribbean newspapers include *The Gleaner*, *The Voice*, *New Nation* and *Caribbean Times*, each published weekly. The *Asian Times* is an English language weekly for people of Asian descent. Publications also appear in other languages, particularly Bengali, Gujarati, Hindi and Punjabi. The fortnightly *Asian Trader* is a successful business publication, while *Cineblitz International* targets those interested in the South Asian film industry.

The periodical press

There are more than 8,000 separate periodical publications that carry advertising. They are generally classified as either 'consumer' titles, offering readers leisure-time information and entertainment, or 'business and professional' titles, which provide people with material relevant to their working lives. Within the former category, there are general consumer titles, which have a wide appeal, and specialist titles, aimed at people with particular interests, such as motoring, sport or music. A range of literary and political journals, appearing monthly or quarterly, caters for a more academic readership. There are also many in-house and customer magazines produced by businesses or public services for their employees and/or clients.

Internet newspapers

Most national newspaper groups have set up websites, building on editorial, directory and advertising services, to develop networks of additional special interest sites to cater for a growing readership. There has also been a growth in the number of websites for regional newspapers, with over 600 online in 2003.

The Audit Bureau of Circulations (ABC) is a UK media organisation that audits more than 1,600 newspapers and 1,400 business and consumer publications. Its role is to assist media trading by providing the market with independently audited and reported circulation data, to standards agreed by its members. ABC ELECTRONIC (ABCE) was established in 1996 and provides an independent auditing service for all forms of electronic media in the United Kingdom and Republic of Ireland. Website traffic is measured by 'page impressions', which record the number of times web pages are accessed by users. ABCE found that in January 2003 there were approximately 75 million page impressions for Guardian Unlimited, the website for *The Guardian* newspaper and that in March 2003 there were approximately 88 million page impressions for the Sun Online, the website for the *Sun* newspaper. Other newspapers whose websites have been audited by ABCE are the *Star*, the *Telegraph* and the *Times*.

Press Complaints Commission

A policy of press self-regulation, rather than statutory control or a law of privacy, operates in the United Kingdom. The Press Complaints Commission deals with complaints about the content and conduct of newspapers and magazines, and operates a Code of Practice agreed by editors covering inaccuracy, invasion of privacy, harassment and misrepresentation by the press. The Commission's jurisdiction also extends to online versions of newspaper and magazine titles by publishers that already subscribe to the Code. It is a non-statutory body whose 16 members are drawn from both the public and the industry.

In 2002 the Commission received 2,630 complaints, a 13 per cent decrease on the previous year. Over half (51 per cent) of the complaints related to national newspapers, 28 per cent to regional newspapers, 7 per cent to newspapers specific to Scotland, 5 per cent to magazines and the remaining 9 per cent to publications in

Northern Ireland and to agencies. Most complaints breaching the Code are resolved by editors. The Commission had to adjudicate on just 36 complaints – upholding 17 and rejecting 19.

The press and the law

There is no state control or censorship of the newspaper and periodical press, and newspaper proprietors, editors and journalists are subject to the law in the same way as any other citizen. However, certain statutes include sections that apply to the press. There are laws governing the extent of newspaper ownership in television and radio companies (see below), mergers involving newspapers, and the right of press representatives to be supplied with agendas and reports of meetings of local authorities.

There is a legal requirement to reproduce the printer's imprint (the printer's name and address) on all publications, including newspapers. Publishers are legally obliged to deposit copies of newspapers and other publications at the British Library (see page 230).

Publication of advertisements is governed by wide-ranging legislation, including public health, copyright, financial services and fraud legislation. Legal restrictions are imposed on certain types of prize competition.

Laws on contempt of court, official secrets and defamation are also relevant to the press. A newspaper may not publish anything that might influence the result of judicial proceedings. The unauthorised acquisition and publication of official information in areas such as defence and international relations, where unauthorised disclosure would be harmful, are offences under the *Official Secrets Acts*. These are restrictions on publication generally, not just through the printed press. Most legal proceedings against the press are libel actions brought by private individuals.

Media ownership

Legislation in 1990 laid down rules enabling the ITC and Radio Authority to keep ownership of the broadcasting media widely spread and to prevent undue concentrations of single and cross-media ownership, in the broader public interest. The *Broadcasting Act 1996* relaxed these rules, both within and across different media sectors, to reflect the needs and aspirations of the industry

against the background of accelerating technological change, by:

- allowing for greater cross-ownership between newspaper groups, television companies and radio stations, at both national and regional levels; and
- establishing 'public interest' criteria by which the regulatory authorities can assess and approve (or disallow) mergers or acquisitions between newspapers and television and radio companies.

The 1996 Act overturned the rule that no one company could own more than two of the ITV (Channel 3) licences; instead, a new limit was set whereby no company could control franchises covering more than 15 per cent of the total television audience. Local newspapers with more than a 50 per cent share of their market may now own a local radio station, providing at least one other independent local radio station is operating in that area. An additional regulation is the Office of Fair Trading's limit of 25 per cent on any company's share of television advertising revenue. Newspaper transfers and mergers are subject to the consent of the Secretary of State for Trade and Industry, usually after reference (where the total paid-for daily circulation of newspapers owned by

Relaxing the media ownership rules

The *Communications Act 2003* makes provisions relating to media ownership:

- to scrap those rules preventing single ownership of ITV, subject to the Competition Commission (see page 346) being satisfied that a merger would not be anti-competitive;
- to continue to disallow any newspaper group with over 20 per cent of the national market having a significant stake in ITV;
- to introduce a parallel, regional rule whereby no one owning a regional Channel 3 licence may own more than 20 per cent of the local/regional newspaper market in the same region;
- to remove ownership rules for Channel 5;
- to introduce a scheme to ensure that at least three commercial local or regional media voices exist in addition to the BBC in almost every local community; and
- to introduce public interest tests which will allow the appropriate Secretary of State to intervene in media mergers which raise public interest considerations.

the proprietors involved is 500,000 or more) to the Competition Commission.

Advertising and sponsorship

Advertising on television accounted for 26 per cent of total expenditure on advertising in the United Kingdom in 2002, while advertising in national and regional newspapers accounted for 12 per cent and 17 per cent respectively (see page 245). New technology such as the Internet, is increasingly being exploited by companies to advertise their products. In 2002 the Internet accounted for 1 per cent (almost £200 million) of the total advertising expenditure in the United Kingdom.

Broadcast media

Advertising and sponsorship are allowed on all commercial television and radio services, subject to controls. The ITC and the Radio Authority operate codes governing advertising standards and programme sponsorship, and can impose penalties on broadcasters that do not comply. In 2002 there were 7,830 complaints to the ITC about advertisements broadcast on UK television (Table 17.6).

Advertisements on independent television and radio are broadcast in breaks during programmes, as well as between programmes, and must be distinct and separate from them. Advertisers are not allowed to influence programme content.

Political advertising and advertisements for betting (other than the National Lottery, the football pools, bingo and amusement arcades) are prohibited. All tobacco advertising is banned on television and radio. Religious advertisements may be broadcast on commercial radio and television, provided they comply with the guidelines issued by the ITC and the Radio Authority.

The BBC may not raise revenue from broadcasting advertisements or from commercial sponsorship of programmes on its public service channels. It must not give publicity to any firm or organised interest except when this is necessary in providing effective and informative programmes. It does, however, cover sponsored sporting and artistic events.

Non-broadcast media

Advertising in non-broadcast media, including newspapers, magazines, posters, sales promotions,

Table 17.6 Reasons for complaints about television advertising in 2002, UK

	Complaints received	Advertisements complained about	Advertisements where complaint was upheld[1]
Misleading	2,213	842	80
Offensive	3,979	880	14
Harmful	1,178	360	3
Miscellaneous	460	170	39
All complaints	7,830	2,252	136

1 Where complaint was upheld wholly or in part.
Source: Independent Television Commission

cinema, direct mail, and electronic media (such as CD Rom commercial emails and paid for advertising on the Internet) is regulated by the Advertising Standards Authority (ASA). The ASA is an independent body set up to ensure that advertisers conform to the British Code of Advertising, Sales Promotion and Direct Marketing. This requires that advertisements and promotions are legal, decent, honest and truthful; are prepared with a sense of responsibility to the consumer and society; and respect the principles of fair competition generally accepted in business.

British Television Advertising Awards
The British Television Advertising Awards (*www.btaa.co.uk*) was originally set up in 1976 as the London Television Advertising Awards. Its ownership is vested in 50 advertising agencies and production companies and from these companies specialists are chosen to judge and reward the best television and cinema commercials of the year. Commercials made by UK production companies (whether transmitted in the United Kingdom or not) are eligible to enter with awards for 41 categories. There is also an award for best commercial of the year. The winner of the 2003 award was a commercial by Saatchi & Saatchi for the National Society for the Prevention of Cruelty to Children (NSPCC), entitled *Cartoon*. The commercial featured a cartoon boy being violently attacked by his father but when he is thrown down the stairs the body of a real boy lies in his place. The final caption reads 'Real children don't bounce back'. Although there were 127 complaints about the commercial, the Independent Television Commission decided it should not be banned.

The ASA monitors compliance with the Code and investigates complaints received. In 2002 it received 13,959 complaints. Pre-publication advice is available to publishers, agencies and advertisers from the Committee of Advertising Practice copy advice team. If an advertisement is found to be misleading or offensive, the ASA can ask the advertiser to change or remove it. Failure to do so can result in damaging adverse publicity from the ASA's weekly publication of its judgements, the refusal of advertising space by publishers, and the loss of trading privileges. Advertisers found guilty of placing irresponsible or offensive posters can face a two-year period of mandatory pre-publication vetting. The ASA can also refer misleading advertisements to the Office of Fair Trading (see page 473), which has the power to seek an injunction to prevent their publication.

Further reading

Department for Culture, Media and Sport: Annual report 2003. Cm 5920. The Stationery Office, 2003.

The Public's View 2002. Independent Television Commission.

Websites

Department for Culture, Media and Sport
www.culture.gov.uk

Department of Trade and Industry
www.dti.gov.uk

British Broadcasting Corporation (BBC)
www.bbc.co.uk

Channel 4
www.channel4.com

Five
www.channel5.co.uk

ITV (Channel 3)
www.itv.co.uk

National Statistics
www.statistics.gov.uk

Office of Communications (Ofcom)
www.ofcom.org.uk

Press Complaints Commission
www.pcc.org.uk

Royal Mail Group plc
www.royalmailgroup.com

UK government portal
www.ukonline.gov.uk

WWW.

18 Sport

The United Kingdom has a long tradition of sporting invention, participation and achievement. In 2002, UK sportsmen and sportswomen held over 50 world titles in a variety of sports, including athletics, professional boxing, sailing, water skiing, snooker and triathlon.[1] In the same year able-bodied UK athletes won 84 medals at world and European championships, while disabled athletes won 161 medals at this level.

Major sporting events in 2002/03

Results of some of the regular sporting events held in the United Kingdom are given in Table 18.1.

England's youngest football player
In February 2003 Wayne Rooney of Everton FC became the youngest footballer ever to play for the senior England team. He was 17 years and 111 days old when he played in a friendly match against Australia. The previous record-holder was James Prinsep of Clapham Rovers, who was 17 years and 252 days old when he played against Scotland in 1879.

In March 2003 Birmingham hosted the World Indoor Athletics Championships. The team from Great Britain and Northern Ireland finished fourth in the medal table, behind the USA, Russia and Sweden. The team collected seven medals, including Golds for Ashia Hansen in the triple jump and Marlon Devonish in the 200 metres.

Over 32,000 runners competed in the London Marathon in April 2003. UK runner Paula Radcliffe set a new women's world record of 2 hours 15 minutes and 25 seconds. This was

1 minute 53 seconds faster than the previous record she set in Chicago in 2002. Each year around three-quarters of the runners are sponsored, raising about £30 million for charities and other good causes.

Michael Watson's marathon
One of the competitors in the 2003 London Marathon was the former boxer Michael Watson, who was raising money for the Brain and Spine Foundation. Watson sustained brain damage during a super-middleweight world title fight against Chris Eubank in 1991. He collapsed in the 12th round, spent 40 days in a coma and had six brain operations. Doctors thought he would never walk again. Although he remains partially paralysed, he covered two miles every morning and afternoon, resting and sleeping in a support bus that followed him along the route. He finished the course at 12.15 pm on Saturday 19 April, more than six days after the winners. Chris Eubank walked with him for the last mile.

In May 2003 the European Champions League Final was played at Old Trafford, the home of Manchester United FC. In June the United Kingdom hosted the World Disabled Badminton Championships in Cardiff, followed by the World Badminton Championships in Birmingham in July and August. Glasgow and Edinburgh hosted the European Junior Swimming and Diving Championships, also in July and August.

The Special Olympics World Summer Games were held in Ireland in June 2003. While the majority of the events were held in the Republic, Northern Ireland staged the rollerskating competition and participated in the Host Town Programme, which gave athletes the opportunity to train and acclimatise before the games. Competing among 7,000 athletes with learning disabilities from over

---

1 A continuous race involving the three disciplines of swimming, cycling and running.

REUTERS / PETER MACDIARMID

6 April 2003 *Top:* Oxford *(right)* wins the 2003 Oxford and Cambridge Boat Race by just 1 foot (30 cm) after one of the most exciting finishes of all time. The race was first held in 1829.

13 April 2003 *Below left:* Paula Radcliffe is the women's winner of the 2003 London Marathon, completing the race in a record 2 hours 15 minutes and 25 seconds.

19 April 2003 *Below right:* Michael Watson *(centre)* as he finishes the London Marathon in six days, two hours, 27 minutes and 17 seconds. Watson started walking again in 2002, having spent a decade in a wheelchair after he was injured in a World Title fight with Chris Eubank *(left)*.

THE LONDON MARATHON LTD

PA PHOTOS

14 April 2003 *Top:* the Bio-Bubble is launched at the Edinburgh Science Festival. It is an inflatable space that forms a giant, scientifically accurate, human cell, magnified 450,000 times. Inside are two interactive shows linked to life in the cell. After the festival, the Bio-Bubble will tour science centres, science festivals and schools across the United Kingdom.

17 April 2003 *Left:* the Saatchi Gallery moves into the former headquarters of the Greater London Council. The collection includes thought-provoking works of contemporary British art. Damien Hirst's shark, *The Physical Impossibility of Death in the Mind of Someone Living,* took six hours and needed an industrial crane to be safely installed in its new home.

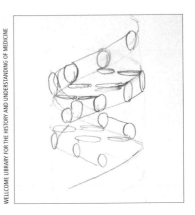

25 April 2003 50th anniversary of an article in the journal *Nature* publicising the discovery of the structure of DNA, the result of research by Francis Crick and James Watson in Cambridge and Rosalind Franklin and Maurice Wilkins in London. An exhibition, *Four Plus: Writing DNA*, that included the first public viewing of Crick's archive, was held in London between April and August 2003. Exhibits included: *(right)* A sketch by Crick of the DNA molecule's double helix shape; and *(below)* the telegram informing Crick that he was to share the 1962 Nobel Prize in Physiology or Medicine with Watson and Wilkins.

POST OFFICE DL — OFFICE STAMP

RECEIVED N 388   TELEGRAM

Prefix. Time handed in. Office of Origin and Service Instructions. Words.
40

At ___ m   At ___ m
From
By

216 GN L1484 STOCKHOLM 67W 18/10 1325

VIA NORTHERN =

DR FRANCIS HARRY COMPTON CRICK INSTITUTE OF

MOLECULAR BIOLOGY CAMBRIDGE

= THE CAROLINE INSTITUTE HAS DECIDED TO AWARD THIS

YEARS NOBEL PRIZE IN PHYSIOLOGY OR MEDICINE

JOINTLY WITH ONE THIRD EACH TO YOURSELF , DR

For free repetition of doubtful words telephone "TELEGRAMS ENQUIRY" or call, with this form B or C at office of delivery. Other enquiries should be accompanied by this form, and, if possible, the envelope. C

POST OFFICE   No. ___ OFFICE STAMP

RECEIVED   TELEGRAM

Prefix. Time handed in. Office of Origin and Service Instructions. Words.
41

At ___ m   At ___ m
From   To
By   By

JAMES DEWAY WATSON , AND DR MAURICE HUGH FREDERICK

WILKINS , FOR YOUR DISCOVERIES CONCERNING THE

MOLECULAR STRUCTURE OF NUCLEAR ACIDS AND ITS

SIGNIFICANCE FOR INFORMATION TRANSFER IN LIVING

MATERIAL = STEN FRIBERG RECTOR +

For free repetition of doubtful words telephone "TELEGRAMS ENQUIRY" at office of delivery. Other enquiries should be accompanied by this form, and, i   TS 784   B or C / C

29 April 2003 *Top:* after-school music workshops with hearing-impaired young people are launched in Huddersfield by the locally-based charity, Music and the Deaf. They are funded through the European Year of Disabled People 2003.

15 May 2003 *Left:* the National Centre for Citizenship and the Law (NCCL) in Nottingham wins the first Gulbenkian Prize for Museums and Galleries, for its Galleries of Justice. The Galleries are housed in a Victorian courtroom and a forbidding 18th century prison. Both form the backdrop for re-enactments of real-life cases that put citizenship and the law into a historical perspective.

Table 18.1 Winners of major sporting events, 2002/03 UK[1]

Athletics
London Marathon (April 2003): *Men* – Gezahegne Abera (Ethiopia); *Women* – Paula Radcliffe

Badminton
All-England Open Championships (February 2003): *Men* – Muhammad Hafiz Hashim (Malaysia); *Women* – Zhou Mi (China)

Cricket
Test matches (summer 2003) – England v Zimbabwe 2–0
England v South Africa 2–2
Frizzell County Championship – Sussex
Cheltenham & Gloucester Trophy – Gloucestershire
Twenty20 Cup – Surrey
Norwich Union League – Surrey

Equestrianism
Badminton three-day event (May 2003) – Pippa Funnell riding Supreme Rock
Hickstead Derby (August 2003) – Michael Whitaker riding Dobels Frechdacks

Football
FA Barclaycard Premiership – Manchester United
AXA-sponsored FA Cup Final – Arsenal beat Southampton 1–0 (May 2003)
Worthington Cup Final – Liverpool beat Manchester United 2–1 (February 2003)
Bank of Scotland Premier League – Glasgow Rangers
Tennents Scottish Cup Final – Glasgow Rangers beat Dundee 1–0 (May 2003)
CIS Insurance Cup Final – Glasgow Rangers beat Celtic 2–1 (March 2003)

Golf
Open Golf Championship (July 2003) – Ben Curtis (USA)
Cisco World Matchplay Championship (October 2002) – Ernie Els (South Africa)

Horse racing
Vodafone Derby (June 2003) – Kris Kin, ridden by Kieren Fallon (Ireland), trained by Sir Michael Stoute
Martell Grand National (April 2003) – Monty's Pass, ridden by Barry Geraghty (Ireland), trained by Jimmy Mangan (Ireland)

Motor racing
British Grand Prix (Formula 1) (July 2003) – Rubens Barrichello (Brazil)
Network Q Rally of Great Britain (November 2002) – Petter Solberg (Norway)

Motorcycling
World Superbike Championship, British Round 1 (June 2003) – Race 1: Neil Hodgson; Race 2: Neil Hodgson; British Round 2 (July 2003) – Race 1: Shane Byrne; Race 2: Shane Byrne

British Motorcycle Grand Prix (July 2003) – 500 cc: Max Biaggi (Italy); 250 cc: Fonsi Nieto (Spain); 125 cc: Hector Barbera (Spain)

Speedway – British Grand Prix (June 2003) – Nicki Pedersen (Denmark)

Rowing
University Boat Race (March 2003) – Oxford

Rugby league
Tetley's Super League Final (October 2002) St Helens beat Bradford Bulls 19–18
Powergen Challenge Cup Final (April 2003) – Bradford Bulls beat Leeds Rhinos 22–20

Rugby union
Lloyds TSB Six Nations Championship – England
Zurich Premiership – Gloucester
Powergen Cup Final (April 2003) – Gloucester beat Northampton 40–22
Celtic League – Munster beat Neath 37–17
WRU Principality Cup Final (May 2003) – Llanelli beat Newport 32–9

Snooker
Embassy World Championship Final (May 2003) – Mark Williams beat Ken Doherty 18–16
UK Championship Final (December 2002) – Mark Williams beat Ken Doherty 10–9

Squash
British Open Championships Finals (October 2003) – *Men:* David Palmer (Australia) beat Peter Nicol 15-13, 15-13, 15-8; *Women:* Rachael Grinham (Australia) beat Cassie Jackman 9-3, 7-9, 9-2, 9-5

Tennis
Wimbledon Finals (July 2003): *Men's singles* – Roger Federer (Switzerland) beat Mark Philipoussis (Australia) 7–6 (7/5) 6–2 7–6 (7/3); *Women's singles* – Serena Williams (US) beat Venus Williams (US) 4–6 6–4 6–2

1 UK sportsmen and sportswomen unless otherwise indicated.

Table 18.2 Medals won by the Great Britain team at the 2003 Special Olympics

	Gold	Silver	Bronze	Total
Gymnastics	35	30	26	91
Powerlifting	26	21	20	67
Equestrian	8	8	9	25
Table tennis	3	7	3	13
Swimming	3	2	6	11
Athletics	3	2	5	10
Tennis	3	2	1	6
Golf	2	4	2	8
Sailing	2	2	0	4
Badminton	1	4	2	7
Cycling	1	3	3	7
Judo	1	1	2	4
Basketball	1	1	0	2
Tenpin bowling	0	2	1	3
Football	0	2	0	2
Total	**89**	**91**	**80**	**260**

Source: Fleishman-Hillard Saunders

150 countries, the 199-strong Great Britain team won a total of 260 medals including four Golds won by powerlifter Gary Haynes. Athletes from Northern Ireland, playing as part of the Ireland team, won 65 medals – 12 Gold, 25 Silver and 28 Bronze.

The national cricket sides of Zimbabwe, Pakistan and South Africa all visited the United Kingdom during 2003. During the visit of the Zimbabwean team, the first new test match ground in 101 years was used – at Durham's Riverside ground.

The Benson & Hedges Cup was replaced in the domestic county cricket calendar by the Twenty20 Cup. Each match consisted of 20 overs a side, lasting less than three hours and played from 5.30 pm to 8.15 pm. The competition featured two weeks of group matches between the 18 counties, with a finals day in July at Trent Bridge.

All four home nations from the United Kingdom sent teams to the Rugby Union World Cup Finals, held in Australia from 10 October to 22 November.

Participation

Watching and participating in sport are two of the most popular forms of leisure activity. Figure 18.3 shows the percentage of people in each age group who had taken part in some kind of sport or physical activity in the four weeks prior to interview during 2000/01. Participation is very high (95 per cent) among the school-age group of 8–15, but tails off as people get older, to fewer than one in three of those aged 65 and over. In every age group, males are more likely to engage in a sport or physical activity than females.

Figure 18.3 Participation[1] in a sport or physical activity by age group, 2000–01, UK

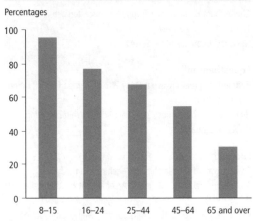

Percentages

1 Percentage reporting taking part in the four weeks prior to interview.
Source: UK 2000 Time Use Survey, Office for National Statistics

Recreational walking or hiking is the form of sport or physical activity most likely to be undertaken by adults of both sexes over the four-week period (Table 18.4). Participation rates for swimming are also relatively high for both men and women.

In the traditional school sports such as gymnastics, athletics, outdoor football, rugby, netball, cricket and tennis, 50 per cent or more of all those who take part in a four-week period are in the 8–15 age group. In contrast, just over half of those participating in squash and in weight training or body building are aged 25–44, while 43 per cent of lawn bowls participants are aged 65 and over.

Football

Recent data for England show that over 42 per cent of 6- to 16-year-olds play football on at least ten days over a 12-month period (outside of school lessons). Between 2000 and 2004, the Government plans to invest, through the Football

Table 18.4 Adult participation¹ in selected sports, 2000–01 UK

Percentages

	Men	Women
Walking/hiking²	22	24
Snooker	17	4
Swimming	15	18
Cycling	14	7
Football	12	1
Golf	10	1
Weights	10	4
Keep fit	9	19
Running/athletics	7	3
Racket sports	7	4
Darts	5	2
Bowls	3	2

1 Percentage of people aged 16 and over reporting participation in the four weeks before the survey.
2 Recreational walking or hiking for two miles or more.
Source: UK 2000 Time Use Survey, Office for National Statistics

Foundation, a total of £67 million to develop grass roots football, community and education initiatives, and essential stadium safety work. The Football Association of Wales Trust will receive around £2 million over the next three years from the Welsh Assembly Government to support their main aims of encouraging more boys and girls of school age to take part in football and to raise the standards of play in Wales.

In England, 310 clubs are affiliated to the Football Association (FA) and about 42,000 clubs to regional or district associations. In Scotland, there are 79 full and associate clubs and nearly 6,000 registered clubs under the jurisdiction of the Scottish Football Association. In Wales there are 155 clubs affiliated to the Football Association of Wales (FAW) and 1,653 clubs affiliated to areas. The Irish Football Association (covering Northern Ireland) has 600 affiliated clubs.

Average attendance at English Premier League games in 2001/02 was 34,300. In comparison, in the German Bundesliga 1 it was 32,600; in Ligue 1 in France, it was 21,450; in Serie A in Italy and Primera division 1 in Spain it was 26,000; while in the Scottish Premier League it was around 15,900.

The Football League is the governing body for the 72 clubs in English Divisions 1, 2 and 3. These clubs attracted a total of 14.9 million attendances

at league matches during the 2002–2003 season – the biggest aggregate attendance for the bottom three divisions of English football for 38 years. Division 1 had an average attendance of about 15,400, which is 50 per cent higher than the equivalent divisions in Italy and Germany and more than double those in Spain and France.

Women's football
In England, girls' and women's football is one of the fastest growing sports in the country, from 80 girls' teams in 1993 to 1,800 in 2000/01, and from 400 to 741 women's teams over the same period.

The top 34 women's teams in the country compete in the FA Nationwide Women's Premier League. The National Division of the League, with ten teams, is the female equivalent of the Barclaycard Premiership, and there are two lower divisions, the Northern and the Southern, each with 12 teams. The current title holders are Fulham LFC.

England has been chosen to host the 2005 UEFA European Women's Championship.

Milk Cup
Every summer, Northern Ireland holds the Milk Cup, an event regarded by many as the world's premier youth football tournament. It celebrated its 21st anniversary in 2003. As well as attracting entries from the English Premiership clubs, teams from as far afield as Argentina, Brazil, New Zealand and India took part.

Horse racing
Some 5.5 million people attended race meetings in Great Britain in 2002. There were 1,158 race meetings and 13,000 horses in training. The cumulative television audience was over 450 million. Horse racing is second to football as the most televised sport on terrestrial channels. In 2002/03, around £8 billion was bet off-course on horse racing, most of it in licensed betting offices.

Tennis
The Lawn Tennis Association (LTA) estimated that about 3.5 million people aged four and upwards played tennis in Great Britain in 2002. The LTA runs a number of international, national and county tournaments, as well as national competitions for British schools. All the profits generated by the Wimbledon Championships – £25.6 million in 2002 – are invested by the LTA in

British tennis. It has embarked on a strategy for developing the game and improving tennis facilities in Great Britain, by expanding participation and club membership, and improving coach education.

> ### Women's cricket
> Records of women's cricket date back to the 18th century. The first Test Match was held in 1934, when the England team defeated Australia. England also won the first World Cup in 1973. In 1998, the Women's Cricket Association, which had been the governing body for 72 years, voted to become part of the England and Wales Cricket Board (ECB). Since then, the number of women's clubs has risen steadily and the ECB estimates that there were over 2 million participants in girls' cricket in 2003.

Sports policy

A 'Sports Cabinet' identifies strategic priorities for sport in the United Kingdom. Its membership comprises the Secretary of State for Culture, Media and Sport (who chairs the 'Cabinet') and the four home country ministers with responsibility for sport. Observers from the national Sports Councils also attend to hear discussions on some of the items.

The Government's Plan for Sport, an action plan for delivery of the strategy set out in *A Sporting Future for All*, was published in March 2001. Progress towards implementation is reported on annually. The latest report, published in April 2003, includes the following objectives and achievements:

For education:
- the creation of 400 specialist sports villages and academies with a sports focus by 2005;
- a minimum of two hours a week of physical education and school sport within and beyond the curriculum to be delivered to 75 per cent of 5- to 16-year-olds by 2006;
- a £459 million investment in PE and school sport between 2003 and 2006; and
- £3 million a year for a new national sports talent scholarship system, from 2004.

For sport in the community:
- community sports clubs can now apply for the financial benefits of charitable status;

- £10 million revenue and £60 million capital funding for community club development over the period 2003/04 to 2005/06; and
- £28 million over three years from 2003/04 to implement the majority of recommendations from the Coaching Task Force.

For the National Governing Body and World Class Programmes:
- an additional £9.4 million over two years from 2004/05 to implement the recommendations of the Elite Sports Funding Review.

As well as the specialist sports colleges, two main schemes are designed to promote sporting excellence.

- The *World Class Performance Programme* provides support to the most talented UK athletes to enable them to improve their performance and win medals in major international competitions.
- The *World Class Events Programme* aims to ensure that major international events can be attracted to, and staged successfully in, the United Kingdom. About £1.6 million a year is available to help support the cost of bidding for, and staging, events.

In December 2002, a strategy for delivering the Government's sport and physical activity objectives in England, entitled *Game Plan*, was published by the Department for Culture, Media and Sport (DCMS) and the Cabinet Office's Strategy Unit. Among the key objectives identified are:
- increasing mass participation in sport and physical activity;
- improving success in popular sports;
- improving the approach to hosting major events;
- simplifying fragmented funding arrangements; and
- reforming the organisational framework.

The Government has implemented one of the key *Game Plan* recommendations. The Activity Coordination Team (ACT), chaired by the Minister for Sport, has brought together eight government departments to coordinate the delivery of policy aims in health, education and community cohesion through sport. The ACT met for the first time in July 2003.

Sport 21 2003–2007 Shaping Scotland's Future, the updated strategy for sport in Scotland, was published in March 2003.

In July 2003 the Welsh Assembly Government launched a consultation strategy, entitled *Sport and Active Recreation in Wales: Climbing Higher, Dringo'n Uwch*, covering the period to 2023.

> **Hunting with dogs**
> Legislation to ban hunting with dogs has been in force in Scotland since August 2002. In England and Wales, the Hunting Bill was introduced into Parliament in December 2002. As originally drafted, this would have allowed some fox hunting to continue under a system of licensing. In June 2003 MPs voted by 362 to 154 for an outright ban on the hunting of wild mammals with dogs, with limited exemptions. The Bill will return to the House of Lords in the autumn. If the Lords reject it or the two Houses do not agree amendments, the Bill might be reintroduced in the next session under the *Parliament Acts* (see page 42).

Organisation and administration

Sports Councils
Government responsibilities and funding for sport and recreation are largely channelled through five Sports Councils:
- the United Kingdom Sports Council, operating as UK Sport;
- the English Sports Council, operating as Sport England;
- the Sports Council for Wales;
- the Scottish Sports Council, operating as **sport**scotland; and
- the Sports Council for Northern Ireland.

UK Sport takes the lead on those aspects of sport and physical recreation that require strategic planning, administration, coordination or representation for the United Kingdom as a whole. Its main functions include:

- coordinating support to sports in which the United Kingdom competes internationally (as opposed to the four home countries separately);
- tackling drug misuse in sport;
- coordinating policy for bringing major international sports events to the United Kingdom; and
- representing UK sporting interests overseas at international level.

All the Sports Councils distribute Exchequer and Lottery funds. UK Sport focuses on elite sportsmen and sportswomen, while the home country Sports Councils are more concerned with the development of sport at the community level by promoting participation, giving support and guidance to providers of sports facilities, and supporting the development of talented sportsmen and women, including disabled people. They also manage the National Sports Centres (see page 257).

Sports governing bodies
Individual sports are run by over 400 independent governing bodies. Some have a UK or Great Britain structure, while others are constituted on an individual home country basis. In Northern Ireland almost half of the sports are part of an all-Ireland structure, which covers both Northern Ireland and the Republic of Ireland. The functions of governing bodies include drawing up rules, holding events, regulating membership, selecting and training national teams, and producing plans for their sports. There are also organisations representing people who take part in more informal physical recreation, such as walking. Most sports clubs in the United Kingdom belong to, or are affiliated to, an appropriate governing body.

Governing bodies that receive funding from the Sports Councils are required to produce development plans, from the grass roots to the highest competitive levels. In order to have access to Lottery funds for their top athletes, they need to prepare 'world-class performance' plans with specific performance targets.

A number of international federations have their headquarters in the United Kingdom: the Commonwealth Games Federation and federations for badminton, billiards and snooker, bowls, cricket, curling, golf, netball, sailing, squash, tennis and wheelchair sports.

Other sports organisations

Central Council of Physical Recreation (CCPR)
The CCPR is the largest sport and recreation federation in the world and works on behalf of 265 national governing and representative bodies of sport and recreation and an estimated 110,000 voluntary sports clubs. The British Sports Trust runs a volunteer sports leadership programme as a charity arm of the CCPR. The Scottish Sports

Association, the Welsh Sports Association and the Northern Ireland Sports Forum are equivalent associations to the CCPR. Their primary aim is to represent the interests of their members to the appropriate national and local authorities, including the Sports Councils, from which they may receive some funding.

British Olympic Association (BOA)

The BOA, comprising representatives of the 35 national governing bodies of Olympic sports, organises the participation of British teams in the Olympic Games, sets standards for selection and raises funds. The BOA is supported by sponsorship and by donations from the private sector and the general public, and works closely with UK Sport. It contributes to the preparation of competitors in the period leading up to the Games, such as arranging training camps, and has programmes to support national governing bodies and their athletes in areas such as acclimatisation, psychology and physiology. Its Olympic Medical Institute at Northwick Park Hospital in Harrow provides medical services for competitors before and during the Olympics. The BOA's educational arm aims to educate youngsters about the Olympic Games and the Olympic movement.

Women in sport

UK Sport organises a UK Coordinating Group on Women in Sport, the overall aim of which is to raise participation by women in sport at all levels, from grass roots to high-performance, and increase the number of women involved in coaching, managing and administering sport.

The Women's Sports Foundation promotes opportunities for women and girls in sport and active recreation. Its activities include advising on key issues and campaigning for changes in policy. Together with Sport England, it has developed a national action plan on women's sport development.

Sport for disabled people

Sport for disabled people is organised by a range of agencies in the United Kingdom. Some organisations promote the needs of people with a particular type of disability across a range of sports. These include the British Amputee and Les Autres Sports Association, British Blind Sport, British Wheelchair Sports Foundation, Cerebral Palsy Sport and the United Kingdom Sports Association for People with Learning Disability. The British Deaf Sports Council organises sporting opportunities for people with hearing

Olympic bid

In May 2003 the Government announced its support for London's bid to host the 2012 Olympic and Paralympic Games. The proposal is likely to include the building of a new stadium near Stratford in East London, where transport links are already being improved by the completion of the Channel Tunnel rail link and the extension of the Docklands Light Railway to the nearby City Airport.

A Bid Company has been established, and will submit an Applicant City Questionnaire to the International Olympic Committee (IOC) in early 2004. If London is successful at that stage, a Candidate Bid Book will be prepared and submitted to the IOC by November 2004. The IOC will announce the result in July 2005. In addition to London, the following cities have confirmed their intention to bid for the Games: Havana, Istanbul, Leipzig, Madrid, Moscow, New York, Paris and Rio de Janeiro.

London has hosted two previous Olympic Games, in 1908 and 1948. On both occasions it was asked to host – the city has never previously made a bid for the Olympics. If the bid is successful, it will be the first time that London has hosted the Paralympic Games.

impairment and coordinates British interests at the World Deaf Games.

In addition, the English Federation of Disability Sport, Disability Sport Cymru, Scottish Disability Sport and Disability Sport Northern Ireland are responsible for the general coordination and development of sport for disabled people. A number of sports already have a degree of integration: archery, athletics, cricket, cycling, equestrianism, football, judo, powerlifting/weightlifting, rugby union, sailing, swimming and wheelchair tennis/table tennis. The Commonwealth Games in Manchester in 2002 was the first major sports event in the world to include an integrated programme of events for disabled people.

The British Paralympic Association (BPA), comprises 26 national governing bodies and disability sport organisations. It ratifies selection, and funds and manages the Great Britain Paralympic Team in the winter and summer Paralympic Games. The BPA's games programme is funded through sponsorship, fund-raising and donations from the public and private sectors.

The separate World-Class Performance Programme of the BPA supports preparation of Britain's elite disabled athletes. It provides sport science and medical advice and develops leading research into performance preparation. In May 2002 UK Sport announced a £1.7 million investment programme to support the British team for the 2004 Paralympic Games in Athens, including multi-sport preparation camps, to be held twice a year, to help the athletes experience similar conditions and climate to those expected in Athens.

Funding

National Lottery

For every Lottery ticket sold, 3.8 pence goes to sport. Between 1994, when the National Lottery started, and June 2003 the Sports Councils awarded 23,175 grants worth around £1.9 billion. Money has been used to improve sporting opportunities, provide new sporting facilities in schools and elsewhere, support current and potential elite performers, and to stage major events. In England, over £1 billion of Lottery funds were invested in over 3,300 community facilities in the first six years. Following a review, the Sport England Lottery Fund will be re-launched in 2004. In Scotland, over 6,000 awards totalling more than £200 million have been made by sportscotland to July 2003. The Sports Council for Northern Ireland has made around 1,000 awards, worth over £50 million.

Sponsorship

Many sports benefit from sponsorship, which may take the form of financing specific events or championships, such as horse races or cricket leagues, or support for sports organisations or individual performers. Motor sport and football receive the largest amounts of private sponsorship. Sponsorship is encouraged by a number of bodies, including the Institute of Sports Sponsorship, which comprises some 100 UK companies involved in sponsoring sport. Sponsors in the United Kingdom now invest more than £1 billion annually in sport.

SportsAid

SportsAid raises funds to help encourage and support young people and disabled people with sporting talent in England. Financial grants are provided on an individual basis, with each application being assessed on the criteria of talent

The Tobacco Advertising and Promotion Act

The *Tobacco Advertising and Promotion Act 2002* (see also page 182) brought in a ban on most forms of tobacco advertising and promotion (including sponsorship of sporting events) across the United Kingdom from 14 February 2003. Transitional arrangements allowed all sports organising bodies until 30 July 2003 to replace any tobacco sponsorship. The Act also allows for longer transitional exemptions until 31 July 2005, provided a sport can demonstrate that it has a global reach.

and need. Those receiving funds must usually be aged between 12 and 18, but there is no age limit for disabled people. Between 1975 and 2003, the charity distributed over £20 million in grants. The Scottish Sports Aid Foundation, SportsAid Cymru/Wales and the Ulster Sports and Recreation Trust have a similar role.

Foundation for Sport and the Arts

The Foundation for Sport and the Arts, set up by the football pools promoters in 1991, has made awards totalling £330 million to schemes benefiting over 100 sports, mainly for small-scale projects. In late 2003 the Trustees will announce the specific areas that will be funded from April 2004 onwards.

Sports facilities

The United Kingdom has a range of world-class sporting facilities including 13 National Sports Centres, operated by the home country Sports Councils. A number of major facilities have been improved in recent years, including the Millennium Stadium in Cardiff, the Wimbledon tennis complex and several football grounds. New facilities were built in Manchester for the Commonwealth Games held in 2002. In September 2002 the Football Association announced the start of work to rebuild the football stadium at Wembley (London), which will seat 90,000 and is due to open in 2006.

United Kingdom Sports Institute

The United Kingdom Sports Institute (UKSI) has been set up under the strategic direction of UK Sport and in partnership with the home country Sports Councils, with funding mainly from the National Lottery. It provides a network of facilities and integrated support services for elite athletes and teams, and those with exceptional potential.

Its Athlete Career and Education (ACE UK) programme is designed to enhance athletes' personal development and sporting performance. All sports have access to the UKSI's services, although it concentrates on Olympic sports and those minority sports that lack a commercial element. UK Sport seeks to maximise the impact of the investment being made in world-class athletes and to ensure there is no duplication of roles within the regional centres in England and the national institutes in Scotland, Wales and Northern Ireland.

In England the UKSI network is managed by the English Institute of Sport (EIS). The EIS provides a nationwide network of world-class training facilities in nine regional multi-sport hub sites together with 35 satellite centres. The network will be fully operational by the end of 2003. It is already helping almost 1,000 world-class athletes. This figure is expected to rise to 3,500, drawn from 30 sports, by 2004.

UKSI centres in Scotland and Wales are already operational. The network supported by **sport**scotland comprises the Scottish Institute of Sport, which opened its new base at Stirling in May 2002, and six area institutes. The centre of the UKSI network in Wales is the Welsh Institute of Sport in Cardiff, which is the premier venue in Wales for top-level training and for competition in many sports.

The Sports Council for Northern Ireland is working in partnership with the University of Ulster to develop a Northern Ireland network centre of the UKSI.

Local facilities

Local authorities are the main providers of basic sport and recreation facilities for the local community, including indoor sports centres, parks, lakes, playing fields, playgrounds, tennis courts, natural and artificial pitches, golf courses and swimming/leisure pools. Commercial facilities include health and fitness centres, tenpin bowling centres, ice-skating and roller-skating rinks, squash courts, golf courses and driving ranges, riding stables and marinas.

Many amateur sports clubs cater for indoor recreation, but more common are those providing outdoor sports facilities, particularly for bowls, cricket, football, rugby, hockey, tennis and golf. For those clubs that cannot, or do not wish to,

become charities, the 2002 Budget included a package of tax measures giving clubs access to tax reliefs similar to those available to charities.

The Government has also announced its intention to allocate £60 million to provide new or refurbished community sports facilities in England through the Community Club Development Programme over the period 2003/04 to 2005/06. Some £20 million of this will come from the Capital Modernisation Fund, which is aimed at improving the delivery of public services.

Everest Golden Jubilee celebrations

On 29 May 1953, New Zealander Edmund Hillary and Tenzing Norgay from Nepal succeeded in reaching the summit of the world's highest mountain, Everest, or Sagarmatha in Nepalese. The British expedition leader, Colonel John Hunt, attributed the successful climb to advice from other mountaineers who had attempted it before, careful planning, excellent open-circuit oxygen equipment and good weather.

Mount Everest was named after Welshman Sir George Everest, the 19th century surveyor-general of India. In the 50 years since 1953, over 1,200 people have scaled the 8,848 metre mountain. To commemorate the 50th anniversary of the first ascent, Nepal invited every living mountaineer who has reached the top to join in celebrations running from 20–29 May.

Support services

Coaching

The organisation Sports Coach UK works closely with sports governing bodies, local authorities, and higher and further education institutions. Supported by the Sports Councils, it provides a comprehensive range of services for coaches in all sports. In 2001 some 30,000 coaches and schoolteachers participated in its programmes. A task force has reviewed coaching in England and in July 2002 produced a report with proposals designed to increase the pool of talented coaches and to introduce a national coaching certificate. The Government is to invest £25 million over the three years from 2003/04 in the development of coaching.

Volunteering

Sport England has developed nine Volunteer Investment Plans, which aim to create a pool of accredited volunteers working in sports clubs. In April 2002 the DCMS Leadership and Volunteering in School and Community Sport programme, known as Step into Sport, began. The first stage of the project, between 2002/03 and 2003/04, is funded by the DCMS and the Home Office and will provide around £7 million to train up to 60,000 people aged 14 to 25 to act as sports leaders in their schools and local sports clubs. It is run by a consortium of the Youth Sport Trust, the British Sports Trust (see page 255) and Sport England. Up to 8,000 older volunteers will train alongside the young volunteers. The Government is providing a further £8 million to develop the project during 2004/05 and 2005/06.

In Scotland, one of the key targets of *Sport 21 2003–2007* is that Scotland should have 150,000 volunteers who are contributing to the development and delivery of Scottish sport.

One of the main priorities of Dragon Sport, a Sports Council for Wales initiative aimed at increasing extra-curricular and sports club membership among 7- to 11-year-olds, is the recruitment and development of volunteers. Since the scheme began, 423 schools have signed up and 132 extra-curricular clubs have been established.

Sports medicine
The National Sports Medicine Institute of the United Kingdom (NSMI) serves as the national focus for all those concerned with sport and exercise medicine. It aims to provide optimum levels of safety and care to enhance the ability of those engaged in exercise and sport from grass roots to international levels. The NSMI is funded through contracts with the Sports Councils and it also generates income from its services, many of which are developed or delivered through collaboration with other organisations.

Modern sports medicine facilities are being set up as part of the UKSI's regional and national network of world-class facilities and services for elite athletes.

Sports science
The development of sports science support services for the national governing bodies of sport is being promoted by the Sports Councils, in collaboration with the BOA and Sports Coach UK, in an effort to raise the standards of

performance of national squads. The type of support provided may be biomechanical (human movement), physiological or psychological.

Drug misuse

UK Sport aims to prevent drug misuse and achieve a commitment to drug-free sport and ethical sporting practices. In January 2002 it launched a national anti-doping strategy, in line with the International Standard for Doping Control endorsed by the World Anti-Doping Agency. The strategy calls on sports bodies to publish a commitment to drug-free sport in their constitution; inform and, where relevant, test their athletes; publicise targets and achievements; and establish an independent disciplinary process. Many leading sports in the United Kingdom, such as football, cricket and rugby union, already comply with the strategy.

UK Sport's Anti-Doping Directorate coordinates an independent drugs-testing programme and is responsible for reporting the results to the appropriate governing body. In 2002/03, 7,240 drug tests were conducted in 40 sports, of which 1.4 per cent were reported to the appropriate sports governing body for further investigation. In January 2002 UK Sport launched a new online drug information service to complement the existing information provided for competitors and officials. The online database draws on information from 102 sports and lists some 3,000 substances and 5,200 products.

Further reading
The Government's Plan for Sport: 2nd Annual Report. Department for Culture, Media and Sport, 2003.

Game Plan: A strategy for delivering Government's sport and physical activity objectives report. Department for Culture, Media and Sport and Cabinet Office Strategy Unit, 2002.

Sport 21 2003–2007 Shaping Scotland's Future, the Updated National Strategy for Sport. sportscotland, 2003.

Sport and Active Recreation in Wales: Climbing Higher, Dringo'n Uwch. Strategy for Consultation. Welsh Assembly Government, Directorate of Culture, Welsh Language and Sport, Sports Policy Unit, 2003.

Websites

Department for Culture, Media and Sport
www.culture.gov.uk

**Department of Culture, Arts and Leisure
(Northern Ireland)**
www.dcalni.gov.uk

British Olympic Association
www.olympics.org.uk

UK Sport
www.uksport.gov.uk
(Includes links to individual governing bodies)

Sport England
www.sportengland.org

sportscotland
www.sportscotland.org.uk

Sports Council for Northern Ireland
www.sportni.org

Sports Council for Wales
www.sports-council-wales.co.uk

Central Council of Physical Recreation (CCPR)
www.ccpr.org.uk

Scottish Sports Association
www.scottishsportsassociation.org.uk

Women's Sports Foundation
www.wsf.org.uk

WWW.

19 The environment

The environment can be defined as anything outside an organism in which that organism lives. It includes not only natural and geological surroundings, but also buildings, the atmosphere and even noise.

The UK environment

The United Kingdom has around 75,000 separate species of plants and animals (excluding micro-organisms), out of a global total estimated at around 30 million. The natural vegetation of much of the country is deciduous forest dominated by oak, lime, elm, ash and beech, with pine locally important in highland areas. However, after many thousands of years of human activity, only scattered woodlands and patches of semi-natural vegetation lie outside enclosed cultivated fields (see Table 19.1). The moorlands and heathlands that occupy around a quarter of the land area of the United Kingdom, while appearing natural, are as much the product of human activity as is farmland.

UK native fauna has also been dramatically affected by human activity, and all native large carnivores, such as wolves and bears, are now

Table 19.1 Land by agricultural and other uses, 2002, UK

Percentages

	Agricultural land			Forest and woodland	Urban land and land not otherwise specified[3]	Total land[4] (=100%) (thousand hectares)
	Crops and bare fallow	Grasses and rough grazing[1]	Other[2]			
England	30	36	5	8	21	13,048
Wales	3	73	1	13	10	2,077
Scotland	7	67	2	17	8	7,879
Northern Ireland	4	77	1	6	12	1,412
United Kingdom	19	51	4	11	16	24,418

1 Includes grasses, and sole right and common grazing.
2 Set-aside and other land on agricultural holdings, such as farm roads, yards, buildings, gardens and ponds. Woodland on agricultural holdings is included in 'Forest and woodland'.
3 Figures are derived by subtracting land used for agricultural and forestry purposes from the land area. Figures include land used for transport and recreation; and non-agricultural, semi-natural environments, such as sand dunes, grouse moors and non-agricultural grasslands; and inland waters.
4 As at January 2001. Includes inland waters.
Source: Department for Environment, Food and Rural Affairs; Forestry Commission; Forest Service

locally extinct. However, small carnivores, such as foxes and stoats, are common in most rural areas, and rodents, birds and badgers are also widespread. Native herbivores include red and roe deer. There are only eight species of amphibian and six species of reptile native to the United Kingdom. In contrast some 550 species of bird have been found, most of which are migratory, with over 200 being regularly seen. Both fresh and salt waters contain a wide variety of fish species.

Land

Protecting countryside and wildlife

The Department for Environment, Food and Rural Affairs (Defra) is responsible for policy on wildlife and the countryside in England. It sponsors three non-departmental public bodies that have particular responsibilities for the environment: the Countryside Agency, English Nature and the National Forest Company. The devolved administrations in Wales and Scotland sponsor similar bodies, while in Northern Ireland, responsibility rests with the Environment and Heritage Service (EHS), an agency within the Department of the Environment (DoE). Defra also sponsors the Joint Nature Conservation Committee (JNCC), a committee of three statutory nature conservation agencies (English Nature, Scottish Natural Heritage and the Countryside Council for Wales).

The *Countryside Agency* is the statutory body in England that aims to improve the quality of life for people in the countryside, and improve the quality of the countryside itself. The Agency is currently working to complete the Countryside Quality Counts project, which will develop national indicators for change in the character and quality of the countryside in England. This project represents the second phase of a new landscape typology database, which, once finalised, will be used to assist planning decisions. The resulting indicators will also contribute to UK quality of life indicators (see chapter 22). The Countryside Agency budget for 2003/04 is £98.6 million.

English Nature promotes the conservation of wildlife and natural features – for example by notifying Sites of Special Scientific Interest (see page 267) – and provides advice to the Government on nature conservation. The Scottish Executive sponsors *Scottish Natural Heritage* (SNH), a body with both the nature conservation

duties and powers of English Nature, and the countryside and landscape powers of the Countryside Agency. The *Countryside Council for Wales* (CCW) has responsibilities for landscape and nature conservation, and for countryside recreation. In Northern Ireland, the EHS protects and manages the natural and built environment. Like English Nature, CCW and SNH are also responsible for providing advice and information to the Government and the public on nature conservation, for notifying land as being of special interest due to its wildlife and geological features, and for establishing National Nature Reserves (NNRs, see page 267).

The JNCC is the statutory committee through which English Nature, CCW and SNH exercise their joint functions. These include providing advice on amendments to the *Wildlife and Countryside Act 1981* and on the development and implementation of policies that affect nature conservation in Great Britain and internationally; establishing common standards for the monitoring of, and research into, nature conservation; and analysis of the information produced. At the international level, the JNCC provides technical advice to government and others to aid implementation of global and European conservation obligations, for example the Convention on Biological Diversity (see page 268) and the Birds and Habitats Directives.

Voluntary organisations

Voluntary organisations are well represented in conservation work. Although they are funded largely by subscription, private donations and entrance fees, many receive government support and grants, sometimes in recognition of statutory responsibilities that they perform.

The *National Trust* (*www.nationaltrust.org.uk*), a charity established in 1895, has over 3 million members. It owns and protects places of historic interest and natural beauty for the benefit of the nation. The Trust cares for around 250,000 hectares of land in England, Wales and Northern Ireland, including forests, fens, moorland, downs, farmland, nature reserves and stretches of coastline. In total, it is responsible for 200 historic houses, 160 gardens, 40,000 ancient monuments and archaeological remains, and 46 villages. Some 12 million people visit National Trust 'pay for entry' properties each year and an estimated 50 million visits are made annually to its coasts and countryside properties.

The separate *National Trust for Scotland* (*www.nts.org.uk*) owns 127 properties and 73,000 hectares of countryside. Established in 1931, it is supported by a membership of nearly 260,000 and over 2 million people visit its properties each year.

National Parks
National Park status recognises the national importance of the area concerned in terms of landscape, biodiversity and as a recreational resource. However, the name National Park does not signify national ownership; most of the land in National Parks is owned by farmers and other private landowners. Each park is administered by an independent National Park Authority.

Following the *National Parks and Access to the Countryside Act 1949*, the first two National Parks in England and Wales, the Lake District and the Peak District, were designated in 1951. There are now 11 parks in all in England and Wales, covering 1.4 million hectares (see map in first colour section), with a further two – the New Forest and the South Downs – in the process of designation.

Scotland's first National Park, Loch Lomond and the Trossachs, was formally inaugurated in July 2002. A second, the Cairngorms, was inaugurated on 1 September 2003.

National Parks and Areas of Outstanding Natural Beauty in England and Wales are designated by the Countryside Agency and the CCW, subject to confirmation by the Secretary of State for Environment, Food and Rural Affairs or the National Assembly for Wales.

Areas of Outstanding Natural Beauty (AONBs)
The primary objective of AONBs is the conservation and enhancement of the natural beauty of the landscape, although many of them also fulfil a wider recreational purpose. Designation started in 1956 with the Gower peninsula in Wales, and the most recent addition was the Tamar Valley in Cornwall in 1995. There are 50 AONBs in the United Kingdom, covering 2.4 million hectares or 10 per cent of the total land area (see Table 19.2).

In Northern Ireland the Council for Nature Conservation and the Countryside (CNCC) advises the Government on natural landscapes and the designation of AONBs. In addition to the nine already designated (covering 285,000 hectares), two more areas – Erne Lakeland and Fermanagh Caveland – have been proposed.

National Scenic Areas
Scotland has 40 National Scenic Areas (NSAs) which, together with four regional parks, cover around 1.1 million hectares. The main purpose of NSAs is to give special attention to the best scenery in Scotland when new development is being considered. Certain developments in the areas are subject to consultation with SNH and, in the event of a disagreement, with the Scottish Executive.

Forest and country parks
There are 17 forest parks in Great Britain, covering nearly 300,000 hectares, which are administered by the Forestry Commission (see page 409). The Countryside Agency recognises 267 country parks in England; there are 35 in Wales, recognised by the CCW, and 36 in Scotland. Northern Ireland has 11 country parks, administered by the EHS or by local authorities. It also has eight forest parks, three forest drives and over 40 minor forest recreation sites, all of which are administered by the Forest Service, an agency of the Department of Agriculture and Rural Development (DARD).

Tree preservation and planting
Tree Preservation Orders enable local authorities to protect trees and woodlands. Once a tree is protected, it is, in general, an offence to cut down or carry out most types of work to it without permission. Courts can impose substantial fines for breaches of such Orders. Replacement trees must be planted where protected trees are felled in contravention of an Order or are removed because they are dying, dead or dangerous.

Some 11,700 hectares of new woodland were planted in Great Britain in 2002/03. Tree planting is sponsored through various grant schemes, including the Forestry Commission's Woodland Grant Scheme, which encourage the planting of species native to the United Kingdom. As a consequence, the planting of broadleaved trees has greatly increased since the 1980s (see Figure 27.11 on page 408).

Major afforestation projects involving the Forestry Commission, the Countryside Agency and 58 local authorities include the creation of 12 Community Forests in and around major cities in England, with a total designated area of 450,000 hectares. These forests help to restore areas marked by industrial dereliction, create sites for recreation, sport and environmental education, and provide new habitats for wildlife. In 2001/02, about

1,000 hectares of new woodlands were created in Community Forest areas, bringing the total created since 1991 to over 9,000 hectares.

Other organisations involved in protecting existing woods and planting new areas of woodland include English Nature and voluntary bodies such as the Woodland Trust, which owns over 1,100 woods across the United Kingdom covering 18,300 hectares. The Trust planted over 3 million trees between 1996 and 2002.

Public rights of way and open country

England has about 190,000 kilometres of rights of way,[1] including 146,600 kilometres of footpaths and 32,400 kilometres of bridleways. There are 15 long-distance walking routes in England and Wales, designated as National Trails. Thirteen have been fully developed and two are in the process of completion. The Hadrian's Wall Path National Trail opened in May 2003. For the first time visitors are able to walk the entire length of the wall along an unbroken path 135 kilometres long. There are five Long Distance Routes in Scotland, which fulfil the same function as National Trails (see map at the end of the first colour section).

In England and Wales local highway authorities are responsible for asserting and protecting the rights of the public to use and enjoy public rights of way, and to ensure any obstructions occurring on them are removed. They have a duty to ensure that all public rights of way are adequately maintained, signposted and waymarked, and for keeping a legal record of all routes. Landowners have responsibility for maintaining stiles and gates in good order. In Scotland, planning authorities are responsible for asserting and protecting public rights of way, while landowners have responsibility both for keeping them clear from obstruction and for maintaining stiles and gates.

Common land[2] in England and Wales totals more than 550,000 hectares. The open character of commons has made them popular for informal recreation, although significant areas are still important for agriculture. Around 80 per cent of

Access to the countryside for people with disabilities

The *Countryside and Rights of Way Act 2000* requires local highway authorities in England and Wales to take account of the needs of people with disabilities when preparing statutory rights of way improvement plans. Relevant authorities must also take into account the needs of all people when planning and implementing footpath and bridleway maintenance and improvements.

The Countryside Agency is producing good practice guidance for countryside managers on how to improve access to the countryside for people with mobility and sensory impairments. The guidance will be based on evidence from six pilot projects, as well as consultation with access bodies. As one of the pilots, Kent County Council has produced *Walks for all in Kent and Medway*, a pack of guides to walks designed particularly for those with mobility impairments. The final version of the Countryside Agency guidance will form part of the *Public rights of way good practice guidance* and be relevant in meeting new requirements of the *Disability Discrimination Act 1995* (see page 99) that come into force in 2004.

common land is privately owned and although only 20 per cent has a legal right of public access, there is also *de facto* access.

Commons are largely unimproved and therefore have high amenity and wildlife value; many are protected by law and by nature conservation designations. For example, around half of the common land in England is found within National Parks and a similar amount is designated as Sites of Special Scientific Interest (SSSIs, see page 267). Ministerial consent is usually required to undertake work on commons or to enclose areas by fencing.

The *Common Land Policy Statement*, published by Defra and the Welsh Assembly Government in July 2002, contained proposals relating to the registration and protection of common land and village greens. Many of these proposals require primary legislation, which the Government hopes to introduce in the 2004/05 parliamentary session.

In England and Wales, the *Countryside and Rights of Way Act 2000* created a public right of access to mountain, moor, heath, down and registered common land. When the new rights come fully into

---

1 Where the general public has legal title to go across someone else's property.

2 The term 'common land' derives from the fact that certain people held rights of common over the land. The different types of rights of common signified different entitlements to the products of the soil of the common – for example to the pasture, or to sand, gravel or peat.

force in 2005, it is estimated that some 1.2 to 1.8 million hectares of land will have been opened up.

The *Land Reform (Scotland) Act 2003* established for the first time a right of responsible access to land and inland water for recreation and passage in Scotland. Part one of the Act places duties on local authorities to uphold the exercise of access rights, to plan for a system of core paths, and to establish local access forums for their area. The Act also requires SNH to draw up a Scottish Outdoor Access Code, setting out guidance on the rights and responsibilities of landowners and those taking access.

The coast

The coastline of Great Britain is 18,843 kilometres in length. It includes 163 estuaries, and is very indented: no location is more than 125 kilometres from tidal waters. About 75 per cent of the European chalk coast is located in the United Kingdom.

Local planning authorities are responsible for planning land use at the coast; they also aim to safeguard and enhance the coast's natural attractions and preserve areas of scientific interest. The policy for the protection of the coastline against erosion and flooding is administered by Defra and the devolved administrations. Operational responsibility lies with local authorities and, in England and Wales, the Environment Agency (see page 285).

Certain stretches of undeveloped coast of particular beauty in England and Wales are defined as Heritage Coast. There are 46 Heritage Coasts, protecting 1,555 kilometres, about 35 per cent of the total length of coastline (see map at the end of the first colour section).

The National Trust (see page 262), through its Neptune Coastline Campaign, raises funds to acquire and protect stretches of coastline of great natural beauty and recreational value. Around £36 million has been raised since 1965 and the Trust now protects around 960 kilometres of coastline in England, Wales and Northern Ireland.

The National Trust for Scotland cares for more than 400 kilometres of the Scottish coastline and protects other stretches through conservation agreements. There are also 29 informal marine consultation areas in Scotland. In addition, SNH has established the Focus on Firths initiative to coordinate management of the main Scottish

Flood and coastal defence

Over 850,000 properties in England and Wales are at risk from flooding and coastal erosion, and the importance of flood and coastal defence was underlined by the flooding in December 2002 and January 2003. The Environment Agency provides and maintains more than 40,000 kilometres of river and coastal defences in the two countries, spending nearly £400 million a year. It operates a flood warning system to over 1.2 million properties which aims to give people at least two hours' notice of impending flooding.

In its Spending Review of July 2002, the Government announced an increase of £185 million in all government spending in England on flood and coastal defence over the period 2003/04 to 2005/06, and an additional £22 million for 2003/04 was announced in February 2003. Much of the new allocation for 2003/04 is for local authorities, to allow for major ongoing coastal defence schemes such as those at Scarborough, West Bay in Dorset, and Brighton.

A coastal realignment project in Essex aims to show how the re-creation of saltmarsh can provide, in some areas, a more cost-effective and sustainable sea defence than traditional arrangements. In November 2002 the sea wall at Abbots Hall Farm was breached, leading to the flooding of 84 hectares of arable land. It is hoped the flooded area will regenerate as natural saltmarsh and saline lagoons – internationally important habitats which will act to protect areas further inland as well as maintain a rich variety of plants and wildlife. The farm is situated on the Blackwater Estuary, which is protected as a Site of Special Scientific Interest (SSSI), a Special Protection Area for Birds (SPA), and a marine Special Area of Conservation (SAC) (see page 268). The project is a partnership between Essex Wildlife Trust, WWF, the Environment Agency, English Nature, the Heritage Lottery Fund and the Wildlife Trusts. There are also three similar managed retreat projects under way in Scotland.

estuaries. In Wales the CCW provides grants to the Arfordir (or Coastal) Group, which is concerned with the sustainable management of the whole coast of Wales.

Wildlife protection

The protection of wildlife is an essential element of the Government's sustainable development agenda (see chapter 22). Defra aims to bring 95 per cent of all nationally important wildlife sites in England into a favourable condition by 2010, compared with the 60 per cent of sites estimated to be in that state when the target was set in 2000.

All wild bird species in Great Britain, except for a few pest and quarry species, are protected under the *Wildlife and Countryside Act 1981*. Certain birds may be killed or taken at specific times of year, or under a licence issued under the Act.

Other species are protected under the Act by Order of the Secretary of State when, in his or her opinion, the animal or plant is in danger of extinction or likely to become so endangered unless conservation measures are taken, or when protection is needed to comply with international legislation. Similar provisions apply under the Nature Conservation and Amenity Lands Order in Northern Ireland.

The JNCC is required to review Schedules 5 and 8 (protected animals and plants respectively) of the Act every five years and consult on the level of protection given to these species. The review produces advice on which the Secretary of State bases his or her decisions. The fourth review was carried out in 2001/02 (see box).

Bird populations are good indicators of the state of wildlife in the countryside, since they are widely distributed and are near the top of the food chain. There are concerns about the declines in certain bird species, as modern land management practices (particularly in agriculture) have altered their habitats and reduced the food supply they need for breeding or surviving the winter. Defra is providing funding up to 2007 for agri-environment schemes to restore farmland habitats (see page 401) and for the development of wild bird indicators using information from annual surveys run by the British Trust for Ornithology (BTO) and other UK bird conservation agencies. It has also funded a study led by the BTO to investigate the long-term declines of the house sparrow and starling, both of which have declined by more than 50 per cent since the 1970s. The UK Biodiversity Action Plan (see page 268) includes targets to reverse declines in bird population. Twenty-six species have been identified for targeting, including the skylark, grey partridge, corn bunting, song thrush and bullfinch.

The fourth review of the species protection Schedules of the *Wildlife and Countryside Act 1981*

Reviews under the Act are required to consider whether those species that are protected should remain so, and whether other endangered species should be legally protected in order to conserve them. A final set of proposals from the fourth review was submitted to the Secretary of State for the Environment, Food and Rural Affairs in September 2002. The report recommended increasing the level of protection to the water vole, giving partial protection to the Roman snail, and giving full protection to seven marine fish and two Burnet moths. No species were recommended for removal from either schedule.

Wildlife crime

Wildlife crime takes many forms and has been increasing in recent years. Examples include theft of eggs from birds of prey, illegal shooting, trapping, poisoning, digging up wild plants, and the illicit trade in endangered species. The most significant organised criminal activities involve the trafficking in endangered species and their by-products, and the taking and keeping of species within the United Kingdom. The extent of such criminality is unknown, but in 2002 HM Customs and Excise seized 8,675 live animals and made 542 separate seizures of endangered species or their by-products.

Defra and the Scottish Executive manage a team of around 100 wildlife inspectors. Their main roles are to verify information submitted in support of applications to keep or trade in wildlife species; and to check that people are complying with the administrative controls contained in certain wildlife legislation. There are also specialist wildlife officers in almost every police force in the United Kingdom.

The Partnership for Action against Wildlife Crime, chaired by the police and Defra (*www.defra.gov.uk/paw*), provides a forum for communication and co-operation between the statutory enforcement authorities and non-governmental organisations which have an active interest in wildlife law enforcement.

The National Wildlife Crime Intelligence Unit, within the National Criminal Intelligence Service (see page 193), provides law enforcement agencies with the information they need to target and disrupt wildlife crimes and the criminals involved. It also acts as a focal point for the gathering and analysing of intelligence on serious wildlife crime at regional, national and international levels.

Much of UK law in relation to wildlife crime is shaped by international regulations. The Convention on International Trade in Endangered Species (CITES) prohibits trade of around 800 species and controls that of a further 23,000. It is implemented in the European Union via the EU Wildlife Trade Regulations, and within the United Kingdom by the Control of Trade in Endangered Species (Enforcement) Regulations 1997. Penalties include terms of imprisonment not exceeding two years.

In January 2003, the Government published a consultation paper on proposals to strengthen the controls on trade in endangered species in the United Kingdom. The paper suggested strengthening the powers of the police and government wildlife inspectors, and increasing the penalty for illegal trade in wildlife within the United Kingdom to a maximum of five years in prison.

Habitat protection
Habitat protection is mainly achieved through the networks of Sites of Special Scientific Interest (SSSIs) in Great Britain, and Areas of Special Scientific Interest (ASSIs) in Northern Ireland. Sites are protected for their plants, animals or geological or physiographical features. Some SSSIs and ASSIs are of international importance and have been designated for protection under the EC Wild Birds and Habitats Directives or the Ramsar Convention (see page 269). In England, the Government's target is to bring 95 per cent of SSSIs into favourable condition by 2010. At the end of February 2003, 55 per cent of assessed SSSIs were in such a condition. Most SSSIs and ASSIs are privately owned, but about 40 per cent are owned or managed by public bodies such as the Forestry Commission, the Ministry of Defence and the Crown Estate.

Conservation agencies in England and Wales have powers to refuse consent for damaging activities on SSSIs, to develop management schemes (in consultation with owners and occupiers of SSSIs), and to serve a management notice to require works to be done where necessary. The maximum penalty for deliberate damage to an SSSI is £20,000 in a magistrates' court, with unlimited fines in the Crown Court. The Environment (Northern Ireland) Order 2002 gave the EHS similar powers in relation to ASSIs in Northern Ireland.

The Wildlife Trusts (*www.wildlifetrusts.org*) and the RSPB (*www.rspb.org.uk*) play an important part in protecting wildlife throughout the United Kingdom. The Wildlife Trusts have over 2,500 nature reserves covering 82,000 hectares. The 47 independent trusts have over 413,000 members in total, and are mainly based in counties in England and Wales, with the whole of Scotland covered by

Table 19.2 Protected areas, 31 March 2003

Type of site[1]	Number of sites	Area ('000 hectares)
National Nature Reserves (NNRs)	399	246
Local Nature Reserves	903	41
Sites of Special Scientific Interest (SSSIs) (Great Britain)	6,586	2,335
Areas of Special Scientific Interest (ASSIs) (Northern Ireland)	196	92
Marine Nature Reserves	3	19
Special Protection Areas (SPAs)	240	1,437
Candidate Special Areas of Conservation	576	2,406
Ramsar Wetland Sites	144	759
Environmentally Sensitive Areas (ESAs)[2]	43	3,190
Areas of Outstanding Natural Beauty (AONBs)	50	2,407
National Scenic Areas (Scotland)	40	1,002

1 Some areas may be included in more than one category.
2 As at 31 March 2002.
Source: JNCC, Department for Environment, Food and Rural Affairs

the Scottish Wildlife Trust. The RSPB manages 182 reserves covering 126,846 hectares. It claims to be the largest voluntary wildlife conservation body in Europe, with over 1 million members.

National Nature Reserves (NNRs)
The year 2002 marked the 50th anniversary of NNRs in England. NNRs are intended to be the best examples of legally protected sites. The anniversary was marked by the declaration of the 223-hectare Sherwood Forest NNR in November.

Biodiversity, species recovery and reintroduction
The United Kingdom is one of 187 Parties to the Convention on Biological Diversity Treaty, agreed at the Rio Earth Summit in 1992 (see page 277). The Parties have agreed to develop national strategies and programmes for the conservation and sustainable use of biological diversity and to ensure the fair and equitable sharing of benefits from the use of genetic resources. While the prime focus for implementation is at national level, much activity is under way internationally to develop the Convention's obligations, share experience and help identify good practice. The next meeting of the Parties will be in 2004.

As part of the UK Biodiversity Action Plan (*www.ukbap.org.uk*), 391 species and 45 habitat action plans have been established and are at various stages of implementation. In addition, over 160 local biodiversity action plans are in preparation or being implemented.

Defra published England's biodiversity strategy, *Working with the grain of nature*, in October 2002. The aim of the strategy is to ensure that the implications for biodiversity are considered as an integral part of policy decisions in key areas – agriculture, water, woodlands, marine and coastal management, and in urban areas. The strategy identifies a new series of indicators for biodiversity, a report on which will be published by the end of 2003 and updated regularly thereafter. The Northern Ireland Biodiversity Strategy was launched by the Assembly in September 2002.

The National Biodiversity Network Trust (*www.searchnbn.net*) is a charity representing 11 voluntary and public organisations across the United Kingdom. The Trust aims to bring together biodiversity information to meet a wide range of conservation, research, educational and public participation needs.

The Royal Botanic Gardens at Kew (see page 274) has been successful for many years in the reintroduction of species. As at August 2003, its Millennium Seed Bank in the Wellcome Trust Millennium Building, at Wakehurst Place, West Sussex, held 7,583 identified species, representing 3 per cent of the world's plants. It also held 97 per cent of UK flora species. The Bank aims to hold 10 per cent of the world's flowering plants, principally from dryland regions, by 2010 and 20 per cent by 2020. The Royal Botanic Garden Edinburgh (RBGE, see page 389) promotes conservation programmes for rare plants in Scotland and for coniferous trees worldwide, maintaining genetically diverse populations in cultivation at many sites as pools for eventual reintroduction to the wild. RBGE's Living Collections consists of 6 per cent of the world's flowering plant species in cultivation, including 1,400 threatened plants.

International action
The EC Habitats Directive, adopted in 1992, aims to promote biodiversity through the conservation of natural habitats and wild flora and fauna. It includes a range of measures relating to the conservation and protection of species and habitats. The most stringent obligations relate to the selection, designation and protection of a series of sites – Special Areas of Conservation (SACs). It is envisaged that these sites will make a significant contribution to conserving the 169 habitat types and 623 species identified by the Directive as being most in need of conservation in a European context. In the United Kingdom 76 such habitat types have been identified, as have 51 species (four of which are now extinct, a further six occurring as vagrants or introductions).

Along with the similar Special Protection Areas set up under the earlier Birds Directive, primarily to protect avian species, SACs will form the UK component of the Europe-wide Natura 2000 network.

Advice to the Government on which sites should be SACs or SPAs has been provided by the statutory conservation agencies (see page 286) and coordinated by the JNCC. As at the end of March 2003, 576 candidate SACs covering 2.4 million hectares had been submitted, and 240 SPAs covering 1.4 million hectares had been classified.

The United Kingdom is also a member of the World Conservation Union and of several

The Darwin Initiative

The Darwin Initiative marked its tenth anniversary in September 2002. The programme provides small grants to fund the use of UK expertise to help countries rich in biodiversity, but poor in resources, with the conservation and sustainable use of their biodiversity. This includes helping them meet their obligations under the Biodiversity Convention (see page 268). Examples of the 270 projects, in 100 countries, funded by the Initiative include:

- conserving Kenya's indigenous forests through certification of sustainably sourced woodcarvings;

- conservation of the critically endangered Gyps vulture in India;

- project Biomap, mapping bird species in Columbia; and

- enabling local people to manage the biodiversity of shade coffee plantations in El Salvador.

international Conventions and Directives, some of which are described below:

- The IUCN – the *World Conservation Union* – is the largest nature conservation body in the world, having a membership of nearly 1,000 governmental and non-governmental organisations. Its purpose is to influence, encourage and help societies throughout the world to conserve the integrity and diversity of nature and to ensure that any use of natural resources is equitable and ecologically sustainable.
- The *Convention on Wetlands of International Importance* (the *Ramsar Convention*) (*www.ramsar.org*) is an intergovernmental treaty covering all aspects of wetland conservation and use. There are 144 Ramsar sites in the United Kingdom.
- CITES (*www.cites.org*) regulates trade in endangered species by means of a permit system (see page 267).
- The *Convention on the Conservation of Migratory Species of Wild Animals* (the *Bonn Convention*) coordinates international action on a range of endangered migratory species.

Land quality, waste, recycling and litter

Land quality

Land quality in the United Kingdom is relatively good, but faces pressure from a range of factors,

including contamination, urbanisation, localised erosion and declining organic content. Contaminated land is the legacy of an industrial age that generated wealth but also caused much pollution. The Environment Agency estimates that there are some 5,000 to 20,000 sites in England and Wales that may be contaminated enough to have an impact on human health or the wider environment. Government policy emphasises the importance of voluntary action to clean up contaminated land, and most attempts to clean up sites occur when they are redeveloped.

Many of the 391 species identified in the UK Biodiversity Action Plan depend on the right type and quality of soil for their survival, and a good balance of soil types is required to support the existing range of ecosystems, landscapes and agriculture. In 2001 the predecessors of Defra jointly published a draft soil strategy for England promoting the sustainable use of soil and raising public awareness of its importance as part of the environment. The Government hopes to publish a full strategy by the end of 2003.

Waste management and disposal

The United Kingdom produces over 400 million tonnes of waste each year, the majority of which comes from agricultural, industrial and construction sources. However, a considerable amount of waste is also produced by households – 89 per cent of an estimated 28.8 million tonnes of municipal waste in England in 2001/02. Commercial activities also produce waste: a further 75 million tonnes a year in England and Wales. Nearly two-thirds of waste from households, commerce and industry is disposed of to landfill, a method which makes little practical use of waste (although some landfill sites produce gas that is used for energy generation). In the case of municipal waste, 13 per cent was recycled or composted in 2001/02; the majority, 77 per cent, was disposed of in landfill.

By 2005 the Government aims to reduce the amount of UK industrial and commercial waste disposed of in landfill sites to 85 per cent of 1998 levels and, in England, to recycle or compost at least 25 per cent of household waste, increasing to 33 per cent by 2015. Between 2000/01 and 2001/02, the amount of household waste recycled increased from 11.2 per cent to 12.4 per cent. Meeting these targets would go some way towards meeting the Government's obligation under the EU Landfill Directive, which requires the United

Table 19.3 Management of municipal waste, England

	1997/98		2001/02	
	Thousand tonnes	%	Thousand tonnes	%
Landfill	21,765	85	22,317	77
Incineration with energy from waste	1,624	6	2,459	9
Refuse-derived fuel manufacture	156	1	84	–
Recycled/composted	2,063	8	3,886	13
Other	102	–	56	–
Total	**25,711**	*100*	**28,801**	*100*

Source: Department for Environment, Food and Rural Affairs

Kingdom to reduce landfill of biodegradable municipal waste to 35 per cent of its 1995 level by 2020. Biodegradable waste consists of materials such as paper, food and green waste, which produce methane, a powerful greenhouse gas, as they degrade.

The Waste and Resources Action Programme (WRAP) aims to overcome market barriers to the recovery and recycling of waste – UK government funding of around £40 million is available to the programme between 2001 and 2004. The Scottish Executive has also allocated around £54 million for this period.

The Waste and Emissions Trading Bill was introduced into Parliament in November 2002. Part one of the Bill would set up a framework that will require local authorities to progressively reduce the amount of biodegradable waste they send to landfill through a system of tradeable landfill allowances. This scheme is believed to be the first of its kind in Europe.

In England, a new Waste Implementation Programme (WIP), initiated by Defra in response to measures called for by the Strategy Unit report (see box), aims to divert biodegradable municipal waste away from landfill.

The landfill tax credit scheme enables landfill site operators in the United Kingdom to channel up to 6 per cent of their landfill tax liability into environmental bodies, to be used for approved projects. Examples include reclamation of polluted land, research and education activities to promote re-use and recycling, provision of public parks and amenities, and restoration of historic buildings.

Waste not, want not

The Government's Strategy Unit (see page 46) published a report, *Waste not, want not*, in November 2002. Predicting that waste volume in England will double, and costs will increase by £1.6 billion a year, between 2002 and 2020, the report outlines a number of possible actions to take. These include:

- raising the level of landfill tax to encourage the development of alternative waste disposal methods;

- tackling waste growth through education and programmes to reduce waste from households and industry; and

- allowing local councils to use discounts and reward schemes to encourage householders to reduce waste and recycle more.

Wales

The Welsh Assembly Government's *Wise about Waste: the National Waste Strategy for Wales*, published in 2002, includes specific targets for public bodies to reduce their waste arisings by 10 per cent from the 1998 level by 2010, and targets for local authorities to have 40 per cent of waste recycled/composted by the same date. In 2000/01, 6.2 per cent of household waste in Wales was collected for recycling/composting. Additional funding is being provided by the Assembly Government to local authorities to help meet the recycling and composting targets and pursue other aspects of the strategy – around £100 million between 2001/02 and 2004/05.

Map 19.4 Household waste recycling: by area, 2000/01, England and Wales

Percentage of
household waste recycled

- 20.0% to 27.0%
- 10.0% to 19.9%
- 0.0% to 9.9%
- no data available

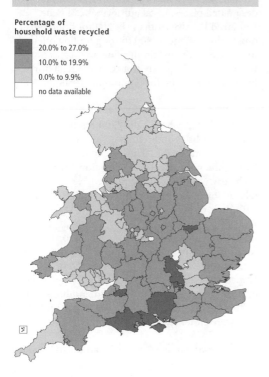

Scotland

The Scottish Executive launched its National Waste Plan in February 2003. The plan contains targets to have 25 per cent of municipal waste recycled or composted by 2006, rising to 55 per cent by 2020, and to reduce the proportion of waste sent to landfill from 90 to 30 per cent by the latter date. It also includes plans for segregated kerbside recycling collection for nine out of ten Scottish homes by 2020. A Strategic Waste Fund has been established to assist local authorities in their implementation of Area Waste Plans. The fund has been allocated £230 million over the three years 2003 to 2006.

Northern Ireland

The primary targets of the DoE's Waste Management Strategy are the recovery of 25 per cent of household waste by 2005, rising to 40 per cent by 2010; reducing the landfilling of industrial and commercial wastes to 85 per cent of 1998 levels by 2005; and reducing the quantities of biodegradable wastes being landfilled to 75 per cent of 1995 levels by 2010, 50 per cent by

2013 and 35 per cent by 2020. The strategy was being reviewed during 2003.

As part of the strategy, district councils have prepared waste management plans to establish a regional network of recycling facilities. The DoE provided grant in aid of £4 million in 2002/03, rising to £10 million in 2003/04, to assist councils in the preparation and implementation of their plans.

Packaging

The first phase of the EC Directive on Packaging and Packaging Waste ended in 2002. The Directive set targets that at least 50 per cent of UK packaging waste should be recovered and at least 25 per cent recycled by 2001. All packaging must be recoverable through recycling, incineration with energy recovery, composting or biodegradation. By the end of 2000, 42 per cent of UK packaging waste was recovered and 36 per cent recycled. For 2003, the Government set a 59 per cent recovery target.

Recycling facilities

Across the United Kingdom, recycling banks are available for the public to deposit various waste materials, including bottles, cans, clothes, paper and plastics. In addition, some local authorities provide kerbside collection of recyclable material. In the United Kingdom in 2001, 63.5 per cent of newsprint was recycled. In comparison, 36 per cent of aluminium cans, 22 per cent of container glass, and only 3 per cent of plastic were recycled in 1998, the most recent year for which data are available for these materials.

Hazardous waste

There is an extensive framework of national and EC legislation on the manufacture, distribution, use and disposal of hazardous chemicals. New and existing chemicals are subject to notification and assessment procedures under EC legislation. Pesticides, biocides and veterinary medicines are subject to mandatory approval procedures. International movements of hazardous waste are controlled by the Basel Convention on the Control of Transboundary Movements of Hazardous Wastes and their Disposal. The United Kingdom is a signatory of the Basel Convention Protocol on Liability and Compensation. Once fully ratified the Protocol will require any exporter of hazardous waste to be insured against any damage caused on the journey to the recycler or disposer of that waste.

Disposal of durable goods

Fridges and freezers: Up to 3 million domestic refrigeration units – fridges, fridge-freezers and freezers – are disposed of in the United Kingdom every year. A European Regulation came into force in 2001 which requires the removal of Ozone-Depleting-Substances (ODS) from refrigeration equipment before such equipment can be scrapped. This led to stockpiling of old units until processing plant came on line. However, by the end of 2002, ten such plants, two mobile and eight static, were in operation.

End-of-life vehicles (ELVs): Approximately 1.8 million ELVs are scrapped every year in the United Kingdom, generating 2 million tonnes of waste material. The scrap vehicle industry has a well-established infrastructure, and ELVs have one of the highest recovery rates of all complex consumer goods: on average, 75 per cent of a vehicle is currently recycled. However, due to falls in scrap steel prices, vehicle dismantlers now charge to collect ELVs, and this has led to an increase in the number of vehicles abandoned in the streets. Local authorities have powers to remove vehicles of no value abandoned on the street after 24 hours, and to destroy them after seven days.

In Great Britain, the Special Waste Regulations 1996 are the centrepiece of hazardous waste controls. As amended, the Regulations seek to ensure that special wastes are managed from the moment they are produced until they are finally disposed of or recovered. Since 1996 the Hazardous Waste List that defines the scope of the EC Hazardous Waste Directive has been refined and increased in length. Furthermore, a number of new Directives have been, or will be, made which will have an impact on the sector, notably the Hazardous Waste Incineration Directive, the Landfill Directive and the IPC Directive (see page 286).

In December 2002 the Government set up a new advisory forum on hazardous waste. Members include government, industry and environmental groups. The forum is intended to play a strategic role in considering the demands on industry made by existing and forthcoming legislation and to consider targets for hazardous waste reduction and recovery.

Litter and dog fouling

It is a criminal offence to leave litter in any public place in the open air or to dump rubbish except in designated places. Local authorities can issue £50 Fixed Penalty Notices (FPNs) for litter and dog fouling offences (£40 for dog fouling offences in Scotland); the maximum fine, upon successful prosecution if FPNs are not paid, is £2,500 for littering and £1,000 for dog fouling (£500 in Scotland).

Local authorities have a duty to keep their public land free of litter and refuse, including dog faeces, as far as is practicable. They spend over £400 million on street cleansing alone in England each year. Members of the public have powers to take action against authorities that fail to comply with their responsibilities.

ENCAMS (*www.encams.org*) is the national agency for litter abatement, working in collaboration with local authorities and the private sector. In 2001 it launched a continuous survey of local environmental quality in England. Findings from its first report indicated that over 18 per cent of sites were either significantly or heavily littered.

The environment agencies, local authorities, police and ENCAMS have been monitoring the incidence of fly-tipping (the illegal dumping of waste) since the introduction of the landfill tax in 1996, and such activity has increased since then. The Environment Agency recorded 5,000 incidents in 2002, and estimates that fly-tipping costs between £100 million and £150 million a year. If indicted to the Crown Court, the maximum penalty for fly-tipping (and other offences relating to waste) is up to five years' imprisonment and/or an unlimited fine. The maximum fine upon successful prosecution in a magistrates' court is up to £20,000. Similar penalties exist in Scotland, where prosecutions would ordinarily proceed before the sheriff court.

Buildings and monuments

In England, lists of buildings of special architectural or historic interest are compiled by the Department for Culture, Media and Sport (DCMS) with advice from English Heritage. In Scotland and Wales, buildings are listed by Historic Scotland and Cadw respectively. In Northern Ireland, the EHS has responsibility for historic buildings, following consultation with the advisory Historic Buildings Council (HBC) and the relevant local district council.

Protecting England's communications heritage

In March 2003 the Government announced the listing of seven historically and architecturally outstanding communications structures, located throughout England. Together the buildings illustrate the rise of British communications technology in the 1950s and 1960s. The most well known of the seven is London's BT Tower, built between 1961 and 1965, and the first purpose-built tower to transmit radiowaves. Other structures listed include the Equatorial Telescopes at Herstmonceux, East Sussex, the British Telecom Earth/Satellite Station antenna number one on Goonhilly Downs, Cornwall, and the ntl Broadcasting Tower on Emley Moor, Yorkshire.

Table 19.5 Listed buildings and scheduled monuments, May 2003

Numbers

	Listed buildings	Scheduled monuments
England[1]	380,097	19,552
Wales[2]	26,431	3,558
Scotland[3]	45,892	7,631
Northern Ireland	8,225	1,615

1 Scheduled monuments as at 30 June 2003.
2 Scheduled monuments at at June 2003.
3 As at 31 March 2003.
Source: Department for Culture, Media and Sport; Cadw: Welsh Historic Monuments; Scottish Executive; EHS

It is a criminal offence to demolish a listed building, or alter or extend it in a way which affects its character, without prior consent from the local planning authority or – on appeal or following call-in – the appropriate government minister. A local planning authority can issue a 'building preservation notice' to protect for six months an unlisted building which it considers to be of special architectural or historic interest and which is at risk, while a decision is taken on whether it should be listed.

There are around 1 million archaeological sites or 'find spots' of all types currently recorded in England, and English Heritage's *Monuments at Risk Survey of England* estimated that there are about 300,000 recorded monuments. Of these, an estimated 12 per cent are prehistoric, 7 per cent Roman, 22 per cent medieval, 34 per cent post-medieval and 3 per cent modern (with 22 per cent being of uncertain date).

English Heritage assesses known archaeological sites in order to identify those that should be afforded statutory protection. It makes its recommendations to the DCMS, which maintains the schedule of ancient monuments[3] (see Table 19.5). The number of entries tends to fluctuate, as some of those sites considered less important are 'descheduled', while others are added. Similar arrangements exist to identify buildings and ancient and historic monuments eligible for statutory protection in Scotland and Wales. In

Northern Ireland the EHS assesses all known archaeological sites in order to identify those sites that should be afforded statutory protection. It then makes recommendations to the Historic Monuments Council (HMC), and also maintains the schedule.

English Heritage is directly responsible for the maintenance, repair and presentation of 409 historic properties in public ownership or guardianship, and gives grants for the repair of other important ancient monuments and historic buildings. In 2002/03 it gave out £39 million in grant aid. Most of English Heritage's properties are open to the public, and there were nearly 5.5 million visits to staffed properties in 2002/03. Government funding for English Heritage in 2003/04 is £122 million.

In Scotland and Wales, Historic Scotland, which cares for over 330 monuments, and Cadw, with 127 monuments, perform similar functions. There were nearly 3 million visitors to Historic Scotland's properties where admission is charged in 2001/02 and 1.1 million visitors to monuments in Wales in 2002/03. The DoE in Northern Ireland has 182 historic monuments in state care or guardianship, managed by the EHS. These received an estimated 150,000 visits in 2002.

Local planning authorities have designated more than 9,000 conservation areas of special architectural or historic interest in England and there are 513 in Wales, around 600 in Scotland and 58 in Northern Ireland. These areas receive additional protection through the planning system, particularly over the proposed demolition of unlisted buildings.

---

3 The word 'monument' in this context covers the whole range of archaeological sites. Scheduled monuments are not always ancient, or visible above ground.

Images of England

Jointly funded by English Heritage and the Heritage Lottery Fund, the *Images of England* project aims to create a 'point in time' photographic record of England's listed buildings, available via the Internet (*www.imagesofengland.org.uk*). A single exterior photograph of each building will be recorded, and when complete the website will provide the first comprehensive visual record of England's listed buildings.

The National Heritage Memorial Fund (NHMF) helps towards the cost of acquiring, maintaining or preserving land, buildings, objects and collections that are of outstanding interest and of importance to the national heritage. In addition, its trustees are responsible for distributing the heritage share of the proceeds from the National Lottery. The first requests for lottery money were received in 1995 and, by March 2003, the Heritage Lottery Fund had made more than 11,500 grants across the United Kingdom, worth over £2 billion.

Many of the royal palaces and all the royal parks are open to the public; their maintenance is the responsibility of the DCMS and Historic Scotland. Historic Royal Palaces, the Royal Household and the Royal Parks Agency carry out this function on behalf of the Secretary of State in England.

Historic monuments and buildings are an important tourist resource. In 2001, 24 per cent of all trips to the countryside were to such heritage sites (including gardens and heritage centres). A survey conducted in 2001 by the English Tourism Council reported over 57.5 million visits to 1,041 responding sites.

Industrial heritage

As the first country in the world to industrialise on a large scale, the United Kingdom has a rich industrial heritage, including such sites as the Ironbridge Gorge (now a World Heritage Site), where Abraham Darby (1677–1717) first smelted iron using coke instead of charcoal.

Several industrial monuments in Scotland are in the care of Scottish ministers, including Bonawe Iron Furnace, the most complete charcoal-fuelled ironworks surviving in the United Kingdom; the working New Abbey Corn Mill, and Dallas Dhu Malt Whisky Distillery.

World Heritage Sites

The World Heritage List was established under the United Nations Educational, Scientific and Cultural Organisation's (UNESCO) 1972 World Heritage Convention in order to identify and secure lasting protection for sites of outstanding universal value (*www.unesco.org/whc*). The United Kingdom currently has 25 World Heritage Sites (see map at the end of the first colour section), including three in Overseas Territories – St George in Bermuda, Henderson Island and Gough Island wildlife reserve. Liverpool's waterfront and commercial centre is the sole UK 2003 nomination to UNESCO for World Heritage status. The proposed site contains 12 surviving historic docks, six dockside warehouses and other important dock structures, as well as the Victorian commercial district.

The Royal Botanic Gardens, Kew – the 25th UK World Heritage Site

The botanic gardens at Kew, were awarded World Heritage status in July 2003. The 132 hectares of gardens represent over 250 years of landscape history, and the site contains more than 40 listed buildings and structures and two ancient monuments. As well as its living collections and herbarium, Kew is an internationally respected scientific organisation, with expertise in plant diversity, conservation and sustainable development.

The first botanic garden at Kew was established in 1759 by Princess Augusta and Lord Bute, and their Physic Garden is the direct ancestor of today's gardens. However, it is Joseph Banks (1743–1820), who became unofficial director of the gardens in 1773, who is credited with guiding Kew towards international significance. Both Banks and his patron, King George III, wanted to develop economic uses for exotic plants. This desire set the course for the gardens' development. Under Banks, the gardens became not simply a collecting house for botanic specimens, but the centre of British economic botany.

Air and the atmosphere

Air quality

Air quality in the United Kingdom has improved considerably since the infamous London smogs of the 1950s. The first step towards these improvements was the introduction of the *Clean Air Act* in 1956, which controlled smoke from industrial and domestic coal burning, a major source of pollution at the time. Since then, the replacement of coal by natural gas and electricity for domestic heating, tighter regulation and structural changes in industry, and the introduction of progressively more stringent standards for vehicle exhaust emissions, have all led to considerable improvements in air quality. For example, in 1970, 8.9 million tonnes of carbon monoxide (CO) and 6.5 million tonnes of sulphur dioxide (SO_2) were emitted into the air in the United Kingdom. By 2001 these emissions had fallen to 3.7 million and 1.1 million tonnes respectively.

Industrial processes with the potential for producing pollutants are subject to regulation under IPC and IPPC (see page 286). Processes with a significant but lesser potential for air pollution require approval, in England and Wales from local authorities, in Scotland from the Scottish Environment Protection Agency (SEPA) and in Northern Ireland from the Chief Industrial Pollution Inspector or relevant district council, depending on the process. Local authorities also control emissions of dark smoke from commercial and industrial premises, and implement smoke control areas to deal with emissions from domestic properties.

Under the provisions of the *Environment Act 1995*, the Government is required to publish an Air Quality Strategy setting out its policies for managing ambient air quality in the United Kingdom, particularly in relation to reducing air pollution and any remaining risks to people's health and the natural and built environment. The current strategy contains air quality standards and objectives for nine pollutants of particular concern to human health: nitrogen dioxide, PM_{10} (particulate matter that is less than 10 microns in diameter), SO_2, CO, ozone, lead, benzene, 1,3-butadiene, and polycyclic aromatic hydrocarbons. Dates for achieving the various objectives across the United Kingdom have been set between 2003 and 2010.

In February 2003[4] Defra and the devolved administrations introduced tighter objectives for benzene, CO and PM_{10}, and an objective for polycyclic aromatic hydrocarbons for the first time. These are the same throughout the United

Kingdom except for benzene and PM_{10}. A tougher PM_{10} objective than elsewhere was proposed for Scotland because air quality there is generally better; conversely, a less stringent objective was proposed for London. Similarly, tighter benzene objectives were set for Scotland and Northern Ireland than for England and Wales.

Monitoring air quality

The United Kingdom has an automatic air quality monitoring network with 116 sites (as at March 2003) covering much of the country, in both urban and rural areas. A number of new sites have been established in recent years, mainly in urban areas in order to provide more comprehensive coverage of air quality in UK towns and cities.

In the United Kingdom in 2002 there was an average of 20 days per monitoring site in urban areas when air pollution was recorded as moderate or higher, compared with 25 days in 2001 and 59 days when the series started in 1993. The main causes of moderate or higher air pollution at urban sites are ground level ozone and PM_{10}. Ground level ozone is formed from chemical reactions of other pollutants such as nitrogen oxides (NO_x) and volatile organic compounds (VOCs) – for example solvents used in industry. As pollution caused by PM_{10}, as well as SO_2, has fallen significantly since 1993, ozone has become the principal cause of pollution in urban areas. In rural areas, air pollution was recorded as moderate or higher on 30 days on average per site in 2002, compared with 34 days in 2001. This series fluctuates from year to year, and there is no clear trend. It reflects variability in levels of ozone, which is overwhelmingly the main pollutant in rural areas. Days of moderate or heavy air pollution are a headline indicator of sustainable development – see page 330.

Air Quality Bulletins provide the public with hourly updates of air pollution data from the national monitoring network. These give the concentrations of the main pollutants, together with a forecast. The information features on television and radio weather reports, and appears in many national and local newspapers. Information can also be accessed through the UK Air Quality Archive website (*www.airquality.co.uk*).

Vehicle emissions

Measures to reduce pollution from road transport are seen as vital to achieving the objectives set out in the UK Air Quality Strategy. Progressively

---

4 These objectives came into force in Scotland earlier than the rest of the United Kingdom, in June 2002.

tighter standards for fuels and vehicle emissions mean that urban road transport emissions of CO, NO_x and particulates are projected to fall by around 70 per cent between 1995 and 2015.

Vehicle emissions standards are governed by a series of EC Directives enforced in the United Kingdom under the Motor Vehicles Construction and Use and Type Approval Regulations. All new petrol-engined passenger cars in the United Kingdom are fitted with catalytic converters, which typically reduce emissions by over 75 per cent. These measures to reduce emissions from new vehicles have been accompanied by improvements in fuel quality with, for instance, reductions in constituents such as benzene and sulphur and the phasing out of leaded petrol. People in the United Kingdom who own vehicles registered after February 2001 pay vehicle excise duty according to the amount of carbon dioxide (CO_2) their car produces and the type of fuel it uses (see page 363).

Compulsory testing of emissions from vehicles is a key element in the UK strategy for improving air quality. Metered emission tests and smoke checks feature in the annual 'MoT' roadworthiness test. Enforcement checks carried out at the roadside or at operators' premises also include a check for excessive smoke. Local councils in England and Wales that have designated air quality management areas have the power to use roadside testing to enforce vehicle exhaust emissions standards in those areas. The Scottish Executive introduced similar powers, available to all Scottish local authorities, in March 2003, and the Welsh Assembly Government is consulting on extending them to local authorities in Wales.

Transboundary air pollution

The pollutant gases SO_2 (mainly from power stations), NO_x (from road transport and power stations), and ammonia (NH_3 – mainly from livestock) can be carried over long distances before being deposited directly onto vegetation and soil or being washed out as acid rain. Acidification results when sensitive ecosystems are not capable of neutralising the deposited acidity. In the United Kingdom, the ecosystems that are most sensitive to acidification are located in the northern and western uplands. The damaging effects of high levels of acid deposition on soils, freshwater, trees and buildings have been demonstrated by scientific research.

The United Kingdom is a party to the UNECE (United Nations Economic Commission for Europe) Convention on Long Range Transboundary Air Pollution, which was set up in 1979 in response to evidence that acidification of lakes in Scandinavia was linked to emissions of SO_2 from other countries in Europe, including the United Kingdom. Under the Convention, there have been a number of protocols to reduce emissions of acidifying pollutants. The latest Gothenburg Protocol, signed in December 1999, tackles the three environmental problems of acidification, eutrophication[5] and ground-level ozone (summer smog). Under the Protocol, the United Kingdom agreed annual emission ceilings, to be achieved by 2010, of 625 kilotonnes for SO_2, 1,181 kilotonnes for NO_x, 297 kilotonnes for NH_3, and 1,200 kilotonnes for VOCs. Current emissions levels are given in Table 19.6.

Running in parallel with the UNECE Gothenburg Protocol is the EC National Emission Ceilings Directive (NECD), which is intended to tackle the harmful effects to human health and the environment from transboundary air pollution. The Regulations came into force in the United Kingdom in January 2003, setting ceilings for 2010 for the same four pollutants. The figures agreed commit the United Kingdom to further cuts in SO_2 and NO_x emissions, reducing the ceilings to 585 kilotonnes and 1,167 kilotonnes respectively.

Table 19.6 Emissions of selected air pollutants, UK

		Kilotonnes
	1990	2001
Carbon monoxide	7,445	3,737
Nitrogen oxides	2,759	1,680
Volatile organic compounds[1]	2,603	1,336
Sulphur dioxide	3,719	1,125
Ammonia[1]	341	290
PM_{10}[2]	332	187

1 Excludes emissions from 'natural' sources such as forests, which are outside the scope of international reporting conventions.
2 Excludes resuspension.
Source: Department for Environment, Food and Rural Affairs

5 The process by which pollution from sewage or fertilisers stimulates excessive growth of algae. Death and decomposition of the algae deplete the oxygen content of the water, resulting in the death of fish and other animals.

Road transport and power stations are two of the most important sources of air pollutants in the United Kingdom. In 2001, road transport accounted for 62 per cent of CO emissions and 46 per cent of NO_x emissions, while power stations accounted for 66 and 23 per cent of SO_2 and NO_x emissions respectively.

Climate change

Several gases naturally present in the atmosphere keep the Earth at a temperature suitable for life by trapping energy from the Sun – the 'greenhouse' effect. However, emissions from human activities are increasing the atmospheric concentrations of several greenhouse gases, causing global warming and climate change.

Defra published its *Global atmosphere research programme bi-annual report 2000–2002* in February 2003. Largely based on work by the Hadley Centre, part of the Met Office, it found that atmospheric concentrations of many greenhouse gases reached their highest ever levels in 2001.

Research at the Hadley Centre is focused on improving climate predictions and investigating the causes of recent climate change. Results from its latest climate model suggest that, with the current levels of increase in greenhouse gases, the global mean sea level will rise by between 9 and 88 centimetres by 2100 and there will be a rise in average global temperature of up to 6°C over the next 100 years.

Possible impacts of climate change in the United Kingdom could include a rise in average temperatures of between 2 and 3.5°C by 2100, with high summer temperatures becoming more frequent and very cold winters becoming increasingly rare. Rainfall will increase during winter, and may decrease during the summer. Relative sea level around the United Kingdom will continue to rise, by as much as 86 centimetres in parts of southern England by the 2080s, and extreme sea levels will be experienced more frequently.

Provisional data released by the Met Office suggest that 2002 was the fourth warmest year in the United Kingdom since records began in 1659. Five of the six warmest years on record in the United Kingdom have occurred since 1990. Globally, 2002 was the second warmest year since records began in 1860, and nine of the ten warmest years worldwide have occurred since 1990. Average

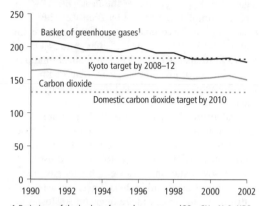

Figure 19.7 Emissions of greenhouse gases, UK

Million tonnes carbon equivalent

1 Emissions of the basket of greenhouse gases (CO_2, CH_4, N_2O, HFCs, PFCs, SF_6) are presented based on their global warming potential.
Source: NETCEN

global temperatures have risen by more than 0.6°C over the last 100 years, and it is thought that the warming over the last 50 years has mainly been due to human activities such as the burning of fossil fuels.

Control of global and regional air pollution requires international co-operation and action. The first international action dealing with climate change dates from the Rio Earth Summit (see page 268), at which the UN Framework Convention on Climate Change (UNFCCC) was adopted. It called for the stabilisation of greenhouse gas concentrations in the atmosphere at a level that would prevent dangerous man-made interference with the climate system. At the third Conference of the Parties to the Framework Convention, held in Kyoto in 1997, richer countries established a Protocol agreeing legally binding targets to reduce emissions of the basket of six main greenhouse gases: CO_2, methane (CH_4), nitrous oxide (N_2O), hydrofluorocarbons (HFCs), perfluorocarbons (PFCs) and sulphur hexafluoride (SF_6). The Protocol committed developed nations to a 5.2 per cent reduction in greenhouse gas emissions below 1990 levels by 2008–12. The European Union subsequently agreed to a collective reduction of 8 per cent by that date. At a further meeting in June 1998, the Member States agreed to share out the EU's target to reflect national circumstances. Individual countries' targets range from a reduction of 28 per cent for Luxembourg to a permitted increase of 27 per cent for Portugal.

The United Kingdom, along with its EU partners, ratified the Kyoto Protocol in May 2002.

The United Kingdom is on course to meet its legally binding target under the Protocol, a reduction of 12.5 per cent by 2008–12. The baseline used for comparison with this target is the sum of the 1990 totals for CO_2, CH_4 and N_2O, and the 1995 totals for HFCs, PFCs and SF_6. Emissions of the basket of greenhouse gases, weighted by global warming potential, fell by 15 per cent from the baseline, to 177 million tonnes carbon equivalent in 2002 (see Figure 19.7). Despite an overall downward trend, there were slight increases in greenhouse gas emissions between 1999 and 2001. These were mainly due to increased use of coal in power stations because of higher gas prices at the end of 2000 and in 2001, lower nuclear output, and lower outside temperatures. However, provisional data for 2002 suggest that the downward trend has resumed, due to lower CO_2 emissions (a result of a decrease in the use of coal relative to oil and gas in power stations), and warmer weather. Emissions of CO_2 and the basket of gases together form one of the headline indicators of sustainable development – see page 330.

Between 1990 and 2001, the EU as a whole achieved a reduction in greenhouse gas emissions of 2.3 per cent, although emissions have increased over the last two years. With the exception of Luxembourg, Germany, the biggest emitter, achieved the largest reduction, at 18.3 per cent, and the United Kingdom, the second biggest emitter, achieved the second largest, at 12.0 per cent.

While the most significant greenhouse gas emitted by the United Kingdom is CO_2, followed by methane and nitrous oxide (N_2O), during the 1990s there was an increase in emissions of HFCs, which have a high global warming potential. Consumption grew in response to the phasing out of ozone-depleting substances under the Montreal Protocol (see page 279). HFCs were virtually unused before 1990, but their emissions accounted for 2.9 per cent of total UK greenhouse gas emissions in 1998 and then fell to about 1.3 per cent in 2001 in response to pollution control regulations. The most significant source of CO_2 emissions in the United Kingdom is the industrial sector (see Table 19.8). Emissions from the industrial sector fell by 37 per cent between 1971 and 2001, while those from the

Table 19.8 Emissions of carbon dioxide: by end user, UK

				Million tonnes
	1971	1981	1991	2001
Industry	92	74	64	58
Domestic	52	47	44	42
Transport	21	25	38	42
Other	14	13	14	11

Source: NETCEN

domestic sector fell by 19 per cent. However, emissions from transport doubled over the 30-year period.

In autumn 2002, the United Kingdom attended the eighth Conference of the Parties (COP) to the UNFCCC in Delhi. The declaration of the COP sought to place climate change in the context of sustainable development (see chapter 22). However, the main focus of the COP was technical. For example, it examined ways in which to implement the Kyoto Protocol, and established the legal and institutional relationship between the Protocol and UNFCCC bodies.

Climate Change: The UK Programme, published in 2000, sets out how the Government and the devolved administrations intend to meet the legally binding UK Kyoto target and move towards a domestic goal of a 20 per cent cut in CO_2 emissions between 1990 and 2010. It seeks to move the United Kingdom towards a more sustainable, lower carbon economy, ensuring that all sectors of the economy and all parts of the United Kingdom play their part. Furthermore, the Energy White Paper (see page 432) accepted the Royal Commission on Environmental Pollution's recommendation that the United Kingdom should put itself on a path to a reduction in CO_2 emissions of 60 per cent from current levels by about 2050.

The integrated package of policies and measures contained in the programme includes the climate change levy, which applies to sales of electricity, coal, natural gas and liquefied petroleum gas to the non-domestic sector (see chapter 29). This aims to encourage business energy efficiency and is expected to save at least 5 million tonnes of carbon emissions by 2010. The package also includes a target to deliver 10 per cent of UK electricity from renewable sources of energy by 2010. In 2002, 3 per cent of UK electricity was generated from such sources.

Emissions trading

Emissions trading schemes – another key element of the climate change programme – are designed to allow businesses to reduce their emissions of greenhouse gases in the most economically efficient way. The UK scheme, launched in April 2002, is the world's first economy-wide greenhouse gas trading scheme. It works by giving individual companies and installations a cap, which when added together form an overall emissions cap for the trading scheme. As long as the aggregate target is achieved, the individual emission contributions do not matter. Participating companies can either meet their individual target by reducing their own emissions; reduce their emissions below their target and sell or bank the excess 'emissions allowances'; or let their emissions remain above target, and buy emissions allowances from other participants. Across the whole scheme those with low-cost emission reduction opportunities will tend to sell allowances to those with higher cost options, thereby minimising the overall cost of delivering a set of environmental benefits.

Thirty-two organisations, including some of the largest businesses, are 'direct participants' in the UK scheme and have legally binding targets to reduce their emissions against 1998–2000 levels. The scheme is also open to around 5,000 further companies with Climate Change Agreements. In the first year of the scheme, nearly 1,000 companies transferred over 7 million tonnes of CO_2. The Waste and Emissions Trading Bill (see page 270) contains provisions to develop the statutory framework for emissions trading schemes. Under part two of the Bill, the financial penalties for direct participants in the trading scheme that fail to comply with their emissions targets would be put on a statutory basis.

The ozone layer

Stratospheric ozone is a layer of gas about 10 to 50 kilometres above the Earth's surface, which protects it from the more harmful effects of solar radiation. UK scientists first discovered ozone losses over much of the globe, including a 'hole' in the ozone layer over Antarctica, in 1985. The 'hole' has been growing steadily, reaching a record 28 million square kilometres in 2000, decreasing slightly to 26 million square kilometres in 2001 (a result of natural meteorological variability). Similar, but less dramatic, thinning of the ozone layer occurs over the North Pole each year as well. Ozone depletion is caused by man-made

chemicals containing chlorine or bromine, such as chlorofluorocarbons (CFCs), hydrochlorofluorocarbons (HCFCs) and halons. These chemicals have been used in aerosol sprays, refrigerators and fire extinguishers.

In an effort to repair this damage, over 170 countries have ratified the Montreal Protocol, an international treaty for the protection of the stratospheric ozone layer. This is enforced in the United Kingdom by an EC Regulation. The implementation of the Protocol has reduced the emissions of ozone-depleting substances. World consumption of CFCs fell by 86 per cent between 1986 and 1999, while in the United Kingdom, production and consumption of CFCs had ceased by 1995, except for certain essential uses such as metered dose inhalers. It is believed that full compliance with the Protocol will result in the recovery of the ozone layer within the next 50 years.

Noise

Noise, whether from the house next door or from aircraft flying overhead, can seriously affect people's quality of life. Defra and the devolved administrations are responsible for the coordination and development of policies and the promotion of initiatives to address the problem.

Local authorities have a duty to inspect their areas for 'statutory nuisances', including noise nuisance from premises and vehicles, machinery or equipment in the street. They must take reasonable steps to investigate complaints, and serve a noise abatement notice where it is judged to be a statutory nuisance. There are specific provisions in law to control noise from construction and demolition sites, to control the use of loudspeakers in the streets and to enable individuals to take independent action through the courts against noise nuisance.

According to the Chartered Institute of Environmental Health, domestic premises were the most common source of noise complaints received by environmental health officers in 2000/01 (see Table 19.9). Overall, the number of such complaints doubled between 1990/91 and 2000/01.

The Government published the results of a consultation on a proposed national ambient noise strategy in December 2002. The strategy will map the main sources and areas of noise, and establish methods that the Government might use to assess

Table 19.9 Noise complaints received by environmental health officers[1] by source, England and Wales

	1990/91	1995/96	Number per million people 2000/01
Industrial/commercial premises	913	1,466	1,381
Road works, construction and demolition[2]	252	229	325
Domestic premises	2,264	4,895	5,001
Vehicles, machinery and equipment in streets[2,3]	n/a	225	365
Total	**3,429**	**6,815**	**7,072**

1 Noise controlled by the *Environmental Protection Act 1990*. Figures relate to those authorities making returns.
2 From 1997/98 complaints about road works and 'noise in the street' are included in 'Vehicles, machinery and equipment in streets'.
3 *Noise and Statutory Nuisance Act 1993*.
Source: Chartered Institute of Environmental Health

its impact on people's lives. The project to map noise across England started in London in the same month. Defra will work with the Greater London Authority and London boroughs to map road traffic noise across the capital. It is hoped the maps generated will identify noise 'hot spots' and be useful in assessing the likely impact of schemes to reduce noise, such as traffic calming.

The Government is also developing a neighbour noise strategy to run in parallel with the ambient noise strategy. The first stage of this will be a study looking at the profiling of the behaviours and attitudes of people who make unacceptably loud noise, and those whose quality of life is affected by noise disturbance, and examining the ways in which noise complaints are resolved, both in England and other European countries.

The Noise Incidence Survey (NIS) and the Noise Attitude Survey (NAS) are undertaken by Defra to establish a baseline for, and monitor changes in, the noise climate in Great Britain. The NIS generates objective assessments of the pattern of the noise exposure of the population. It found that between 1990 and 2000 there were only small changes in outdoor noise level and exposure to noise. Typical outdoor sound levels were lower in 2000 than in 1990, while levels during the night were slightly worse in 2000.

Compensation may be payable for loss in property values caused by physical factors, including noise from new or improved public works such as roads, railways and airports. Highway authorities (in Scotland, local road authorities and the Scottish Executive; in Wales, the Assembly Government and local authorities) are required to make grants available for the insulation of homes when they

are subject to specified levels of increased noise caused by new or improved roads. Equivalent regulations exist for railways.

Radioactivity

Man-made radiation represents about 15 per cent of the total exposure to ionising radiation of the UK population – most radiation occurs naturally (for example from the radon gas given off by some rock formations, particularly granite). A large proportion of the exposure to man-made radiation comes from medical sources, such as X-rays. This and other man-made radiation is subject to stringent control. Users of radioactive materials must be registered by the Environment Agency, SEPA or the Chief Radiochemical Inspector in Northern Ireland as appropriate. The Health and Safety Executive (HSE – see page 141) is responsible for regulating safety at civil nuclear installations. The National Radiological Protection Board (NRPB) advises on health risks posed by radiation and how to guard against them.

Radioactive waste management

The United Kingdom currently has over 10,000 tonnes of solid, long-lived radioactive waste in storage. This will rise to over 500,000 tonnes over the next century as nuclear reactors and other facilities come to the end of their lives. All solid radioactive waste in the United Kingdom is either disposed of in suitable facilities on land or safely stored pending the adoption of a final management strategy.

In 2001 the Government and devolved administrations started a major programme of consultation and research, *Managing radioactive waste safely*, which aims to arrive at such a strategy. After considering the results of a consultation exercise, the Government announced in July 2002 that it was setting up an independent body to oversee a review process, in which there will be a programme of public debate backed by research into various options. This second stage of the strategy will effectively assess the options for the disposal of radioactive waste, and produce recommendations for ministers to consider. The third stage, scheduled to occur around 2006, will consist of a public debate on how the decisions reached should be implemented, while the fourth, in 2007, will be the start of the implementation process.

Radioactive wastes vary widely in nature and level of activity, and the methods of current management reflect this. Most solid waste – of low radioactivity – is disposed of at the shallow disposal facility at Drigg in Cumbria. Some small quantities of very low-level waste are disposed of at authorised landfill sites. Some intermediate-level waste is stored at nuclear licensed sites (usually those sites where it is generated) but most of the United Kingdom's inventory is at Sellafield in Cumbria. High-level or heat-generating waste is stored in either raw (liquid) or vitrified (glass-like) form. Once vitrified it will be stored for at least 50 years to allow it to cool to a safe temperature for final management.

International commitments
An EC Directive lays down basic standards for the protection of the health of workers and the general public against the dangers arising from ionising radiation. The provisions of the Directive are implemented in the United Kingdom through a number of Acts including the *Radioactive Substances Act 1993*. The United Kingdom is also a contracting party to the International Joint Convention on the Safety of Spent Fuel Management and on the Safety of Radioactive Waste Management.

The contracting parties to the Oslo and Paris Convention on the Protection of the Marine Environment of the North East Atlantic (OSPAR), including the United Kingdom, have agreed to reduce radioactive discharges to the North East Atlantic so that by 2020 concentrations of radioactive substances in the marine environment would be almost reduced to natural levels. The *UK Radioactive Discharge Strategy 2001–2002* sets out how the United Kingdom will implement OSPAR. The Government is also consulting on new statutory guidance to the Environment Agency on the regulation of radioactive discharges from

licensed nuclear sites in England. Similar arrangements will apply in Scotland and Wales (there are no nuclear licensed sites in Northern Ireland).

Water

Freshwater environment
Freshwater habitats in the United Kingdom include rivers, lakes and ponds, and wetlands such as fens, bogs and reedbeds. Many invertebrates and all amphibians native to the United Kingdom are dependent on these habitats, and there are 38 native species of freshwater fish. In addition, a large number of bird species, and two 'rare or threatened' mammals, the otter and water vole, depend on aquatic habitats.

Despite the high rainfall in the United Kingdom, there are limited natural and man-made capacities for storage, and the country's high population density means there is relatively little water per person. Available resources of water include rivers, reservoirs and underground aquifers, but these must be carefully managed. The Environment Agency's strategy for water resource management considers both environmental and socio-economic factors (see chapter 29).

Marine environment
The seas around the United Kingdom support a wide variety of plants and animals, and are a source of both food and fuel. It is estimated that around 50 per cent of UK biodiversity is to be found in the sea. However, marine life and the food chain can be put at risk by pollution and overfishing. Defra and the devolved administrations have responsibility for protecting UK seas and coastal waters.

In November 2002 Defra published the consultation document *Seas of change*. Following on from *Safeguarding our seas*, the first marine stewardship report, *Seas of change* is intended to form the basis for discussion on how to develop the ideas set out in the stewardship report, which outlined a conservation and sustainable development approach to managing the seas.

Government policy is not to permit any deposit of waste in the sea when there is a safe land-based alternative, unless it can be demonstrated that disposal at sea is the best practicable option. Disposal of sewage sludge at sea ceased at the end of 1998. The only types of waste that are now routinely considered for deposit in the sea are dredged material from ports and harbours, and small quantities of fish waste.

Through the OSPAR Convention, the United Kingdom and other contracting parties have put in place strategies which aim to protect the biodiversity of the North-East Atlantic and tackle the threats posed to the marine environment by hazardous substances, eutrophication and offshore industries.

Decisions about which areas of the UK Continental Shelf should be made available for petroleum licensing are made by the Secretary of State for Trade and Industry, taking account of advice from the JNCC. Where areas are made available for exploration and development, special conditions, agreed with the JNCC, may be imposed on the licence holders to minimise or avoid any impact on the marine environment.

The Maritime and Coastguard Agency (see page 322) is responsible for dealing with spillages of oil or other hazardous substances from ships at sea. The various counter-pollution facilities for which it is responsible include remote-sensing surveillance aircraft; aerial and seaborne spraying equipment; stocks of oil dispersants; mechanical recovery and cargo transfer equipment; and specialised beach cleaning equipment. The Agency has an Enforcement Unit at its headquarters in Southampton for apprehending ships making illegal discharges of oil and other pollutants off the British coast. In England, the maximum fine for pollution from ships is £250,000 in cases heard in magistrates' courts.

Water quality

The quality of UK inland waters is generally good. In 2001, around 95 per cent of the river network was classified as being of good or fair chemical quality. A similar proportion of the network was classified as being of good or fair biological quality. However, nitrate concentrations are a cause of specific concern, with higher levels found particularly in central and eastern England, and parts of eastern Scotland (see page 283). River quality is a headline indicator of sustainable development (see page 331).

About 96 per cent of the UK population live in properties connected to a sewer, and the waste water from the majority of these properties is

given secondary treatment[6] or better. Continued investment in the sewerage system and improving sewage treatment standards will be made up to 2005, and is expected to deliver improvements including at least secondary treatment for all significant discharges from sewage treatment works.

The Government published *Directing the flow – priorities for future water policy* in November 2002. It aims to produce an integrated strategy for water that pulls together policies for all its uses, natural, domestic and industrial. Potential benefits of such integration are:

- better integration with agricultural policy, which will enable action to be taken to reduce diffuse river and coastal pollution, preventing algal blooms from excess manure and fertilisers;
- better water management, which can aid flood storage and low-flow water demand as well as biodiversity; and
- better integration with recreation and tourism, which benefit from water resources but which in turn have impacts on those resources.

In Scotland, the *Water Environment and Water Services Act*, approved by Parliament in January 2003, introduced a 'source-to-sea' planning framework for river basin management that is designed to reduce levels of pollution and protect water resources and habitats associated with rivers and lochs. It includes provision for the protection of the environment through regulations over water pollution, the abstraction of water, engineering works and fish farming.

Discharges to inland waters, coastal waters and groundwaters

All discharges to water in the United Kingdom are regulated. In England and Wales the Environment Agency controls water pollution by issuing legally binding documents, known as consents, for all effluent discharges into controlled waters (groundwaters, inland and coastal waters). The effluent quality is monitored against the conditions set within the consents. The Agency maintains public registers containing information

---

6 The preliminary treatment of sewage involves screening to remove rags, grit and other solids. Primary treatment involves a physical and/or chemically enhanced settlement of suspended solids not removed by preliminary treatment. Secondary treatment involves 'biological' treatment – using bacteria to break down the biodegradable matter in waste water.

Table 19.10 Water pollution incidents:[1] by source, England and Wales

	2001	2002
Sewage and water industry	171	168
Agriculture	174	150
Industry	142	105
Domestic/residential	n/a	43
Transport	43	36
Waste management facilities	38	18
Other	410	346
Total	**978**	**866**

1 Incidents where the source was identified.
  Category 1 (most serious) and Category 2 (serious) incidents.
Source: Environment Agency

about water quality, performance and compliance, consents, authorisations and monitoring. Both SEPA, in Scotland, and the EHS, in Northern Ireland, have similar responsibilities.

Trade effluent discharges to the public sewers are controlled by the water companies in England, Wales and Scotland, and by the Department for Regional Development's Water Service in Northern Ireland.

In 2002, the Environment Agency substantiated almost 30,000 pollution incidents to water, land and air in England and Wales. Of these, 866 incidents had a serious impact on water, a decrease of over 10 per cent on the previous year (see Table 19.10). The sewage and water industry and agriculture are the most common sources of such serious water pollution incidents.

In 2001/02, SEPA recorded and investigated 2,016 water pollution incidents in Scotland, of which 187 were classified as significant. A total of 2,434 reports of water pollution were made to the EHS in Northern Ireland in 2002, of which 1,510 were substantiated.

Under the 1998 Groundwater Regulations, certain listed dangerous substances may be disposed of to land only after investigation and authorisation. An authorisation will not be granted if the investigation reveals that List I substances could enter, or List II substances could pollute, groundwater. The regulations also give the Environment Agency (in England and Wales) and SEPA (in Scotland) powers to control or stop activities which might indirectly

cause groundwater pollution. Similar legislation applies in Northern Ireland, where the prior investigation and authorisation of disposals are undertaken by the EHS.

Diffuse pollution from agriculture

Agricultural nutrients, pesticides, microbes from livestock manure, and soil erosion from farmland can all cause water pollution. *Directing the flow* identified diffuse pollution from agriculture as the single biggest problem facing water quality in England.

One aspect of this wider problem is nitrate pollution arising from the application of inorganic fertiliser, livestock manures and other organic wastes on farmland. The designation of Nitrate Vulnerable Zones (NVZs), under the EC Nitrates Directive, is intended to reduce or prevent this pollution. An area is designated as an NVZ when the nitrate concentrations in its ground or surface water exceed, or are likely to exceed, 50 mg/litre. A total of 55 per cent of England was designated as NVZs in October 2002 (this figure includes eight areas originally designated in 1996). Also in 2002, the Scottish Executive announced the designation of some 14 per cent of the total area of Scotland as NVZs, while in Wales around 3 per cent of the total area was designated.

Farmers in NVZs are required to follow rules (known as 'Action Programme measures'), controlling the timing and rate of application of fertilisers and organic manure, and the storage of slurry. These measures both aim to help safeguard drinking water supplies and to curtail wider ecological damage, including eutrophication of freshwater, estuarine or tidal waters.

Bathing waters and coastal sewage discharges

Bathing water quality is influenced by natural factors (such as temperature, salinity and sunlight), discharges from coastal sewerage treatment works, storm water overflows, river-borne pathogens (that is, pollutants that could affect human health), and run-off from urban and agricultural land. Over recent years the overall quality of UK bathing waters has continued to improve (see Table 19.11, which shows compliance with standards on coliform bacteria).

In Scotland, the Executive aims to meet European bathing water standards at all 60 Scottish bathing

Table 19.11 Bathing waters complying with EC Bathing Waters Directive coliform standards[1]

United Kingdom		Percentages
	1998	2002
Coastal bathing waters		
England	90	99
Wales	94	100
Scotland	52	91
Northern Ireland	94	94
United Kingdom	89	98
Inland bathing waters		
United Kingdom	100	100

1 At least 95 per cent of samples must have counts not exceeding the mandatory limit values for total and faecal coliforms during the bathing season.
Source: Department for Environment, Food and Rural Affairs

waters. It has identified nine bathing waters as sensitive under the EC Urban Waste Water Treatment Directive. The Welsh Assembly has identified 24 Welsh bathing waters, Defra has declared 180 such coastal areas in England, and there are 16 identified bathing waters in Northern Ireland. The identification confirms that advanced treatment has been or will be provided to discharges into the bathing waters from local waste water treatment works.

In 2003 ENCAMS (see page 272) gave Seaside Awards (*www.seasideawards.org.uk*) to 317 beaches in the United Kingdom for meeting appropriate standards of water quality and beach management. The Awards are given to beaches that comply with the EC Bathing Waters Directive mandatory standards, are clean, safe and well managed; and that provide appropriate information about water quality.

The European Blue Flag Campaign (*www.blueflag.org*) is an initiative of the Foundation of Environmental Education in Europe and is administered in the United Kingdom by ENCAMS. To be considered, a beach must have attained the guideline standard of the EC Bathing Waters Directive before being assessed for 24 other criteria, including beach cleanliness, dog control, wheelchair access, the provision of life-saving equipment and other facilities. In 2003, 105 beaches in the United Kingdom were awarded a 'Blue Flag', compared with 83 in 2002, and 12 marinas won recognition in the 'Blue Flag' for marinas category.

Business and the consumer

Business has an important role to play in environmental matters. A Defra survey found that UK industry spent an estimated £3.9 billion on environmental protection in 2001. This is spending by companies where the primary aim is to reduce environmental pollution, for example reducing emissions to air or water, to protect soil and groundwater or to prevent noise and vibration.

The Envirowise (*www.envirowise.gov.uk*) programme promotes the use of better environmental practices that reduce business costs for industry and commerce. It provides information and advice on environmental technologies and techniques by means of publications, events and a freephone UK helpline. In 2001 it helped businesses generate savings of £217 million and reduce solid waste by 1.5 million tonnes. Between 1994 (when the programme started) and the end of 2001, the total savings made by business as a result of advice from Envirowise was nearly £800 million. It works in partnership with Action Energy (see page 446), which supports energy efficiency measures.

Other government initiatives to encourage environmentally sound practices include:

- the Advisory Committee on Business and the Environment (ACBE) (*www.defra.gov.uk/environment/acbe*), which provides a forum for government and business to discuss environmental issues;
- the Sustainable Technologies Initiative (STI), which provides financial support for developing new technologies that will help businesses to be more efficient in their use of resources, and produce less waste and pollution;
- the Trade Union Sustainable Development Advisory Committee, which acts as the main forum for consultation between the Government and the trade unions on sustainable development and environmental issues; and
- the Advisory Committee on Consumer Products and the Environment, which provides advice to the Government on policies to reduce the environmental impacts associated with the production and consumption of goods and services.

Environmental management systems

An environmental management system provides organisations with a tool to help them control and minimise the impact of their products, services and activities on the environment. Recognised models include the international management system ISO 14001, and the EU Eco-Management and Audit Scheme (EMAS). The latter is based on the ISO, but additionally requires the reporting of environmental performance. Both require auditing by an accredited independent third party. In the United Kingdom accreditation is provided by the UK Accreditation Service (UKAS).

A new British Standard (BS 8555, see page 380), designed primarily for small and medium-sized enterprises, was published in 2003. It allows companies to implement environmental management in stages, to eventually achieve full certification under ISO 14001 or EMAS.

Many leading companies now address environmental issues in their annual reports and over half of the FTSE 100 listed companies (see page 461) now report publicly on their environmental performance. To encourage organisations to report publicly on their major environmental impacts, the Government has produced guidance to help companies measure and report on greenhouse gas emissions, water consumption and waste.

The Government has also issued proposals for company reporting in the White Paper *Modernising company law*. These would require the leading 1,000 companies to report on a range of non-financial issues, including their policies and performance on environmental issues, where directors judge them to be relevant to an understanding of the business.

Environmental labelling

Consumers often rely on the information given on product labels when trying to choose environmentally friendly goods. To help them, the Government encourages accurate and relevant environmental labelling, as part of an integrated approach to reduce the environmental impact of consumer products. The mandatory EU A–G energy label on household appliances is one well-known environmental information label. Through Defra, the Government also administers the voluntary EU ecolabelling award scheme in the United Kingdom. The voluntary Green Claims Code sets out guidance for businesses that make environmental claims about their products, and provides an introduction to ISO 14021 – the international standard on

environmental labelling. The Government's Market Transformation Programme aims to encourage the take-up of more energy-efficient domestic appliances. Among other areas, it covers technical standards, consumer product information, and minimum standards.

Responsibility for environmental affairs

Government departments and agencies with overall responsibility for countryside policy and environmental protection are shown in the boxes (see page 286). In England, Wales and Scotland (but not in Northern Ireland) non-departmental environment agencies are responsible for regulation and enforcement matters.

Environment Agency

The Environment Agency is a non-departmental public body, accountable to ministers, whose aim is to protect and improve the environment. With a budget of approximately £800 million in 2003/04, it is responsible in England and Wales for regulating and controlling pollution, managing water resources, and improving flood defence. It also carries out conservation, and manages and maintains fisheries and waterways. The Scottish Environment Protection Agency carries out many of the same responsibilities north of the border.

Many local authorities, voluntary organisations and charities are also involved in environmental conservation and protection.

Pollution control

Executive responsibility for pollution control is divided between local authorities, central government and the devolved administrations. Central government and the devolved administrations make policy, promote legislation and advise pollution control authorities on policy implementation. Local authorities are responsible for:

- collection and disposal of domestic waste;
- keeping the streets clear of litter;
- controlling air pollution from domestic premises and, in England and Wales, from many industrial premises;
- reviewing, assessing and managing local air quality; and
- noise and general nuisance abatement.

Main non-departmental public bodies with responsibility for the environment

England
Environment Agency
www.environment-agency.gov.uk

Countryside Agency
www.countryside.gov.uk

English Nature
www.english-nature.org.uk

English Heritage
www.english-heritage.org.uk

Wales
Environment Agency Wales
www.environment-agency.gov.uk/regions/wales

Countryside Council for Wales
www.ccw.gov.uk

Cadw: Welsh Historic Monuments Executive Agency
www.cadw.wales.gov.uk

Scotland
Scottish Environment Protection Agency
www.sepa.org.uk

Scottish Natural Heritage
www.snh.org.uk

Historic Scotland (an agency of the Scottish Executive
Education Department)
www.historic-scotland.gov.uk

Council for Nature Conservation and the Countryside

Northern Ireland
Environment and Heritage Service
www.ehsni.gov.uk

Great Britain
Joint Nature Conservation Committee
www.jncc.org.uk

Industrial pollution control

There are two pollution control regimes for the United Kingdom: Local Air Pollution Control (LAPC), which regulates emissions to air; and Integrated Pollution Control (IPC), which regulates emissions to land and water, as well as air.

A new Pollution Prevention and Control (PPC) regime, which implements an EC Directive on Integrated Pollution Prevention and Control (IPPC), has been introduced. It succeeds IPC and part of LAPC, and will be fully established by 2007.

Under both old and new regimes, regulators are required to ensure that pollution from industry is prevented or reduced through the use of best available techniques, subject to assessment of costs and benefits. The characteristics of each installation and its local environment must be considered.

Under PPC, the issuing of integrated permits will apply to more industrial activities than was previously the case. These include animal rendering, the food and drink industry, and intensive livestock installations. Regulators are also required to take into account a wider range of environmental impacts (including noise, energy efficiency and site restoration) when issuing integrated permits.

A Pollution Inventory for England and Wales, administered by the Environment Agency, provides details of emissions to air, water and land from processes regulated under IPC, and their contributions to national emission levels. The data are updated annually and can be found on the Agency's website. The implementation of the IPPC Directive will increase the number of sites reporting to around 7,000 in 2003.

In 2003 the United Kingdom made its first report to the European Commission on emissions of 50 key pollutants from installations covered by the IPPC Directive. This will feed into an EU-wide European Pollutant Emissions Register. In Scotland, the data are being used as the basis for the first phase in the development of a comprehensive pollution inventory to be completed by 2005.

Environmental legislation

Conservation and the countryside (see pages 262–9)

The primary conservation legislation in Great Britain is the *Wildlife and Countryside Act 1981*, which provides for a range of measures to protect plants and animals from damage and destruction. It was strengthened by the *Countryside and Rights of Way Act 2000*, which gave ministers and government departments in England and Wales a statutory duty to have regard to the conservation of biological diversity in carrying out their functions, and contained new measures for the conservation and protection of habitats and wildlife. It also created a new statutory right of access, giving people greater freedom to explore the open countryside, while also providing safeguards for landowners.

The Scottish Executive published the draft *Nature Conservation (Scotland) Bill* in March 2003. It includes proposals to strengthen the protection of SSSIs in Scotland; to place a duty on public organisations to promote biodiversity; and for new legislation to tackle wildlife crime. The Environment (Northern Ireland) Order 2002 includes measures which allow for the increased protection and management of ASSIs.

Waste management (see pages 269–72)

Waste management in Great Britain is governed by the *Environmental Protection Act 1990* (as amended) and the Waste Management Licensing Regulations 1994, with similar legislation existing in Northern Ireland. A licence is required by anyone wanting to deposit, recover or dispose of waste. Licences are issued by the Environment Agency and SEPA. In Northern Ireland the responsibility for waste disposal licensing will transfer from district councils to the EHS by the end of 2003. A duty of care requires waste producers, and anyone else with responsibility for waste, to take all reasonable steps to keep their waste safe. If they give their waste to someone else they must be sure that those people are authorised to take it and can transport, recycle or dispose of it safely. Failure to comply with either the licensing requirements or a duty of care is an offence.

Local authorities are responsible for the collection and disposal of all household waste and some commercial waste. In 'two-tier' areas (see page 9), district councils are responsible for collection, and county councils for disposal, while in unitary areas the council has both roles.

The disposal of radioactive waste in the United Kingdom is regulated by the *Radioactive Substances Act 1993*. This Act makes the Environment Agency in England and Wales and SEPA in Scotland responsible for regulating the safe use and storage of radioactive materials and the management of waste. The DoE is responsible for regulating radioactive waste in Northern Ireland.

Air pollution (see pages 274–6)

Ambient air pollution is controlled and regulated by a number of different pieces of legislation, depending on the source of emissions.

Noise (see pages 279–80)

In Great Britain, the primary legislation used to take action against the producers of noise that causes nuisance is the *Environmental Protection Act 1990*. Under the *Housing Act 1996*, local authorities in England and Wales have powers to deal with anti-social behaviour by tenants, including noise. In Scotland, action against noisy neighbours is taken under earlier legislation. The *Crime and Disorder Act 1998* introduced Anti-Social Behaviour Orders in England, Scotland and Wales, which can be used against any person who is causing harassment, alarm or distress to others, including noise nuisance. An EC Directive specifies the maximum noise level of certain new equipment for use outside.

Further reading

Climate Change: The UK Programme. DETR, 2000.

Digest of Environmental Statistics. Defra. Available only on the Internet: *www.defra.gov.uk/ environment/statistics/des/index.htm*

Environment in your Pocket 2002. Defra, 2002.

Global Atmosphere Research Programme Bi-annual report 2000–02. Defra, 2003.

Municipal Waste Management Survey 2001–2002. Defra, 2003.

State of the Historic Environment Report 2002. English Heritage, 2002.

The State of the Countryside 2003. Countryside Agency, 2003.

Working with the grain of nature. Defra, 2002.

Websites

Department for Environment, Food and Rural Affairs (Defra)
www.defra.gov.uk

Welsh Assembly Government
www.wales.gov.uk

Scottish Executive Environment and Rural Affairs Department (SEERAD)
www.scotland.gov.uk

Department of the Environment (DoE)
www.doeni.gov.uk

Department of Agriculture and Rural Development (DARD)
www.dardni.gov.uk

WWW.

20 Housing, planning and regeneration

The United Kingdom is a relatively densely populated country with 2.4 people per hectare in 2002. At the time of the 2001 Census there were almost 24.5 million households. Compared with 1991, the average household size had declined from 2.51 to 2.36 people.

Increasing demand for housing and recent economic trends such as low interest rates have led to a buoyant UK housing market. In 2002, the average UK dwelling price was just over £128,000, a 14 per cent increase on the previous year and more than twice the average price ten years earlier. Various measures have been introduced to help certain groups of key workers, such as nurses, to buy homes in areas where accommodation is particularly expensive (see page 293).

The combination of a growing population and the declining size of households places increasing pressure on land use. Throughout the United Kingdom a number of programmes continue to work to regenerate areas that have been in decline and are in need of investment.

Housing

Housing policy
The Office of the Deputy Prime Minister (ODPM) has responsibility for determining housing policy in England and supervising the housing programme. Responsibility for housing policy in Wales, Scotland and Northern Ireland rests with the devolved administrations. They all work with local authorities (which are responsible for preparing local housing strategies) and with the private and voluntary sectors. Social housing (housing at below market rent) is provided by local authorities, registered social landlords (RSLs) (see page 296) – most of which are housing associations – and the Northern Ireland Housing Executive (NIHE). RSLs are registered by the Housing Corporation (in England), the Welsh Assembly Government and Communities Scotland, through which bodies they also receive government funding. In Northern Ireland, the Housing Division of the Department for Social Development funds the NIHE and the housing association movement, and has regulatory powers over both.

In March 2003 a draft Housing Bill was published for consultation. The main areas of legislation for England and Wales set out in the Bill are:

- replacing the existing housing fitness standard with the Housing Health and Safety Rating System (see page 296);

- improving the controls on houses in multiple occupation, including a mandatory national licensing scheme to tackle poor physical and management standards of these properties;

- empowering local authorities to license landlords in areas of low housing demand or similar areas where the growth and poor management of the private rented sector frustrates efforts to create sustainable communities;

- requiring sellers of residential property, or their agents, to assemble a home information pack so that the information needed by sellers is available when the property is marketed; and

- modernising the Right to Buy scheme (see page 293) by tackling profiteering and emphasising purchasers' responsibilities.

Supporting People programmes were introduced across the United Kingdom in April 2003. The programmes provide a funding and policy framework for the delivery of housing support

---

Sustainable Communities Plan

In a statement to the House of Commons in February 2003 the Deputy Prime Minister launched the Sustainable Communities Plan (*Sustainable Communities: Building for the Future*). The Plan sets out a 15 to 20 year programme of action which will include £22 billion of investment to improve housing and communities in England. It covers a wide agenda, which recognises that to develop communities in which people wish to live, housing policy needs to be linked to improving economies, public services, transport and the environment at a local level. In particular the Plan aims to:
- provide more high-quality and affordable housing in areas of high demand;
- regenerate declining communities;
- tackle social exclusion and homelessness;
- improve the efficiency of the planning system (see page 299); and
- decentralise housing policy and planning by empowering local and regional government.

To meet demand for affordable housing in the South East, the Plan has identified four substantial sites where land can be accessed relatively inexpensively so that large quantities of homes can be built. The sites are centred around Ashford in Kent; Milton Keynes; the M11 corridor from London to Stansted; and the Thames Gateway, a 64-kilometre strip to the east of London. In many towns and cities in the North and Midlands the decline in traditional manufacturing industries has left a surplus of homes. The plan will provide £500 million to tackle failing housing markets in these areas through widespread demolition and rebuilding.

---

services for vulnerable people, such as the homeless, older people, people with mental health problems or physical disabilities, and victims of domestic violence. The programmes aim to prevent crises, such as hospitalisation, institutional care or homelessness, by providing early support when it is most effective so that vulnerable people become and remain independent in the community, in all types of accommodation.

In the first year 150 local authorities in England will receive a total of £1.4 billion in local government grants towards delivering the programmes. The grants will be based on the transfer of funding from a number of other sources including elements of: Transitional Housing Benefit; the Supported Housing Management Grant; Income Support; and Jobseeker's Allowance. Local authorities will run the programmes through partnerships with local housing and social services, as well as the health and probation services.

In Wales, Supporting People funds for the elderly and those people receiving a care service are administered by local authorities. The Welsh Assembly Government retains a grant scheme to pay for other forms of supported housing.

The Scottish Executive is responsible for implementing the Supporting People programme in Scotland. Provisions included in the *Housing (Scotland) Act 2001* enable grants to be made to local authorities for housing support services. The Act also allows for secondary legislation and guidance to specify how the grant is to be used. The Scottish Executive has set up a Stakeholders' Group, representing local authorities, housing support providers and service users' groups to guide the development and overall direction of the programme. For the first time services will be subject to quality monitoring and contract compliance procedures, through registration by the Scottish Commission for the Regulation of Care (see page 146).

In Northern Ireland the Supporting People programme is administered by the Northern Ireland Housing Executive, in partnership with the four Health and Social Services Boards and the Probation Board.

Housing stock and housebuilding

In 1951 there were 14.1 million dwellings in the United Kingdom. By 2002 the number had

Figure 20.1 Housebuilding completion rates, 2001/02, UK

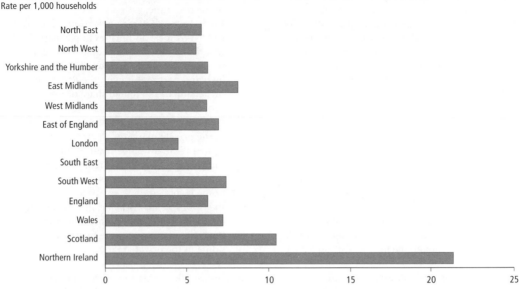

Rate per 1,000 households

Source: Office of the Deputy Prime Minister

increased to 25.5 million. The housebuilding peak was in 1968 when total completions amounted to 426,000 dwellings, 53 per cent completed by private enterprises, and 47 per cent by the social sector (primarily local authorities). In all there were 183,100 dwellings completed in 2002, of which 86 per cent were completed by private enterprise. While local authorities are no longer major developers of new social sector housing, they still play an important role as landlords. RSLs (predominantly housing associations) dominate building in the social sector, and in 2002 accounted for 99 per cent of completions in this sector.

In 2001/02, Northern Ireland had the highest overall rate of completions in the United Kingdom at 21.4 dwellings per 1,000 households (see Figure 20.1). London had the lowest rate of completions with 4.5 per 1,000 households. Compared with 1991/92, Northern Ireland and Scotland were the only parts of the United Kingdom where there was an increase in the rate of completions.

The type of dwellings built has changed over the last century. Terraced housing was the norm before the First World War and over a third of the current stock of terraced housing dates from before 1919. Between 1919 and 1944 there was an expansion in the number of semi-detached dwellings. After 1965 the private sector began to build more detached houses, while a large number

Figure 20.2 Households, by type of dwelling occupied, 2001/02, UK

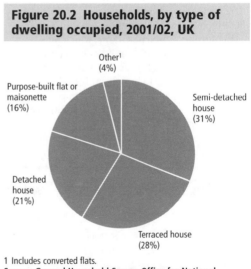

1 Includes converted flats.
Source: General Household Survey, Office for National Statistics; Continuous Household Survey, Northern Ireland Statistics and Research Agency

of purpose-built flats were provided in the public sector. Figure 20.2 illustrates the mix of accommodation in 2001/02.

To minimise greenfield development (that is, building on land that has not previously been developed) and to encourage urban regeneration, the Government wishes to see unoccupied homes brought back into use. The number of empty homes in England fell from 868,600 in 1993 to 732,000 in 2002. About four-fifths of vacant dwellings are private housing, with about half of these having been vacant for six months or more. Some dwellings are vacant for short periods between purchase and sale or re-let (known as transactional vacancies), but others may be vacant for longer pending demolition or renovation.

Home ownership

Between 1981 and 2001 the number of owner-occupied dwellings in the United Kingdom increased by more than 40 per cent to 17.6 million, while the number of rented dwellings fell by around 15 per cent to 7.8 million.

Within the United Kingdom, Northern Ireland had the highest proportion of owner-occupied dwellings in 2002, and Scotland the lowest (see Table 20.3).

Since the 1980s the increase in the proportion of dwellings that are owner-occupied has in part been due to a number of schemes that aim to increase low-cost home ownership. In England these include the Right to Buy, Right to Acquire and Voluntary Purchase Grants, which offer tenants in social housing a discount against the market value of the homes they rent if they are eligible and choose to buy them. In addition, funding to support low-cost ownership is provided through the Housing Corporation and local authorities, including:

- *Conventional Shared Ownership*, which allows people to part buy and part rent homes

developed by RSLs. The scheme allows people to increase their share of ownership in their home over time;

- *Do-It-Yourself Shared Ownership*, which is funded by local authorities in partnership with RSLs and enables people to select a house in the private market and then part own and part rent it, with the RSL taking on ownership of the rented share of the property;

- *Homebuy*, which allows people to buy a home in the private market with an equity loan from an RSL for 25 per cent of the value of the property. The loan is repayable, at 25 per cent of the current market value, when the home is sold; and

- the *Cash Incentive Scheme*, in which local authorities offer cash grants to existing tenants, to be used for the purchase of a home in the private market.

In February 2003, as part of the Sustainable Communities Plan (see page 290), the Government established the Home Ownership Task Force. The task force will consider a number of the schemes currently available to potential homeowners on low or modest incomes, and identify the most effective ways of promoting sustainable home ownership, particularly among key workers and young families. It will look at the housing market as a whole and assess what other approaches can be taken to provide more affordable home ownership without reducing the stock of social housing in the longer term. The task force will report its recommendations in autumn 2003.

Table 20.3 Tenure of dwellings, 2002,[1] in the UK

Percentages

	Owner-occupied[2]	Rented from local authority[3]	Rented privately or with job or business	Rented from registered social landlord
England	70	13	10	7
Wales	73	14	9	4
Scotland	64	23	7	6
Northern Ireland	75	17	5	3
United Kingdom	70	14	10	7

1 As at 31 March 2002 for England, Wales and Northern Ireland. Figures for Scotland are for 31 December 2001.
2 Including dwellings purchased with a mortgage or loan as well as those owned outright.
3 Including the Northern Ireland Housing Executive.
Source: Office of the Deputy Prime Minister; National Assembly for Wales; Scottish Executive; and Department for Social Development, Northern Ireland

In Wales, local authorities and housing associations operate a low-cost home ownership scheme allowing purchasers to buy a home for 70 per cent of its value, or 50 per cent in rural areas, the balance being secured as a charge on the property. In Northern Ireland, over 102,500 NIHE tenants had bought their homes by March 2003. The Northern Ireland Co-ownership Housing Association administers a 'buy half, rent half' (shared ownership) scheme which, by June 2003, had helped 17,600 people become homeowners.

Communities Scotland administers a Housing Association Grant for low-cost home ownership. The grant is used to bridge the shortfall between the cost of provision and locally assessed market value. Communities Scotland also administers the Grant for Rent and Owner Occupation. The purpose of this grant is to widen the choice of housing for those who seek to become home owners. The grants are targeted at areas of wholly social sector housing and areas of high demand.

Right to Buy discounts

Since 1980, 1.6 million social housing tenants in England have acquired their homes through Right to Buy. Tenants qualify for Right to Buy after two years, and can obtain discounts of up to 32 per cent on houses and 44 per cent on flats, capped at a cash limit varying by region, from £22,000 in the North East to £38,000 in London and the South East. Up to 100 per cent of the discount is repayable if the purchaser sells the property within three years. To tackle severe housing pressures and discourage exploitation of the rules, the maximum Right to Buy discounts were reduced in 41 local authority areas in London and southern England in March 2003. The maximum discount available to tenants in these areas is now £16,000.

Key workers

The Starter Home Initiative (SHI), set up in 2000, aims to help key workers in England, particularly teachers, police officers, nurses, and other essential health workers, to buy homes within a reasonable distance of their workplace in areas where high house prices are undermining recruitment and retention. The Government has made £250 million available over the years 2001/02 to 2003/04 in support of the scheme, mainly through RSLs. Types of assistance vary and include equity loans, interest-free loans and shared ownership. By June 2003, over 3,300 key workers had bought their first homes under the scheme.

London Housing Strategy 2003

Demand for housing in London is rising sharply, with the number of households estimated to increase by 20,400 a year until 2016. The London Housing Strategy 2003, *Homes and Communities in London for London*, sets out the key housing issues and a programme of action to address them. The five priority issues identified are:

- to increase the supply of affordable housing;
- to reduce homelessness and the use of inappropriate temporary accommodation;
- to modernise the private rented sector;
- to bring social housing up to a decent standard; and
- to promote regeneration to achieve sustainable communities.

Mortgage loans

A feature of home-ownership in the United Kingdom is the relatively high proportion of homes purchased with a mortgage. Approximately three-quarters of house purchases are financed in this way. In 2002, 76 per cent of loans for home purchase were obtained through banks and 17 per cent through building societies, with 7 per cent through other lenders.

Those who are buying a house can choose from a variety of different types of mortgage, the most common being repayment and interest-only. With repayment mortgages, the debt and the interest are both repaid during the life of the mortgage (typically 25 years). Around 81 per cent of all new mortgages were standard repayment mortgages in 2002. Interest-only mortgages, usually involving endowment policies, ISAs (individual savings accounts, see page 461) or personal pensions, account for the bulk of other mortgages. Since the late 1980s there has been a decrease in the popularity of endowment mortgages because of the possibility that investments may not grow fast enough to repay the capital borrowed. In 1988, 83 per cent of new mortgages for house purchase were endowment mortgages, but by 2002 this had fallen to 5 per cent.

In the first quarter of 2003 UK base rates fell to their lowest level since the early 1960s. However, due to rising house prices, first-time buyers accounted for just 31 per cent of loans for house purchases during this period, the lowest proportion since records began in 1969. The proportion of fixed (as opposed to variable) rate mortgages is markedly lower in the United

Kingdom than in many other countries. In the April 2003 Budget, the Chancellor of the Exchequer announced that a review would be undertaken to identify the factors underlying the low take-up of fixed rate mortgages in the United Kingdom. The report and recommendations are due in spring 2004.

The average price of dwellings bought and sold in the United Kingdom in 2002 was £128,265 (see Table 20.5), although there were marked regional variations with buyers in London and the South East paying the most for their property. However, between 2001 and 2002 the East Midlands and South West of England recorded the largest percentage increases in house prices. Dwelling prices also vary according to type, with detached houses being the most expensive.

Rented housing

As owner-occupation has increased, the number of dwellings that are rented has decreased. In 2002, 21 per cent of UK households were renting from the social sector (local authorities and housing associations), while 10 per cent were renting privately (Table 20.3).

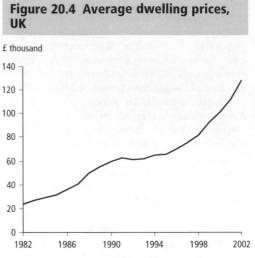

Figure 20.4 Average dwelling prices, UK

£ thousand

Source: Office of the Deputy Prime Minister

Private rented sector

During the past 60 years the size and nature of the private rented sector in the United Kingdom has changed significantly. Prior to the Second World War 57 per cent of the population lived in private rented accommodation. Most tenancies were

Table 20.5 Average dwelling prices by region, 2002

£

	Bungalow	Detached house	Semi-detached house	Terraced house	Flat/ maisonette	All dwellings	% increase on 2001
North East	96,408	137,732	70,015	54,620	53,688	78,971	13
North West	112,979	162,284	84,477	58,747	84,863	92,074	12
Yorkshire and the Humber	107,984	156,551	75,140	59,247	89,784	88,126	15
East Midlands	116,521	162,789	83,150	70,110	74,992	104,835	20
West Midlands	157,053	186,841	94,727	73,761	79,245	112,313	15
East	147,399	237,160	140,042	117,610	90,598	151,330	18
London	250,759	356,421	244,236	217,327	173,619	207,246	14
South East	197,101	293,538	171,483	136,270	112,972	180,243	15
South West	162,220	221,574	127,442	108,518	98,895	142,403	20
England	150,597	212,314	119,723	105,739	128,380	137,278	15
Wales	96,073	150,136	76,845	59,577	69,401	88,261	11
Scotland	98,718	140,555	71,108	55,118	61,656	77,655	6
Northern Ireland	93,475	129,576	79,927	56,379	81,532	83,829	5
United Kingdom	**138,299**	**201,815**	**113,299**	**99,150**	**113,492**	**128,265**	**14**

Source: Survey of Mortgage Lenders; Office of the Deputy Prime Minister

unfurnished, subject to rent control and occupied by the same tenants for many years. For many people today, private renting has become a more temporary tenure, occupied by those such as students and young professionals who may need to move frequently, and by people who are saving to buy. There are, in addition, people who have no other option because they cannot afford to buy and do not qualify for social rented accommodation. About a quarter of households in the private rented sector receive rent assistance in the form of Housing Benefit.

'Assured' and 'shorthold' (in Scotland, 'short assured') tenancies are the most common forms of arrangement for the letting of houses and flats by private landlords. If the tenancy is shorthold, the landlord can regain possession of the property six months' after the beginning of the tenancy, provided that he or she gives the tenant two months, notice requiring possession. If the tenancy is assured, the tenant has the right to remain in the property unless the landlord can prove to the court that he or she has grounds for possession. In an assured tenancy, the landlord does not have an automatic right to repossess the property when the tenancy comes to an end. In both types of tenancy the landlord can charge a full market rent.

The National Approved Lettings Scheme (NALS) is a voluntary accreditation scheme for private sector landlords in England that aims to promote best practice among lettings agencies. It sets minimum standards for service and financial probity of agents in handling clients' money.

Social housing

Much of the Government's expenditure on social housing is provided as subsidies to local authorities to help pay for the costs of nearly 3.7 million rented council homes in the United Kingdom. More than 2,000 housing associations, most of them RSLs, provide other social housing.

Since the late 1980s government policy has aimed to promote a wider range of social landlords through stock transfers. In England a Large Scale Voluntary Transfer (LSVT) Programme has been running since 1988. By April 2003, almost 787,000 dwellings had been transferred from local authorities to RSLs with the support of tenants and the approval of the appropriate Secretary of State. The transfers generated £5.5 billion in capital receipts, and raised over £12 billion in

private finance. In Scotland, three local authorities transferred their entire stock of around 101,000 dwellings to RSLs in 2002/03.

Proposals to reform the funding of local authority housing services in England were included in the *Local Government Act 2003*. This allows a greater proportion of local authorities' housing capital receipts to be invested in new housing rather than debt repayment, and provides for a proportion of receipts to be pooled for redistribution by the Government to areas where they are most needed. Seventy-five per cent of receipts from Right to Buy and other sales of dwellings will be pooled, and 50 per cent of receipts from the sale of other Housing Revenue Account property such as bare land, shops, garages and surplus vacant dwellings. The amounts to be pooled may, however, be reduced if all of the receipts used for capital expenditure on affordable housing and regeneration. Receipts from large-scale and small-scale voluntary transfers (including preserved rights to buy) are excluded.

Local authorities in Wales own around 200,000, or approximately 14 per cent, of all Welsh homes. By law they have to manage their own stock efficiently and, in consultation with their tenants, address current housing needs and demands.

In March 2003 the Scottish Executive published a consultation paper, *Modernising Scotland's Social Housing*. This outlined a package of measures aimed at improving the quality of the social housing stock. The main proposals included:

- developing a national Scottish social housing standard to deliver a minimum set of quality standards for all tenants of social landlords;
- establishing a community ownership programme to facilitate the transfer of further council stock to RSLs and unlock resources for future investment; and
- introducing a 'prudential borrowing regime' for housing investment allowing councils to borrow outside government controls.

Under the *Housing (Scotland) Act 2001*, the Scottish Executive has powers to place government investment in housing under council control, thus enhancing the role of local authorities. It is planned that Glasgow City Council will be the first local authority to receive this funding.

In Northern Ireland the Government's contribution to housing of £226 million in 2002/03, supplemented by rental income and capital receipts, meant that gross resources available were £601 million. The Northern Ireland Housing Executive (NIHE), the regional strategic housing authority for Northern Ireland, is the landlord of 116,000 properties, nearly one-third of rented properties in Northern Ireland. It is responsible for assessing the need for, and arranging the supply of, social housing.

Registered social landlords

Registered social landlords (RSLs) are the major providers of new subsidised homes for those in housing need. They range from almshouses to large housing associations, managing thousands of homes. They also include large-scale voluntary transfer and local housing companies, set up to own and manage council houses transferred from local authorities.

The Housing Corporation, which regulates RSLs in England, gives capital grants to provide homes for rent and for sale under shared ownership terms, primarily from the Approved Development Programme (ADP). Planned ADP for 2003/04 is £1.5 billion, including a £300 million Challenge Fund to provide 4,000 new homes for rent or low-cost sale in London and the south-east of England.

In 2003/04 Communities Scotland will invest £237 million on housing projects, helping to complete more than 4,400 new and improved homes already under way and allowing work to start on another 6,000, mainly for rent through

---

New single inspectorate for social housing

In April 2003 a new Housing Inspectorate for social housing in England was established, bringing together the functions of the previous Housing Inspectorate (which was responsible for local authority housing services) and the inspection role of the Housing Corporation (which was responsible for housing associations). The new inspectorate, which is located at the Audit Commission, will report the results of its inspection of housing associations to the Housing Corporation, as the statutory regulator, and both will work to ensure inspection and regulatory activity are properly coordinated, in order to avoid unnecessary burdens on housing associations.

In Scotland, Communities Scotland is responsible for the regulation and inspection of both RSLs and local authority landlords.

---

housing associations. In addition, Communities Scotland will assist the Scottish Executive in delivering a range of policy initiatives.

In Northern Ireland, the NIHE has continued to transfer its new-build programme to registered housing associations. The 2003/04 programme will provide 1,575 new homes.

Improving existing housing

The English House Condition Survey showed that the number of dwellings failing to provide a decent standard of accommodation (see page 297) fell from 9.4 million (or 46 per cent of the total) in 1996 to 7.0 million (33 per cent) in 2001. Although primary responsibility for maintaining a property rests with the owner, the Government can provide help to improve housing quality across all tenures and accepts that some people, especially the elderly and most vulnerable, do not have the resources to keep their homes in good repair.

The Government intends to reform the legislation on housing fitness for England. The current statutory housing fitness standard (set out in the *Housing Act 1985*) is based in part on criteria first introduced approximately 80 years ago. To reflect a more modern approach to health and safety hazards in the home, the Government has developed the Housing Health and Safety Rating System (HHSRS). Measures to introduce this system were included in the draft Housing Bill which was published for consultation in March 2003 (see page 289). HHSRS will assess 24 broad categories of housing hazard and provide a rating for each one. The assessment is based on the risk to the potential occupant who is most vulnerable to each specific hazard, for instance, stairs constitute a greater risk to the elderly so for this hazard they would be considered as the most vulnerable group. Subject to legislation, local housing authorities will in future base enforcement decisions on assessments made under the HHSRS.

Disabled Facilities Grant

Disabled people in all tenures can apply for grants to ensure they continue to live independent lives in their own homes. The Disabled Facilities Grant (DFG) is allocated to eligible applicants through local authorities in England, and pays for essential adaptations for better access into and within the home. For 2003/04 the Government allocated a DFG budget of £99 million, a 12.5 per cent increase on the previous year.

Private housing

Local authorities in England have discretionary grant-giving powers to help home-owners and tenants to repair their properties and assist in the regeneration of communities. Local authorities use these powers to fund around £250 million of repairs for some 70,000 home-owners and tenants a year. The Regulatory Reform (Housing Assistance) Order, which came into force in 2002, gives local authorities a general power to deliver private sector housing renewal through grants, loans, loan guarantees and equity release schemes.

Local authorities have similar powers in Scotland. In 2001 the Scottish Executive announced modifications to the legislation so that new types of work could become eligible for grant, and a national test of resources could be introduced, enabling those on the lowest incomes to receive full grant funding for necessary repairs and improvements. The Housing Improvement Task Force was established in March 2001 to undertake a comprehensive examination of the issues affecting the condition and quality of private sector housing and the process of buying and selling houses in Scotland. Its work included an examination of the statutory and strategic framework for improving private sector housing. The final report of the Task Force, *Stewardship and Responsibility: A Policy Framework for Private Housing in Scotland*, was published in March 2003.

In Northern Ireland, funding is allocated through the house renovation grants scheme, administered by the NIHE, on a similar basis to that in England. In rural areas of Northern Ireland, financial assistance to replace isolated dwellings that cannot be restored is also available.

Social housing

Most capital expenditure on local authority housing goes towards major repairs and renovations. In 2000 the Government set a target to bring all social housing in England up to a decent standard by 2010 (see box) and in March 2003 it published a review of how this target will be met. The review recommended three approaches to securing additional investment in council owned housing:

- stock transfer to RSLs;
- arms-length management companies set up by local authorities with responsibility for management of their housing stock; and
- private finance initiative (PFI, see below).

The Sustainable Communities Plan launched in February 2003 (see page 290) announced funding of £2.8 billion over three years from 2003/04 to improve council housing and £685 million of Housing Revenue Account PFI credits. The PFI for local authority housing uses private sector funding to refurbish council houses and thereafter to provide housing services, with tenants remaining tenants of the local authority. In 1999 eight authorities in England were selected as 'pathfinders' to pilot the Housing Revenue Account PFI scheme. In March 2003 Manchester City Council became the first authority to sign a PFI contract. In addition to the eight pathfinders, a further ten schemes are in progress with the aim of refurbishing a total of 30,000 council houses across England.

The decent home standard

The Government's key housing target is for all housing rented from social landlords in England to meet the decent home standard by 2010. A decent home is one that:

- meets the current statutory minimum for housing, which at present is the 'fitness standard';
- is in a reasonable state of repair;
- has reasonably modern facilities; and
- provides a reasonable degree of thermal comfort through effective insulation and efficient heating.

Results from the 2001 English House Condition Survey, published in July 2003, showed that:

- the number of non-decent homes in the social sector fell from 2.3 million in 1996 to 1.6 million in 2001; and
- the single main reason why these homes did not meet the standard was the failure to provide a reasonable degree of thermal comfort.

Rural housing

The Housing Corporation finances a special rural programme to build houses in villages with a population of 3,000 or less across England. The Sustainable Communities Plan (see page 290) included a government target for the Corporation to provide a total of 3,500 affordable homes in small villages between 2004/05 and 2005/06. This was in addition to the target of 1,600 for 2003/04. The plan also included measures to make it easier for local authorities to limit the resale of ex-council housing in rural areas so that it is reserved for local people.

The National Assembly for Wales supports the development of housing in rural areas if it is regarded as a strategic priority by the local authority.

Communities Scotland's Rural Development Programme provided 1,350 new and improved homes across Scotland in 2002/03 and aims to approve a further 1,440 in 2003/04.

In Northern Ireland, a strategic target has been set that allocates a minimum of 10 per cent of all new social housing to areas outside of district and larger towns. During 2002/03, 277 new social rented homes were provided in rural areas while just over 300 private properties benefited from replacement grant assistance.

Homelessness

Local housing authorities in England and Wales have a statutory duty to ensure that suitable accommodation is available for applicants who are eligible for assistance, have become homeless through no fault of their own, and who fall within a priority need group (this is the 'main homeless duty'). Among the priority need groups are families with children, and households that include someone who is vulnerable, for example because of pregnancy, domestic violence, old age, or physical or mental disability.

Where applicants are homeless but not owed the main duty (for example, because they do not fall within a priority need group) the housing authority must ensure that they are provided with advice and assistance in their own attempts to find accommodation. Authorities also have a general duty to ensure that advice about homelessness and the prevention of homelessness is available free of charge to everyone in their district. In most areas, advice about homelessness is available from housing aid centres, Shelter (a charity that offers housing advice to homeless and badly housed people), Citizens Advice and other local agencies.

From July 2003 local authorities in England and Wales also have a duty to carry out reviews of homelessness within their area and produce strategies for tackling and preventing homelessness.

The number of households accepted as homeless by local authorities in England increased by 10 per cent to 129,320 during 2002/03. Figure 20.6 shows the trend in the number of homeless households

Figure 20.6 Homeless households[1] in temporary accommodation,[2] England

Thousands

1 Excludes 'homeless at home' cases who have remained in their existing accommodation after acceptance but have the same rights to suitable alternative accommodation as those in accommodation arranged directly by authorities.
2 Data are at end year and include households awaiting the outcome of homeless enquiries.
Source: Office of the Deputy Prime Minister

in temporary accommodation in recent years. There were nearly 85,000 such households at the end of 2002, about 15 per cent of whom were in bed and breakfast (B&B) accommodation.

Some £260 million has been allocated over the three years from 2003/04 to help English local authorities sustain reductions in rough sleeping, end the use of B&B hotels as a form of temporary accommodation for homeless families with children, and develop new approaches to tackle homelessness more effectively. The Government's target is that by March 2004 no homeless family with children should have to live in B&B accommodation, except in an emergency and then for no more than six weeks.

Domestic violence accounted for 15 per cent of all local authority homelessness acceptances in England in 2002. In April 2003 the Government announced £18.8 million funding for 2003/04 to build and develop refuges to help women and children fleeing violent partners. The money will be used in partnership with local refuge groups, RSLs and local authorities to ensure better availability of safe accommodation.

In Wales, the Homelessness Commission was established in 2001 to advise the National Assembly on the measures that should be introduced to reduce homelessness. Recommendations made in the Commission's final report led to the Assembly developing the National Homelessness Strategy and action plan, which were both published in March 2003. The strategy identified 23 objectives that it expects to be covered within local homelessness strategies. Assembly funding for voluntary sector schemes aimed at tackling homelessness and rooflessness in Wales increased from £650,000 in 1999/2000 to £4.7 million in 2003/04.

Scotland and Northern Ireland have similar legislation on homelessness. In Scotland, the Scottish Executive has allocated funds of £37 million in 2003/04, rising to £45 million in both 2004/05 and 2005/06 to deliver the recommendations of the Homelessness Task Force. The task force published its final report in February 2002, making 59 recommendations covering homelessness policy and practice, all of which have been accepted by the Scottish Executive.

The *Homelessness (Scotland) Act 2003* takes forward the legislative recommendations of the Homelessness Task Force and sets a target that by 2012 all homeless people will be entitled to permanent accommodation. The main provisions in the Act include:

- widening the categories of people who will be assessed as being in priority need and therefore entitled to permanent accommodation;
- allowing homeless people to apply to any local authority without having to demonstrate a local connection;
- requiring landlords to inform local authorities of repossession cases so that early action may be taken to prevent homelessness; and
- improving the way in which intentionally homeless people are assisted through the provision of housing and practical support.

In Northern Ireland there were 16,426 applications under the homeless persons legislation during 2002/03 and the number of acceptances increased by 14 per cent to 8,580. In September 2002 the NIHE published the *Homelessness Strategy for Northern Ireland*. This focuses on helping people avoid homelessness, helping people out of homelessness and supporting people when they get a home.

People sleeping rough

The Rough Sleepers Unit (RSU), established in April 1999, was set the target of reducing rough sleeping in England to as near to zero as possible and by at least two-thirds by 2002. In December 2001 it announced that the latter target had been met. In order to sustain the reduction, the RSU is working to prevent people ending up on the streets in the first place as well as rebuilding the lives of former rough sleepers through education, training and employment.

Over the three years to 2004, £3.5 million is available to support projects whose aim is to reduce the number of people sleeping rough in Wales. In Scotland, the Executive has set a target to remove the need for anyone to have to sleep rough by 2003. This programme was allocated £4 million in capital funding between 2002 and 2004 and will also receive £9.5 million a year in revenue funding up to 2006.

Land use planning

Planning systems regulate development and land use, and contribute to the Government's strategy for promoting a sustainable pattern of physical development in cities, towns and the countryside.

In Great Britain land use planning is the direct responsibility of local authorities. They prepare development plans and determine most planning applications. The ODPM and the devolved administrations have overall responsibility for the operation of the system. They issue national planning policy guidance, approve structure plans (except in Wales where unitary authorities have this role), decide planning appeals and determine planning applications that raise issues of national importance. In England the ODPM operates through the Government Offices for the Regions and the Planning Inspectorate.

In Northern Ireland, the Department of the Environment (DoE) functions as the single planning authority. The Planning Service, an executive agency within the DoE, is responsible for issuing operational planning, policy and guidance, determining planning applications and preparing development plans.

England

There are just over 400 planning authorities in England – including county councils, district councils, unitary authorities and National Park authorities. The first planning laws were enacted in 1909 and the modern system dates from the *Town and Country Planning Act 1947* and subsequent legislation in 1990 and 1991. The Government's national policy is set out in 25 Planning Policy Guidance notes (PPGs) – covering issues such as housing, transport, sport and recreation – and in 15 Minerals Policy Guidance notes (MPGs) as well as circulars and other guidance.

There are several tiers to the planning system. Central government issues national planning guidance to local authorities and also Regional Planning Guidance (RPG) based on advice from regional planning conferences. Upper-tier local authorities (such as county councils) produce 'structure plans', which indicate where development should be focused, while lower-tier local authorities (such as district councils) produce 'local plans' with more detailed and site-specific information. Local authorities decide individual planning applications with reference to these plans. In London the Mayor has responsibility for production of a 'spatial development strategy' covering development, regeneration and transport issues in the capital.

In December 2002 the Planning and Compulsory Purchase Bill was introduced into Parliament. The Bill aims to make the planning system fairer, faster and more predictable by simplifying the way decisions are made. The Bill applies to Wales as well as England, with specific sections for the different development planning arrangements in the two countries (see page 302).

Proposals included in the Bill aim to:
- simplify the planning development system with a new two-tier system whereby Regional Spatial Strategies are prepared by each English region and Local Development Frameworks (see page 301) by unitary and district councils;
- introduce a requirement for local planning authorities to consult with local communities through the preparation of a statement of community involvement;
- speed up the process of major infrastructure projects requiring decision by central government;
- introduce Business Planning Zones to aid regeneration by fast-tracking developments in areas where jobs are needed most; and

- make the compulsory purchase system faster and clarify local authority powers in relation to the acquisition of land for planning and regeneration.

Planning Policy Guidance Note 3: Housing (PPG3) sets out the Government's planning policies for housing in England. It encourages planning authorities to recycle brownfield (previously developed) sites within urban areas, bring empty homes back into use and convert existing buildings in preference to the development of greenfield sites. It also encourages planning authorities to use land more efficiently; assist with the provision of affordable housing in both rural and urban areas; and promote mixed-use developments that integrate housing with shops, local services and transport.

The Government's national target is that, by 2008, 60 per cent of additional housing in England should be provided on brownfield land or by re-using existing buildings. In 2002, 64 per cent of new housing was built on brownfield land. Proportions varied between regions, with London having the highest (90 per cent), while in the North East, South West and East Midlands less than 50 per cent of additional homes were built on brownfield sites.

Wales
Issues covered in *Planning Policy Wales* (PPW), published in March 2002, include: keeping development away from flood risk areas; the possible establishment of Wales' first Green Belt areas; development of land and buildings in a way that creates a more accessible environment, including for people with limited mobility; guidance on the sustainable use of previously developed land beyond housing needs alone; encouraging both rural and farm diversification; and proposals to relax the control of developments in the open countryside so that development on farm complexes can be permitted (subject to controls to prevent adverse environmental and transport effects).

In November 2002, the Minister for Environment launched a programme to improve the planning system in Wales. Based on proposals contained in the consultation paper *Planning: Delivering for Wales*, the programme will involve the Welsh Assembly Government working in collaboration with the 25 local planning authorities and the Planning Inspectorate in Wales to ensure that the planning system will be open, fair and transparent; deliver improved quality and speed; and integrate with other plans and processes. Some of the proposals require primary legislation.

Scotland

There are 33 planning authorities in Scotland comprising 32 local authorities and the Loch Lomond and Trossachs National Park Authority which became fully operational in July 2002. Scotland's second National Park, the Cairngorms, became a planning authority in relation to certain functions in September 2003.

Legislation for planning policy in Scotland is contained in the *Town and Country Planning (Scotland) Act 1997*. Scottish Planning Policies (SPPs) provide statements of Scottish Executive policy on nationally important land use and other planning matters, supported where appropriate by a locational framework. To date there are three – SPP1 the Planning System, SPP2 Economic Development and SPP3 Land for Housing – updating the relevant National Planning Policy Guidelines (NPPGs) on these topics. The remaining 16 NPPGs have continued relevance to decision-making, until such time as they are replaced by a SPP. The *Review of Strategic Planning Conclusions and Next Steps*, published in June 2002, outlined the intention to review and update the remainder of the NPPG series by 2007 with the aim of making documents more concise and the policy content more explicit.

As a result of a review of strategic planning (see also page 302), a national planning framework is to be prepared. This will cover:

- settlement pattern, land resources and infrastructure capacity;
- population and household change;
- economic prospects and the implications for planning;
- environmental challenges and the role of the planning system; and
- strategic priorities for transport and other infrastructure investment.

Northern Ireland

The Planning Service in Northern Ireland has embarked on a comprehensive programme of change. In February 2002 a consultation paper, *Modernising Planning Processes*, presented a wide range of proposals for improving the planning system in Northern Ireland. The Implementation Plan, launched in February 2003, identifies specific issues and the action the Planning Service intends to achieve to modernise and improve the development control process, the formulation of planning policy for Northern Ireland and the preparation of development plans for local council areas.

Development plans

Development plans play an integral role in shaping land use and provide a framework for consistent decision-making. Planning applications are determined in accordance with relevant development plan policies unless 'material considerations' indicate otherwise. Proposals included in the Planning and Compulsory Purchase Bill (see page 300) would require unitary and district councils in England to prepare Local Development Frameworks (LDFs). LDFs would replace structure plans, local plans and unitary development plans and contain:

- a statement of core policies setting out the local authority's approach to development;
- a statement of community involvement setting out the planning authority's policy for involving the community in the development and revision of LDFs and in significant development control decisions;
- site-specific policies and proposals, including area action plans for smaller local areas; and
- a map showing existing and revised designations, such as conservation areas, sites for particular future land uses or developments and locations of any proposed or actual area action plans.

Local planning authorities would be able to produce, by agreement, joint LDFs between two or more districts and between two or more districts and counties, under a joint committee. The continual updating and review of LDFs will become a requirement for all local authorities.

To ensure that all local authorities have LDFs in place the Government is providing £350 million between 2003 and 2006 through the Planning Delivery Grant. The grant is performance-based and is being allocated to local authorities that have made significant improvements in their handling of development control planning applications. The Government is developing the proposals for the grant in 2004/05, building on those for 2003/04, which included additional funding for growth areas and areas of high housing demand. Funding will also be allocated to the regional planning bodies for their work on new regional

Green Belts

Green Belts are areas of land that are intended to be left open and protected from development. The aim is to control the unrestricted sprawl of large built-up areas, prevent towns from merging with one another, preserve the heritage of historic towns and encourage the recycling of derelict and other urban land, thereby encouraging urban regeneration. Not all Green Belt land is countryside. It can cover small villages comprising a mixture of residential, retail, industrial and recreational land as well as fields and forests. Development on Green Belts is only permitted under exceptional circumstances.

The first major Green Belt was established around the fringes of Greater London following legislation in 1938. Green Belts have also been established around Glasgow, Edinburgh, Aberdeen, Greater Manchester, Merseyside and the West Midlands, as well as several smaller towns. In 1997, there were 14 separate designated Green Belt areas in England, amounting to 1.65 million hectares (about 13 per cent of the land area).

Between 1997 and 2000 some 3 per cent of new dwellings were built within Green Belts, but around 60 per cent of these were on previously developed land. The Sustainable Communities Plan, published in February 2003 (see page 290), includes a government commitment that in each region of England Green Belt land will be maintained or increased.

In Scotland there are seven Green Belt areas totalling 159,000 hectares. A further three Green Belts are now approved in principle at St Andrews, Dunfermline and Perth. There are 245,000 hectares of Green Belt in Northern Ireland; this represents about 18 per cent of the total land area. There are no Green Belts at present in Wales, but their creation is under consideration.

spatial strategies and reviews of existing planning guidance.

The Bill includes specific clauses for Wales that include the introduction of Local Development Plans (LDPs), which would replace Unitary Development Plans. LDPs would be subject to independent examination, with local planning authorities being obliged to act on any recommendations of the inspector prior to formally adopting the plan. The Welsh Assembly

Government would have the power to intervene in the production of a LDP, prior to adoption, if it felt it was unsatisfactory.

In Scotland, development plans are prepared by local authorities and consist of structure and local plans. In the case of National Parks, the Park Authorities have responsibility for the preparation of a National Park Plan and for local planning, and are statutory consultees on structure planning for the area. Following the Review of Strategic Planning, the Scottish Executive outlined a new approach to development planning. It proposed that in the four main cities (Aberdeen, Dundee, Edinburgh and Glasgow), there should be two tiers of development plan: a City Region Plan (CRP) and a Local Development Plan (LDP). Elsewhere there should be a single tier LDP. Councils not involved in CRP should include an explanation of their strategy in the LDP. Certain aspects of the modernisation programme will require legislative change which, subject to parliamentary priorities, will be taken forward through a Planning Bill.

The Scottish Executive's Planning Audit Unit works with planning authorities to establish best practice in development control and development planning, and to highlight areas where improvements could be made to processes and services. By August 2003 two-thirds of Scottish councils had had a planning audit.

In Northern Ireland, the *Modernising Planning Processes Implementation Plan* of February 2003 (see page 301) will reduce the number of development plans by grouping local council areas together, and will provide complete development plan coverage for Northern Ireland by the end of 2006.

Development control

Development control is the process for regulating the development of land. Most forms of development, such as the construction of new buildings, alterations of existing buildings or changes of land use, require permission from the relevant planning authority. Applications are dealt with on the basis of the development plans and other material considerations, including national and regional guidance.

In 2002/03 district planning authorities in England received 634,000 applications for permission, and made 586,000 decisions, granting permission to 86 per cent of applications. Householder developments accounted for 52 per cent of all decisions in 2002/03, compared with 11 per cent for new dwellings and 16 per cent for commercial and industrial developments. Other decisions involved listed buildings or conservation areas, advertisements, or change of use.

Planning authorities in Scotland received a total of 47,600 applications for permission in 2002/03 and granted permission to 94 per cent of these.

In 2002/03, 67 per cent of all planning decisions in England were made within the statutory eight-week period. The Government's target is for 80 per cent of applications to be dealt with within this timeframe. Similar targets apply in Wales, Scotland and Northern Ireland.

In England, Wales and Scotland, a small number of planning applications are referred for decision to the Secretary of State, the Welsh Assembly, or Scottish ministers, rather than being decided by the local planning authority. In general, this only occurs where the planning issue is of more than local importance. A small number are referred for consideration at a public inquiry, such as the Terminal 5 inquiry at London Heathrow Airport, which concluded with government approval for the project.

If a local authority refuses to grant planning permission, grants it with conditions attached or fails to decide an application within eight weeks (or two months in Scotland), the applicant has a right of appeal to the Secretary of State, the Welsh Assembly or Scottish ministers. In Scotland, a consultation paper on modernising public local inquiries was published in June 2003 aimed at improving the inquiry process and identifying best practice. The Executive's White Paper, *Your Place, Your Plan* published in March 2003, sets out the commitment to consult on broadening the right of appeal in planning cases.

The Planning Inspectorate serves both the Deputy Prime Minister in England and the National Assembly for Wales on appeals and other casework on planning, housing, the environment, highways and related legislation. It also provides information and guidance to appellants and other interested parties about the appeal process. In 2002/03, over 15,000 planning appeal cases were determined in England and Wales.

In Scotland, the Scottish Executive Inquiry Reporters Unit is responsible for the determination of the majority of planning appeals and organises public local inquiries into planning proposals and related matters. A total of just over 1,000 cases were determined in Scotland in 2001/02. In Northern Ireland, the applicant has the right of appeal to the Planning Appeals Commission. Major planning applications can be referred to a public inquiry in certain circumstances.

Regeneration

Regeneration policies aim to enhance both the economic and social development of communities through a partnership between the public and private sectors, with a substantial contribution from the latter. They support and complement other programmes tackling social and economic decline, and initiatives such as Sure Start (see page 152), Health Action Zones (see page 166), the Crime Reduction Partnerships (see page 191) and the work of the Social Exclusion Unit (see page 100). Rundown areas in the United Kingdom benefit from European Union Structural Funds, which assist a variety of projects in the least prosperous industrial, urban and rural areas of the European Union. Over £10 billion of Structural Funds, including £3 billion covering Objective 1 areas (see page 345), have been allocated to the United Kingdom for the period 2000–06.

England

In England, the Government and the nine Regional Development Agencies (RDAs, see page 344) set out the priorities for regeneration and ensure that new programmes enhance and complement those already in place. RDA strategies, alongside Regional Planning Guidance overseen by Government Offices (for the Regions), provide a regional framework for economic development and regeneration.

The Department of Trade and Industry is the lead sponsor of the RDAs, with the Government Offices responsible for day-to-day issues. The ODPM and a number of other departments are responsible for financing RDAs and for advising them on the implementation of regional strategies.

RDAs are now supporting regeneration schemes from a single budget worth £1.7 billion in 2003/04 and £2 billion in 2005/06, giving them greater budgetary flexibility and freedom. Under this new framework they will be required to deliver targets set collectively by government departments.

English Partnerships (EP) is sponsored by the ODPM and together with the RDAs form the Government's main regeneration agencies. EP is a key contributor to delivering the Government's *Living Communities* strategy, which was set out in July 2002 and seeks to create new jobs and investment through sustainable economic regeneration and development in the English regions. EP's funding programme will increase from £163 million in 2003/04 to £179 million in 2004/05 and 2005/06.

As well as delivering the *Living Communities* strategy, EP has responsibility for: the Greenwich Peninsula; the National Coalfields Programme; Millennium Communities; support for urban regeneration companies (URC); the English Cities Fund; the National Land Use Database; and the production and maintenance of a national brownfield strategy. Measures announced in the Sustainable Communities Plan in February 2003 (see page 290) will additionally involve EP in working alongside the Forestry Commission and the Environment Agency to create a land restoration trust to provide for the long-term sustainable management of cleaner and safer public open space and forestry across England. EP will also be creating a register of surplus public sector land.

Neighbourhood renewal
In 2001, *New Commitment to Neighbourhood Renewal: A National Strategy Action Plan* set out the Government's plans for delivering economic prosperity, safe communities, high-quality education, decent housing and better health to the poorest parts of the country. At the national level the plan is implemented by the Neighbourhood Renewal Unit in the Office of the Deputy Prime Minister.

Funding for neighbourhood renewal is provided via a number of programmes, including the Neighbourhood Renewal Fund (NRF) and the New Deal for Communities. The NRF provides extra resources for 88 of the most deprived local authority districts in England. The Government announced in April 2003 that the 88 areas would continue to be funded in 2004/05 and 2005/06 at the 2003/04 level. This will amount to £800 million of the £975 million additional resources that have been allocated to the NRF over the two-year period.

Sustainable Communities Award
In March 2003 the Government announced the launch of an award for England's most innovative regeneration schemes. Nominations for the Award for Sustainable Communities are invited from projects that are contributing to making towns and cities better places to live and work. The qualifying criteria include:
- improving the quality of life for local people, by addressing a need or challenge identified by the community;
- demonstrating a high quality of design for spaces and/or buildings;
- demonstrating imaginative ways of creating employment and affordable homes for key workers and the local community; and
- demonstrating the creation of appropriate high-density housing.

The first award will be announced in November 2003.

New Deal for Communities has been running since 1998 and since 1999 has covered 39 neighbourhoods across England. It is a ten-year programme with funding of £1.9 billion. In each area, partnerships have been established between local communities, service providers and other agencies, and the lessons learned from trying out new ideas and policy initiatives are passed on to the wider renewal programme. Each partnership covers a neighbourhood of between 1,000 and 4,000 households and has between £30 million and £60 million to spend over ten years.

Urban renaissance
The Partners in Urban Renaissance project, launched in 2001, is also seeking to develop new ways of dealing with urban problems. Ideas from the project were brought together in a report published in 2002 at the Urban Summit (see page 305). The report provided an assessment of progress on urban regeneration in the 24 towns and cities involved in the project across England and sets out good practice guidelines for drawing up regeneration strategies.

Urban regeneration companies
The first urban regeneration companies (URCs) were formed in England in 1999. URCs are independent partnerships established by local authorities, RDAs, EP and the private sector to produce strategies on physical and economic regeneration. The emphasis of the URCs is on

Urban Summit
The Urban Summit, which took place in autumn 2002, was the largest regeneration conference ever held in England. The summit looked at a wide variety of topics that impact on urban living, such as housing, transport, open spaces and jobs. It brought together an extensive range of delegates including community groups, councils, house builders, architects and designers. The summit aimed to promote a government-wide commitment to urban regeneration, identify progress that had been made by individual towns and review progress on the commitments made in the 2000 Government White Paper on urban policy *Our Towns and Cities: The Future – Delivering an Urban Renaissance*. Ideas arising from the summit were used to inform the development of the Sustainable Communities Plan (see page 290).

physical and economic regeneration. However, they have each produced strategies that cover more than just physical issues and that reflect local circumstances. By April 2003 14 URCs had been established in England.

Parks and open spaces
Good quality parks and green spaces make an important contribution to the quality of life in towns and cities by promoting healthy living and providing play areas and educational benefits for children. In 2002 at the Urban Summit (see box) the Government published the report *Living Places – Cleaner, Safer, Greener*. The report highlighted litter, graffiti and the fear of crime as the reasons people stay away from public spaces. These issues are to be the subject of a five-year improvement programme. Additionally, in February 2003 the Government announced funding of £201 million to improve parks and public spaces. The Commission for Architecture and the Built Environment (CABE) will receive £18 million of this over three years. Part of this funding will be used to set up a green spaces unit (CABE space) with the aim of ensuring good quality design, management and maintenance of public spaces.

Rural regeneration
Although most problems arising from dereliction and unemployment occur in urban areas, some rural areas have also been affected by declining employment in traditional sectors, such as mining, agriculture and rurally-based defence establishments. Even in areas that appear relatively prosperous, some individuals within these areas may be disadvantaged by poor local services, poor public transport and low wages or seasonal unemployment.

The RDAs outside London are responsible for rural regeneration. The Countryside Agency promotes and advises on conserving and enhancing the countryside, on access to the countryside for recreation, and on the economic and social development of England's rural areas. It also administers a number of grants designed to help meet village needs for transport, shops or other services.

Wales
Following the reduction in steel-making capacity and consequent redundancies, announced in 2001, the Welsh Assembly Government announced funding of £76 million to help stimulate the regeneration of the affected communities. Projects include the reopening of the Ebbw Vale rail line for passenger transport, a Community Learning Network and an urban regeneration company for Newport.

Wales is receiving up to £1.2 billion from the European Union to fund a variety of programmes until 2006. These include Objective 1 Funds (see page 345) for West Wales and the Valleys. By March 2003 some £1 billion of Objective 1 Funds had been allocated to almost 800 projects in Wales. The programmes are aimed at developing a stronger, more sustainable economy (especially with an expanded small and medium-sized company sector), better infrastructure, a more highly skilled workforce, and the regeneration of urban and rural communities.

The Welsh Assembly Government has allocated £33 million to the Local Regeneration Fund (LRF) in 2003/04. The purpose of the Fund is to support sustainable regeneration or development within, or benefiting, the most deprived areas, including the Objective 1 area in West Wales and the Valleys. Some of the money is used to match funding provided by European structural funds.

Communities First is an area-based regeneration programme that will benefit the 100 most deprived electoral wards, and other communities including 32 pockets of deprivation. The programme emphasises the involvement of local people in decision-making through a community-based partnership. The Welsh

Llanhilleth regeneration scheme

The Llanhilleth regeneration scheme, launched in March 2003, aims to help alleviate the impact of steel closures on the local community. The Welsh Assembly Government is investing £6 million in the £10 million project, with other funding being provided from Objective 1, Communities First and the Welsh Development Agency. The scheme will cover the building of a combined school and institute, a road junction, industrial units, a village square, and associated infrastructure.

Assembly Government has allocated £152 million to the programme between 2001 and 2006.

The Welsh Development Agency also contributes to economic regeneration across Wales. Its programmes include physical and environmental regeneration activities, such as land reclamation and environmental improvements; activities to provide site development work to assist with business infrastructure; and financial support for community initiatives, such as the Market Towns Initiative and the Small Towns and Villages programmes.

Scotland

The Social Inclusion Partnership (SIP) programme, established in 1999, involves 48 local partnerships tackling the problems that disadvantaged groups and communities face across rural and urban Scotland. The SIPs are multi-agency partnerships, consisting of all relevant local public agencies, the voluntary and private sectors, and representatives from the community. The SIPs are supported over three years from 2001/02 by £169 million from the Social Inclusion Partnership Fund.

Scottish Enterprise is the main economic development agency for Scotland, covering 93 per cent of the population from Grampian to the Borders. Communities Scotland also has a responsibility for regeneration. It works closely with a number of partners, in particular local authorities. The planned budget for Communities Scotland for regeneration schemes in 2003/04 is over £90 million.

Northern Ireland

The Department for Social Development (DSD) has a lead role in addressing social need and social inclusion in Northern Ireland. It does this through its main business areas – housing, social security, child support, urban regeneration and community development.

The DSD uses a combination of public and private sector investment as well as contributions from the European Union's Structural Funds and the International Fund for Ireland to carry out regeneration of Northern Ireland's towns and cities.

Physical development schemes have been one of the most important elements of urban regeneration policy in Northern Ireland. The most frequently used initiatives are:

- the Urban Development Grant (UDG), which aims to encourage physical and economic regeneration in targeted areas and seeks to promote job creation, inward investment and environmental improvement through the development of vacant derelict or underused land and buildings;
- Comprehensive Development Schemes which contribute to the regeneration of disadvantaged areas through development or redevelopment; and
- Environmental Improvement Schemes which help to improve the appearance of public spaces in town and city centres across Northern Ireland.

Social, community and economic regeneration have also been major strands of regeneration policy since the late 1980s. *Making Belfast Work* and the *Londonderry Regeneration Initiative* were introduced at that time to direct more government funding into the most disadvantaged part of these two cities. The Laganside Corporation has been a model for brownfield regeneration in Belfast and has successfully transformed the waterfront area. Outside these cities the Community Regeneration and Improvement Special Programme (CRISP) has regenerated run-down town and village centres.

The Neighbourhood Renewal Strategy, launched in June 2003, sets out the long-term direction for the renewal of the most deprived neighbourhoods in urban areas of Northern Ireland. The *Heart of the City* (August 2003) is an integrated urban design strategy for Londonderry, which will inform the future planning and design of key development sites. The strategy places an emphasis on high-quality architecture, public open spaces and landscaped areas.

The consultation document *Belfast City Centre Regeneration Policy Framework*, published in July 2003, outlines the direction needed to guide and maximise the regeneration potential of investment in the city centre for the benefit of Belfast and Northern Ireland as a whole.

Further reading

ODPM Annual Report 2003. Cm 5906. The Stationery Office, 2003.

The Housing Corporation: Annual Review. The Housing Corporation.

2001 English House Condition Survey. Office of the Deputy Prime Minister. The Stationery Office, 2003.

English Partnerships: Annual Report and Financial Statements. English Partnerships, 2003.

Housing Statistics (annual). Office of the Deputy Prime Minister. The Stationery Office.

Sustainable Communities: Building for the Future. Office of the Deputy Prime Minister, 2003.

Social Trends (annual). Office for National Statistics. The Stationery Office.

Websites

Office of the Deputy Prime Minister
www.odpm.gov.uk

National Assembly for Wales
www.wales.gov.uk

Scottish Executive
www.scotland.gov.uk

Northern Ireland Executive
www.nics.gov.uk

English Partnerships
www.englishpartnerships.co.uk

Council of Mortgage Lenders
www.cml.org.uk

Housing Corporation
www.housingcorp.gov.uk

Communities Scotland
www.communitiesscotland.gov.uk

Northern Ireland Housing Executive
www.nihe.gov.uk

WWW.

21 Transport

Introduction

British residents travelled on average around 11,000 kilometres a year within Great Britain between 1999 and 2001, about 50 per cent further than in the early 1970s. Both the number and length of trips have increased. In 1975–76 the average British resident made 935 trips a year, with an average length of 8.2 kilometres per trip. By 1999–2001 these figures had increased to 1,019 trips and 10.8 kilometres respectively.

Travel by car or van is by far the dominant form of transport in Great Britain, accounting for 85 per cent of passenger-kilometres in 2001 (see Table 21.1). Nearly three-quarters of households have access to at least one car or van. In 2001, 44 per cent had one only, 29 per cent had two or more, and 27 per cent had no car.

Table 21.1 Passenger transport, by mode,[1] Great Britain

	Billion passenger-kilometres		
	1991	2000	2001
Buses and coaches	44	45	46
Cars, vans and taxis	582	618	624
Motorcycles, mopeds and scooters	6	5	5
Pedal cycles	5	4	4
All road	**637**	**672**	**679**
Rail[2]	39	47	47
Air[3]	5	8	8
All modes[4]	**681**	**726**	**734**

1 Since 2000 figures have been produced on a different basis and are not directly comparable with earlier years.
2 Financial years. Includes urban rail systems and underground railways.
3 Excludes air taxis, private flying and passengers paying less than 25 per cent of the full fare. Includes Northern Ireland and the Channel Islands.
4 Excludes travel by water within the United Kingdom.
Source: Department for Transport

Leisure was the most common reason for travel in Great Britain between 1999 and 2001, accounting for 31 per cent of all trips made. Shopping was the reason for 21 per cent of trips, and commuting for a further 15 per cent. Despite the increase in both the distance travelled and the number of trips taken, there have been reductions in the death rates from accidents involving most forms of transport since the 1980s (Table 21.2). For example, the death rate from accidents involving cars more than halved between 1981 and 2001.

Roads

The length of the total road network in Great Britain in 2001 was 392,408 kilometres. Trunk motorways (motorways that are the direct responsibility of central government rather than the local authority) accounted for 3,428 kilometres of this, less than 1 per cent, and other trunk roads for 11,726 kilometres, or 3 per cent. However,

Table 21.2 Passenger death rates: by mode, Great Britain

	Rate per billion passenger-kilometres		
	1981	1991	2001
Motorcycle	115.8	94.7	122.7
Walk	76.9	69.3	46.9
Pedal cycle	56.9	46.5	34.5
Car	6.1	3.7	2.9
Van	3.8	2.1	0.9
Water[1]	0.4	0.0	0.5
Bus or coach	0.3	0.6	0.2
Rail[2]	1.0	0.8	0.1
Air[1]	0.2	0.0	0.0

1 Data are for the United Kingdom.
2 Financial years. Includes train accidents and accidents occurring through movement of railway vehicles.
Source: Department for Transport

motorways carry 20 per cent of all traffic, and trunk roads another 16 per cent. Combined, they carry over two-thirds of all goods vehicle traffic in Great Britain. In Northern Ireland the road network was 24,788 kilometres in length at the end of 2001/02, of which 114 kilometres was motorway.

Motor vehicles

The number of licensed vehicles on Great Britain's roads increased by 55 per cent between 1982 and 2002, reaching nearly 30.6 million (Table 21.3). This increase is more than accounted for by the rise in the number of private cars. The number of some types of vehicle, such as goods vehicles and motorcycles, fell between 1982 and 2002.

Despite the increase in the number of cars in Great Britain over the last 20 years, in 1999 there were fewer cars per person in Great Britain than the EU average (Figure 21.4) – 414 passenger cars per 1,000 people, compared with 460.

Driving licences and driver standards

Over 71 per cent of adults in Great Britain hold a full car driving licence – some 32.3 million people between 1999 and 2001. New drivers of motor vehicles must pass both a computer-based touch screen theory test and a practical driving test in order to acquire a full driving licence. In 2001/02, 1.3 million car driving tests were conducted in Great Britain by the Driving Standards Agency (DSA), the national driver testing authority. The pass rate for the tests has fallen from 65 per cent to 50 per cent in recent years. The DSA also supervises professional driving instructors, the compulsory basic training scheme for learner motorcyclists and a voluntary register for instructors of drivers of large goods vehicles.

Figure 21.4 Passenger cars per thousand inhabitants, 1999

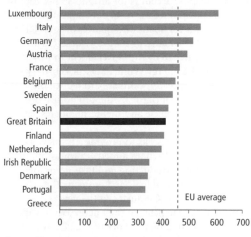

Numbers

Source: Eurostat

Minimum ages for driving in the United Kingdom are:

- 16 for riders of mopeds, drivers of small tractors, and disabled people receiving a mobility allowance;
- 17 for drivers of cars and other passenger vehicles with nine or fewer seats (including that of the driver), small motorcycles, and goods vehicles not over 3.5 tonnes maximum authorised mass (MAM);
- 18 for goods vehicles weighing over 3.5, but not over 7.5, tonnes MAM; and
- 21 for passenger-carrying vehicles with more than nine seats, goods vehicles over 7.5 tonnes MAM and large motorcycles.

Vehicle standards

Before most new cars and goods vehicles are allowed on the roads, they must meet safety and environmental requirements, based primarily on standards drawn up by the European Union (EU). The Vehicle Certification Agency is responsible for ensuring these requirements are met, through a process known as 'type approval'.

The Vehicle Inspectorate is responsible for ensuring the roadworthiness of vehicles, through annual testing. It also uses roadside and other enforcement checks to ensure that drivers and vehicle operators comply with legislation. In Northern Ireland the Driver and Vehicle Testing

Table 21.3 Motor vehicles licensed in Great Britain

			Thousands
	1982	1992	2002
Private cars	15,264	19,870	24,543
Goods vehicles	477	432	425
Motorcycles	1,370	684	941
Buses	n/a	72	92
Total¹	**19,762**	**24,577**	**30,557**

1 Total includes Crown and exempt vehicles, and other vehicles.
Source: Department for Transport

Agency is responsible for testing both vehicles and drivers.

New vehicle and fuel technologies

Road transport accounts for around 85 per cent of the transport sector's carbon emissions, which in turn account for about one-quarter of total UK emissions. The *Powering Future Vehicles* (PFV) strategy, launched by the Government in July 2002, and the Energy White Paper of February 2003 (see chapter 29) both seek to reduce the negative effects of traffic by the promotion of better, cleaner vehicle and fuel technologies.

The PFV strategy seeks to provide a framework for decisions and action, aimed at promoting the development, introduction and take-up of low-carbon vehicles and fuels and ensuring the involvement of UK industry in the new technologies. Elements of the Energy White Paper intended to build on the work of the PFV strategy and promote the development of alternative fuels include encouraging manufacturers to develop Liquid Petroleum Gas (LPG) powered vehicles, and reducing the duty on biodiesel and bioethanol to 20 pence per litre less than the standard diesel rate.

Traffic and congestion

Estimated traffic levels in Great Britain rose by 2.5 per cent between 2001 and 2002, to 486 billion vehicle kilometres. This increase partly reflected the impact of foot and mouth disease (see page 404) on traffic in 2001, and it is estimated that the underlying increase was between 1 and 2 per cent.

About 7 per cent of the network of the Highways Agency (see page 315) in England experiences regular heavy peak and occasional non-peak congestion, and a further 13 per cent sees heavy congestion on at least half the days in the year. Research by the Department for Transport (DfT) suggests that during the morning peak, drivers on England's trunk roads lose an average of nine seconds for every kilometre travelled due to congestion. For drivers in London, this rises to 66 seconds.

Traffic management schemes aim to reduce congestion through measures such as traffic-free shopping precincts, bus lanes and other bus priority measures, red routes with special stopping controls, and parking controls. The DfT has a target to reduce congestion on the inter-urban road network and in large urban areas in England to below 2000 levels by 2010, as part of its commitment to the Government's Sustainable Development Programme (see chapter 22).

Congestion charging

Local authorities in England and Wales can introduce congestion charging schemes for road users or a levy on workplace parking. The net revenue generated from charges can be retained for at least ten years, provided that it is used to fund local transport improvements. Authorities must consult local people and businesses, make improvements to public transport and obtain ministerial approval before starting schemes.

Great Britain's first congestion charging scheme, in the historic centre of Durham, began in 2002. The revenue is being used to fund improvements to the city's bus services.

A congestion charging scheme in central London went into operation in February 2003. The congestion charging zone is 21 square kilometres, with 174 entry and exit points around its boundary. The owners of cars entering or moving around the zone are charged £5, payable in advance or up until 10.00 pm on the day by telephone, Internet, post or at retail outlets (residents within the zone receive a 90 per cent discount). Around 100,000 payments are received each weekday, while evening and weekend travel remain uncharged. Penalties for non-payment range from £5 if the charge is paid late on the day of travel to £120 for late payment of the Penalty Charge Notice that is issued for non-payment. The scheme is expected to raise £70 million a year.

The original aim of the scheme was to reduce traffic in central London by 10 to 15 per cent, and

Table 21.5 Motor vehicle traffic: by road class, Great Britain

			Billion vehicle-kilometres
	1993	2001	2002
Motorways	68.2	90.7	92.4
Urban major roads[1]	77.3	81.5	81.8
Rural major roads	113.3	133.2	136.5
Minor roads	153.3	168.5	175.2
All roads	412.2	473.9	485.9

1 Urban roads are those within an urban settlement with a population of more than 10,000 people.
Source: Department for Transport

journey delays by 20 to 30 per cent. Observations from the first six weeks of operation suggested that levels of traffic have stabilised at around 16 per cent lower within the zone across the charging day, and congestion reduced by some 40 per cent.

Traffic information

Traffic information is provided throughout Great Britain by a variety of means, such as the media, roadside signs and in-vehicle systems. Information sources include roadside sensors, the traffic police and highway authorities, and data are collated by organisations such as the Automobile Association (AA) and the Royal Automobile Club (RAC), and by information service providers like Integrated Traffic Information Services (ITIS), Metro Networks and Trafficmaster.

Local traffic control centres across Great Britain help to manage traffic and provide information about conditions. The Highways Agency has entered into a public-private partnership (PPP, see page 357) with Traffic Information Services to set up and run the Traffic Control Centre (TCC). The TCC is intended to provide a coordinated national information service to travellers in England by early 2004. Up-to-the-minute details will be available via variable message signs, the Highways Agency information line, the Internet, the media and commercial driver-information services.

Scotland operates a national network control centre and Wales has two regional traffic control centres. These provide a broad range of services that include both the work undertaken by English control centres and the forthcoming TCC.

The blue badge scheme

The blue badge scheme provides parking concessions for people with severe walking difficulties who travel as either car drivers or passengers. It also applies to registered blind people and people with very severe upper limb difficulties. Badge holders are allowed to park close to their destination. For example, cars displaying a blue badge may park free of charge and without time limit at parking meters, or in special parking bays near the exits of car parks. Blue badges also enable holders to park in areas where there are concessions for disabled people in any European Members States.

Road safety

In 2002 there were 0.5 per cent fewer road deaths, and 21 per cent fewer people killed or seriously injured, in Great Britain compared with the average for the years 1994 to 1998. Road traffic increased by 10 per cent over the same period. In 2002 there were 221,751 road accidents involving personal injury in Great Britain, 3 per cent fewer than in 2001, of which 33,645 involved death or serious injury. There were 3,431 deaths in road accidents, 35,976 serious injuries and 263,198 slight injuries.

Overall, Great Britain has one of the best road safety records in the world. Even so, the Government has set a target of reducing the number of people killed or seriously injured on the roads by 40 per cent by 2010, compared with the average level for 1994–98. A higher target reduction, of 50 per cent, has been set for deaths and serious injuries to children. Measures taken include creating more 20 mph zones around schools and in residential areas. Road safety education is also being improved, for example through a network of road safety schemes for children, and improvements in child pedestrian training.

Research has found that children from disadvantaged backgrounds are five times more likely to be killed or seriously injured on the roads than children in the highest socio-economic group. In October 2002 the Government announced £18 million of funding to help councils in deprived areas of England that have high incidences of child pedestrian casualties to develop strategies to tackle the problem. Possible measures include improved play areas, more road safety education and re-examining after-school care.

20th anniversary of compulsory seat belts

Wearing seat belts when driving or sitting in the front seat of a car was made mandatory in 1983. The DfT estimates that in the 20 years since then, front seat belts have saved 50,000 lives, and prevented 590,000 serious casualties and 1.5 million minor casualties. It became mandatory for child rear seat passengers to wear a seat belt in 1989, and for adult rear passengers in 1991.

Motoring offences

The number of motoring offences dealt with by official police action or penalty charge notice (including those issued by traffic wardens and local authority traffic attendants) in England and Wales in 2001 was 10.5 million. This was 5 per cent more than in 2000 and the highest number recorded. There were 389 offences per 1,000 licensed vehicles, compared with 403 in 1997 and 370 per 1,000 in 1991. A total of 19 per cent of offences were dealt with by court proceedings in 2001, while 79 per cent were dealt with by a fixed penalty notice or penalty charge notice.

Obstruction, waiting and parking offences together accounted for 6.7 million offences, while speed limit offences accounted for 1.4 million. Nearly 624,000 screening breath tests for alcohol were carried out in 2001 – 16 per cent of these tests were positive or refused, the highest proportion since 1992.

Cameras provided evidence for 1.1 million offences dealt with in England and Wales in 2001, including 72 per cent of speeding offences. Research carried out for the DfT suggests that between April 2000 and March 2002 there was a 35 per cent reduction in deaths and serious injuries from road accidents at sites where speed cameras were in operation. The number of vehicles speeding at camera sites was 67 per cent lower than at comparable sites without cameras.

Road haulage
Most freight in Great Britain is carried by road, which accounts for over four-fifths of goods by tonnage and more than two-thirds in terms of tonne-kilometres.

An operator's licence is required for operating goods vehicles over 3.5 tonnes gross weight in the United Kingdom. About 88 per cent of the 107,000 licences in issue are for fleets of five or fewer vehicles, and there are around 430,000 heavy goods vehicles (HGVs) in the United Kingdom. Road haulage traffic by HGVs amounted to 150 billion tonne-kilometres in Great Britain in 2002, 24 per cent more than in 1992. Road hauliers are tending to use larger vehicles carrying heavier loads – 87 per cent of the traffic, in terms of tonne-kilometres, is now carried by vehicles of over 25 tonnes gross weight.

International road haulage has grown rapidly. In 2002 about 2.5 million road goods vehicles travelled by ferry or the Channel Tunnel to mainland Europe, a 5 per cent increase over 2001. Of these, around 490,000 were powered vehicles registered in the United Kingdom. UK vehicles

carried 13.3 million tonnes internationally and 96 per cent of this traffic was with the EU.

The Government's long-term strategy for freight in the United Kingdom seeks to reduce the extent to which economic growth generates additional lorry movements, by improving efficiency, making the most of rail, shipping and inland waterways, and improving interchange links between the different types of transport. Measures include an increase in the maximum weight of lorries on domestic journeys to 44 tonnes in 2001. The Freight Facilities Grant scheme provides assistance towards capital costs associated with moving freight by inland waterway, coastal and short sea routes rather than road.

Bus services
In 2001/02, 4,347 million passenger journeys were made on local bus services in Great Britain, 1 per cent more than in the previous year. Passenger journeys on local buses had been in decline for decades, reaching a low of 4,248 million in 1998/99, but have been increasing in recent years. The number of passenger journeys in London grew from the mid-1990s, and reached 1,434 million in 2001/02, a 5.5 per cent increase on the previous year. About one in three of all passenger journeys on local buses now occur in London. There has also been an increase in bus use in Scotland, with passenger journeys rising by 6 million to 441 million in 2001/02. The ten-year plan (see page 323) target for bus use in England is for a growth of 10 per cent in passenger numbers between 2000 and 2010.

There are over 93,000 buses and coaches in Great Britain in public service. Of these about one-third are small buses with up to 35 seats, while around a fifth are double-deckers. The proportion of single deck buses has increased in recent years, particularly those of low floor design, while the proportion of double-deckers has fallen.

Operators
Almost all bus services in Great Britain are provided by private sector concerns, apart from 17 bus companies owned by local authorities. Transport for London is responsible for providing or procuring public transport in the capital. It oversees approximately 700 bus routes run by about 25 companies under contract.

Five main groups operate bus services: Arriva, FirstGroup, Go-Ahead Group, National Express

Group and Stagecoach. All also run rail services and some have expanded into transport services in other countries.

In Northern Ireland almost all road passenger services are operated by subsidiaries of the publicly owned Northern Ireland Transport Holding Company (NITHC), collectively known as 'Translink'. Citybus Ltd operates services in Belfast, and Ulsterbus Ltd runs most of the services in the rest of Northern Ireland, accounting for 20 million and 46 million passenger journeys a year respectively.

50th anniversary of Routemaster buses

The year 2004 is the 50th anniversary of the Routemaster bus. A familiar sight on the streets of London, nearly 2,900 of these buses were built between 1954 and 1968, and over 600 are still in service. Routemasters differ from modern buses in that the entrance is at the back of the bus and has no door, allowing passengers to jump on and off. A conductor collects fares, which means less congestion is caused by buses remaining stationary while passengers pay the driver. However, Routemaster buses are difficult to access for disabled passengers or those carrying child buggies, as well as being expensive to operate. They are being replaced on several routes with single deck articulated low floor buses. The replacement buses are cashless: the fare must be paid in advance via methods such as travelcards or stored value cards, or at roadside ticket machines.

Services

Most local bus services are provided commercially, although local authorities may subsidise services that are not commercially viable but are considered socially necessary. Over 80 per cent of bus services in Great Britain outside London were operated commercially in 2001/02.

Bus fares in Great Britain increased by 2 per cent in real terms (after allowing for inflation) in the year ending March 2002. However, fares in London fell by 3 per cent. Overall, bus fares have risen by 21 per cent in Great Britain over the last decade, while those in London rose by 15 per cent.

Local authorities in England and Wales are required to develop bus strategies as part of their Local Transport Plans (LTPs – see page 323). In Scotland, local authorities are expected to set out their views on bus services in their Local Transport Strategies. Outside London statutory backing also exists for 'bus quality partnerships' and 'quality contracts' between local authorities and bus operators. Similar partnerships have already been developed voluntarily in around 130 towns and cities, and have led to better services with higher-quality buses, and typically 10 to 20 per cent greater passenger use. Authorities have powers to promote joint ticketing and to work with Train Operating Companies on bus/rail ticketing.

Bus priority measures, such as bus lanes, are becoming more extensive, while in some areas innovative measures, such as guided busways (with buses travelling on segregated track) are being adopted. Over 80 park and ride schemes – in which car users park on the outskirts of towns and travel by bus to the centre – are in operation in England and Scotland, and are being increasingly used to relieve traffic congestion. Over 120 new schemes are envisaged in England over the next ten years. Similar schemes operate in Wales and Northern Ireland.

A number of schemes are in operation which provide funds for improving local bus services. In England, the Rural Bus Subsidy Grant has funding of £136 million between 2001/02 and 2003/04 for the provision of new and enhanced local bus services. The Urban Bus Challenge plays a similar role in towns and cities, and has been allocated £46 million over the same period. In addition, the Rural Bus Challenge is an annual competition in which local authorities bid for project funding. It has been allocated £60 million between 2001/02 and 2003/04. The Welsh Assembly Government is allocating more than £8 million in 2003/04 to increase the number and range of subsidised bus services and support community transport projects, while in Scotland, the Executive's Rural Transport Fund has provided for over 400 new or improved rural bus services since its introduction in 1998/99.

Local authorities in England are required by law to offer, as a minimum, half price bus travel concessionary schemes for the elderly and disabled. In 2001, 94 per cent of local authorities offered a half fare concessionary scheme. The remainder either had flat-fare schemes or schemes offering free travel, such as in London. Travel on local bus services in Wales is free for pensioners and disabled people, while in Scotland, there is a national minimum standard of free off-peak local bus fares for elderly and disabled people. Travel on public transport in Northern Ireland is free for registered blind people and for everyone over the age of 65. In February 2003 people with a range of specified disabilities became eligible to travel at half fare.

Coaches account for much of the non-local mileage operated by public service vehicles, which totalled 1,590 million vehicle-kilometres in 2001/02. Organised coach tours and holiday journeys account for about 60 per cent of coach travel in Great Britain. High-frequency scheduled services, run by private sector operators, link many towns and cities, and commuter services run into London and some other major centres each weekday. The biggest coach operator, National Express, has a national network of scheduled coach services and carries about 12 million passengers each year.

Taxis

There are about 63,000 licensed taxis in England and Wales (mainly in urban areas), around 9,600 in Scotland, and over 3,700 in Northern Ireland. In London (which has over 20,000 taxis) and several other major cities, taxis must be purpose-built to conform to strict requirements. In many districts, taxi drivers have to pass a test of their knowledge of the area.

Private hire vehicles (PHVs or 'minicabs') have increased in number in recent years and there are now over 79,000 PHVs in England and Wales, over 9,000 in Scotland and around 2,000 in Northern Ireland. PHVs may only be booked through the operator and not hired on the street. Licences are required for PHV operators in England and Wales. In London, licensing of PHV operators is under way, and there are now 2,100 licensed operators. Since April 2003 all PHV drivers in London have been obliged to meet licensing standards set by the Public Carriage Office, in order to trade legally in the capital.

Cycling and motorcycling

After a long period of decline, the use of two-wheeled transport in Great Britain has stabilised in the last decade, albeit at a low level. In 2001, cycling and motorcycling accounted for 1 per cent each of total passenger-kilometres travelled in Great Britain. However, there has been a revival in interest in motorcycling over the last few years. The number of licensed motorcycles rose from a low of 594,000 in 1995 to 941,000 in 2002, the highest figure since 1987.

The National Cycling Strategy aims to increase the number of pedal cycle journeys fourfold by 2012 (based on 1996 figures). The Cycling Forum for England is coordinating the implementation of the Strategy, which has been endorsed by the Government. The Scottish Cycle Forum coordinates implementation in Scotland, and Wales and Northern Ireland also have their own strategies. The DfT announced its own target of trebling the number of cycling journeys by 2010, as part of the Government's ten-year plan. Cycling strategies form part of Local Transport Plans and Strategies, and include measures to make cycling safer and more convenient.

The National Cycle Network comprised 10,460 kilometres of cycling and walking routes throughout the United Kingdom in 2003. Developed by the transport charity Sustrans (*www.sustrans.org.uk*), the network will cover 16,000 kilometres when it is completed in 2005. Over a third of the network will be entirely free from motor traffic by utilising old railway lines, canal towpaths, river paths and derelict land, as well as new infrastructure. The remainder will follow existing roads, with traffic calming and cycle lanes being implemented where necessary. An estimated 97 million trips were made on the network in 2002, and around 50 per cent of users are cyclists and 48 per cent pedestrians. Sustrans estimates that more than half of all network users making functional journeys could have chosen a car instead of cycling or walking.

Walking

People in the United Kingdom are walking less than in the past, with fewer journeys on foot and many more by car. The Government wishes to reverse this trend, and expects local authorities to give more priority to walking. Almost all local authorities included walking in their Local Transport Plans and Strategies, many identifying targets to encourage walking, through a variety of initiatives. LTP funding can be used to make walking safer and more accessible, for example by improving pavement and footway maintenance, removing obstructions and improving pedestrian crossings.

Home Zones are residential streets in which the road space is shared between the drivers of motor vehicles and other road users, with the wider needs of residents (including people who walk or cycle, and children) in mind. The aim is to change the way that streets are used, for example by

23 May 2003 Hadrian's Wall National Trail opens to the public.
The 135-kilometre path takes an average seven days to complete.

29 May 2003 50th anniversary of the British-led expedition to the summit of Mount Everest. This photograph of the late Tenzing Norgay was taken at the summit by Sir Edmund Hillary.

30 May 2003 closure of the Royal Mail's 75-year-old miniature MailRail that ran under the streets of central London. Cutbacks over the years had reduced the number of stations from nine to three: Paddington, Mount Pleasant and Whitechapel. MailRail carried around 4 million letters and parcels a day.

31 May 2003 the AXA English FA Cup Final was held at the all-weather Millennium Stadium in Cardiff, where Arsenal defeated Southampton.

Above: two weeks earlier Glasgow Rangers beat Dundee at Hampden Park to win the Tennents Scottish FA Cup Final; 2002/03 was a good season for Rangers, which became the first football club to win 50 League championships.

2 June 2003 the British space probe, Beagle 2, is launched in a rocket from Kazakhstan. It is part of the European Space Agency's mission to try to discover if there is life on Mars.

2 June 2003 50th anniversary of the coronation of Queen Elizabeth II is celebrated with a special service at Westminster Abbey and a children's tea party in the garden at Buckingham Palace *(below)* complete with a fairground, clowns and a bouncy castle. The children were invited by a number of charities.

encouraging people to walk rather than use their cars, and to improve the quality of life of local residents. Thirteen pilot schemes are in operation across the United Kingdom; one, in Northmoor, Manchester, has already seen a significant drop in car speeds, by up to 10 mph. In addition, £30 million has been allocated under the Home Zones Challenge to a total of 61 projects, which include wholly new zones as well as extensions of the pilot schemes.

Safe routes to school projects aim to encourage and enable children to walk and cycle to school (*www.saferoutestoschool.org*). They combine practical measures, such as redesigns of roadspace to provide for cyclists and pedestrians and 20 mph speed limits near schools, with educational measures, for example cycle training for children and an emphasis on the health benefits of walking and cycling.

The road programme

The maintenance, operation and improvement of the motorway and trunk road network in England is the responsibility of the Highways Agency (*www.highways.gov.uk*), an executive agency of the DfT. In London, responsibility for most major roads lies with the Greater London Authority. In Wales, Scotland and Northern Ireland responsibility for the motorway and trunk road network rests with the devolved administrations.

The Highways Agency operates England's 9,380 kilometres of strategic, or trunk, road network. Its budget for programme expenditure (which excludes the costs of administration and costs associated with network investment, such as depreciation and the cost of capital) is £1.7 billion in 2003/04, with a planned increase to £1.9 billion in 2005/06. In addition, local authorities have a budget of nearly £2.6 billion in 2003/04 for maintaining non-trunk roads. In Scotland the motorway and trunk road programme for 2003/04 will cost £250 million.

The Highways Agency's 2003/04 programme includes plans to spend £748 million on maintenance; £680 million on major road projects, including 11 projects intended to ease congestion and improve safety; and £242 million on smaller improvement schemes, including the use of new technology.

A £5.5 billion package of major national and local transport measures was announced in December 2002. It included plans to widen the M6 between Manchester and Birmingham and the M1 in the East Midlands from three to four lanes, as well as proposals to protect the Stonehenge World Heritage Site (see page 274) alongside the A303 in Wiltshire. A further £7 billion (£4 billion of which is allocated 10-year-plan money) of funding for improvements to some of Great Britain's most congested roads was announced in July 2003. This funding is intended to ensure that better use is made of existing roads, for example by building new capacity along particularly busy stretches and making improvements to public transport. Key elements include widening sections of the M25, M1 and M11, and funding of up to £1 billion for a package of major public transport and road improvements to the West Midlands conurbation.

The M6 toll, Great Britain's first toll motorway, is due to open in January 2004. Built and operated by a private sector company, the 43-kilometre, three lane road will bypass the busiest section of the existing M6 in the West Midlands, one of the most congested roads in Western Europe. The standard charge for using the motorway will be £3 for cars, while Heavy Goods Vehicles will pay £10.

In Scotland, the motorway and trunk road network extends to almost 3,500 kilometres, around 6 per cent of the total road network. The 2002 Scottish budget allocated around £300 million a year to the motorway and trunk road network over the period 2003/04 to 2005/06. The current programme includes a number of major improvement projects, including the completion of the M74 in Glasgow.

Railways

Network Rail (*www.networkrail.co.uk*) is responsible for operating all track and infrastructure in Great Britain. Its assets include 33,800 kilometres of track; 40,000 bridges, tunnels and viaducts; 2,500 stations; and connections to over 1,000 freight terminals. It took over Railtrack plc, the previous track and infrastructure operating company, after that company was placed into administration in 2002. Network Rail is a company limited by guarantee – a private company without shareholders, run along commercial lines. It aims to make surpluses from its operations and, instead of paying dividends, invest profits in improvements in the rail infrastructure.

Table 21.6 Passenger traffic on rail,[1] underground and selected light rail services, Great Britain

Million passenger-kilometres

	1992/93	2001/02	2002/03
National railways	31,700	39,100	39,700
London Underground	5,758	7,451	7,367
Glasgow Underground	39	44	43
Docklands Light Railway (London)	33	207	232
Greater Manchester Metro	53	161	165
Tyne and Wear Metro	271	238	275
Croydon Tramlink (London)	.	99	100
Centro (West Midlands)	.	50	50
Stagecoach Supertram (Sheffield)	.	39	40

1 Excludes Heathrow Express.
Source: Department for Transport

Most railway services in the United Kingdom are now operated by the private sector. Apart from 15 major stations operated directly by Network Rail, nearly all stations and passenger depots are leased to the passenger Train Operating Companies (TOCs) that run passenger services under franchise. There are currently 25 TOCs. Many franchises are for seven years, but some are for 10, 12 or 15 years.

The TOCs, such as First Great Western, South West Trains and GNER, lease their rolling stock from the three main rolling stock companies: Angel Trains, HSBC Rail and Porterbrook Leasing. Freight services are run by five companies, and there are a number of infrastructure maintenance companies.

There are also over 100 other passenger-carrying railways, often connected with the preservation of steam locomotives. Services are operated mostly on a voluntary basis and cater mainly for tourists and railway enthusiasts.

Rail regulation and strategy

The regulation of Great Britain's railways is the responsibility of two organisations: the Strategic Rail Authority (SRA) and the Office of the Rail Regulator (ORR). The two organisations have common statutory purposes but different powers to achieve them. The SRA is subject to directions and guidance from the Government, while the ORR is independent.

The SRA is responsible for providing strategic leadership to the rail industry; allocating government funding to the railways; negotiating, awarding and monitoring the franchises for operating rail services; and a number of other statutory functions, in particular relating to customer protection. Government support to the rail industry amounted to approximately £1.8 billion in 2001/02.

The Rail Regulator provides independent economic regulation of the monopoly and dominant elements of the rail industry, particularly Network Rail's stewardship of the national rail network. In addition, the Regulator licenses the railway operators, approves or directs agreements governing access to track, stations and depots, and enforces competition law in connection with the provision of rail services.

The SRA's ten-year plan for the railways, published in 2002, set out the changes required by 2010 to meet the Government's targets for rail – a 50 per cent increase in passenger-kilometres, reductions in overcrowding, and an 80 per cent increase in freight tonne-kilometres. The Authority published its second *Strategic Plan* in January 2003. The plan seeks to tackle the short-term challenges facing the industry while also taking a longer-term view. Priorities identified for the short term include the modernisation of the West Coast route and the upgrading of the Southern power supply, while longer-term plans include a possible North-South high speed line and the Crossrail project in London.

The SRA has embarked on a new refranchising programme, designed to help deliver the Government's ten-year plan targets. Wherever franchises are replaced or extended, new contracts will prioritise provision of better facilities, higher performance incentives for operators and better compensation arrangements for passengers when things go wrong. The Authority also intends that in the future each major London terminal will have only one operator. The first such combined franchise, 'Greater Anglia', operating from London Liverpool Street, will be awarded from 2004.

Rail safety

There have been a number of high-profile fatal rail accidents in recent years, including incidents at Southall (London) in 1997, Ladbroke Grove, near Paddington (London), in 1999, Hatfield (Hertfordshire) in 2000 and Potters Bar (Hertfordshire) in 2002. Nevertheless, there is evidence that overall trends in railway safety are improving (see Table 21.2). Health and Safety Executive (HSE) figures for Great Britain show that in 2001/02 there were 92 significant train incidents (that is, most collisions and derailments involving passenger trains). This is the second lowest number of incidents on record. Five people were killed in train accidents in 2001/02, compared with 17 in 2000/01.

Measures being taken to improve the safety of the railway network include:

- the fitting of the train protection and warning system (TPWS) to the national network by the end of 2003 (99 per cent of passenger trains and 66 per cent of freight trains had been fitted by May 2003);
- the development of plans to fit the new European automatic train protection (ATP) system as lines that are included in the European high-speed network are upgraded; and
- the development of a new national safety plan to improve safety management and ensure best practice.

Passenger services

The passenger network (see map in the first colour section) comprises a fast inter-city network, linking the main city-centres of Great Britain; local and regional services; and commuter services in and around the large conurbations, especially London and the South East. Passenger traffic is growing (see Table 21.6) and on the national railways rose by 1 per cent in 2002/03 to 39.7 billion passenger-kilometres, representing some 976 million passenger journeys.

According to the SRA's Public Performance Measure, an average of 79 per cent of scheduled services ran to timetable in 2002/03.

Northern Ireland

Northern Ireland Railways, a wholly owned subsidiary of the NITHC (see page 313), operates the railway service on about 467 kilometres of track and handled 6.3 million passenger journeys in 2002/03. The NITHC is currently undertaking a programme to improve the railway network, with increased expenditure provided by the Department for Regional Development.

Freight

Rail freight traffic in Great Britain totalled an estimated 18.7 billion tonne-kilometres in

2002/03, representing the carriage of 87.0 million tonnes. Most traffic by volume is in bulk commodities, mainly coal, coke, iron and steel, building materials and petroleum. The two largest operators are English, Welsh & Scottish Railway (EWS), which also runs trains through the Channel Tunnel; and Freightliner, which operates container services between major ports and inland terminals.

The Government and the devolved administrations are keen to encourage more freight to be moved by rail, to relieve pressure on the road network and to bring environmental benefits. Grants are available to encourage companies to move goods by rail or water rather than by road. The SRA operates the Rail Freight Facilities grant, which in 2002/03 provided funds for 22 schemes.

Channel Tunnel

The Channel Tunnel, which celebrates its tenth anniversary in 2004, is operated by the UK-French group Eurotunnel under a concession from the British and French Governments. As well as managing the infrastructure of the Channel Tunnel – tunnels, terminals and track – Eurotunnel operates a drive-on, drive-off shuttle train service between terminals near Folkestone and Calais. In 2002 the service carried 2.3 million cars (down 8 per cent on 2001), over 1.2 million goods vehicles (up by 3 per cent) and 72,000 coaches (down by 5 per cent). Volumes of cars and buses have been falling in recent years, while goods vehicle numbers have been increasing.

Eurostar high-speed train services are operated jointly by Eurostar (UK) Ltd, French Railways and Belgian Railways under the commercial direction of Eurostar Group Ltd. Frequent services connect London (Waterloo) and Paris or Brussels, taking approximately 3 hours and 2 hours 40 minutes respectively. Trains also serve Ashford International (Kent), Calais, Lille, Disneyland Paris, Bourg St Maurice in the French Alps (in the winter) and Avignon (in the summer). Eurostar carried 6.6 million passengers in 2002.

Channel Tunnel Rail Link

The first section of the Channel Tunnel Rail Link (CTRL), between the Channel Tunnel terminal and Fawkham Junction (Kent), was completed in autumn 2003. Construction work on the second section to St Pancras (London) is in progress, and is due to become operational in 2007. The whole project is forecast to cost an estimated £5.2 billion.

Eurostar trains will be able to travel in the United Kingdom at speeds of up to 185 mph, reducing journey times by 35 minutes. High-speed domestic services will also operate from Kent to London. New international stations for the CTRL will be built at Stratford in east London and Ebbsfleet in Kent.

Underground railways

The world's first underground railway opened in London in 1863, and the 'Tube' network now serves 275 stations on 408 kilometres of track. It is run by London Underground Ltd (LUL, *www.tfl.gov.uk/tube*), which is part of Transport for London (see page 324). In 2002/03, 953 million passenger journeys were made on the network. The Glasgow Underground, the United Kingdom's only other such system, is a heavy rapid-transit system operating on an 11-kilometre circle in central Glasgow.

Responsibility for maintaining and upgrading LUL's infrastructure has been transferred to the private sector under a public-private partnership (PPP, see page 357), while LUL continues to have responsibility for safety and for all aspects of operating passenger services across the network. Under the PPP, three private sector infrastructure companies (Infracos) will work under contract to LUL for a 30-year period. Ownership of LUL's assets – for example, trains, stations, track and tunnels – remains within the public sector; the Infracos will lease the assets for the period of the contracts. The PPP is expected to provide about £16 billion of investment over 15 years.

The Tube map
The year 2003 marked the 70th anniversary of London's famous Tube map, originally designed by Harry Beck. An electrical draughtsman working for the Underground, Beck based the map on the circuit diagrams he drew for his day job. His revolutionary design, with some modifications and improvements, survives to the present day.

Light railways and tramways
There has been a revival in interest in tram/light rail services in recent years, and a number are now in operation (see Table 21.7). Government plans indicate a growing role for tramways, with the provision of up to 25 new lines in major cities and conurbations.

Table 21.7 Light rail systems in operation in 2003, UK

	Number of stations	Length of route (km)
Tyne and Wear Metro	58	77
Greater Manchester Metro	36	39
Stagecoach Supertram (Sheffield)	47	29
Croydon Tramlink (London)	38	28
Docklands Light Railway (London)	34	27
Centro (West Midlands)	23	20
Nottingham Express Transit[1]	26	14

1 Expected to open in November 2003.
Source: Department for Transport

The £180 million Nottingham Express Transit system, which will run for 14 kilometres, is expected to open in late 2003. The Leeds Supertram system was approved in 2003, along with a light rail system in south Hampshire. The north Edinburgh loop, one of three tram lines intended for the city, will be completed by 2009.

Air travel

Both the number of passengers and the tonnes of freight carried into and out of UK airports have trebled in the last 20 years, while air transport movements more than doubled. According to the DfT, these trends look set to continue, as the number of air passengers is growing by between 4 and 5 per cent a year and the freight market by 7 per cent. The number of UK residents visiting abroad by air has grown rapidly (Figure 21.8). In 1982, 12.0 million such visits were made; by 2002, this number had grown to 44.5 million.

Traffic on UK-owned airlines, 2002

Aircraft-kilometres flown	1,502 million
Passengers uplifted[1]	107 million
Passenger-kilometres flown	246 billion
Cargo and mail uplifted[1]	939,065 tonnes
Cargo- and mail-kilometres flown	5,472 million

1 Passenger and cargo movements are counted every time an aircraft takes off, that is, on every stage of a journey rather than once for the whole journey.

Figure 21.8 Trips abroad by air, UK residents

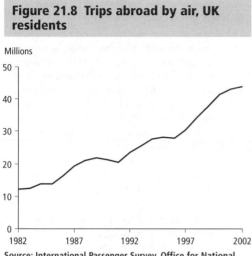

Millions

Source: International Passenger Survey, Office for National Statistics

UK airlines are entirely in the private sector, as are most of the major airports. Day-to-day responsibility for the regulation of civil aviation rests with the Civil Aviation Authority (CAA, *www.caa.co.uk*).

In May 2002, the Government set up an independent review to examine the arrangements for security at UK airports, and how improvements might be implemented, particularly in the light of the terrorist attacks of 11 September 2001. The Government accepted in principle all the recommendations of the review in October 2002, including strengthening the strategic direction and coordination of security at airports, and re-examining police powers.

The Government further announced in December 2002 that specially trained armed police officers would henceforth be allowed to travel on UK flights.

Airlines

British Airways is one of the world's largest international airlines. During 2001/02 the British Airways group carried over 32 million passengers on its fleet of 331 planes, achieving an occupancy of 71 per cent on its main scheduled services. This compares with 34 million passengers, and an occupancy rate of 72 per cent, in 2000/01. The airline's worldwide network covers 172 destinations in 77 countries, and its main operating bases are London's Heathrow and Gatwick airports.

BMI, formerly British Midland, is the second largest scheduled carrier and operates an extensive network of scheduled services with 54 jet aircraft, carrying 7.5 million passengers in 2002. Britannia Airways is the world's biggest charter airline and carried 8 million passengers in 2002 on its 32 aircraft. Virgin Atlantic operates scheduled services to 20 overseas destinations with 35 aircraft, and carried over 3.5 million passengers in 2002. In recent years low-cost or 'no-frills' airlines have become increasingly popular. Those based in the United Kingdom include bmibaby, flybe and easyJet.

Concorde

In April 2003, British Airways announced the retirement of its fleet of seven Concordes, with effect from the end of October. The primary reason for this decision was the global downturn in all forms of premium travel in the airline industry.

Concorde is the world's only supersonic passenger aircraft, with a cruising speed of around 1,350 mph at an altitude of over 18,000 metres. Travelling at twice the speed of sound, it can cross the Atlantic in just over three hours. The Concorde project was an Anglo-French partnership, and the plane's first flight was from Toulouse in March 1969, while the first commercial flights took off from London and Paris in January 1976. Air France was the only other airline to operate Concordes; the last flight of a French plane was in May 2003.

Airports

Of the 150 or so licensed civil aerodromes in the United Kingdom, nearly a quarter handle more than 100,000 passengers a year each. In 2002 UK civil airports handled a total of 189.8 million passengers (188.8 million terminal passengers and over 1 million in transit), and 2.2 million tonnes of freight. Heathrow is the world's busiest international airport, handling 63 million passengers (excluding those in transit) and 1.2 million tonnes of freight in 2002, while Gatwick is the world's busiest single runway airport, handling some 30 million passengers a year.

Ownership and control

BAA plc is the world's largest commercial operator of airports. It handled 128 million passengers in its seven UK airports – which include Heathrow and Gatwick – in 2002. Overseas, BAA international division has interests in 12 airports, including six in

Table 21.9 Passenger traffic at the UK's main airports[1]

	Million passengers		
	1992	2001	2002
London Heathrow	45.0	60.5	63.0
London Gatwick	19.8	31.1	29.5
Manchester	11.7	19.1	18.6
London Stansted	2.3	13.7	16.0
Birmingham	3.7	7.7	7.9
Glasgow	4.7	7.2	7.8
Edinburgh	2.6	6.0	6.9
London Luton	1.9	6.5	6.5
Belfast International	2.2	3.6	3.6
Newcastle	1.9	3.4	3.4
Bristol	1.0	2.7	3.4
Aberdeen	2.2	2.5	2.5

1 Terminal passengers, excluding those in transit.
Source: Civil Aviation Authority

Australia, handling around 78 million passengers a year. The second largest UK operator is TBI, which has an interest in 41 airports worldwide.

Highland and Islands Airports Ltd (HIAL) owns ten airports in Scotland. These airports receive considerable investment from the Scottish Executive to ensure the continued provision of 'lifeline' services to remote areas.

All UK airports used for public transport must be licensed by the CAA for reasons of safety. Stringent requirements, such as adequate firefighting, medical and rescue services, have to be satisfied before a licence is granted.

Airport development
The rapid increase in air travel in recent years is a trend which is forecast to continue, with the DfT predicting that terminal passenger numbers will be over twice 2002 levels by 2020. At the same time, however, some of the UK airports are reaching their capacity limits, with those in south east England being under particular pressure. In 2002 the DfT launched a major consultation to examine and decide on the ways in which the UK air services and airports should develop over the next 30 years. The Government wishes to develop a long-term, sustainable framework that will maximise the benefits of air travel and minimise the negative effects. The consultation, which closed in the summer of 2003, will be key in the

formulation of an Air Transport White Paper, which will set out such a framework.

Investment to expand passenger facilities is already in progress at many UK airports. At Heathrow, BAA is investing £6.6 billion on new and existing facilities, including £3.2 billion on Terminal 5. Phase one of the new terminal will open to the travelling public in 2008, and, by 2016, it will increase Heathrow's passenger handling capacity by around 30 million passengers a year. A £1 billion investment at Gatwick over the next 11 years is designed to raise annual capacity to around 40 million passengers.

Among other large-scale projects at UK airports are an £800 million programme at Stansted over the next 11 years, to develop the airport to serve 25 million passengers a year, and a £360 million expansion plan at Birmingham Airport, which will increase capacity to around 10 million passengers a year.

Air traffic control
Civil and military air traffic control over the United Kingdom and the surrounding seas, including much of the North Atlantic, is undertaken by National Air Traffic Services Ltd (NATS – *www.nats.co.uk*), working in collaboration with military controllers. NATS is a PPP, in which the Government's partners are the Airline Group, a consortium of seven UK airlines, and BAA. The CAA retains responsibility for air safety regulation, and also regulates NATS air traffic control charges.

To cope with the long-term forecast growth in air traffic, NATS is in the process of replacing the three previous UK centres for civil and military en route air traffic control operations with two major new centres. Swanwick (Hampshire) replaced the old West Drayton (London) centre, and opened in 2002, while a new Scottish centre at Prestwick will replace the existing one in 2009. Controlling around 322,000 square kilometres of airspace above England and Wales, Swanwick handles up to 6,000 flights a day during busy periods.

A financial restructuring of NATS was agreed with the CAA in March 2003. Formulated in response to the sharp fall in revenue following 11 September 2001, the plan is designed to protect NATS from further market fluctuations and safeguard its investment programme, and includes the provision of new shareholder capital. The first phase of a £1 billion investment plan – the replacement of its entire UK radar network – was announced by NATS in April 2003. The investment plan is intended, among other things, to enable the company to handle a 50 per cent increase in flights, from 2 million to 3 million, by 2010/11, and reduce NATS-attributable delays to less than one minute per flight.

Air safety

The CAA is responsible for safety standards on UK airlines. It certifies aircraft and crews, licenses air operators and air travel organisers, and approves certain air fares and airport charges. To qualify for a first professional licence, a pilot must pass a full-time course of instruction approved by the CAA or have acceptable military or civilian flying experience. Every company operating aircraft used for commercial air transport purposes must possess an Air Operator's Certificate, which the CAA grants when it is satisfied that the company is competent to operate its aircraft safely. All aircraft registered in the United Kingdom must be granted a certificate of airworthiness by the CAA before being flown. The CAA works closely with the Joint Aviation Authorities, a European grouping of aviation safety regulation authorities.

The DfT's Air Accidents Investigation Branch (AAIB) investigates accidents and serious incidents in UK airspace and those that occur overseas to aircraft registered or manufactured in the United Kingdom. In 2002 the AAIB was involved in the investigation of 343 civil aviation accidents or

Table 21.10 Top ten destinations for UK residents visiting abroad

			Thousands
	1997	2001	2002
Spain	8,281	11,790	12,606
France	11,149	11,959	11,707
Irish Republic	3,613	3,930	4,043
USA	3,028	3,990	3,665
Greece	1,512	3,215	3,000
Italy	1,801	2,471	2,649
Germany	2,023	2,242	2,243
Netherlands	1,756	2,095	2,110
Portugal	1,304	1,598	1,796
Belgium	1,419	1,738	1,726

Source: International Passenger Survey, Office for National Statistics

incidents worldwide and provided technical assistance to military aircraft accident investigations on ten occasions.

Shipping and ports

It is estimated that about 95 per cent by weight (75 per cent by value) of UK foreign trade is carried by sea. The UK fleet has declined considerably in tonnage terms in the last 25 years, reflecting changing trade patterns, removal of grants, and greater competition, although there has been a slight revival in recent years. International revenue (including freight revenue) earned by the UK shipping industry in 2001 was £3.7 billion and represented over 5 per cent of the total export of services from the United Kingdom.

At the end of 2002 there were 590 UK-owned merchant trading ships of 100 gross tonnes or more, with a total tonnage of 12.3 million deadweight tonnes, an increase of 0.3 million tonnes on 2001. There were 140 vessels totalling 4.7 million deadweight tonnes used as oil, chemical or gas carriers, and 450 vessels totalling 7.6 million deadweight tonnes employed as dry-bulk carriers, container ships or other types of cargo ship. In addition there were 40 passenger ships. In all, 78 per cent of UK-owned vessels are registered in the United Kingdom, the Channel Islands, the Isle of Man or British Overseas Territories, such as Bermuda.

Cargo services

International revenue earned by the UK shipping industry in 2002 was £3.7 billion: £2.8 billion from freight (£2.2 billion on dry cargo and passenger vessels and £0.7 billion on tankers and liquefied gas carriers); £0.3 billion from charter receipts; and £0.6 billion from passenger revenue. Nearly all scheduled cargo-liner services from the United Kingdom are containerised. UK tonnage serving these trades is dominated by a relatively small number of companies. Besides the carriage of freight by liner and bulk services between the United Kingdom and the rest of Europe, many roll-on, roll-off services carry cars, passengers and commercial vehicles.

Passenger services

Around 30 million passenger journeys a year take place on international and domestic ferry services linking Great Britain with Ireland and mainland Europe. A further 19 million passengers are carried on ferry services to many of Great Britain's offshore islands, such as the Isle of Wight, Isle of Man, Orkney and Shetland, and the islands off the west coast of Scotland.

P&O Ferries is the largest UK ferry operator, with a fleet of about 50 ships operating on 18 routes around the UK coast. Cross-Channel services are operated by roll-on, roll-off ferries, high-speed catamarans and high-speed monohulls.

Maritime safety

The DfT's policies for improving marine safety and pollution control are implemented by the Maritime and Coastguard Agency (MCA), which inspects UK ships and foreign ships using UK ports, to ensure that they comply with international safety, pollution prevention and operational standards. In 2002, 120 foreign-flagged ships were detained in UK ports.

In an emergency, HM Coastguard coordinates facilities, such as its own helicopters; cliff rescue teams; lifeboats of the Royal National Lifeboat Institution (RNLI, a voluntary body); aircraft, helicopters and ships from the armed forces; and merchant shipping and commercial aircraft. In 2002 the MCA was alerted to 13,395 incidents and 19,984 people were assisted, including 5,851 who required rescuing. This represents an increase from 2001, almost entirely due to an expansion of HM Coastguard's search and rescue responsibilities, particularly on the River Thames.

Some locations around the United Kingdom are potentially hazardous for shipping. There are over 1,000 marine aids to navigation around the UK coast and responsibility for these rests with three regional lighthouse authorities. Measures to reduce the risk of collision include the separation of ships into internationally agreed shipping lanes. This applies, for example, in the Dover Strait, one of the world's busiest seaways, which is monitored by radar from the Channel Navigation Information Service at the MCA's Dover base. A new Vessel Traffic Management Information System for tracking ships in the Strait was introduced at the base in May 2003, one of the first of its kind in the world.

Ports

There are over 100 ports of commercial significance in Great Britain, while several hundred small harbours cater for local cargo,

Table 21.11 Traffic through the principal ports of Great Britain

			Million tonnes
	1992	2001	2002
Grimsby and Immingham	40.8	54.8	56.1
London	48.9	50.7	51.2
Tees and Hartlepool	43.4	50.8	50.5
Forth	23.3	41.6	42.0
Milford Haven	35.6	33.8	34.5
Southampton	29.8	35.7	34.1
Liverpool	27.8	30.3	30.4
Sullom Voe	41.4	31.2	29.4
Felixstowe	18.0	28.4	25.1
Dover	13.1	19.1	20.0

Source: Department for Transport

fishing vessels, island ferries or recreation. There are three broad types of port: those owned and run by boards constituted as trusts; those owned by local authorities; and company-owned facilities.

Associated British Ports (ABP) is the largest UK port owner and operates 21 ports, including Cardiff, Grimsby and Immingham, Hull, Ipswich, Newport, Port Talbot, Southampton and Swansea. Other major facilities owned by private sector companies include Felixstowe, Harwich and Thamesport (all owned by the Hong Kong group Hutchison Whampoa).

The Government intends to assist ports in maintaining competitiveness, and to develop nationally agreed safety standards; to promote environmental best practice; and to build on the approach detailed in its ten-year plan for transport, which recognised the importance of port hubs within integrated transport systems.

Port traffic

A total of 558 million tonnes (Mt) of freight traffic was handled in UK ports in 2002, a 1 per cent reduction on 2001. Traffic through the 52 major UK ports (generally those handling over 1 million tonnes a year) accounted for 97 per cent (542 Mt) of the total. Inwards traffic fell by 8 Mt to 321 Mt while outward traffic was virtually unchanged at 238 Mt.

The main ports, in terms of total tonnage handled, are shown in Table 21.11. Forth, Milford Haven and Sullom Voe mostly handle oil, while the principal destinations for non-fuel traffic are London, Felixstowe, Grimsby and Immingham, Tees and Hartlepool, and Liverpool. Crude oil now accounts for one-third of all port traffic.

By far the most important port for container traffic is Felixstowe (which handles about two-fifths of this type of traffic), while Dover is the leading port for roll-on, roll-off traffic. Dover is also the major arrival and departure point for sea passengers, handling well over half of all international movements to and from the United Kingdom. The top four UK ports are among the ten largest ports in northern Europe.

Northern Ireland has four main ports, at Belfast, Larne, Londonderry and Warrenpoint. Belfast handles around three-fifths of Northern Ireland's seaborne trade.

Inland waterways

Inland waterways are now used mainly for leisure and general recreation, but they have a number of other important roles: as a heritage and environmental resource, as a catalyst for regeneration, and in land drainage and water supply.

Some inland waterways still carry freight. In 2001, 53.5 million tonnes of goods were carried on inland waters in the United Kingdom, an increase of 9 per cent on the previous year. The volume of goods moved was 1.9 billion tonne-kilometres. Crude petroleum and petroleum products dominate waterborne freight movement, accounting for 74 per cent of the total in 2001. The River Thames is the busiest inland waterway route in the United Kingdom.

The United Kingdom's waterways are managed by about 30 different navigation authorities. British Waterways (*www.britishwaterways.co.uk*), a public corporation sponsored by the Department for Environment, Food and Rural Affairs and the Scottish Executive, is the largest, responsible for some 3,200 kilometres of navigable waterways, over half the UK total.

British Waterways has embarked on the United Kingdom's biggest ever programme of waterway restorations, in which over 480 kilometres of canals and waterway structures will be restored or built in two phases. Funding for the programme comes from a wide range of partnerships and public support. The first phase, which opened over

350 kilometres of canals and structures in eight projects, was completed in 2002. The second phase, covering ten further projects, includes the first new canal to be designed in a century – the Bedford and Milton Keynes Waterway. The route of the proposed canal was announced in February 2003 and the 32-kilometre waterway is expected to cost £150 million to build, with work starting in 2007 and completing in 2010.

The cross-border body Waterways Ireland is responsible for the management, maintenance, development and restoration of the inland navigable waterways system throughout Ireland, which is principally used for recreational purposes.

Transport policy

Underpinning the Government's transport policy is its ten-year transport spending plan, launched in 2000, which currently envisages public spending and private investment of some £180.6 billion in the decade to 2010/11, including: £64.1 billion for railways in Great Britain; £59.3 billion for local transport in England; £26.9 billion for transport in London; £20.8 billion for strategic roads in England and £9.7 billion on future projects and other transport areas. The plan will be subject to a review alongside the Government's spending review in 2004. Public spending by the DfT in 2002/03 is given in Figure 21.12.

The Government published its first progress report on the ten-year plan in December 2002. While the report acknowledged that much remained to be done, it also highlighted improvements made since the instigation of the plan, including the completion of five major new road schemes, the commencement of work on the M6 toll road and 17 other major road improvements, and growth in bus, and especially light rail, patronage.

Under the *Transport Act 2000*, Local Transport Plans (LTPs) have been drawn up by local transport authorities in England (outside London), and by Welsh authorities. In Scotland all local authorities have produced Local Transport Strategies and Strathclyde Passenger Transport has a public transport strategy.

Each year, capital allocations to English authorities are made in the LTP capital settlement. Funding

Figure 21.12 Total Department for Transport public spending, 2002/03[1]

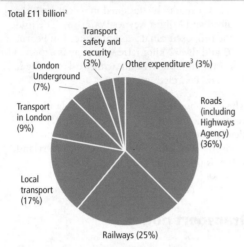

Total £11 billion[2]

- Transport safety and security (3%)
- Other expenditure[3] (3%)
- London Underground (7%)
- Transport in London (9%)
- Local transport (17%)
- Railways (25%)
- Roads (including Highways Agency) (36%)

1 Percentages based on resource and capital expenditure, provisional outturn.
2 Resource budget plus capital budget, less depreciation.
3 Includes logistics and maritime, transport strategy, aviation and central administration.
Source: Department for Transport

totalling £8.4 billion is envisaged from 2001/02 to 2005/06, and the 2003/04 settlement distributed £1.6 billion to local authorities, including funds for:

- around 5,500 local road safety and traffic calming schemes, including around 900 safe routes to school schemes (see page 315);
- new bus stations in Norwich, North Manchester and Warrington;
- over 1,000 kilometres of cycle tracks and over 1,750 new cycle parking facilities; and
- up to 200 kilometres of new footpaths, footway improvements or pedestrianisation.

The London Mayor is responsible for transport in the capital with the exception of mainline rail. The Mayor's Transport Strategy recognises that an increase in the capacity of London's transport system cannot be based on the private car. It aims to increase the capacity of the Underground and rail systems by up to 50 per cent over the 15 years from 2002, although two-thirds of this is due to come from major mainline rail projects. The Strategy also aims to increase the capacity of the bus system by 40 per cent over ten years. Authorities in London produce Local Implementation/Borough Spending Plans in line with the Strategy, the funding for which was

£130 million in 2003/04. Transport for London will be responsible for delivering the Strategy.

The Government published the *Railways and Transport Safety Bill* in January 2003. The Bill would set up a new Rail Accident Investigation Branch, introduce alcohol testing in relation to shipping and civil aviation, modernise the structure of the British Transport Police, and restructure the Office of the Rail Regulator.

Wales

The *Transport Framework for Wales* sets the context within which the Assembly Government makes decisions relating to transport. It aims to provide a better coordinated and sustainable transport system, including improved public transport. Programmes have been set out under the framework for rail, roads and local transport.

The Assembly Government's Transport Directorate has a budget of around £260 million for 2003/04. It is responsible for maintaining and improving motorways and trunk roads in Wales, and administering grants to local authorities and other bodies to fund capital transport schemes and transport services.

A £77 million package of transport investment for Wales for 2003/04 was announced in January 2003. It includes measures to improve bus services and facilities for walkers and cyclists, as well as confirming commitments to road and rail improvements made in the Framework.

Scotland

Expenditure on transport of £1.4 billion is planned in 2003/04, compared with £1.2 billion in 2002/03. The Scottish Executive set out its priorities for transport in *Building a better Scotland*, its spending proposals for the period 2003–06. These include increasing capacity and services on the rail network, for example by investing in rail links to Glasgow and Edinburgh airports; and tackling inter-urban congestion in central Scotland, including improvements to the trunk road network such as upgrading the A8 and A80 to motorway standard.

The Executive is also attempting to take a longer-term strategic approach to financial planning for public transport infrastructure, and announced plans for funding of £3 billion over ten years in March 2003.

The first piece of private rail legislation to go before the Scottish Parliament since devolution was presented in February 2003. The Bill relates to the re-opening of the Stirling-Alloa-Kincardine rail link, part of the Executive's proposed improvements to the Scottish rail network.

Northern Ireland

The *Regional Transportation Strategy for Northern Ireland 2002–2012* identifies strategic transportation investment priorities and considers potential funding sources and the affordability of planned initiatives over the next ten years. Funding of £3.5 billion is envisaged over the ten years of the strategy, for initiatives which include:

- upgrading existing rail network and services, and providing new trains and increased capacity;
- improving bus services;
- building a rapid transit system in the Belfast metropolitan area; and
- strategic highway improvements to provide, for example, up to 13 bypasses and 85 kilometres of dual carriageways.

Further reading

Department for Transport Annual Report 2003. Cm 5907. The Stationery Office.

National Travel Survey: 1999/2001 Update. Department for Transport, 2002.

Transport 2010: The Ten-Year Plan. Department of the Environment, Transport and the Regions, 2000.

Transport Statistics Great Britain, annual report. The Stationery Office.

Websites

Department for Transport
www.dft.gov.uk

Northern Ireland Department for Regional Development
www.drdni.gov.uk

Scottish Executive
www.scotland.gov.uk

Transport for London
www.transportforlondon.gov.uk

Welsh Assembly Government
www.wales.gov.uk

Strategic Rail Authority
www.sra.gov.uk

The Office of the Rail Regulator
www.rail-reg.gov.uk

WWW.

22 Sustainable development

Introduction

A widely used definition of sustainable development is 'development that meets the needs of the present without compromising the ability of future generations to meet their own needs'.

The UK Government defines the aim of sustainable development as 'ensuring a better quality of life for everyone, now and for the generations to come'. It notes that four key objectives, relevant to both the United Kingdom and the world as a whole, need to be met simultaneously in order to reach this goal:

- social progress that recognises the needs of everyone;
- effective protection of the environment;
- prudent use of natural resources; and
- maintenance of high and stable levels of economic growth and employment.

In September 2002 the World Summit on Sustainable Development (WSSD) was held in Johannesburg, South Africa (*www.johannesburgsummit.org*). It marked the tenth anniversary of the UN Conference on Environment and Development, held in Rio de Janeiro, Brazil (the Rio 'Earth' summit). WSSD focused on implementation, recognising that progress since Rio had been limited, and that success in the future would be measured by how agreements reached are translated into action. Outcomes from the summit contained commitments on a wide range of issues: making the links between good environmental and natural resource management; international development and poverty eradication, international trade; and sustainable patterns of production and consumption.

The most important domestic commitment made by the United Kingdom at WSSD was accepting the importance of working towards sustainable patterns of production and consumption, including increasing energy efficiency and the use of renewable energy sources (see page 443). The Government believes economic, social and environmental objectives must be met through more efficient use of resources, and that the link between economic growth and environmental degradation be broken. Breaking this link is a key feature of the Government's *Sustainable Consumption and Production Strategy*, to be published in autumn 2003.

Sustainable development in the UK

The UK Government's sustainable development strategy, *A Better Quality of Life*, was launched in 1999. It identifies a core set of around 150 indicators of sustainable development with a subset of 15 headline indicators to provide an overview of progress. The headline indicators cover economic and social, as well as environmental, concerns. The Government reports annually on progress towards sustainable development, and the 2002 report, *Achieving a Better Quality of Life*, was published in February 2003 (see page 328).

A Better Quality of Life sets out ten guiding principles and approaches for sustainable development.

- *Putting people at the centre.* The Declaration made at Rio stated that 'human(s) are at the centre of concerns for sustainable development. They are entitled to a healthy and productive life in harmony with nature'.

- *Taking a long term perspective.* Thinking and policy must be viewed in terms of decades, not years.

- *Taking account of costs and benefits.* These cannot be viewed purely in cash terms. In pursuing any one objective, disproportionate costs should not be imposed elsewhere.

- *Creating an open and supportive economic system.* Sustainable development requires a global economic system, which supports economic growth in all countries.

- *Combating poverty and social exclusion.*

- *Respecting environmental limits.* Serious or irreversible damage to some aspects of the environment could threaten global society – for example, major climate change or overuse of freshwater stocks. In such cases there are likely to be natural limits that should not be breached.

- *The precautionary principle.* Defined in the Rio Declaration, the principle states: 'where there are threats of serious or irreversible damage, lack of full scientific knowledge shall not be used as a reason for postponing cost-effective measures to prevent environmental degradation'.

- *Using scientific knowledge.*

- *Transparency, information, participation and access to justice.*

- *Making the polluter pay.* Wherever possible, the costs created by environmental pollution and resource depletion should be borne by the polluter, or ultimately the consumer, rather than society as a whole.

The Government Sustainable Development Unit within the Department for Environment, Food and Rural Affairs (Defra) encourages and promotes action on sustainable development in the United Kingdom. The Sustainable Development Commission, an advisory non-departmental public body reporting to the Prime Minister and leaders of the devolved administrations, acts as an advocate and helps to build consensus on the actions needed.

Defra also funds the Sustainable Development Research Network (SDRN, *www.sd-research.org.uk*), which was set up to contribute to sustainable development in the United Kingdom by facilitating the better use of evidence and research in policy making.

The Royal Commission on Environmental Pollution (*www.rcep.org.uk*) is an independent standing body that advises the Government on dangers to the environment, suggesting ways of integrating environmental objectives with other economic and social objectives in order to achieve sustainable development. Established in 1970, it has produced 24 in-depth reports so far, on a variety of topics such as climate change and environmental standards.

The environmental impact of air travel
The Royal Commission on Environmental Pollution published a special report, *The Environmental Effects of Civil Aircraft in Flight*, in November 2002. The report expressed concern about the global impacts of the rapid growth in air travel. It stated that, unless action is taken, emissions from aircraft are likely to become a major contributor to global warming. A key message of the report was that short-haul flights, such as UK domestic and European journeys, make a disproportionately large contribution to the global environmental impacts of air transport, and that these impacts are very much larger than those for rail travel over the same point-to-point journey.

The devolved administrations
The devolved administrations of the United Kingdom are responsible for their own programmes, which are intended to reflect local situations and priorities. Similarly, each English region has developed a sustainable development framework.

Wales
The National Assembly for Wales has a legal duty to promote sustainable development in its functions. It has adopted a sustainable development scheme, Learning to Live Differently, to provide the framework for this duty, which is also reflected in the Welsh Assembly Government's corporate strategy document *Plan for Wales 2001* and other key strategies.

The Welsh Assembly Government has also adopted its own list of sustainable development indicators. This is a headline list rather than the detailed UK set (see below), and includes: the percentage of Welsh speakers, reflecting the importance of the language for Welsh identity and communities; the amount of electricity used in Wales produced by renewable sources; and Wales' global ecological footprint, which provides a measure of the burden imposed on the natural environment.

Scotland

Meeting the Needs, published in 2002, set out the Scottish Executive's goals for sustainable development. It included 24 indicators for Scotland, and identified resource use, energy and travel as the main priority areas. Action on sustainable development within the Executive is led by the Cabinet Sub-committee on Sustainable Scotland, chaired by the First Minister.

Sustainable development was one of the main cross-cutting themes in the Scottish Executive's 2002 spending review. Departments were asked to produce statements on how their spending contributed to sustainable development, which were then published collectively in a document, *Building a Sustainable Scotland*.

The Scottish Executive has adopted a number of targets with regard to sustainable development. These include increasing the amount of waste that is recycled or composted, and a plan to have 40 per cent of electricity generated from renewable sources by 2020. Progress towards the targets will be measured via the indicators set out in *Meeting the Needs*. These include:

- Waste recycling – the proportion of household waste recycled.
- Population structure – the proportion of the population that is of working age.
- Sea fisheries – the proportion of fish stocks that are within safe biological limits.
- Fuel poverty – the total number of households living in fuel poverty (defined as those having to spend more than 10 per cent of their income on fuel use).

Northern Ireland

In its *Programme for Government* the Northern Ireland Executive stated that 'sustainable development will be a key theme running throughout work and priorities'. Some specific strategies include: the *Regional Development Strategy for Northern Ireland 2025*, which seeks to provide a development framework that will work towards balanced and sustainable development in the region, with 12 headline indicators reported each year; the *Growing for a Green Economy* strategy, which seeks to achieve sustainable economic development through more efficient business practices; and the *Northern Ireland Biodiversity Strategy*.

These commitments continued under the interim arrangements put in place after the suspension of the Northern Ireland Assembly (see page 26). A sustainable development strategy is being developed, which will include a set of indicators designed specifically to reflect concerns in Northern Ireland.

Measuring progress

The 15 headline indicators for the United Kingdom, reported each year in *Achieving a Better Quality of Life*, are the main way of assessing progress towards sustainable development. Many have related public service agreement targets (see chapter 24).

The indicators are divided into three groups – economic, social and environmental. Progress on each indicator is measured against two base years, 1990 and 1999 – when the strategy was launched (although in most cases the data that were available in 1999 refer to the situation one or two years before the launch). The indicators relate to the United Kingdom as a whole, wherever possible.

Economic indicators

H1 – Economic output

Between 1990 and 2002, the output of the UK economy, measured in terms of gross domestic product (GDP) per head grew by 2.1 per cent a year on average (see also chapter 23). The

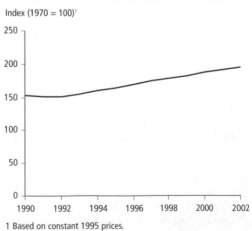

Figure 22.1 Economic output: GDP per head, UK

Index (1970 = 100)[1]

1 Based on constant 1995 prices.
Source: Office for National Statistics

Government aims to maintain high, stable economic growth that does not conflict with social and environmental goals.

H2 – Investment

Total investment at constant prices as a percentage of GDP fell from 18.1 per cent in 1990 to 16.3 per cent in 1995, but increased to 18.9 per cent in 1998 before falling back to 17.6 per cent in 2002. See chapter 22 for more on investment.

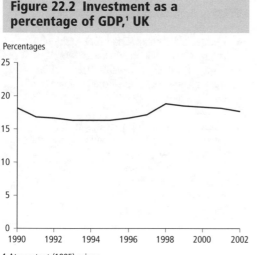

Figure 22.2 Investment as a percentage of GDP,[1] UK

Percentages

1 At constant (1995) prices.
Source: Office for National Statistics

H3 – Employment

This indicator focuses on the proportion of people of working age who are in work. This figure was 74.7 per cent in 1990; it fell to 70.4 per cent in 1993, but has increased steadily since then, reaching 74.6 per cent in 2002 (see also chapter 11).

Social indicators

H4 – Poverty and social exclusion

A number of separate indicators are grouped together under H4. The overall assessment of these indicators is that there has been no significant change since 1990. However, worsening in the levels of some indicators in the mid-1990s, followed by improvements toward the end of the decade, means that there have been improvements since the initiation of the sustainable development strategy.

- The proportion of working age people in Great Britain who live in households where no one works fell from a peak of 14 per cent in the mid-1990s to 12 per cent in 2002.

- The proportion of working age people in Great Britain without qualifications fell from 27 per cent in 1993 (when the series started) to 15 per cent in 2002.

- The proportion of single elderly households experiencing fuel poverty in England fell from 77 per cent in 1991 to 50 per cent in 1998, the latest year for which data are available.

- The proportion of children living in households in Great Britain with relative low incomes after housing costs (see glossary) was 31 per cent in 1994. It rose to 34 per cent in 1996 before falling back to 30 per cent in 2001.

H5 – Education

The indicator used for education is the percentage of 19-year-olds with NVQ level 2 qualifications (see chapter 10). In 1990, 52 per cent of 19-year-olds had these qualifications; by 2003, this figure was 76 per cent. However, since the start of the strategy, the proportion has remained relatively constant.

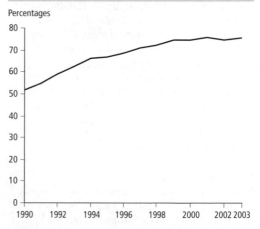

Figure 22.3 Proportion of 19-year-olds with NVQ level 2 qualifications or above,[1] UK

Percentages

1 NVQ level 2 is equivalent to one GCE A level, or five or more GCSE grades A* to C.
Source: Department for Education and Skills

H6 – Health

The health indicator is healthy life expectancy (see glossary). Between 1990 and 1999 healthy life expectancy in Great Britain increased, from

66.1 to 66.6 years for men and from 68.3 to 68.9 years for women.

H7 – Housing conditions

The indicator used is the percentage of households in England living in non-decent housing stock (see glossary and chapter 20). Between 1991 and 1996 there was no significant change across a broad range of condition measures. However, since 1996 there have been significant improvements. In 1996, 46 per cent of homes were non-decent, compared with 33 per cent in 2001.

H8 – Crime

Robbery, theft of or from vehicles, and domestic burglary constitute the crime indicator. Theft of or from vehicles and domestic burglary both fell by nearly a fifth in England and Wales between 1990 and 2000, while robberies more than tripled over the same period.

Environmental indicators

H9 – Climate change

Emissions of the 'basket' of six greenhouse gases (see page 276) are recorded for this indicator. UK emissions fell by 8 per cent between 1990 and 1997 and by 7 per cent between 1997 and 2002.

H10 – Air quality

The average number of days each year when air pollution was moderate or high at monitoring sites forms the basis of indicator H10. Sites are grouped into urban and rural areas. Urban air quality has improved significantly since 1993 (when monitoring started), from 59 days of moderate or higher air pollution in 1993 to 20 days in 2002. Rural air quality has also improved over the period. Year-on-year variations in air quality are considerable, however, meaning that it is difficult to assess progress since the introduction of the strategy.

H11 – Road traffic

Road traffic is measured both in terms of overall volume (see Figure 22.4) and traffic intensity, which measures vehicle-kilometres travelled per unit of GDP. Historically there has been a very strong link between road traffic, which has many negative effects on the environment and people's health, and economic growth.

Total road traffic volume in Great Britain grew by 18 per cent between 1990 and 2002. In the earlier year it was 411 billion vehicle-kilometres. By 1998

Community Energy Programme

The Government's £50 million Community Energy Programme was set up to help reduce energy bills and combat greenhouse gases and fuel poverty. It provided grants to bidders in six allocations in 2002 and 2003 for energy-saving projects targeted at low-income households, hospitals and other public buildings.

In February 2003, funding was announced for ten schemes, which are expected to cut carbon emissions by 4,000 tonnes a year. They included:

- Chesterfield Borough Council's Poolsbrook community heating network that, when complete, will use renewable fuel – methane gas from a landfill site – to serve 176 homes and other buildings;

- replacing Edinburgh University's steam infrastructure with a combined heat and power system (see page 443); and

- refurbishing, upgrading or expanding community heating networks in Rotherham, Midlothian, Woking and Portsmouth.

Figure 22.4 Road traffic,[1,2] Great Britain

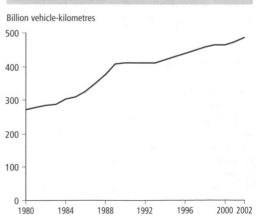

Billion vehicle-kilometres

1 Does not include pedal cycles.
2 Figures from 1999 are calculated on a different basis and are not directly comparable with earlier years. 2000 figure affected by September fuel protest.
Source: Department for Transport

road traffic volume was 460 billion vehicle-kilometres, and by 2002 this figure had increased to 486 billion vehicle-kilometres (a change in the way the data are calculated in 1999 mean that comparisons between earlier and later years are not precise).

Road traffic intensity fell by 10 per cent between 1990 and 2001, and by 4 per cent between 1998 and 2001. This suggests that the link between growth in road traffic volume and economic growth may be weakening.

H12 – River water quality
This indicator records the percentage of river lengths of good or fair chemical and biological quality in each part of the United Kingdom. River water quality is good across the United Kingdom, and the situation is similar for both chemical quality (see Table 22.5) and biological quality. The most significant improvement in both measures between 1990 and 2001 was in English rivers, bringing more of them up to the quality found in the rest of the United Kingdom.

Table 22.5 Rivers[1] of good or fair chemical quality[2]

	Percentage of total river lengths		
	1990[3]	1998	2001
England	83	89	94
Wales	98	99	98
Northern Ireland	95	96	96
Scotland[4]	97	98	96

1 Excludes tidal rivers in England and Wales.
2 Figures are three-year averages ending in year shown.
3 1991 in Northern Ireland.
4 Owing to different methodologies, figures from Scotland are not directly comparable with the rest of the UK. In addition, a new classification system was introduced in Scotland in 2000.
Source: Department for Environment, Food and Rural Affairs

H13 – Wildlife
Indicator H13 examines the populations of British woodland and farmland birds, which have been in long term decline since the end of 1970s. Between 1990 and 2000, the population of farmland birds fell by 17 per cent and that of woodland birds fell by 7 per cent. In contrast, the overall population of British birds remained fairly constant over the same period. Since the introduction of the strategy, it appears that populations of farmland

birds may have stabilised somewhat, while those of woodland birds may be increasing, reaching their highest level since 1990, in 2000.

H14 – Land use
The percentage of newly built or converted homes on previously developed land is covered by this indicator. Re-using previously developed land protects the countryside and encourages urban regeneration. In England, this percentage increased from 54 per cent in 1990 to 64 per cent in 2002, but there were some fluctuations in the intervening years (see Figure 22.6).

Figure 22.6 Proportion of new homes[1] built on previously developed land, England

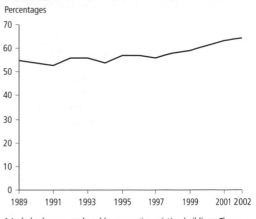

Percentages

1 Includes homes produced by converting existing buildings. These contribute an estimated three percentage points.
Source: Department for Environment, Food and Rural Affairs

H15 – Waste
Both household waste, in terms of waste generated per person that is not recycled or composted, and all waste arisings and management, are covered by indicator H15. However, due to a lack of data there is no realistic assessment of progress in the latter case – it is hoped new data will be available in 2004.

The amount of household waste generated per person has increased since 1991/92, when the amount not recycled or composted was 417 kilogrammes per person. By 1997/8 this figure was 441 kilogrammes, and by 2001/02, 457 kilogrammes. However, the proportion of household waste recycled or composted rose from 3 to 12 per cent over the same period.

The non-headline indicators

The non-headline core indicators are arranged in a framework of five groups:

- sustainable economy – which includes indicators for improving resource efficiency, developing skills, and rewarding work;
- building sustainable communities – including indicators for health, travel and access (for example access to services for disabled people or those who live in rural areas);
- managing the environment and resources – including indicators for freshwater, seas, oceans and coasts, and landscape and wildlife;
- 'sending the right signals' – which includes indicators which examine both government and individual actions for sustainable development; and
- international co-operation and development – including indicators for global poverty, population and pollution.

Reviewing progress and developing the indicators

In its original sustainable development strategy, the Government envisaged a full review of both the strategy and the indicators after five years. A full review of progress on the core indicators will be produced in 2004, and a wider review of the strategy and indicators will follow. This will assess the usefulness of the indicators in measuring progress towards sustainable development, as well as issues such as how they are presented and interpreted.

Sustainable development in government
The first annual report on *Sustainable Development in Government* was published in November 2002. It measured departmental performance against environmental targets, and progress on making sustainable development a key factor in all policy making. It found, for example, that all 19 central departments covered by the report exceeded the target for a 1 per cent reduction in greenhouse gas emissions for all buildings in both 2000/01 and 2001/02. Six departments now recover more than 40 per cent of their office waste, with five more recovering between 29 and 40 per cent.

International co-operation and development

Sustainable development in the United Kingdom cannot be considered in isolation from sustainable development elsewhere, as the actions of consumers and policy makers in the United Kingdom impact on the rest of the world. The Government identifies four key areas when considering sustainable development in an international context:

- working with others to eliminate global poverty and raise living standards in developing countries;
- working with others to tackle global pressures on the environment and resources;
- promoting a fair and open trade system which respects the environment; and
- strengthening the place of sustainable development in the work of international organisations.

The Government seeks to work in these areas within a number of international organisations; not only WSSD, but also the World Trade Organisation (see page 371), the G8 group of industrialised nations (see page 64) and other bodies and conventions. Some recent international developments are outlined below.

Overseas aid and trade

During 2002 the UK Government committed to increase its overseas aid budget (see page 73). This will result in aid rising from 0.26 per cent of gross national income (GNI) in 1997 and 0.32 per cent in 2001, to 0.40 per cent of GNI by 2005/06.

In April 2003 the Export Credits Guarantee Department (see page 374) announced that it will make available at least £50 million of guarantees each year for the UK renewable-energy sector to help it assist developing countries limit greenhouse gas emissions. It is hoped this initiative will encourage UK companies to export renewable-energy goods and services, by offering them insurance against the risks of non-payment, and aid developing countries meet their power generation requirements in a sustainable way by providing finance linked to UK involvement.

Outcomes from WSSD

These included:

- a statement by world leaders underlining their commitment to global sustainable development;
- a plan of implementation – the main focus of negotiations at the summit – which sets out

Fairtrade

Fairtrade is a trading partnership that aims towards greater equity in international trade by offering better trading conditions to, and securing the rights of, marginalised farmers and workers in the developing world, helping reduce poverty and improve living standards. More than 130 products now carry the Fairtrade Mark, including coffee, tea, cocoa, fresh fruit and snack products. In 2002 Fairtrade food sales in the United Kingdom reached an estimated retail value of £63 million.

The Fairtrade Foundation certifies and promotes Fairtrade. It was set up in the early 1990s by a number of agencies, including the charities Cafod, Christian Aid, Oxfam, Traidcraft Exchange and the World Development Movement.

the priority actions needed to achieve global sustainable development; and

- a wide range of partnerships for action, which involve governments, businesses, non-governmental organisations and other stakeholders, for example the Sustainable Tourism Initiative.

Further reading

A Better Quality of Life: a Strategy for Sustainable Development for the UK. The Stationery Office, 1999.

Achieving a Better Quality of Life 2002. Defra, 2003.

Regional Quality of Life Counts, 2002. Defra, 2003.

Indicators of Sustainable Development for Scotland. Scottish Executive, 2003.

Meeting the Needs. Scottish Executive, 2002.

Sustainable Development Indicators for Wales, 2003. National Assembly for Wales, 2003.

Websites

Government Sustainable Development Unit
www.sustainable-development.gov.uk

Sustainable Development Commission
www.sd-commission.gov.uk

Sustainable Development Team, Scottish Executive
www.sustainable.scotland.gov.uk

Sustainable Development Team, Welsh Assembly Government
www.wales.gov.uk/themessustainabledev

WWW.

23 Economic and business framework

National accounts figures contained in this chapter and any commentary on them do not reflect data released on 30 September, consistent with the 2003 edition of the *United Kingdom National Accounts – the Blue Book*, as they were not available until after this publication went to print.

Growth in the UK economy continued for the 11th consecutive year in 2002 (see Figure 23.1). Gross domestic product (GDP) at constant 1995 market prices (see glossary) rose by 1.9 per cent, a little below its post-war average of around 2½ per cent a year.

Growth in output in 2002 was strongest in agriculture, forestry and fishing, which recovered most of the sharp decline in output in 2001. The construction sector also grew strongly in all its sub-sectors except industrial projects. In recent decades growth has been dominated by the service sector (see chapter 30), but in 2002 this had its lowest increase since 1992. The deceleration was most pronounced in telecommunications and post, business services, and transport and storage. However, activity picked up within distribution and government services.

Figure 23.1 Annual percentage change in GDP at 1995 market prices, UK

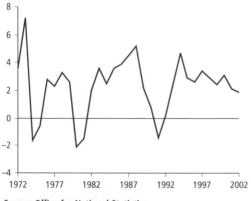

Source: Office for National Statistics

In 2002 expenditure by households (at constant 1995 prices) remained buoyant and government expenditure also continued to pick up. In contrast, gross fixed capital formation (see glossary) fell by 1.0 per cent, the worst performance since 1991, and inventories held by manufacturers continued to decline. General government investment rose by 14.0 per cent, while business investment fell by 6.1 per cent. The volume of trade was weaker than in recent years. Exports of goods and services fell for the first time since 1991, while imports grew by only 2.1 per cent.

Structure and performance

The value of all goods and services produced in the UK economy for final consumption is measured by GDP. In 2002 GDP at current market prices – 'money GDP' – totalled £1,044 billion (see Table 23.2), the first year it has exceeded the trillion mark. Average annual growth in GDP at 1995 market prices over the past five years has been 2.5 per cent.

According to the Organisation for Economic Co-operation and Development (OECD), the United Kingdom experienced lower economic growth than all its major competitors in the 1970s and also, apart from Germany and France, in the 1980s. In the 1990s, UK growth was just above the European Union average but behind that of Canada and the United States (see Table 23.3).

In the 2003 Budget, HM Treasury expected GDP to grow by between 2 and 2½ per cent in 2003 and to increase by 3 to 3½ per cent in both 2004 and 2005, with the economy returning to its long-term trend of 2¾ per cent by the end of 2005.

The trend in UK living standards, as measured by GDP per head at 1995 market prices, has grown steadily over the last 30 years. Since 1995 the annual rate of growth has been between 1.9 per cent and 3.1 per cent.

Table 23.2 Gross domestic product and gross national income, UK

£ million

	1992	1997	2000	2001	2002
Final consumption expenditure					
Households	379,758	503,374	603,557	633,867	662,079
Non-profit institutions	10,806	19,602	23,027	24,258	25,685
General government	129,195	149,147	177,801	191,506	209,621
Gross capital formation					
Gross fixed capital formation	100,583	134,163	158,918	164,338	167,534
Changes in inventories	−1,937	4,621	5,595	1,441	−416
Acquisitions less disposals of valuables	17	−26	5	366	213
Total exports	144,091	231,622	265,135	267,733	269,637
Gross final expenditure	**762,513**	**1,042,503**	**1,234,038**	**1,283,509**	**1,334,353**
less Total imports	−151,659	−231,436	−283,623	−289,943	−290,660
Statistical discrepancy	0	0	0	−442	−70
GDP at current market prices	**610,854**	**811,067**	**950,415**	**993,124**	**1,043,623**
Net income from abroad[1]	−4,125	1,301	5,620	13,148	18,316
Gross national income at current market prices	**606,729**	**812,368**	**956,035**	**1,006,272**	**1,061,939**
GDP at 1995 market prices	651,566	763,459	829,517	847,022	863,325
GDP index at 1995 market prices (1995=100)	90.6	106.2	115.3	117.8	120.0

1 Includes employment, entrepreneurial and property income.
Source: Quarterly National Accounts, Office for National Statistics

Table 23.3 Annual average GDP growth, G7 countries and EU

Percentages

	1970s	1980s	1990s
United Kingdom	2.4	2.3	2.1
United States	3.3	3.0	3.0
Japan	5.2	3.8	1.7
Germany	3.1	1.8	3.0
France	3.7	2.2	1.7
Italy	3.3	2.4	1.5
Canada	4.4	3.0	2.4
G7 average	3.6	2.9	2.4
EU average	3.4	2.2	2.0

Source: National Accounts of OECD countries

Output

The output of production industries fell by 3.5 per cent in 2002. Within this there were falls of 4.1 per cent in manufacturing output (its second successive year-on-year decline), 0.7 per cent in the electricity, gas and water industries and 1.9 per cent in mining and quarrying, including oil and gas extraction. Within manufacturing there was a significant fall of 17.0 per cent in the output of the electrical and optical equipment industries. Manufacturing as a proportion of GDP has continued to decline, contributing only 18 per cent to gross value added (GVA, see glossary) in 2001, compared with over a third in 1950.

The service sector's contribution to GVA grew from 55 per cent in 1985 to 71 per cent in 2001. In 2002 its output rose by 2.6 per cent. Agriculture, forestry and fishing output increased by 9.7 per cent and construction sector output rose by 7.5 per cent in 2002.

Table 23.4 shows changes in output since 1995. At constant 1995 prices, four sectors – agriculture, mining, manufacturing, and hotels and restaurants – have declined over this period.

Household income and expenditure

In 2002 UK household final expenditure (see glossary) rose by 3.7 per cent at constant 1995 prices to £589 billion, representing 76.3 per cent of the total £772 billion final consumption

Table 23.4 Output by industry – gross value added,[1] UK

	At current basic prices			% change 1995–2001 at 1995 basic prices
	1995 (£ million)	2001[2] (£ million)	% contribution 2001[2]	
Agriculture, forestry and fishing	11,766	8,241	0.9	−2.1
Mining and quarrying	16,369	25,665	2.9	−0.4
Manufacturing[3]	139,789	153,132	17.5	−1.5
Electricity, gas and water supply	15,586	15,713	1.8	13.0
Construction	33,005	47,327	5.4	22.2
Wholesale and retail trade	74,612	106,766	12.2	33.6
Hotels and restaurants	18,252	29,359	3.4	−3.7
Transport, storage and communication	51,340	70,252	8.0	49.4
Financial intermediation[4]	40,089	46,034	5.3	31.0
Adjustment for financial services	−23,215	−39,367	−4.5	51.8
Real estate, renting and business activities	119,052	209,837	24.0	40.7
Public administration and defence	39,756	42,096	4.8	1.5
Education	34,208	52,659	6.0	8.6
Health and social work	42,051	61,410	7.0	23.9
Other services	27,247	45,101	5.2	27.4
Total gross value added	**639,908**	**874,227**	**100**	**19.1**

1 Represents the difference between the value of the output of goods and services produced by a company and its intermediate consumption – the value of the goods and services or raw materials used up in the production of such output.
2 Figures for 2002 were not available at the time of going to print.
3 See Table 28.4 for an industry breakdown.
4 The activity by which an institutional unit acquires financial assets and incurs liabilities on its own account, by engaging in financial transactions on the market.
Source: **Quarterly National Accounts** and *United Kingdom National Accounts 2002 – the Blue Book*, **Office for National Statistics**

expenditure. This was the seventh consecutive year of strong growth. Expenditure on semi-durable and durable goods rose by 9.2 per cent and 8.4 per cent respectively, while growth in services was limited to 1.2 per cent.

Table 23.5 shows the pattern of household final consumption expenditure. Since 1995, in real terms, growth was strongest in the durable and semi-durable goods categories, and weakest in non-durable goods and services. Communication (postal services, and telephone and fax equipment and services), recreation and culture, and clothing and footwear showed the most significant growth. Spending on housing, alcohol and tobacco, and restaurants and hotels showed the smallest increase.

Total resources (income) of the UK household sector – including non-profit institutions serving households[1] – rose by 3.2 per cent in 2002 to

£1,036 billion. Gross disposable income – after deductions, including taxes and social contributions – totalled £710 billion. In 1995 prices, real household disposable income (RHDI, see glossary) rose by 2.1 per cent to £630 billion. RHDI has more than doubled since 1978. Wages and salaries increased by 3.8 per cent during 2002 to £497 billion, accounting for nearly 60 per cent of household primary income. The household saving ratio[2] fell from 5.7 per cent in 2001 to 4.7 per cent in 2002. This represented a modest growth in wages and salaries and a fall in net property income, while final expenditure rose more strongly.

The net worth[3] of the household sector has grown strongly in recent years, rising by an average of 8.9 per cent a year between 1987 and 2000, although falling by 4.6 per cent in 2001 to £4,573 billion. Of the total, non-financial assets increased

---

1 These include bodies such as charities, universities, churches and trade unions.

2 The percentage of total available resources saved during the year.

3 The value of assets after deducting for any liabilities.

Table 23.5 Household final consumption expenditure, UK

	At current market prices			% change 1995–2002 at 1995 basic prices
	1995 (£ million)	2002 (£ million)	% contribution 2002	
UK domestic				
Food and drink	49,790	61,711	9.3	14.5
Alcohol and tobacco	18,776	26,314	4.0	9.8
Clothing and footwear	28,030	39,759	6.0	68.0
Housing	81,412	118,968	18.0	8.8
Household goods and services	26,287	38,005	5.7	36.2
Health	6,835	11,062	1.7	12.6
Transport	62,733	94,463	14.3	30.1
Communication	9,067	14,701	2.2	98.2
Recreation and culture	51,075	80,235	12.1	74.7
Education	6,197	10,423	1.6	16.1
Restaurants and hotels	50,383	75,387	11.4	11.8
Miscellaneous	52,329	80,716	12.2	24.5
Total	442,914	651,744	98.4	29.7
of which:				
Durable goods	51,092	80,131	12.1	82.8
Semi-durable goods	50,848	79,974	12.1	74.7
Non-durable goods	124,466	156,279	23.6	11.3
Services	216,508	335,360	50.7	17.1
Net tourism	453	10,335	1.6	
Total UK national	**443,367**	**662,079**	100	32.9

Source: Quarterly National Accounts, Office for National Statistics

by 7.3 per cent to £2,562 billion, while financial assets fell by 16.4 per cent to £2,011 billion.

Investment

The 1.0 per cent fall in UK gross fixed capital formation at constant 1995 prices in 2002 was the first fall since 1992 and followed a 1.0 per cent rise in 2001. The 6.1 per cent decline in business investment was the first fall since 1993. As a percentage of GDP, business investment declined from 13.7 per cent in 2001 to 12.6 per cent in 2002 – the lowest proportion since 1997. For 2003, business investment is forecast by HM Treasury to decline by 1 to 1½ per cent, but then to grow by 4¾ to 5½ per cent in 2004 and by 5¼ to 6 per cent in 2005. The general government investment rise of 14.0 per cent in 2002 follows a 3.8 per cent increase in 2001.

In 2002, by asset type, there were increases of 18.9 per cent in dwellings, 3.8 per cent in transport equipment, 2.5 per cent in intangible fixed assets and 0.8 per cent in other buildings and

structures; in contrast, other machinery and equipment fell by 8.9 per cent.

UK whole economy investment accounted for a smaller share of GDP than for other industrialised countries – 15.8 per cent of GDP (at current prices) in 2002, compared with a G7 average of 18.0 per cent.

International trade

The United Kingdom was the third largest trading nation in 2002 (behind the United States and Germany) with exports of goods and services accounting for 26 per cent of GDP. See chapter 25 for details of the UK balance of payments position.

Mergers and acquisitions

In 2002 expenditure on acquisitions abroad by UK companies fell sharply, by 36 per cent, continuing the fall from the record high of £181.3 billion set in 2000 (see also Table 23.6). A significant

Table 23.6 Mergers and acquisitions involving UK companies

	1992	1997	2002
Acquisitions abroad by UK companies			
Number	679	464	262
Value (£ billion)	7,264	19,176	26,626
Acquisitions in the UK by foreign companies[1]			
Number	210	193	117
Value (£ billion)	4,139	15,717	16,798
Acquisitions in the UK by UK companies			
Number	432	506	430
Value (£ billion)	5,941	26,829	25,236

1 Includes acquisitions by foreign companies routed through their existing UK subsidiaries.
Source: Office for National Statistics

transaction in 2002, for a reported £2.1 billion, was the acquisition of Niagara Mohawk Holdings by National Grid Group. Expenditure on acquisitions in the United Kingdom by foreign companies also fell sharply (by 31 per cent in 2002) for the second successive year, from the record level of £64.6 billion in 2000. The most significant reported acquisition in 2002 was of Powergen by E.On AG of Germany for a reported £5.2 billion. Expenditure on acquisitions in the United Kingdom by UK companies fell by 13 per cent in 2002. A significant transaction was the acquisition of Homebase by GUS for a reported £0.9 billion.

Prices

Three main measures of retail price inflation are used in the United Kingdom:

- the all items Retail Prices Index (RPI), which is the main domestic measure of UK prices. RPI inflation measures the average change from month to month in the prices of goods and services purchased by most UK households and is commonly called 'headline' inflation;
- the RPI excluding mortgage interest payments (RPIX), which is used to calculate 'underlying' inflation, the target measure set by the Government, although the Bank of England has the task of meeting the target (see page 453); and
- the harmonised index of consumer prices (HICP), calculated in each Member State of the European Union for the purposes of European comparisons; it is also used by the European Central Bank as the measure of price stability across the euro area.

Retail Prices Index
The RPI is compiled using a large and representative 'basket' of 650 goods and services sampled each month to see how prices are changing. Each year a review of the composition of the basket is undertaken. New items are added to represent new or increasing areas of spending, while other items are deleted as spending on them falls. For the 2003 review, some of the changes included:

In	**Out**
Dried potted snacks	Lead replacement petrol
Diet-aid drink powder	Tinned spaghetti
Draught premium lager	Brown ale
Takeaway café latte	Fixed telephones
Hair gel	Vinyl floor covering
Shower gel	Women's shoe repair
Slimming clubs	Launderette charges

Figure 23.7 Annual percentage change in the Retail Prices Index, UK

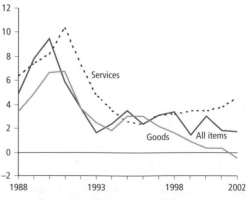

Source: Office for National Statistics

Table 23.8 Consumer and producer prices, UK

	1992	1997	2000	2001	2002
Consumer prices					
RPIX (January 1987=100)	136.4	156.5	167.7	171.3	175.1
RPI (January 1987=100)	138.5	157.5	170.3	173.3	176.2
HICP (1996=100)	90.9	101.8	105.6	106.9	108.3
Producer prices (1995=100)					
Output prices					
Manufactured products	90.2	103.5	108.0	108.2	108.5
of which:					
Food, beverages and tobacco	89.4	103.9	107.8	110.1	111.5
Petroleum products	84.7	113.9	149.7	142.0	136.7
Input prices[1]					
Materials purchased	83.8	90.9	94.2	92.8	89.8
Fuels purchased	104.6	88.3	86.7	94.6	91.7

1 Includes climate change levy from April 2001.
Source: Monthly Consumer Price Indices, Producer Prices, Office for National Statistics

The Chancellor of the Exchequer intends, subject to confirmation when the autumn 2003 Pre-Budget Report is published, to change the inflation target at that time to one based on the HICP definition. This will not affect pensions or benefits, which will continue to be linked to changes in the RPI.

Annual underlying inflation (RPIX) has fluctuated considerably in the last 25 years or so, peaking at 20.8 per cent in May 1980. However, it was much lower in the 1990s, and since 1993 has been in a relatively narrow range, from around 2 per cent to 3½ per cent. It averaged 2.2 per cent in 2002, and was generally close to the Government's current target of 2½ per cent – set in May 1997 – from April 1999 to October 2002. RPIX increased in November 2002 and remained above the Government's target into the first half of 2003. HM Treasury forecast it would remain a little above this target for a few months but then ease back.

In 2002 the all items RPI averaged 1.7 per cent. Goods inflation averaged –0.5 per cent, the first time the annual change has ever been negative, since the series began in 1987; services inflation was 4.6 per cent (see also Figure 23.7). On the HICP measure UK inflation was 1.3 per cent, equal with Germany as the lowest in the EU. This was significantly below the EU average of 2.1 per cent and it has remained below this average in the first half of 2003.

Producer input prices for materials and fuels purchased by manufacturing industry fell by 3.2 per cent in 2002, the largest fall since 1998. Producer output price inflation was 0.3 per cent in 2002, little changed from the 0.2 per cent recorded in 2001.

The experimental ONS Corporate Services Price Index (CSPI), which aims in the long run to be the services sector equivalent of the manufacturing Producer Prices Index, showed a 2.3 per cent increase in 2002, compared with 4.8 per cent in 2001. Above average increases occurred in business air fares, waste disposal, property rental payments and security services, whereas sea and coastal water freight, and freight forwarding showed declines. The aggregate CSPI currently has 31 component indices and covers 50 per cent of the corporate services sector.

Labour market

UK employment reached a record level of 27.91 million in the three months to May 2003, 254,000 higher than in the same period a year earlier, and representing an employment rate of 59.9 per cent. According to the International Labour Organisation measure, unemployment was 1,474,000 in the three months to May 2003, 50,000 lower than a year earlier. This represented 5.0 per cent of the workforce, well below the figure of 8.1 per cent for all EU countries (see chapter 11).

Economic strategy

The main elements of the Government's economic strategy, designed to deliver high and stable levels of economic growth and employment, are as set out in the 2003 Budget:

- maintaining macroeconomic stability;
- meeting the productivity challenge;
- increasing employment opportunity for all;
- building a fairer society;
- delivering high-quality public services; and
- protecting the environment.

HM Treasury is the department with prime responsibility for the Government's monetary and fiscal policies – in particular money supply, taxation and spending. It is also responsible for wider economic policy, which it carries out in conjunction with other government departments, such as Trade and Industry, Education and Skills, Work and Pensions, and Transport.

Economic and monetary union (EMU)

Government policy on EMU (see page 61) was originally set out by the Chancellor of the Exchequer in October 1997. The Government is in favour of UK membership providing the economic conditions are right. The determining factor is the national economic interest and whether the economic case for joining is clear and unambiguous. The Government has set out five economic tests which must be met before any decision to join can be made. The five tests are:

- sustainable convergence between the United Kingdom and the economies of a single currency;
- whether there is sufficient flexibility to cope with economic change;
- the effect on investment;
- the impact on the UK financial services industry; and
- whether it would be good for employment.

The assessment of the five economic tests in June 2003 concluded that at the present time a decision to join EMU would not be in the national economic interest. The Government has announced a number of reforms – that are in the UK economic interest and appropriate to help meet the five tests – for which there is a realistic prospect of making significant progress over the next year. If a decision to recommend joining is taken by the Government, it will be put to a vote in Parliament and then to a referendum of the UK people.

Economic stability

The Government has established frameworks for the operation of both monetary and fiscal policy to achieve low and stable inflation and sound public finances. It seeks to ensure the coordination of monetary and fiscal policy by setting mutually consistent objectives for both.

The Bank of England's Monetary Policy Committee (see page 453) sets interest rates to meet the Government's inflation target of 2½ per cent, as defined by the 12-month change in RPIX. Since the introduction of the new monetary framework in May 1997, official interest rates peaked at 7½ per cent in 1998, compared with a peak of 15 per cent in 1989 in the previous economic cycle. More recently, they were held at 4 per cent from November 2001 to February 2003, when they were reduced to 3¾ per cent, and in July 2003 they were further reduced to 3½ per cent. Concern over the faltering international economy and its hesitant recovery has been the main reason behind these recent interest rate cuts. Between February 2000 and July 2003, interest rates were cut by 2½ percentage points, mainly in response to the global economic slowdown.

Figure 23.9 shows sterling's effective exchange rate against other major currencies since 1997.

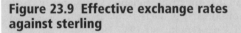

Figure 23.9 Effective exchange rates against sterling

Indices 1997=100

Source: Bank of England

Fiscal policy framework

The *Code for Fiscal Stability* sets out the five key principles of fiscal management at the heart of the

Government's fiscal policy framework:

- *transparency* in the setting of fiscal policy objectives, the implementation of fiscal policy and the publication of the public accounts;
- *stability* in the fiscal policy-making process and in the way fiscal policy impacts on the economy;
- *responsibility* in the management of the public finances;
- *fairness*, including between generations; and
- *efficiency* in the design and implementation of fiscal policy and in managing both sides of the public sector balance sheet.

The Code also requires the Government to state both its objectives and the rules through which policy will be operated. These objectives are:

- over the medium term, to ensure sound public finances and that spending and taxation impact fairly within and between generations; and
- over the short term, to support monetary policy and, in particular, to allow the 'automatic stabilisers' to help smooth the path of the economy.

These objectives are implemented through the Government's two fiscal rules, against which the performance of fiscal policy can be judged:

- *the golden rule* – over the economic cycle, the Government will borrow only to invest and not to fund current spending; and
- *the sustainable investment rule* – public sector net debt as a proportion of GDP will be held over the economic cycle at a stable and prudent level. Other things being equal, net debt will be maintained below 40 per cent of GDP over the economic cycle.

The fiscal rules are designed to ensure sound public finances in the medium term They allow flexibility in two key respects:

- the rules are set over the economic cycle, allowing fiscal balances to vary between years in line with the cyclical position of the economy; and
- the rules work together to promote capital investment while ensuring sustainable public finances in the longer term.

The fiscal policy framework also recognises the uncertainty that is inherent in projecting public finances. Projections are therefore based on cautious assumptions for key economic variables, including the trend rate of growth, equity prices

and the level of unemployment. This approach builds a safety margin into the public finances and minimises the need for unexpected changes in taxation or spending. The assumptions are audited by the Comptroller and Auditor General as part of a three-year rolling review to ensure they remain reasonable and cautious.

Sound public finances are a prerequisite for sustainable investment in public services. The fiscal rules are the foundation of the *public spending framework* (see chapter 24) and have important consequences for the structure of the budgeting regime.

The Budget

The Budget is presented annually by the Chancellor of the Exchequer in a major speech to Parliament. Budget day in 2003 was on 9 April and the 2003 Budget Report comprised two documents:

- the Economic and Fiscal Strategy Report (EFSR), setting out the Government's long-term goals and the comprehensive strategy it is pursuing to achieve them, the progress that has been made so far, and the further steps the Government is taking in the 2003 Budget to advance its long-term goals; and
- the Financial Statement and Budget Report (FSBR), providing a summary of each of the main Budget measures and how they affect the Budget arithmetic, and updated forecasts of the economy and the public finances.

Origins of the Budget

The origins of the Exchequer go back to the Norman period in the 11th century. The Norman system was based on two departments to deal with finance: the first, the Treasury, received and paid out money on behalf of the Monarch; the second, the Exchequer, had a lower office connected to the Treasury which received money, and an upper office, a court of law concerned with regulating the King's accounts. The word 'exchequer' comes from the Latin *scaccarium* meaning a chessboard. The name was given to the court because counters were moved on a square table. The word 'budget' comes from an old French word *bougette* which means little bag.

Under the Code for Fiscal Stability (see page 353), the Government is committed to publishing a Pre-Budget Report (PBR) at least three months before the Budget (usually in the previous November). The PBR sets out updated forecasts for the economy and the public finances, reports on how the Government's policies are helping to deliver its long-term goals, and describes the reforms that the Government is considering ahead of the forthcoming Budget and on which it will be consulting in the months ahead.

Industrial and commercial policy

The Department of Trade and Industry (DTI) aims to increase UK competitiveness and scientific excellence to generate higher levels of sustainable growth and productivity.

Competitiveness

UK performance in improving productivity is assessed in the DTI's productivity and competitiveness indicators. The latest full update of indicators was published in October 2002 and is available on the DTI website (*www.dtistats.net/competitiveness*); it includes international comparisons with other members of the G7 and the OECD. The 2002 indicators showed that the United Kingdom:

- had the fastest growth in GDP per head in the G7 over the past decade, largely due to strong labour market performance;
- had a macroeconomic environment that was becoming less volatile;
- was well-regulated compared with other G7 countries;
- had an excellent science base and a rapidly expanding number of university 'spin-out' companies; and

Table 23.10 Productivity and unit wage costs, UK

			1995=100
	1992	1997	2002
Output per job			
Whole economy	91.0	103.1	110.3
Production	88.3	100.8	115.4
Manufacturing	92.2	100.7	114.9
Output per hour worked			
Whole economy	n/a	103.3	113.5
Production	n/a	101.1	118.1
Manufacturing	n/a	100.5	116.4
Unit wage costs			
Whole economy	99.4	104.5	120.4
Manufacturing	94.5	108.0	116.4

Source: Office for National Statistics

- was one of the leading countries for inward research and development (R&D) investment.

On the other hand:
- UK productivity continued to lag;
- innovation performance remained disappointing;
- there were relatively low levels of investment; and
- there were low rates of female entrepreneurship.

In 2002 UK whole economy productivity growth (measured by output per job) was 1.5 per cent, slightly higher than the 1.1 per cent increase recorded in 2001. The alternative measure, output per hour worked, showed a 1.7 per cent increase in 2002, compared with 0.9 per cent in 2001.

Enterprise, innovation and business support

The DTI promotes enterprise and innovation to increase productivity. It does this by encouraging business start-ups, and by increasing the capacity of business, including small and medium-sized enterprises (SMEs) to grow, invest, develop skills, adopt best practice, and exploit opportunities abroad.

Following a reorganisation of its business support programmes, the DTI launched a number of new products in the first half of 2003, including an extension of the Small Firms Loan Guarantee. The first three of these are specifically aimed at SMEs:

- a grant to support R&D projects;
- a grant to help prepare business for innovation;
- Knowledge Transfer Partnerships for business development (see chapter 26);
- supply chain groups for the automotive industry; and
- an initiative to promote development in the metals technology industries.

Business Link (*www.businesslink.org*) is the national business advice service, delivering independent advice, business information and access to a wide network of business support organisations throughout England. It reports to the Small Business Service (*www.sbs.gov.uk*), an agency of the DTI, which is responsible for organising the delivery of help to SMEs. Similar business support arrangements apply in other parts of the United Kingdom, via the Business Gateway (*www.sbgateway.com*) for lowland Scotland, Highlands and Islands Enterprise (*www.hie.co.uk*), Welsh Development Agency National Gateway (*www.wda.co.uk*) and Invest Northern Ireland (*www.investni.com*).

Business finance

The Government is working in partnership with the private sector to help address weaknesses in the finance market for SMEs. Examples of funding include:

- Small Firms Loan Guarantee;
- Enterprise Investment Scheme;
- Venture Capital Trusts;
- Regional Venture Capital Funds (England only);
- Early Growth Funding Programme (England only);
- UK High Technology Fund;
- University Challenge Fund;
- Bridges Community Development Venture Fund; and
- community investment tax relief.

The Queen's Awards for Enterprise

The Queen's Awards for Enterprise (*www.queensawards.org.uk*) are the top UK annual awards for business performance. Successful organisations are entitled to use the Queen's Award emblem on their stationery, packaging, goods and advertising. Valid for five years, they are awarded for outstanding achievement in three categories: international trade, innovation and sustainable development. All UK organisations operating regularly as a 'business unit', and that can meet the criteria, are eligible to apply. In 2003 a total of 123 Awards were conferred – 62 for international trade, 51 for innovation and 10 for sustainable development.

Information and communications technology

The Government's e-commerce strategy is being taken forward by the Office of the e-Envoy (OeE), within the Cabinet Office. The e-Envoy is responsible for ensuring that all government services are available electronically by the end of 2005. Forty-seven per cent of adults who have used the Internet have accessed a government or public sector website.

By the end of 2002, 63 per cent of government services were online. The Government portal (*www.ukonline.gov.uk*) gives access to all UK Government information and services. The site has been awarded the Royal National Institute of the Blind's 'See it Right' logo. In April 2003 the Delivering on the Promise infrastructure initiative was launched by OeE. This is designed to make access to government services more customer friendly.

The United Kingdom has experienced strong growth in Internet take-up in recent years. According to the OeE, 99 per cent of schools and over 91 per cent of businesses were online in 2002.

Results from the second annual ONS e-commerce survey of UK businesses show that, excluding the financial sector, £18.4 billion of sales were made online in 2001 – £11.8 billion to business and £6.6 billion to households. This represented 1 per cent of total sales by the non-financial sectors of the UK economy. The majority of online orders were received from within the United Kingdom (81 per cent), with 12 per cent coming from other EU countries and 7 per cent

Table 23.11 Online sales by UK businesses in the non-financial sectors, by broad sector[1]

			£ billion
	2000	2001	2001
	10 or more employment	10 or more employment	All businesses
Manufacturing, electricity, gas and water supply, and construction	3.7	4.2	4.5
Wholesale, retail, catering, travel and telecommunications	6.9	11.1	11.7
Computing and other business services	1.4	1.4	1.9
Other services	n/a[2]	0.3	0.3
Total	**12.0**	**17.0**	**18.4**

1 Firms with fewer than ten in employment were excluded from the 2000 survey.
2 Coverage was increased for the 2001 survey to include other services.
Source: Office for National Statistics

from outside the EU. Purchases online by businesses amounted to £23.4 billion – the majority (80 per cent) were placed with other UK businesses. Sales by UK businesses in 2001 in the non-financial sectors over electronic networks other than the Internet were provisionally estimated at £182 billion.

Regional policy and development

Government regional policy aims to build economic success in the regions and boost regional capacity for innovation and enterprise. The Office of the Deputy Prime Minister (ODPM) has overall responsibility for regional policy in England, while responsibility for Regional Development Agencies rests with the DTI.

The DTI provides direct financial assistance to business through Regional Selective Assistance (RSA). This is a discretionary grant awarded in accordance with European Community law to secure employment opportunities and increase regional competitiveness and prosperity in areas where there are significant disparities from the national average in unemployment, the employment rate, or in the area's dependency on manufacturing. Grants awarded in 2002/03 amounted to over £72 million. In 2002 there were 435 offers of RSA grants accepted, valued at £190 million.

GVA per head in 2001 ranged from £14,800 in England to £11,300 in Northern Ireland (Table 23.12). Scotland, however, showed the smallest increase in GVA over the two years to 2001, growing by 6.7 per cent on a per head basis, compared with 8.4 per cent in England.

England

There are nine Regional Development Agencies (RDAs) in England – one for each region (see map on page 12). Each RDA has five statutory purposes:

- to further economic development and regeneration;
- to promote business efficiency, investment and competitiveness;
- to promote employment;
- to enhance the development and application of skills relevant to employment; and
- to contribute to sustainable development.

The RDAs are supported by, and work with, regional Government Offices and their work is scrutinised by voluntary regional chambers (see page 11).

RDAs are financed through a single funding programme with money from five contributing departments – the DTI (the lead sponsoring department), the ODPM, DfES, Defra and DCMS. This money is available to spend as the RDAs see fit, to achieve the regional priorities in their economic strategies and the targets in their corporate plans. Total funding is £1,864 million in 2003/04, rising to £2,045 million in 2005/06.

Scotland

The Scottish Executive's Enterprise, Transport and Lifelong Learning Department (ETLLD) (*www.scotland.gov.uk/who/etlld*) supports Scottish ministers in developing and promoting an environment that encourages business and enterprise in Scotland. It provides direct grant assistance to a wide range of businesses.

Table 23.12 Gross value added at current basic prices, UK

| | £ billion | | | £ thousand | | |
| | Gross value added | | | Gross value added per head | | |
	1999	2000	2001	1999	2000	2001
England	668.6	698.7	730.0	13.7	14.3	14.8
Wales	30.7	31.9	33.1	10.6	11.0	11.4
Scotland	64.9	67.2	69.2	12.8	13.3	13.7
Northern Ireland	17.7	18.4	19.1	10.5	10.9	11.3
United Kingdom[1]	**781.8**	**816.1**	**851.4**	**13.4**	**13.9**	**14.5**

1 Excludes compensation of employees and gross operating surplus (which cannot be assigned to regions) and statistical discrepancy.
Source: Office for National Statistics

Its objectives are promoted in collaboration with Scottish Enterprise and Highlands and Islands Enterprise, the lead economic development agencies in lowland and highland Scotland respectively. Most of the services for which they are responsible are delivered through a network of 22 Local Enterprise Companies (LECs). LECs provide support to business start-ups, venture capital, and a range of business services.

Wales

The Welsh Development Agency (WDA) (*www.wda.co.uk*) plays a key role in the economic development of Wales. It aims to attract world-class companies to invest in the country and works with local communities to encourage prosperity. The WDA is accountable to the Welsh Assembly Government.

Implementation of the Welsh Assembly Government's national economic development strategy, 'A Winning Wales', is coordinated by the Economic Development Department (EDD). It provides policy advice on a broad range of economic development matters and works closely with the National Assembly's economic development agencies, other public and voluntary bodies, and social partner organisations.

The EDD administers RSA grants and the Assembly Investment Grant, which offer small grants to small and medium-sized enterprises.

Northern Ireland

Invest Northern Ireland was established in April 2002 to encourage innovation and entrepreneurship in the Northern Ireland economy. It took on the functions previously carried out by five other bodies. In its first year of operation, it made offers of financial assistance of £138 million, which are expected to result in total investment of about £600 million.

EU regional funding

Structural Funds, which account for over one-third of the EU budget, are the main instruments for supporting social and economic restructuring across the EU. The UK allocation for the period 2000–06 is over £10 billion. Regions may have access to up to four funds, depending on their Objective status (see below). These funds comprise the European Regional Development Fund (ERDF), European Social Fund, European Agricultural Guidance and Guarantee Fund, and the Financial Instrument for Fisheries Guidance.

The ERDF aims to improve economic prosperity and social inclusion by investing in projects to promote development and encourage the diversification of industry into other sectors. This fund is available in Objective 1 and 2 areas.

Objective 1 status is the highest level of regional funding available from the EU. Eligible areas are those with less than 75 per cent of EU average GDP. Funding is aimed at promoting development and structural adjustment. In the United Kingdom, the qualifying areas are:

- Cornwall and the Isles of Scilly;
- Merseyside;
- South Yorkshire; and
- West Wales and the Valleys.

In addition to these areas, the United Kingdom also has two transitional[4] Objective 1 areas: the Scottish Highlands and Islands, and Northern Ireland (which also qualifies for the PEACE programme, see page 31). In total, the United Kingdom will receive over £3.9 billion of Objective 1 money between 2000 and 2006.

Objective 2 status is the second highest level of funding available from the EU. It aims to support the economic and social conversion of areas facing structural difficulties. Areas qualify under four main strands – industrial, rural, urban and fisheries. This objective covers nearly 14 million people in the United Kingdom. Over 5 million more are covered by transitional programmes. The United Kingdom will receive over £3.1 billion for Objective 2 (including transitional arrangements) over the period 2000–06.

Between March and July 2003 the DTI, HM Treasury and the ODPM held a joint UK-wide consultation process on the future of the Structural Funds after 2006. The Government is expected to give a full statement in autumn 2003.

Competitive markets

Enterprise Act 2002

The *Enterprise Act 2002* includes a range of measures designed to strengthen UK competition law and consumer enforcement frameworks, transform its approach to bankruptcy and corporate rescue, and empower consumers. The Act builds on the *Competition Act 1998*, recent

---

4 Areas that were eligible in 1994–99 but which are no longer eligible in the period 2000–06.

insolvency reforms and measures already implemented from the 1999 White Paper *Modern Markets: Confident Consumers*. The Office of Fair Trading (OFT) became a corporate body on 1 April 2003 and the role of Director General of Fair Trading was replaced by a new statutory board. The Act also established an independent Competition Appeal Tribunal. Most of the substantive consumer and competition provisions of the Act came into force on 20 June 2003.

The main reforms include:

- competition measures – removing the need for ministerial involvement from most decisions on mergers and references for market investigation, new criminal sanctions with a maximum penalty of five years in prison to deter cartels engaging in serious forms of anti-competitive behaviour, disqualification of directors for breaches of competition law, and greater opportunities for victims of anti-competitive behaviour to gain redress;
- consumer protection measures – extending the Stop Now Orders[5] approach to protect consumers from traders who do not meet their legal obligations, the OFT to approve consumer codes of practice, and provisions for designated consumer bodies to be able to make 'super-complaints' to the OFT and certain sector regulators (see page 473); and
- insolvency reforms – see page 351.

Office of Fair Trading

The OFT (*www.oft.gov.uk*) plays a leading role in promoting and protecting consumer interests throughout the United Kingdom, while ensuring that markets are fair and competitive.

Its work is structured into three areas:

- markets and policy initiatives – carrying out studies to explore how markets and market practices operate, considering super-complaints and liaising with interested parties, including through the OFT's enquiries unit;
- consumer protection – tackling rogue traders, eliminating unfair trading practices, approving consumer codes of practice and licensing certain traders (see also chapter 30); and

- competition enforcement – safeguarding vigorous and open competition by enforcing competition legislation, including action under the *Competition Act 1998* against anti-competitive behaviour and agreements, and decisions on mergers.

Each quarter, around 200 UK trading standards departments provide data to the OFT on the number of complaints received; the top ten types of complaint are shown in Table 23.13 below. The home maintenance, repair and improvement category was again the highest in 2002, increasing by 1.2 per cent over 2001.

Table 23.13 Top ten consumer complaints received by trading standards departments, UK

	2001	2002
Home maintenance, repair and improvement	78,524	79,464
Second-hand motor vehicles	67,710	62,807
Other personal goods and services	46,913	47,439
Upholstered furniture	38,664	35,195
Radio, TV and audiovisual equipment	36,306	34,971
Large white goods[1] and major fixed appliances	33,837	33,843
Personal computers and related hardware	39,820	33,604
Clothing and clothing fabrics	34,131	30,418
Food and drink	31,917	29,110
Double glazing products and installation	27,534	27,613

1 Such as fridge freezers, washing machines and dishwashers.
Source: Office of Fair Trading

Competition Commission

The Competition Commission (*www.competition-commission.org.uk*) is an independent public body established under the *Competition Act 1998*, replacing the Monopolies and Mergers Commission. It conducts in-depth inquiries into:

- mergers (both anticipated and completed);
- markets (the successor to scale monopoly and complex monopoly[6] inquiries); and

---

5 The Stop Now Orders (EC Directive) Regulations 2001 create a new enforcement system under which the OFT and ten other enforcement partners have strengthened powers to stop businesses from breaching a wide range of UK consumer protection laws.

6 A scale monopoly exists where a single company (or a group of interconnected companies) supplies or acquires at least 25 per cent of the goods or services of a particular type in all or part of the United Kingdom. A complex monopoly exists where a group of companies which are not connected, together account for at least 25 per cent of the supply of, or acquisition of, any particular description of goods or services in all or part of the United Kingdom and engage in conduct that has, or is likely to have, the effect of restricting, distorting or preventing competition.

4 June 2003 Liverpool is chosen from six short-listed cities to be European Capital of Culture in 2008 and promises a year-long festival featuring art, architecture, ballet, comedy, cinema, food, fashion, literature, music, opera, science and theatre. *Below right:* Liverpool's new arts centre, the Foundation for Art and Technology (FACT), opened in February 2003. Costing £10 million, FACT comprises three cinemas and two galleries.

7 June 2003 the British Museum celebrates its 250th anniversary.
It was the first museum to belong to a nation, rather than to a monarch
or a public patron, and was originally located in Montague House
(above), designed by Robert Hooke. Its exhibits represent cultures
from around the world and date from prehistory to the present.
Below: Carved from whale teeth and walrus ivory, the Lewis chessmen
were found buried on the Isle of Lewis off the west coast of Scotland
in 1831. They were probably made by Vikings in the late 12th century.

*' First we saw Egyptians that
had been dead 3,000 years ago.
Next we saw the skull of an
elephant. . . There was a piece
of the wall of Babylon and the
headdress of a lady 5,000 years
ago. . . There were thousands
of other things . . . and indeed
we could not stay to look at
half of them.'*

John Coltman aged 12 to his brother,
aged 8 (1780)

10 June 2003 art student Charlotte Harris wins the BP Portrait Award for her portrait *Untitled*, which was of her 83-year-old grandmother, Doris Davis. The portrait was chosen from a record 858 entries.

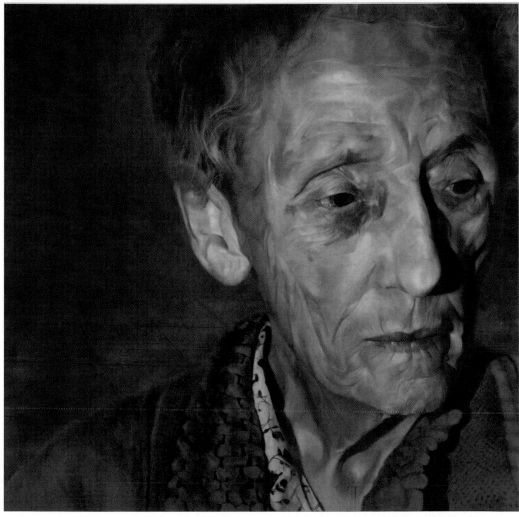

21–29 June 2003 the Special Olympics World Games (for athletes with learning disabilities) are held in Dublin, in the Republic of Ireland. Towns across the whole of Ireland were involved as host towns, welcoming delegations and giving them the opportunity to acclimatise and train before the competition began.

Top left: the Special Olympic 'Flame of Hope' torch arrives at Stormont, Northern Ireland on its way from Athens to Dublin. It is carried by teams of police officers running in relays.

Top right: Gary Haynes, winner of four Golds for Great Britain for powerlifting, with Muhammad Ali.

Centre left: Paul Wilson wins the Gold medal for power lifting in the squat 67.5 kilogram class.

Centre right: Christina McSherry wins a Gold after lifting 135 kilograms, almost twice her own weight.

Bottom left: Emma Stokes wins a Gold in the artistic gymnastics.

- the regulation, including price regulation, of the major regulated industries.

Every inquiry the Commission undertakes is in response to a reference made to it by another authority. This is usually the OFT, but references may also be made by the Secretary of State for Trade and Industry, or by the sectoral regulators under special legislative provisions. The Commission has no power to conduct inquiries on its own initiative.

The *Enterprise Act 2002* (see page 345) has enhanced the role of the Commission in most merger and market investigation inquiries, making it responsible for decisions on the competition questions and for taking and implementing decisions on appropriate remedies.

Mergers and markets
Most merger references are referred to the Competition Commission by the OFT. The mergers may be either anticipated or completed. The OFT has a duty to make a reference to the Commission if it believes there is or may be a relevant merger situation[7] that has resulted or may be expected to result in a substantial lessening of competition within any market or markets in the United Kingdom for goods and services.

Exceptionally, the Secretary of State can intervene in the consideration of a merger if this might raise a 'public interest consideration' specified by the *Enterprise Act 2002*, such as national security. The Secretary of State can serve a European intervention notice in cases where the competition issues have an EC dimension and fall under the EC Merger Regulation. This might occur if consideration was being given whether to take appropriate measures to protect legitimate interests (under Article 21(3) of the ECMR) such as public security.

The special provisions for newspaper mergers and for water enterprise mergers in England and Wales under the *Fair Trading Act 1973* are still in place. In the latter case, the OFT is obliged to refer mergers between two or more enterprises if the gross assets of the target and at least one of the water enterprises of the acquirer exceed £30 million.

---

7 A merger qualifies for investigation if either the value of the UK turnover of the enterprise acquired (or to be acquired) exceeds £70 million or if the share of supply of goods or services in the United Kingdom (or a substantial part of the United Kingdom) is at least 25 per cent as a result of the merger.

The OFT and those utility regulators that have concurrent powers also examine markets and may make a reference to the Competition Commission to establish whether a feature or combination of features of a market is, or appears to be, preventing, restricting or distorting competition.

Sectoral regulators
A number of bodies regulate particular industries or sectors formerly in public ownership, including gas, electricity, water, telecommunications and the railways. Each regulator has the power to apply and enforce the *Competition Act 1998* to deal with anti-competitive agreements or abuse of market dominance relating to relevant activities in their designated sector.

EU Single Market
The Government works with the European Commission and other Member States to ensure effective competition within the Single Market (see page 61). It is looking to improve the way the market operates through wide-ranging economic reforms which target 'weak areas'. By May 2003, 98.5 per cent of Single Market measures had been incorporated into UK law.

Corporate affairs

There were 3.86 million UK enterprises in the whole economy in 2002, including many large companies.

According to a *Financial Times* survey of the world's 500 largest companies in March 2003, 39 were UK-based and 34 were UK-owned, with a market capitalisation of US$1,051 billion. Of the top ten UK companies by market capitalisation, four were banks and there were two each in oil and gas, and in pharmaceuticals and biotechnology (see Table 23.15). BP, the biggest UK company, was the ninth largest in the world and the third largest oil and gas company. In the other most valuable sectors, by market capitalisation:

- the United Kingdom had three representatives in the world's top ten banks – HSBC Holdings, Royal Bank of Scotland and HBOS;
- GlaxoSmithKline was the world's fourth largest pharmaceuticals and biotechnology company, and AstraZeneca ranked eighth; and
- Vodafone was the world's largest telecommunication services company.

Table 23.14 Business enterprises,[1] UK, 2002

	Number of enterprises	% of enterprises	% of employment	% of turnover
Enterprises with employees	1,167,530	30.7	87.0	93.0
Number of employees:				
1–4	760,525	20.0	10.0	8.9
5–9	206,135	5.4	6.5	6.0
10–19	113,580	3.0	7.0	7.2
20–49	53,440	1.4	7.3	7.8
50–99	18,020	0.5	5.5	6.7
100–199	7,605	0.2	4.7	6.2
200–249	1,635	0.0	1.6	2.1
250–499	3,175	0.1	4.9	7.5
500+	3,415	0.1	39.6	40.6
Enterprises with no employees[2]	2,630,195	69.3	13.0	7.0
All enterprises	**3,797,725**	**100**	**100**	**100**

1 Private sector. For statistical purposes public corporations and nationalised bodies are included. Around 63,000 central and local government enterprises and non-profit organisations are excluded.
2 Sole proprietorships, partnerships comprising only the self-employed owner-manager(s), and companies comprising only an employee director.
Source: Small Business Service

In the private sector over 3,400 UK enterprises employed 500 or more people (see Table 23.14), accounting for just 0.1 per cent of total enterprises, but representing 40 per cent of total employment and 41 per cent of turnover.

Small firms play an important part in the UK economy. Around 44 per cent of the private sector workforce in 2002 were in companies employing

Table 23.15 Top ten UK companies by market capitalisation, 2003[1]

	Market capitalisation (US$ billion)[2]
BP/oil & gas	144.4
Vodafone/telecommunication services	122.9
GlaxoSmithKline/pharmaceuticals & biotechnology	107.1
HSBC Holdings/banking	98.0
Royal Bank of Scotland/banking	69.4
Shell Transport & Trading/oil & gas	59.6
AstraZeneca/pharmaceuticals & biotechnology	59.1
HBOS/banking	40.0
Barclays/banking	38.4
Diageo/beverages	32.6

1 As at 28 March.
2 Market capitalisation represents the number of shares issued multiplied by their market value.
Source: *FT 500 Survey*

fewer than 50 people. Just over 2.6 million enterprises were sole proprietorships or partnerships without employees, while a further 761,000 enterprises employed one to four people (see Table 23.14). Together these 3.4 million enterprises accounted for over 89.3 per cent of the total number of enterprises, 23 per cent of employment and 16 per cent of turnover.

The number of enterprises in the United Kingdom registering for VAT fell by 4 per cent to 175,500 between 2000 and 2001, while those de-registering fell by 8 per cent to 162,700 (see Table 23.16). The net gain of 12,700 enterprises over the year represents a rise in the total business stock for the sixth consecutive year. Only two sectors, construction, and hotels and restaurants, recorded an increase in registrations in 2001, while all sectors except mining, energy and water showed a decrease in de-registrations. During 2001 the largest net losses were in wholesale, retail and repairs and in manufacturing, while the largest net gain was in business services. This sector had grown by over 140,000 in the eight years to 2001 to 452,500, or one in four UK VAT-registered businesses at the start of 2002.

Company profitability

Company profitability for all UK private non-financial companies, in terms of the net rate of

Table 23.16 Business start-ups and closures,[1] UK

	Thousands and rate per 10,000 resident adults		
	1999	2000	2001
Registrations			
Number	178.5	183.3	175.5
Rate	38	39	37
De-registrations			
Number	172.0	177.1	162.7
Rate	37	37	34
Businesses registered at end year	1,658.1	1,664.4	1,677.1

1 Those registering and de-registering for VAT. There are separate registration and de-registration thresholds.
Source: Small Business Service

Figure 23.17 Profitability of UK companies

Annual net rate of return (%)

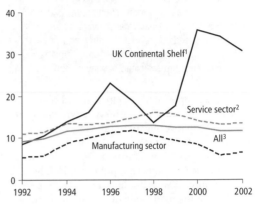

1 Those involved in the exploration for, and production of, oil and natural gas from the UK Continental Shelf (UKCS).
2 Excludes financial service sector companies.
3 Includes other sectors (such as construction, electricity and gas supply, agriculture, mining and quarrying).
Source: Office for National Statistics

return on capital employed, was 11.6 per cent in 2002, similar to the 11.7 per cent recorded in 2001 (see Figure 23.17). Among the individual sectors:

- manufacturing companies' net rate of return increased to 6.4 per cent, compared with 5.7 per cent in the previous year (the latter being the lowest annual rate of return since 1992);
- service companies' net rate of return was estimated at 13.4 per cent, similar to their profitability in 2001;
- the net rate of return of UK Continental Shelf (UKCS) companies in 2002 was 30.6 per cent, compared with 34.2 per cent in 2001. Rates of return between 2000 and 2002 were at much higher levels than in previous years and reflected high levels of production and the high oil price in these years; and
- non-UKCS companies' net rate of return in 2002 was 10.9 per cent, compared with 10.7 per cent in 2001.

Corporate structure

At the end of September 2003 there were 1,754,475 companies on the active register in Great Britain, maintained by Companies House (*www.companieshouse.gov.uk*). This includes companies incorporated overseas with a place of business or branch in Great Britain. Most corporate businesses are 'limited liability' companies – the liability of members is restricted to contributing an amount related to their shareholding (or to their guarantee where companies are limited by guarantee). Since April

2001 businesses can also be incorporated as limited liability partnerships, with the organisational flexibility and tax status of a partnership but with limited liability for their members. In Northern Ireland, the Companies Registry reported 22,730 companies on their active register at the end of March 2003.

Companies may be either public or private – at the end of September 2003 there were 11,658 public limited companies (plcs) on the active register in Great Britain. Certain conditions must be satisfied before they can become plcs – they must be limited by shares and meet specified minimum capital requirements. Private companies are generally prohibited from offering their shares to the public.

Company law and corporate governance

Company law is designed to meet the need for proper regulation of business, to maintain open markets and to create safeguards for those wishing to invest in companies or do business with them. It takes account of EC Directives on company law, and on company and group accounts and their auditing.

A fundamental revision of British company law has been under way following an independent three-year review. The aim of the review was to

In April 2003 Business Link published *The No-Nonsense Guide to Government rules and regulations for setting up your business* (available via the Business Link and DTI websites). This includes information on tax, National Insurance, VAT, health and safety, employment law, trading regulations, and intellectual property, and explains the forms a business can take – for example sole trader, partnership or limited liability company.

develop a simple, modern, efficient and cost-effective framework for business activity in Great Britain. The Government published its response to the review's major recommendations and set out its core proposals for reform in a White Paper, *Modernising Company Law,* published in July 2002. In July 2003 it announced its intention to legislate on the main body of reforms as soon as practicable. Some more urgent issues, aimed at restoring investor confidence following a number of corporate failures in the United States, such as the Enron and Worldcom failures, will be brought forward as soon as parliamentary time allows.

New regulations came into force in August 2002 giving shareholders the right to an annual vote on company directors' pay, with the intention of strengthening accountability, transparency and the links between pay and company performance. A quoted company is required, as part of the annual reporting cycle, to publish a report on directors' remuneration. This must include full details, including the performance criteria for share options and long-term incentive schemes, a justification of any compensation payments when a contract is terminated, and a graph showing company performance. A company must put a resolution to shareholders on this remuneration report at each annual general meeting.

In April 2002 the Government commissioned an independent review of the role and effectiveness of company non-executive directors. The Higgs Review reported in January 2003. It recommended changes to the 'Combined Code' on corporate governance to require a greater proportion of independent, better-informed individuals on a company's board. The new Code will require greater transparency and accountability in the boardroom, formal performance appraisal, and closer relationships between non-executive directors and shareholders. The report calls for all boards to put in place a significantly more rigorous appointments process. The Financial Reporting Council (*www.frc.org.uk*) agreed the final text of the new Code, which will come into effect for reporting years beginning on or after 1 November 2003.

Table 23.18 Insolvencies, Great Britain

	2000	2001	2002
England and Wales			
Company insolvencies[1]			
Compulsory liquidations	4,925	4,675	6,230
Creditors' voluntary liquidations	9,392	10,297	10,075
Total	14,317	14,972	16,305
Individual insolvencies			
Bankruptcy orders	21,550	23,477	24,292
Individual voluntary arrangements[2]	7,978	6,298	6,295
Total	29,528	29,775	30,587
Scotland			
Companies			
Compulsory liquidations	344	378	556
Creditors' voluntary liquidations	239	224	232
Total	583	602	788
Individuals			
Sequestrations	2,965	3,048	3,215

1 Including partnerships.
2 Including deeds of arrangement.
Source: Department of Trade and Industry Insolvency Service

Insolvency

The Insolvency Service, an executive agency of the DTI (*www.insolvency.gov.uk*), operates in England and Wales mainly under the *Insolvency Act 1986*, the *Company Directors Disqualification Act 1986* and the *Companies Act 1985*. It provides the means for dealing with individual and corporate financial failure, and investigates fraud and misconduct in insolvencies. In Scotland, Accountant in Bankruptcy (*www.aib.gov.uk*) an executive agency of the Scottish Executive Justice Department, operates principally under Section 1 of the *Bankruptcy (Scotland) Act 1985*, as amended. The Northern Ireland Insolvency Service (*www.insolvency.detini.gov.uk*) operates under the Insolvency (Northern Ireland) Order 1989 and the Companies (Northern Ireland) Order 1989.

There was an 8.9 per cent increase in company insolvencies in England and Wales in 2002; in Scotland, where insolvencies are defined differently, the increase was 30.9 per cent (see also Table 23.18).

The *Enterprise Act 2002* contained provisions to modernise insolvency law in the areas of both individual and corporate insolvency. These provisions included:

- reducing the discharge period for most bankrupts and removing outdated statutory restrictions;
- introducing tighter restrictions on bankrupts whose conduct has been irresponsible or reckless;
- changing the provisions relating to the treatment of the bankrupt's home;
- for companies, restricting administrative receivership and streamlining administration;
- abolishing the Crown's preferential right to recover unpaid taxes ahead of other creditors; and
- modernising the financial regime of the Insolvency Service.

Regulation of business

The Cabinet Office's Regulatory Impact Unit (RIU) (*www.cabinet-office.gov.uk/regulation*) aims to ensure all new and existing regulation is necessary, to meet the principles of better regulation, and to impose the minimum burden. The RIU reports to the Minister for the Cabinet Office and assists government ministers to ensure that regulations are fair and effective. It takes an overview of regulations impacting on business, the voluntary sector, charities and the public sector.

The Unit's work involves promoting the principles of good regulation; removing unnecessary or over-burdensome legislation under the *Regulatory Reform Act 2001*; improving assessment, drawing up and enforcement of regulation; taking account of the needs of business identifying risk and assessing options to deal with risk; responsibility for the Cabinet Office Code of Practice on Written Consultation; and supporting the Better Regulation Task Force.

This Task Force (*www.brtf.gov.uk*) is an independent body that makes recommendations to the Government, to ensure that regulation and its enforcement accord with the five principles of good regulation: proportionality; accountability; consistency; transparency; and targeting. The Task Force comments on the quality of existing or proposed regulations, and carries out studies of particular regulatory issues.

Industrial associations

Trade associations represent companies that produce or sell a particular product or group of products. They exist to supply common services, regulate trading practices and represent their members in dealings with government departments. A range of other organisations exists to represent the views of business and to provide advice and assistance.

The CBI (Confederation of British Industry) (*www.cbi.org.uk*) was founded in 1965 and is the largest business organisation in the United Kingdom. Membership is corporate, comprising companies and trade associations – its direct corporate members employ over 4 million people, and its trade association membership represents over 6 million people in some 200,000 firms. The CBI's objective is to help create and sustain the conditions in which business can compete and prosper, both in the United Kingdom and overseas. It is the UK member of the Union of Industrial and Employers' Confederations (UNICE) and has offices in Brussels and Washington as well as 12 UK regional offices.

The British Chambers of Commerce (BCC) (*www.chamberonline.co.uk*) is the national network for chambers of commerce, which are local, independent, non-profit-making and organisations funded by membership subscriptions. In 2003 over 135,000 businesses were members of Chambers in its accredited network. With over 2,500 staff covering more than

100 locations, the network provides a support team to businesses throughout the United Kingdom. The BCC represents business views to the Government at local, regional and national levels and is also part of the global network of Chambers of Commerce. It publishes a quarterly economic survey of UK businesses.

The Institute of Directors (IoD) (*www.iod.com*) was established in 1903 and granted a Royal Charter in 1906. It provides advice on matters affecting company directors, such as corporate management, insolvency and career counselling, and represents the interests of members to authorities in the United Kingdom and EU. It has around 55,000 members.

The Federation of Small Businesses (FSB) (*www.fsb.org.uk*) was formed in 1974 and is the largest campaigning pressure group promoting and protecting the interests of the self-employed and small firms. It has over 174,000 members, and provides them with information and guidance on subjects such as taxation, employment, health and safety, and insurance.

Enterprise Insight (*www.enterpriseinsight.co.uk*) was launched in 2000 as a government-supported initiative and is a joint venture between the BCC, CBI, FSB and IoD. It aims to encourage more positive attitudes to enterprise among young people aged 5 to 30 and to develop their entrepreneurial skills.

Further reading

Budget 2003. Building a Britain of economic strength and social justice. Economic and Fiscal Strategy Report and Financial Statement and Budget Report April 2003. HM Treasury. The Stationery Office, 2003.

Champions of Better Regulation: Better Regulation Task Force Annual Report 2001/02. The Stationery Office, 2003.

Companies in 2002–2003. Department of Trade and Industry. The Stationery Office, 2003.

Modern Company Law for a Competitive Economy. Final Report of the Company Law Review Steering Group. 2 vols. Department of Trade and Industry, 2001.

Modernising Company Law. Cm 5553. 2 vols. Department of Trade and Industry. The Stationery Office, 2002.

Productivity and Enterprise: A World Class Competition Regime. Cm 5233. Department of Trade and Industry. The Stationery Office, 2001.

Productivity and Enterprise: Insolvency – A Second Chance. Cm 5234. Department of Trade and Industry. The Stationery Office, 2001.

Trade and Industry: Departmental Report 2003. Cm 5916. The Stationery Office, 2003.

United Kingdom National Accounts – the Blue Book (annual). Office for National Statistics. The Stationery Office.

Websites

Department of Trade and Industry
www.dti.gov.uk

HM Treasury
www.hm-treasury.gov.uk

National Statistics
www.statistics.gov.uk

WWW.

24 Public finance

Total UK government spending is expected to be around £456 billion in 2003/04, and public sector current receipts are forecast to be £428 billion (see Table 24.1). Social protection is the biggest single element of public spending, involving expenditure of £133 billion (29 per cent of total public spending) in 2003/04, followed by spending on the National Health Service (NHS) of £72 billion and on education of £59 billion.

In 2002/03 there was a deficit of £10.9 billion on the public sector current budget, compared with a surplus of £10.0 billion in 2001/02 (see Table 24.2). Global uncertainty affected the fiscal balances, as receipts weakened as a result of cyclical or otherwise temporary factors and the Government made a special contingency provision of £3 billion to cover the cost of UK military obligations in Iraq (see page 80). Public sector net borrowing was £22.2 billion and public sector net investment totalled £11.3 billion in 2002/03 (see Table 24.2).

Fiscal policy framework

The fiscal policy framework is designed to ensure sound public finances, which are a prerequisite for sustainable investment in public services. The *Code for Fiscal Stability* sets out the five principles of fiscal management – transparency, stability, responsibility, fairness and efficiency – and government objectives are implemented through two fiscal rules which are the foundation of the spending framework and are designed to promote economic stability:

- *the golden rule* – over the economic cycle, the Government will borrow only to invest and not to fund current spending; and
- *the sustainable investment rule* – public sector net debt as a proportion of gross domestic product (GDP) will be held over the economic cycle at a stable and prudent level – generally below 40 per cent of GDP.

The fiscal framework recognises that projections of the current budget and net debt involve a

Table 24.1 UK government expenditure and revenue 2003/04

	£ billion	Percentages
Expenditure by function		
Social protection	133	*29*
NHS	72	*16*
Education	59	*13*
Law and protective services	27	*6*
Defence	26	*6*
Debt interest	22	*5*
Housing and environment	20	*4*
Other health and personal social services	17	*4*
Industry, agriculture and employment	16	*4*
Transport	15	*3*
Other[1]	47	*10*
Total Managed Expenditure	**456**	***100***
Receipts		
Income tax	122	*29*
National Insurance	75	*18*
VAT	67	*16*
Excise duties	38	*9*
Corporation tax	31	*7*
Business rates	19	*4*
Council tax	19	*4*
Other[2]	58	*14*
Total receipts	**428**	***100***

1 Other expenditure includes spending on central administration; culture, media and sport; international co-operation and development; public service pensions; and spending yet to be allocated and some accounting adjustments.
2 Other receipts include capital taxes, stamp duties, vehicle excise duties and some other tax and non-tax receipts.
Source: *Budget Report 2003,* HM Treasury

considerable element of uncertainty. Projections of the public finances are therefore based on cautious assumptions for key economic variables, including the trend rate of growth, equity prices and the level of unemployment. This minimises the need for unexpected changes in taxation or spending. The assumptions are audited by the National

Table 24.2 Key fiscal indicators, UK

	1997/98	1998/99	1999/2000	2000/01	2001/02	2002/03
Public sector						
Surplus on current budget (£ billion)	−1.6	10.1	20.0	21.5	10.0	−10.9
Net investment (£ billion)	4.9	6.0	4.4	5.2	9.7	11.3
Net borrowing (£ billion)	6.5	−4.1	−15.7	−16.3	−0.3	22.2
Net debt (£ billion)	352.0	348.5	340.9	306.8	311.4	333.0
Net debt as a percentage of GDP	41.5	39.1	36.3	31.3	30.2	30.8

Source: *Financial Statistics,* Office of National Statistics

Audit Office (NAO, see page 356) under a three-year rolling review to ensure they remain reasonable and cautious.

Public spending framework

Public expenditure is measured across the whole public sector using aggregate Total Managed Expenditure (TME). TME is the sum of public sector current expenditure, public sector net investment and public sector depreciation. For budgeting purposes TME is split into:
- Departmental Expenditure Limits (DELs), which are three-year spending limits for departments; and
- Annually Managed Expenditure (AME), which covers those elements of spending that cannot reasonably be subject to firm multi-year pre-set limits and are instead subject to annual scrutiny as part of the Budget process (see chapter 23).

To improve long-term planning and protect capital investment, DELs are further divided into capital and resource (current) budgets, and these are managed separately.

Other features of the framework include:
- a five-year plan for spending on health (see page 172) and a ten-year plan for transport (see page 323);
- Public Service Agreements, through which each department is committed to deliver challenging targets that focus on outcomes;
- a National Asset Register to improve the utilisation of the public sector asset base;
- flexibility to allow departments to retain resources not fully spent by the end of the financial year, so assisting them in managing their budgets and avoiding wasteful end-of-year spending surges; and

- Resource Accounting and Budgeting (RAB), whereby public expenditure is planned, controlled and reported on a full resource basis, with DELs reflecting the full economic costs of delivering services. RAB aims to improve the efficiency of resource use and increases the focus on departmental objectives and outputs.

Public expenditure

Total Managed Expenditure rose from £223.5 billion in 1972/73 to £408.6 billion in 2002/03 (see Table 24.3) in terms of constant (2001/02) prices, taking account of the effects of inflation. During this period TME peaked as a proportion of GDP at 49.9 per cent in 1975/76, but by 1999/2000 this had fallen to 37.4 per cent, before rising to 39.9 per cent in 2002/03.

Spending priorities

In July 2002 the Government published its 2002 Spending Review, setting plans and targets for the period 2003/04 to 2005/06, and spending on the NHS to 2007/08. The plans envisage:
- current expenditure rising by 3.1 per cent in real terms in 2004/05 and 3.8 per cent in 2005/06;
- public sector net investment rising from its target of 1.8 per cent of GDP in 2003/04 to 2 per cent by 2005/06 and to 2¼ per cent by 2007/08;
- over 75 per cent of planned additional spending allocated to the key priority areas of health, education, criminal justice, housing and transport; and
- spending on the NHS growing by an annual average of 7.3 per cent in real terms until 2008.

Total Managed Expenditure is planned to grow by 4.3 per cent a year in real terms between 2002/03

Table 24.3 Trends in Total Managed Expenditure, UK

	1972/73	1982/83	1992/93	1997/98	2001/02	2002/03
In cash terms (£ billion)	28.1	137.5	272.1	323.6	389.6	421.0
In real terms (£ billion)[1]	223.5	293.9	340.9	356.9	389.6	408.6
Percentage of GDP	*41.8*	*48.5*	*44.2*	*39.3*	*38.8*	*39.9*

1 At 2001/02 prices.
Source: *Public Expenditure Statistical Analyses 2003*, HM Treasury

Table 24.4 Components of Total Managed Expenditure, UK

£ billion

	Outturn	Estimated outturn	Plans		
	2001/02	2002/03	2003/04	2004/05	2005/06
Resource Budget	215.8	241.6	249.1	263.8	283.4
Capital Budget	18.0	20.6	25.1	26.8	29.1
less depreciation	−9.6	−18.3	−10.3	−11.1	−11.8
Departmental Expenditure Limits	**224.1**	**243.9**	**263.8**	**279.5**	**300.7**
Annually Managed Expenditure	**165.5**	**177.1**	**191.8**	**205.2**	**215.8**
of which:					
Social security benefits	104.9	109.6	114.7	117.7	122.1
Tax credits[1]	5.2	5.8	8.2	11.2	12.5
Locally financed expenditure	19.8	20.7	23.0	24.6	26.1
Central government gross debt interest	22.1	20.8	21.8	23.2	24.3
Total Managed Expenditure	**389.6**	**421.0**	**455.7**	**484.7**	**516.5**

1 Includes working tax credits, stakeholder pension credits and, from 2003/04, child tax credits previously included as child allowances in Income Support and Jobseeker's Allowance.
Source: *Public Expenditure Statistical Analyses 2003*, HM Treasury

and 2005/06. Over this period spending on transport is set to grow by 8.3 per cent a year and on education by 5.7 per cent a year, while spending on debt interest and on social security is forecast to grow by 2.5 and 2.3 per cent a year respectively.

New Public Service Agreements for all government departments were published as part of the Government's spending plans in July 2002. The agreements set targets for the outcomes that each department is committed to achieving, and there are independent audit and inspection arrangements to monitor progress. Departments publish details of progress against their targets twice a year, and regular web-based reporting against the targets was introduced on the HM Treasury website (*www.hm-treasury.gov.uk/performance*) in April 2003.

Measures announced in the 2003 Budget included:

- £332 million to invest in further counter-terrorism measures over the next three years, to ensure that UK citizens are protected within the United Kingdom from the threat of international terrorism (see page 192);
- key issues to be investigated in the run-up to the next Spending Review in 2004, including a new study into the scope for relocating public service staff from London and the South East to other areas; and
- action to increase regional and local flexibility in public service pay systems and to increase transparency about performance.

UK local authorities are estimated to have spent nearly £106 billion in 2002/03 (see page 54), around a quarter of Total Managed Expenditure.

Table 24.5 Main Departmental Expenditure Limits[1]

£ billion

	Outturn	Estimated outturn	Plans		
	2001/02	2002/03	2003/04	2004/05	2005/06
Total Departmental Expenditure Limits	**224.1**	**243.9**	**263.8**	**279.5**	**300.7**
of which:					
Education and Skills	19.0	23.2	25.3	27.4	29.9
Health	53.5	59.1	65.6	71.6	78.7
of which: National Health Service	52.3	56.7	63.3	69.4	76.4
Transport	6.8	8.7	10.3	10.8	11.3
Office of the Deputy Prime Minister	4.5	5.6	6.6	7.2	7.5
Local government	37.0	37.6	41.3	44.4	48.3
Home Office	10.7	11.9	12.6	12.5	13.2
Defence	30.7	32.3	29.2	29.8	30.7
Trade and Industry	5.4	4.9	5.1	5.0	5.4
Work and Pensions	6.3	7.6	7.9	8.2	8.1
Scotland[2]	17.1	19.0	20.1	21.3	22.7
Wales[2]	8.6	9.7	10.4	11.0	11.9
Northern Ireland Executive[2,3]	5.9	6.7	6.8	7.1	7.6

1 Resource and net capital DELs on a full resource basis, net of depreciation.
2 Allocations within DEL totals may be subject to final decisions in allocation by the devolved administrations.
3 There is a separate DEL for the Northern Ireland Office.
Source: *Public Expenditure Statistical Analyses 2003*, HM Treasury

The main categories of local government expenditure are education, law and order, health and personal social services, social security, housing and other environmental services, and transport.

Public expenditure is planned and controlled on a departmental basis, except where devolved responsibility lies with the Scottish Parliament, the National Assembly for Wales or the Northern Ireland Assembly. The Scottish Parliament has limited financial authority to vary tax revenue in Scotland (see page 22). In 2002/03 the estimated outturn for the current and capital budgets of the devolved administrations totalled £18.1 billion in Scotland, £9.6 billion in Wales and £7.4 billion in Northern Ireland. Table 24.6 shows expenditure in 2001/02 when non-devolved expenditure has been allocated. England accounted for 80 per cent of expenditure, Scotland 10 per cent, Wales 6 per cent and Northern Ireland 4 per cent.

The Office of Government Commerce (OGC), an independent office of HM Treasury, is responsible for improving the efficiency and effectiveness of the commercial activities of central civil

government. In 2003/04 it has taken on a new role in assisting departments to set up project and programme management centres of excellence. The OGC is expected to have achieved its initial primary target of delivering value-for-money gains of £1 billion in the three years to the end of 2002/03. Between 2003/04 and 2005/06 its target is to deliver £3 billion of value-for-money gains.

Examination of public expenditure

Examination of public expenditure is carried out by select committees of the House of Commons. The committees study in detail the activities of particular government departments and question ministers and officials. The Public Accounts Committee considers the accounts of government departments, executive agencies and other public sector bodies, and examines reports by the Comptroller and Auditor General (C&AG) on the way in which these bodies have used their resources.

Audit of the Government's spending is conducted by the C&AG, an officer of the House of Commons and the head of the National Audit Office (NAO) (*www.nao.gov.uk*). The C&AG and

Table 24.6 Identifiable expenditure on services¹ 2001/02

	Expenditure (£ billion)	£ per head
England	246.5	5,012
Scotland	31.6	6,246
Wales	17.1	5,882
Northern Ireland	11.2	6,626
Total identifiable expenditure, UK	306.4	5,207
Non-identifiable expenditure,² UK	47.0	799
Total expenditure on services, UK	353.4	6,006

1 Expenditure on services differs from Total Managed Expenditure in that it excludes debt interest payments, net public service pensions and a number of accounting adjustments.
2 Expenditure, such as on defence and overseas aid, that is incurred on behalf of the United Kingdom as a whole.
Source: *Public Expenditure Statistical Analyses 2003,* HM Treasury

the NAO are independent of government. The Comptroller certifies the accounts of all government departments and executive agencies, and those of many other bodies receiving public funds. The Comptroller also has statutory authority to report to Parliament on the economy, efficiency and effectiveness with which departments and other public bodies have used their resources.

New audit powers
In May 2003 the C&AG's powers were extended by two Orders made under the *Government Resources and Accounts Act 2000*. One Order provides for the C&AG to become the statutory auditor of some 25 additional non-departmental public bodies (NDPBs – see page 50). The other Order gives the C&AG stronger rights of access to information relating to the spending of public money by a range of bodies, including train operating companies, registered social landlords, private contractors and their subcontractors that do business with government, and most recipients of government grants.

Public-private partnerships
The Government sees public-private partnerships (PPPs) as an important part of the delivery of high-quality public services. The aim is to improve the value for money, efficiency and quality of these services by bringing in private

sector management with the incentive of having private capital at risk. PPPs cover a variety of arrangements, including joint ventures; outsourcing; the sale of equity stakes in government-owned businesses; and the Private Finance Initiative (PFI), in which the public sector specifies the service needed and the private sector competes for the opportunity to deliver the service in a way that offers better value for money over the whole life of the asset than through conventional procurement. Contracts for over 560 PFI projects had been signed by mid-2003 and are expected to bring in some £35.5 billion of investment in schools, hospitals, roads and other public services.

Partnerships UK (*www.partnerships.org.uk*), owned jointly by the public and private sectors, supports public authorities in the development and implementation of PPP and PFI projects.

Debt and reserves management

The Government meets its borrowing needs by selling debt to the private sector. In 2002/03 UK public sector net debt was £333 billion (see Table 24.2), £22 billion higher than in 2001/02. Net debt represented 30.8 per cent of GDP, slightly higher than in the previous year but well below the level of 41.5 per cent in 1997/98. In 2002 the United Kingdom had the lowest debt-to-GDP ratio of any G7 country.

The objective of the Government's debt management policy is to minimise, over the long term, the cost of meeting the Government's financing needs, taking into account risk while ensuring that debt management policy is consistent with the aims of monetary policy. Operational responsibility for managing government debt rests with a Treasury agency, the United Kingdom Debt Management Office (DMO) (*www.dmo.gov.uk*).

Gilt-edged stock
The major debt instrument, government bonds, is known as gilt-edged stock ('gilts'), as government securities are judged by the market as having the lowest risk of default. Gilts include 'conventionals', which generally pay fixed rates of interest and redemption sums; and index-linked stocks, on which both principal and interest payments are linked to movements in the Retail Prices Index.

The annual *Debt and Reserves Management Report* sets out the framework for issuing gilts for the forthcoming fiscal year. The DMO, on behalf of the Government, is aiming for gilts sales of about £47.4 billion in 2003/04. Gilts will continue to be issued primarily by auction, and the DMO plans to hold 15 auctions of conventional gilts and eight of index-linked gilts in 2003/04.

At the end of March 2003 holdings of central government marketable securities were estimated at £308 billion. This comprised £215 billion of conventional gilts, £78 billion of index-linked gilts and £15 billion of Treasury Bills (short-term securities issued as part of the DMO's cash management operations). Insurance companies and pension funds held 66 per cent of gilts at the end of December 2002, other UK financial institutions 5 per cent, UK households 10 per cent, local authorities and public corporations 1 per cent and holders in the rest of the world 18 per cent.

Official reserves

The United Kingdom holds official reserves of gold, foreign currency assets and International Monetary Fund (IMF) Special Drawing Rights (SDRs). Apart from those SDR assets that constitute the United Kingdom's reserves tranche at the IMF, these are held in the Exchange Equalisation Account (EEA). The Bank of England, acting as the Treasury's agent, manages the EEA by carrying out day-to-day tasks, such as foreign exchange dealing and portfolio investment, within the framework of an annual remit set by the Treasury.

At the end of 2002 UK gross official holdings of international reserves totalled US$42.4 billion, including US$8.7 billion of US dollars, US$18.6 billion of euro, US$5.1 billion of Japanese yen, US$6.5 billion of SDRs and US$3.5 billion of gold. After deducting liabilities of US$26.8 billion, the net reserves totalled US$15.6 billion, compared with US$13.5 billion a year earlier.

Main sources of revenue

Government revenue is forecast to be £428 billion in 2003/04. The main sources (see Table 24.1) are:
- taxes on income (together with profits), which include personal income tax,

corporation tax and petroleum revenue tax (see page 434);
- taxes on expenditure, which include VAT (value added tax) and customs and excise duties;
- National Insurance contributions (NICs – see chapter 12); and
- taxes on capital, which include inheritance tax, capital gains tax, council tax and non-domestic rates (also known as business rates).

Taxation policy

The primary aim of tax policy is to raise sufficient revenue for the Government to pay for the services that its policies require and to service its debt, while keeping the overall burden of tax as low as possible. The Government has based its tax policy on the principles of encouraging work and saving, raising investment, and promoting fairness and opportunity. It has taken measures designed to improve productivity, secure employment opportunities, and protect the environment. It is reforming the tax and benefit system with the intention of guaranteeing decent family incomes and tackling child poverty. As part of these reforms, child tax credit and working tax credit were introduced in April 2003 (see chapter 12).

Collection of taxes and duties

The Inland Revenue assesses and collects taxes on income, profits and capital, and stamp duty. In 2002/03 its net receipts were £152 billion (see Table 24.7), 1.2 per cent less than in 2001/02, mainly reflecting a fall of 8.1 per cent in receipts of corporation tax. Its National Insurance Contributions Office (*www.inlandrevenue.gov.uk/nic*) is responsible for collecting NICs. HM Customs and Excise collected nearly £109 billion in taxes and duties in 2002/03 (see Table 24.8), 3.7 per cent higher than in 2001/02. Local authorities collect the main local taxes, such as council tax.

Under the self-assessment system for collecting personal taxation, around 9.3 million people – primarily higher-rate taxpayers, the self-employed and those receiving investment income – are required to complete an annual tax return for the Inland Revenue. Such taxpayers may calculate their own tax liability, although they can choose to have the calculations done by the Inland Revenue if they return the form by the end of September.

Tax measures in the Budget

Among the tax measures contained in the Budget in April 2003 were:

- measures to protect tax revenues (see below);
- a new regime for stamp duty (see page 364);
- changes to support a modern and competitive business tax system, including further reforms to VAT for small business and extensions to research and development tax credits; and
- a series of measures to improve waste management and protect the environment.

Review of Inland Revenue and Customs and Excise

In July 2003 the Government announced a major review of the organisations dealing with tax policy and administration. The review, which will report to the Chancellor of the Exchequer, will examine the best organisational arrangements to achieve the Government's present and future tax objectives, and a primary focus will be to make public service delivery more effective and efficient. The initial conclusions of the review will be announced by the Chancellor in the 2003 Pre-Budget Report.

Table 24.7 Inland Revenue taxes and duties

£ billion

	1997/98	1998/99	1999/2000	2000/01	2001/02	2002/03
Net receipts by Board of Inland Revenue						
Income tax and capital gains tax combined[1]	78.3	88.5	96.0	108.4	111.0	111.6
Corporation tax	30.4	30.0	34.3	32.4	32.0	29.4
Inheritance tax	1.7	1.8	2.0	2.2	2.4	2.4
Stamp duties	3.5	4.6	6.9	8.2	7.0	7.6
Petroleum revenue tax	1.0	0.5	0.9	1.5	1.3	1.0
Windfall tax	2.6	2.6	–	–	–	–
Total	**117.4**	**128.1**	**140.2**	**152.7**	**153.7**	**151.9**

1 From 1999/2000 receipts are net of payments of Working Families' Tax Credit and Disabled Person's Tax Credit.
Source: Inland Revenue

The United Kingdom has agreements governing double taxation with over 100 countries. They are intended to avoid double taxation arising, to deal with cross-border economic activity, and to prevent fiscal discrimination against UK business interests overseas. They also include provisions to counter tax avoidance and evasion. Among recent agreements signed is a new double taxation treaty with the United States, which replaces an existing treaty from 1975.

The Tax Law Rewrite Project, established in 1996, involves rewriting UK primary direct tax legislation so that it is clearer and easier to use, but without changing its general effect. Two Acts have been implemented using clearer language: the *Capital Allowances Act 2001* and the *Income Tax (Earnings and Pensions) Act 2003*. Proposals to modernise the legislation for Pay-As-You-Earn (PAYE) were issued for consultation in April 2003, involving the first complete overhaul of PAYE

since the regulations were implemented in 1944. Under PAYE, most wage and salary earners have their income tax deducted and accounted for to the Inland Revenue by their employer, in a way which enables most employees to pay the correct amount of tax during the year.

Protecting tax revenues

The 2003 Budget contained a series of measures designed to tackle tax fraud and avoidance. This included a new compliance and enforcement package for direct tax and NICs. An extra £66 million is being provided to the Inland Revenue over the next three years and this package of measures is expected to produce an extra £1.6 billion over this period. Additional staff will be deployed in three areas where significant risks to revenue have been identified:

- protecting the Exchequer from non-payment of tax and NIC debts and from failure to file tax returns;

Table 24.8 Customs and Excise taxes and duties

£ billion

	1997/98	1998/99	1999/2000	2000/01	2001/02	2002/03
Payments by HM Customs and Excise into the Consolidated Fund[1]						
VAT	50.6	52.3	56.4	58.5	61.0	63.5
Duties on:						
hydrocarbon oils	19.5	21.6	22.5	22.6	21.9	22.1
tobacco	8.4	8.2	5.7	7.6	7.8	8.1
spirits	1.5	1.6	1.8	1.8	1.9	2.3
beer	2.7	2.7	2.8	2.9	2.9	2.9
wine and made wine	1.4	1.5	1.7	1.8	2.0	1.9
cider and perry	0.1	0.1	0.2	0.2	0.2	0.2
betting, gaming and lottery	1.6	1.5	1.5	1.5	1.4	1.3
air passengers	0.5	0.8	0.9	1.0	0.8	0.8
Customs duties and agricultural levies	2.3	2.1	2.0	2.1	2.0	1.9
Insurance premium tax	1.0	1.2	1.4	1.7	1.9	2.1
Landfill tax	0.4	0.3	0.4	0.5	0.5	0.5
Climate change levy	–	–	–	–	0.6	0.8
Aggregates levy	–	–	–	–	–	0.2
All payments	**89.8**	**94.0**	**97.3**	**102.2**	**104.9**	**108.7**

1 Excluding shipbuilder's relief.
Source: HM Customs and Excise

- tackling fraud involving concealing undeclared income or profits offshore; and
- countering avoidance of corporation tax and of NICs and tax on employment income.

A further range of measures is being introduced to tackle instances of direct tax avoidance, protecting around £250 million a year. The measures include action to prevent tax and NICs avoidance through the payment of share-based remuneration, prevent tax avoidance in connection with life insurance policies held in trust, and action to prevent tax and NICs avoidance by those engaging domestic workers through a service company.

In addition, the Government is taking action aimed at tackling losses in the indirect tax regimes. The 2003 Budget introduced further measures designed to reduce VAT fraud and avoidance, and HM Customs and Excise is consulting on regulatory measures to reduce opportunities for alcohol fraud.

Taxes on income

Income tax
Income tax is charged on all income originating in the United Kingdom – although some forms, such

as child benefit, are exempt – and on all income arising abroad of people resident in the United Kingdom. Income tax is imposed for the year of assessment beginning on 6 April. The tax rates and bands for 2002/03 and 2003/04 are shown in Table 24.9. In 2002/03 there were around 29.4 million income taxpayers, including 3.1 million at the starting rate (10 per cent), 22.5 million at the basic rate (22 per cent), 3.1 million at the higher rate of 40 per cent (32.5 per cent on dividends) and over 800,000 with a marginal rate at the 20 per cent lower rate for savings income or the 10 per cent ordinary dividend rate.

Allowances and reliefs reduce an individual's income tax liability. All taxpayers are entitled to a personal allowance against income from all sources, with a higher allowance for the elderly (see Table 24.9). This higher allowance is only given in full to people with incomes up to a certain limit (£18,300 in 2003/04). One of the most significant reliefs, which is designed to encourage people to save towards their retirement, covers contributions to pension schemes. Personal tax-free saving is encouraged through the Individual Savings Account (ISA) (see page 461), while the 2003 Budget gave details of a new Child Trust Fund, which will provide every child born from September 2002 onwards with an endowment at birth of £250, rising to £500 for children in the poorest one-third of families that qualify for the full child tax credit.

Taxation of pensions

In December 2002 the Government announced proposals to simplify the taxation of pensions, at the same time as publishing its Green Paper on pensions (see page 149). Following consultation, it announced in June 2003 that it would introduce legislation in 2004 with the intention of implementing the changes in April 2005. The main features involve:

- abolishing the existing tax regimes governing pensions, including the eight different sets of tax rules, and introducing a single, unified set of rules;

- replacing the current limits on annual pension contributions by a single lifetime limit on the amount of pension saving that can benefit from tax relief – the Government intends to set the initial limit at £1.4 million on the scheme's proposed introduction in 2005;

- establishing a 'light touch' compliance regime, including an annual limit on inflows of value to an individual's pension fund – this limit would initially be £200,000 from 2005;

- encouraging flexible retirement, which would allow people to continue working while drawing an occupational pension; and

- allowing scope for more innovation in the market for annuities.

Corporation tax

Corporation tax is payable by companies on their income and capital gains. The main rate of corporation tax in the United Kingdom, 30 per cent, is lower than any other major European country. This rate is levied on companies with annual profits of over £1.5 million. The small companies' rate is 19 per cent, levied on firms with annual profits of between £50,000 and £300,000. There is a zero starting rate, so that companies with annual profits of up to £10,000 do not pay corporation tax. A sliding scale of relief is allowed for companies with annual profits of between £10,000 and £50,000 and between £300,000 and £1.5 million, so that the overall average rate paid by these firms is up to 19 per cent and between 19 per cent and 30 per cent respectively.

Table 24.9 Income tax allowances and bands, UK

	2002/03	2003/04
Income tax allowances		
Personal allowance		
age under 65	4,615	4,615
age 65–74	6,100	6,610
age 75 and over	6,370	6,720
Married couple's allowance[1]		
age 65 before 6 April 2000	5,465	5,565
age 75 and over	5,535	5,635
Income limit for age-related		
allowances	17,900	18,300
Blind person's allowance	1,480	1,510
Bands of taxable income[2]		
Starting rate of 10 per cent	0–1,920	0–1,960
Basic rate of 22 per cent	1,921–29,900	1,961–30,500
Higher rate of 40 per cent	over 29,900	over 30,500

1 Tax relief for this allowance is restricted to 10 per cent. The minimum amount for the allowance is £2,150 in 2003/04 (£2,110 in 2002/03).
2 The rate of tax applicable to savings income in the basic rate band is 20 per cent. For dividends the rates applicable are 10 per cent for income below the basic rate upper limit and 32.5 per cent above that.
Source: Inland Revenue

In August 2002 the Government issued a consultative document containing proposals to reform and modernise the corporation tax regime. It is proposing change in three areas: the tax treatment of capital assets not covered by earlier reforms; rationalisation of the way in which various types of income are taxed; and differences in the tax treatment of trading and investment companies. A further round of consultation was launched in summer 2003.

Some capital expenditure – on plant and machinery, industrial buildings and agricultural buildings, for example – may qualify for relief in the form of capital allowances. There is a 40 per cent first-year allowance for expenditure on plant or machinery by small or medium-sized businesses. Small businesses can also claim 100 per cent first-year allowances on investments in information and communications technology (ICT) between 1 April 2000 and 31 March 2004, enabling them to write off immediately the entire cost against their taxable profit. In April 2002 a new research and development (R&D) tax credit, giving additional tax relief of 25 per cent of qualifying R&D expenditure, was introduced for large companies, complementing a similar credit for small and medium-sized firms. The April 2003 Budget introduced a series of reforms to this tax credit, including reducing the minimum expenditure threshold from £25,000 to £10,000.

There are 100 per cent first-year allowances for investments in qualifying environmental technologies (including allowances introduced as part of the climate change levy package – see page 363). Expenditure from 1 April 2003 on designated water-efficient technologies will qualify for this 100 per cent first-year allowance. The designated energy-efficient technologies that qualify for the allowance will be expanded later in 2003.

Taxes on capital

Capital gains tax
Capital gains tax (CGT) is payable by individuals, personal representatives of deceased people, and trusts on gains realised from the disposal of assets. It is payable on the amount by which total chargeable gains for a year exceed the exempt amount (£7,900 for individuals and £3,950 for most trusts in 2003/04, up from £7,700 and £3,850 respectively in 2002/03). Subject to conditions, gains on some types of asset are exempt from CGT, including the principal private residence, UK government gilt-edged securities, certain corporate bonds, and gains on assets held in a Personal Equity Plan or an Individual Savings Account (see page 461). For individuals, CGT in 2003/04 will be payable at 10, 20 or 40 per cent, depending on a person's marginal income tax rate.

CGT taper relief reduces the amount of the chargeable gain depending on how long an asset has been held since April 1998, with a higher rate of relief for business assets than for non-business assets. The current CGT taper relief reduces the percentage of the gain that is chargeable for a business asset from 100 per cent for assets held for less than one year to 25 per cent for assets held for two years or more. For non-business assets the chargeable gain falls from 100 per cent for assets held for less than three years to 60 per cent for assets held for ten years or longer. A series of measures to simplify CGT was introduced in April 2003, designed to reduce compliance burdens and allow some capital losses arising on the disposal of certain rights to be carried back and set off against related gains of earlier tax years.

Inheritance tax
Inheritance tax is essentially charged on estates at the time of death and on gifts made within seven years of death; most other lifetime transfers are not taxed. There are several important exemptions, including transfers between spouses, and gifts and bequests to UK charities, major political parties and heritage bodies. In general, business assets and farmland are exempt from inheritance tax, so that most family businesses can be passed on without a tax charge.

Tax is charged at a single rate of 40 per cent above a threshold (£255,000 in 2003/04, up from £250,000 in 2002/03). Only about 5 per cent of estates each year become liable for an inheritance tax bill.

Taxes on expenditure

Value added tax (VAT)
VAT is a tax on consumer expenditure and is collected at each stage in the production and distribution of goods and services. The final tax is payable by the consumer. The standard rate is 17.5 per cent, while certain goods and services are relieved from VAT, either by being charged at a zero rate or by being exempt, and there is a reduced rate of 5 per cent on certain goods and services:

- The reduced rate of 5 per cent applies to a number of goods and services, including domestic fuel and power, certain types of property conversion, children's car seats, women's sanitary products, the installation of energy-saving materials in homes and grant-funded installation of heating equipment.
- Under zero rating, a taxable person does not charge tax to a customer but reclaims any VAT paid to suppliers. Among the main categories where this applies are goods exported to other EU countries; most foods; water and sewerage for non-business use; passenger transport; books, newspapers and periodicals; construction of new residential buildings; young children's clothing and footwear; drugs and medicines supplied on prescription; specified aids for handicapped people; and certain supplies by or to charities.
- For exempt goods or services, a taxable person does not charge any VAT but is not entitled to reclaim the VAT on goods and

services bought for his or her business. The main categories where this applies are many supplies of land and buildings; financial services; postal services; betting and gaming (where there are some exemptions); lotteries; much education and training; and health and welfare.

Recent Budgets have contained measures designed to help new and small businesses, allowing them to manage their entry into the VAT system, reduce their VAT administrative burden and improve their cash flow. From April 2003 the annual level of turnover above which traders must register for VAT was raised from £55,000 to £56,000. The optional VAT flat-rate scheme was extended to small businesses with an annual turnover of up to £150,000, compared with the previous limit of £100,000. Under this scheme, businesses do not have to account for VAT on each purchase and sale but are able to calculate their net VAT liability by applying a flat-rate percentage to their total annual turnover. The 2003 Budget also contained a number of measures designed to modernise and simplify the VAT system, such as simplifying the VAT treatment of business gifts, and measures to tackle VAT fraud and avoidance.

Environmental and transport taxes

Vehicle excise duty (VED): since March 2001 VED for new cars has been determined according to the carbon dioxide (CO_2) emissions of the vehicle and the type of fuel used. There are now six VED bands for new cars (see Table 24.10). For cars registered before 1 March 2001 VED is determined according to engine size. The standard rate is £165, with a lower rate of £110 for cars up to 1,549 cc. VED for goods vehicles ranges from £165 to £1,850 a year (£160 to £1,350 for lorries with reduced pollution certificates). Duty on buses varies according to seating capacity.

Road fuel duties: these are charged on mineral oils used as road fuel, with lower rates for more environmentally friendly fuels, such as ultra low-sulphur fuels and road fuel gases.

Air passenger duty: for flights within the United Kingdom and for those to destinations in the European Economic Area (EEA), those countries applying to join the EU (see page 63) and Switzerland, the duty is £5 for the lowest class and £10 for any other class; the equivalent rates to other destinations are £20 and £40 respectively. All

flights *from* airports in the Scottish Highlands and Islands are exempt from duty in recognition of their remoteness and dependence on air travel.

Landfill tax: this is levied at £14 a tonne, with a lower rate of £2 a tonne for inert waste.

Table 24.10 Vehicle excise duty rates for cars registered after 1 March 2001

£

CO_2 emissions (g/km)	Petrol car	Diesel car	Cars using alternative fuels
100 and below	65	75	55
101 to 120	75	85	65
121 to 150	105	115	95
151 to 165	125	135	115
166 to 185	145	155	135
186 and over	160	165	155

Source: *Budget Report 2003,* HM Treasury

Aggregates levy: this is applied at £1.60 a tonne on the extraction of sand, gravel and rock for use as aggregate.

Climate change levy: since April 2001 this has been levied on the non-domestic use of energy. All revenues are recycled back to business through a reduction in employers' National Insurance contributions and additional support for energy efficiency measures (see page 445). An 80 per cent discount is available to energy-intensive business sectors that meet targets agreed with the Government for increasing energy efficiency and reducing greenhouse gas emissions.

Other indirect taxes and duties

As well as duties on tobacco and beer, wines and spirits (see box on page 364), other indirect taxes and duties include:

Insurance premium tax: this is levied at 5 per cent on most general insurance, with a higher rate of 17.5 per cent on travel insurance and on insurance sold by suppliers of cars and domestic appliances.

Betting and gaming duties: these are charged on off-course betting, pool betting, gaming in casinos, bingo and amusement machines. Rates vary with the particular form of gambling. The Government has modernised the structure of gambling taxation with the intention of reducing

Changes on indirect taxes and duties in the Budget

The main announcements on environmental and transport taxes and on other indirect taxes and duties in the April 2003 Budget included:

- an increase in tobacco, beer and wine duties in line with inflation and a freeze in the duty on spirits, sparkling wine and cider;
- deferring the annual revalorisation of the main road fuel duties until 1 October 2003 following the high and volatile levels of oil prices that occurred as a result of the military conflict in Iraq (see page 80). In addition, further duty differentials were announced to encourage the use of more environmentally friendly fuels, such as sulphur-free petrol and diesel;
- a new band of vehicle excise duty for the least polluting cars, while other car VED rates increased from 1 May 2003 (see Table 24.10), although the rates for lorries and motorcycles were frozen;
- no change in the climate change levy and the aggregates levy;
- higher rates of increase for the landfill tax, which encourages efforts to minimise the amount of waste generated – the rate will rise to £15 a tonne from April 2004, to £18 a tonne by 2005/06 and by at least £3 a tonne in subsequent years, on the way to a medium- to long-term rate of £35 a tonne; and
- abolition of the duty on bingo (from 27 October 2003) and its replacement by a 15 per cent tax on the gross profits of bingo companies.

administrative complexity, improving efficiency and helping the UK gambling industry to compete more effectively. Reforms have included replacing general betting duty by a 15 per cent tax on bookmakers' gross profits, and a similar arrangement is being implemented for bingo (see above).

Lottery duty: on the National Lottery there is a 12 per cent duty on gross stakes, but no tax on winnings.

Stamp duty

Some transfers are subject to stamp duty. Transfers of shares generally attract duty at 0.5 per cent of the cost, while certain types of document, such as declarations of trust, generally attract a small fixed duty of £5. Transfers by gift and transfers to charities are exempt. Duty on

Modernisation of stamp duty

Following consultation, the Government announced in the April 2003 Budget details of a major reform of stamp duty on UK land and buildings. Under the new regime, which will be introduced from December 2003, stamp duty land tax will replace the existing stamp duty on UK land and buildings. The new regime is intended to modernise administrative arrangements, close loopholes, remove distortions in the system and pave the way for the introduction of e-conveyancing systems. Subject to further consultation, new arrangements will apply to the charge on the grant of new leases. In addition, the exempt threshold for non-residential purchases and for new leases of non-residential property will rise from £60,000 to £150,000.

The existing stamp duty regime will continue to apply to other transfers, such as those of stocks and marketable securities, as well as interests in partnerships.

land and property is payable at 1 per cent of the total price when above £60,000, 3 per cent above £250,000 and 4 per cent over £500,000. Property transfers of up to £150,000 in the most disadvantaged areas in the United Kingdom are exempt from stamp duty, and since April 2003 stamp duty on certain non-residential transfers in these areas has no longer been payable.

Local authority taxation

Domestic property in Great Britain is subject to the council tax, one of the main sources of income for local authorities (see page 54). Each dwelling is allocated to one of eight valuation bands, based on its capital value (the amount it might have sold for on the open market) in April 1991. Discounts are available for dwellings with fewer than two resident adults or which are second homes, and those on low incomes may receive council tax benefit of up to 100 per cent of the tax bill (see page 158). In 2003/04, in England, the average council tax for a Band D dwelling (occupied by two adults) is £1,102 (compared with £976 in 2002/03): £1,058 in London, £1,098 in other metropolitan areas and £1,114 in shire areas. In Scotland the average Band D dwelling council tax is £1,009 and in Wales £837.

Non-domestic rates (also known as business rates) are a tax on the occupiers of commercial property.

The rateable value is assessed by reference to annual rents and reviewed every five years. Separate non-domestic rates are set for England, Wales and Scotland, and collected by local authorities. They are paid into separate national pools and redistributed to local authorities in proportion to their population.

In Northern Ireland, rates – local taxes on domestic and non-domestic properties – are based on the value of the property. For 2003/04 the average domestic rates bill in Northern Ireland is £471.

Further reading

2002 Spending Review. Opportunity and security for all: Investing in an enterprising, fairer Britain. New Public Spending Plans 2003–2006. Cm 5570. HM Treasury. The Stationery Office, 2002.

Budget 2003. Building a Britain of economic strength and social justice. Economic and Fiscal Strategy Report and Financial Statement and Budget Report April 2003. HM Treasury. The Stationery Office, 2003.

Inland Revenue Statistics. Contains statistics on taxes administered by the Inland Revenue. Available only on the Internet at *www.inlandrevenue.gov.uk/stats*

Annual Reports
Debt and Reserves Management Report. HM Treasury.

Public Expenditure Statistical Analyses. HM Treasury. The Stationery Office.

Websites

HM Treasury
www.hm-treasury.gov.uk

Inland Revenue
www.inlandrevenue.gov.uk

HM Customs and Excise
www.hmce.gov.uk

WWW.

25 International trade and investment

In July 2003 the Office for National Statistics published revised statistics for imports of goods from the rest of the EU. The revisions include initial adjustments to take account of the effect of fraud arising from traders importing goods and then reselling them without paying VAT on these sales. This fraud led to imports being under-recorded. The revisions amount to £1.7 billion in 1999, £2.8 billion in 2000, £7.1 billion in 2001 and £11.1 billion in 2002.

The balance of payments figures and commentary contained in this chapter do not reflect these revisions, nor do they reflect data consistent with the 2003 edition of the *UK Balance of Payments –* the *Pink Book*, which was not available until after this publication went to print.

The United Kingdom had a 4.4 per cent share of world trade in exports of goods and a 5.3 per cent share of imports of goods in 2002, according to the Organisation for Economic Co-operation and Development (OECD). Fifty-two per cent of UK export trade in goods and services and 53 per cent of its import trade was with the European Union, the world's largest established trading group. The United Kingdom exports more per head than either the United States or Japan. Sales of goods and services abroad accounted for 26 per cent of UK gross domestic product at market prices in 2002.

The United Kingdom experienced its biggest ever surpluses in both trade in services and in investment income in 2002. Together these accounted for 51 per cent of current account credits and for 41 per cent of debits. The United Kingdom consistently runs large surpluses on these accounts.

However, the United Kingdom experienced a record annual deficit on trade in goods in 2002. Table 25.1 shows how this deficit compared with other G7 countries.

Table 25.1 International trade in goods balances, G7 countries

			US$ billion
	1992	1997	2002
Canada	7.4	18.6	34.5
France	2.4	26.6	10.9
Germany	28.2	71.3	123.3
Italy	−1.0	40.1	17.1
Japan	124.7	101.6	93.8
United Kingdom	−22.8	−20.2	−52.0
United States	−96.9	−198.1	−484.4

Source: OECD Economic Outlook

Balance of payments

The balance of payments (see Table 25.2) is an account of all economic transactions between the United Kingdom and the rest of the world. It records inward and outward transactions, the overall net flow of transactions between UK residents and the rest of the world, and how that flow is funded. Economic transactions include:

- *exports and imports of goods*, such as oil, chemicals and other semi-manufactured goods and finished manufactured goods;
- *exports and imports of services*, such as international transport, travel, and financial and business services;
- *income flows*, such as dividends and interest earned by non-residents on investments in the United Kingdom and by UK residents investing abroad;
- *financial flows*, such as investment in shares, debt securities, loans and deposits; and
- *transfers*, such as payments to, and receipts from, EU institutions, foreign aid and funds brought by migrants to the United Kingdom.

The balance of payments is made up of the following accounts:

- the *current account* – trade in goods and services (see Table 25.3), income (investment income and compensation of employees – for example, locally engaged staff in UK embassies and military bases abroad) and current transfers (such as food aid);

■ the *capital account* – capital transfers and the acquisition and disposal of non-produced, non-financial assets (such as copyrights);

■ the *financial account* – the flow of direct, portfolio and other investment and reserve assets; and

■ the *international investment position* – the UK stock of external financial assets and liabilities.

Table 25.2 summarises the UK balance of payments position. The annual current account for 2002 was in deficit by £9.6 billion, compared with a £12.5 billion deficit in 2001. There was a slight improvement in the deficit on goods and services from the record sum in 2001, and the surplus on the income account was the highest ever. However, there was a fall in the surplus on the capital account, from £1.5 billion in 2001 to £1.1 billion in 2002.

Trade in goods and services

Table 25.3 summarises UK trade in goods and services at current prices and Figure 25.4 shows the trend in these balances over the past 30 years. Although the deficit from trade in goods and the surplus from trade in services were both at record levels in 2002, the growth in the latter was more significant and narrowed the overall trade deficit.

Table 25.2 Balance of payments summary,[1] UK

£ million

	1992	1997	2000	2001	2002
Current account					
Trade in goods and services	−7,568	186	−18,488	−22,210	−21,023
Income	128	3,906	9,400	16,404	20,646
Current transfers	−5,534	−5,812	−10,032	−6,679	−9,247
Current balance	−12,974	−1,720	−19,120	−12,485	−9,624
Capital account	421	804	1,823	1,512	1,096
Financial account	5,089	−5,066	13,172	15,277	7,188
Net errors and omissions[2]	7,464	5,982	4,125	−4,304	1,340

1 Balance of payments basis.
2 Amount necessary to bring the sum of all balance of payments entries to zero.
Source: ONS Balance of Payments

Table 25.3 External trade in goods and services,[1] UK

£ million

	1992	1997	2000	2001	2002
Exports of goods	107,863	171,923	187,936	190,050	186,170
Exports of services	36,228	59,699	77,199	77,683	83,467
Exports of goods and services	144,091	231,622	265,135	267,733	269,637
Imports of goods	120,913	184,265	218,262	223,560	221,352
Imports of services	30,746	47,171	65,361	66,383	69,308
Imports of goods and services	151,659	231,436	283,623	289,943	290,660
Balance of trade in goods	−13,050	−12,342	−30,326	−33,510	−35,182
Balance of trade in services	5,482	12,528	11,838	11,300	14,159
Balance of trade in goods and services	**−7,568**	**186**	**−18,488**	**−22,210**	**−21,023**

1 Balance of payments basis.
Source: ONS Balance of Payments

Figure 25.4 UK balance of payments in goods and services

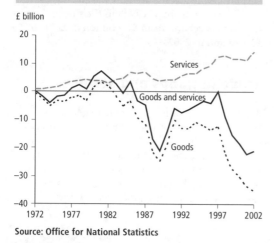

Source: Office for National Statistics

Figure 25.5 UK trade in goods 2002[1]

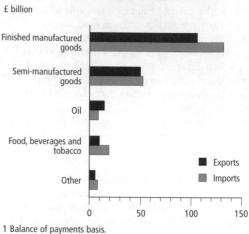

1 Balance of payments basis.
Source: ONS Balance of Payments

Commodity composition of goods

UK exports of goods are dominated by manufactures (Figure 25.5) – finished manufactures and semi-manufactured goods – which accounted for a similar proportion of exports in 2002 (84 per cent) as they did in 1972 (83 per cent). Oil exports, which rose as a proportion of total exports from 4 per cent in 1972 to 21 per cent in 1984, have subsequently declined, to 8 per cent in 2002.

Historically the United Kingdom was predominantly an importer of foods and basic materials. Over the last 30 years, however, imports of manufactures have grown rapidly. Between 1972 and 2002 the share of finished manufactures in total imports rose from 31 per cent to 60 per cent. The United Kingdom has not had a surplus on manufactured goods since 1982. Basic materials fell from 11 per cent of total imports by value in 1972 to 3 per cent in 2002. Food, beverages and tobacco accounted for 21 per cent of imports in 1972, compared with 9 per cent in 2002. Intermediate goods, such as car parts, computer chips and semi-conductors, accounted for 21 per cent of exports and 18 per cent of imports in 2002.

Sectors with significant positive trade balances in 2002 included crude oil, chemicals and capital goods, while those with large negative balances included consumer goods (including cars) and food, beverages and tobacco. Trade in motor cars has been in deficit for many years, with the deficit

widening very sharply between 2000 and 2001 because production was disrupted by restructuring in UK industry. In 2002 there was a reduction of the deficit in this sector as exports grew more strongly than imports.

Geographical breakdown of goods

UK trade in goods is mainly with other developed countries (see Figure 25.6). In 2002, 85 per cent of UK exports were to fellow member countries of the OECD, and 81 per cent of imports came from these countries.

Figure 25.6 Distribution of UK trade in goods, 2002[1]

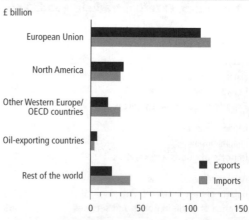

1 Balance of payments basis.
Source: ONS Balance of Payments

Table 25.7 Trade in goods – main export and import markets, 2002, UK[1]

	Value (£ million)	% share of UK trade in goods
Main export markets		
United States	28,192	15.1
Germany	22,010	11.8
France	18,707	10.0
Irish Republic	15,363	8.3
Netherlands	13,979	7.5
Belgium and Luxembourg	10,530	5.7
Italy	8,489	4.6
Spain	8,468	4.5
Sweden	3,863	2.1
Japan	3,587	1.9
Main import markets		
Germany	30,371	13.7
United States	24,973	11.3
France	18,886	8.5
Netherlands	14,979	6.8
Belgium and Luxembourg	13,075	5.9
Italy	10,378	4.7
Irish Republic	9,215	4.2
Japan	8,247	3.7
Spain	8,122	3.7
China	6,695	3.0

1 Balance of payments basis.
Source: ONS Balance of Payments

The United States remained the largest single UK export market in 2002 but was overtaken by Germany as its largest single supplier (see Table 25.7). The majority of the main UK trading partners are EU Member States.

Trade in services

A surplus has been recorded for trade in services (see glossary) in every year since 1966, and in 2002 this rose to a record £14.2 billion, £2.9 billion higher than in the previous year. Exports rose sharply by 7.4 per cent to £83.5 billion in 2002, with imports rising by 4.4 per cent to £69.3 billion. There were strong surpluses in financial and business services and in insurance, while travel and transport contributed the largest deficits (see Table 25.8).

The travel sector recorded its largest ever deficit in 2002. This deficit has widened substantially in recent years – in the early 1990s exports were between 24 and 27 per cent of the total trade in services, compared with 17 per cent in 2002, although imports were only slightly lower than the 40 per cent recorded in 2002. Increasing numbers of UK citizens travelling abroad and a slow recovery in US visitors to the United Kingdom in the aftermath of the 11 September 2001 attacks have contributed to this deficit.

Income and transfers

Earnings on UK investment abroad fell by 13.6 per cent to £122.3 billion in 2002. Debits

Table 25.8 Trade in services, ranked by exports, 2002, UK

	Value (£ million)			% change on 2001	
	Exports	Imports	Balance	Exports	Imports
Business services[1]	24,437	10,778	13,659	6.2	2.1
Travel	13,995	27,847	−13,852	6.8	5.6
Financial services	12,450	3,543	8,907	−1.3	16.7
Transport	11,905	16,360	−4,455	−2.3	4.1
Insurance	7,008	715	6,293	83.9	−7.9
Royalties and licence fees	5,126	3,986	1,140	−10.8	−6.4
Computer and information services	3,785	1,720	2,065	29.3	59.4
Personal, cultural and recreational services	1,577	798	779	38.8	18.8
Government	1,554	1,897	−343	2.1	−3.9
Communications	1,443	1,586	−143	−2.8	−13.4
Construction	187	78	109	27.2	−22.8
Total	**83,467**	**69,308**	**14,159**	**7.4**	**4.4**

1 Includes merchanting, operational leasing and consultancy services such as advertising, engineering and legal services.
Source: ONS Balance of Payments

(earnings of foreign-owned assets in the United Kingdom) also fell, by 18.8 per cent, to £101.8 billion, giving a £20.6 billion surplus, slightly higher than in 2001. A record surplus on direct investment income of £29.9 billion in 2002 reflected record profits from UK companies' direct investment abroad; this was partly offset by a £9.2 billion deficit on other investment income (including earnings on reserve assets).

The deficit on current transfers increased from £6.7 billion in 2001 to £9.2 billion in 2002.

Outward and inward investment

With an open economy, the United Kingdom has no restrictions on the outward flow of capital.

Initial estimates of investment in 2002 suggest that there was a net inflow of £7.2 billion. UK direct investment abroad, at £7.3 billion, was the lowest since 1984 and direct investment in the United Kingdom, at £18.5 billion, the lowest since 1996. There was net portfolio investment abroad of £0.1 billion in 2002, the lowest since 1994.

The UK stock of external liabilities amounted to £3,245 billion at the end of 2002 and its stock of assets to £3,220 billion. Direct investment abroad stood at £626 billion, while direct investment in the United Kingdom was £398 billion – giving a net balance of £228 billion, slightly less than in 2001.

International direct investment

According to the United Nations Conference on Trade and Development (UNCTAD) *World Investment Report 2003*, the United Kingdom was ranked seventh at attracting inward investment in 2002 and fourth in its outward investment (see Table 25.9). Over 20,000 foreign-owned companies operate in the United Kingdom, employing over 2 million people; North American companies account for over a quarter of the total.

Recent inward investment announcements in the United Kingdom have included:
- Irish company Quinn Direct Insurance is investing approximately US$12 million to establish a new centre in Enniskillen, Northern Ireland, expected to create around 350 jobs by 2006;

Table 25.9 Largest foreign direct investment sources and recipients, 2002

	Value (US$ billion)	World share (%)
Outward investment		
Luxembourg[1]	154.1	23.8
United States	119.7	18.5
France	62.5	9.7
United Kingdom	39.7	6.1
Japan	31.5	4.9
Canada	28.8	4.4
Netherlands	26.3	4.1
Germany	24.5	3.8
Spain	18.5	2.9
Hong Kong	17.7	2.7
European Union	394.1	60.9
World	**647.4**	**100**
Inward investment		
Luxembourg[1]	125.7	19.3
China	52.7	8.1
France	51.5	7.9
Germany	38.0	5.8
United States	30.0	4.6
Netherlands	29.2	4.5
United Kingdom	24.9	3.8
Spain	21.2	3.3
Canada	20.6	3.2
Irish Republic	19.0	2.9
European Union	374.4	57.5
World	**651.2**	**100**

1 Luxembourg is home to a large number of holding companies and corporate headquarters established by trans-national corporations.
Source: UNCTAD, *World Investment Report 2003*

- Los Angeles-based ticketing agency Ticketmaster plans to expand its call centre in Manchester, creating 350 jobs over three years;
- Irish glass manufacturer Quinn Glass is to establish an advanced production and distribution facility in Ince, Cheshire, creating more than 300 jobs by 2007; and
- New York-based financial services firm JP Morgan is creating up to 150 jobs for skilled software engineers at its European Technology Centre in Glasgow.

International trade policy

The Department of Trade and Industry (DTI) represents UK interests in international trade policy, working closely with EU partners and drawing on UK bilateral relations and membership of international organisations such as the World Trade Organisation.

European Union

The free movement of goods, people, services and capital is a fundamental principle of the EU. These four freedoms, set out in the Treaties of Rome, form the basis of the Single European Market (see page 60).

The EU Common Commercial Policy (CCP) establishes uniform principles covering trade between all Member States. These include changes in tariff rates, the conclusion of tariff and trade agreements with non-member countries, uniformity in trade liberalisation measures, export policy, and instruments to protect trade such as anti-dumping measures and subsidies.

Since 1993 the EU has formed a single territory without internal borders within which the free movement of goods is guaranteed. However, the EU does restrict imports of textiles and clothing, steel, footwear and ceramics from certain countries using licensing controls; these are also used to monitor imports and deter quota fraud.

In May 2003 the European Commission published the new medium-term Internal Market Strategy for 2003 to 2006. This is a ten-point plan to make the internal market work better and build on jobs and wealth that have been created since the free movement of goods within the EU took effect. The Strategy aims to take account of the effects of enlargement in 2004 (see page 63) and of an ageing population, and aims for the EU to become the world's most competitive economy by 2010. Particular priorities include implementing the free movement of services, removing the remaining obstacles to trade in goods, and improving the regulatory framework.

EU initiatives for simplifying national and Community rules include SLIM (simpler legislation for the internal market) and the European Business Test Panel, which allows for consultation with business during the drafting stage of new legislation.

A framework for ensuring the even-handed and effective enforcement of single market rules has been established. This involves encouraging co-operation between national administrations, setting up contact points for businesses and citizens, and improving the efficiency of the European Commission's complaints procedure. The Commission has set up an additional dispute mechanism called SOLVIT. This operates through a network of centres based in each Member State. It aims to resolve problems arising from the misapplication of EU rules, informally and speedily, without the need for legal action. Details are held on an online database system. In the United Kingdom, the DTI's Action Single Market/UK SOLVIT Centre (*www.dti.gov.uk/ewt/diff.htm*) acts not only as a contact point for UK business and citizens but also as a first port of call for similar centres in other Member States when single market problems arise.

Spring 2003 was the deadline set by EU Heads of Government for Member States to meet the 1.5 per cent implementation deficit target[1] for internal market Directives. Only five Member States met this target by May 2003 – the United Kingdom, at 1.5 per cent, was in fifth place. An average 2.4 per cent of Directives had not been implemented over all Member States, an increase of 0.6 percentage points on the figure for May 2002. Heads of Government also set a target for the full implementation of all Directives two or more years overdue. The United Kingdom met that target in May 2003, one of only four Member States to do so and one of only three Member States to have met both targets.

World Trade Organisation (WTO)

The WTO (*www.wto.org*) was established in 1995 to succeed the General Agreement on Tariffs and Trade. Its main functions are to act as a forum for trade negotiations, administer trade agreements and handle disputes. The key principle is non-discrimination, ensuring that similar products from different countries must be treated in the same way. As at April 2003 there were 146 member countries, with 28 negotiating to join. At the fourth Ministerial Conference in Doha, Qatar, in November 2001, members agreed to accept China and Taiwan into the WTO. The Ministerial Declaration, the *Doha Development Agenda*, adds new negotiations on industrial goods, the environment, subsidies and anti-dumping to existing ones on agriculture and services. More negotiations are envisaged after two years' study on investment, competition, transparency in government procurement and trade facilitation. The fifth Ministerial Conference was due to be held in Cancun, Mexico, in September 2003.

---

1 This is the percentage of Directives that have not been written into national law after the deadline for doing so has passed.

WTO disputes

Up to 11 September 2003 the WTO had recorded 301 disputes. The most recent disputes brought against the EC had been:

- measures affecting the approval and marketing of biotechnology products (by Argentina, Canada and the United States);
- protection of trademarks and geographical indications for agricultural products and foodstuffs (by Australia);
- customs classification of frozen boneless chicken cuts (by Thailand); and
- export subsidies on sugar (by Thailand).

In turn the EC had brought disputes against:

- Australia, relating to its quarantine regime for imports; and
- India, on import restrictions maintained under the export and import policy, 2002–07.

The WTO provides an arbitration service for countries involved in trade disputes through its dispute settlement system, although ideally, the countries concerned should discuss their problems and settle any dispute mutually. The trade policy review mechanism within the WTO allows members to discuss an individual country's trade regime.

Although the United Kingdom is a member of the WTO in its own right, for all practical purposes it works through membership of the EU, as required by the CCP (see page 371).

Developing countries

The DTI works closely with the Department for International Development (DFID) and other government departments to ensure that developing countries participate in, and benefit from, the world trade system. An inter-departmental Working Group on Trade and Development, chaired by the DTI, meets regularly to ensure consistency of approach.

The *Generalised System of Preferences* (GSP) exists to promote the better integration of developing countries into the world trading system. It aims to encourage them to increase exports by allowing their products preferential access to the markets of developed countries. The United Kingdom is party to the EC GSP, operated by all Member States. The current scheme took effect in January 2002 and will run until the end of 2004.

The *Cotonou Partnership Agreement*, signed in June 2000 in Cotonou, Benin, replaced the Lomé Convention. This had provided a framework for trade, aid and political relations between the EU and 77 sub-Saharan African, Caribbean and Pacific (ACP) countries. Under the new agreement, the ACPs have unrestricted access to the EU market for substantially all industrial goods and for a wide range of agricultural products. One of the agreement's main objectives is the integration of ACP states into the global economy. Current trade arrangements with the ACP will be allowed to continue during an eight-year transitional period – the EU obtained a waiver from WTO rules to cover this period. Before 2008, new WTO-compatible arrangements will have to be agreed. Negotiations on these new trading arrangements began in September 2002.

Controls on trade

Import controls

In addition to EU-wide restrictions (see above), certain goods are prohibited from import into the United Kingdom or are restricted for reasons of health and safety, or to protect the environment.

Prohibited goods include unlicensed drugs; offensive weapons; indecent and obscene material; counterfeit and pirated goods, and goods that infringe patents; and meat, milk and their products from outside the EU (with some exceptions).

Restricted goods, which cannot be imported without authority such as a licence, include firearms, explosives and ammunition; animals outside the Pet Travel Scheme (see page 404); live birds; endangered species and derived products (under the CITES Convention, see page 267); certain plants and their produce; and radio transmitters not approved for use in the United Kingdom.

Import licences

The DTI's Import Licensing Branch (ILB) has responsibility for issuing import licences in accordance with UK and EC law. In 2002/03 ILB issued 353,632 licences; a similar number of licences is expected to be issued in 2003/04.

Export controls

Governments control the export of goods and technology for a variety of reasons. Licences for goods subject to strategic export control are issued by the DTI acting through its Export Control Organisation (ECO). These controls apply to a wide range of goods, components and spare parts, and technology, including:

- military equipment, such as arms, ammunition, bombs, tanks, imaging devices, military aircraft and warships;
- nuclear-related items, including nuclear materials, nuclear reactors and processing plant;
- dual-use items – goods designed for civil use but which can be used for military purposes – such as machine tools, electronic equipment, computers, telecommunication equipment, cryptographic goods, sensors and radar, navigation and avionics equipment, marine equipment, and space and propulsion equipment;
- chemical weapons precursors, and related equipment and technology;
- certain micro-organisms, biological equipment and technology; and
- goods used in programmes involved in weapons of mass destruction and missiles used for their delivery.

The ECO also issues licences for the export or supply of goods and certain activities subject to control as a result of the imposition of UN trade sanctions or a UN embargo against particular countries or regions.

The *Export Control Act 2002* sets out a new legislative framework for the control of strategic goods and technology. It is an enabling Act and will come into force when the powers given under the Act are implemented through secondary legislation. The draft secondary legislation is being finalised following the consideration of responses to the public consultation that took place between January and April 2003.

Exports subject to control under legislation other than that administered by the ECO include: certain live animals and protected species of wildlife and flowers (under CITES); antiques and works of art; and drug precursors.

Government services

The Government provides a wide range of advice and practical support to meet the needs of overseas inward investors and exporters. *British Trade International* (BTI) delivers its services

through *Trade Partners UK*, which is responsible for trade development and *Invest UK,* which is responsible for inward investment. The *Export Credits Guarantee Department* (ECGD) helps UK exporters win business and helps firms to invest overseas.

British Trade International[2]

BTI brings together the work of the Foreign & Commonwealth Office and the DTI on international trade and investment. It enhances the competitiveness of companies in the United Kingdom through promoting exports and overseas investment and aims to maintain a high level of inward direct investment. Each of the devolved administrations, through Wales Trade International (*www.walestrade.com*), Invest Northern Ireland (*www.investni.com*), and Scottish Development International (*www.scottishdevelopmentinternational.com*), is represented on the BTI Board.

Responsibilities of BTI

- Trade development and promotion work in the English regions, by international trade teams working with the Regional Development Agencies (RDAs, see page 344), the Small Business Service (SBS) and the Business Link network, as well as with private sector partners.
- Trade support services provided nationally.
- Inward investment development work within the United Kingdom in collaboration with the national development agencies and the English RDAs.
- Trade and inward investment work of embassies and other diplomatic posts.

Trade Partners UK

Trade Partners UK (*www.tradepartners.gov.uk*) provides national coordination across government departments, the devolved administrations and the English regions on international trade, and a voice within government for exporters and companies investing overseas.

Trade UK

Trade UK (*www.tradeuk.com*) is a free online service for overseas customers to help find products and services from UK companies. Over 60,000 UK businesses can be searched by name, product or service, with links to 34,000 websites and 50,000 email addresses.

---

2 From November 2003 British Trade International will be changing its name to UK Trade and Investment.

Table 25.10 Invest UK decisions notified, 2002/03

Country	Projects	% of total	New jobs[1]
United States	283	40	17,271
Canada	73	10	1,946
Germany	50	7	2,768
Japan	49	7	1,108
France	45	6	2,144
China	22	3	234
Irish Republic	20	3	1,397
India	19	3	316
Italy	15	2	733
Australia	14	2	453
Rest of the EU	62	9	4,483
Rest of the World	57	8	1,543
Total	**709**	**100**	**34,396**

1 Jobs expected to be created.
Source: Invest UK

Invest UK

Invest UK (*www.invest.uk.com*) is the government agency promoting the whole of the United Kingdom as an inward investment location. Its principal aim is to attract, retain and add value to investment by communicating the benefits of the United Kingdom as the first choice in Europe for potential investors. Invest UK identifies and approaches potential investors and assists them with all aspects of locating and expanding in the United Kingdom. It operates through a network of offices in British diplomatic posts abroad, and with partners in development agencies throughout the United Kingdom.

Figures for 2002/03 on inward investment decisions notified to Invest UK by its national and regional development agency partners, and new jobs expected to be created, are shown in Table 25.10. New investments accounted for 44 per cent of these projects and expansions for a further 33 per cent. Investment in industries linked to the knowledge-driven economy – computer software, IT, Internet, e-commerce, electronics and telecommunications sectors – formed the largest category of inward investment, with 232 projects (33 per cent). Other major sectors for UK inward investment were the automotive sector, financial services and pharmaceuticals.

Export Credits Guarantee Department

ECGD (*www.ecgd.gov.uk*) is the official UK export credit agency. Its role is to help UK manufacturers

and investors trade overseas by providing them with insurance and/or backing for finance to protect against non-payment. It complements the insurance that is available from the private sector. ECGD insurance is available both for UK exporters of goods and services, and investors in overseas projects. The largest part of its operation involves underwriting finance packages to support the sale of capital goods, such as aircraft, machinery and services, and to help UK companies take part in overseas projects, such as hospitals, airports and power stations.

Including overseas investment insurance and reinsurance, the total business supported by

Table 25.11 Top ten markets for ECGD guarantees, 2002/03

	Value (£ million)	% share of total market
Saudi Arabia	1,013	28.7
Oman	348	9.9
Malaysia	225	6.4
Chile	225	6.4
Turkey	161	4.6
Indonesia	148	4.2
Nigeria	127	3.6
Sweden	118	3.3
Romania	107	3.0
Qatar	100	2.8
Sub-total	2,574	72.9
World	**3,532**	**100**

Source: ECGD

Table 25.12 ECGD guarantees by main civil business sector

	Per cent	
	2001/02	2002/03
Water	27	34
Power generation and transmission	25	23
Energy (oil and gas)	13	13
Manufacturing, process plant and equipment	10	8
Telecommunications	5	7
Mining	2	2
Education and medical	1	1
Transport	12	0
Other	5	12

Source: ECGD

ECGD in 2002/03 was £3,532 million. The top ten markets, representing 73 per cent of business in the year, are shown in Table 25.11.

ECGD's main civil business sectors are shown in Table 25.12. Power generation and transmission business remained fairly consistent at 23 per cent of activity in 2002, while business in the water sector increased from 27 per cent in 2001 to 34 per cent in 2002. The energy sector (oil and gas) remained at 13 per cent of all new business in 2002. The main area of reduced business was in the transport sector, with only one small piece of business.

Further reading

Trade and Industry. Departmental Report 2003. Cm 5916. The Stationery Office, 2003.

British Trade International. Departmental Report 2003. Cm 5915. The Stationery Office, 2003.

United Kingdom Balance of Payments – the Pink Book (annual publication). Office for National Statistics. The Stationery Office, 2003.

Export Credits Guarantee Department. Annual Review and Resource Accounts 2002/03. The Stationery Office, 2003.

Websites

Department of Trade and Industry
www.dti.gov.uk

National Statistics
www.statistics.gov.uk

WWW.

26 Science, engineering and technology

The United Kingdom has been at the forefront of many world-class advances in science, engineering and technology. Notable areas of UK achievement include biotechnology, biomedicine, materials, chemicals, electronics and aerospace. In the past 50 years UK scientists have won 46 Nobel Prizes.

Sydney Brenner and Sir John Sulston
In 2002 Sydney Brenner and Sir John Sulston were awarded the Nobel Prize for Medicine, sharing the award with US scientist Robert Horvitz. The award is in recognition of their work into how genes control the division of the body's cells and the development of organs. This work has helped understanding of the development of many diseases. Among their discoveries is the genetic mechanism controlling the programmed death of cells at the end of their lives. The work was carried out on a species of nematode worm, 40 per cent of whose genes are closely related to humans.

Achievements by UK scientists in the last 30 years have included:

- the development of *in vitro* fertilisation leading to the birth of the world's first 'test-tube baby' in 1978;
- the development of DNA fingerprinting in 1985;
- discovery of the hole in the ozone layer over the Antarctic, also in 1985;
- the invention of the Internet address system and layout in 1990;
- pioneering work on nuclear transfer, which resulted in the birth of the world's first cloned mammal, Dolly the sheep, in 1996;[1] and
- contributing to the completion of the Human Genome Project in 2003 (see page 392).

Fifty years of the double helix
On 25 April 1953 a letter from two scientists at the Cavendish Laboratory in Cambridge was published in the science journal *Nature*.

We wish to discuss a structure for the salt of deoxyribose nucleic acid (D.N.A). This structure has novel features which are of considerable biological interest . . . It has not escaped our notice that the specific pairing we have postulated immediately suggests a possible copying mechanism for the genetic material.

With these now famous words, Francis Crick and James Watson, an American, announced one of the most celebrated scientific breakthroughs of the 20th century. Fifty years later, the complete human genome has been sequenced, DNA fingerprinting has become commonplace and DNA technology is beginning to influence the treatment of disease.

Watson, Crick, and Maurice Wilkins from King's College, London went on to receive the Nobel Prize. In 2003 a prize for women in science (see page 390) was established in memory of Rosalind Franklin, whose experimental work at King's had crucially informed the model-building in Cambridge.

Research and development expenditure

Gross domestic expenditure in the United Kingdom on research and development (R&D)[2] in 2001 was £18.8 billion, almost 2 per cent of gross domestic product (GDP, see page 334). Of this,

---

1 Dolly the sheep died in February 2003. Her body has been preserved and put on display at the Royal Museum in Edinburgh.

2 R&D is defined by the Organisation for Economic Co-operation and Development (OECD) as 'creative work undertaken on a systematic basis in order to increase the stock of knowledge, including knowledge of man, culture and society and the use of the stock of knowledge to devise new applications'.

Figure 26.1 Gross domestic expenditure on R&D in the UK, 2001

Total: £18.8 billion

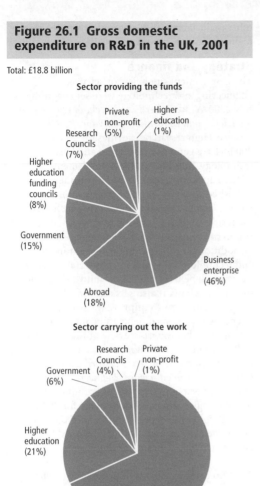

Sector providing the funds

Higher education (1%)
Private non-profit (5%)
Research Councils (7%)
Higher education funding councils (8%)
Government (15%)
Abroad (18%)
Business enterprise (46%)

Sector carrying out the work

Research Councils (4%)
Private non-profit (1%)
Government (6%)
Higher education (21%)
Business enterprise (68%)

Source: Office for National Statistics

£16.1 billion was on civil R&D, with the rest going to defence projects. In real terms, gross domestic expenditure on R&D increased by 5 per cent between 2000 and 2001.

Business enterprise is the largest source of funding, providing 46 per cent of expenditure in 2001 (see Figure 26.1). Contract research organisations often carry out R&D for companies and are playing an increasingly important role in the transfer of technology to UK industry. Business enterprise also supports university research and finances contract research at government establishments. Some charities have their own laboratories as well as offering grants for research.

R&D Scoreboard

The R&D scoreboard is used as an international benchmarking tool to help companies decide if they are investing in R&D at the right level. It contains details of R&D investment, sales, profits, and employee numbers for certain UK and international companies. The dataset includes 600 UK based companies (40 from the FTSE 100, see page 461) with R&D investments totalling £16 billion. The international section comprises the top 600 R&D investing companies with R&D totalling £206 billion.

The 2002 Scoreboard conclusions suggests that the challenges facing the United Kingdom are to:

- maintain its leading position in pharmaceuticals and biotechnology, health, and aerospace and defence;
- increase the intensity[3] of R&D in other sectors, where average intensity and distribution compare less favourably with other major economies; and
- encourage middle-sized companies (those with a turnover of £70 million to £500 million) in all sectors, but particularly high R&D sectors, to increase their R&D intensity.

Business enterprise carried out R&D worth some £12.7 billion in 2001, an increase of 8 per cent on 2000 in real terms. Business enterprises own funds accounted for 64 per cent of this work, with 12 per cent coming from government and most of the remaining 24 per cent from overseas. Expenditure on R&D within the pharmaceuticals product group accounted for 24 per cent of all spending, followed by aerospace and the radio, television and communication equipment sectors, where it accounted for 10 per cent and 8 per cent respectively.

Government role

The Secretary of State for Trade and Industry, assisted by the Minister for Science, has overall responsibility for science, engineering and technology (SET). They are supported by the Office of Science and Technology (OST), part of the Department of Trade and Industry (DTI). The

---

3 R&D intensity is R&D as a percentage of sales.

Ministerial Committee on Science Policy provides the framework for the collective consideration of, and decisions on, major science policy issues.

The OST, headed by the Government's Chief Scientific Adviser, is responsible for policy on SET, both nationally and internationally, and coordinates science and technology policy across government departments. The Chief Scientific Adviser also reports directly to the Prime Minister.

An independent Council for Science and Technology advises the Prime Minister on the strategic policies and framework for science and technology in the United Kingdom. Its members are drawn from academia, business and charitable foundations/institutions.

The term 'science and engineering base' (SEB) is used to describe the research and postgraduate training capacity based in the universities and colleges of higher education and in establishments operated by the Research Councils (see pages 382–386). Also included are the national and international central facilities (such as CERN – see page 390) supported by the Research Councils and available for use by UK scientists and engineers. There are also important contributions from private institutions, chiefly those funded by charities. The SEB is the main provider of basic research and much of the strategic research (research likely to have practical applications) carried out in the United Kingdom. It also collaborates with the private sector in the conduct of specific applied research.

The OST, through the Director General of Research Councils, has responsibility for the Science Budget, and for the government-financed Research Councils. Through the Research Councils, the Science Budget supports research by:

- awarding research grants to universities, other higher education establishments and some other research units;
- funding Research Council establishments to carry out research or provide facilities;
- paying subscriptions to international scientific facilities and organisations; and
- supporting postgraduate research students and postdoctoral fellows.

The Science Budget also funds programmes of support to the science and engineering base through the Royal Society (see page 392) and the Royal Academy of Engineering (see page 392). The other main sources of funds for universities are the higher education funding councils.

Strategy and finance

The Government's policies for science, engineering and technology were set out in the July 2000 White Paper *Excellence and Opportunity – a science and innovation policy for the 21st century*. High research priorities for 2001/02 to 2003/04 are genomics, e-science and basic technology. Building on the commitments in the White Paper, in July 2002 the Government published *Investing in innovation: a strategy for science, engineering and technology*, which included the results of a cross-cutting review of science and research (see page 386). The strategy sets out how an additional £1.25 billion investment in science and technology allocated from the 2002 Spending Review will be used by schools, universities and the research base. It also sets out how the Government plans to improve the way it manages science within government, and contains its response to the Roberts Review of the supply of skilled scientists and engineers (see page 389). The DTI/OST publication *The Forward Look 2003: Government funded science, engineering and technology* sets out government spending on science, engineering and technology for 2002 to 2005. It contains reports and financial data from departments, Research Councils, learned bodies and the devolved administrations.

The SEB is chiefly financed through two funding streams, which together are known as the Dual Support system. One stream is provided by the Education Departments through their higher education funding councils. The other stream is provided by the DTI/OST through the Research Councils, which award programme and project grants for specific research programmes, both to universities and to their own institutions. The OST is examining ways to implement changes to the Dual Support system, as recommended by the cross-cutting review of science and research.

Planned total government expenditure on SET (both civil and defence) in 2003/04 is £7.9 billion (see Figure 26.2). In the 2002 Spending Review the Government announced that the OST's Science Budget would increase by 10 per cent a year between 2002/03 and 2005/06, from £2.0 billion in 2002/03 to £2.9 billion in 2005/06. This includes an extra £436 million over the three years to fund an expansion in science and engineering research activities.

Figure 26.2 Planned net government expenditure on SET, 2003/04, UK

Total: £7.9 billion

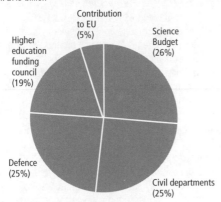

Source: Office for National Statistics

Additional resources will be available for knowledge transfer from the SEB, with funding of £90 million a year by 2005/06 for an enlarged Higher Education Innovation Fund.

Departmental responsibilities

Department of Trade and Industry

In 2003/04 the DTI's planned expenditure (excluding the OST) on SET is £417 million. Expenditure covers innovation and technology for a number of industrial sectors, including aeronautics, biotechnology, chemicals, communications, engineering, environmental technology, IT, space, and nuclear and non-nuclear energy.

Funding for innovation embraces the development, design and financing of new products, services and processes, exploitation of new markets, creation of new businesses and associated changes in the management of people and in organisational practices. Through its Innovation Unit, a mixed team of business secondees and government officials, the DTI seeks to promote a culture of innovation in all sectors of the economy.

Aeronautics

The DTI's aeronautics research programme (formerly known as CARAD – the Civil Aircraft Research and Technology Demonstration Programme) is part of the national aeronautics research effort. The supported research work is led

Foresight Programme

The Government's Foresight programme (*www.foresight.gov.uk*) encourages the public and private sectors to work together to identify opportunities in markets and technologies likely to emerge over the next 10 to 20 years. The programme is coordinated by a joint industry/academic steering group, headed by the Chief Scientific Adviser.

The current round of Foresight – launched in April 2002 – operates through a rolling programme that looks at three or four areas at any one time. The starting point for a project area is either a key issue where science holds the promise of solutions, or an area of science where the potential applications and technologies have yet to be considered and articulated.

The four current projects are:
- flood and coastal defence;
- cognitive systems;
- cyber trust and crime prevention; and
- exploiting the electromagnetic spectrum.

The fifth Foresight project will be brain science and drugs.

by industry with significant involvement of QinetiQ (see page 381) and the science base. Projects funded by the programme include aluminium and composite airframe structures and materials, more efficient and environmentally friendly engines, and advanced aircraft systems.

National Measurement System

The DTI is responsible for the National Measurement System (NMS), which funds science and technology programmes in measurement science, including materials metrology. In 2003/04 the DTI expects to invest £68 million on the NMS. The system provides world-class measurement standards and calibration facilities, enabling businesses and public authorities to make accurate measurements that are nationally and internationally accepted. Although most of the work is carried out at the National Physical Laboratory, LGC (formerly the Laboratory of the Government Chemist), NEL (formerly the National Engineering Laboratory) and the National Weights and Measures Laboratory, the DTI is taking steps to increase competition in these programmes and to work more

Technology and knowledge transfer

The DTI aims to increase collaboration and the flow of knowledge between the SEB and businesses through a number of programmes:

LINK

LINK (*www.ost.gov.uk/link*) is the Government's main mechanism for promoting partnership in pre-commercial research between companies and the research base. Government departments and Research Councils fund up to 50 per cent of the cost of research projects, with companies providing the balance. Recent programmes include, health technology devices, information storage and display, and basic technologies for industrial applications.

International Technology Service

The DTI's International Technology Service (ITS) (*www.globalwatchonline.com*) helps UK businesses improve their competitiveness by assisting them to identify and learn from the latest technological developments employed by leading organisations around the world. ITS encourages bilateral international science and technology activities, including high-technology forums, seminars and workshops.

Knowledge Transfer Partnerships (KTPs)

KTPs are part-funded by the DTI and facilitate technology and knowledge transfer between businesses and universities, colleges or research organisations that have expertise relevant to their industry. They also provide business-based training and experience for high-calibre graduates. KTPs are managed by the Small Business Service (see page 342).

Faraday Partnerships

The Faraday Partnerships scheme (*www.faradaypartnerships.org.uk*) is intended to improve the exploitation of SET in the United Kingdom. A Faraday Partnership is an alliance of organisations and institutions, which can include research and technology organisations, universities, professional institutes, trade associations and firms. Faraday Partnerships are sponsored for core funding by the DTI, the Scottish Executive and several of the Research Councils. The national network consists of 24 Faraday Partnerships focused on technologies of major importance to the United Kingdom.

closely with business in order to identify its future needs.

British Standards Institution

The DTI works closely with the British Standards Institution (BSI), the national standards body that is independent of the Government, to promote UK trade and technology interests. DTI support for BSI is directed particularly towards European and international standards, which account for over 90 per cent of the Institution's work. It also provides support for the United Kingdom Accreditation Service (UKAS), the sole national body recognised by the Government to accredit organisations that test, calibrate, inspect and certify against standards. The DTI contribution to BSI and UKAS was £6.4 million in 2002/03.

Intellectual property

The Government supports innovation through the promotion of national and international systems for the establishment of intellectual property rights. These matters are the responsibility of the Patent Office, an executive agency of the DTI. The Office is responsible for the granting of patents, and registration of designs and trade marks. In 2002 it received almost 30,000 applications for patents and over 80,000 applications for trade marks.

The Patent Office encourages worldwide harmonisation of rules and procedures, and the modernisation and simplification of intellectual property law. International patenting arrangements include the European Patent Convention and the Patent Co-operation Treaty. For trade marks the European Community Trade Mark System and the Madrid Protocol provide means of acquiring rights beyond UK borders. The Patent Office Central Enquiry Unit and the website (*www.patent.gov.uk*) offer detailed information about intellectual property rights. To raise awareness of the value and importance of intellectual property throughout the United Kingdom, the Patent Office runs seminars and workshops for business advisers, small and medium-sized enterprises (SMEs) and academics.

Ministry of Defence (MoD)

The Government invests about £450 million a year in research to ensure that UK armed forces stay ahead of threats from potential adversaries. The MoD has a research budget and also a much larger equipment procurement budget. Planned net expenditure on SET for 2003/04 is almost £2 billion. MoD research is carried out by two organisations: Defence Science and Technology Laboratory (Dstl) and QinetiQ plc. Dstl carries out research in key areas, provides a high-level overview of defence science and technology, acts as an in-house source of impartial advice and manages international research collaboration.

A third of QinetiQ plc was sold to the Carlyle Group in December 2002. The MoD plans to sell its remaining stake in QinetiQ within three to five years.

Department of Health (DH)

The DH supports R&D to provide the evidence needed to inform policy and practice in public health, healthcare and social care. It delivers this objective through:

- National Health Service (NHS) R&D funding, which supports projects funded by other non-commercial R&D sources (including charities) carried out in the NHS, and also specific health and social care projects meeting the identified research needs of the DH and the NHS;
- a Policy Research Programme (PRP), directly commissioned by the DH; and
- ad hoc project funding from other DH R&D budgets and support for non-departmental public bodies (NDPBs).

The DH expects to spend some £573 million on research in 2003/04: £505 million on NHS R&D, £36 million on the PRP and about £32 million involving the NDPBs and ad hoc budgets.

Home Office

Some scientific and medical research, as well as the regulatory safety and efficacy testing of new drugs and other substances, involves the use of live animals. In Great Britain this is regulated through a licensing system administered by the Home Office under the *Animals (Scientific Procedures) Act 1986*, and in Northern Ireland the system is regulated by the Department of Health, Social Services and Public Safety, under the same Act. Animals may only be used for specified permitted purposes, when the benefits are judged likely, on expert assessment, to outweigh the cost to their welfare. There also has to be full application of what are known as the '3Rs': replacement of animals with non-animal

alternatives whenever practicable; where animals have to be used, reduction of their number to the minimum; and refinement of the procedures to minimise their suffering. Prescribed standards of animal housing and care also have to be maintained in the establishments concerned.

In 2002, 2.75 million such procedures were performed, mostly on mice and other rodents. The number of regulated procedures has fallen considerably since 1987 (when the legislation was introduced), when 3.6 million procedures were performed.

Scottish Executive

The Scottish Higher Education Funding Council disburses the majority of the Scottish Executive's support for the science base. In total this amounts to some £190 million in 2003/04 – £139 million for research and £51 million to support the strategic development of the sector. The Scottish Executive spends about £160 million a year directly on agricultural and fisheries research, health, biological, environmental, economic and social science. A large proportion of this goes to the Scottish Agricultural and Biological Research Institutes, the Fisheries Research Service and the Scottish Agricultural College. In addition, the UK Research Councils contribute around £200 million to Scottish research institutions and around £120 million is contributed by other UK government sources.

In August 2001 the Executive launched *A Science Strategy for Scotland*. In accordance with the strategy, the Executive has established an independent Scottish Science Advisory Committee, to advise it on strategic science matters.

Northern Ireland Executive

In addition to participating in the Dual Support system (see page 378) and other UK-wide

National e-Science Centre

The UK National e-Science Centre, run jointly by Edinburgh and Glasgow universities, will coordinate the activities of eight regional centres. The aim of the e-Science Centre is to develop a global computing network that will one day replace the world wide web. The Centre will use the Grid, a highly developed computer system with massive processing power, to underpin its activities.

initiatives, the Northern Ireland Executive is part-funding the Support Programme for University Research (SPUR). This is a joint public/private programme, the first phase of which (SPUR 1) will invest some £44 million into the university research infrastructure over the period 2001/02 to 2004/05. The second phase (SPUR 2) will similarly invest £50 million between 2003 and 2007. About two-thirds of expenditure is for science-related projects. In Northern Ireland, Invest NI has a similar role to that of the DTI's Innovation Unit, supporting industrial R&D, technology transfer and innovation.

Space activities

The UK civil space programme is brought together through the British National Space Centre (BNSC) (*www.bnsc.gov.uk*), a partnership of government departments and the Research Councils. BNSC's policy and aims were set out in *Space Strategy 1999–2002: New Frontiers*. A draft strategy for the next three years was published for consultation in January 2003. It proposed three key objectives for the space industry:

- to enhance UK standing in astronomy, planetary and environmental sciences;
- to stimulate increased productivity by promoting the use of space in government, science and commerce; and
- to develop innovative space systems, to deliver sustainable improvement in quality of life.

Through BNSC, the Government spends around £160 million a year on space activities. Nearly 60 per cent of this is channelled through the European Space Agency (ESA) for collaborative programmes such as Earth observation, telecommunications, and space science, much of which returns to the United Kingdom through contracts awarded to UK industry. The remainder of the space budget is spent on international meteorological programmes carried out through the European Meteorological Satellite Organisation (EUMETSAT); developing experiments (such as the Beagle 2 Mars Lander – see box) for ESA satellites; and on the national programme, which is aimed at complementing R&D supported through ESA. Around half of the UK space programme is concerned with satellite-based Earth observation (remote sensing) for commercial and environmental applications.

The United Kingdom is also a major contributor to ESA's Earth observation satellite, ENVISAT,

Mars Express/Beagle 2
Launched in June 2003, the Mars Express spacecraft is ESA's first independent planetary mission. It carries seven scientific instruments that will study the geology of the planet and search for water under the Martian surface. On board the spacecraft is Beagle 2, the first space lander to look specifically for evidence of life since the two Mars Viking probes of the 1970s. Beagle 2 was designed and built in the United Kingdom and named after the ship on which Charles Darwin sailed to South America before developing his theory of evolution. Beagle 2 will send the results of its research to the Open University and the National Space Centre in Leicester. The nine-note call sign to announce its arrival on Mars has been composed by the British pop group Blur, and the probe carries a work of art by artist Damien Hirst, which is used to synchronise its visual instruments.

launched in March 2002. This carries a new generation of radar and radiometer systems as well as other scientific environmental instruments, some of which have been either designed or constructed in the United Kingdom.

A third of the UK space budget is devoted to space science led by the Particle Physics and Astronomy Research Council, in support of astronomy, planetary science and geophysics. The United Kingdom is contributing substantially to the SOHO mission to study the Sun; to the Cluster mission launched in 2000 to study solar-terrestrial relationships; to the Infrared Space Observatory, which is investigating the birth and death of stars; and to the Cassini Huygens mission, a seven-year programme to send a probe, launched in 1997, to Saturn and its moon Titan. It is also participating in XMM, ESA's X-ray spectroscopy mission to investigate X-ray emissions from black holes, and ESA's SMART-1 Mission (Small Missions in Advanced Research Technology), which was launched from Kourou in French Guiana in September 2003. This will be the first European spacecraft to travel to and orbit the Moon.

Research Councils

The UK Research Councils are independent public bodies responsible to the Office of Science and Technology. They are funded through the

Government Science Vote,[4] and had a total budget of £1.6 billion in 2002/03. There are currently seven Research Councils in the United Kingdom, each with members of its governing council drawn from universities, the professions, industry and government. Following a government announcement in January 2003, the current Arts and Humanities Research Board (AHRB) should take on the status of a fully fledged Research Council funded by the OST by 2005. The Councils support research, study and training in universities and other higher education institutions. They also carry out or support research, through their own institutes and at international research centres, often jointly with other public sector bodies and international organisations. They provide awards to about 15,000 postgraduate students in science, social sciences, engineering and technology.

The Research Councils deploy a range of initiatives to encourage academics to commercialise their findings, to work with industry and to enhance the entrepreneurial culture in the UK research base. They also work with the public, promoting awareness and listening to their views on issues in which research plays a part.

Research Councils UK

Following the Quinquennial Review of the Research Councils in 2001, a new strategy group, Research Councils UK (RCUK), was launched in May 2002 to develop a stronger strategic framework for science, engineering and technology. It is supported by the seven UK Research Councils and the AHRB, and aims to:

- create a common framework for research, training and knowledge transfer;
- provide a single focus for dialogue with stakeholders;
- provide the focus for independent scientific advice from the Research Councils to the Government;
- promote collaboration to deliver scientific and strategic goals; and
- harmonise procedures to give stakeholders a more efficient service.

The RCUK strategy group is chaired by the Director General of Research Councils and includes the chief executives of the seven Councils.

Engineering and Physical Sciences Research Council (EPSRC)

The EPSRC (*www.epsrc.ac.uk*) promotes and supports high-quality basic, strategic and applied research and related postgraduate training in engineering and the physical sciences. It also provides advice, disseminates knowledge and promotes public understanding in these areas. Its remit is delivered through ten programme areas: engineering; infrastructure and the environment; innovative manufacturing; chemistry; physics;

Research funded by the Science Budget

The allocation of the Science Budget (see page 378) to the Research Councils includes funding for a number of key areas:

- *developing life-saving health techniques* – £136 million to build on existing genomics and proteomics research, £40 million for research into stem cells, and £15 million to take advantage of recent advances in brain science;
- *using science to help rural Britain* – £20 million for research to examine the impact of the changing role of the countryside on the rural economy;
- *developing a sustainable energy economy* (see page 384).
- *developing the Grid* – £115 million for e-science to continue research into the next generation of distributed computing technology; and
- *finding the next generation of 'leading edge' technologies* – £60 million to develop new leading edge technologies, including vision machines that mimic the human eye and imaging techniques that can find tumours in the body or buried objects.

Rail research

EPSRC recently launched a multidisciplinary centre for railway systems research, bringing together researchers, representatives from industry and policy makers. The £7 million centre, Rail Research UK, involves 12 research groups from seven universities. It will provide an engineering base for railway systems research in the United Kingdom and aim to improve the safety, reliability and capacity of the rail network, reduce the impact of railways on the environment and make rail travel more attractive for passengers.

---

4 The Director General of Research Councils, located in OST, has overall responsibility for advising ministers on the resources needed by the Research Councils, the Royal Society and the Royal Academy of Engineering (the Science Vote).

mathematics; information and communications technologies; materials; the boundary between the EPSRC and the life sciences; and public awareness of SET. The EPSRC also manages programmes in basic technology and e-science on behalf of all the Research Councils.

Medical Research Council (MRC)

The MRC (*www.mrc.ac.uk*) (see also chapter 13, page 185) is the main source of public funds for biomedical, health services and related research and training aimed at maintaining and improving public health. The Council has three major institutes: the National Institute for Medical Research, the Laboratory of Molecular Biology and the Clinical Sciences Centre. It has 29 smaller MRC Units, an MRC Health Services Research Collaboration (a collaborative arrangement based in the Department of Social Medicine in Bristol University and involving groups in seven other universities) and five grant-funded Centres. Most of these are attached to higher education institutions or hospitals throughout the United Kingdom. The MRC also has laboratories overseas in The Gambia and Uganda.

About half the MRC's research expenditure is allocated to its own institutes and units, with the rest going mainly on grant support and research training awards to teams and individuals in higher education institutions. The Council works closely with the health departments, the major charities, industry and international collaborators.

Stem cell discovery

MRC scientists have made an important discovery about the essential role of a gene known as Sox2, in the earliest stages of the developing mammalian embryo. They have been able to show that the presence of Sox2 is vital in allowing the embryonic stem cells to maintain their ability to become virtually any cell type when grown in the laboratory, or to achieve full embryo development and generate any of the cell types found in adult mammals.

Natural Environment Research Council (NERC)

NERC (*www.nerc.ac.uk*) funds and carries out scientific research in the sciences of the environment. *Science for a sustainable future 2002–2007* is the strategy document that identifies priority areas for NERC, including:

- *Earth's life-support systems* – water, biogeochemical cycles and biodiversity;
- *climate change* – predicting and mitigating the effects; and
- *sustainable economies* – identifying and providing sustainable solutions to the challenges associated with energy, land use and the effects of natural hazards.

NERC provides training for the next generation of environmental scientists. It also provides a range of facilities for use by the wider environmental science community, including a marine research fleet. NERC's wholly owned research centres are the British Geological Survey, the British Antarctic Survey, the Centre for Ecology and Hydrology, and the Proudman Oceanographic Laboratory. NERC also supports 15 collaborative centres in UK universities.

Towards a Sustainable Energy Economy

NERC is leading the coordination of a £28 million cross-council programme *Towards a Sustainable Energy Economy*, of which £8 million to 12 million will be used to set up a UK Energy Research Centre. The research will address the challenge of how to supply energy in a secure and affordable way while minimising carbon dioxide emissions and helping the United Kingdom to meet its targets on renewable energy.

Biotechnology and Biological Sciences Research Council (BBSRC)

The BBSRC (*www.bbsrc.ac.uk*) is the principal UK public funding agency for basic and strategic research in non-clinical biosciences. The scientific themes of its research committees are biomolecular sciences; genes and developmental biology; biochemistry and cell biology; plant and microbial sciences; animal sciences; agri-food; and engineering and biological systems. As well as funding research in universities and other research centres, the BBSRC sponsors eight research institutes.

Particle Physics and Astronomy Research Council (PPARC)

PPARC (*www.pparc.ac.uk*) directs, coordinates and funds UK research, education and postgraduate training in four broad areas of science: particle physics, astronomy, solar system science and particle astrophysics. This includes funding novel

Combating virus diseases in livestock

International trade in animals and the speed of movement of animals and people means that there is an increased risk of the transmission of infectious diseases. Recent events have highlighted the global threats to UK farming from viruses. In July 2003 the BBSRC invited proposals for research that will contribute to a greater understanding of the pathophysiology and epidemiology of animal viral disease. The £9 million initiative will support studies of the fundamental biology of the interactions of a range of viruses with their hosts, especially viral persistence, the epidemiology of animal infectious diseases and related investigations in support of improved diagnostics and vaccines. The initiative is coordinated with a parallel Department for Environment, Food and Rural Affairs invitation. The Scottish Executive Environment and Rural Affairs Department is also supporting the initiative by providing funding for Scottish Institutes participating in the initiative through collaborative projects.

technology development, and encouraging its exploitation by industry; an e-science programme that will meet the data acquisition requirements from new facilities in coming years; and promoting public understanding and engagement in PPARC science. PPARC directly manages three scientific establishments in support of its ground-based astronomy programmes: the UK Astronomy Technology Centre in Edinburgh, the Isaac Newton Group of telescopes on La Palma and the Joint Astronomy Centre in Hawaii. Access to other facilities is provided on a national and international basis, the latter through bodies such

Gravitational wave detectors

PPARC is investing in the new field of gravitational wave astronomy. The aim is to detect gravitational waves for the first time, and then to use them as new probes of violent cosmic events and to test theories of fundamental physics. It will build upon UK success in enhancing the performance of the UK/German GEO 600 detector and the US Laser Interferometric Gravitational-Wave Observatory (LIGO) experiment.

Working with the most sensitive array of detectors built to date, UK scientists have helped to set new upper limits on the strengths of gravitational waves, and thus provided initial benchmarks against which to measure future improvements in sensitivity.

as the European Organisation for Nuclear Research (CERN), the European Southern Observatory and the European Space Agency.

Economic and Social Research Council (ESRC)

The role of the ESRC (*www.esrc.ac.uk*) is to promote and support high-quality basic, strategic and applied research and related postgraduate training in the social sciences. Research funded by the ESRC is conducted in higher education institutions or independent research establishments. It aims to focus economic and social research on scientific and national priorities; enhance the capacity for the highest quality in social science research; and increase the impact of research on policy and practice.

Sustainable Technologies Programme

Launched in 2002, this £3 million ESRC programme (*www.sustainabletechnologies.ac.uk*) is part of the Government's Sustainable Technologies Initiative. It aims to fund innovative social and economic research into the shaping, development and use of more sustainable technologies. Six projects and one fellowship are funded under the first phase of the programme, examining topics such as policy for and barriers to sustainable development, and the role of consumers and consumption.

Council for the Central Laboratory of the Research Councils (CCLRC)

The CCLRC (*www.cclrc.ac.uk*) promotes scientific and engineering research by providing facilities and technical expertise, primarily to meet the needs of the research communities supported by the other Research Councils. Under the strategic direction of the RCUK strategy group, it acts as the focus for large-scale facilities for neutron scattering, synchrotron radiation and high-power lasers. It also coordinates the development of policies and strategies to provide access for UK scientists to large-scale facilities in these scientific areas, both nationally and internationally.

The CCLRC is responsible for the Rutherford Appleton Laboratory (RAL) in Oxfordshire; the Daresbury Laboratory (DL) in Cheshire; and the Chilbolton Facility in Hampshire. These centres provide facilities too large or complex, and technologies too specialised, to be housed by individual academic institutions.

RAL is the home of the DIAMOND project, a new synchrotron light source due to be operational in 2007. Among other resources, RAL also hosts ISIS (the world's leading source of pulsed neutrons and muons); the high-power Central Laser Facility with some of the world's brightest lasers; and specialist e-science, instrumentation, accelerator and space technology centres. In April 2003 the Government announced a grant of £100 million to fund a new target station at the ISIS neutron facility. Daresbury Laboratory hosts the Synchrotron Radiation Source and advanced computing facilities, and Chilbolton provides infrastructure for experimental work undertaken by the CCLRC's Radiocommunications Research Unit.

Fourth generation light source

In April 2003 the Government agreed funding for an exploratory phase of a project to build a fourth generation light source (4GLS) at DL. If constructed, it would produce very short pulses of light, over a million, million, million times brighter than a household light bulb. This would allow researchers to study molecules in real time, follow chemical reactions as they happen, look at potential drug molecules as they interact with cells and examine the spin of electrons. The research carried out on 4GLS would help develop the next generation of computer memories, pharmaceuticals and catalysts.

Research in higher education institutions

Universities carry out most of the United Kingdom's long-term strategic and basic research in science and technology. The higher education funding councils (HEFCs) provide the main general funds to support research in universities and other higher education institutions in Great Britain. These funds pay for the salaries of permanent academic staff (who usually teach as well as undertake research) and contribute to the infrastructure for research. The quality of research performance is a key element in the allocation of funding. In Northern Ireland institutions are funded by the Department for Employment and Learning.

The Research Councils also finance basic and strategic research in higher education institutions.

The other main channels of support are industry, charities, government departments and the EU.

Cross-cutting review of science and research

The cross-cutting review of science and research was part of the 2002 Spending Review. It found that the UK university research base was declining. Among the reasons set out in the review were:

- chronic overtrading in research leading to reliance on internal cross-subsidies from uncertain income sources and a neglect of physical infrastructure;
- lack of clarity of the Dual Support system about the purposes for which HEFC support for research was intended;
- a shift in the balance between the two sides of the Dual Support system with funding provided by Research Councils increasing faster than that provided by the HEFCs; and
- an increase over the previous decade in the volume of research being performed which was funded at less than full economic cost.

Government actions aimed at tackling these problems include: £500 million a year in capital funding from 2004/05, to deal with the effects of under-investment in research infrastructure; and £120 million a year from 2005/06 to allow the Research Councils to pay a larger contribution of the full economic costs of research in universities. The amount universities will have to contribute to the costs of projects will be reduced from 25 per cent to 10 per cent.

Science Parks

Science Parks encourage and support the start-up, incubation and growth of knowledge-based businesses. They have formal or operational links to a higher education institution or other major research centre. In 2003 there were 63 fully operational Science Parks in the United Kingdom belonging to the UK Science Park Association (*www.ukspa.org.uk*), hosting almost 1,700 firms which were employing 41,000 people.

Public engagement in science

The Government seeks to raise the status of SET among the general public, and to increase awareness of the contribution of SET to the United Kingdom's economic wealth and quality of life. To this end, it supports activities such as the annual Festival of Science, and National Science Week – both organised by the British Association for the Advancement of Science (BA). It also offers grants to science communicators through a scheme administered by the Royal Society. In November 2002 the BA produced the report *Science in Society* for the OST. It made recommendations on how the Government could obtain an overview of the range and quality of scientific communication activities across the United Kingdom, and whether they meet the needs of the public. In response, the OST consulted on a number of proposals, including:

- holding a biennial national public survey to establish the public's participation in existing activities, the barriers to participation, their awareness of, and interest in, specific areas of science, and its attitudes towards science and scientists; and
- producing an annual summary of media coverage of science.

Science festivals

Science festivals are a growing feature of local efforts to further the understanding of the contribution made by science to everyday life.

The BA Festival of Science

In September 2003 the BA's Festival of Science took place at the University of Salford, near Manchester. The theme was Sustainable Science, spanning all aspects of how and whether science is sustainable, how science is working towards sustainability, and how science and technology can help society achieve and maintain a higher standard of living.

Edinburgh International Science Festival

This is the longest established annual science festival to be held in a single location. The festival held in April 2003 was attended by an estimated 69,000 people. Its aim is to communicate science and technology, and the wonder of discovery, to the widest possible audience.

Cheltenham Festival of Science

The second Cheltenham Festival of Science was held over five days in June 2003. The theme of the 2003 festival was time and space, including subjects such as exploring the cosmos and the science of ageing. The festival also included discussions on organic food, alternative medicine, the future of the health service, the science of Harry Potter and the Discovery Zone, an interactive science space.

Scottish Space School

The Scottish Space School offers gifted and able young people an opportunity to undertake workshops and distance learning modules on space science developed by the American National Aeronautics and Space Administration (NASA). The project has the support of the Scottish Executive and is a partnership between Careers Scotland and Johnson Space Center in Houston, Texas. Twenty-six young people, who completed the NASA modules, were selected by the Scottish Space School Foundation to attend the winter Space Camp in Houston in January 2003.

Science and Engineering Ambassadors (SEAs)

The Science and Engineering Ambassadors project was launched by the Department for Education and Skills (DfES) and the DTI in January 2002. Individuals with backgrounds in science, engineering, technology and mathematics go into schools to help teachers develop the curricula and to act as role models for the young. SEAs are administered across the United Kingdom by SETNET – the Science, Engineering, Technology and Mathematics Network (*www.setnet.org.uk*) – and delivered through a network of 53 SET points.

Planet Science

Planet Science was launched in September 2002 as an extension to science year, running until July 2003. A UK-wide education initiative, it was managed by the National Endowment for Science, Technology and the Arts and funded by the DfES. It focused particularly on those aged 10 to 19 and the adults around them (especially their teachers) and was aimed at raising awareness of the wide range of subjects and careers that are underpinned by science and technology.

National Science Week

The tenth National Science Week, coordinated by the BA and held throughout the United Kingdom, took place in March 2003. Organisations participating included hospitals, schools, industry and museums. Events included 'Bug Brother', based on the TV show *Big Brother*, a science quiz, an online survey to find the healthiest town in Wales, and productions of *The Ig Nobels: The Annals of Improbable Research – celebrating scientific research that cannot or should not be reproduced.*

Bio Bubble – the amazing inflatable cell
Launched during National Science Week, the Bio Bubble is an inflatable replica of a human cell. It is aimed at schoolchildren and allows them to 'shrink' half a million times and transport themselves inside a giant, scientifically accurate human cell. Once inside the Bio Bubble children experience 'Snog' – a theatrical show about young love and the invasion of the Epstein-Barr virus (glandular fever). The Bio Bubble is touring schools and science festivals throughout 2003/04.

Aventis Prize for Science Books
The winner of the 15th international science book prize in 2003 was Chris McManus for *Right Hand, Left Hand*. Chris McManus is currently Professor of Psychology and Medical Education at University College London and one of the world's foremost experts on handedness and lateralisation.

The prize for the best science book for children under 14 was awarded to Dr Frances Dippe for the *Dorling Kindersley Guide to the Oceans*.

Scientific museums
The Natural History Museum (*www.nhm.ac.uk*) is one of the most popular UK visitor attractions (see page 473). It has exhibitions devoted to the Earth and the life sciences and is also a leading centre in the fields of taxonomy and biodiversity. It is founded on collections of 70 million specimens from the natural world, and has 500,000 historically important original works of art. The museum employs 350 scientists, and is active in research projects in 60 countries. The museum also offers an advisory service to foreign institutions.

The Darwin Centre
In September 2002 the opening of phase one of the Darwin Centre made a further 12 million specimens accessible to the public for the first time. They range from animals collected by Charles Darwin on his 19th century voyages, to a barracuda found in UK waters in 2001. Phase two is expected to open in 2007 and will result in almost 80 per cent of the Natural History Museum's exhibits being on display.

The Science Museum (*www.sciencemuseum.org.uk*) promotes public understanding of the history of science, technology, industry and medicine. The collections contain many of the icons of the scientific age with objects as diverse as Crick and Watson's DNA model and Stephenson's *Rocket*.

These two museums are in South Kensington, London. Other important collections include those at the Museum of Science and Industry in Manchester, the Museum of the History of Science in Oxford, and the Royal Scottish Museum, Edinburgh.

Discovery centres
The Deep (*www.thedeep.co.uk*) in Hull attracted over 1 million visitors in the first 14 months since it opened in March 2002. The *submarium* includes one of Europe's deepest aquariums, featuring marine life from the equator to the poles and including the world's longest underwater lift ride. The Deep also includes a business centre, a lifelong learning centre and a research facility.

In Belfast, the W5 Interactive Discovery Centre (*www.w5online.co.uk*) is located within Northern Ireland's Millennium project, Odyssey. It has over 140 hands-on, high-technology exhibits and attracts around 200,000 visitors a year.

Zoological gardens
The Zoological Society of London (ZSL) (*www.zsl.org*), an independent conservation, science and education charity founded in 1826, runs London Zoo in Regent's Park. It also owns and runs Whipsnade Wild Animal Park in Bedfordshire. ZSL is responsible for the Institute of Zoology, which carries out research in support of animal conservation. The Institute's work covers topics such as ecology, reproductive biology and conservation genetics. ZSL also operates in overseas projects concerned with practical field conservation, primarily in East and Southern Africa, the Middle East and parts of Asia. Other well-known zoos in the United Kingdom include those in Edinburgh, Bristol, Chester, Dudley and Marwell (near Winchester).

Botanic gardens
The Royal Botanic Gardens, Kew (see page 274, *www.kew.org.uk*), founded in 1759, are based at Kew in south-west London and at Wakehurst Place (Ardingly, in West Sussex). They contain one of the largest collections of living and dried plants in the world. Research is conducted into all aspects of plant life, including physiology, biochemistry, genetics, economic botany, and the conservation of habitats and species.

The Royal Botanic Garden in Edinburgh (*www.rbge.org.uk*) was established in 1670 and is the national botanic garden of Scotland. Together with its three associated specialist gardens, it has become an internationally recognised centre for taxonomy; for the conservation and study of living and preserved plants and fungi; and as a provider of horticultural education.

A National Botanic Garden and research centre for Wales was opened in 2000 (*www.gardenofwales.org.uk*) on a site on the Middleton Hall estate at Llanarthne, near Carmarthen.

The SET workforce

The DTI report *Maximising Returns – to science, engineering and technology careers*, published in January 2002, estimated that the number of SET graduates in the working age population increased between 1992 and 2000 by 19 per cent, from 1.1 million to 1.3 million. However, owing to the increase in the number of graduates overall, the proportion holding a SET degree declined from 32 per cent to 25 per cent. Although the number of women SET graduates is increasing, in 2000 men outnumbered women by more than four to one.

The study found that less than half of male SET graduates and approximately a quarter of female SET graduates were employed in key SET occupational groups (as defined by the study), such as engineers, scientists and computer programmers. They may, however, be engaged in related occupations such as sales and marketing.

According to the 2001 ONS Business R&D Survey, the number of staff employed on R&D in UK businesses increased by 7 per cent between 1996 and 2001, to 152,000. Scientists and engineers accounted for almost two-thirds of the staff.

In 2000/01 there were 84,000 full-time SET staff employed in higher education: including just over 48,000 working in teaching and research, and just over 32,500 working only in research. In all, 32 per cent were women.

Roberts Review
The 'Roberts Review' was published in *SET for Success, the supply of people with science,*

technology, engineering and mathematical skills in April 2002. It found that, compared to other countries, the United Kingdom has a relatively large and growing number of students studying for scientific and technical qualifications. This growth primarily reflected increases in those studying IT and the biological sciences, and there were downward trends in the numbers studying mathematics, engineering and the physical sciences. The review made recommendations to deal with a number of issues including:

- poor experiences of science and engineering education, coupled with a negative image of careers in the sector;
- a shortage of women choosing to study subjects such as mathematics, engineering and the physical sciences;
- insufficiently attractive career opportunities in research; and
- science and engineering graduates and postgraduates not having the transferable skills required by R&D employers.

The 2002 Spending Review provided for additional investment of £100 million a year by 2005/06 paid via the Science Budget. This is to enable the OST to take forward the key recommendations of the Roberts Review. Measures include attracting students in schools and universities to science through improved pay and training for PhD students and postdoctoral researchers, together with better teaching and research facilities.

Women in SET
In April 2003 the Government published *A Strategy for Women in Science, Engineering and Technology* in response to Baroness Greenfield's report, *SET Fair* published in November 2002, which examined the status of women in SET in the United Kingdom and overseas. The aim of the strategy is to improve the participation of women in SET in employment, education and policy making in the United Kingdom and it is aimed equally at academia, industry and public service. New initiatives will include a resource centre to support and advise SET employers and professional bodies, and funds to help support new schemes, for example for mentoring and networking or to help with mobility needs.

The strategy also sets out a new role for the Promoting SET for Women Unit, which was set up in 1994. Its tasks will include:

Rosalind Franklin Award

In March 2003 Professor Susan Gibson was presented the first Rosalind Franklin Award. The award commemorates the scientist whose work contributed to the discovery of the double helix structure of DNA (see page 376) and rewards excellence in SET. Professor Gibson is Daniell Professor of Chemistry at King's College London, and works in the field of synthetic chemistry.

- setting up and managing the new resource centre;
- working across government departments to ensure that they follow good practice in their employment of women scientists;
- working with the DfES to ensure that mainstream policies on science in schools, careers advice and information, and higher education take account of women in SET;
- ensuring all aspects of mainstream science policy do not disadvantage women in SET; and
- setting up and supporting a new implementation group to oversee the strategy's progress and impact.

International collaboration

European Union

The EU's Sixth Framework Programme for Research and Technical Development (FP6), published in June 2002, has a budget of €17.5 billion for the four years to 2006. Framework programmes are the EU's main instrument for funding research. There are seven key areas within FP6: research in genomics and biotechnology for health; information society technologies; nanotechnologies and nanosciences; aeronautics and space; food safety; sustainable development; and economic and social sciences. Framework programmes also provide support for mobility, fellowships, infrastructures and the continuation of nuclear research under Euratom.

FP6 is a key mechanism in realising a European Research Area, which aims to regroup all EC support for better coordination of research and innovation policies, at national and EU levels. The United Kingdom is actively engaged in the development of a common European Space Strategy involving ESA, the EU and others.

The six grant-giving Research Councils, in association with UK universities, maintain the UK Research Office in Brussels that aims to promote UK participation in European research programmes. The CCLRC receives funds from the EU to make its facilities available to researchers from other Member States.

Other international activities

The COST programme (European co-operation in the field of scientific and technical research) is a multilateral agreement involving 34 countries (including all the EU Member States, many Mediterranean, Central European and Eastern European countries plus Israel as an associated state). Its purpose is to encourage co-operation in national research activities across Europe, with participants from industry, academia and research laboratories. The United Kingdom participates in the majority of COST actions and in the management of the programme.

Another example of international collaboration is CERN, home to the European laboratory for particle physics, based in Geneva, where the Large Hadron Collider is due to be completed by 2007. Scientific programmes at CERN aim to test, verify and develop the 'standard model' of the origin and structure of the Universe. There are 20 member states. PPARC leads UK participation in CERN, and the CCLRC coordinates several aspects of research community involvement. The CCLRC provides the UK contribution to the costs of access by UK researchers to the high-flux neutron source at the Institute Laue-Langevin and to the European Synchrotron Radiation Facility, both in Grenoble. The United Kingdom is a member of the European Space Agency, providing PPARC researchers entry to the Cosmic Vision 2020 space missions programme. In 2002 the United Kingdom also joined the multinational European Southern Observatory, giving PPARC-funded scientists access to a suite of 8-metre VLTs (Very Large Telescopes) in Chile.

PPARC is a partner in the European Incoherent Scatter Radar Facility within the Arctic Circle, which conducts research on the ionosphere. NERC has a major involvement in international programmes of research into global climate change organised through the World Climate Research Programme and the International Geosphere-Biosphere Programme. It also supports the UK subscription to the Ocean Drilling Program.

The Medical Research Council pays the UK subscription to the European Molecular Biology Laboratory (EMBL), which has its home research base at Heidelberg. The European Bioinformatics Institute, an outstation of the EMBL, at Hinxton, near Cambridge, provides access to important molecular biology, sequencing and structural databases. The MRC is also responsible for UK subscriptions to the International Agency for Cancer Research, Lyon.

The BBSRC and the MRC pay the UK subscription to the Human Frontiers Science Program, which promotes international collaboration in two areas: brain functions and biological functions through molecular level approaches.

The Research Councils have a number of bilateral arrangements to promote international collaboration. For example, the BBSRC has agreements with its equivalent organisations in Canada, China, France, India, Japan, the Republic of Korea, the Netherlands, and the United States, and supports travel, workshops and other activities to encourage international links.

The United Kingdom is a member of the science and technology committees of such international organisations as the Organisation for Economic Co-operation and Development (OECD) and North Atlantic Treaty Organisation (NATO), and of various specialised agencies of the United Nations, including the United Nations Educational, Scientific and Cultural Organisation (UNESCO). The Research Councils and the Royal Society are members of the European Science Foundation – an association of 76 major national funding agencies in 29 European countries.

The UK Government also enters into bilateral agreements with other governments to encourage closer collaboration in SET. The Foreign & Commonwealth Office has established a network of Science & Technology (S & T) attachés in posts overseas:

- to help capitalise on and enhance the UK science base;
- to help companies access overseas innovation and technology;
- to facilitate high-technology trade and attract foreign investment; and
- to use S & T as a vehicle to maximise UK impact abroad.

The British Council promotes 'cutting edge' UK science through events, partnership programmes, seminars, exhibitions and information provision.

Other organisations

Charitable organisations

Medical research charities are a major source of funds for research in the United Kingdom. According to the Association of Medical Research Charities, its members spent more than £600 million in support of medical research in the United Kingdom in 2002/03. The two largest contributors are the Wellcome Trust and Cancer Research UK.

The Wellcome Trust (*www.wellcome.ac.uk*) is an independent charity, established under the will of Sir Henry Wellcome in 1936. Its mission is 'to foster and promote research with the aim of improving human and animal health'. To this end, it supports 'blue sky' research and applied clinical research, and encourages the exploitation of research findings for medical benefit. The Trust also seeks to raise awareness of the medical, ethical and social implications of research and to promote dialogue between scientists, the public and policy makers.

Centre for auditory research

In February 2003 University College London announced the creation of a centre for auditory research. Its main aims will be to restore hearing to the Deaf and to prevent deafness in those at risk. The centre will be the largest of its kind in the United Kingdom and has been funded by a £9 million award from the Wellcome Trust.

To complement the programme of resources announced in the 2002 Spending Review, the Wellcome Trust is committing an additional £280 million between 2002 and 2007 for new programmes of science research and improved training for science teachers.

Professional and learned institutions

There are numerous technical institutions, professional associations and learned societies in the United Kingdom, many of which promote their own disciplines or the education and professional well-being of their members. The

Completion of the Human Genome Project
The international Human Genome Project was completed in April 2003, two years ahead of schedule. The Wellcome Trust Sanger Institute was the only UK organisation involved in the project. It carried out nearly one-third of the work and contributed £150 million, making it the largest single contributor. The project has led to the discovery nearly 100 per cent of the 2.9 billion letters of the human DNA code. Knowing virtually the entire genetic sequence gives scientists the chance to explore everything that is genetically determined about human life. The work has helped accelerate the search for genes involved in diabetes, leukaemia and childhood eczema.

Council of Science and Technology Institutes has ten member institutes representing biology, biochemistry, chemistry, the environment, food science and technology, geology, hospital physics and physics.

Science

Royal Society
The Royal Society (*www.royalsoc.ac.uk*), founded in 1660, has 1,248 Fellows and 118 Foreign Members. The Society has three roles: as the national academy of science, as a learned society and as a funding agency for the scientific community. It offers independent advice to government on science matters, acts as an international forum for discussion of ground-breaking scientific research, supports many of the best young scientists and engineers in the United Kingdom, facilitates dialogue between scientists and the public, and promotes science education. Its government grant for 2003/04 is £29.2 million.

Other societies
In Scotland the Royal Society of Edinburgh (*www.ma.hw.ac.uk*), established in 1783, promotes science by offering postdoctoral research fellowships and studentships, awarding prizes and grants, organising meetings and symposia, and publishing journals. It also acts as a source of independent scientific advice to the Government and others.

Three other major institutions publicise scientific developments by means of lectures and publications for specialists and schoolchildren. Of these, the British Association for the Advancement of Science (*www.the-ba.net*), founded in 1831, is mainly concerned with the sciences, while the Royal Society of Arts (*www.rsa.org.uk*), dating from 1754, deals with the arts and commerce as well as science.

The Royal Institution (*www.rigb.org*), founded in 1799, arranges a large and varied public programme of events to bring science to a wider audience, including the *Christmas Lectures* and the *Friday Evening Discourses*. Over 100 events are organised each year, attracting around 70,000 visitors of all ages. The *Christmas Lectures* (started by Michael Faraday) have been running since 1825. As well as being broadcast in the United Kingdom, the lectures are transmitted to other parts of Europe, Japan and Korea.

Engineering

Engineering Council (UK)
EC[UK] – the Engineering Council (UK) – (*www.engc.org.uk*) was created in March 2002 as the successor of the chartered body first established in 1982 to promote and regulate the engineering profession in the United Kingdom. It is responsible for the Register of Chartered Engineers, Incorporated Engineers and Engineering Technicians. EC[UK] is supported by 35 professional engineering institutions and 14 professional affiliates. In partnership with the institutions, the Council accredits higher and further education courses and advises the Government on academic, industrial and professional issues.

Engineering and Technology Board (ETB)
Created in January 2002, the Engineering and Technology Board (*www.etechb.co.uk*) promotes SET in order to support the supply of appropriately skilled individuals to meet present and future needs in the United Kingdom. It works in partnership with business and industry, government, education and the engineering profession.

Royal Academy of Engineering
The national academy of engineering in Great Britain is the Royal Academy of Engineering (*www.raeng.org.uk*), which has 1,236 Fellows and 91 Foreign Members. It promotes excellence in engineering for the benefit of society, and advises government, Parliament and other official organisations. The Academy's programmes are

aimed at attracting students into engineering, raising awareness of the importance of engineering design among undergraduates, developing links between industry and higher education, and increasing industrial investment in engineering research in higher education institutions. It has a government grant of £5.3 million in 2003/04.

Further reading

Excellence and Opportunity – a science and innovation policy for the 21st century. Cm 4814. The Stationery Office, 2000.

The Forward Look 2003 Government-funded science, engineering and technology. DTI/OST. Cm 5877. The Stationery Office, 2003.

Invest in Innovation – A strategy for science, engineering and technology. DTI/HMT/DfES, 2002.

Maximising Returns – to science, engineering and technology careers. DTI, 2002.

SET for success, the supply of people with science, technology, engineering and mathematical skills. HM Treasury, 2002.

A Strategy for Women in Science, Engineering and Technology. DTI, 2003.

Campaign to Promote Engineering

The Campaign to Promote Engineering (CPE) is an industry-led organisation, recently integrated into the ETB. Its main aim is to increase public awareness of the role engineering plays in life and promote engineering as a career. Recent events have included:

- Imagineering 2002 – an event designed to introduce 8- to 16-year-olds to engineering and manufacturing through fun and hands-on activity; and

- Flying Challenge II – an event held in March 2003 at the Fleet Air Museum in Yeovil, at which local aerospace companies came together to demonstrate the principles behind aerospace engineering in order to promote it as a career choice to young people.

Websites

Office of Science and Technology
www.ost.gov.uk

Research Councils UK
www.rcuk.ac.uk

Council of Science and Technology
www.cst.gov.uk

WWW.

27 Agriculture, fishing and forestry

Agriculture accounted for only around 0.8 per cent of the total UK economy, in terms of gross value added, in both 2001 and 2002. However, issues such as the outbreak of foot-and-mouth disease in 2001, and the on-going debate around genetically modified food (see pages 404 and 397 respectively) meant that its profile across the United Kingdom was far greater. Agriculture's share of the total economy has fallen from 1.6 per cent in 1995 and 2.9 per cent in 1973, mainly because of a long-term fall in agricultural prices.

The United Kingdom was about 62 per cent self-sufficient for all food and about 75 per cent for indigenous food in 2002. This was the lowest level recorded since the current method of calculating self-sufficiency was first applied in 1988. Although the ban on UK meat exports that followed the outbreak of foot-and-mouth disease was lifted in February 2002, exports of meat did not recover and imports continued to increase slightly. There was also a small increase in imports of indigenous fruit and vegetables.

The United Kingdom, along with Belgium, has the joint lowest percentage of its workforce employed in agriculture, fishing and forestry of any country in the European Union (EU), at just 1.4 per cent – see Figure 27.1.

Agriculture

In 2002 UK agriculture contributed £7.1 billion to the economy and employed some 550,000 people. Agricultural land represents 77 per cent of total land area in the United Kingdom, compared with around 40 per cent for the EU as a whole. Most agricultural land in the United Kingdom is

Figure 27.1 Employment in the agriculture, forestry, hunting and fishing sector:[1] EU, 2001

Percentages

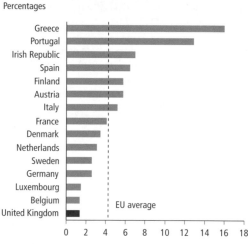

1 Share of employed civilian working population.
Source: Eurostat

grassland or rough grazing, with only a quarter used to grow crops (see Figure 27.2).

In June 2002 there were 303,000 farm holdings in the United Kingdom, with an average area of 56.6 hectares. Nearly half were smaller than the minimum size considered by the EU to be necessary for full-time holdings. About two-thirds of all agricultural land was owner-occupied; the rest was tenanted or rented.

Total income from farming rose in real terms by 14 per cent between 2001 and 2002, to £2.4 billion. However, this was still 62 per cent below its peak in 1995. The value of output (including subsidies

Figure 27.2 Agricultural land use, 2002, UK

Total area on agricultural holdings

18.4 million hectares

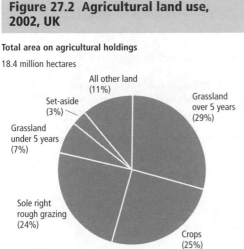

Source: Department for Environment, Food and Rural Affairs

Figure 27.3 Producer prices for agricultural products,[1] UK

Index (1995=100)

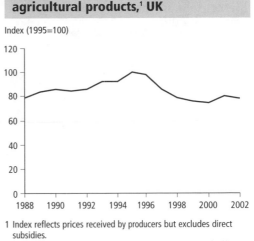

1 Index reflects prices received by producers but excludes direct subsidies.

Source: Department for Environment, Food and Rural Affairs

directly related to products) rose by 1.1 per cent, or £168 million. Volume was 4.8 per cent higher, but prices received were 3.6 per cent lower. There were notable increases in the value of output of cereals and livestock, but decreases in the value of output of potatoes and milk. Income per full-time worker from agriculture in the United Kingdom increased by 3.5 per cent in 2002, compared with an EU average increase of 3.1 per cent.

Productivity measures how efficiently inputs are converted into outputs. Since 1973 the productivity of the agriculture industry in the United Kingdom has increased by more than a third. Total factor productivity increased by 7.4 per cent in 2002 – outputs increased and inputs (including labour) declined slightly. This was a large gain when compared with 2001, when productivity fell due to foot-and-mouth disease and unusually wet weather.

Between the 1995 peak and 2002, the prices received by agricultural producers for their products fell by 22 per cent (see Figure 27.3). The largest falls were in the prices of root crops (55 per cent) and cereals (43 per cent). The main reason for the overall fall has been the relatively high level of sterling since the mid-1990s, which made exports more expensive and imports cheaper.

Agricultural tenure

About 35 per cent of agricultural land (excluding common rough grazing) in England and 21 per cent in Wales is rented. Since 1995 a simplified

legal framework for new tenancies, known as farm business tenancies, has allowed landowners to benefit from full inheritance tax relief.

There is a similar proportion of rented land in Scotland, much of it under crofting tenure. Crofting is a system of land tenure regulated through the *Crofting Acts* and found only in the Highlands and Islands of Scotland. A croft is a unit of land subject to these Acts; there are around 17,700 in total, and croft land covers some 106,000 hectares (excluding common grazing land). The *Land Reform (Scotland) Act 2003* gave crofting communities the right to buy their crofts at any time. The Scottish Executive has also changed the law relating to agricultural tenure, and the *Agricultural Holdings (Scotland) Act 2003* aims to stimulate the rental sector and offer tenants the opportunity to manage their land more flexibly.

Most farms in Northern Ireland are owner-occupied, but the conacre system allows owners not wishing to farm all their land to let it annually to others. Conacre land, about 30 per cent of agricultural land, is used mainly for grazing.

Production

Home production of the principal foods is shown in Table 27.4 as a percentage by weight of total new supplies.

Livestock

About 40 per cent of farms are devoted mainly to dairy farming or to beef cattle and sheep. Most of

Table 27.4 Home production as a percentage of total new supply[1] for use in the UK

Percentages

	Average 1991–93	1997	2002
Wheat	124	121	103
Barley	124	124	115
Oats	109	112	121
Oilseed rape	93	94	86
Linseed	143	83	53
Sugar (as refined)	59	70	63
Potatoes	90	91	87
Vegetables	78	71	66
Fruit	19	11	9
Beef and veal	97	77	72
Mutton and lamb	107	97	84
Pork	104	109	76
Bacon and ham	46	51	40
Poultrymeat	94	96	91
Milk[2]	101	101	102
Butter	67	79	69
Cheese	68	67	68
Eggs	96	95	87

1 Total new supply is home production plus imports less exports.
2 Includes milk used in the production of dairy products.
Source: Department for Environment, Food and Rural Affairs

the beef animals and sheep are reared in the hill and moorland areas of the United Kingdom. Among world-famous British livestock are the Hereford, Welsh Black and Aberdeen Angus beef breeds, the Jersey, Guernsey and Ayrshire dairy breeds, the Large White pig breed and a number of sheep breeds. Data on livestock products are given in Table 27.5.

Cattle and sheep constitute 34 per cent of the value of UK gross agricultural output. Dairy production is the largest part of the sector, followed by cattle and calves, and then sheep and lambs.

Between June 2001 and June 2002 the UK cattle population declined by 2.4 per cent to 10.3 million. In 2002 the average size of dairy herds in England was 87, in Wales 66, and in Scotland 92. The average yield of milk for each dairy cow in the United Kingdom was 6,531 litres.

The total value of production of milk and milk products for human consumption fell by 12 per

cent in 2002, to £2.5 billion. This was primarily due to a fall in the value of milk sold for processing to dairy companies resulting from a 2 pence fall, to 17 pence per litre, in the average milk price received by farmers in 2002.

Almost all home-fed beef production originates from specialist beef suckler herds – since 1996, almost all beef from dairy cows has been removed from the food chain. The remainder derives from suckler herds producing high-quality beef calves. The value of cattle and calf production rose by 14 per cent in 2002 to £2 billion, mainly because of a 12 per cent increase in the value of home-fed production of beef and veal, and a 13 per cent increase in direct subsidy and other payments to beef producers.

The number of sheep and lambs in the United Kingdom fell by 2.4 per cent, to 35.8 million, between June 2001 and June 2002. The value of production of sheep and lambs rose by 34 per cent to £840 million in 2002, mainly as a result of a 42 per cent increase in the value of home-fed production and a 31 per cent increase in subsidy payments. The United Kingdom has more than 60 native sheep breeds and many cross-bred varieties.

Between June 2001 and June 2002 the total number of pigs in the United Kingdom fell by 4.4 per cent, to 5.6 million. The value of production of pigs fell by 8.3 per cent in 2002 to £687 million, half the peak value of £1.4 billion in 1996. The main reason was a 6.7 per cent fall in the value of home-fed production of pigmeat.

The UK poultry population in June 2002 comprised 105 million chickens and other table fowls; 29 million birds in the laying flock; 11 million fowls for breeding; and 11 million turkeys, ducks and geese. The size of the breeding flock fell by 11 per cent between June 2001 and June 2002. The value of production of poultrymeat fell by 7.9 per cent in 2002 to £1.2 billion. There were falls in average producer prices for both broiler meat and turkey meat.

Crops
Farms devoted primarily to arable crops are found mainly in eastern and central southern England and eastern Scotland. The main crops are shown in Figure 27.6 and Table 27.7. In 2002, 3.2 million hectares were planted to *cereals* – predominantly wheat, barley and oats – an increase of 7.7 per cent on 2001, although this was still 3 per cent less

Table 27.5 Livestock products, UK

Thousand tonnes

	Average 1991–93	1997	2000	2001	2002
Beef and veal	963	698	706	645	692
Mutton and lamb	408	342	382	266	306
Pork	809	888	725	610	628
Bacon and ham	199	239	209	197	185
Poultrymeat	1,232	1,520	1,513	1,565	1,533
Milk (million litres)[1]	14,033	14,135	13,801	14,009	14,213
Eggs (million dozen)[2]	805	794	747	806	854

1 For human consumption; includes milk used in the production of dairy products.
2 For human consumption only; does not include eggs for hatching.
Source: Department for Environment, Food and Rural Affairs

than in 2000. More normal sowing patterns were evident in 2002, following the very wet planting conditions of the previous year's crops. The total volume of cereal production rose by 22 per cent and the total value by 8 per cent.

The value of production of *oilseed rape* increased by 6.8 per cent in 2002. Better yields led to an overall increase in the volume of production of 24 per cent compared with 2001. Prices remained strong, while overall subsidy payments fell by 22 per cent. The value of *sugar beet* production rose by 6.3 per cent – although the area of contracted sugar beet decreased, an increase in yield led to a 13 per cent increase in the volume of production.

Large-scale *potato* and *vegetable* cultivation takes place on fertile soils throughout the United Kingdom. The total area for all potato cultivation fell by 4.1 per cent in 2002, and the value of production fell by 27 per cent, because the average price paid to registered growers was lower than in 2001.

Horticulture

Table 27.8 gives details of the main horticultural products. As at June 2002 the total area devoted to horticulture (excluding mushrooms, potatoes, and peas for harvesting dry) amounted to 176,000 hectares, compared with 173,000 hectares in 2001. This area relates to field area and does not take into account the number of crops in the year.

The value of production of vegetables decreased by 8 per cent to £948 million in 2002. However, the value of production of ornamentals, such as

Figure 27.6 Area under crops, 2002, UK

4.6 million hectares

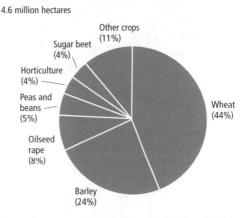

Source: Department for Environment, Food and Rural Affairs

flowers and shrubs, rose by 7 per cent to £726 million, and the value of fruit increased by 9 per cent to £257 million.

Genetically modified crops

An estimated 59 million hectares of genetically modified (GM) crops were grown in 16 countries across the world in 2002. In the United Kingdom, the year 2002 witnessed the continuation of a four-year UK programme of farm-scale evaluations (FSEs) of GM crops, in which independent researchers are studying the effects that the management of the crops might have on farmland wildlife, when compared with equivalent non-GM crops. The crops involved, all of which are modified to be resistent to specific herbicides, are oilseed rape (both spring and autumn sown),

Table 27.7 Cereals and other crops in the UK

	Average 1991–93	1997	2002
Cereals			
Wheat			
Production ('000 tonnes)	13,783	15,018	16,053
Yield (tonnes per hectare)	7.1	7.4	8.0
Value of production (£ million)	1,718	1,851	1,490
Barley			
Production	7,010	7,828	6,192
Yield	5.4	5.8	5.6
Value	805	977	623
Oats			
Production	501	577	758
Yield	5.1	5.8	6.0
Value	61	71	71
Total for cereals[1]			
Production	21,398	23,534	23,114
Yield	6.4	6.7	7.1
Value	2,587	2,907	2,192
Other crops			
Oilseed rape			
Production	1,193	1,527	1,437
Yield	2.8	3.2	3.3
Value	358	406	294
Sugar beet			
Production	9,505	11,084	9,435
Yield	48.3	56.6	55.8
Value	350	329	272
Potatoes			
Production	7,085	7,128	6,375
Yield	40.2	43.0	40.1
Value	484	390	463

1 Includes rye, mixed corn and triticale.
Source: Department for Environment, Food and Rural Affairs

Table 27.8 Horticulture in the UK

	Average 1991–93	1997	2002
Vegetables[1,2]			
Area ('000 hectares)	178	153	143
Value of production (£ million)	944	959	948
Fruit			
Area	44	39	33
Value	279	199	257
of which:			
Orchard fruit			
Area	31	28	25
Value	140	80	79
Soft fruit			
Area	13	11	9
Value	138	111	162
Ornamentals[2]			
Area	19	20	20
Value	539	671	726

1 Includes peas harvested dry for human consumption.
2 Areas relate to field areas multiplied by the number of crops in the year.
Source: Department for Environment, Food and Rural Affairs

Following advice from the Agriculture and Environment Biotechnology Commission (AEBC), the Department for Environment, Food and Rural Affairs (Defra) announced a UK-wide public debate on GM issues in July 2002. Managed by an independent steering board, the main phase of the debate featured a series of conferences, debates and meetings held throughout the summer of 2003. The steering board will report people's views to the Government at the end of the process.

Complementing the GM debate were submissions from a review of the science behind GM, conducted by a panel of independent scientists, in May 2003, and a study of the costs and benefits of GM crops, conducted by the Strategy Unit (see page 46), which was published in July 2003. The Strategy Unit report concluded that existing GM crops could offer some cost and convenience advantages to UK farmers. However, any economic benefit to the United Kingdom is likely to be limited, at least in the short term, since only a narrow range of GM crops are currently suited to UK conditions, and consumer demand is weak. In the long term, the overall spread of costs and benefits will depend on public attitudes, and the ability of the regulatory system to manage uncertainties.

beet, and maize. The project has involved between 60 and 75 fields of each crop and also monitored gene-flow, including cross-pollination. The results will be reported, made publicly available and considered by the Government in 2003/04. The Government has a voluntary agreement with the industry that no GM crops will be grown commercially in the United Kingdom before the results of the FSEs have been fully assessed.

The findings of the GM debate and the two reports will, along with the FSE results, help inform future decisions on commercialisation of GM crops in the United Kingdom.

Food safety

The Food Standards Agency (FSA – see chapter 13) aims to ensure that the food consumers eat is safe, and to offer independent, balanced advice to government throughout the United Kingdom. The Meat Hygiene Service, an executive agency of the FSA, is responsible for enforcing legislation on meat hygiene, inspection, animal welfare at slaughter and the control of specified risk materials in all licensed abattoirs and cutting premises in Great Britain. In Northern Ireland this role is carried out by the Department of Agriculture and Rural Development (DARD) on behalf of the FSA.

The FSA conducts the annual *Consumer Attitudes to Food* survey each autumn. The 2002 survey found that there have been falls in the levels of concern over food safety in recent years – in 2002, 45 per cent of respondents (aged 16 and over) said that they were 'very' or 'fairly' concerned about Bovine Spongiform Encephalopathy (BSE), compared with 61 per cent in 2000. For GM food these figures were 36 per cent and 43 per cent respectively.

A revised action plan on illegal meat imports, which takes account of an assessment of the risk of foot-and-mouth disease, was published in April 2003. Under the plan, HM Customs and Excise took responsibility for anti-smuggling controls on illegal imports of meat and other animal products from non-EU countries.

Pesticides

The Pesticides Safety Directorate (PSD), an executive agency of Defra, administers the regulation of agricultural, horticultural, forestry, food storage and home garden pesticides. Its principal functions are to evaluate and process applications for approval of pesticide products for use in Great Britain and provide advice to government on pesticides policy. The PSD aims to:

- ensure the safe use of pesticides, for both people and the environment;
- reduce negative impacts of pesticides, encourage reductions in their use, and encourage the development and introduction of alternative control measures as part of the

strategy for sustainable farming and food (see page 400); and
- harmonise pesticide regulation within Europe.

Exports, marketing and promotion

Exports of food, drink and animal feed were around £8.9 billion in 2002, compared with £18.9 billion for imports. EU countries accounted for 62 per cent of all UK food and drink exports; the main markets were the Republic of Ireland (£1.4 billion) and France (£1.1 billion).

The value of British food and drink exports was 4 per cent higher in 2002 than in 2001. Added value products accounted for 63 per cent of these exports. Sales of alcohol, breakfast cereals, tea and cheese all increased.

Food from Britain (FFB), an organisation funded by Defra on behalf of the four UK agricultural departments and by the food and drink industry, provides specialist marketing and international business development services to the industry. It has a network of 11 international offices, each with local food industry expertise and trade contacts. It also fosters the development of the speciality food and drink industry in the United Kingdom through a range of tailored business development and marketing services, delivered nationally by FFB and locally by regional and county food groups.

The British Farm Standard red tractor logo, administered by Assured Food Standards and owned by the National Farmers' Union, is intended to be an authoritative mark to identify food that meets independently verified assurance standards covering food safety, animal welfare and environmental issues.

Agricultural shows

Several major agricultural shows are held annually across the United Kingdom, including:

- the Royal Show, Stoneleigh, Warwickshire (early July), where visitors can see the latest techniques and improvements in British agriculture;

- the Royal Highland Show, Edinburgh (June), with around 4,000 head of livestock on show and the largest trade exhibition of agricultural machinery in Great Britain;

- the Royal Welsh Show, Llanelwedd, Builth Wells (late July);

- the Royal Welsh Agricultural Winter Fair, Llanelwedd, Builth Wells, for livestock and carcases (December);

- the Royal Ulster Agricultural Society Show, Belfast (May); and

- the Royal Smithfield Show, London (every other year), for agricultural machinery, livestock and carcases.

Farmers' markets

Around 460 farmers' markets operate in the United Kingdom, selling produce directly to consumers. The National Association of Farmers' Markets (NAFM – *www.farmersmarkets.net*) sets the criteria that such markets should meet, which include:

- food must be locally produced (each market has a definition of local);

- all produce sold must be grown, reared or otherwise produced by the stallholder; and

- information should be available to customers at each market about the rules of the market and the production methods of the producers.

Government role

Defra has responsibility for agriculture, fisheries, food, animal welfare issues, environmental protection, and wildlife and the countryside in general. It also administers support policies agreed in Brussels, which provide around £3 billion a year to UK agriculture from the EU budget.

The Scottish Executive Environment and Rural Affairs Department (SEERAD), the Welsh Assembly Government's Agriculture and Rural Affairs Department (ARAD), and DARD have varying degrees of responsibility for agriculture and fisheries affairs.

UK agriculture strategy

The Government's policy is to secure a more competitive agriculture industry with a stronger market orientation. It aims to help farming become more competitive, diverse, flexible, responsive to consumer wishes and environmentally responsible. In the short-term, it offers support to those sectors hit hardest by the continuing farming crisis and in the longer-term encourages industry restructuring and adaptation.

The Government launched its *Strategy for Sustainable Farming and Food* for England in December 2002. This aims to secure a profitable and internationally competitive future for the industry while maintaining and improving the environment and improving nutrition and public health. Expenditure of £500 million is planned over the three years of the strategy, key elements of which include:

- continued expansion of agri-environment schemes such as Countryside Stewardship, including the introduction of new, simpler 'entry level' schemes (see page 401);

- a 'whole farm' approach to management and regulation, helping farmers plan their business as a whole to meet commercial and regulatory needs;

- a new *Agricultural Development Scheme* to improve competitiveness and marketing;

- new funding to assist small regional food producers; and

- a network of demonstration farms to share best practice and experience.

The devolved administrations have strategies to meet priorities in their own areas. The Welsh Assembly Government's *Farming for the Future: A New Direction for Farming in Wales*, published in 2001, contains many elements similar to the *Strategy for Sustainable Farming and Food*, as does the Scottish Executive's *Forward Strategy for Scottish Agriculture*, also published in 2001. *A Vision for the future of the Northern Ireland agri-food industry*, produced by the 'Vision' group set up by the Minister of Agriculture and Rural Development, was published in the same year.

Agri-industrial materials (AIMS)

The AIMS section in Defra is responsible for the development of crops that provide renewable raw materials for energy and industry. Such crops can help meet sustainable development, climate change and renewable energy targets, as well as provide new commercial opportunities for the agriculture sector. Defra also provides the secretariat for a government/industry forum on non-food uses of crops. Crops for the production of heat and power are supported through the Energy Crops Scheme, part of the England Rural Development Programme.

Rural Development Programmes (RDPs)

Although each is different, RDPs have the general aims of conserving and improving the environment, and creating productive and sustainable rural economies. Developing more diverse and competitive rural industries are also central themes. The RDPs will run from 2001 to 2006, investing around £3 billion in the UK rural economy.

The *England Rural Development Programme* is investing £1.6 billion in rural development and agri-environment measures. These include the Environmentally Sensitive Areas and Countryside Stewardship Scheme; the Rural Enterprise Scheme; the Energy Crops Scheme; the Processing and Marketing Grant; and the Vocational Training Scheme.

The *Scottish Rural Development Programme* (SRDP) concentrates on complementing the Common Agricultural Policy (see page 402) and provides support for less favoured areas (LFAs), agri-environment measures, and afforestation. Around £685 million is being spent over the lifetime of the programme. In addition to the SRDP measures, the Agricultural Business Development Scheme provides support to farmers and crofters and their families in the Highlands and Islands. SEERAD will provide £50 million towards supporting diversification elsewhere in Scotland between 2001 and 2006.

The *Rural Development Plan for Wales* involves investment of around £450 million. The programme makes funds available for schemes such as the *Tir Gofal* (Land in Care) whole farm agri-environment scheme and the Processing and Marketing Grant Scheme. It includes support for hill farming and a range of forestry and farm woodland initiatives.

The *Rural Development Regulation Plan for Northern Ireland*, which is running from 2000 to 2006, is worth £266 million. It includes the new LFA support scheme and an enhanced agri-environment programme. DARD also manages

a Rural Development Programme targeted at the broader rural community that is expected to be worth about £80 million between 2001 and 2007.

Land based schemes

Land based schemes are a major part of the RDPs. Within them, agri-environment schemes make payments for the management of land to maintain, enhance and extend wildlife habitats; conserve historic or geological features; encourage public access; and restore traditional aspects of the countryside. Aiming to make conservation part of management practice, agri-environment schemes are funded by the EU and the Government, and include:

- The *Environmentally Sensitive Areas* (ESA) scheme, which offers incentives to farmers to adopt agricultural practices that will safeguard and enhance parts of the country of particularly high landscape, wildlife or historic value. The scheme operates as Tir Gofal in Wales.

- The *Countryside Stewardship* scheme, the main scheme for the wider countryside in England. Farmers and land managers enter ten-year agreements to manage land in an environmentally beneficial way in return for annual payments. The *Countryside Management* scheme fulfils a similar role in Northern Ireland.

- In Scotland, the *Rural Stewardship* scheme, which has replaced both the ESA and Countryside Premium schemes as the main scheme for encouraging environmentally friendly farming practice.

- *Organic farming* schemes, which offer payments to farmers – in the form of financial help during the conversion process – to aid them in converting to organic farming and thereafter to continue to manage their land in an environmentally beneficial way.

- In England, Wales and Northern Ireland, simplified *Entry Level* agri-environment schemes are being considered. A trial of one such scheme is taking place in England.

Other land based schemes include:

- the *Farm Woodland Premium* scheme (partly funded by the EU), which aims to encourage

Organic farming in the United Kingdom
Anyone involved in the production, processing or import (from outside the EU) of organic food must be registered with an approved organic certification body, of which there are 14 in the United Kingdom, and subject to at least annual inspection. The European Commission (EC) Regulation controlling the industry sets out the principle that organic farming aims to be self-sufficient, and fertility should come principally from the farm itself, for example in the use of animal and plant manures and crop rotation systems, although other, mostly natural, fertilisers and pesticides are allowed.

As at December 2002, there were nearly 725,000 hectares of land registered as being in conversion or farmed organically in the United Kingdom, an increase of 6 per cent on the previous year. There were 4,060 farmers and growers and 1,940 processors and importers registered with the various certification bodies. It is estimated that the UK market for organic food was worth around £920 million in 2001/02.

The Organic Conversion Information Service, funded by Defra in England, provides free advice to farmers and growers considering conversion to organic farming methods. Similar services are operated in Wales through the Farming Connect Organic Development Centre, while in Scotland SEERAD funds the Scottish Agricultural College to operate a telephone helpline. Standards of organic food production in the United Kingdom are set by the UK Register of Organic Food Standards.

farmers to convert productive agricultural land to woodlands by providing payments to help offset consequent falls in agricultural income; and

- the *Hill Farm Allowance* scheme, which provides support to hill farmers in specified areas of England, in recognition of the difficulties they face and the vital role they play in maintaining landscape and community in upland areas. The scheme operates as Tir Mynydd in Wales.

Project based schemes
These schemes are intended to benefit the wider rural economy. Those operating in England include the *Rural Enterprise Scheme*, which assists farmers and other rural businesses adapt to

changing markets; and the *Vocational Training Scheme*, which is aimed at improving the occupational skills of farmers and foresters.

Common Agricultural Policy (CAP)
The CAP was introduced in 1962, driven by a need to ensure food security in Europe. However, recent reforms emphasise a more market-oriented approach to agriculture. Total UK expenditure under the CAP and on national grants and subsidies in 2002/03 is forecast to fall by some £1.5 billion compared with 2001/02, to £3.1 billion (see Figure 27.9). Expenditure was much greater in 2001/02 because of foot-and-mouth disease; in 2000/01, total UK expenditure was £3.0 billion.

Expenditure under the CAP arable and livestock schemes is protected by the Integrated Administration and Control System (IACS). Controls to prevent and detect fraud and irregularity are major features of the system. These include verification checks of claimed land and animals, including on-the-spot inspections and remote sensing by observation satellites.

Member States not participating in the European single currency have the opportunity to offer producers, processors and traders the option of CAP payments in euros. The UK Government

Figure 27.9 Public expenditure[1] under the CAP and on national grants and subsidies, 2002/03, UK

Total: £3.1 billion

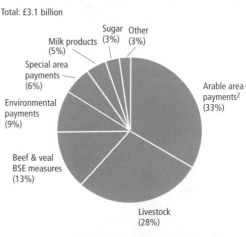

Milk products (5%)
Sugar (3%)
Other (3%)
Special area payments (6%)
Environmental payments (9%)
Arable area payments[2] (33%)
Beef & veal BSE measures (13%)
Livestock (28%)

1 Forecast expenditure by the Rural Payments Agency and agricultural and other departments.
2 Includes set-aside.
Source: Department for Environment, Food and Rural Affairs

offers CAP market support measures, such as export refunds, to traders and processors, and intends to extend this option to direct aid recipients.

EU legislation permits Member States to recycle, or *modulate*, a proportion of payments made direct to farmers under CAP commodity regimes. Modulation was introduced in 2001 at a flat rate of 2.5 per cent, to help fund the RDPs (see page 401). This means that 2.5 per cent of subsidy payments will be reallocated to agri-environment and forestry schemes such as Countryside Stewardship, Tir Gofal and ESAs. The Government is matching the sum reallocated to provide further funding for the RDPs. Modulation is estimated to have reduced arable and livestock subsidies by £43 million in 2002. To secure a significant increase in funds for rural development measures, all direct payments made under CAP commodity regimes between 2001 and 2006 will be modulated.

In June 2003 the Council of Agriculture Ministers agreed a package of proposals to reform the CAP. The reforms are intended to make European agriculture more competitive and market-oriented, promote simplification of the CAP, facilitate the EU enlargement process (see page 63) and increase flexibility, while guaranteeing farmers income stability. Key elements include:
- a single farm payment, not linked to production;
- linking payments to environmental, food safety, animal welfare, health and occupational safety standards, as well as a requirement to keep all farmland in good condition; and
- a stronger rural development policy.

The UK Government supports these reforms, and predicts overall economic benefits to the United Kingdom of about £400–600 million a year if they are implemented.

The World Trade Organisation (WTO) fourth ministerial conference, held in November 2001 in Doha (see page 371), contained an important text on agriculture, which committed WTO members to substantial cuts in market protection and domestic subsidies such as the CAP, as well as reductions in export subsidies. It also committed members to take account of environmental, rural development and animal welfare concerns, and negotiate special treatment for developing countries.

Arable Area Payments Scheme
Under this scheme – part of the CAP – farmers may claim area payments on cereals, oilseeds, proteins and linseed, and on flax and hemp for fibre. A condition for claiming area payments is that farmers (excluding small producers) must 'set aside', and not use, a certain percentage of their land, thereby avoiding overproduction, and must comply with the strict rules for managing set-aside. The minimum rate for set-aside for 2003 was 10 per cent of the total area claimed.

In 2002 there were around 56,000 claims for area payments in the United Kingdom in respect of 4.5 million hectares of land. After allowing for modulation, payments for claims made in 2002 are expected to total over £1 billion.

Professional, scientific and technical services
A number of organisations are active in service provision:

- in England the Rural Development Service of Defra provides scheme implementation services for the England Rural Development Programme, involving professional and technical work in relation to the enhancement and protection of the environment, including biodiversity and rural development;

- in Wales, similar services are provided by Farming Connect and ARAD's divisional offices while DARD has a similar remit in Northern Ireland;

- in Scotland SEERAD agricultural staff provide professional and technical scheme implementation services, and the Scottish Agricultural College (SAC) provides professional, business, scientific and technical services in the agriculture, rural business, food and drink, and environmental markets;

- the Farm Business Advice Service, which aims to help farmers in England increase profitability and examine the possibility of diversification; and

- Lantra, which is the UK Sector Skills Council (see page 119) for the industry, receives government support under contracts from Defra and the Scottish Executive.

Animal health and welfare

Professional advice and action on the statutory control of animal health and the welfare of farm livestock are the responsibility of the State Veterinary Service in Great Britain. It is supported in England and Wales by the Veterinary Laboratories Agency (*www.defra.gov.uk/corporate/ vla*), which also offers its services to the private sector on a commercial basis. Similar support is provided in Scotland by the Scottish Agricultural College. In Northern Ireland, DARD's Veterinary Service carries out a similar role to the State Veterinary Service, supported by its Veterinary Sciences Division.

Defra aims to ensure priority is given to maintaining standards of welfare for animals during all stages of production. Together with the devolved administrations in Wales and Scotland, it launched the *Ten year Animal Health and Welfare Strategy* in January 2003. Key goals of the strategy include achieving consistently high standards of animal health and welfare, improved public health, and a capacity to deal swiftly and effectively with any disease emergency. The Northern Ireland *Animal Health and Welfare Strategy* will, when finalised, be closely linked to the ten-year strategy.

A draft Animal Welfare Bill was published by Defra in October 2002, and is intended to update a number of pieces of legislation. It covers the welfare of all farmed, wild or exotic animals in captivity, domestic animals, and animals in entertainment and sport. The Bill proposes a new statutory duty of care on the owners of animals, as well as powers to make regulations banning mutilations of animals, such as the docking of dogs' tails.

The United Kingdom enforces controls on imports of live animals and genetic material, including checks on all individual consignments originating from outside the EU and frequent checks at destination points on those from other EU Member States. Measures can be taken to prevent the import of diseased animals and genetic material from regions or countries affected by disease. Veterinary checks also include unannounced periods of surveillance at ports.

The Pet Travel Scheme (PETS) allows cats and dogs (including guide and hearing dogs) from certain countries, and animals returning from a period abroad, to enter the United Kingdom without quarantine. Certain criteria must be met in order for an animal to be eligible – these include having a microchip implanted under its skin so it can be identified. The scheme started in 2000, covering European countries only. It has since been extended to cover certain long-haul destinations, for example Jamaica, Australia, Japan, the USA and Canada.

A European Commission (EC) Directive on welfare standards for laying hens stopped the installation of conventional barren battery cages after 1 January 2003, and will ban them altogether from January 2012. Currently farmers are still able to use 'enriched cages', which have more space for each bird and a nest, perch and litter, although the EC will report in 2005 on the various systems for rearing laying hens, and make proposals as to which should be allowed in the future.

Foot-and-mouth disease

A significant outbreak of foot-and-mouth disease (FMD) occurred in the United Kingdom during 2001. The disease is highly virulent in pigs, cattle, sheep and other ungulates, spreading rapidly by contact between animals, transmission via people or transport, or through the air. There were 2,030 confirmed cases in total, and during the year over 4 million animals, on 10,075 premises, were slaughtered for disease control purposes.

The Treasury has estimated that the net economic effect of the outbreak was under £2 billion (0.2 per cent of GDP), less than was originally expected because expenditure, for example on tourism, was diverted elsewhere in the economy.

Part of the Government's response to the outbreak was the *Animal Health Act 2002*, which included provision of new powers of entry to farms for vaccination, serology or slaughter in the event of an outbreak of animal disease. It also included additional powers to cull animals to prevent the spread of disease. A requirement of the Act, Defra's foot-and-mouth disease contingency plan, was laid before Parliament in March 2003. It set out the operational arrangements Defra intends to put in place to deal with any occurrence of foot-and-mouth disease, and records the policy on which they are based. The Northern Ireland contingency plan is also being revised to take account of lessons learned from FMD.

Cattle tracing system (CTS)

The British Cattle Movement Service (BCMS) was launched in 1998 to record all cattle on a CTS database. Cover has been extended to over 98 per cent of the 10 million cattle in the Great Britain herd. Work is in hand to collect the remaining data and apply checks to help ensure that information held on the database is accurate and complete. There is a legal requirement to notify the BCMS of all movements. In Northern Ireland, all cattle and cattle movements are recorded on the Animal and Public Health Information System (APHIS), which has been approved by the EU since 1999 as a fully operational database for cattle traceability.

Tuberculosis (TB) in cattle

The Government's strategy is to find a science-based policy to control TB in cattle. An annual £5 million research programme is in place to find out how the disease is spread among cattle and wildlife, including research into improved diagnostic tests and the development of a TB vaccine. An on-farm epidemiological survey, known as TB99, is starting to provide data to help understand the disease and focus future research. Defra is also investigating the role that husbandry might play in reducing TB risk. An important element of the Government's strategy in Great Britain is the badger culling trial, designed to establish the contribution that badgers, as opposed to other factors, make in spreading TB to cattle. It is hoped that the trial will start yielding results by 2004.

Fur farming

Keeping animals solely or primarily for slaughter for their fur became illegal across the United Kingdom on 1 January 2003.

Veterinary medicinal products

The *Veterinary Medicines Directorate* (*www.vmd.gov.uk*), an executive agency of Defra, aims to protect public health, animal health and the environment, and to promote animal welfare, by ensuring the safety, quality and efficacy of all aspects of veterinary medicines in the United Kingdom. The Government is advised by the independent scientific *Veterinary Products Committee* on standards to be adopted in the authorisation procedures for veterinary medicines.

The fishing industry

The United Kingdom has a major interest in sea fisheries, reflecting its geographical position in the North East Atlantic, and is one of the EU's largest fishing countries, taking about a fifth of the total catch in major species. It has an interest in more than 100 'Total Allowable Catches' set by the European Commission (see page 58). In 2002 total UK fish supplies amounted to some 687,000 tonnes, with the UK fishing industry supplying around 67 per cent by quantity. Household consumption of fish in the United Kingdom in 2002 was estimated at 491,000 tonnes.

Fisheries Departments, in partnership with the European Commission, are responsible for the administration of legislation concerning the fishing industry, including fish and shellfish farming. The *Sea Fish Industry Authority* (*www.seafish.co.uk*), a largely industry-financed body, undertakes research and development, provides training and promotes the marketing and consumption of sea fish. There are also two government laboratories specialising in fisheries research – one in Aberdeen and one in Lowestoft.

The Prime Minister announced a Strategy Unit study into the UK fishing industry in March 2003. The study will examine the medium and long-term problems facing the industry, and attempt to develop a long-term strategy for sustainable sea fishing in the United Kingdom. A report is due to be published at the end of 2003.

Fish caught and the fishing fleet

United Kingdom fishing industry statistics are shown in Table 27.10. Altogether, some 538,000 tonnes of sea fish, with a total value of £490 million, were landed into the United Kingdom by both the UK fleet and foreign fishing vessels in 2002. Another major source of supply is the bulk import into the United Kingdom of fish caught by other countries.

In 2002 demersal fish (living on or near the bottom of the sea) accounted for 38 per cent by weight of total landings by British fishing vessels, pelagic fish (living in mid water) for 34 per cent and shellfish for 28 per cent. Landings of all types of fish (excluding salmon and trout) by British fishing vessels into the United Kingdom totalled 465,600 tonnes. Cod and haddock represented 18 and 17 per cent of the total value of demersal fish landed respectively. The quayside value of landings of all sea fish, including shellfish, by British vessels in 2002 was £415 million.

Catches of crabs, lobsters, nephrops (for example langoustines) and other shellfish have increased to supply a rising demand. In 1985 British fishermen

Table 27.10 UK fishing industry: summary table

	1991	1996	2000	2001	2002
Fleet size at end of year					
Number of vessels	11,411	8,667	7,818	7,721	7,578
Employment					
Number of fishermen	n/a	19,044	15,121	14,645	12,746
Total landings by UK vessels[1]					
Quantity ('000 tonnes)	787	892	748	738	685
Value (£ million)	496	635	550	574	546
Household consumption					
Quantity ('000 tonnes)	418	471	442	492	491

1 Figures relate to landings both in the UK and in other countries.
Source: Department for Environment, Food and Rural Affairs

landed 75,000 tonnes of shellfish worth about £65 million. By 2002 landings were 130,700 tonnes worth £164 million.

Some of the species caught by UK fishing vessels find a more favourable market overseas and these species are usually exported or landed directly abroad. In 2002 UK vessels landed 219,800 tonnes of sea fish directly into non-UK ports, with a value of £131 million.

The United Kingdom is contributing to the EU objective of reducing the fishing fleet by both cutting numbers and limiting the time some vessels spend at sea. At the end of 2002 the UK fleet consisted of 7,578 vessels (including 372 greater than 24.39 metres or 80 feet), and there were around 12,700 professional fishermen (see Table 27.10).

There is a substantial fish processing industry in the United Kingdom. Based on a survey of activity conducted in 2000, there are around 540 businesses, which employ some 22,000 people. At the retail level, there are approximately 1,400 fishmongers. An increasing proportion of all fish (69 per cent by volume and 67 per cent by value, excluding canned produce) is sold through supermarkets. A small proportion of the catch is used to make fish oils and animal feeds.

Aquaculture
Fish farming is a significant industry in remote rural areas on the west coast of Scotland, as well as in Orkney, Shetland and the Western Isles, producing primarily salmon. In addition, species such as cod, halibut and turbot are entering commercial production. Trout is also farmed as a freshwater species, and various shellfish species are produced all round the coast of the United Kingdom. In 2000, the total value at first sale of farmed fish was estimated at over £350 million, and the industry employed over 3,000 people.

Aquaculture is subject to a comprehensive regulatory regime covering such issues as fish and shellfish health and disease control, control of discharges into the marine and riverine environment, site leasing and planning, and the use of medicines and other chemicals.

Common Fisheries Policy (CFP)
Management of the United Kingdom's sea fisheries is subject to the EU Common Fisheries Policy. Under the policy, UK vessels have exclusive rights to fish within 6 miles of the UK coast. Certain other EU Member States have historic rights in UK waters between 6 and 12 miles. UK vessels have similar rights in other Member States' 6 to 12 mile belts. Between 12 and 200 miles, EU vessels may fish wherever they have access rights. Non-EU countries' vessels may fish in these waters if they negotiate reciprocal fisheries agreements with the EU. UK fishery limits extend to 200 miles or the median line (broadly halfway between the UK coast and the opposing coastline of another coastal state) measured from baselines on or near the coast of the United Kingdom.

The primary aim of the CFP is to ensure rational and sustainable exploitation of fish stocks through conservation and management policies designed to protect resources and reflect the needs of the fishing industry. The CFP aims to improve the balance between catching capacity and available resources by regulating the amount of fishing and the quantities of fish caught, through a system of Total Allowable Catches (TACs), based on scientific advice, which are then distributed to Member States. Catch limits are complemented by a series of technical conservation measures intended to achieve more selective fishing, for example by setting rules on minimum landing sizes, minimum mesh sizes and gear design, as well as defining areas of seasonal closures, methods of fishing and target species. Opportunities to fish in third country waters are also secured through the CFP.

The EU Fisheries Council announced a revised CFP in December 2002. Key elements include:

- a more long-term approach to fisheries management, including the setting of 'multi-annual' catch limits to replace the previous annual allocations;

- recovery plans for depleted stocks;

- from 31 December 2004, ending state aid for fishing vessels and stopping aid for the transfer of EU fishing vessels to third countries; and

- improvements in enforcement arrangements.

Conservation of fish stocks

Stocks of some fish in EU waters, notably cod and hake, have been depleted through a combination of overfishing, low numbers of fish surviving to a size where they are taken commercially, and possible environmental factors.

Measures have been put in place that aim to halt and ultimately reverse the decline in EU cod stocks, which is recognised as a serious problem. Previously, these measures have included restrictions on cod fishing in the Irish Sea, the North Sea and the West of Scotland during the key spring spawning periods, along with cuts in the numbers of cod that could be caught in those areas. The revised CFP contained an interim measure that limited the number of days each month fishermen could spend at sea catching cod. The Fisheries Council will produce a long-term plan for cod recovery during 2003.

An aid package of over £60 million has been made available to UK fishermen affected by the North Sea cod recovery measures. In addition to money

for the voluntary decommissioning of boats, which is expected to bring about a 15–20 per cent reduction in activity from boats in the sector, it contains money to be allocated in consultation with the fishing industry on joint projects between fishermen and scientists to improve understanding of fisheries science.

Fish quotas

EU fisheries ministers set TACs for a wide range of stocks each year, and the TACs are divided into quotas for each Member State. UK quotas are then allocated among various groups within the UK fishing fleet. Some allocations are managed by fishermen's organisations, known as Producer Organisations. However, overall responsibility for managing UK quotas rests with Defra and the other Fisheries Departments in the United Kingdom. Quotas, technical conservation and other management measures aim to restore balance to fish populations and allow them to renew themselves.

The 2003 quotas were decided at the EU Fisheries Council in December 2002. Because of the high risk to some cod stocks and the difficulty of controlling low catch limits, scientists from the International Council for the Exploration of the Sea and the Scientific, Technical and Economic Committee on Fisheries advised a moratorium on the fisheries concerned. Owing to the economic and social impact of such a measure, however, the EC proposed a package of measures as an alternative to a moratorium. This included substantially reduced quotas for cod and cod-related fisheries, fishing effort limitations and control measures to ensure implementation. The Fisheries Council eventually agreed on temporary recovery measures for cod and set TACs at levels generally higher than those proposed by the EC.

Restrictive licensing system for fishing vessels

A restrictive licensing system is operated by the four Fisheries Departments in the United Kingdom. It controls the activities of the UK fishing fleet in accordance with the EU and UK objectives on fleet and catch management. All engine-powered UK-registered vessels which fish for profit for sea fish (other than salmon, migratory trout and eels) are required to hold a licence issued by one of the Departments. To constrain the size of the fleet, additional licences are not granted. Licences may, however, be transferred or aggregated in accordance with detailed rules. A national licensing scheme for shellfish is being introduced which, from 2004 onwards, will limit the number of vessels permitted to catch crabs and lobsters.

Sea Fisheries Committees

There are 12 Sea Fisheries Committees (SFCs) which regulate local sea fisheries around virtually the entire coast of England and Wales out to 6 miles. SFCs were established in the 19th century and are empowered to make by-laws for the management and conservation of their districts' fisheries. In Scotland, inshore fisheries are regulated by Scottish legislation, and local management bodies may also be established in statute to regulate specific shellfish fisheries.

Forestry

Land area covered by woodland in 2003 amounted to 17 per cent in Scotland, 14 per cent in Wales, 9 per cent in England and 6 per cent in Northern Ireland. This represents 11.6 per cent for the United Kingdom, or 2.81 million hectares, almost double the cover in 1947. This compares with 37 per cent for the EU as a whole. The composition of UK woodland is shown in Table 27.11.

In 2002/03, 25,300 hectares of trees were planted in Great Britain, including both new planting and restocking. This total included some 8,300 hectares of new broadleaf planting and 3,400 hectares of new conifer planting (see Figure 27.12). Since the early 1990s, incentives for planting broadleaves and native pinewood, and for planting on former agricultural land, have led to a growth in the number of broadleaved trees planted; previously, timber production was the key priority, resulting in the planting mainly of fast growing conifer trees.

The United Kingdom uses a large amount of timber, paper, board and other wood products each year, equivalent to about 50 million cubic metres under bark. Around 85 per cent of this has to be imported, at a cost of about £9 billion a year. The timber industry, using wood from sustainable forests, has received considerable investment in recent years. The volume of wood supplied from Great Britain's forests each year has more than doubled from 4 million cubic metres over bark standing in the 1970s to over 10 million in 2001. This is forecast to increase to over 15 million cubic metres by 2020, offering scope for further substantial investment in the processing industry.

Table 27.11 Area of woodland by ownership and forest type: 31 March 2003, UK

Thousand hectares

	Conifers	Broadleaves[1]	Total productive woodland
Forestry Commission/ Forest Service			
England	156	51	207
Wales	99	11	110
Scotland	445	25	470
Northern Ireland	56	5	61
United Kingdom	755	92	848
Private woodland[2]			
England	216	687	904
Wales	64	112	176
Scotland	607	250	857
Northern Ireland	10	14	24
United Kingdom	897	1,063	1,960
Total			
England	372	739	1,110
Wales	163	123	285
Scotland	1,052	275	1,327
Northern Ireland	66	19	85
United Kingdom	1,652	1,155	2,807

1 Broadleaves include coppice and coppice with standards.
2 Private woodland figures for England, Scotland and Wales are based on the 1995–99 National Inventory of Woodland and Trees (NIWT) adjusted to reflect subsequent changes (although at present no adjustment is made for woodland converted to another land use). The NIWT did not include Northern Ireland.
Source: Forestry Commission

Very few woodlands in Great Britain are planted without some form of grant. The Forestry Commission offers grants through the *Woodland Grant Scheme* (WGS), and in England is closely involved with the operation of Defra's *Farm Woodland Premium Scheme* (FWPS), which shares a joint application process with the WGS. In Wales, there is a joint application form for farmers who enter land into the WGS and FWPS, which is administered by the Welsh Assembly Government, and similar schemes are operated by the Forestry Commission and SEERAD in Scotland. These grants aim to encourage the creation of new woodlands and the management of existing woodlands by providing money towards the cost of the work involved. In England, expenditure of £139 million between 2001 and 2006 on the WGS

Figure 27.12 New woodland creation,[1] Great Britain

Thousand hectares

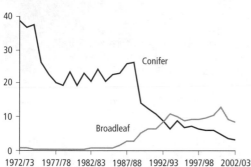

1 Excluding areas of new private woodland created without grant aid.
Source: Forestry Commission

is provided for under the England Rural Development Programme.

The new National Forest (*www.nationalforest.org*) covers 520 square kilometres of the English Midlands, covering parts of Derbyshire, Leicestershire and Staffordshire. The aim is to increase woodland cover to about one-third of the total area, with another third remaining in agriculture. A total of 5 million trees had been planted by the end of March 2003, and 30 million will eventually be planted. See page 263 for community forests.

The Forestry Commission and forestry policy

The Forestry Commision operates as a cross-border public body within Great Britain (for Northern Ireland see below). In each country it serves as the forestry department of the administration, advising on forestry policies and, working with partners, putting those policies into practice. In particular, it gives grant aid for the stewardship of existing woodlands and woodland expansion in the private sector, and manages the national forests of England, Wales and Scotland. The work of the Commission in each country is overseen by a National Committee which has responsibility for giving strategic direction to all of the Commission's activities in that country. The Forest Ministers' Group discusses matters of common interest, such as the UK Forestry Standard, which sets out the criteria and standards for the management of all forests and woodland in the United Kingdom.

In each country, ministers have agreed strategies for forests and woodlands. *A new focus for*

England's woodlands, published in 1998, contains four programmes, the objectives of which include increasing the contribution of forest and woodland to local economies and rural development; expanding the role of woodland in supporting economic regeneration of former industrial land and disadvantaged communities; and promoting access to woodland. Some of the key targets for Forestry Commission England for 2003–06 are planting 15,000 hectares of new woodland, harvesting 38 per cent of annual timber growth each year to promote the sustainable use of woodland resource, and creating 2,700 hectares of new woodland in coalfield areas and deprived wards to encourage economic regeneration.

Forests for Scotland (2000) aims to maximise the value to the Scottish economy of wood resource, create a diverse forest, ensure that forestry in Scotland makes a positive contribution to the environment, and improve access to woods and forests, while *Woodlands for Wales* (2001) is based on five strategic objectives covering similar areas.

Progress on the Forestry Commission's task of developing and promoting sustainable forest management will be measured by the UK Indicators of Sustainable Forestry. The indicators were first published in October 2002, and number 40 in total, grouped into six themes: woodland; biodiversity; condition of forest and environment; timber and other forest products; people and forests; and economic aspects.

Forest Research is the principal organisation in the United Kingdom involved in forestry and tree-related research. An agency of the Commission, it produces scientific research and surveys, both to inform the development of forestry policies and practices and to promote high standards of sustainable forest management. The priorities for forestry research are agreed between England, Wales and Scotland at the meetings of the forestry ministers.

Forestry in Northern Ireland

The Forest Service is an executive agency within DARD and promotes the interests of forestry through sustainable management and expansion of state-owned forests. It encourages private forestry through grant aid for planting. It manages over 60,000 hectares of forest land.

The Service offered over 400,000 cubic metres of timber for sale in 2001/02, with receipts of

£4.6 million. Forestry and timber processing employ about 1,050 people. It is estimated that some 2 million people visited Northern Irish forests during the year.

Further reading

Agriculture in the United Kingdom 2002. Defra, SEERAD, DARD and ARAD. The Stationery Office, 2002.

Forestry Statistics. Forestry Commission, 2003.

Strategy for Sustainable Farming and Food. Defra, 2002.

Scottish Agriculture Facts and Figures 2002. Scottish Executive, 2003.

United Kingdom Sea Fisheries Statistics. Defra. The Stationery Office.

Statistical Review of Northern Ireland Agriculture 2002. Department of Agriculture and Rural Development, 2003.

Departmental report of the Department for Environment, Food and Rural Affairs, Forestry Commission and the Office of Water Services 2003. Cm 5919. The Stationery Office, 2003.

Websites

Department for Environment, Food and Rural Affairs
www.defra.gov.uk

Department of Agriculture and Rural Development (Northern Ireland)
www.dardni.gov.uk

National Assembly for Wales
www.wales.gov.uk/subiagriculture

Scottish Executive Environment and Rural Affairs Department
www.scotland.gov.uk/who/dept_rural.asp

Food from Britain
www.foodfrombritain.com

Food Standards Agency
www.foodstandards.gov.uk

Forestry Commission
www.forestry.gov.uk

The Forest Service
www.forestserviceni.gov.uk

WWW.

21 June 2003 Prince William, second in line to the throne, celebrates his twenty-first birthday.

26 June 2003: *Below:* some 4,000 children queue outside the Royal Albert Hall in London to meet author, J K Rowling. Her long-awaited *Harry Potter and the Order of the Phoenix*, the fifth book in the 'Harry Potter' series, went on sale at midnight on 20 June. Nearly 2 million copies were sold on the first day, and over 1 million orders taken by one Internet retailer alone.

28 June 2003 *Left:* 300th anniversary of the birth of John Wesley (1703–91), spiritual leader of the Methodist revival. He began outdoor preaching in 1739, covering thousands of miles of Great Britain.

1 July 2003 *Top right:* the month-long Cardiff festival opens with a mix of street theatre, live music, visual arts, funfairs and theatre. Highlights included:

26 July *Centre right:* the Masquerade Carnival, which attracted more than 400 costumed revellers, samba bands, dance troupes and stilt walkers; and

1–3 August *Below:* the festival's 'Big Weekend' finale featuring three days of live music attracting more than 250, 000 people.

Cardiff Festival

3 July 2003 the Royal Botanic Gardens at Kew in south-west London is awarded World Heritage Site status by UNESCO. The 132 hectares of landscaped gardens contain over 40 listed buildings and other structures, including the Palm House (pictured here in autumn).

KEW GARDENS

All Climates, all Floras, at your choice,
Water and Woods for walks and shade,
Good Teas, Fancy Ducks, Scented Air.

UNDERGROUND STATION

Top right: illustration of a rhododendron by artist Walter Hood Fitch (1817–92). Fitch worked as a botanical illustrator at Kew for a number of years and his illustrations helped to raise public awareness of newly discovered and imported plants. He was a prolific worker, drawing more than 200 botanical plates in 1845 alone.

Centre right: engraving of British explorer and naturalist Sir Joseph Banks (1743–1820) by N Schiavoretti. As honorary director of Kew, Banks encouraged botanists to travel overseas and bring back plants of economic, scientific or horticultural interest, and so greatly extended the Garden's collection.

Left: a 1927 London Underground poster by artist Clive Gardiner.

21 July 2003 *Top:* champion freediver Tanya Streeter breaks the world record by descending on a single breath to 400 feet (122 metres). She surfaced after 3 minutes, 58 seconds. Behind, her husband Paul punches the air in celebration.

26 July 2003 *Left:* Katy Sexton wins Gold in the 200 metres women's backstroke competition at the World Championships in Barcelona, Spain. *Below:* Two days later, on her return to the United Kingdom Sexton displays her Gold medal at Heathrow airport with James Gibson, winner of the 50 metres breaststroke.

28 Manufacturing and construction

Manufacturing continues to play an important but declining role in the UK economy, accounting for 18 per cent of gross value added (GVA, see glossary) at current basic prices in 2001, and for 14 per cent of employment (3.6 million people) in December 2002. Manufacturing generated only 25 per cent of the amount that service industries contributed to GVA in 2001, and 17 per cent of employment in December 2002.

The regions with the highest proportion of employees in manufacturing in December 2002 were the East Midlands and West Midlands (both 19 per cent). London had the lowest at 6 per cent.

The recession in the early 1990s led to a decline in manufacturing output. It began to rise again between 1993 and 2000, but declined in 2001 and fell by 4.7 per cent in 2002. Productivity (measured as output per job) in 2002 was 25 per cent above the 1992 level.

The construction industry accounted for 5 per cent of GVA in 2001. Following a period of marked decline as recession affected the industry in the early 1990s, output has picked up and was 25 per cent higher in 2002 than in 1992, well above pre-recession levels. The growth in output in 2002 was 7.5 per cent. There were 1,896,000 workforce jobs in the construction industry in December 2002, about 2.5 per cent more than ten years earlier.

Manufacturing

The number of manufacturing enterprises declined by 3 per cent between 1999 and 2001 (Table 28.1). Over half have an annual turnover of less than £250,000 and employ fewer than five people (Tables 28.2 and 28.3). In contrast, there are 1,140 enterprises with a turnover of at least £50 million and 925 that employ 500 or more people.

GVA, output, employment and productivity are shown in Tables 28.4 to 28.7. Output in the chemicals and man-made fibres industry has grown by 33 per cent since 1992. Electrical and optical equipment, although 39 per cent higher than in

The Government's manufacturing strategy

In 2002 the Government published a manufacturing strategy for the United Kingdom. This sets out the current position and trends, and identifies seven key issues for the Government, companies and the workforce:

- macroeconomic stability;
- investment;
- science and innovation;
- best practice;
- raising skills and education levels;
- modern infrastructure; and
- having the right market framework.

The Department of Trade and Industry (DTI) will be carrying out further analyses and ensuring that Regional Development Agencies (see page 344) reflect the importance of manufacturing in their future economic strategies.

Table 28.1 Manufacturing in the UK

	Number of enterprises	Total turnover (£ million)
1999	170,196	461,771
2000	167,289	469,146
2001	164,718	461,899

Source: Annual Business Inquiry, Office for National Statistics

Table 28.2 Manufacturing – size of UK businesses by turnover, 2003

Annual turnover (£ thousand)	Number of businesses	Percentages
0–49	22,670	15.8
50–99	23,805	16.6
100–249	31,400	21.9
250–499	20,230	14.1
500–999	16,085	11.2
1,000–1,999	11,220	7.8
2,000–4,999	9,035	6.3
5,000–9,999	3,805	2.7
10,000–49,999	3,785	2.6
50,000+	1,140	0.8
Total	**143,170**	**100**

Source: *Size Analysis of United Kingdom Businesses*, Office for National Statistics

Table 28.3 Manufacturing – size of UK businesses by employment, 2003[1]

Employment size	Number of businesses	Percentages
0–4	77,475	54.2
5–9	25,090	17.6
10–19	17,095	12.0
20–49	12,765	8.9
50–99	5,190	3.6
100–249	3,145	2.2
250–499	1,150	0.8
500–999	550	0.4
1,000+	375	0.3
Total	**142,835**	**100**

1 Not all businesses have been allocated by employment size, so the total differs from that given in Table 28.2.
Source: *Size Analysis of United Kingdom Businesses*, Office for National Statistics

Table 28.4 Gross value added at current basic prices in UK manufacturing, 2001[1]

1992 Standard Industrial Classification (SIC) category	£ million	% contribution
Food, drink and tobacco	21,102	13.8
Textiles, leather and clothing		
Textiles and textile products	5,076	3.3
Leather and leather products	702	0.5
Wood and wood products	2,368	1.5
Pulp, paper and paper products; publishing and printing	21,242	13.9
Coke, refined petroleum products and nuclear fuel	3,258	2.1
Chemicals, chemical products and man-made fibres	16,419	10.7
Rubber and plastic products	7,512	4.9
Other non-metallic mineral products	5,228	3.4
Basic metals and fabricated metal products	15,906	10.4
Engineering and allied industries		
Machinery and equipment not elsewhere classified	12,708	8.3
Electrical and optical equipment	19,732	12.9
Transport equipment	15,242	10.0
Manufacturing not elsewhere classified	6,635	4.3
Total	**153,132**	**100**

1 Figures for 2002 were not available at the time of going to print.
Source: *United Kingdom National Accounts 2002 – the Blue Book*, Office for National Statistics

Table 28.5 Index of manufacturing output, UK

1995=100

1992 SIC category	1992	1997	2002
Food, drink and tobacco	98.9	103.2	102.4
Textiles, leather and clothing			
Textiles and textile products	101.9	95.9	62.4
Leather and leather products	95.8	103.5	72.2
Wood and wood products	97.8	95.5	91.7
Pulp, paper and paper products; publishing and printing	93.0	98.2	97.8
Coke, refined petroleum products and nuclear fuel	88.6	93.8	81.0
Chemicals, chemical products and man-made fibres	88.5	102.4	117.5
Rubber and plastic products	85.1	98.5	91.2
Other non-metallic mineral products	94.7	99.3	93.4
Basic metals and fabricated metal products	96.0	101.1	88.4
Engineering and allied industries			
Machinery and equipment not elsewhere classified	94.7	95.7	85.6
Electrical and optical equipment	79.0	108.1	110.1
Transport equipment	99.9	112.1	109.6
Manufacturing not elsewhere classified	97.2	104.0	105.9
Total manufacturing	**92.8**	**102.0**	**98.5**

Source: Office for National Statistics

Table 28.6 Employee jobs, UK manufacturing industries

Thousands, seasonally adjusted, June

1992 SIC category	1992	1997	2002
Food, drink and tobacco	500	500	473
Textiles, leather and clothing	442	388	217
Wood and wood products	85	88	83
Pulp, paper and paper products; publishing and printing	452	464	443
Chemicals, chemical products and man-made fibres	270	251	231
Rubber and plastic products	198	252	222
Other non-metallic mineral products; basic metals and			
fabricated metal products	736	720	589
Engineering and allied industries			
Machinery and equipment not elsewhere classified	414	389	338
Electrical and optical equipment	445	508	424
Transport equipment	408	394	377
Coke, refined petroleum products and nuclear fuel;			
manufacturing not elsewhere classified	203	236	232
Total manufacturing	**4,155**	**4,191**	**3,629**

Source: *Labour Market Trends*, Office for National Statistics

Table 28.7 Output per job in UK manufacturing industries

1992 SIC category	1992	1997	1995=100 2002
Food, drink and tobacco	92.9	100.5	107.3
Textiles, leather and clothing	93.5	101.1	114.5
Pulp, paper and paper products; publishing and printing	94.6	98.1	108.0
Chemicals, chemical products and man-made fibres	84.1	103.1	126.9
Rubber and plastic products	100.3	92.0	100.2
Other non-metallic mineral products	89.1	101.0	113.2
Basic metals and fabricated metal products	94.2	100.9	103.9
Engineering and allied industries			
Machinery and equipment not elsewhere classified	89.9	95.6	104.4
Electrical and optical equipment	84.5	102.4	130.8
Transport equipment	93.0	105.2	115.6
Wood and wood products; coke, refined petroleum products and nuclear fuel; manufacturing not elsewhere classified	97.2	93.7	94.7
Total manufacturing	**92.2**	**100.7**	**114.9**

Source: Office for National Statistics

1992, has shown a marked short-term decline – it fell by 24 per cent between 2000 and 2002. Output of some other sectors remains below the 1992 level – output of textiles and textile products, for example, was 39 per cent lower.

An outline of the major manufacturing sectors follows, in order of their significance to the economy in terms of GVA. For each sector a table shows the number of enterprises and turnover at current prices for the latest available three years. These data are collected by the ONS Annual Business Inquiry (ABI), which in 2001 sampled about 73,000 businesses. On occasion, statistics in the text and in some of the later tables come from sources other than National Statistics, such as trade associations. Any variations usually reflect differences in coverage of the industry concerned.

Table 28.8 Pulp, paper and paper products, publishing and printing, UK

	Number of enterprises	Total turnover (£ million)
1999	32,884	43,387
2000	32,588	45,291
2001	32,493	44,903

Source: Annual Business Inquiry, Office for National Statistics

Paper, printing and publishing

In 2001 the UK pulp, paper and paper products industry had a turnover of £11.3 billion and the publishing and printing industry had a turnover of £33.6 billion. Total industry output rose by 0.6 per cent in 2002 and was 5 per cent higher than in 1992. Exports in 2002 were £4.8 billion – the largest contributors were paper and paperboard, and publishing of books (both 26 per cent), and publishing of journals and periodicals (10 per cent).

Paper

The paper and board sector is dominated by a small number of medium and large firms. In 2002 there were 83 pulp, paper and board mills in the United Kingdom, employing around 16,200 people and concentrated in north Kent, Lancashire, the West Country and central Scotland. These mills produce hundreds of different grades of paper and board, which are converted into a wide range of products for use in industry, commerce, education, communications, distribution and in the home. They also produce a host of speciality papers for industrial use, for example filters and papers, which are subsequently coated, sensitised or laminated.

There has been a continuing trend towards waste-based packaging grades. Recycled paper made up 65.1 per cent of the raw material for UK newspapers in 2002, compared with 63.5 per cent in 2001 (including imports). UK papermaking production in 2002 was 6.2 million tonnes, 0.2 per cent higher than in 2001, and 21.2 per cent higher than in 1992. In 2002, 1.2 million tonnes were exported, 1.8 per cent more than in 2001 but 18 per cent lower than in 1992. Exports to the EU fell in 2002 to 0.8 million tonnes; total imports fell by 1.2 per cent to 7.5 million tonnes.

Printing and publishing

Unlike the paper and board sector, the UK printing and publishing industry has many small businesses – only 3.4 per cent of enterprises employed 50 or more people and over 91 per cent of enterprises employed fewer than 20 people in 2003. Much publishing and printing employment and output are carried out in firms based in south-east

Table 28.9 UK printing and publishing industry: top ten export categories

		£ million
	2001	2002
Books, booklets and brochures	1,028.3	1,019.5
Newspapers and periodicals	394.2	496.5
Single sheets	103.1	132.8
Trade advertising	101.6	96.6
Cartons, boxes, etc	55.6	79.6
Printed labels	56.5	69.8
Postcards and greetings cards	62.6	63.7
Security printing	35.8	40.8
Transfers	23.1	32.9
Dictionaries and encyclopedias	16.3	30.9

Source: HM Customs and Excise

Table 28.10 Top ten UK export destinations for books

	£ million		% share
	2001	2002	in 2002
United States	213.1	214.0	17.4
Irish Republic	83.8	91.9	7.5
Germany	79.8	81.7	6.7
Netherlands	69.8	68.4	5.6
Australia	66.9	60.9	5.0
Spain	58.1	59.6	4.9
France	44.2	52.1	4.2
Japan	39.2	45.9	3.7
Italy	36.5	38.3	3.1
Singapore	28.4	33.4	2.7
Total exports	**1,204.2**	**1,227.2**	**100**

Source: Department of Trade and Industry

England. Mergers have led to the formation of large groups in newspaper, magazine and book publishing. The main export categories for the printing and publishing industry are shown in Table 28.9.

The UK book-publishing industry is a major exporter, with exports of over £1.2 billion in 2002, 1.9 per cent higher than in 2001 (see Table 28.10). The United States maintained its place as the largest export market, with over one-sixth of the total; the Irish Republic was in second place. The total number of new and revised titles published in the United Kingdom rose by 5.4 per cent to 125,390 in 2002.

The UK printing industry had a turnover of £14.4 billion and employed an average of 201,000 people in 2001. It has continued to take advantage of technological changes. The use of digital technology has improved both automation and personalisation, and is one way in which printers have been able to add value to clients. Direct exports were worth £426 million in 2002.

Food, drink and tobacco

There were around 7,700 enterprises in the UK food and drink manufacturing and processing industry, with a combined turnover of £66.1 billion in 2001. The industry has accounted for a growing proportion of total domestic food supply since the 1940s.

Table 28.11 Food products, drink and tobacco, UK

	Number of enterprises	Total turnover (£ million)
1999	8,124	73,655
2000	7,888	73,872
2001	7,706	74,804

Source: Annual Business Inquiry, Office for National Statistics

The largest concentration of enterprises is in the production of bread, cakes and fresh pastry goods, followed by those engaged in processing and preserving meat and meat products. Spirits production gives Scotland the highest concentration of employment in the alcoholic and soft drinks manufacturing industry, with a significant proportion of jobs in its economically deprived rural areas.

The biggest food and drink export category in 2002 was alcoholic drinks, with exports of £3.3 billion, accounting for 39 per cent of the total value of food and drink sales overseas. The largest food-exporting sectors were dairy products and cheeses, and cocoa, chocolate and confectionery, worth £549 million and £532 million respectively. As well as the leading companies involved in food and drink manufacturing and processing, there are many specialist small and medium-sized firms, supplying high-quality 'niche' products, often to small retail outlets, such as delicatessens.

Frozen foods and chilled convenience foods, such as frozen potato products and ready-prepared meals, fish and shellfish dishes, salads and pasta, together with yogurts, desserts and instant snacks, have formed some of the fastest-growing sectors of the food market. Many low-fat and fat-free items have been introduced, ranging from dairy products to complete prepared meals. Organic foods are also widely available and the organic sector is a mainstream sector of the UK food market, worth over £850 million in 2002. There has been a substantial rise in sales of vegetarian foods (both natural vegetable dishes and vegetable-based substitutes of meat products).

Bread and morning goods
The market for bread and morning goods is one of the largest sectors in the UK food industry. The two largest bread producers are Allied Bakeries and British Bakeries, with 26 manufacturing sites in Great Britain and three in Northern Ireland between them. Sandwiches are the most frequently consumed snack food in the United Kingdom and have a wider range of distribution outlets than other bread sales. The sandwich market was estimated at £3.3 billion in 2002.

Dairy products
Of total UK household purchases of milk, 79 per cent was bought from shops and supermarkets in 2002, with the remaining 21 per cent delivered to the doorstep. This latter proportion has been in decline for some time – in 1992 the figure was 60 per cent, falling to 35 per cent by 1997. Household consumption of liquid milk per head – 2.2 litres a week – is among the highest in the world. Semi-skimmed (containing between 1.5 and 1.8 per cent fat) and skimmed milk (not more than 0.5 per cent fat) consumption continues to grow, and accounted for 70 per cent of total milk sales in 2002.

The UK dairy industry accounted for 69 per cent of butter and 68 per cent of cheese supplies to the domestic market in 2002, and achieved significant sales overseas. Over 400 different types of cheese are produced in the United Kingdom. Household purchases of Leicester and Red Leicester cheese rose sharply by 40 per cent in 2002, but Cheddar remained the most popular. Other well-known varieties include Caerphilly, Cheshire, Double Gloucester, Stilton and Wensleydale.

Beer
UK consumers spent £2.9 billion on beer in 2002, 4 per cent more than in 2001. Beer (including lager) production in 2002, at 56.7 million hectolitres, was 0.2 per cent lower than in 2001; beer released for home consumption amounted to 59.4 million hectolitres, 2 per cent higher than in 2001. Exports were valued at around £280 million in 2002, amounting to 4.2 million hectolitres.

Lager accounted for 68 per cent of all sales, but there is still a strong demand for traditional cask-conditioned and brewery-conditioned ales and stouts. The UK brewing industry has six major national brewery groups, 43 regional/family brewers and about 300 micro-breweries. Throughout the world brewers use UK malt, made almost entirely from home-grown barley.

Table 28.12 UK alcoholic drink production

			Thousand hectolitres
	1992	1997	2002
Beer	57,617	59,139	56,672
Potable spirits			
Home-produced whisky	3,915	4,801	3,906
Other	304	496	603
Released for home consumption			
Beer	60,973	61,114	59,384
Wine of fresh grapes			
Still	6,511	7,976	11,864
Sparkling	292	382	589
Made wine	872	1,637	1,974
Cider and perry	4,398	5,513	5,939
Spirits			
Home-produced whisky	356	312	321
Other[1]	505	533	737

1 Includes imported spirits.
Source: HM Customs and Excise

Spirits

UK expenditure on spirits rose by 4 per cent in 2002 to £2.7 billion. Home-produced whisky production in 2002 was 3.9 million hectolitres, a 6 per cent increase on 2001. The Scotch whisky industry is one of the top UK export earners, with overseas sales worth nearly £2.3 billion in 2002. although the volume of exports fell by 7 per cent because of global economic difficulties. The industry exports to 200 countries worldwide – the top ten overseas markets are shown in Table 28.13. In September 2002, some 10,400 people worked in the Scotch whisky industry and a further 30,000 were employed in Scotland in associated sectors, for instance supplying ingredients and materials. Most Scotch consumed is a blend of malt and grain. There are around 80 malt whisky distilleries in Scotland, the majority in Speyside and in the Highlands, with a further seven on Islay and three in the Lowlands. In addition, seven distilleries produce grain whisky. Some of the best-known single malt Scotch whiskies include Glenfiddich, Glen Grant, Glenmorangie and Macallan.

Gin and vodka production is another important part of the spirits industry, with some 70 per cent bottled in Scotland. Around 70 per cent of UK-produced gin and 20 per cent of vodka were exported in 2002, worth £205 million – about the same as in 2001. The largest overseas market was the United States, worth £80 million.

Table 28.13 Top ten overseas markets for Scotch whisky

		Thousand bottles	
Country	2001	2002	% share in 2002
France	153,941	148,111	15.7
Spain	137,428	109,224	11.6
United States	110,018	108,216	11.5
Japan	70,139	50,223	5.3
South Korea	45,381	46,597	4.9
Venezuela	43,779	42,688	4.5
Greece	38,015	34,980	3.7
Thailand	34,015	32,351	3.4
Germany	34,000	31,537	3.3
Australia	25,674	29,627	3.1
Total exports	**1,012,970**	**942,036**	**100**
of which:			
European Union	448,732	416568	44.2

Source: Scotch Whisky Association

Wine, cider and perry

UK consumers spent £5.4 billion on wine in 2002, 8 per cent more than in 2001. There were 333 commercial vineyards at the end of 2002, covering 812 hectares of land, nearly all in the southern half of England and Wales. Most of the production is white wine, mainly from Germanic vines. Quality continues to improve with a combination of more experienced winemakers, modern technologies and better winemaking equipment. Cider and perry are made predominantly in the west and south-west of England, notably in Herefordshire, Somerset and Devon. Bulmers, one of the two big UK producers, is the world's largest cider maker. In 2003 it was acquired by Scottish & Newcastle, one of the major UK national brewery groups.

Soft drinks

The soft drinks industry produces still and carbonated drinks, dilutable drinks, fruit juices and juice drinks, and bottled waters. The UK market was worth £10.2 billion by retail value in 2002, with Coca-Cola Enterprises the largest supplier. Soft drinks are one of the fastest-growing sectors of the grocery trade. In 2002, UK consumption of soft drinks was 13.1 billion litres, compared with 12.4 billion litres a year earlier. Sales of bottled waters – natural mineral waters, spring and table waters – reached over £1 billion in 2002. Carbonates registered the smallest increase in sales in 2002, with 4 per cent growth.

Tobacco

UK consumers spent £15.1 billion on tobacco products in 2002, 3 per cent more than in 2001. These figures include spending on smuggled tobacco products. The Tobacco Manufacturers' Association estimates that spending on legitimate tobacco products in 2002 was £12.5 billion, of which £10.0 billion was accounted for by excise duty (£8.1 billion) and VAT (£1.9 billion). The figures in Table 28.14 show a substantial decline in sales, which in recent years has been exacerbated by the rapid growth in smuggling and legitimate cross-border shopping. Government estimates of revenue lost through tobacco smuggling in 2001/02 were £3.3 billion, compared with £3.5 billion in 2000/01.

The industry achieved significant export sales – £956 million in 2002 – with Europe, the Middle East and Africa important overseas markets. The UK tobacco industry remains one of the top ten balance of payments earners in the UK economy.

In 2002 around 6,850 people were directly employed in tobacco manufacturing, with a further 125,000 jobs indirectly supported in supplier industries and associated jobs in distribution and retailing. Three major manufacturers supply the UK market, including British American Tobacco, the second largest tobacco company in the world.

Table 28.14 Tobacco – UK sales to trade[1]

	1992	1997	2002
Cigarettes (billion)	89.6	76.9	56.0
Handrolling tobacco (tonnes)	3,840	1,875	2,805
Pipe tobacco (thousand kg)	1,600	890	535
Cigars (million)	1,305	1,025	872

1 Based on UK manufacturers' sales to the wholesale and retail trade and estimates of imported goods.
Source: Tobacco Manufacturers' Association

Electrical and optical equipment

In 2001, 33 per cent of turnover in this UK industry was in the radio, TV and communications equipment sector; 24 per cent in electrical machinery; 23 per cent in office machinery and computers; and 21 per cent in medical, precision and optical equipment and watches. Total output rose sharply up to 2000, and then fell by 24 per cent by 2002. Nevertheless, it was 39 per cent higher than in 1992. Production of office machinery and computers nearly trebled between 1992 and 2002, while radio, TV and communications equipment output was up by 55 per cent. However, output of medical and optical instruments was only 2 per cent higher in 2002 than in 1992, while that of electrical machinery and apparatus fell by 10 per cent over the same period. Of the total exports of £44.7 billion in 2002, computers and process equipment accounted for £10.3 billion, TV and radio

Table 28.15 Electrical and optical equipment, UK

	Number of enterprises	Total turnover (£ million)
1999	16,618	64,891
2000	16,418	69,110
2001	16,141	63,660

Source: Annual Business Inquiry, Office for National Statistics

transmitters for £10.2 billion and electronic components for £7.4 billion.

A substantial proportion of employment in these sectors (especially sales and administrative jobs) is based in southern England, with Scotland and Wales important areas for inward investors. Scotland's electronics industry ('Silicon Glen' – in effect all of central Scotland) directly employed 40,400 people in 2000. In 2002 electrical and instrument engineering accounted for Scottish exports worth £6.7 billion, 39 per cent less than in 2001, but worth 46 per cent of Scotland's total manufactured exports.

Many of the world's leading overseas-based multinational electronics firms have substantial manufacturing investment in the United Kingdom. The main electronic consumer goods produced are television sets – 2.3 million were manufactured in 2002 – with UK production concentrated in the high-value market, increasingly in widescreen and digital sets. High-fidelity audio and video equipment are also produced, including 3.0 million VCRs in 2002.

The UK computer industry produces a range of systems for all uses – 10 million personal computers were produced in 2002. Many multinational computer manufacturers operate in the United Kingdom, although since 2000 production of computers has declined by about 30 per cent.

A range of other electrical machinery and apparatus is produced in the United Kingdom by both UK and foreign companies, including electric motors, generators, transformers, switchgear, insulated wire and cable (including optical fibre cables for telecommunications), and lighting equipment, but many of these industries are in decline.

In recent years there has been a reduction in the number of electronic service providers – contract electronic manufacturers – manufacturing and assembling products to the specification of other companies. Some multinationals located in the United Kingdom have been encouraged by the shift abroad of contract electronics manufacture to move into service precision, for example design and/or integration of electronic equipment. The United Kingdom is the leading location in Europe for electronics and semi-conductor design.

Communications equipment

Domestic telecommunications equipment manufacturers have invested heavily in facilities to meet rapidly increasing demand for telecommunications services (see chapter 17). The main products are switching and transmission equipment, telephones and terminals. Transmission equipment and cables for telecommunications and information networks include submarine and high-specification data-carrying cables.

The United Kingdom is among Europe's leading markets and research bases for mobile communications (see page 236) and some producers have UK design centres. Fibre optics were a UK invention. There has been a general downturn in the telecommunications sector due mainly to the downturn in the world economy. This has led to rationalisation and job losses across the sector.

Another sector of the industry manufactures radio communications equipment, radar, radio and sonar navigational aids for ships and aircraft, thermal imaging systems, alarms and signalling apparatus, public broadcasting equipment and other capital goods. Radar was invented in the United Kingdom and UK firms are still in the forefront of technological advances. Solid-state secondary surveillance radar is being supplied to numerous overseas civil aviation operators.

Medical electronics

The high demand for advanced medical equipment in the United Kingdom stems from its comprehensive healthcare system and extensive clinical research and testing facilities in the chemical, biological, physical and molecular sciences. UK scientists and engineers have made important contributions to basic research and development (R&D) in endoscopy, computerised tomography scanning, magnetic resonance imaging (which was pioneered in the United Kingdom), ultrasonic imaging, coronary artery diagnosis and renal analysis. Total exports in this sector were £1.8 billion in 2002.

Instrumentation and control

The instrumentation and control sector covers the design, development and manufacture of scientific and industrial equipment and systems for analysis, measurement, testing and control. The instrumentation sector is generally broken down into six specific categories: navigation and

surveying; electronic and electrical testing; laboratory/analytical; process monitoring and control; automotive; and drafting and dimensional measurement. The UK instrumentation and control sector has an estimated annual turnover of £8.1 billion, with a trade surplus of £3.2 billion in 2002. The sector is diverse, with around 3,350 enterprises, employing 91,000 people in 2001.

Chemicals and chemical products

The chemicals industry is one of the primary manufacturing sectors in the United Kingdom, accounting for 11 per cent of manufacturing industry's GVA in 2001. Over 36 per cent of turnover in 2001 was in the manufacture of basic chemicals, with a further 29 per cent in pharmaceutical products.

Table 28.16 Chemicals, chemical products and man-made fibres, UK

	Number of enterprises	Total turnover (£ million)
1999	4,029	46,282
2000	3,952	47,544
2001	3,864	47,575

Source: Annual Business Inquiry, Office for National Statistics

The sector underpins the UK manufacturing industry, with chemicals being essential supplies for most other industrial processes. Output growth slowed in 2002 (1.5 per cent compared with 3.6 per cent in 2001), but output was still 33 per cent higher than in 1992. The industry is a leading UK exporter, with an annual trade surplus in 2002 of £4.9 billion. Exports totalled £28.7 billion, of which £10.7 billion were pharmaceuticals and £9.3 billion basic chemicals. Sales for a range of chemical products are shown in Table 28.17.

The industry is diverse, with important representation in all principal chemical sectors – ranging from bulk petrochemicals to low-volume, high-value specialised organics. It includes key industrial materials, such as plastics and synthetic rubber (both in primary forms), and other products such as man-made fibres, soap and detergents, cosmetics, adhesives, dyes and inks, and intermediate products for the pharmaceutical and a range of other downstream industries.

Table 28.17 Chemicals – UK manufacturers' sales by industry[1]

£ million

	2000	2001	2002
Basic chemicals and pesticides			
Industrial gases	n/a	538	514
Dyes and pigments	1,095	1,073	1,103
Other inorganic basic chemicals	1,155	1,148	1,107
Other organic basic chemicals	5,412	5,716	5,761
Fertilisers and nitrogen compounds	714	592	568
Plastics in primary forms	3,775	3,640	3,092
Synthetic rubber in primary forms	351	322	n/a
Pesticides and other agrochemical products	1,049	1,137	497
Pharmaceutical products			
Basic products	666	679	860
Preparations	7,264	8,004	8,234
Soaps, detergents; cleaning and polishing preparations	1,917	1,963	1,989
Perfumes and essential oils			
Perfumes and toilet preparations	2,656	2,640	2,479
Essential oils	n/a	582	548
Other chemical products			
Paints, varnishes and similar coatings; printing ink and mastic	2,600	2,530	2,618
Explosives	109	n/a	n/a
Glues and gelatines	318	376	348
Photographic chemical material	605	342	310
Prepared unrecorded media	131	n/a	124
Other chemical products not elsewhere classified	2,382	2,078	1,962
Man-made fibres	739	656	601

1 Where indicated as not available, data have been suppressed to avoid identifying individual enterprises.
Source: PRODCOM (PRODucts of the European COMmunity), Office for National Statistics

Bulk chemicals

North Sea oil and gas provide accessible feedstocks for the large UK organics sector, including products such as ethylene, propylene, benzene and paraxylene. These provide the building blocks for the manufacture of many chemical products, including plastics that are strong, durable, and lightweight, and are increasingly used in transport and packaging applications; and synthetic fibres, such as nylon and polyester, used in textiles, clothing and home furnishings.

There is substantial inorganics production, including sulphuric acid, chlorine and caustic soda, based on minerals such as salt, sulphur, and phosphate ores, or on reaction between gases. These also serve many other chemical processes.

Formulated products

The United Kingdom is strong in formulated consumer products, such as decorative paint, home laundry and cleaning products, and personal care items like toothpaste, shampoos and skincare products, as well as a wide range of industrial speciality products, such as adhesives, inks and lubricants.

Fine chemicals

Fine chemicals meet specific needs through highly sophisticated product and process development. Active ingredients for the pharmaceutical and agrochemical sectors are at the forefront of this kind of innovation. In recent years, the application of chirality[1] in synthesis has allowed firms to make

1 Chiral compounds are mirror images of each other, analogous to left- and right-handed forms. One form may be more effective, or safer, than the other.

drugs and agrochemicals more closely tailored to specific targets. Leading-edge research by international pharmaceutical and agrochemical companies in the United Kingdom is supported both by a strong academic research capability and a network of specialist manufacturers of fine chemicals. The latter specialise in the highly skilled processes needed to produce commercial quantities of the complex molecules identified by the pharmaceutical and agrochemical companies' research.

Pharmaceuticals

The UK pharmaceuticals industry, largely based in the South East, North West and North East of England, is the world's fifth largest pharmaceuticals sector earner by trade surplus, equating to £2.1 billion in 2002. Research-driven, it is one of the most dynamic UK industries, of key importance to the economy. Principal overseas markets are Western Europe, North America and Japan. Recently, the largest growth has been in medicines acting on the cardiovascular system, followed by central nervous system and alimentary tract remedies. The UK pharmaceuticals sector had an estimated total UK market value of about £10.3 billion in 2002, of which prescription medicines accounted for 83 per cent.

Around 365 pharmaceuticals companies operate in the United Kingdom, with indigenous and US-owned multinationals dominating production. GlaxoSmithKline and AstraZeneca (Anglo-Swedish) are the two largest UK-based companies, followed by Pfizer (United States), the world's largest pharmaceuticals company.

Some 71,000 people are directly employed in the UK pharmaceuticals industry, with another 250,000 in related sectors. About a third are engaged in R&D, with the industry investing £3.2 billion in UK-based R&D in 2002, around 25 per cent of total UK industrial R&D. AstraZeneca and GlaxoSmithKline are the top two UK-based companies in terms of R&D expenditure, with the US companies Pfizer, Merck and Eli Lilly and Company, the European companies Novartis (Switzerland), Organon (Netherlands) and Sanofi-Synthelabo (France) also significant investors.

Major developments pioneered in the United Kingdom include semi-synthetic penicillins and cephalosporins, both powerful antibiotics, and new treatments for ulcers, asthma, arthritis,

meningitis C, cancer, migraine, HIV/AIDS, coronary heart disease, hypertension, fungal infections, erectile dysfunction and schizophrenia. The UK pharmaceuticals industry is second only to the US in the discovery and development of leading medicines, including 15 of the world's current top 75 best-selling drugs. Among the best-selling drugs produced by the two largest UK-based companies are:

- GlaxoSmithKline – Seretide/Advair (respiratory), Seroxat/Paxil (central nervous system: depression), Augmentin (anti-bacterial) and Avandia (metabolic/diabetes); and
- AstraZeneca – Nexium (the successor to Losec), Losec/Prilosec (gastro-intestinal), Seroquel (schizophrenia/Parkinson's disease/Alzheimer's disease) and Crestor (cholesterol).

Significant manufacturing R&D investment in the United Kingdom in 2002 included:

- the announcement by Novartis of a £134 million primary manufacturing expansion for Grimsby, Lincolnshire; and
- AstraZeneca's announcement of a £40 million R&D expansion (new screening centre) for Alderley Park, Macclesfield, Cheshire.

Biotechnology

The United Kingdom has the leading biotechnology sector in Europe, with over 480 companies, employing over 23,000 people in 2002. UK companies have a particular strength in healthcare, which includes some of the largest biotechnology companies in Europe, such as Celltech, Cambridge Antibody Technology, Antisoma and Acambis. Of the potential new drugs under development in Europe, around 43 per cent are from publicly quoted UK companies. Companies are clustered particularly around Cambridge, Oxford and London, and there are also concentrations of companies in parts of the South East, the North West and Scotland. The industry benefits strongly from the UK science base. Bioscience research in UK universities is of world renown, and the major research laboratories of leading pharmaceuticals multinationals are based in the United Kingdom. The United Kingdom has a number of world-class research institutes, such as the Sanger Centre in Cambridge, which played an important part in the Human Genome Project (see page 392), the Laboratory of Molecular Biology (also in Cambridge) and the Roslin Institute in Edinburgh.

Basic metals and fabricated metal products

The Industrial Revolution in the United Kingdom was based to a considerable extent on the manufacture of iron and steel and heavy machinery. These sectors remain important but, with the exception of products for the construction industry, they are declining. Output of basic metals and fabricated metal products fell by 4.6 per cent in 2002 and exports totalled £10.2 billion.

The major areas of steel production are concentrated in south Wales and northern England, with substantial processing in the Midlands and Yorkshire. Major restructuring in the steel industry took place during the 1980s and 1990s, and has continued into the 21st century with the ending of steelmaking at the Corus Llanwern site in south Wales and a number of plant closures by smaller UK producers.

Table 28.18 Basic metals and fabricated metal products, UK

	Number of enterprises	Total turnover (£ million)
1999	32,451	40,879
2000	32,058	41,028
2001	31,629	40,765

Source: Annual Business Inquiry, Office for National Statistics

Total UK crude steel production was 11.7 million tonnes in 2002, 1.8 million tonnes lower than in 2001 and the fifth successive year of decline. UK producers delivered 13.1 million tonnes of finished steel in 2002. The main UK markets for steel are in the engineering (24 per cent), construction (22 per cent), automotive (17 per cent) and metal goods industries (14 per cent). The UK steel industry exported 5.6 million tonnes (around 47 per cent of its output) in 2002, 4.0 million tonnes of which went to other EU countries, with Germany the biggest market. Annual steel industry exports peaked in 1997 at 8.5 million tonnes.

Corus is Europe's second largest steelmaker and the sixth biggest in the world. It employed 25,400 people in the United Kingdom at the end of December 2002 and produced 85 per cent of its total crude steel. It produces carbon steel by the basic oxygen steelmaking method at its plants in Port Talbot, Teesside and Scunthorpe and a wide range of other materials at sites across Great Britain.

Products manufactured by other UK steel companies include reinforcing bars for the construction industry, wire rods, hot rolled bars, bright bars, tubes, and wire and wire products. Production of special steels is centred on the Sheffield area and includes stainless and alloy special steels for the aerospace and offshore oil and gas industries.

Steel has had a notable success in the UK construction industry, with its market share in buildings of two or more storeys more than doubling from 30 per cent in the early 1980s to more than 67 per cent in 2002. It has 95 per cent of the single-storey market. The market mix is changing, with a fall in the construction of London multi-storey offices and an increase in hospitals, schools, car parks and high-rise residential accommodation. Total iron and steel sales to the construction sector were £2.5 billion in 2002. Consumption of constructional steelwork was 1.2 million tonnes of hot rolled steel and a similar tonnage of cold rolled steel.

Steel is a fully recyclable product and, following its initial life cycle, can be reclaimed from, for example, end-of-vehicles, demolished buildings and discarded cabs. Scrap recycled in this way is treated and cleaned, and then used as a raw material by steelmakers in the making of new steel. The UK steel recycling industry currently reclaims around 9 million tonnes of steel scrap each year, 4 million tonnes of which is sold to UK steelmakers and 5 million tonnes exported to steelmakers overseas.

Non-ferrous metals in the United Kingdom are produced from both primary and recycled raw materials. Including precious metals, exports totalled £3.1 billion in 2002. The main sectors and their uses are:

- aluminium, supplying customers in the aerospace, transport, automotive and construction industries;
- copper and copper alloys, used for electrical wire and cables, power generation, and electrical and electronic connectors, automotive components, plumbing and building products, and components for industrial plant and machinery;
- lead, for lead acid batteries and roofing;
- zinc, for galvanising to protect steel;

- nickel, used principally as an alloying element to make stainless steel and high-temperature turbine alloys; and

- titanium, for high-strength, low-weight aerospace applications.

Fabricated metal products include those made by forging, casting, pressing, stamping and roll forming of a variety of metals. They are used in applications varying from automotive, aerospace and railway components to construction, domestic appliances, packaging and general hardware. Many of these products are subjected to surface engineering processes, which improve their working performance. These include electroplating, galvanising, anodising and heat treatment.

Transport equipment

This sector covers the production of cars and commercial vehicles, vehicle components, shipbuilding, marine engineering, railway equipment, aerospace and defence.

Table 28.19 Transport equipment, UK

	Number of enterprises	Total turnover (£ million)
1999	5,921	63,239
2000	5,745	60,440
2001	5,665	61,018

Source: Annual Business Inquiry, Office for National Statistics

Motor vehicles

UK car production, at 1.6 million, was 9 per cent higher in 2002 (recovering nearly all of the fall that took place in 2001) and 26 per cent higher than in 1992. Traditional home markets no longer dominate production by vehicle manufacturers – exports accounted for 64 per cent of production in 2002, compared with 46 per cent in 1992. There were just over 1 million passenger cars produced for export in 2002, a 17 per cent increase on 2001, with growth in worldwide Mini sales a significant contributory factor. Commercial vehicle production in 2002 fell slightly, by 0.8 per cent to 191,000; almost 60 per cent, or 114,000 units, was for export. The sector is dominated by light commercial vehicles (mainly vans and minibuses). In total, the UK motor vehicle export market was worth £13.7 billion in 2002.

Table 28.20 UK car and commercial vehicle production

Percentages

	2000	2001	2002
Passenger cars			
Total production ('000s)	1,641	1,492	1,628
of which:			
1,000 cc and under	6	6	5
1,001 cc to 1,600 cc	41	42	44
1,601 cc to 2,500 cc	44	43	44
2,501 cc and over	9	9	7
Production for export ('000s)	1,063	894	1,047
of which:			
1,000 cc and under	5	6	3
1,001 cc to 1,600 cc	35	37	42
1,601 cc to 2,500 cc	48	45	45
2,501 cc and over	11	12	9
Commercial vehicles			
Total production ('000s)	172	193	191
of which:			
Light commercial vehicles	85	88	88
Rigid trucks	7	6	6
Motive units	2	1	1
Buses, coaches and minibuses	7	4	5
Production for export ('000s)	76	96	114
of which:			
Light commercial vehicles	86	91	92
Rigid trucks	5	5	4
Motive units	–	–	–
Buses, coaches and minibuses	8	4	4

Source: Motor Vehicle Production Inquiry, Office for National Statistics

With investment of £80 million, the new Astra is to be built at Vauxhall's Ellesmere Port (Cheshire) factory, safeguarding 3,000 jobs. The first of an expected 190,000 cars annually will come off the production line in 2004.

In 2002 around 246,000 people were employed in vehicle and component production and manufacturing activities in the United Kingdom. This was around 17,000 down on 2001, a trend similar to UK manufacturing as a whole, and driven mainly by improvements in manufacturing efficiency.

The United Kingdom has always been an important location for manufacturing cars and commercial vehicles. In addition to the independent MG Rover, eight global companies manufacture cars in the United Kingdom: Nissan, Honda, Toyota, BMW, Ford, General Motors, Volkswagen and Peugeot. Nissan's Sunderland plant is the most productive in Europe in terms of vehicles produced per employee, with Honda and Toyota also in the top ten. However, Peugeot's Ryton (West Midlands) factory makes the most intensive use of capacity, with four shifts manufacturing the popular 206 model. A range of smaller producers, such as Morgan, Noble, Bristol and TVR, target specialist markets such as sports and luxury cars. London Taxis International produces the world-famous London taxi at its Coventry factory and is developing a hybrid variant that will make a significant improvement to air quality in London and other cities. The latest model, the TXII, was launched in early 2002.

The main UK truck manufacturer is Leyland Trucks, based in Lancashire. Medium-sized vans are manufactured by LDV at Birmingham, Ford at Southampton and by the General Motors/Renault joint venture at the IBC plant in Luton, Bedfordshire. Transbus is the main UK bus and coach manufacturer, producing both chassis and complete vehicles. Accessibility is an important issue and the company is one of the world leaders in the design of low-floor chassis and variable height suspension.

The United Kingdom is an increasing force in engine production. Two major decisions announced in 2002 and early 2003 were the creation of Ford's global centre of excellence in diesel engines at Dagenham and the expansion of BMW's new Hams Hall (West Midlands) plant to produce engines for the next generation Mini and forthcoming BMW 1-series. When all planned investments are in place, the United Kingdom will have the capacity to manufacture 4.5 million vehicle engines each year.

Seventeen of the world's top 20 suppliers of vehicle components have UK manufacturing facilities and a further 2,800 firms in the wider supply base provide a range of manufacturing and engineering services.

Shipbuilding and marine engineering

In 2001 there were around 760 enterprises employing 27,000 people engaged in the building and repairing of ships in the United Kingdom,

with a turnover of over £1.9 billion. A further 785 enterprises employing 10,000 people were engaged in building and repairing of pleasure and sporting boats, with a turnover of £755 million. In aggregate, exports in 2002 were worth £571 million. Approximately 20 companies are engaged in this sector. In the merchant sector, UK shipyards face a difficult market, but in the naval sector, dominated by BAe Systems Marine and VT Shipbuilders, the future is more secure. In 2002 naval sector orders were placed through yards in Glasgow, Barrow-in-Furness and Portsmouth.

Civil shipbuilding is predominantly located in Scotland and northern England. The 17 yards produce a range of specialist vessels and platforms, from tugs to ferries and support craft for the offshore and exploration industry. The industry's 2003 order book was for ten ships. The ship repair and conversion industry comprises over 60 companies and provides the United Kingdom with a strong presence and a high level of expertise in this field.

Oil and gas production development in the North Sea has generated a major international offshore industry (see page 433). Shipbuilders and fabricators design and build semi-submersible units for drilling, production and emergency/ maintenance support; drill ships; jack-up rigs; modules; and offshore loading systems as well as undertaking 'floating production storage and offload' vessel (FPSO) conversions. Harland and Wolff of Belfast is a typical example in the offshore sector, specialising in drill ships. Many other firms supply equipment and services to the industry, such as metering systems, both diving expertise and diverless intervention techniques, down-hole technologies, consultancy, design, project management and R&D. A number have used their experience of North Sea projects to develop business in world oil and gas producing areas, particularly in deeper waters in the Gulf of Mexico and off the coast of West Africa.

The UK marine equipment industry had a turnover of some £1.7 billion in 2002. It comprises about 690 companies, which produce marine equipment for commercial seagoing vessels, warships and naval auxiliaries (excluding weapons and associated equipment), yachts over 30 metres and large workboats. Approximately 62 per cent of turnover is exported. There are around 16,600 employees engaged in marine equipment manufacture. Faced with a diminishing home market, this sector has been particularly successful in targeting the Korean, Japanese and Chinese markets. All aspects of marine equipment – propulsion, electrical and electronic equipment, navigational, as well as safety and accommodation products – are supplied to naval and civil yards worldwide.

In 2002 the leisure boatbuilding sector had turnover of £579 million, with exports of £412 million. The top four powerboat builders (measured by value of sales) account for approximately 60 per cent of industry turnover and between 70 and 80 per cent of total exports. The sector employs some 7,850 people, primarily in small and medium-sized enterprises.

Railway equipment

A number of UK enterprises are engaged in manufacturing railway equipment for both domestic and overseas markets, mainly producing specialist components and systems for use in rolling stock, signalling, track and infrastructure applications. Employment in the industry averaged 14,000 in 2001, with turnover of £1.4 billion. In 2002 exports were worth £161 million. About 4,000 firms are involved in the supply chains, and UK expertise extends to technical consultancy and project management. The Canadian-owned Bombardier Transportation is the largest company in this sector and assembles and maintains passenger rolling stock in the United Kingdom. All new trains being introduced in the United Kingdom have a number of foreign-made components, and UK input varies from 5 to 75 per cent of total value. Privatised train operating companies have placed orders for around 4,000 new passenger carriages since 1997, while many older trains have been refurbished. An extensive programme of infrastructure modernisation is also being undertaken.

Aerospace and defence

The UK aerospace industry is one of the few in the world with a complete capability across the whole spectrum of aerospace products and technology. An average of 115,000 people were employed in 769 enterprises in 2001 and turnover was £17.5 billion. The industry achieved exports of £11.6 billion in 2002.

Industry activities cover designing and constructing airframes, aero-engines, guided weapons, simulators and space satellites, materials, flight controls including 'fly-by-wire' and 'fly-by-

light' equipment (see below), and avionics and complex components, with their associated services. The United Kingdom also has one of the largest defence manufacturing industries in the Western world.

Among the leading companies are BAe Systems and Rolls-Royce. BAe Systems is an international company engaged in the development, delivery and support of advanced defence and aerospace systems in the air, on land, at sea and in space. The company designs, manufactures and supports military aircraft, surface ships, submarines, radar, avionics, communications, electronics and guided weapons systems. It had annual sales of £12 billion in the United Kingdom in 2002 and an order book of £43 billion.

Engines

Rolls-Royce is the world's second largest manufacturer of aero-engines, with a turnover in 2002 of £5.8 billion, including £2.7 billion for its aerospace business and £1.4 billion for defence. As at June 2003, there were more than 37,000 Rolls-Royce civil engines in service. Customers include more than 500 airlines, 4,000 corporate, utility and helicopter operators, and 160 armed forces. In civil aerospace, the Trent family of engines have won a 50 per cent share of business in the new generation wide-bodied aircraft produced by Airbus and Boeing. In the defence sector, Rolls-Royce participates in two of the world's major combat programmes:

- Eurofighter – where it has a 36 per cent share in the EJ200 engine and assembles all engines for the RAF; and
- Joint Strike Fighter (JSF) – where it provides the short take-off and vertical landing (STOVL) technology and has a 40 per cent share in the F136 engine.

Equipment

A number of UK companies manufacture aerostructures (doors, windows and aircraft body parts), equipment and systems for engines, and other products. UK firms have made important advances in, for example, developing the technology in which control surfaces on the wings and elsewhere are moved by means of automatic electronic signalling (fly-by-wire) and by fibre optics (fly-by-light). UK companies provide radar and air traffic control equipment and ground power supplies to airports and airlines all over the world.

Civil aircraft

Airbus is jointly owned by BAe Systems (with a 20 per cent stake) and EADS (European Aeronautic Defence and Space Company). Airbus UK designs and manufactures the wings for the whole range of Airbus airliners. By the end of June 2003, over 4,800 Airbus aircraft had been ordered and around 3,300 delivered. They are operated by nearly 200 airlines worldwide. Airbus is now engaged in the design and manufacture of the wings for the new A380 'super jumbo' – the world's only twin-deck, four-aisle airliner, with capacity for 555 passengers – which is due to enter service in 2006. Firm orders and commitments had been received for 129 aircraft from 11 customers by July 2003.

Bombardier Aerospace of Canada, the third largest civil aircraft manufacturer in the world, produces a wide range of turboprop and regional jet aircraft and business jets. At its Belfast site, Bombardier Aerospace Northern Ireland designs and manufactures major civil aircraft sub-assemblies, advanced engine nacelles and flight controls, as well as providing aviation support services.

Military aircraft and missiles

BAe Systems, along with EADS and Alenia of Italy, has built the Eurofighter Typhoon, a swing-role aircraft for the RAF and for the German, Italian and Spanish air forces. The company is also a partner with Lockheed Martin of the US in the JSF programme. BAe Systems also has the Harrier jump-jet, Tornado combat aircraft and Hawk fast-jet trainer.

Europe's main guided weapons business, MBDA, is co-owned by BAe Systems, EADS and Italy's Finmeccanica. The French-owned Thales, including Thales Air Defence in Belfast, is another major company operating in the UK guided weapons sector.

Helicopters

AgustaWestland, a joint venture company owned equally by GKN and by Finmeccanica, produces the multi-role EH101 medium-lift helicopter for civilian and military markets. There are two UK variants – the Royal Navy's Merlin HM.1 advanced anti-submarine warfare helicopter and the RAF's Merlin HC.3 combat transport helicopter. It also manufactures the Super Lynx light battlefield and naval helicopter, and is building and supporting the WAH-64 Apache attack helicopter for the UK Army, under licence

from Boeing. It has a joint venture with Bell in the US, and their Bell Agusta AB139 helicopter had its maiden flight in 2001.

Land systems

The United Kingdom's main armoured fighting vehicle capability is concentrated in two companies: Alvis Vickers (formed from the acquisition by Alvis of Vickers Defence in 2002) and RO Defence (part of BAe Systems), created in 2000 by the integration of the former Land and Systems business of Marconi with Royal Ordnance. RO Defence is also the main UK artillery and ordnance company.

Space equipment and services

Around 400 organisations employing about 5,000 people were engaged in industrial space activities, with turnover of £389 million in 2002. UK participation in the European Space Agency, and the British National Space Centre's (BNSC) role in coordinating UK space policy (see page 382), has enabled UK-based companies to participate in many leading space projects. The industry's strengths are in the development and manufacture of civil and military communications satellite systems, small satellites, radar and antennae, and software. In the field of Earth observation, BNSC has played a major role in programmes which have led to the development of platforms, space radar and meteorological satellite hardware, and in the exploitation of space data imaging products.

EADS became 100 per cent owners of Astrium, Europe's leading space company, in January 2003. As EADS Astrium, its satellite business activities cover civil and military communications and Earth observation, science and navigation programmes, avionics and equipment.

Construction

In 2002 the total value of work done in the construction industry in Great Britain was £83.6 billion, of which £45.4 billion was new work and £38.2 billion repair and maintenance (see Table 28.22). There was an additional £2.4 billion of work done in Northern Ireland. The volume of output in Great Britain at constant prices grew by 8 per cent in 2002, and was the highest annual increase since 1988. New work increased by 11 per cent and repair and maintenance by 5 per cent. The main areas of construction work within the

Table 28.21 Construction in the UK

	Number of enterprises	Total turnover (£ million)
1999	188,304	111,365
2000	190,550	121,549
2001	192,960	131,132

Source: Annual Business Inquiry, Office for National Statistics

industry in Great Britain covered by these statistics are:

- building and civil engineering – ranging from major private sector companies with diverse international interests to one-person enterprises carrying out domestic repairs; and
- specialist work – companies or individuals undertaking construction work ranging from structural steelwork and pre-cast concrete structures to mechanical and electrical services (including the design and installation of environmentally friendly building control systems).

Table 28.22 Value of construction output by type of work at current basic prices, Great Britain

	2000	2001	£ billion 2002
New work			
New housing			
Public	1.3	1.4	1.7
Private	8.7	8.8	10.4
Other new work			
Infrastructure	6.5	7.1	8.1
Other public	4.9	5.3	6.9
Other private industrial	3.7	3.7	3.4
Other private commercial	12.7	13.6	15.0
Total	37.7	40.0	45.4
Repair and maintenance			
Housing			
Public	6.6	6.6	6.4
Private	10.4	11.0	12.8
Other work			
Public	5.7	6.1	6.7
Private	9.4	11.0	12.3
Total	32.0	34.7	38.2
All work	**69.7**	**74.7**	**83.6**

Source: Department of Trade and Industry

Other areas of construction work not covered in the above statistics include:

- the supply of building materials and components (see Table 28.23 for production details) – ranging from large quarrying companies, and those engaged in mass production of manufactured items, to small, highly specialised manufacturers; and
- consultancy work – companies or individuals engaged in the planning, design and supervision of construction projects. Estimated earnings by engineering consultants on projects in the United Kingdom in 2002 were £3.7 billion. This figure accounted for 30 per cent of all income earned by UK professional services firms.

In 2002 the total value of new orders in Great Britain was £33.4 billion, of which £9.2 billion was

Table 28.23 Production of building materials and components, Great Britain

	2000	2001	2002
Bricks (million)	2,864	2,754	2,750
Concrete building blocks (thousand sq m)	90,219	87,922	91,474
Cement (thousand tonnes)[1]	11,894	11,090	11,089
Sand and gravel (thousand tonnes)[2]	89,234	88,210	85,513
Ready mixed concrete (thousand cu m)[1,3]	23,043	23,008	22,597
Slate (tonnes)[4]	85,858	93,125	94,954
Concrete roofing tiles (thousand sq m)	26,765	24,825	25,023

1 UK figures.
2 Sales.
3 Deliveries.
4 Excluding slate residue used for fill.
Source: *Construction Statistics Annual 2003*, Department of Trade and Industry

new housing and £24.2 billion other new work (see Table 28.24). The volume of new orders at constant prices grew by 9 per cent over the year, the highest growth since 1993.

Housing

The volume of new housing orders in Great Britain in 2002 rose by 9 per cent at constant prices, with the private sector accounting for almost 84 per cent of the total. Construction

Table 28.24 Value of new orders by type of work, current prices, Great Britain

£ billion

	2000	2001	2002
New housing			
Public and housing association	0.9	1.1	1.1
Private	6.1	6.5	8.1
Total	7.0	7.6	9.2
Other new work			
Infrastructure	5.0	5.2	5.6
Public	3.8	4.1	5.9
Private industrial	2.6	2.5	2.2
Private commercial	9.7	10.2	10.5
Total	21.1	22.0	24.2
All new work	**28.1**	**29.6**	**33.4**

Source: Department of Trade and Industry

Table 28.25 New dwellings completed by sector, Great Britain

Thousands

	1992	1997	2002
Private enterprise	141	153	150
Registered social landlords	26	28	19
Local authorities	5	-	-
Total	**172**	**181**	**169**

Source: Office of the Deputy Prime Minister

started on 183,000 dwellings: 165,200 by the private sector; 17,600 by registered social landlords; and 200 by local authorities. New dwellings completed by sector are shown in Table 28.25.

Project procurement, management and financing

Private and public sector projects are managed in a variety of ways. Most clients invite construction firms to bid for work by competitive tender, having used the design services of a consultant. The successful contractor will then undertake on-site work with a number of specialist subcontractors. Alternative methods of project procurement have become more common – for example, contracts might include subsequent provision of building maintenance, or a comprehensive 'design-and-build' service where a single company oversees every stage of a project from conception to completion.

Financing of major projects has also been changing. Traditionally, clients raised the finance to pay for schemes themselves. Today, they often demand a complete service package that includes finance. As a result, larger construction companies are developing closer links with banks and other financial institutions. In public sector construction, the Government's Private Finance Initiative (PFI)/public-private partnerships (see

Major construction projects in the United Kingdom

Some recent and current construction projects include:

- Birmingham Bull Ring redevelopment, including the new Selfridges 'Armadillo' store, which opened in September 2003;
- Swiss Re Headquarters ('The Gherkin'), City of London, due for completion in late 2003;
- M6 Toll road, 43 kilometres long, bypassing the congested West Midlands, due for completion by January 2004;
- Docklands Light Railway 4.4 kilometre extension to London City Airport and North Woolwich, due for completion by late 2005;
- the new Wembley Stadium, featuring a 130-metre arch supporting the retractable roof, due to open in 2006;
- Terminal 5, Heathrow Airport, due to open in 2008; and
- the Channel Tunnel Rail Link – section 1 (74 kilometres) from the Channel Tunnel to Fawkham Junction, North Kent, opened in September 2003, and section 2 (39 kilometres) to London St Pancras is due to open in early 2007.

page 357) have also heralded a move away from traditional financing.

Overseas contracting and consultancy

UK companies operate internationally and in any one year British consultants work in almost every country in the world.

UK contractors have pioneered management contracting and design and build, and also the financing mechanisms developed in the domestic market through innovations such as the PFI. During 2002 they won new international business valued at £4.3 billion, 9 per cent less than in 2001 (see Table 28.26). Contractors were particularly

Table 28.26 Overseas construction activity by UK companies – new contracts

| | £ million | | % |
| | | | share in |
	2001	2002	2002
Europe	870	701	16
of which:			
European Union	773	595	14
Middle East	334	416	10
Far East	734	527	12
of which:			
Hong Kong	325	375	9
Africa	535	162	4
Americas	1,931	2,112	49
of which:			
North America	1,778	2,053	48
Oceania	308	353	8
Total	**4,712**	**4,271**	**100**

Source: *Construction Statistics Annual 2003,* Department of Trade and Industry

successful in North America, the most valuable market, which accounted for 48 per cent of all new contracts. Current contracts include:

- constructing the Lok Ma Chau Rail Terminus complex in Hong Kong;
- construction and maintenance of highways and toll roads in Texas;
- the construction of North America's deepest mine shaft at the Kidd Mine, Canada; and
- tunnelling on the Narrangansett Bay Tunnel project, Los Angeles.

The main categories of work in which UK consultants are involved include structural commercial (roads, bridges, tunnels and railways); electrical and mechanical services; chemical, oil and gas plants; and water supply.

Further reading
The Government's Manufacturing Strategy. Department of Trade and Industry, 2002.

Websites

Department of Trade and Industry
www.dti.gov.uk

National Statistics
www.statistics.gov.uk

www.

29 Energy and natural resources

Energy

The energy industries in the United Kingdom play a central role in the economy by producing, transforming and supplying energy in its various forms to all sectors. In 2002 they accounted for 4.3 per cent of gross domestic product (GDP, see glossary). The energy industries are also major contributors to the UK balance of payments through the export of crude oil and oil products – in 2002 the UK trade surplus in fuels was £6 billion.

Figure 29.1 Production of primary fuels, UK

Million tonnes of oil equivalent

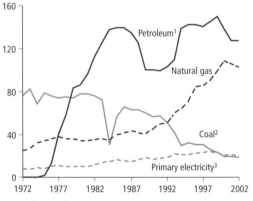

1 Includes crude oil, natural gas liquids and feedstocks.
2 Includes colliery methane.
3 Nuclear, natural flow hydro-electricity and, from 1988, generation at wind stations.
Source: Department of Trade and Industry

Production and resources

Production of primary fuels (Figure 29.1) was 1.7 per cent lower in 2002 than 2001, at 272.8 million tonnes of oil equivalent (including electricity generated from renewables and waste sources). Production of gas (including gaseous renewables) was 103.6 million tonnes of oil equivalent, 2.1 per cent lower than in 2001. This contrasts with a sharp increase in natural gas production in the 1990s.

Petroleum production in 2002 was 127.0 million tonnes of oil equivalent, down by 0.6 per cent on 2001, and stocks of crude oil and petroleum products were 4.0 per cent lower at the end of 2002 than a year earlier.

Coal production in the United Kingdom has followed a long-term downward trend. This decline continued between 2001 and 2002, with a fall of nearly 6 per cent. Despite this, coal still supplies a significant proportion of the country's primary energy needs: 32 per cent of the electricity supplied in 2002 was from coal. However, gas is the main fuel for generating electricity, accounting for 39.7 per cent of supply in 2002, an increase of 2.3 percentage points on the previous year. In contrast, nuclear energy supplied 21.6 per cent of electricity in 2002, a fall of half a percentage point.

The United Kingdom had a trade surplus in fuels of 41 million tonnes of oil equivalent in 2002. In volume terms, imports of fuel in 2002 were 3.8 per cent lower than in 2001, while exports were 1.5 per cent higher.

Overall the UK trade surplus (on a balance of payments basis) in crude oil and petroleum products was £5.4 billion. Total imports of fuels in 2002 were 6.7 per cent lower in value terms than in 2001, largely owing to a 27 per cent decrease in the value of imports of coal and other solid fuel. Exports were 5.5 per cent higher, with the value of exports of natural gas increasing by 16.0 per cent, reflecting high world gas prices during 2002.

The United Kingdom has an obligation under European Union (EU) law to maintain stocks of key oil products at or above a certain level, to ensure adequate supplies would exist for any international oil supply emergency. These obligations are based on UK annual consumption of the key products such as motor spirit, diesel-engined road vehicle (DERV) fuel and other gas diesel oils, aviation fuel, and other kerosenes and fuel oils. These obligations are updated every July as consumption data for the previous year are finalised. The current overall UK obligation based on 2001 consumption data is to hold a total of 11 million tonnes of these products, equal to around 67 days of consumption. At the end of 2002 the United Kingdom held stocks equal to 77 days of consumption.

Consumption

Total UK inland energy consumption was 2.9 per cent lower in 2002 than in 2001, at 230 million tonnes of oil equivalent (based on primary fuel input). Between 2001 and 2002 consumption of coal fell by 8.3 per cent, while oil and gas fell by 2.9 per cent and 0.6 per cent respectively (Table 29.2). On a temperature corrected basis, which shows what annual intake might have been if the average temperature during the year had been the same as the average for 1961–90, overall consumption fell by 1.5 per cent.

Final energy consumption is consumption by the final user rather than that which is used for transformation into other energy. It shows a strong seasonal pattern with more energy being consumed in the winter months and less in the summer, particularly in the domestic and service sectors. Final consumption by sector and end use are shown in Figures 29.3 and 29.4. Non-energy purposes include fuel used for chemical feedstock, solvents and road-making material.

Between 2001 and 2002 energy consumption in the service, transport and domestic sectors fell by

Table 29.2 Inland consumption for energy use (in terms of primary sources), UK

Million tonnes oil equivalent

	1992	2001	2002
Natural gas	55.1	95.3	94.7
Oil	77.5	75.3	73.1
Coal	63.0	41.2	37.8
Nuclear electricity	18.5	20.8	20.1
Hydro electricity[1]	0.5	0.4	0.5
Renewable and waste	0.8	2.5	2.7
Net electricity imports	1.4	0.9	0.7
Total[2]	**216.7**	**236.4**	**229.6**

1 Excludes pumped storage. Includes generation at wind stations.
2 Total includes losses of electricity during transmission and distribution.
Source: Department of Trade and Industry

Figure 29.3 Final energy consumption by sector, 2002, UK

Total: 168 million tonnes of oil equivalent[1]

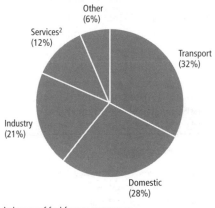

1 Includes use of fuel for non-energy use.
2 Includes agriculture.
Source: Department of Trade and Industry

9.6 per cent, 0.7 per cent and 1.3 per cent respectively, but consumption in the industrial sector rose, by 0.9 per cent.

International energy issues

EU countries vary considerably in the amount of energy each person uses at home due to many factors, such as climate, house size, energy efficiency and prices. Among EU countries household energy use per person ranged from

Figure 29.4 Final energy consumption by end use, 2002, UK

Total: 157 million tonnes of oil equivalent[1]

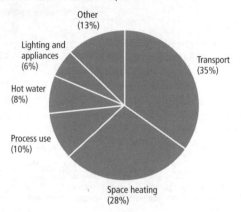

Other (13%)

Lighting and appliances (6%)

Hot water (8%)

Process use (10%)

Transport (35%)

Space heating (28%)

1 Excludes use of fuel for non-energy use.
Source: Department of Trade and Industry

0.29 tonnes of oil equivalent per person in Portugal to 1.52 in Luxembourg, with the United Kingdom, at 0.76, in the middle of the range (Figure 29.5).

Energy policy

In February 2003 the UK Government published a White Paper, outlining its proposals for future energy policy.

Figure 29.5 Household energy consumption per person in EU countries, 2001

Tonnes of oil equivalent per person

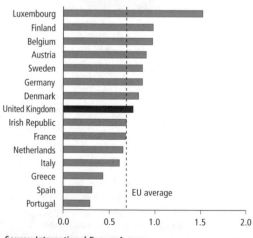

Luxembourg
Finland
Belgium
Austria
Sweden
Germany
Denmark
United Kingdom
Irish Republic
France
Netherlands
Italy
Greece
Spain
Portugal

EU average

0.0   0.5   1.0   1.5   2.0

Source: International Energy Agency

Our energy future – creating a low carbon economy identified three major challenges confronting the UK energy system. These are climate change, declining indigenous energy supply and keeping the UK energy infastructure up to date with changing technologies and needs. To address these challenges the new energy policy has four goals:

- to cut UK carbon dioxide (CO_2) emissions by about 60 per cent between 1990 and 2050;
- to maintain the reliability of energy supplies;
- to promote competitive markets in the United Kingdom and beyond, helping to raise the rate of sustainable economic growth and improve productivity; and
- to ensure that every home is adequately and affordably heated.

Many of the policies set out in the White Paper have built on the Cabinet Office Performance and Innovation Unit's Energy Review of February 2002 and the Royal Commission on Environmental Pollution's 22nd Report of June 2000. The Department of Trade and Industry (DTI) also conducted a consultation on energy policy in 2002, which took into account the views of the public, experts and industry. At the same time detailed analytical work was undertaken on areas such as assessing the costs of a low carbon economy in the future, energy security, and the implications for the energy system of using additional renewable sources.

The Government aims to ensure that market framework and policy instruments reinforce each other to achieve these goals. It believes that energy efficiency is likely to be the cheapest and safest way of addressing all four goals, and that renewable energy will play an important part in reducing carbon emissions, while also strengthening energy security and improving industrial competitiveness. It is investing a further £60 million in renewable energy projects, bringing total support for renewables to around £350 million between 2002/03 and 2005/06.

Climate change levy

The climate change levy (CCL) was introduced in April 2001 as an environmental tax on the use of energy by business and the public sector. Its purpose is to encourage the efficient use of energy, in order to help meet UK targets for cutting emissions of greenhouse gases.

The revenue raised by the levy is recycled back to business, primarily through the 0.3 percentage point reduction – worth around £1.7 billion in 2003–04 – in employers' National Insurance contributions. Revenue from the levy also provides support for investment in energy efficiency measures by businesses through 100 per cent enhanced capital allowances, and support for the Carbon Trust, which provides advice for business and supports the development of low carbon technologies. The levy and package of associated measures form part of the Government's strategy for moving the burden of tax from 'beneficial' activity, such as employment, to 'detrimental' activity, such as pollution.

Since the introduction of CCL, 44 eligible energy intensive sectors of industry have been able to enter into agreements to improve their energy efficiency and reduce emissions, in return for an 80 per cent discount from the levy. Facilities that have been certified by the Department for Environment, Food and Rural Affairs (Defra) as having met their 2002 targets can continue to benefit from the levy discount from April 2003 to March 2005. Carbon dioxide (CO_2) emissions fell by 9 per cent between 1990 and 2001, achieving the climate change programme goal (see page 278).

An extra-statutory concession was introduced in 2002 which exempts energy used for certain environmentally-friendly industrial recycling processes from the CCL. This exemption applies to recycling processes competing with processes that use fuels for non-energy purposes or for dual energy/non- energy use (for example coke used in steel blast furnaces).

International developments
Since 1999 the EU's Sixth Framework Programme (FP6) of Research and Technological Development has been the focus of research, development and demonstration of energy technologies in the European Union. The overall budget covering the four-year period from 2003 to 2006 is €17.5 billion, representing an increase of 17 per cent from the Fifth Framework Programme.

The European Commission has proposed a new energy action programme, Intelligent Energy for Europe, to run from 2003 to 2006. It aims to implement the strategy outlined in the 2001 Green Paper *Towards a European Strategy for the security of energy supply*, in which renewable energy and energy savings play a strategic role. It also aims to promote renewable energies (ALTENER) and

energy saving (SAVE), and at the same time to bring international action into line with these two priorities (COOPENER). Finally, it proposes to introduce new measures on the energy aspects of transport (STEER), in line with the Common Transport Policy.

The International Energy Agency (IEA), based in Paris, is an autonomous agency linked with the Organisation for Economic Co-operation and Development (OECD). It monitors world energy markets on behalf of industrialised countries and promotes reform of energy markets, both among its members and internationally. The IEA is the energy forum for 26 member countries, including the United Kingdom. IEA member governments are committed to taking joint measures to meet oil supply emergencies and agree to share information, coordinate their energy policies and co-operate in the development of rational energy programmes.

EU Energy Products Directive
Agreement was reached on the EU Energy Products Directive in March 2003. From January 2004 the Directive will increase the existing EU minimum rates of duty on oils, with a second increase on diesel from January 2010. It will also provide a Community framework with minimum rates of duty for the taxation of other energy products, including electricity, natural gas, coal and other solid fuels. Those Member States that do not currently tax these fuels will be required to introduce such taxes.

Oil and gas exploration and production
In 2002 oil and gas accounted for about three-quarters of total UK energy consumption, either through direct use or as a source of energy for electricity generation. Total UK production of crude oil and natural gas liquids (NGLs) in 2002 was 0.6 per cent lower than in 2001, at 115.9 million tonnes. UK production accounted for 95 per cent of gas available for consumption in 2002, a decrease from 97 per cent in 2001 reflecting UK ability to import additional supplies from the Norwegian sector of the North Sea through the Vesterled pipeline.

The UK Continental Shelf (UKCS) comprises those areas of the seabed and subsoil up to and beyond the territorial sea over which the United Kingdom exercises sovereign rights of exploration and exploitation of natural resources. Exports from the UKCS rose by 9 per cent in 2002 to

Table 29.6 Oil statistics, UK

Million tonnes

	1992	2001	2002
Oil production			
Land	4.0	2.9	2.7
Offshore	85.2	105.5	104.7
Refinery output	85.8	77.0	79.8
Deliveries	75.4	70.9	70.4
Export			
Crude, NGL, feedstock	57.6	86.7	86.8
Refined petroleum	20.2	19.0	22.8
Imports			
Crude, NGL, feedstock	57.7	53.5	56.7
Refined petroleum	10.6	17.0	13.7

Source: Department of Trade and Industry

14.2 billion cubic metres. Gas was exported to the Netherlands from the UK share of the Markham transboundary field and the neighbouring Windermere field, to the Republic of Ireland, and to Belgium through the UK–Belgium interconnector. About 5.7 billion cubic metres were imported from Norway and from Belgium via the interconnector, representing 5.8 per cent of total supplies in 2002, compared with 2.9 per cent in 2001.

Taxation

The North Sea fiscal regime is a major mechanism for gaining economic benefit for the United Kingdom from its oil and gas resources. The Government grants licences to private sector companies to explore for, and exploit, oil and gas resources (see right). Its main sources of revenue from oil and gas activities are petroleum revenue tax, levied on profits from fields approved before 16 March 1993, and corporation tax, charged on the profits of oil and gas companies. Since the 2002 Budget, companies have paid a 10 per cent supplementary charge on North Sea profits and received a 100 per cent first-year allowance for capital expenditure in the North Sea.

As part of the modernisation of the North Sea fiscal regime, the Government abolished royalty on North Sea oil and gas production with effect from January 2003. Royalty was charged at 12.5 per cent of the value of oil and gas produced after deduction of an allowance for initial transport, treatment and storage. It only applied to North Sea fields granted development consent prior to 1 April 1982 as it was abolished for all other fields in the 1980s.

Licensing

The main type of offshore licence is the Traditional Seaward Production Licence and it covers the full life of a field from exploration to decommissioning. Onshore production licences are called Petroleum Exploration and Development Licences and are similar to the offshore production licences. A new type of licence called the 'Promote' was introduced in February 2003, and is designed to increase oil and gas production in the North Sea, and offer opportunities to smaller producers.

In February 2003 the 21st offshore and 11th onshore licensing rounds were launched, along with the first application offer for Promote licences. As a result, 30 offshore and 8 onshore production licence applications were received, along with 40 new Promote licence applications covering 140 blocks in total. This is an increase of over 100 blocks on the previous round in 2002 and the largest number of blocks applied for since the early 1970s.

In May 2003 the DTI introduced a new oil and gas database for the onshore sector. The new data available include technical sections of licence applications for the first to sixth onshore licensing rounds, together with technical licence reports more than six years old. The database is an important resource that will be useful to companies already operating in the United Kingdom as well as to newcomers.

Production and reserves

Some 244 offshore fields were in production at the end of 2002: 124 oil, 99 gas and 21 condensate (a lighter form of oil). During 2002 five new developments were approved. Offshore, these comprised four gasfields and one condensate field. In addition, approval for three incremental offshore developments and one incremental onshore development was granted.

Cumulative production of oil and natural gas liquids to the end of 2002 was 2.8 billion tonnes. In 2002 oil and gas production is estimated to have been some 4.7 million barrels of oil equivalent per day (boepd), a decline of some 61,000 boepd on 2001.

The value of UK recoverable oil and gas reserves mainly depends upon the estimated physical amounts remaining, the current rate of extraction and the assumed future price per unit of oil and gas, net of the cost of extraction. Since 1993 the estimated stock of reserves has fallen as a result of extraction, but the value of reserves has generally risen because of a long term increase in oil prices. By the end of 2001 oil reserves were valued at £52 billion, while gas reserves were estimated to be worth £39 billion.

Offshore gas

Natural gas now accounts for over 41 per cent of total inland primary fuel consumption in the United Kingdom. In 2002 indigenous production amounted to a record 113 billion cubic metres (bcm), 2.1 per cent up on 2001.

The first significant discovery of offshore gas in the United Kingdom was in 1965, and cumulative gas production to the end of 2002 was 1,826 bcm. Maximum possible remaining gas reserves in present discoveries now stand at just under 1,595 bcm.

Oil and gas income

Since 1965 the UK oil and gas production industry has generated operating surpluses of some £306 billion, of which about £115 billion (including £25 billion of exploration and appraisal expenditure) has been reinvested in the industry, £106 billion paid in taxation, and about £85 billion retained by the companies. Total annual income of the oil and gas sector fell slightly to £24 billion in 2002.

Pipelines

Some 10,900 kilometres of major submarine pipelines transport oil, gas and condensate from one field to another and to shore. Nine landing places on the North Sea coast bring gas ashore to supply a national and regional high- and low-pressure pipeline system some 273,000 kilometres long, which transports natural gas around Great Britain.

A 40-kilometre pipeline takes natural gas from Scotland to Northern Ireland; exports to the Republic of Ireland are conveyed by the Britain–Ireland interconnector. The pipeline from Bacton in Norfolk to Zeebrugge in Belgium (232 kilometres), which was opened in 1998, has an annual export capacity of 20 bcm of gas, or

about 15 per cent of UK peak demand. Although a smaller volume of gas can flow into the United Kingdom at present, the interconnector's owners are proceeding with plans to increase import capacity from the current 8.5 bcm a year to 16.5 bcm a year in 2006.

Economic and industrial aspects

World oil prices declined in 2002; the average price received by producers from sales of UKCS oil was £124 a tonne, compared with £126 in 2001. Total revenues from the sale of production from the UKCS in 2002 remained similar to 2001, with oil (including NGLs) at some £14.5 billion and gas at £8.2 billion. Taxes and royalty receipts attributable to UKCS oil and gas fell slightly to some £4.9 billion in 2002/03.

PILOT, now in its third year, is an initiative promoting industry co-operation with the Government to develop recovery of UK oil and gas resources and prolong indigenous supplies.

Among PILOT's targets for 2010 are to:
- prolong self-sufficiency in oil and gas for the United Kingdom;
- maintain production levels of three million boepd;
- sustain investment levels of £3 billion a year;
- deliver a 50 per cent increase in the value of industry-related exports by 2005 (from the 1999 level);
- sustain 100,000 more jobs than there would have been; and
- ensure that the United Kingdom is the safest place to work in the worldwide oil and gas industry.

Production investment in the UK oil and gas extraction industry in 2002 remained similar to that in 2001 at some £4.0 billion, including exploration and appraisal investment of around £0.4 billion. It formed about 16 per cent of total UK industrial investment and some 2.4 per cent of gross fixed capital investment. In 2002 some 32,000 people were engaged in extraction, while the industry supported some 265,000 in other sectors.

The offshore environment

All new developments are assessed under the Offshore Petroleum Production and Pipelines (Assessment of Environmental Effects) Regulations, the Environmental Impact Assessment (EIA) Regulations and the Offshore

Petroleum Activities (Conservation of Habitats) Regulations 2001. The EIA Regulations apply to the drilling of wells, the installation of pipelines, extended well tests and the development of new fields. Environmental Statements are required for projects that could have a significant impact on the marine environment. The Habitats Regulations additionally apply to activities that are not covered by the EIA Regulations, such as offshore oil and gas surveys, well abandonment and decommissioning operations.

In addition to these assessment procedures, permits are required for a number of offshore activities. The Offshore Combustion Installations (Prevention of Control of Pollution) Regulations 2001 control emissions from offshore combustion installations, that is, gas turbines and diesels burning natural gas or diesel fuel which are predominantly used to generate electricity. Permits are also required for the use and discharge of chemicals during all offshore operations under the Offshore Chemicals (Pollution Prevention and Control) Regulations 2002. A comprehensive review of the application procedures for environmental consents has taken place, and application systems are being developed that will allow operators to apply for all the required permits using a single application system administered online via the UK Oil and Gas Portal.

The amount of oil spilled around the United Kingdom and offshore is small in relation to total oil production. The total amount of oil spilled offshore during 2001 was 94 tonnes. The number of oil spills recorded increased from 349 in 1997 to 436 in 2001. About 96 per cent of reports were for a spill of less than 1 tonne. Since 1986 the United Kingdom has carried out surveillance flights in accordance with international obligations under the Bonn Agreement. These flights are unannounced and cover all offshore installations on the UKCS. The DTI uses a computer link to the aircraft, which transmits photographic images of possible pollution incidents and enables it to investigate these as they happen. In addition, the DTI has conducted an initial study into the potential for satellite surveillance, complemented by aerial surveillance.

Decommissioning

The *Petroleum Act 1998* places a decommissioning obligation on the operators of every offshore installation and the owners of every offshore pipeline on the UKCS. Companies have to submit a decommissioning programme for ministerial approval and ensure that its provisions are carried out. In 1998 the OSPAR Convention (see page 282) agreed rules for the disposal of defunct offshore installations at sea. Under the terms of this decision, there is a prohibition on the dumping and leaving in place of such installations. Derogations, however, are possible for concrete platforms and for the footings of steel installations with a jacket weight above 10,000 tonnes. All installations put in place after 9 February 1999 must be completely removed. The Government encourages the re-use of facilities and expects operators to show that they have investigated such a course. It also encourages free trade in mature offshore oil and gas assets, as a means of extending field life and maximising economic recovery. By August 2003, 24 decommissioning programmes, covering 25 redundant installations, had been approved by the DTI.

Offshore safety

Offshore health and safety are the responsibility of the Health and Safety Executive (HSE, see page 141). The Offshore Division (OSD) within the HSE ensures that risks to people who work in oil and gas extraction are properly controlled. OSD's regulatory tasks range from providing advice and guidance on operational and technical matters, to working with industry on reducing releases of hydrocarbons.

OSD's work includes:
- inspecting and auditing offshore operations, and onshore oil and gas well operations;
- investigating accidents and complaints;
- assessing safety cases and other notifications, including well operations and some construction operations; and
- providing technical information and statistics.

The Offshore Petroleum Industry Training Organisation and the Norwegian Oil Industry Association have approved the Warsash Maritime Centre in Southampton as a recognised training centre. It offers a range of basic safety and emergency training courses for those employed in the offshore oil and gas industry. The course is a prerequisite that satisfies UK Offshore Operators Association guidelines on environmental health.

Suppliers of goods and services

As the UK offshore oil and gas sector matures, UK supply and manufacturing companies have increasingly turned to work in other industrial sectors and in overseas hydrocarbon producing areas. The Oil and Gas Industry Development Group in the DTI works with the PILOT (see page 435) initiative and takes other action to help the industry realign to changing market circumstances. The UK supply chain database (*www.og.dti.gov.uk/portal*), maintained by the DTI, contains contact details of over 3,000 companies in the UK oil and gas supply chain, and is available for global buyers who seek information on the capabilities and contact details of UK-based companies in this sector.

Gas supply industry

Structure

The holder of a gas transporter's licence in Great Britain may not also hold licences for supply or shipping in a fully competitive market.[1] Three entirely separate companies have been formed from the demerged British Gas plc. The supply business is now part of the holding company Centrica plc (which still trades under the British Gas brand name in Great Britain). In October 2000 BG Group plc demerged into a separately listed company, Lattice Group plc, while the rest of the group continue as BG Group plc. Lattice Group merged with National Grid plc in October 2002 to create National Grid Transco plc (NGT). It is an international energy delivery business, whose main activities are in the regulated electricity and gas industries.

Transport, telecommunications, research and technology (R&T) and other businesses are part of NGT, while the pipeline and storage businesses, most exploration, and production are part of the BG Group plc.

NGT is the owner, operator and developer of the majority of Britain's gas transport system. Its network supplies 40 per cent of the country's energy needs and it is responsible for dealing with gas leaks and emergencies. It has also had a monopoly in gas metering, which the energy regulator, the Office of Gas and Electricity Markets (Ofgem, see page 438), plans to open to competition.

---

1 Suppliers sell piped gas to consumers; public gas transporters (PGTs) operate the pipeline system through which gas will normally be delivered and shippers arrange with PGTs for appropriate amounts of gas to go through the pipeline system.

Shippers participate in balancing supply and demand in the pipeline network, within a regime partly driven by commercial concerns, and utilising gas trading arrangements, which include a screen-based on-the-day commodity market for trading in wholesale supplies of gas. In addition, there are auctions for the allocation of entry capacity into the high-pressure national transmission system and commercial incentives for NGT to operate and balance the system efficiently. Because of the increasing use of gas for electricity generation, the energy regulator is considering changes to the way gas supply is matched to demand.

In Northern Ireland supplies of natural gas have been available since 1996, when the Scotland to Northern Ireland gas pipeline was brought into operation. Phoenix Natural Gas Ltd has a combined licence for the conveyance and supply of gas in Greater Belfast.

Bord Gais Eireann (BGE – based in the Republic of Ireland) is responsible for the development and maintenance of Ireland's natural gas transport network. It is constructing the North West and South/North gas transmission pipelines. The company intends to complete the gas transmission pipeline to the North West by autumn 2004 and the connecting South–North pipeline by 2006.

Competition

Since deregulation of the industry in 1994 suppliers other than British Gas have captured 83 per cent of the industrial and commercial gas market. Some 60 companies are licensed to sell gas to the commercial sector.

By December 2002 about 7.4 million (out of 20 million) domestic customers no longer took their gas supply from British Gas and were supplied by one of 27 other companies now in the domestic market. In 2002 a standard credit customer could save, on average, £53 on his or her annual gas bill by changing supplier. (The average annual bill in the United Kingdom was £310 in 2002, including VAT.) Only companies that have been granted a supplier's licence are allowed to sell gas. Licence conditions include providing gas to anyone who requests it and is connected to the mains gas supply. Special services must be made available for elderly, disabled and chronically sick people. Suppliers must offer customers a range of payment options and, although they are able to set their own charges, must publish their prices and

other terms so that customers can make an
informed choice. In 2001 UK average domestic gas
prices were the second lowest within the European
Union.

Ofgem acts to ensure that Great Britain's
competitive retail market works for all customers
and that anti-competitive practices do not take
place. It also works to prevent continuing
problems caused by doorstep selling, which
undermine customer confidence.

Consumption and the market
In the United Kingdom, gas has been mainly used
as a fuel for the domestic, commercial and
industrial markets. During the 1990s a new
market for gas opened up, using the fuel for power
generation, which offered higher generation
efficiency, fewer carbon emissions and lower fuel
costs than conventional coal-fired technology. The
increase of gas-fired generation caused rapid
growth in UK gas use, so that by 2000 demand
had risen to 283 million cubic metres per day.
In 2002 gas represented around 42 per cent of
UKCS hydrocarbon production, 38 per cent of
UK energy production and 4.3 per cent of world
production, making the United Kingdom the
fourth largest gas producer.

UK demand for natural gas in 2002, at 1,105
terawatt hours (TWh), was 1.3 per cent lower than
in 2001. Consumption in the domestic sector fell
by 0.7 per cent to 376.3 TWh in 2002, while
consumption in the public administration,
commerce and agriculture sectors fell by 4.5 per
cent. Consumption in the industrial sector fell by
6.6 per cent to 181.3 TWh. Gas used for
electricity generation in 2002, at 326.2 TWh, was
5.3 per cent higher than in 2001, largely due to
lower gas prices during 2002.

Between the first quarters of 2002 and 2003 prices
paid by industry (excluding the CCL) fell by 6 per
cent in real terms. This compares with a 42 per
cent increase between the same quarters of 2000
and 2002.

Downstream oil

Oil consumption
Deliveries of petroleum products for inland
consumption (excluding refinery consumption) in
2002 included 19.8 million tonnes of petrol for
motor vehicles, 17.6 million tonnes of DERV fuel,

10.3 million tonnes of aviation turbine fuel, 6.7
million tonnes of gas oil (distilled from petroleum)
and 2.1 million tonnes of fuel oils (blends of heavy
petroleum).

Oil refineries
In 2002 the 12 UK refineries processed 85 million
tonnes of crude and process oils, about the same
as in 2001. About 80 per cent of UK output by
weight is in the form of lighter, higher-value
products, such as gasoline, DERV and jet
kerosene. Petrol production is more important in
the United Kingdom than in its European
counterparts, accounting for about a third of each
barrel of crude oil compared with the European
average of just over a fifth.

In 2002 UK exports of refined petroleum products
rose by 10 per cent to £4.1 billion. Virtually all
exports went to partners in the European Union
and in the International Energy Agency, especially
the Netherlands, France, Germany and the United
States.

Coal
The UK coal industry is entirely in the private
sector. The main deep mine operators in the
United Kingdom are UK Coal plc (formerly
known as RJB Mining), in England, Tower
Colliery in South Wales, and Hatfield Colliery in
South Yorkshire. UK Coal, Scottish Coal Company
Ltd, H J Banks and Company and Celtic Energy,
which operates in Wales, are the main opencast
operators. In May 2003 there were 22
underground mines in production, including 14
major deep mines, employing around 8,600
workers (including contractors), and 42 opencast
sites, employing some 2,600 workers. Opencast
production accounts for most of the relatively
low-sulphur coal mined in Scotland and South
Wales and contributes towards improving the
average quality of coal supplies. Opencast mining
is subject to approval by local authorities and can
take place only where it can comply with strict
environmental guidelines.

Market for coal
Imports of coal into the United Kingdom in 2002
fell by 19 per cent from the record level in 2001 to
28.7 million tonnes, of which just over 6 million
tonnes were for the iron and steel sector. The
decline in the level of imports was due to lower
demand for coal which fell by 8.5 per cent. Major
sources of imports include Australia, Colombia,
Poland, South Africa and the United States. Very

little UK coal is exported, usually less than
1 million tonnes a year.

Clean coal

Cleaner coal technologies reduce the
environmental impact of coal used for power and
industrial applications by increasing the efficiency
of its conversion to energy and reducing harmful
emissions, which is one of the causes of acid rain.
Improvements in the efficiency of coal-fired
power stations lead directly to reductions of
carbon dioxide, a major contributor to climate
change.

The DTI is supporting a programme of research
and development into cleaner coal technology,
covering a number of technologies in advanced
power generation and emissions reduction. In the
longer run it should be possible for UK project
developers to benefit from carbon credits through
international trading under the Kyoto Protocol
(see page 277) clean development mechanism.

The current Cleaner Coal Technology Programme
has a total budget of £25 million over three years.
It has two components: to support research and
development into new cleaner coal technologies;
and to facilitate the transfer of cleaner coal
technology to other countries and promote the
exports of UK expertise and products.

Coal Authority

The Coal Authority is a public body sponsored by
the DTI. It has five main responsibilities: licensing
coal-mining operations; repairing coal subsidence
damage; managing coalfield property; managing
minewater pollution and other environmental
problems associated with coal-mining; and
providing information to house buyers, other
purchasers of property and local authorities about
mining activity near property.

Nuclear power

Nuclear power substantially reduces the use of
fossil fuels that would otherwise be needed for
electricity generation. It generates about one-sixth
of the world's energy and over a third of Europe's.
In the United Kingdom, nuclear stations generated
88 TWh in 2002 and contributed around a quarter
per cent of total electricity generation. The private
sector company British Energy owns and operates
seven advanced gas-cooled reactor stations and
the pressurised water reactor (PWR) at Sizewell B.
British Energy's reactors have a declared net

capacity of 7,140 megawatts (MW) in England
and 2,440 MW in Scotland. British Nuclear Fuels
operates six magnox power stations, and five more
which are being decommissioned.

Existing nuclear stations are expected to continue
to contribute to UK energy requirements provided
they do so to the high safety and environmental
standards currently observed. Government
projections suggest that nuclear power generation
could represent about 17 to 18 per cent of total
generation by 2010 and about 7 per cent of total
generation by 2020. These projections assume no
new stations will be built, and recognise that plant
lifetimes are dependent on safety and economic
factors.

In September 2002, as a result of experiencing
financial difficulties, British Energy asked the
Government for financial support, and it received
a short-term loan. In March 2003 sufficient
proceeds had been received from the sale of BE's
stake in Bruce Power, a Canadian subsidiary, to
enable it to repay all the outstanding amount of
£215 million, including interest and commission.
The Government confirmed that it would
continue to fund BE's operation while its
restructuring plan was agreed and implemented,
and extended the credit facility on a contingency
basis to September 2004 or the date on which the
restructuring plan becomes effective. The
maximum amount available was reduced from
£650 million to £200 million. At the same time the
Government applied for state aid approval from
the European Commission for the restructuring
plan.

British Nuclear Fuels (BNFL)

BNFL is the primary UK provider of nuclear
products and services, including spent fuel
management, recycling, reprocessing oxide fuel,
decommissioning and cleaning up redundant
nuclear facilities, and treating historic wastes for
both UK and international customers. The
company's turnover in 2002/03 was £2.22 billion.
In July 2003 the Government announced that it
would conduct a joint review with BNFL to
evaluate options for alternative strategies for the
company. The review will be conducted against
the framework of the Government's policy
objectives set out in the White Paper *Managing the
Nuclear Legacy – a strategy for action*. The
organisational structure now in place and the
review of forward strategy will prepare the

company for the market-place after the establishment of the NDA.

Managing the nuclear legacy

The UK nuclear legacy has to be managed safely, securely and cost effectively in ways that protect the environment. The draft Nuclear Sites and Radioactive Substances Bill, which was published in June 2003, follows on from *Managing the Nuclear Legacy – A strategy for action* (published in July 2002). The Bill would provide for the creation of the NDA, a non-departmental public body that would take responsibility for discharging the historic liabilities currently owned and managed by BNFL and the UK Atomic Energy Authority (UKAEA) (see below). It is estimated that the costs of cleaning up this legacy, which are already being met by the taxpayer, will amount to £48 billion over the next century.

The NDA would be responsible for developing a long-term strategy for decommissioning and cleaning up designated sites. In doing so, it would work closely with the nuclear regulators (the Environment Agency, the Scottish Environment Protection Agency, the HSE Nuclear Installations Inspectorate and the Office for Civil Nuclear Security) to ensure that its clean-up plans are carried out in line with environmental and international obligations. The NDA would also have a duty to maintain the skills base necessary to meet the challenges of decommissioning over the long term and would seek to use the best skills available through promoting competitive markets for clean-up contracts. It is expected that the new authority would be functioning by 1 April 2005.

UK Atomic Energy Authority

UKAEA is responsible for managing the decommissioning and environmental restoration of its former nuclear research sites at Dounreay (Scotland), Windscale (Cumbria), Harwell (Oxfordshire), and Winfrith (Dorset). It also manages the UK contribution to the fusion energy programme at Culham, Oxfordshire.

By summer 2003 UKAEA had dismantled 18 major radioactive facilities including six research reactors. It had also produced plans for the restoration of all its sites. It is a non-departmental public body, funded mainly by the DTI. The estimated cost of its liabilities is £8.9 billion.

Fusion research

The Office of Science and Technology (see page 377) and Euratom (the European Atomic Energy Community) fund nuclear fusion research in the United Kingdom. In 2003/04 UK government spending on research is expected to be £15.6 million, of which the main focus is magnetic confinement, based at Culham. UKAEA operates Europe's leading fusion facility – JET (Joint European Torus) on behalf of its European partners in the European Fusion Development Agreement – as well as the UK domestic programme. Through the European Union, the Euratom/UKAEA Fusion Association (*www.fusion.org.uk*) contributes to the International Thermonuclear Experimental Reactor, the international partnership between Canada, China, Europe, Japan, Russia, South Korea and the United States to demonstrate the principle of power production from fusion.

Nuclear safety

The safety of nuclear installations is the responsibility of the nuclear operators within a system of regulatory control enforced by the HSE. Regulation of nuclear safety is primarily achieved through a system of licensing that requires the licensees to demonstrate to the HSE that they meet 36 licence conditions. The HSE assesses and inspects sites to satisfy itself that the licensees meet their responsibilities for safety.

The International Convention on Nuclear Safety has been ratified by 53 countries, including the United Kingdom and other members of the European Union. Each signatory is required to submit a report showing how it meets the articles of the Convention, and such reports are the subject of peer review by the other countries that are party to the Convention. The latest UK report for the Convention on Nuclear Safety was prepared in April 2002.

The Nuclear Safety Directorate acting for the HSE gives specialist assistance to the International Atomic Energy Agency (IAEA), the Organisation for Economic Co-operation and Development's nuclear energy agency, and Euratom. The main UK contribution to the international effort to improve safety in Central and Eastern Europe and in the former Soviet republics is channelled through the European Union's nuclear safety programmes.

Electricity

England and Wales
In December 2002, 72 companies held generation licences in England and Wales. The largest generators are Innogy, Powergen, AES, British Energy, American Electric Power, Edison Mission Energy, and BNFL's Magnox Generation Group. The National Grid Transco (NGT) owns and operates the transmission system, and is responsible for balancing electricity supply and demand.

There are 12 Distribution Network Operators (DNOs) that are responsible for transferring electricity from the high-voltage National Grid to consumers via local networks. Supply – the purchase of electricity from generators and its sale to end-users – has been fully open to competition since 1999. All retail consumers in Great Britain are free to choose their electricity supplier.

Cross-border acquisitions and takeovers have become a feature of the European power market. The Regional Electricity Companies (RECs), that were formed when the electricity industry was privatised in 1990, effectively no longer exist. This is because the franchise market has been abolished while distribution and supply have typically been sold off as separate activities. Most of the companies involved are now overseas-owned. All but one of the main UK generators are now vertically integrated through the ownership of supply businesses.

The New Electricity Trading Arrangements (NETA) came into effect in England and Wales in March 2001, replacing the Electricity Pool that had operated since privatisation. NETA was designed to introduce more competition into wholesale electricity trading and to create a commodity-based market. For instance, generators, suppliers, traders and customers are encouraged to enter into bilateral contracts in forwards and futures markets and short-term power exchanges. Participants are free to trade electricity for any half-hour period until one hour ahead of real time 'gate closure'. From that point until real time, the market operates through the Balancing Mechanism, run by the NGT, because of the need to balance the system on a second-by-second basis. NETA took effect through conditions inserted into generation, supply and transmission licences.

Scotland
Scottish Power and Scottish and Southern Energy transmit and distribute electricity within their respective franchise areas, and generate and supply electricity throughout the United Kingdom. They are also contracted to buy all the output from British Energy's two Scottish nuclear power stations (Hunterston B and Torness) until 2006 at the latest. All major suppliers compete in the retail market in Scotland.

In January 2003 the UK Government published a draft Bill setting out its proposals for the British Electricity Trading and Transmission Arrangements (BETTA) in Great Britain. In essence, BETTA would extend NETA to Scotland, thus creating a wholesale electricity market throughout Great Britain for the first time, which it is hoped would increase competition in Scotland and across Great Britain more generally. BETTA is scheduled to be introduced by April 2005, subject to parliamentary time being available to pass the necessary legislation.

Northern Ireland
Three private sector companies – AES Kilroot Power Ltd, Premier Power Ltd and Coolkeeragh Power Ltd – generate electricity in Northern Ireland. Most of the electricity generated is sold to Northern Ireland Electricity plc (NIE), which has a monopoly of transmission and distribution, and a right to supply. The Northern Ireland Authority for Energy Regulation, a non-ministerial government department, regulates the electricity and natural gas industries in Northern Ireland. It is supported by the Office for the Regulation of Electricity and Gas.

The electricity market has been gradually opened up to competition since 1999. In 2001 the right to choose a supplier was extended to 35 per cent of the total market (mainly large industrial consumers). In addition, a number of second-tier suppliers are now operating. In February 2003 the Electricity Regulator proposed to extend NIE's supply price control until 2007.

In April 2002 NIE, the grid operator for Northern Ireland and ESB National Grid, the transmission system operator in the Republic of Ireland opened three upgraded electricity interconnectors linking the electricity system of Northern Ireland with the Republic. The main North–South interconnector has a capacity to trade 2 x 600 MW of power, enough electricity to power several major towns.

The interconnectors enable trade of electricity between Northern Ireland and the Republic of Ireland and, through the Moyle Interconnector (Northern Ireland– Scotland) with Great Britain.

Regulation and other functions

The electricity and gas markets in Great Britain are regulated by Ofgem, which is governed by an authority whose powers are provided under the *Gas Act 1986*, the *Electricity Act 1989* and the *Utilities Act 2000*. Ofgem's principal objective is to protect the interests of gas and electricity customers, wherever appropriate, by promoting effective competition. Other duties and objectives include ensuring that reasonable demands for electricity are met and that electricity and gas licensees are able to finance their statutory obligations. Ofgem is responsible for setting performance standards for gas and electricity companies, and for price regulation of companies where competition has not yet fully emerged or where there is a natural monopoly.

The Offices of Director General of Electricity Supply and Director General of Gas for Northern Ireland were merged in April 2003 to form the Northern Ireland Authority for Energy Regulation.

Consumption

In 2002 final consumption of electricity in the United Kingdom (332.8 TWh) remained unchanged from 2001. Industrial and household consumption each accounted for around a third of this total, with the transport and service sectors accounting for the remainder. The sales of electricity through the public distribution system in the United Kingdom amounted to 319.8 TWh. The average price of electricity for domestic customers in the United Kingdom fell by 27 per cent in real terms (including VAT) between 1991 and 2002. Over the same period industrial customers saw prices drop by 34 per cent in real terms (37 per cent excluding the climate change levy, see page 432, which came into effect in April 2001).

The UK market is increasingly competitive. The number of companies generating electricity had risen from six at the time of privatisation to over 30 by October 2002. By December 2002, 9.2 million domestic electricity customers (37 per cent of total domestic customers) had changed from the electricity supplier they had at the time of deregulation. In 2002 these customers saved an average of £23 on their annual bill over customers who had not changed supplier. The average annual domestic electricity bill in the United Kingdom for a customer paying by standard credit (paying monthly in advance by cheque or cash, at a bank or post office) was estimated at £249 in 2002. As a result of the competitive market, industrial customers have saved £1.5 billion and domestic customers £500 million in lower electricity prices. In 2001 UK average domestic electricity prices including taxes were the fourth lowest in the European Union.

Energywatch

Energywatch was established under the *Utilities Act 2000* as an independent adviser for consumers in the gas and electricity markets in Great Britain. Working closely with Ofgem, it:

- investigates and resolves consumer complaints about energy companies;
- helps the energy companies improve their complaint and enquiry handling; and
- produces consumer information and advice.

The Government is working with Ofgem, Energywatch and the industry to ensure that the market works better and to improve consumers' confidence. Energywatch will also be seeking to ensure that both the industry as a whole and individual companies improve their performance in a range of other areas of customer contact, administration of companies and the management of accounts. It receives a grant from the DTI, which is derived from the licence fee that energy companies have to pay to the Government.

Generation

Non-nuclear power stations owned by the major UK power producers consumed 55 million tonnes of oil equivalent in 2002, of which coal accounted for 52 per cent and natural gas for 46 per cent. Other power companies (for which gas is the most widely used fuel) and over 2,000 small autogenerators (which produce power for their own use) have equal access with the major generators to the grid transmission and local distribution systems.

Combined cycle gas turbines (CCGTs)

In 2002 CCGT stations accounted for 35 per cent of the electricity generated by major power producers, compared with 16 per cent in 1995. This increase has been balanced by a fall in coal- and oil-fired generation. CCGT stations, favoured by the smaller, independent producers and using natural gas, offer cheap generation, and give out

Table 29.7 Generation by power stations owned by the major power producers in the UK

| | Electricity generated (GWh) | | | % in |
	1992	2001	2002	2002
Nuclear plant	73,269	89,870	88,043	*25*
Other conventional steam plant	217,149	136,154	132,922	*38*
Gas turbines and oil engines	410	2,472	2,011	*1*
Pumped storage plant	1,697	2,356	2,652	*1*
Natural flow hydro-electric plant	4,591	3,215	3,925	*1*
CCGTs	3,010	117,966	123,893	*35*
Renewables other than hydro	52	737	762	*–*
Total	**300,178**	**352,770**	**354,208**	***100***
Electricity supplied (net)[1]	282,301	333,781	334,785	

1 Electricity generated less electricity used at power stations (both electricity used on works and that used for pumping at pumped storage stations).
Source: Department of Trade and Industry

almost no sulphur dioxide and some 55 per cent less CO_2 per unit of electricity than coal-fired plant. At the end of March 2002 the United Kingdom had 27 such stations, with a total registered capacity of 20.5 GW (gigawatts).

Combined heat and power (CHP)

CHP plants are designed to produce both electricity and usable heat. They convert about 80 per cent of fuel input into useful energy, while conventional generation wastes at least half the energy content of the fuel and emits considerably more CO_2. CHP thus benefits the environment and contributes to UK climate change targets by reducing emissions of greenhouse gases. It is also used for cooling and chilling.

CHP can be fuelled by a variety of energy sources. It offers particular benefits where there is a regular need for heat as well as electricity – in hospitals, leisure centres and housing developments, for example – and can be provided on a local scale. About 84 per cent of CHP plants are less than 1 MW capacity. However, large-scale plants (above 10 MW) produce around 80 per cent of total CHP capacity. In 2002 over 1,500 CHP schemes supplied more than 4,700 MW of generating capacity and produced a total of 24.2 TWh. This represents nearly 7 per cent of UK total electricity generated (and 13 per cent of electricity consumption in the commercial and industrial sectors).

The Government aims to have at least 10,000 MW of CHP generating capacity by 2010. EU strategy is to double CHP's share of the EU electricity

market from 9 per cent in 2001 to 18 per cent by 2010. The Government promotes CHP by administering a quality assurance programme under the Energy Efficiency Best Practice Programme (EEBPP, see page 446), to assess CHP schemes for exemption from the climate change levy and for other benefits.

Trade

NGT and Electricité de France run a 2,000 MW cross-Channel cable link, allowing transmission of electricity between the two countries. The link has generally been used to supply 'baseload' power – which needs to be generated and available round the clock – from France to England. Imports met just over 2 per cent of UK electricity needs in 2002.

Scotland has a peak winter demand of under 6 GW and generating capacity of over 9 GW. The additional available capacity is used to supply England and Wales through transmission lines linking the Scottish and English grid systems. This interconnector's capacity is now 1,600 MW, with plans to increase it to 2,200 MW. The 60-kilometre 500 MW undersea interconnector between Scotland and Northern Ireland (see page 435) allows exports of power from Scotland.

Renewable energy

Renewable electricity can be generated from wind, water (hydro, wave and tidal power), sunlight (the direct conversion of solar radiation into electricity, called photovoltaics or PV), biomass (energy from forestry, crops or the biodegradable portion of waste) and from the earth's heat (geothermal energy). None of these forms of generation, except biomass, involves the production of carbon, and biomass generation produces only the carbon that the material has absorbed from the atmosphere while growing. The extensive coastline of the United Kingdom is highly exposed to ocean winds and currents, and offers particularly strong potential for the expansion of wind, wave and tidal power. See Table 29.8 for details of renewable energy sources.

Heat, as well as electricity, can be generated from renewable sources. Solar energy can heat water directly, either for hot water or for space heating in buildings. Heat from the ground, river water, sewage and even the air can be put through a heat exchange for both water and space heating.

The Government is putting in place measures designed to ensure that the United Kingdom exceeds its commitment to reduce emissions of greenhouse gases by 12.5 per cent below 1990 levels by 2010 (see page 278).

Growth in the proportion of electricity generated from renewable sources will play a vital role in these efforts. The United Kingdom produced much less of its electricity from renewable sources than most other countries in the European Union (Figure 29.9).

The Government's key measure to encourage renewable energy generation in the United

Figure 29.9 Proportion of electricity produced by renewable sources[1] in EU countries, 2001

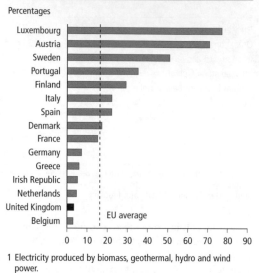

Percentages

1 Electricity produced by biomass, geothermal, hydro and wind power.
Source: Eurostat

Kingdom is the Renewables Obligation. The Orders for the Renewables Obligation for England and Wales and the associated Scottish Renewables Obligation came into force in April 2002. These Orders oblige all licensed electricity suppliers to ensure that a specified and growing proportion of their electricity comes from renewable sources. Initially set at 3.0 per cent for 2002/03, the level of the Obligation rose to 4.3 per cent for 2003/04 and will rise by annual steps to 10.4 per cent for 2010/11. Suppliers may meet their Obligation by supplying eligible renewable electricity to customers in Great Britain, by buying renewable obligation certificates reflecting renewable generation by others, or by paying a buy-out price to the electricity regulator, Ofgem, rather than supplying renewables electricity. The buy-out price is set at a level intended to make the last option unattractive.

By 2010 it is estimated that support from the Renewables Obligation and the benefit of exemption from the climate change levy will be worth around £1 billion a year to the UK renewable energy industry.

In addition the Government has allocated £348 million over the period 2001–04 for a direct support programme to bring forward newer forms

Table 29.8 Total use of renewables, UK

		Percentages	
	1990	2001	2002
Active solar heating and photovoltaics	1	0	1
Wind and wave	0	3	3
Hydro (small and large scale)	41	12	13
Landfill gas	7	28	28
Sewage gas	13	6	6
Wood (domestic and industrial)	16	16	15
Waste combustion	15	22	23
Other biofuels	9	13	12
Total (thousand tonnes of oil equivalent) (=100%)	**1,103**	**2,974**	**3,201**

Source: Department of Trade and Industry

of renewable energy through capital grants and research grants for offshore wind power, energy crops and small-scale biomass; a photovoltaics demonstration and installation scheme; support for wave and tidal demonstration projects; and a wide-ranging research and development programme.

A new government unit, Renewables UK, was established as part of the DTI in 2002 to help manufacturers of renewable equipment and technology. It seeks to raise awareness of the industry and to take advantage of transferable skills from the established oil and gas industry.

Wind energy

Wind energy generated at both onshore and offshore installations is expected to make the largest contribution to the expansion of renewable energy in the United Kingdom by 2010. At the end of 2002 UK wind generating capacity was 534 MW, up from 427 MW at the end of 2001. In 2002 these wind generators produced 1,256 gigawatt hours (GWh) of electricity, up from 965 GWh in 2001.

The first UK offshore wind farm, off the Northumberland coast at Blyth, consists of two 2 MW turbines and began generating power in 2000. In December 2000 the Government announced a first round of leasings of areas of the UK seabed for offshore wind farms. This resulted in 17 proposals from developers, and two wind farms are already under construction: at North Hoyle, near Rhyl, and Scroby Sands near Great Yarmouth. In total, this first round should result in more than 500 turbines, generating 1.5 GW, which is enough to power all the households in a city the size of Manchester.

A second round of offshore leasings, on a much larger scale was announced in July 2003, with each wind farm expected to comprise hundreds of turbines. Three strategic areas of shallow coastal waters, the ideal environment for siting offshore wind turbines, have been identified by the Crown Estate and the DTI as appropriate for development: the Thames Estuary; the Greater Wash; and the coastal waters of the North West of England.

It is estimated that by 2010 UK offshore wind farms could provide up to 6 GW of energy, enough to power 15 per cent of all households in the United Kingdom.

Biomass and waste

Agricultural biomass embraces both agricultural wastes, such as straw, and crops such as coppice wood grown specifically for electricity generation (energy crops).

Elean power station at Sutton (Cambridgeshire) is the first UK straw-fired power plant. With a potential output of 36 MW, it burns 200,000 tonnes of straw a year and generates enough power for 80,000 homes.

The Government is supporting biomass projects through a £66 million Bioenergy Capital Grants Scheme and a £29 million Energy Crops Scheme to help farmers and foresters establish energy crops.

Wave and tidal power

While their longer-term potential may be great, wave and tidal power are some way from commercialisation, with a number of competing designs. The United Kingdom is at the forefront of research in this field and, recognising this, the Government is supporting industry to develop prototype wave and tidal technologies in projects off the Western Isles, Orkney Islands and Devon coasts.

Photovoltaics (PV)

The costs of solar PV technology have fallen substantially over the last 25 years and are expected to fall further as global markets expand. However, costs continue to present a barrier to large-scale commercialisation. Under the first phase of its major PV demonstration programme, the Government is making £30 million available for projects of all sizes to install PV systems in buildings such as private homes, social housing, schools, offices, and community and visitor centres. It also supports PV field trials, and clusters of residential properties and large-scale public buildings have received around £15 million in grants to install and monitor PV systems.

Energy efficiency

The Government funds a number of energy efficiency programmes in the United Kingdom. These initiatives are an essential part of the UK strategy for reducing greenhouse gas emissions.

The Carbon Trust is a government-backed organisation that provides UK business and industry with advice on reducing carbon emissions. The Trust's funding is around £50 million a year from the Government – partly from recycled receipts from the climate change levy. It has taken over the non-domestic part of the Energy Efficiency Best Practice Programme (EEBPP) (see page 443), renamed as Action Energy and designed to provide free energy efficiency information and advice to business and public sector organisations.

The Energy Saving Trust is a non-profit organisation funded by the Government and the private sector. Its network of advice centres provide free and impartial energy efficiency advice to households and small businesses across the United Kingdom, including advice on grants available locally as well as general advice on how to make homes more energy efficient.

Under the Energy Efficiency Commitment (EEC) for 2002–05, electricity and gas suppliers must meet targets for the promotion of improvements in domestic energy efficiency. They do this by encouraging and assisting consumers to take up energy efficiency measures, such as insulation and heating measures, and energy efficiency appliances and light bulbs. As outlined in the Energy White Paper, the Government will consult on an expansion of the EEC to run from 2005 to at least 2008.

The Government's Market Transformation Programme (MTP), launched in 1998, aims to promote product systems and services which do less harm to the environment, using less energy, water and other resources. The MTP's focus has been on improving the delivered energy performance of domestic and non-domestic products, especially appliances, equipment and components. It seeks to achieve this by providing strategic support to a growing set of 'product' policies, which aim to encourage resource efficiency through measures such as reliable product information and raising minimum standards.

Fuel poverty

A household is considered to be living in fuel poverty when it needs to spend at least 10 per cent of its income on household fuel use in order to keep warm. Fuel poverty is generally more significant in the United Kingdom than in the rest of Europe, where homes have traditionally been built to high energy efficiency standards.

The UK Fuel Poverty Strategy was published in November 2001. It sets out policies for ending fuel poverty by 2010 in vulnerable households. In March 2003 the Government's first Annual Report on progress towards the objectives set out in the Fuel Poverty Strategy was published. The report suggests that fuel poverty fell by over 40 per cent across the United Kingdom between 1996 and 2001, from 5.5 million households to around 3 million. Falling fuel prices and increases in incomes are thought to be the main factors responsible for the reduction, with a smaller contribution from improved energy efficiency.

The Fuel Poverty Advisory Group is a non-departmental public body jointly sponsored by Defra and the DTI. Its primary task is to advise the Government on practical measures needed to achieve its target of eradicating fuel poverty in England.

The main programme for the provision of energy efficiency measures in England is the Warm Front Team (WFT). WFT has a budget of over £600 million for the period 2000–04 and is targeted specifically at vulnerable households in the private sector in receipt of an income-related benefit. It offers grants of up to:

- £1,500 for packages of insulation and heating improvements (except central heating) for low-income families with children under the age of 16 and for people who receive a disability benefit; and
- £2,500, including packages of insulation and central heating, for those aged 60 and over who receive an income-related benefit.

About 310,000 households received financial help from the WFT between April 2001 and March 2002.

The Welsh Assembly Government's fuel poverty programme, the Home Energy Efficiency Scheme (HEES), made over £12 million available during 2002/03 to tackle fuel poverty among an estimated 220,000 affected households. While broadly similar to Warm Front, there are a number of differences. Grant rates are £1,500 for a basic insulation package and £2,700 for heating and insulation. The heating package is available to single parents, to chronically sick or disabled people and to households including an occupant over 60 years of age.

Warm Deal, the Scottish Executive's insulation grant scheme, has provided energy efficiency packages to over 128,000 households since 1999, exceeding the Executive's target of assisting 100,000 homes. In addition, the Scotland Central Heating Programme has installed free central heating systems to over 10,000 households since 2001 and will provide a further 10,000 in 2003/04. People are eligible for the programme if they are over 60 years old, receive benefits or are on a low income.

In Northern Ireland, the Warm Homes Scheme (introduced in April 2001) has provided insulation and heating measures to nearly 10,000 homes in the private sector. By 2006 it is hoped that the scheme and initiatives to address fuel poverty in the social rented sector will have assisted at least 40,000 households.

Water supply

About three-quarters of the UK water supply is obtained from mountain lakes, reservoirs and river intakes, while a quarter is from underground sources (stored in layers of porous rock). South East England and East Anglia are more dependent on groundwater than any other parts of the United Kingdom. Scotland and Wales have a relative abundance of unpolluted water from upland sources. Northern Ireland also has plentiful supplies for domestic use and for industry.

Water put into the public water supply system (including industrial and other uses) in England and Wales averaged 15,783 megalitres a day (Ml/d) in 2001/02. An average of 2,409 Ml/d was supplied in Scotland, and for Northern Ireland the figure was 735 Ml/d. The average daily consumption per head in the United Kingdom was 149 litres.

Some 59,990 Ml/d were abstracted from all surface and groundwaters (for example, rivers and reservoirs) in England and Wales in 2000, of which public water supplies accounted for 17,052 Ml/d. About 13 per cent was used by households through the public water supply network. The electricity supply industry took 31,544 Ml/d and agriculture 151 Ml/d (excluding spray irrigation which accounted for a further 291 Ml/d).

England and Wales
The 26 water companies across England and Wales have statutory responsibilities for public water

supply, including quality and sufficiency. Ten of these companies are also responsible for public sewerage and sewage treatment.

The *Water Industry Act 1999* prohibits water companies from disconnecting households and other premises deemed vital to the community. It also makes provision for the protection of water customers on metered supplies who are vulnerable to hardship because of high usage for essential household purposes. These include a large number of low-income families, and elderly and disabled people.

In February 2003 the Government issued a consultation paper discussing a range of options for amending the Vulnerable Groups Regulations. The main recommendations are to extend assistance to include children up to the age of 18, instead of 16 as at present, and to extend the list of qualifying medical conditions. Any changes made to the regulations as a result of the consultation will come into effect in April 2004.

The average household bill in 2003/04 is £236. Since privatisation in 1989 average household bills for water have increased by 21 per cent.

The Water Bill, published in February 2003, commits the Government to the sustainable management and use of water resources within the United Kingdom. It would update the framework for abstraction licensing, and aims to promote greater water conservation and planning for the future by water companies. It would also introduce provisions to improve the regulatory regime and to extend the opportunity for competition in the water industry by allowing new entrants to supply non-household customers who consume large volumes of water.

The Director General of Water Services, who heads OFWAT (the Office of Water Services) is the economic regulator of the water industry in England and Wales. For the period 2000–05 the Director has set maximum prices for water and sewerage services. These price limits assumed water companies would deliver a capital investment programme of £15.6 billion at May 1999 prices during this period. This capital investment will maintain the water and sewerage systems, improve customer services, and cope with growth in demand. It also includes £7.4 billion on improving drinking water and environmental

447

water quality, chiefly to meet new EU and national standards.[2]

About 22 per cent of households and 90 per cent of commercial and industrial customers are currently charged for water on the basis of consumption measured by meter. Most homes are still charged according to the rateable value of their property. Provisions made in the *Water Industry Act 1999* have given customers increased choice over whether or not to have their bills based on a water meter. As a result, all water companies now supply and install free meters to households on request. In 2003/04 the average unmeasured bill for water is £116 and for sewerage it is £129. The average measured bill in 2003/04 is £96 for water and £113 for sewerage.

WaterVoice provides independent representation for all customers of the water and sewerage companies in England and Wales. Operating through regional committees, it represents the interests of customers in respect of price, services and value for money, and investigates complaints. The ten committee Chairmen form the WaterVoice Council, which deals with issues at national and European levels.

The Drinking Water Inspectorate (DWI) is responsible for ensuring that water companies in England and Wales supply wholesome water and comply with the requirements of the Regulations governing water supply. In 2002, 99.87 per cent of the 2.97 million drinking water samples taken met the quality standards. The Regulations were introduced to implement an EU Directive on drinking water quality. This Directive required new standards to be met by 2003, with the exception of the final standard for lead, which needs to be met by 2013.

The UN World Water Development Report, published in March 2003, found that the United Kingdom had the fourth best water quality of 122 selected countries, behind Finland, Canada and New Zealand.

Competition

In July 2002 the UK Government and the National Assembly for Wales issued a joint consultation paper seeking views on the possible extension of opportunities for competition, including the licensing of new entrants into the market for production and retail activities.

In March 2000 the *Competition Act 1998* (see page 346) came into force and strengthened regulators' powers against anti-competitive behaviour. The Act has enabled the shared use of distribution networks (often referred to as common carriage). By March 2002 nine 'inset appointments' had been made, under which a water company can seek to be appointed to supply a customer in another appointed water company's area.

Water leakage

Targets are set each year for water companies in England and Wales to reduce leakage. In 2001/02, 3,414 megalitres a day of water put into the supply in England and Wales were lost through leakage – 33 per cent lower than in the peak year of 1994/95 but 5 per cent higher than in 2000/01.

Scotland

Scottish Water was created from the merger of the three former water authorities in Scotland as a result of the *Water Industry (Scotland) Act 2002*. It provides water and waste water services to household and business customers across one-third of the land area in Britain. Scottish Water remains in the public sector and is answerable to the Scottish Parliament.

Scottish Water is the fourth largest water service provider in the United Kingdom and the 12th biggest business in Scotland by turnover. Its assets are valued at £13 billion, and the company serves over 5 million customers with drinking water and also provides sewerage services. It supplies approximately 2.5 billion litres of water a day.

Scottish Water is accountable to three regulatory bodies: the Water Industry Commissioner for Scotland, the Scottish Environment Protection Agency, and the Drinking Water Quality Regulator for Scotland.

Northern Ireland

The Water Service is an executive agency of the Department for Regional Development. It is responsible for the supply and distribution of drinking water and the provision of sewerage services to over 730,000 domestic, agricultural, commercial and business customers throughout

---

2 The 2000–05 programme includes tightening sewage effluent quality standards to improve river estuaries and coastal waters, reducing the impact of storm overflows from the sewerage system and renovating iron water mains to reduce discoloured water.

Non-energy minerals in the United Kingdom

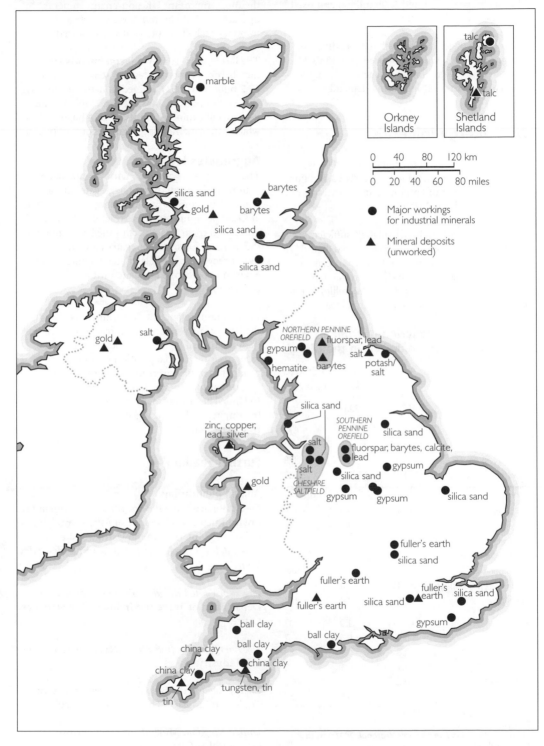

Northern Ireland. It has an annual budget, before capital charges, of around £300 million and fixed assets valued at £4.9 billion.

The Water Service envisages that expenditure of around £3 billion will be required over 15 to 20 years to bring water and sewerage services up to standard and to meet increasing demand.

Non-energy minerals

UK output of non-energy minerals in 2001 was 312.8 million tonnes, valued at nearly £2.5 billion. The total number of employees in the extractive industry was about 25,000.

The United Kingdom is virtually self-sufficient in construction minerals, and produces and exports several industrial minerals, notably china clay (kaolin), ball clay, potash and salt. Production of china clay, the largest export, was 2.2 million tonnes in 2001, of which 88 per cent was exported.

Table 29.10 Production of some of the main non-energy minerals in the UK

	Million tonnes		Production value 2001
	1991	2001	(£ million)
Sand and gravel	106.4	101.4	677
Silica sand	4.2	3.8	54
Igneous rock	53.9	51.5	328
Limestone and dolomite	114.3	102.6	702
Chalk	10.3	8.2	69
Sandstone	16.6	20.0	119
Gypsum	2.5	1.7	15
Salt comprising rock salt, salt in brine and salt from brine	6.8	6.1	152
Common clay and shale[1]	13.1	10.4	19
China clay[2]	2.5	2.2	187
Ball clay	0.7	1.0	47
Fireclay[1]	0.9	0.5	7
Potash	0.8	0.9	80
Fluorspar	0.1	0.1	5
Fuller's earth[2]	0.2	0.1	5
Slate	0.4	0.6	30

1 Great Britain only.
2 Moisture-free basis.
Source: *United Kingdom Minerals Yearbook 2001*, British Geological Survey

The Boulby potash mine in north-east England is the most important UK non-energy mineral operation. Production in 2002 was 900,000 tonnes, of which 50 per cent was exported.

The largest non-energy mineral imports are metals (ores, concentrates and scrap – valued at £2.2 billion in 2001), refined non-ferrous metals (£3.9 billion), iron and steel (£2.3 billion), and non-metallic mineral products (£6.4 billion, of which rough diamonds accounted for £4.2 billion).

Aggregates levy

The aggregates levy is an environmental tax on the commercial exploitation of aggregates in the United Kingdom. It was introduced in April 2002 at £1.60 per tonne on the extraction of sand, gravel and rock. The object of the levy is to reduce the demand for such aggregates and encourage the use of recycled materials, thereby reducing the environmental costs associated with quarrying operations.

In Northern Ireland the Government is phasing in the levy over five years for aggregates used in the manufacture of processed products. This relief recognises the special position of processed product manufacturers in Northern Ireland, because of the land boundary with the Republic of Ireland. The Government is continuing to review the impact of the phasing-in of the levy in Northern Ireland.

Further reading

Annual publications

Digest of Environmental Statistics. Department for Environment, Food and Rural Affairs. Available only on the Internet on the Defra website (*www.defra.gov.uk/environment/statistics/des/index. htm*).

Digest of United Kingdom Energy Statistics. Department of Trade and Industry. The Stationery Office.

UK Energy Sector Indicators. Department of Trade and Industry.

Energy Report (the Blue Book). Department of Trade and Industry. The Stationery Office.

United Kingdom Minerals Yearbook. British Geological Survey.

Other

Our energy future: creating a low carbon economy.
Cm 5761. Department of Trade and Industry. The
Stationery Office, 2003.

*Managing the Nuclear Legacy – a strategy for
action.* Cm 5552. Department of Trade and
Industry. The Stationery Office, 2002.

*Water Resources (Environmental Impact
Assessment) (England and Wales) Regulations 2003*
SI No. 164. Defra, 2003.

Websites

Department of Trade and Industry
www.dti.gov.uk

**Department for Environment, Food and Rural
Affairs**
www.defra.gov.uk

Northern Ireland Executive
www.northernireland.gov.uk

Scottish Executive
www.scotland.gov.uk

National Assembly for Wales
www.wales.gov.uk

British Geological Survey
www.bgs.ac.uk

BGS Minerals website
www.mineralsuk.com

Energywatch
www.energywatch.org.uk

Natural Environment Research Council
www.nerc.ac.uk

Office of Gas and Electricity Markets
www.ofgem.gov.uk

The Coal Authority
www.coal.gov.uk

The UK Atomic Energy Authority
www.ukaea.org.uk

European Commission energy website
www.europa.eu.int/comm/energy

WWW.

30 Financial and other services

The service sector in the United Kingdom continues to grow and accounted for 71 per cent of gross value added (GVA, see glossary) at current basic prices in 2001. There were over 23.2 million workforce jobs in the sector in December 2002, representing 79 per cent of all jobs.

Financial services and the economy

The financial services sector accounted for around 5 per cent of GVA in 2001, and over 1.0 million employee jobs in December 2002. UK financial sector net exports reached a record £15.3 billion in 2002.

Historically, UK financial services have been centred on the 'Square Mile' in the City of London, and this remains broadly the case. Major financial institutions and markets in the City include the Bank of England, the London Stock Exchange and Lloyd's insurance market. London is one of the three main financial centres in the world, along with New York and Tokyo, and is the premier financial centre in Europe. Scotland (Edinburgh and Glasgow) is the second financial centre in the United Kingdom, and one of the main European centres for institutional fund management – at the end of 2002 nearly £300 billion of funds were under management in Scotland. Other sizeable UK financial centres are Leeds, Manchester, Bristol and Birmingham.

International Financial Services London (IFSL) (*www.ifsl.org.uk*) promotes the international activities of UK-based financial institutions and

Table 30.1 Index numbers of gross value added[1] at basic prices, service industries, UK

1995=100

	2001	2002	% change
Wholesale and retail trade	127.2	133.6	5.0
Hotels and restaurants	97.4	96.3	−1.1
Transport, storage and communication	147.2	149.4	1.5
Financial intermediation[2]	127.8	131.0	2.5
Real estate, renting and business activities	136.9	140.7	2.8
Public administration and defence	99.6	101.5	1.9
Education	107.6	108.6	0.9
Health and social work	118.7	123.9	4.4
Other services	125.2	127.4	1.8
Adjustment for financial services	144.8	151.8	4.8
Total service industries	124.9	128.2	2.6

1 See glossary.
2 Operations of institutions such as banks, building societies, insurance companies, pension funds, unit trusts and investment trusts.
Source: Office for National Statistics

professional and business services. It also seeks to raise awareness of the United Kingdom's leading role in international financial markets and highlight the major contribution of financial services to the UK economy.

Bank of England

The Bank of England, sometimes known as the 'Old Lady of Threadneedle Street', was founded in 1694 and nationalised in 1946. It gained operational independence in 1997 when it was given responsibility for setting the United Kingdom's official interest rate (see page 340). It is the UK central bank and is responsible for promoting and maintaining a stable and efficient monetary and financial framework. In pursuing this goal, it has three main purposes:

- maintaining the integrity and value of the currency;
- maintaining the stability of the financial system; and
- seeking to ensure the effectiveness of the financial services sector.

Under the *Bank of England Act 1998*, the Court of Directors is responsible for managing the affairs of the Bank, apart from the formulation of monetary policy. The Court comprises the Governor, two Deputy Governors and 16 non-executive directors. It is required to report annually to the Chancellor of the Exchequer.

Monetary policy framework
The Bank's monetary policy objective is to deliver price stability and, subject to that, to support the Government's economic policy, including its growth and employment objectives. Price stability is defined by the Government's inflation target (see page 338). Responsibility for meeting this target and for setting interest rates rests with the Bank's Monetary Policy Committee, comprising the Governor, the two Deputy Governors, two further Bank executives and four external members appointed by the Chancellor of the Exchequer. The Committee meets every month and decisions on interest rates are announced at noon immediately after the meeting; minutes of the meetings, including a record of any vote, are normally published on the second Wednesday after each meeting. The Committee is accountable to the Bank's Court of Directors, to the Government and to the public through Parliament.

Financial stability
Under the Memorandum of Understanding between HM Treasury, the Bank and the Financial Services Authority (FSA), the Bank is responsible for the overall stability of the UK financial system as a whole, and its Financial Stability Committee oversees its work in this area. In exceptional circumstances, in consultation with the FSA and HM Treasury as appropriate, the Bank may provide, or assist in arranging, last-resort financial support where this is needed to avoid systematic damage to the financial system. It also oversees the effectiveness of the financial sector in meeting the needs of customers and in maintaining the sector's international competitiveness.

Other main functions
Through its daily operations in the money market, the Bank supplies the funds that the banking system as a whole needs to achieve balance at the end of each day. By setting the interest rate for these operations, the Bank influences the general level of interest rates, as the interest rate at which the Bank deals is quickly passed on through the financial system. This in turn affects the whole pattern of interest rates across the UK economy.

The Bank provides banking services to its customers, principally the Government, the banking system and other central banks. It plays a key role in payment and settlement systems.

Banknotes and coins
The Bank is the sole issuer of currency notes in England and Wales, and although banks in Scotland and Northern Ireland[1] issue their own notes, most of these must be covered, pound for pound, by Bank of England notes or other assets. Net profits from the Bank of England note issue are paid over to the Government.

The provision of UK coinage is the responsibility of the Royal Mint (*www.royalmint.com*), based at Llantrisant, mid-Glamorgan. At the end of 2002 there were an estimated 24.8 billion coins in circulation in the United Kingdom, with a face value of £3.0 billion. The number of coins issued during 2002/03 amounted to 1.6 billion.

---

1 In Scotland these comprise the Bank of Scotland, Royal Bank of Scotland and Clydesdale Bank, and in Northern Ireland the Bank of Ireland, First Trust Bank, Northern Bank and Ulster Bank.

Recent banknote issues
A new Bank of England £20 note was issued on 22 June 1999 featuring a portrait of Sir Edward Elgar. This was followed on 7 November 2000 by a new £10 note, featuring Charles Darwin, and on 20 May 2002 by a new £5 note, featuring Elizabeth Fry.

Table 30.2 Banknotes in circulation, UK

	Value of notes in circulation end-February 2003 (£ billion)	Number of new notes issued in year to end-February 2003 (million)
£5	1.1	222
£10	5.9	390
£20	18.1	405
£50	5.4	12
Other notes[1]	3.3	–
Total	**33.9**	**1,029**

1 Includes higher value notes used internally in the Bank, for example, as cover for the note issues of banks of issue in Scotland and Northern Ireland in excess of their permitted issues.
Source: Bank of England

Banking services

The United Kingdom is a major banking centre, and UK banking sector assets were valued at £3,600 billion at the end of 2002. This was about three times the level in 1991, with just over half being owned by overseas banks, mostly from the EU. At the end of March 2003 there were 185 authorised banks incorporated in the United Kingdom, 92 banks authorised in the European Economic Area (EEA) and a further 103 authorised branches of banks incorporated outside the EEA. In addition, 284 branches of European-authorised institutions, though not located in the United Kingdom, were entitled to accept deposits in the United Kingdom.

'Retail' banking primarily caters for personal customers and small businesses. Nearly all banks also engage in some 'wholesale' activities, which involve taking larger deposits, deploying funds in money-market instruments, and making corporate loans and investments, while some concentrate on wholesale business. Banks feature strongly among the top UK companies. Four of the top ten companies by market capitalisation on 28 March 2003 were banks: HSBC, Royal Bank of Scotland, HBOS and Barclays.

Retail bank services include current accounts, savings accounts, loan arrangements, credit and debit cards, mortgages, insurance, investment products, share-dealing services and 'wealth management' services. Around 93 per cent of households in Great Britain have at least one adult member with a bank or building society or other savings account (see Table 30.3).

The universal banking programme, giving access to basic bank accounts and a Post Office card account, became available through post offices from April 2003. These services are intended to tackle financial exclusion and bring those people without bank accounts into the financial mainstream, while ensuring that benefit recipients and pensioners can continue to receive their money in cash at their local post office when such payments are automated. Automated payments commenced in April 2003 and will be completed by October 2005. The major financial institutions have agreed to contribute by making their own basic bank accounts – 17 currently – accessible at post offices and by making a contribution of £182 million to the cost of running the Post Office card account.

Table 30.3 Households[1] by type of saving in 2001/02, Great Britain

	Percentages
Type of account	
Current account	88
Post Office account	7
Tax Exempt Special Savings Account (TESSA)	11
Individual Savings Account (ISA)	29
Other bank or building society accounts (excluding current accounts, ISAs and TESSAs)	57
Stocks and shares/member of a share club	25
Personal Equity Plans	10
Unit trusts or investment trusts	6
Gilt-edged stock	1
Premium Bonds	24
National Savings Bonds	4
Company share scheme/profit-sharing scheme	5
Save as you earn	1
Any type of account	93

1 Households in which at least one adult member has an account.
Source: Family Resources Survey, Department for Work and Pensions

The major retail banks have traditionally operated through local branches, although the number of such branches has declined by around 12 per cent in the five years to 2001. The British Bankers' Association estimates that 30 per cent of personal accounts are accessed by telephone and 12 per cent via the Internet. According to APACS (see page 456), over 16 million people in the United Kingdom used the telephone, the Internet or interactive digital television to access their current accounts in 2002. About a third of these used remote banking to initiate 72 million payments, the most popular application being the settlement of credit card bills. The United Kingdom is the largest European online banking market. Internet banking is offered either as an additional option for customers or as a separate stand-alone facility.

Supervision

The Financial Services Authority (see page 464) is responsible for regulating banks. They are required to meet minimum standards on the integrity and competence of directors and management, the adequacy of capital and cash flow, and the systems and controls to deal with the risks they experience. Should a bank fail to meet the criteria, its activities may be restricted, or it may be closed. These arrangements are intended to strengthen, but not guarantee, the protection of bank depositors, thereby increasing confidence in the banking system as a whole.

The Banking Code is an additional, voluntary, arrangement, under which the relationship between banks and building societies and their customers is improved. The independent Banking Code Standards Board assesses compliance with the Code.

Competition

In March 2002 the Competition Commission issued a report on small business banking, which found that there was a complex monopoly in the supply of banking services to small and medium-sized enterprises (SMEs). It identified practices carried out by the main UK clearing groups that restricted or distorted competition and operated against the public interest. It recommended a number of changes to the banks' practices with the intention of reducing barriers to entry, improving choice for SMEs and making it easier to switch accounts between banks. The Competition Commission also identified the four main clearing groups in England and Wales as acting against the public interest through excessive

pricing. The Commission recommended that these banks be required to offer interest-free money transmission services on business current accounts. The Government accepted the Commission's report and recommendations, and the Office of Fair Trading (see page 346) has negotiated undertakings from the banks on the proposed remedies.

Investment and private banking

London is a major international financial centre for investment banking, accounting for an estimated 50 per cent of such activity in Europe. Global banks dominate the international market, and most have headquarters or a major office in London.

Investment banks offer a range of professional financial services, including corporate finance and asset management. Advice on mergers and acquisitions accounted for 57 per cent of investment banking revenue originating in the United Kingdom in 2001. Equity underwriting accounted for a further 25 per cent, and banks facilitate a wide range of equity finance transactions, such as flotations, the issue or placing of new shares, and management buy-outs.

The United Kingdom, along with the United States and Switzerland, is one of the top centres for private banking. Some £280 billion of private client securities were being managed by banks, fund managers and stockbrokers in the United Kingdom in 2002.

Building societies

Building societies are mutual institutions, owned by, and run for, their members. As well as their retail deposit-taking services, they specialise in housing finance, making long-term mortgage loans against the security of property – usually private dwellings purchased for owner-occupation. In recent years a number of building societies have diversified and now offer a wide range of personal financial services. The chief requirements for societies are that:

- their principal purpose is making loans which are secured on residential property and are funded substantially by their members;
- at least 75 per cent per cent of lending has to be on the security of housing; and
- a minimum of 50 per cent of funds must be in the form of deposits made by individual members.

At the end of 2002 there were 65 building societies in the United Kingdom, all of which were members of the Building Societies Association (BSA) (*www.bsa.org.uk*), with total assets of over £185 billion. They employed over 38,000 full-time and part-time staff in head offices and had around 2,100 branches. About 15 million adults had building society savings accounts and over 2.5 million were buying their own homes with the help of building society loans. The largest society is the Nationwide, with group assets of £85 billion in April 2003, followed by the Britannia and Yorkshire (£19 billion and £14 billion respectively at the end of 2002).

The number of societies has fallen from 273 in 1980 to 101 in 1990 and 65 in 2002 as a result of mergers. In addition, several large societies – starting with the Abbey National in 1989 – have given up their mutual status and become banks. Many of the remaining societies have taken steps to defend their mutual status, for example by requiring new members to assign to charity any 'windfall' payments arising from a conversion.

Payment systems

Apart from credit and debit card arrangements, three companies manage the major UK payment clearing systems, operating within the UK trade association for payments, APACS (Association for Payment Clearing Services) (*www.apacs.org.uk*):

- Cheque and Credit Clearing Company, responsible for the bulk clearing of cheques and paper credits throughout Great Britain – cheque and credit payments in Northern Ireland are processed locally;
- CHAPS (Clearing House Automated Payment System), an electronic transfer system for same-day payments from bank to bank; and
- BACS (Bankers' Automated Clearing Services), responsible for bulk electronic clearing of direct credits, direct debits and standing orders.

A total of 26 banks and building societies are members of one or more clearing companies, while several hundred others obtain access to APACS clearing through agency arrangements with one of the members.

The Government plans legislation to establish a new regulatory framework governing UK payment systems. As a result, the Office of Fair Trading (see page 346) would have new powers to promote competition in payment systems.

Trends in financial transactions

The nature of financial transactions has undergone major changes since the first plastic cards appeared in 1966. Most small non-regular payments are still made by cash, but the trend is away from cash and cheques towards greater use of plastic cards (see Table 30.4).

Consumers now acquire more than half their cash through withdrawals from automated teller machines (ATMs), which in 2002 dispensed £136 billion in 2.3 billion transactions. About two-thirds of adults use ATMs regularly, making on average 70 withdrawals a year.

In 2002 direct debit and standing order payments accounted for 62 per cent of regular bill payments in the United Kingdom, and 73 per cent of adults have set up at least one direct debit or standing order. Many mortgage and other loan repayments and life insurance contributions are made by this means, as are the majority of utility and council tax bills. Direct debit payments rose by 6 per cent to reach 2.3 billion in 2002.

Table 30.4 Transaction trends in the UK

	1992	1997	2002
Transaction volumes (million)			
All plastic card purchases	1,316	2,759	4,814
of which:			
Debit card	522	1,503	2,994
Credit and charge card	724	1,128	1,687
Plastic card withdrawals at			
ATMs and counters	1,199	1,809	2,342
Direct debits, standing orders,			
direct credits and CHAPS	1,962	2,826	3,929
Cheques	3,728	3,083	2,393
of which:			
For payment	3,332	2,838	2,246
For cash acquisition	396	245	147
Total non-cash transactions	8,205	10,477	13,478
Cash payments[1]	27,845	25,540	26,601
Post Office Order Book payments			
and passbook withdrawals	1,108	1,066	687
Total transaction volumes	**37,158**	**37,083**	**40,766**
UK ATM network			
Number of ATMs	18,700	23,200	40,800
ATM withdrawals (million)	1,169	1,745	2,268
ATM cards (million)	49	60	83

1 Estimated figures.
Source: Association for Payment Clearing Services

Plastic cards

According to APACS, there were 147.5 million plastic cards in issue in 2002 and 7.2 billion plastic card transactions in the United Kingdom, when 91 per cent of adults held one or more cards.

Debit cards, where payments are deducted directly from the purchaser's bank or building society account, were first introduced in the United Kingdom in 1987. At the end of 2002, 59.4 million were in issue. They are usually combined with other facilities such as ATM and cheque guarantee functions. The total number of debit card purchases was almost 3.0 billion in 2002, averaging £36 per transaction. Over 40 per cent of these payments were made at supermarkets.

At the end of 2002 there were 58.8 million *credit cards* and 4.3 million *charge cards* in use in the United Kingdom. There are many credit card providers and over 1,000 different brands of card. Increasingly popular as a source of consumer credit, they are also the most common way for adults to buy goods and services using the Internet.

UK plastic card fraud reached a record level of £425 million in 2002, with counterfeit cards, at 35 per cent, accounting for the largest category of fraud. To combat this, banks are investing in new systems, in which information is contained on a microchip embedded in the card. By the end of 2002, more than 42 million of the new cards had been issued. Cash machines and point-of-sale terminals are also being upgraded. The first UK 'chip and PIN' (personal identification number) transaction trials started in Northampton in May 2003. This is the first phase of a nationwide programme that will see more than 850,000 retailer terminals and 40,000 cash machines upgraded, and 120 million cards issued over 18 months. By 2005, the vast majority of face-to-face UK credit and debit card transactions will be verified by the customer keying in his or her PIN rather than by signing a receipt.

National Savings and Investments

National Savings and Investments (NS&I) (*www.nationalsavings.co.uk*), formerly National Savings, is an executive agency of the Chancellor of the Exchequer. It is a source of finance for government borrowing, offering personal savers a range of savings and investments. The *Finance Act 2003* includes a number of provisions in respect of NS&I. For example, it should soon be able to issue

plastic cards so that customers can make cash withdrawals from ATMs.

Gross sales of NS&I products (including accrued interest) were £12 billion in 2002/03 and £63 billion was invested in NS&I products at March 2003. Savings products include Premium Bonds (see box), Savings Certificates (both Fixed Interest and Index-linked), Pensioners Guaranteed Income Bonds, Capital Bonds, Children's Bonus Bonds, cash mini ISAs (see page 461), Ordinary and Investment Accounts (where deposits and withdrawals can be made at post offices) and the Guaranteed Equity Bond, launched in 2002, where the investor's return is linked to the performance of the FTSE 100 index.

Premium Bonds

These offer tax-free prizes – instead of interest – in a monthly draw. Originally launched in the 1956 Budget, the maximum individual holding was set at £500. The first draw took place on 2 June 1957, with winning numbers picked by ERNIE (Electronic Random Number Indicator Equipment), an early computer, which took ten days to complete the first draw. The latest ERNIE takes just six hours. The maximum holding was increased in May 2003 from £20,000 to £30,000. Prizes each month range from £50 to the £1 million top prize. Premium Bonds are held by around 23 million people in the United Kingdom and abroad. At the end of June 2003 there were 385,000 unclaimed prizes, worth £23 million.

Friendly societies

Friendly societies are mutual organisations – set up and owned by their members and run for their benefit – providing a wide range of savings, assurance, insurance and healthcare products, often tax-free. The representative body for the United Kingdom is the Association of Friendly Societies (*www.afs.org.uk*). There were 232 friendly societies at the end of November 2002.

Credit unions

Credit unions are financial co-operatives, established under the *Credit Unions Act 1979*, owned and controlled by their members, who save in a common fund. The money saved is used to make low-interest loans to other credit union members. The Association of British Credit Unions Ltd (ABCUL) (*www.abcul.org*) is the main trade association in Great Britain. Around 686 credit unions are registered, with membership of about 366,000 and savings balances of around £224 million. In Northern Ireland, credit unions are served by the Irish League of Credit Unions, which covers the whole of Ireland.

Responsibility for registration and supervision of credit unions lies with the Financial Services Authority (see page 464) and a new regulatory regime took effect in July 2002. Among its key features are the need to meet a basic test of solvency and maintain a level of initial capital and a minimum liquidity ratio, while for the first time members have protection for their deposits through the Financial Services Compensation Scheme (see page 464).

Private equity/venture capital
Private equity/venture capital companies offer medium- and long-term equity financing for new and developing businesses, management buy-outs and buy-ins, and company rescues. The British Venture Capital Association (BVCA) (*www.bvca.co.uk*) represents private equity and venture capital sources in the United Kingdom. According to its report on investment activity for 2002 (based on data provided by 160 of the 164 firms that were then members), UK private equity and venture capital firms invested in 1,459 businesses worldwide, to a value of £5,466 million. Of this investment, £4,480 million (82 per cent) was in the United Kingdom. The Government is encouraging the further development of venture capital, including new Regional Venture Capital Funds.

Other credit and financial services
Finance houses and leasing companies provide consumer credit, business finance and leasing, and motor finance. There are 106 full and 81 associate members of the Finance and Leasing Association (*www.fla.org.uk*), achieving new business worth £81 billion in 2002, £58 billion of which was credit granted to private individuals.

Factoring and invoice discounting comprises a range of financial services, including credit management and finance in exchange for outstanding invoices. Member companies of the Factors & Discounters Association (*www.factors.org.uk*) handled business worth £104 billion in 2002, 18 per cent higher than in 2001, of which £83 billion was domestic invoice discounting. They had over 33,500 clients at the end of 2002.

Insurance

The UK insurance industry is the largest in Europe and the third largest in the world. In 2002 it employed 360,000 people in insurance and reinsurance companies, Lloyd's of London, insurance brokers and other related activities, representing a third of all financial services jobs. About 50,000 of these jobs are supported by the London Market, a unique international wholesale insurance market.

Net worldwide premiums generated by the UK insurance industry reached £161 billion in 2002, according to the Association of British Insurers (ABI) (*www.abi.org.uk*). UK risks were £126 billion and overseas risks £35 billion. The industry has over £1,000 billion invested in company shares and other assets.

Main types of insurance
Insurance can be long-term, such as life insurance, pensions and savings, where contracts may be for many years; and general, such as motor, household and commercial insurance, where contracts are usually for up to one year only. Most insurance companies reinsure their risks; this performs an important function in spreading losses and in helping companies manage their businesses.

UK long-term insurance has been rising more rapidly than general insurance, accounting for £122 billion of net worldwide premiums by UK industry in 2002, compared with £39 billion of general insurance. Life insurance accounted for 37 per cent of long-term premium income, occupational pensions 32 per cent and individual pensions 29 per cent. About 49 per cent of households have life insurance cover.

Motor insurance accounts for over a third of UK company market general insurance premiums. Other important areas are property insurance, and accident and health insurance. Independent intermediaries distributed 55 per cent of general insurance premiums in 2002, direct selling 20 per cent, company agents 8 per cent, and banks and building societies 7 per cent. Direct selling in motor insurance has increased, reflecting the growth of insurers offering telephone-based and Internet-based services.

Structure of the industry
At the end of 2002, 806 companies were authorised to conduct insurance business in the

United Kingdom. Almost 600 companies carry on general business only, 160 are authorised for long-term business and 54 are authorised to conduct both types of business. About 400 companies belong to the ABI.

The industry includes both public limited companies and mutual institutions (companies owned by their policyholders), although the mutual sector has gradually contracted. The biggest insurance group in the United Kingdom in 2002 was Aviva, with net premium income of nearly £14 billion.

Insurance firms and markets have been affected by weak equity markets and by events such as the destruction of the New York World Trade Centre in September 2001. The Financial Services Authority has relaxed some of its requirements on solvency to ease the position for insurance companies. Its prime focus in these market conditions is on life insurance companies maintaining financial resources sufficient to meet their responsibilities to policyholders, including their ability to absorb any market falls that may occur.

The London Market

The London Insurance Market (London Market) is a distinct part of the UK insurance and reinsurance industry centred on the City of London. It is the main centre for world reinsurance business and for energy, marine, aviation, satellite and other forms of transport insurance. It comprises insurance and reinsurance companies, Lloyd's syndicates, Protection and Indemnity clubs (mutual insurers for shipowners) and brokers who handle most of the business. The business traded is mainly non-life (general) insurance and reinsurance, with an increasing emphasis on high-exposure risks.

Estimated gross premiums of the London Market from reported returns were £22 billion in 2002. Virtually all companies participating in its company sector are members of the International Underwriting Association of London (IUA) (*www.iua.co.uk*), which in August 2003 had 56 members. Over three-quarters of companies operating in the London Market are overseas-owned.

Lloyd's of London

Lloyd's of London (*www.lloydsoflondon.com*) is the world's leading insurance market, with a capacity to accept premiums of over £14 billion in 2003. It provides specialist insurance services to businesses in over 120 countries and is the world's second largest commercial insurer and sixth largest reinsurance group. In 2003, 71 syndicates were underwriting insurance at Lloyd's, covering many speciality areas, including marine, aviation, catastrophe, professional indemnity and motor. Syndicates, staffed by underwriters, compete for business and cover either all or a portion of the risk. They are run by managing agents who have a franchise to operate within the Lloyd's market.

Lloyd's is not a company but an incorporated society of insurers. It is administered by the Council of Lloyd's and a Franchise Board; the latter replaced its Regulatory and Market Boards in January 2003.

In 2002 Lloyd's reported a profit of £0.8 billion on an annually accounted basis, and an initial projection of profit of £1.5 billion on a three-year accounted basis for the 2002 underwriting year. The total resources of the society and its members increased by 23 per cent from £21.9 billion in 2001 to £27.0 billion in 2002.

Investment

The United Kingdom has considerable expertise in fund management, which involves managing funds on behalf of investors, or advising them how best to invest their money. The main institutional groups and asset types are shown in Table 30.5. The assets of these institutions were valued at £1,838 billion at the end of 2001, compared with £1,920 billion at the end of 2000.

The Myners review of institutional investment was published in 2001 and the Government subsequently confirmed that it would take forward all the review's recommendations, including revised Codes of Investment Principles to encourage diversity in investment approaches. Since then:
- the Institutional Shareholders' Committee (ISC) has published guidance for fund managers (and their clients) on shareholder activism, helping them to maximise the value of their clients' equity holdings and the productivity of the companies they own. In 2004 the Government will review the extent to which the ISC's statement of principles has

Table 30.5 Assets and net investment by UK insurance companies, pension funds and trusts

£ billion

	Holdings at end of 2001 (market values)	Net investment in 2002 (cash values)
Long-term insurance funds	925.0	30.0
General insurance funds	95.3	11.3
Self-administered pension funds	713.6	4.0
Investment trusts	58.1	−1.9
Unit and property unit trusts[1]	215.3	15.5
Consolidation adjustment[2]	−169.0	−6.6
Total	**1,838.3**	**52.3**
of which:		
UK company securities	871.9	20.7
Government sterling securities (gilts)	223.7	10.7
Overseas company and government securities	420.3	29.8

1 Including open-ended investment companies (OEICs).
2 Adjustment to take account of investment of one institutional group in another.
Source: Office for National Statistics

been successful in delivering behavioural change;

- the Green Paper on pensions (see page 149), published in December 2002, restated the Government's commitment to legislate to require more expertise in pension scheme trustees, with the aim of improving the investment decisions taken for the huge blocks of capital controlled by the occupational pension scheme sector;
- the Government has launched a major review, to run to the end of 2003, of the effectiveness of the Myners principles in driving changes in investment decision-making by occupational pension schemes. The review will inform future decisions on the need for further action to improve the operation of the institutional market; and
- the Financial Services Authority is consulting on proposals on 'soft commission' (the practice by which a broker agrees to pay for the supply of services from a third party to a fund manager in return for an agreed volume of business at an agreed commission rate) and 'bundling' (the provision by brokers of other in-house services, such as research, together with dealing in securities in a single

commission charge) of transaction costs by brokers, following discussions of these issues in the Myners report.

Pension funds

At the end of 2001 total holdings of UK self-administered pension funds were £714 billion, compared with £768 billion at the end of 2000. Pension funds are major investors in securities markets, holding around 17 per cent of securities listed on the London Stock Exchange. Funds are managed mainly by the investment management houses.

Unit trusts and open-ended investment companies (OEICs)

Authorised unit trusts and OEICs pool investors' money in funds divided into units or shares of equal size, enabling people with relatively small amounts of money to benefit from diversified and managed portfolios. Most unit trusts are general funds, investing in a wide variety of UK or international securities, but there are also many specialist funds. OEICs, set up in 1997, are similar to unit trusts, but investors buy shares in the fund rather than units.

At the end of 2002 there were a total of 1,957 funds in the United Kingdom, of which 931 were OEICs, and 130 companies, of which 71 were OEIC providers. Total funds under management were valued at £195 billion, compared with £236 billion at the end of 2001. OEICs accounted for £106 billion at the end of 2002, Personal Equity Plans £35 billion and Individual Savings Accounts (ISAs) £23 billion.

The Investment Management Association (IMA) (*www.investmentuk.org*) represents the UK asset management industry. It was formed in February 2002 following the merger of the Association of Unit Trusts and Investment Funds and the Fund Managers' Association.

Investment trusts

Investment trusts are companies that invest in the shares of other companies. They are listed on the London Stock Exchange and their shares can be bought and sold in the same way as other companies. Assets are purchased mainly out of shareholders' funds, although investment trusts are also allowed to borrow money for investment.

At the end of March 2003 there were 372 investment trusts, forming the largest listed sector of the London Stock Exchange, with assets worth £46 billion and market capitalisation of £31 billion. Members of the Association of Investment Trust Companies (*www.aitc.co.uk*) accounted for 274 of the total listed trust companies.

Share ownership

Results from the Office for National Statistics (ONS) share ownership survey for 2002 (see Table 30.6) show that over 49 per cent of all ordinary shares listed on the UK Stock Exchange were owned by insurance companies, pension funds and other institutional shareholders. About 25 per cent of households have at least one adult owning shares (see Table 30.3).

According to ProShare, an independent organisation founded in 1992 to promote wider share ownership, there are over 10,000 investment clubs – groups of individuals, usually about 15 to 20 people, who regularly invest in shares.

Tax-free savings

Tax-free saving is encouraged by Individual Savings Accounts (ISAs), launched in April 1999 for an initial ten-year period as the successor to Personal Equity Plans (PEPs) and TESSAs (Tax Exempt Special Savings Accounts). Until April 2006, £7,000 can be invested every tax year. There are three main elements of an ISA:

- cash – up to £3,000 each year – such as in a bank or building society ISA account;
- stocks and shares – up to £7,000 a year in a maxi ISA and £3,000 in a mini ISA (see below); and
- life insurance – up to £1,000 a year.

In addition, savers can roll over capital from a matured TESSA into a cash ISA or a special TESSA-only ISA.

There are two main types of ISA: a maxi ISA, which can include all three elements in an ISA with a single manager up to the value of £7,000; and mini ISAs, which allow savers to have different managers, for the cash, stocks and shares, and life insurance components up to the value of £5,000. Savers can choose to put money into mini ISAs or a maxi ISA, but not both, in each tax year.

In 2002/03 subscriptions were made to about 12.5 million ISAs – 10.5 million mini ISAs and 2.0 million maxi ISAs – attracting £27.9 billion (see Table 30.7).

Financial markets

London Stock Exchange

The London Stock Exchange, founded in 1801, is one of the world's leading equity exchanges and a leading provider of services that facilitate the raising of capital and the trading of shares, with around 470 companies from 60 countries admitted to trading on its markets. A market for smaller, fast-growing companies – AIM, the Alternative Investment Market – opened in 1995. In 1999, techMARK, a market for innovative technology companies was launched, followed in 2001 by techMARK mediscience, the world's first international market for healthcare companies. The number of companies operating in these markets and the equity market value of each market are shown in Table 30.8.

A range of indices track share price movements on the Stock Exchange. The most widely quoted is the FTSE 100 index (the 'Footsie'), which relates to the 100 largest UK companies, by market capitalisation, listed on the Exchange. Figure 30.9 shows monthly closing levels for the FTSE 100 since its inception in January 1984.

Table 30.6 Ownership of UK ordinary shares[1]

	£ billion		%
	2001	2002	2002
UK shareholders			
Insurance companies	310.6	230.1	19.9
Pension funds	250.0	180.1	15.6
Individuals	229.9	165.5	14.3
Unit trusts	27.6	18.9	1.6
Investment trusts	34.9	20.6	1.8
Other financial institutions	153.2	121.4	10.5
Banks	19.8	24.2	2.1
Charities	16.1	13.1	1.1
Private non-financial companies	15.3	9.1	0.8
Public sector	0.7	1.3	0.1
Total UK shareholders	1,058.0	784.2	67.9
Rest of the world	496.0	370.4	32.1
Total	**1,554.0**	**1,154.6**	**100**

1 As at 31 December.
Source: Share Ownership Survey, Office for National Statistics

Table 30.7 Subscriptions to ISAs, UK

	Subscriptions in 2001/02 (£ million)	Subscriptions in 2002/03 (£ million)	% of subscriptions in 2002/03
Mini ISAs			
Stocks and shares	1,772	1,704	6.1
Cash	16,831	18,359	65.9
Life insurance	153	190	0.7
Total invested in mini ISAs	**18,756**	**20,252**	**72.7**
Maxi ISAs			
Stocks and shares	9,547	7,419	26.6
Cash	227	167	0.6
Life insurance	20	18	0.1
Total invested in maxi ISAs	**9,794**	**7,605**	**27.3**
Total invested in ISAs	**28,549**	**27,857**	**100**

Source: Inland Revenue

Several other products for raising capital are handled, including Eurobonds, warrants, depositary receipts and gilt-edged stock (see page 357). The London Stock Exchange provides a secondary or trading market where investors can buy or sell UK Government securities (gilts). Turnover in UK gilts on the Exchange was £2,158 billion in 2002, compared with £2,030 billion in 2001.

The CREST computerised securities settlement system, operated by CRESTCo (*www.crestco.co.uk*),

Table 30.8 London Stock Exchange selected statistics

	2001	2002
UK		
Number of companies	1,809	1,701
Equity market value (£ billion)	1,524	1,148
AIM		
Number of companies	629	704
Equity market value (£ billion)	12	10
techMARK		
Number of companies	243	210
Equity market value (£ billion)	414	246
techMARK mediscience		
Number of companies	47	44
Equity market value (£ billion)	192	117
International		
Number of companies	453	419
Equity market value (£ billion)	2,580	1,902

Source: London Stock Exchange

settled over 296,000 transactions a day in 2002 with a value of £440 billion. In September 2002 CRESTCo merged with Euroclear to form Europe's largest system for both equity and fixed income transactions.

Other equity exchanges

There are three other, relatively small markets in the City of London for trading equities: Virt-x, OFEX and OM London. A new equities derivatives business, EDX London Ltd, jointly owned by the London Stock Exchange and OM AB, began trading Scandinavian equity derivatives at the end of June 2003.

Bond markets

London is at the centre of the Euromarket (a major market in a variety of currencies lent outside their domestic markets) and houses most of the leading international banks and securities firms. According to IFSL, bookrunners based in London are estimated to account for about 60 per cent of the primary and 70 per cent of the secondary market in Eurobonds.

Foreign exchange market

A Bank for International Settlements (BIS) survey in 2001 showed that daily foreign exchange turnover in the United Kingdom was US$504 billion and that London was the world's biggest trading centre, handling nearly a third of global net daily turnover. Trading was down by a fifth since the previous survey in 1998, mainly

Figure 30.9 FTSE 100 index[1]

January 1984 = 1,000

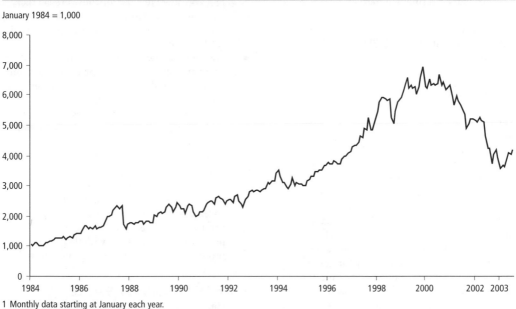

1 Monthly data starting at January each year.
Source: London Stock Exchange

reflecting the overall fall in global foreign exchange trading. One factor was the introduction of the euro in 1999, which eliminated cross-trading between the former euro currencies. Dealing is conducted by telephone and electronic links between the banks, other financial institutions and a number of firms of foreign exchange brokers which act as intermediaries.

Bullion markets

London is the world's most liquid 'spot' (immediate) market for gold and the global clearing centre for gold and silver. Around 60 banks and other financial trading companies participate in the London gold and silver markets. World gold prices are fixed twice a day and the world silver price once a day in London, through the members of the London Bullion Market Association (*www.lbma.org.uk*).

Derivatives

Financial derivatives, including 'futures' and 'options', offer a means of protection against changes in prices, exchange rates and interest rates. The United Kingdom is the most important 'over the counter' market-place, as measured by booking location. According to the BIS, the UK share of world turnover rose from 27 per cent in 1995 to 36 per cent in 2001, representing average daily turnover of US$275 billion.

Euronext.liffe is the international derivatives business of Euronext, comprising the Amsterdam, Brussels, LIFFE, Lisbon and Paris derivatives markets. It was formed following the purchase in 2001 of LIFFE, the London International Financial Futures and Options Exchange (*www.liffe.com*), and is the world's leading exchange for euro short-term interest rate derivatives and equity options. Euronext.liffe is creating a single market for derivatives, by bringing all its derivatives products together on a single electronic trading platform LIFFE CONNECT. It traded a record 697 million futures and options contracts in 2002, 13 per cent more than in 2001, representing an underlying value of €183 trillion.

Other exchanges

Other important City exchanges include:

- the *London Metal Exchange* (LME) – the primary non-ferrous metals market in the world, trading contracts in aluminium, aluminium alloy, copper, lead, nickel, tin and zinc. It traded 58.6 million futures and options lots in 2002;

- the *International Petroleum Exchange* (IPE), a subsidiary of Intercontinental Exchange Inc (ICE) of the United States, and Europe's leading energy futures and options exchange; and

- the *Baltic Exchange*, the world's leading international shipping market.

The London Clearing House (LCH) clears and settles business at the LSE, LIFFE, LME, IPE and Virt-x.

Regulation

The *Financial Services and Markets Act 2000*, which came fully into force in December 2001, created the current framework for the regulation of financial services. It formally established the Financial Services Authority (FSA) (*www.fsa.gov.uk*) – already in operation since 1997 – as the single regulator for the industry. The FSA became responsible for the regulation of investment business and exchanges, banks, building societies and insurance companies previously handled by nine regulatory bodies. In May 2001 it acquired responsibility from the London Stock Exchange for acting as the competent authority for listing companies in the United Kingdom. A new single Financial Services Compensation Scheme and a single Financial Ombudsman Service were also set up (see below).

FSA objectives and functions

The FSA's main aims are maintaining confidence in, and promoting public understanding of, the UK financial system; securing the right degree of protection for consumers; and helping to reduce financial crime.

From October 2004 the FSA will be responsible for statutory regulation of mortgage advice and from January 2005 for the sale of general insurance products, replacing the present voluntary arrangements. The Mortgage Code Compliance Board is the current regulator for the UK home loans market – most lenders and intermediaries are signatories to its voluntary Mortgage Code. The General Insurance Standards Council sets standards for selling general insurance products.

Compensation

The Financial Services Compensation Scheme (FSCS) (*www.fscs.org.uk*) pays compensation if an authorised firm is unable, or likely to be unable, to pay claims against it. The Scheme became operational in December 2001, replacing eight previous compensation schemes, and covers:
- *deposits* – when authorised deposit-taking firms (such as banks, building societies or

credit unions) go out of business or when the FSA considers they are unable to repay their depositors or are likely to be unable to do so. The maximum level of compensation payable is £31,700 per customer;
- *investments* – two kinds of loss are covered: when an authorised investment firm goes out of business and cannot return investments or money, and a loss arising from bad investment advice or poor investment management. The maximum compensation is £48,000; and
- *insurance* – when an insurance firm goes out of business or into liquidation. Compulsory insurance, such as third-party motor insurance, is covered in full; the first £2,000 is covered for non-compulsory and long-term insurance, such as home insurance, pension plans and life assurance, with 90 per cent protection for amounts above this threshold.

Financial Ombudsman Service

The Financial Ombudsman Service considers complaints about a wide range of financial matters from firms in the insurance, mortgage, pensions and investments business. Consumers must first complain to the firm – if the matter is not satisfactorily resolved, the Ombudsman can be asked to look at the case. All firms authorised by the FSA are subject to the Ombudsman's procedures. In 2002/03 the Service received a total of 62,170 complaints, of which 13,570 related to mortgage-linked endowment policies.

Non-financial services

Non-financial services covered in this chapter include the motor, wholesale and retail trades; hotels, restaurants and bars; travel agents and tour operators; real estate, renting, computer and related activities, such as software consultancy; and a host of business services, such as market research, business and management consultancy, and advertising. See Table 23.3 for the contribution these industries make to the UK economy.

Table 30.10 shows turnover for a range of non-financial services.

Consumer spending on personal and leisure services has increased considerably with rising income levels. Long-term growth in tourism has benefited UK travel, hotel and restaurant services.

Table 30.10 Turnover in selected non-financial services[1], Great Britain

£ billion

	2001	2002	% change
Motor trades	125.4	135.0	7.7
Wholesale trades	376.2	382.9	1.8
Hotels and restaurants	56.4	59.1	4.8
Transport and postal services[2]	121.1	124.9	3.1
Renting	18.3	19.0	3.5
Computer and related activities	46.3	45.8	−1.0
Business services	159.2	158.4	−0.5

1 Annual data derived from short-term turnover inquiries. Retailing is covered by a separate sales inquiry.
2 Only travel agents and tour operators are covered in this chapter.
Source: Office for National Statistics

The United Kingdom is one of the world's leading tourist destinations, even though the foot-and-mouth outbreak in 2001, the aftermath of 11 September 2001 and the war in Iraq have caused a temporary decline in visitor numbers (see also page 471).

Distributive trades

Motor trades

In December 2002 there were 589,000 employee jobs in the United Kingdom in retailing motor vehicles and parts, and in petrol stations. Turnover in Great Britain in 2002 was 7.7 per cent higher than in 2001 (see Table 30.11).

Most businesses selling new vehicles are franchised by the motor manufacturers. Vehicle components are on sale at garages that undertake servicing and repair work and also at retail chains and independent retailers. Drive-in fitting centres sell tyres, exhaust systems, batteries, clutches and other vehicle parts. At the end of 2002 there were 11,423 petrol stations in the United Kingdom; the top three companies accounting for 34 per cent. The number of petrol stations declined by 17 per cent between 1999 and 2002, reflecting intense competition in the sector, relatively low profit margins and consolidation among operators. This particularly affected rural areas.

Many petrol stations offer other retail services, such as shops, car washes and fast-food outlets (there were 672 'quick-serve' restaurants attached to forecourts at the end of 2002). Approximately 27 per cent of petrol sold in the United Kingdom comes from supermarket forecourts, 1,084 of which were operating at the end of 2002.

Wholesaling and retailing

In 2003 over 106,000 enterprises (see Table 30.12) were engaged in *wholesaling* in the United Kingdom; 23 per cent were sole proprietors and 14 per cent partnerships. There were 1.1 million employee jobs in the United Kingdom in this sector in December 2002 and turnover in 2002 in Great Britain amounted to £383 billion, 1.8 per cent higher than in 2001.

Almost all large retailers in the food and drink trade have their own buying and central distribution operations. Many small wholesalers and independent grocery retailers belong to voluntary 'symbol' groups, which provide access to central purchasing facilities and coordinated promotions. This helps smaller retailers to remain relatively competitive; many local and convenience

Table 30.11 Turnover[1] in the motor trades industry, Great Britain

£ billion

	2001	2002	% change
Sale of motor vehicles	85.5	95.0	11.1
Maintenance and repair of motor vehicles	9.9	11.3	13.4
Sale of motor vehicle parts and accessories	11.7	11.0	−6.1
Sale, maintenance and repair of motorcycles and related parts and accessories	1.8	1.9	5.5
Retail sale of automotive fuel	16.6	16.0	−3.6
Total	**125.4**	**135.0**	7.7

1 Annual data derived from short-term turnover inquiries.
Source: Office for National Statistics

Table 30.12 Wholesale and retail VAT-based[1] enterprises, 2003, UK

Number of enterprises

Turnover[2] (£ thousand)	Wholesale Total	of which: Sole proprietors	Partnerships	Retail Total	of which: Sole proprietors	Partnerships
0–49	16,600	7,375	2,230	18,520	10,110	3,810
50–99	15,005	6,195	2,400	41,475	23,795	10,990
100–249	21,330	6,480	3,870	65,560	28,465	23,555
250–499	14,235	2,575	2,515	34,120	10,080	13,670
500–999	12,890	1,310	1,785	17,300	3,375	5,730
1,000+	26,220	810	1,785	11,895	1,065	2,295
Total	**106,285**	**24,750**	**14,585**	**188,870**	**76,895**	**60,050**

1 Excludes units with zero VAT turnover and all enterprises without a VAT basis.
2 Turnover figures relate mainly to a 12-month period ending in early 2002.
Source: *Size Analysis of UK Businesses,* Office for National Statistics

stores and village shops would otherwise not be able to stay in business.

The *retail sector* accounted for 2.9 million UK employee jobs in December 2002. In 2003 there were nearly 189,000 retail enterprises in the United Kingdom (see Table 30.12); 41 per cent were sole proprietors and 32 per cent partnerships.

In 2001 total retail turnover (including repair of personal and household goods) in the United Kingdom amounted to £226 billion, almost 4 per cent higher than in 2000.

The volume of retail sales rose by 34 per cent between 1995 and 2002 (see also Table 30.13).

London's wholesale markets

An independent review of London's wholesale markets was published in November 2002. The report recommended (among other things) that the markets should be consolidated to provide three composite markets, each providing facilities for the sale of fruit and vegetables, meat and fish. New Covent Garden Market at Nine Elms should provide a particular service to the Central London catering trade. The other two consolidated markets should be New Spitalfields in East London and Western International, near Heathrow. The report also recommended that legislation restraining trade and limiting competition between markets should be removed. A three-month consultation period ended in February 2003 and a Written Ministerial Statement was issued in June giving the Government's broad support to the report and detailing future action.

Growth in non-food stores (47 per cent) was higher than in predominantly food stores (22 per cent), with the greatest increase (69 per cent) in household goods stores.

Many of the large food retailers sell electrical goods, household wares and clothing. Some of the larger supermarkets include in-store pharmacies, post offices, cafeterias and dry-cleaners. Several retail chains offer personal finance facilities and others have diversified into banking and financial services. Some supermarkets are now open 24 hours a day from Monday to Saturday.

Small independent retail businesses and co-operative societies have been in relative decline for some time. To help their competitive position, under the *Sunday Trading Act 1994*, small shops (under 280 square metres) have no restrictions on Sunday opening, while large shops (over 280 square metres) are restricted (except in Scotland) to six hours only between 10.00 am and 6.00 pm.

The Co-operative Group (CWS) Limited is the largest UK mutual retail group, with total food sales of £2.6 billion in 2002. As well as food retailing, the Group's operations include funeral businesses, travel retailing, motor trading and non-food department stores.

The Co-operative Group is the principal supplier of goods and services to the Co-operative Movement – comprising 41 independent retail societies and 3,030 stores – and was a founder member of the Co-operative Retail Trading Group

Table 30.13 Volume of retail sales, Great Britain

1995=100

	1992	1997	2000	2001	2002
Predominantly food stores	93.1	105.9	113.6	117.7	121.6
Predominantly non-food stores					
Non-specialised stores	93.6	111.5	122.2	129.0	134.7
Textile, clothing and footwear stores	89.1	111.2	124.7	137.3	150.8
Household goods stores	86.5	117.2	148.6	161.6	169.0
Other stores	93.8	105.7	117.0	124.4	129.7
Total	90.3	111.2	127.9	138.1	146.6
Non-store retailing and repair	103.8	105.7	115.6	119.2	125.7
All retailing	92.4	108.5	120.8	128.0	134.3

Source: Office for National Statistics

(CRTG). The CRTG acts as a central marketing, buying and distribution partnership for retail co-operative societies, and now controls all Co-op food trade. Retail co-operative societies are voluntary organisations controlled by their members, membership being open to anyone paying a small deposit on a minimum share.

Franchising is the granting of a licence by one company (the franchiser) to another (the franchisee), usually by means of an initial payment with continuing royalties. Franchised activities operate in many areas, including cleaning services, film processing, print shops, fitness centres, courier delivery, car rental, engine tuning and servicing, and fast-food retailing. About 220 franchisers are members of the British Franchise Association (*www.british-franchise.org*) which conducts an annual survey of franchising. Its findings for 2003 estimated that there were 677 business-format franchises, with around 34,400 outlets, accounting for about 326,000 direct jobs in the United Kingdom and with annual turnover of £9.5 billion.

Shopping facilities

There are eight regional out-of-town shopping centres in the United Kingdom, located at sites offering good road access and ample parking facilities. Opened between 1985 and 1999, they range in size from 56,000 square metres (Braehead, near Glasgow) to 160,000 square metres (Bluewater, in Kent, which is the largest such development in Europe).

Since 1996, social, economic and environmental considerations have led the Government and local planning authorities to limit new retail developments outside town centres. Out-of-town superstores, retail warehouses and shopping centres were felt to be undermining the vitality and viability of existing town and district centres. Government policy is now to focus new retail development in existing centres and so revitalise them. This is to ensure that everyone has easy access to a range of shops and services, whether or not they have a car, and to enable businesses of all types and size to prosper.

All new retail development requires planning permission from the local planning authority, which must consult central government before granting permission for most developments of 2,500 square metres or more.

Home shopping

Traditionally, all kinds of goods and services are purchased through mail-order catalogues. The largest-selling items are clothing, footwear, furniture, household textiles and domestic electrical appliances. Internet sales and electronic home shopping, using a television and telephone, have grown rapidly. Online sales by UK businesses in the non-financial sector were estimated at £18.4 billion in 2001, with the wholesale, retail, catering, travel and communications sector accounting for the largest share (£11.7 billion or 64 per cent); £5.3 billion of this sector's online sales were to households.

Hotels, restaurants and catering

There were 1.8 million employee jobs in the hotel and restaurant trades in the United Kingdom in December 2002. This includes public houses (pubs), wine bars and other licensed bars in addition to all kinds of businesses offering accommodation and prepared food. Turnover in 2002 in Great Britain, at £59.1 billion, was 4.8 per cent higher than in 2001.

In 2001 there were 52,600 enterprises in the United Kingdom in the licensed restaurant industry (including fast-food and takeaway outlets), an increase of 2.4 per cent on 2000. Total turnover in 2002 in Great Britain was £19.1 billion, 5.0 per cent higher than in 2001. UK restaurants offer cuisine from all over the world, and several of the highest-quality ones have international reputations. Chinese, Indian, Italian, French, Greek and Thai restaurants are among the most popular. Fast-food restaurants are widespread, many of them franchised, and specialise in selling burgers, chicken, pizza and a variety of other foods. Traditional fish and chip shops are another main provider of cooked takeaway food. Sandwich bars are common in towns and cities, especially in areas with high concentrations of office workers.

There were an estimated 48,750 pubs in the United Kingdom in 2002, a decline of nearly 10 per cent since 1990. They accounted for 56 per cent of all fully licensed premises, compared with 65 per cent in 1990. Turnover was estimated at £14.0 billion in 2001, an annual average of around £287,000 per pub. Although brewers still own many pub chains, their share has declined to 25 per cent of UK pubs. The breweries either provide managers to run the pubs or offer tenancy agreements, and tend to sell only their own brands of beer, although some also offer 'guest' beers. Multiple pub-owning 'pub companies' and venture capital companies account for 40 per cent of the ownership. The remaining 35 per cent of pubs, called 'free houses', are independently owned and managed – these frequently serve a variety of different branded beers.

Real estate, renting and business activities

Exhibition and conference centres

The United Kingdom is one of the world's leading centres for international conferences. Many UK towns and cities have conference and exhibition facilities, including several traditional seaside resorts that have adapted to the growing business tourism market.

Key exhibition venues include the National Exhibition and International Conference Centres

in Birmingham; the ExCel exhibition and conference centre in Docklands; Earls Court and Olympia Conference Centres, Wembley Arena and Queen Elizabeth II Conference Centre in London; SECC (Scottish Exhibition & Conference Centre) in Glasgow; Cardiff International Arena; and the Belfast Waterfront Hall. Smaller regional venues include, in England, Brighton (East Sussex), Harrogate (North Yorkshire), Bournemouth (Dorset), Manchester, Nottingham, and Torquay (Devon) and, in Scotland, Edinburgh and Aberdeen. Other important exhibition facilities in London are at the Barbican, Business Design Centre and Alexandra Palace.

The Association of Exhibition Organisers (*www.aeo.org.uk*) is the UK trade body representing organisers of trade exhibitions and consumer events. The AEO estimates that between 1999 and 2001 spending by exhibitors on exhibitions rose from £1.8 billion to £2.0 billion.

Table 30.14 Exhibitions and attendance[1], UK

	2001	2002
Number of events	823	855
of which:		
Trade (%)	56	55
Public and consumer (%)	42	44
Trade and public (%)	2	1
Number of visitors (million)	9.1	10.3
of which:		
Trade (%)	27	25
Public and consumer (%)	69	74
Trade and public (%)	4	1

1 Excludes one-day public events; covers only venues of 2,000 square metres and over.
Source: Association of Exhibition Organisers

In addition to the figures in Table 30.14 above, there were 5 million visitors to 50 exhibitions held in outdoor venues in 2002. A further 787 exhibition events (mainly smaller and often regional) took place in 336 venues, attracting an estimated 5.5 million visitors.

The Department of Trade and Industry (DTI), via its Trade Partners UK operating arm, sponsors the website (*www.exhibitions.co.uk*), which offers a comprehensive listing of all consumer, public, industrial and trade exhibitions held in major UK venues.

Rental services

A varied range of rental services, many of which are franchised, are available across the United Kingdom. These include hire of cars and other vehicles; televisions, video recorders and camcorders; household appliances such as washing machines; tools and heavy decorating equipment such as ladders and floor sanders; and videos, DVDs and computer games. Retailing of many types of service is dominated by chains, although independent operators are still to be found in most fields. In December 2002 there were 161,000 employee jobs in the United Kingdom in the rental sector, with turnover in 2002 in Great Britain amounting to £19.0 billion, 3.5 per cent higher than in 2001.

Computing services

The computing software and services industry comprises businesses engaged in software development; systems integration; IT consultancy; IT 'outsourcing'; processing services; and the provision of complete computer systems. It also includes companies that provide IT education and training; independent maintenance; support, contingency planning and recruitment; and contract staff.

In December 2002 there were around 500,000 employee jobs in the United Kingdom in computer and related activities. Turnover of companies in this sector amounted to £45.8 billion in 2002 in Great Britain, 1.0 per cent lower than in 2001. UK firms and universities have established strong reputations in software R&D and a number of international IT conglomerates, such as Microsoft, have set up R&D operations in the United Kingdom. Academic expertise is especially evident in such areas as artificial intelligence (AI), neural networks, grid computing, formal programming for safety-critical systems, and parallel programming systems.

Software firms have developed strengths in sector-specific applications, including systems for retailing, banking, finance and accounting, the medical and dental industries, and the travel and entertainment industries. Specialist 'niche' markets in which UK software producers are active include AI, scientific and engineering software (especially computer-aided design), mathematical software,

geographical information systems, and data visualisation packages. Some firms specialise in devising multimedia software. Distance learning, 'virtual reality' and computer animation all benefit from a large pool of creative talent.

One of the biggest users of software is the telecommunications industry (see page 235). The provision of almost all new telecommunications services, including switching and transmission, is dependent on software.

A one-off survey by ONS in 2001 estimated the size of the computer services market in Great Britain in 2000 as £32.0 billion (including exports). Sales activity in non-computer (but related) services accounted for an additional £5.4 billion, with wholesaling or retailing of goods worth £3.1 billion, and telecommunications services £1.2 billion.

Business services

In December 2002 a total of 2.8 million employee jobs in the United Kingdom were in the other business activities sector, which includes market research, business and management consultancy activities and advertising. Turnover in 2002 in Great Britain amounted to £158.4 billion, 0.5 per cent lower than in 2001.

Market research

The British Market Research Association (BMRA) (*www.bmra.org.uk*) aims to promote good practice in market research in the United Kingdom and to cater for the professional and trade needs of UK market research companies. Its members' turnover grew by 2.6 per cent in 2002 to an estimated £1.2 billion, following growth of 7.1 per cent in 2001. UK-owned market research companies include the largest international customised market research specialists. The top ten companies by turnover are shown in Table 30.15.

Management consultancy

The 70,000 UK management consultants supply technical assistance and advice to business and government clients. In 2002 revenues for the industry were estimated at £9 billion, with exports worth £1 billion. The 40 member firms of the Management Consultancies Association (MCA) (*www.mca.org.uk*), which account for roughly half of UK revenues, generated £4.7 billion in fee income in 2002, 9 per cent more than in 2001 (see Table 30.16). Income from outsourcing activities accounted for 27 per cent of all UK fee income.

Table 30.15 Top ten market research companies[1] by turnover, UK

	£ million	
	2001	2002
Taylor Nelson Sofres	120	113
NOP World	72	77
NFO Worldgroup	45	47
Ipsos (UK)	41	44
MORI	34	36
Information Resources	34	35
Maritz/TRBI	24	25
Martin Hamblin GfK	31	19
ISIS Research	14	17
Synovate[2]	.	16

1 BMRA members only.
2 Not included in 2001 data.
Source: British Market Research Association

Table 30.16 Management consultancy income[1], UK

	£ million	
	2001	2002
Outsourcing	1,188	1,273
Strategy	502	289
IT consultancy	956	1,069
Financial systems	391	200
Production management	155	239
Human resources	115	398
Project management	401	622
Marketing	40	55
Other	32	71
Total UK fee income	3,780	4,216
Overseas fee income	565	528
Total	**4,345**	**4,743**

1 MCA firms only.
Source: Management Consultancies Association

Advertising and public relations

The United Kingdom is a major centre for creative advertising, and multinational companies often use advertising created in the United Kingdom for marketing their products globally. UK agencies have strong foreign links through overseas ownership and associate networks. UK television advertising has received many international awards. According to the Advertising Association (*www.adassoc.org.uk*), total UK advertising expenditure rose by 1.2 per cent in 2002 to

£16.7 billion, following a slight decline in 2001 (see also Table 30.17).

There were around 1,570 advertising agencies in 2002. As well as their creative, production and media-buying roles, some offer integrated marketing services, including consumer research and public relations. Many agencies have sponsorship departments, which arrange for businesses to sponsor products and events, including artistic, sporting and charitable events.

Table 30.17 UK advertising revenue by medium

	£ million		%
	2001	2002	2002
Press	8,504	8,306	49.6
of which:			
National newspapers	2,062	1,930	11.5
Regional newspapers	2,834	2,870	17.2
Consumer magazines	779	785	4.7
Business and professional magazines	1,202	1,088	6.5
Directories	959	990	5.9
Press production costs	669	643	3.8
Television	4,147	4,326	25.9
Direct mail	2,228	2,378	14.2
Outdoor and transport	788	802	4.8
Radio	541	545	3.3
Cinema	164	180	1.1
Internet	166	197	1.2
Total all media	**16,537**	**16,734**	**100**

Source: *Advertising Statistics Yearbook 2003*, World Advertising Research Center

Government advertising campaigns – in areas such as crime prevention, health promotion and armed services recruitment – are often organised by COI Communications (see page 477), an executive agency of the Government.

The UK public relations industry has developed rapidly, and there are now many small specialist firms as well as some quite large ones. The Public Relations Consultants Association (*www.prca.org.uk*) membership accounts for 70 per cent of UK fee income. It has over 120 members employing around 6,500 people and generates more than £400 million each year in fees from clients.

Travel and tourism

Overseas travel

Spain and France were the top countries visited by UK residents in 2002, each with over 12 million visits. Long-haul holidays have remained popular, despite recent global events. The United States is still the top long-haul destination, with Australia, New Zealand, South Africa and Thailand also maintaining their popularity. Short breaks have increased rapidly over the last few years and accounted for 15 per cent of overseas holidays.

In 2002 total turnover in the travel agency and tour operator businesses in Great Britain amounted to £18.2 billion, 2.4 per cent lower than in 2001. Around 70 per cent of high street travel agencies are members of the Association of British Travel Agents (ABTA) (*www.abta.com*). Although most are small businesses, a few large firms have hundreds of branches. ABTA's 800 tour operators and nearly 1,600 travel agency companies have 6,700 offices and are responsible for the sale of some 80 per cent of UK-sold holidays.

ABTA operates financial protection schemes to safeguard customers and maintains a code of conduct drawn up with the Office of Fair Trading. It also offers a free consumer affairs service to help resolve complaints against its members, and a low-cost independent arbitration scheme for customers.

Tourism in the UK

Tourism is one of the key UK long-term growth sectors, with total spending in 2002 estimated at £76.0 billion (see Table 30.18). The bulk of tourism services are provided by 128,000 mainly independent small businesses, such as hotels and guest houses, restaurants, holiday homes, caravan and camping parks.

The British Incoming Tour Operators Association (*www.bitoa.co.uk*) represents the commercial and political interests of incoming tour operators and suppliers to the British inbound tourism industry.

There were an estimated 24 million overseas visitors to the United Kingdom in 2002, an increase of 6 per cent on the previous year. The earnings they generated increased by an estimated 5 per cent to £11.9 billion (see Tables 30.18 and 30.20). These figures are still below 2000 levels, but they suggest a partial recovery from the effects

Table 30.18 Spending on tourism, UK

£ billion

	2000	2001	2002
Spending by:			
Overseas residents			
Visits to the UK	12.8	11.3	11.9
Overseas fares to UK carriers	3.5	3.2	3.2
Domestic tourists			
Trips of one night or more	26.1	26.1	26.7
Day trips	32.7	33.4	34.2
Total	**75.1**	**74.0**	**76.0**

Source: Overseas travel and tourism, Office for National Statistics; VisitBritain

Table 30.19 Employment in tourism-related industries, June 2002, Great Britain

	Thousands
Hotels and other tourist accommodation	418
Restaurants, cafés, etc.	545
Bars, public houses and nightclubs	536
Travel agencies/tour operators	134
Libraries/museums and other cultural activities	81
Sport and other recreation activities	413
Total	**2,127**
of which: Self-employment jobs	163

Source: Department for Culture, Media and Sport

of the foot-and-mouth outbreak and the 11 September 2001 attacks. Holiday visits, however, were still 17 per cent down on 2000 levels.

The number of visitors from the European Union rose by 10 per cent in 2002, and those from North America and from all other areas by 1 per cent. Table 30.21 shows that the United States was in top place for overseas visitors to the United Kingdom.

Business travel, which includes attendance at conferences, exhibitions, trade fairs and other business sites, accounted for almost 30 per cent of all overseas visits in 2002. Nearly 71 per cent of visitors arrived by air, principally at London's Heathrow and Gatwick airports. The other main points of entry are the port of Dover and the Channel Tunnel.

Domestic tourism expenditure was estimated to be nearly £61 billion in 2002. Short holiday breaks

Table 30.20 Overseas visits to the UK

Million

	2000	2001	2002
By area			
North America	4.9	4.2	4.3
European Union	14.0	12.9	14.1
Non-EU Europe	2.1	2.0	2.1
Other countries	4.3	3.8	3.7
By purpose			
Holiday	9.3	7.6	7.7
Business	7.3	6.8	7.2
Visiting friends or relatives	5.8	5.9	6.4
Miscellaneous	2.8	2.6	2.9
All visits	**25.2**	**22.8**	**24.2**

Source: Overseas travel and tourism, Office for National Statistics

Table 30.21 Top ten countries of origin of overseas visitors to the UK

Visits (thousands)

	2001	2002
United States	3,580	3,611
France	2,852	3,077
Germany	2,309	2,556
Irish Republic	2,039	2,439
Netherlands	1,411	1,419
Spain	856	1,010
Italy	857	977
Belgium	916	966
Australia	694	702
Canada	647	660

Source: Overseas travel and tourism, Office for National Statistics

(up to three nights), valued at £8.7 billion in 2002, accounted for half of all spending on holidays (excluding day trips).

Historic towns and cities and the scenic rural and coastal areas of the United Kingdom continue to have great appeal for domestic and overseas tourists alike. Their popularity reflects a growing interest in UK heritage, arts and culture. There are more than 6,400 visitor attractions in the United Kingdom, which in 2001 attracted over 257 million visits. Museums, galleries and historic properties make up just over half of the attractions. Tourism plays an increasingly important role in supporting UK national heritage and creative arts, in addition to the large financial

contribution it makes to hotels, restaurants, cafés and bars, and public transport.

Activity holidays are often based on walking, cycling, canoeing, mountain climbing, or artistic activities. The Youth Hostel Association operates a comprehensive network of around 310 hostels in the United Kingdom, offering a range of facilities, including self-catering, to families and people of all ages. Theme parks attract millions of visitors every year. Attractions in these parks include spectacular 'white knuckle' rides and overhead cable cars and railways, while some also feature domesticated and wild animals.

Table 30.22 Top tourist attractions charging admission[1], UK

Visits (million)

	2001	2002
British Airways London Eye[2]	3.85	4.09
Tower of London	2.02	1.94
Eden Project, St Austell[3]	1.70	1.83
Legoland, Windsor	1.63	1.45
Flamingo Land Theme Park & Zoo, Kirby Misperton, North Yorkshire[4]	1.32	1.39
Windermere Lake Cruises, Ambleside, Cumbria	1.24	1.27
Drayton Manor Theme Park, Tamworth, Staffordshire[4]	0.96	1.20
Edinburgh Castle	1.13	1.15
Chester Zoo	1.06	1.13
Canterbury Cathedral[4]	1.15	1.11

1 Attractions that responded to the survey and gave permission for their information to be published.
2 Estimated numbers in 2001.
3 Estimated numbers in 2002.
4 Estimated numbers.
Source: Survey of Visits to Tourist Attractions

The British Airways London Eye was the most popular UK attraction charging admission in 2002 (see Table 30.22). With the abolition of admission charges to several museums and galleries, London's Natural History, Victoria & Albert and Science Museums recorded sharp increases in visitor numbers. The largest tourist attraction with free admission (and also the largest overall attraction) was Blackpool Pleasure Beach in Lancashire (see Table 30.23).

Tourism promotion

Tourism is the responsibility of the Department for Culture, Media and Sport and the devolved

Table 30.23 Top free tourist attractions[1], UK

	Visits (million)	
	2001	2002
Blackpool Pleasure Beach	6.50	6.20
Tate Modern, London	3.55	4.62
British Museum, London	4.80	4.61
National Gallery, London[2]	4.92	4.13
Natural History Museum, London[3]	1.70	2.96
Victoria & Albert Museum, London[3]	1.45	2.66
Science Museum, London[3]	1.35	2.63
Pleasureland Theme Park, Southport[2]	2.00	2.00
Eastbourne Pier[2]	2.00	1.90
York Minster[2]	1.60	1.57

1 Attractions that responded to the survey and gave permission for their information to be published.
2 Estimated numbers.
3 Admission policy changed from paid admission to free admission.
Source: Survey of Visits to Tourist Attractions

assemblies. The government-supported British Tourist Authority (BTA) and the English Tourism Council merged in April 2003 to form an organisation called VisitBritain (*www.visitbritain.com*), which promotes the United Kingdom to an international audience as well as promoting England domestically. VisitBritain has a network of 27 overseas offices, located in markets offering the best potential return and which cover 88 per cent of all visitors to the United Kingdom. There are separate national tourist boards – in Scotland (*www.visitscotland.com*), Wales (*www.visitwales.com*) and Northern Ireland (*www.discovernorthernireland.com*) – which support domestic tourism and work with VisitBritain to promote the United Kingdom overseas. Since April 2003 the Regional Development Agencies in England have been playing a stronger role and are required to develop and implement regional sustainable tourism strategies, working with regional and local partners as well as with VisitBritain on marketing.

VisitBritain and the national tourist boards inform and advise the Government on issues of concern to the industry. They also research and publicise trends affecting the industry and work closely with regional tourist boards, on which local government and business interests are represented. There are several hundred local Tourist Information Centres in the United

Kingdom. The national tourist boards, in conjunction with the AA and the RAC, administer the National Quality Assurance Standards (NQAS) schemes for accommodation.

Consumer protection

The Government aims to maintain and develop a clear and fair regulatory framework that gives confidence to consumers and contributes to business competitiveness. It works closely with outside bodies that have expert knowledge of consumer issues to develop policies and legislation. The 1999 White Paper, *Modern Markets: Confident Consumers*, set out a range of initiatives aimed at improving consumer protection. Many of the government proposals have been implemented. There are new consumer councils for the energy and postal industries, and a stronger National Consumer Council (see page 475). Information and redress have been improved with the launch of consumer support networks and there are plans to pilot new helplines on consumer advice and debt.

The regulatory regime has been strengthened with the implementation of the *Enterprise Act 2002* (see page 345) to tackle rogue traders for whom existing sanctions are not a sufficient deterrent.

The functions of the Office of Fair Trading (OFT) (*www.oft.gov.uk*) are now managed by a new corporate body that reflects the interests, among others, of consumers (see page 346). The OFT has also been given a new range of duties:
- to promote competition;
- to approve industry codes of practice;
- to educate consumers; and
- to consider 'super-complaints' about markets that are failing consumers (see page 346).

EU consumer programme covers activities such as health and safety, protection of the consumer's economic interests, promotion of consumer education and strengthening of consumer representation. The interests of UK consumers on EU matters are represented by a number of organisations, including the Consumers' Association and the National Consumer Council (see page 475).

Consumer advice and information

Citizens Advice provide advice from approximately 2,000 outlets across England, Wales and Northern

Consumer legislation

- The *Trade Descriptions Act 1968* makes it an offence for a trader to apply, by any means, false or misleading statements, or to knowingly or recklessly make such statements about goods and services.

- The Consumer Credit Act 1974 regulates consumer credit and consumer hire agreements for amounts up to £25,000. Its provisions apply to agreements between traders and individuals, sole traders, partnerships and unincorporated associations, but not agreements made between traders and corporate bodies such as limited companies. The Act lays down rules covering the form and content of agreements; credit advertising; the method of calculating the annual percentage rate (APR) of the total charge for credit; the procedures to be adopted in the event of default, termination or early settlement; and extortionate credit bargains. The Act also requires all traders who make regulated agreements to obtain licences from the OFT (see page 346). Credit brokers, debt advisers and others may also require licences.

- The *Sale of Goods Act 1979* implies certain terms into contracts for the sale of goods. For example, goods must be as described, of satisfactory quality, and fit for any purpose which the consumer makes known to the seller. If they are not of satisfactory quality, the buyer is entitled, if he or she acts within a reasonable time, to reject the goods and get his or her money back.

- The *Weights and Measures Act 1985* and its secondary legislation regulate most transactions in goods by weight or measure and the measuring instruments used in those transactions.

- The *Consumer Protection Act 1987* covers misleading indications about prices of goods. It also makes it a criminal offence to supply unsafe products, and provides product liability rights for consumers. The regulatory framework to control product safety is a mixture of EU and UK legislation, voluntary safety standards and industry codes of practice.

- The *Doorstep Selling Regulations* (1987 and 1998) give consumers the right to a seven-day cooling-off period during which they may cancel an agreement to buy goods or services worth more than £35 from a trader whose visit is unsolicited. The same right to a seven-day cooling-off period applies where a visit by a trader follows an unsolicited doorstep or telephone approach.

- The *Control of Misleading Advertisements Regulations 1988* are aimed at protecting the interest of consumers and traders from the effects of misleading advertisements, including representations made orally, in print or on the Internet.

- The *Unfair Terms in Consumer Contracts Regulations 1999* protect consumers against unfair standard terms in contracts they make with businesses, in particular from terms that reduce their rights under normal contract or general law, and from terms that seek to impose unfair burdens upon the consumer over and above the obligations of ordinary rules of law.

- The *Distance Selling Regulations 2000* give rights to consumers in the area of home shopping. Under the Regulations, consumers shopping for goods or services by telephone, mail order, fax, digital television, the Internet and other types of distance communication have the right to clear information, a seven-day cooling-off period and protection against fraudulent use of a credit card.

- The *Enterprise Act 2002* enables the OFT and specified consumer bodies to take swift action against traders in the United Kingdom and other EU Member States who breach one of ten EC Directives or 52 pieces of UK legislation, where the collective interests of consumers are harmed. The Act covers all UK markets for both goods and services, including consumer credit, unfair contract terms, distance selling, misleading and comparative advertising, doorstep selling, timeshare, package travel and sale of goods.

Ireland. They handled 5.7 million new enquiries during 2001/02 (see Table 30.24). Their work is coordinated by the National Association of Citizens Advice Bureaux (*www.nacab.org.uk*)

linked to local and regional committees. In 2001/02 an additional 405,000 problems were handled by Citizens Advice Scotland (*www.cas.org.uk*). Similar assistance is provided by

Table 30.24 Citizens Advice new enquiries, England, Wales and Northern Ireland

Thousands

Category	2000/01	2001/02	% change[1]
Benefits	1,723	1,629	−5.5
Consumer and utilities	1,175	1,194	1.6
Employment	632	601	−4.8
Housing	600	573	−4.5
Legal	479	460	−4.0
Relationships	388	390	0.5
Tax	154	150	−2.9
Other	707	721	1.9
Total	**5,858**	**5,718**	−2.4

1 Based on unrounded data.
Source: Citizens Advice

trading standards and consumer protection departments of local authorities in Great Britain and, in some areas, by specialist consumer advice centres.

The National Consumer Council (*www.ncc.org.uk*) is a consumer policy and research organisation with a special focus on the needs of disadvantaged consumers. It is a non-profit-making company limited by guarantee and most of its funding is from the DTI. It works with associate organisations in Wales and Scotland – the Welsh and Scottish Consumer Councils – and the General Consumer Council of Northern Ireland to represent all consumer interests to policy makers, regulators and suppliers in the United Kingdom and in the EU.

Consumer bodies for privatised utilities investigate questions of concern to the consumer.

Some trade associations have set up codes of practice. In addition, several organisations work to further consumer interests by representing the consumer's view to government, industry and other bodies. The largest is the Consumers' Association, with 642,000 members in July 2003, funded largely by subscriptions to *Which?* magazine (*www.which.net*). Over 69,000 subscribers have online access to the complete range of *Which?* publications.

Further reading

Competition in UK Banking: A Report to the Chancellor of the Exchequer. HM Treasury. The Stationery Office, 2000.

Bank of England Annual Report. Bank of England.

Financial Services Authority Annual Report. FSA.

Websites

Bank of England
www.bankofengland.co.uk

British Bankers' Association
www.bba.org.uk

Financial Services Authority
www.fsa.gov.uk

London Stock Exchange
www.londonstockexchange.com

National Statistics
www.statistics.gov.uk

www.

Appendix A UK Parliament and devolved administrations, government departments and agencies

This appendix gives contact details for the main government departments and describes their principal functions. It is divided into the following sections:

- non-devolved functions (including matters 'reserved' to the UK Government); and

- devolved administrations – Wales, Scotland and Northern Ireland.

The entries for departments responsible for non-devolved functions give a broad indication of their geographical remit, but details may vary.

Executive agencies are listed at the end of the entry for their sponsor department. Those marked with an asterisk* also have an entry in their own right.

Following the entry for the UK Parliament, the listing within each section is alphabetical, except that words like 'the' 'and' 'of' and 'for' are ignored, as is the 'HM' before Customs and Excise, Land Registry, and Treasury.

A complete listing of government departments, executive agencies, non-departmental public bodies, and a range of related organisations, such as museums, galleries and research establishments, is published in the *Civil Service Year Book*; and there is further information in *Public Bodies 2003*, published by HMSO.

Houses of Parliament
House of Commons and House of Lords

Westminster
London SW1A 0AA (Commons) and
SW1A 0PW (Lords)
Tel: 020 7219 3000
Website: *www.parliament.uk*

Responsible for examining the work of Government (see chapter 6) and for all legislation for England, primary legislation for Wales, and legislation for the whole of the United Kingdom on areas not devolved to the National Assembly for Wales, Scottish Parliament and Northern Ireland Assembly (when it is sitting). This includes constitutional affairs; the franchise (including at local government elections, and the conduct and funding of parliamentary elections); defence, national security and official secrets; foreign policy; overall economic, fiscal and monetary policy; competition policy; international trade policy; consumer safety and protection; some elements of health; home affairs including the police (except Scotland); asylum, immigration and extradition; misuse of drugs and firearms; the legal system (except Scotland); human rights, anti-discrimination, equal opportunities and data protection; the Post Office; energy; telecommunications; control over broadcasting and the National Lottery; and power over the regulation and safety of aviation and shipping.

The House of Commons also decides what taxes should be collected and in broad terms how the money should be spent.

Non-devolved functions and England

Cabinet Office (CO)

70 Whitehall
London SW1A 2AS
Tel: 020 7276 3000
Website: *www.cabinet-office.gov.uk*
Status: Ministerial department

Supports the Government in transacting its
business, including the reform of public services.
Also coordinates on matters of national security.

Executive agencies
COI Communications*
Government Car and Despatch Agency

Charity Commission

Harmsworth House
13–15 Bouverie Street
London EC4Y 8DP
Tel: 0870 333 0123
Website: *www.charitycommission.gov.uk*
Status: Non-ministerial department

Responsible for registering bodies qualifying for
charitable status in England and Wales, advising
charities and their trustees, monitoring the
activities of charities and investigating
maladministration and abuse.

Child Support Agency (CSA)

Benton Park View
Benton Park Road
Newcastle upon Tyne NE98 1YX
Tel: 08457 133 133
Website: *www.csa.gov.uk*
Status: Executive agency of the Department for
Work and Pensions

Assesses the financial support required for
children in Great Britain whose parents do not
live together, and ensures that this is paid.

COI Communications

Hercules Road
London SE1 7DU
Tel: 020 7928 2345
Website: *www.coi.gov.uk*
Status: Non-ministerial department and executive
agency of the Cabinet Office

Consultancy, procurement and project management
of marketing and communications activity on
behalf of government departments, agencies and
other public sector clients across the UK.

Companies House

Crown Way
Cardiff CF14 3UZ
Tel: 0870 33 33 636
Website: *www.companieshouse.gov.uk*

Status: Executive agency of the Department of
Trade and Industry

Incorporates and dissolves companies, registers
the information they are required to supply under
companies and related legislation, and makes that
information available to the public.

Court Service

7th Floor
Southside
105 Victoria Street
London SW1E 6QT
Tel: 020 7210 2266
Website: *www.courtservice.gov.uk*
Status: Executive agency of the Department for
Constitutional Affairs

Provides administrative support to the courts in
England and Wales (excluding magistrates' courts)
and to a number of tribunals.

Crown Prosecution Service (CPS)

50 Ludgate Hill
London EC4M 7EX
Tel: 020 7796 8000
Website: *www.cps.gov.uk*
Status: Non-ministerial department

Prosecutes people in England and Wales who have
been charged by the police with a criminal
offence. The CPS is headed by the Director of
Public Prosecutions, who is accountable to
Parliament through the Attorney General.

HM Customs and Excise (HMCE)

New King's Beam House
22 Upper Ground
London SE1 9PJ
Tel: 0845 010 9000 (UK local rate)
+44 (0) 20 8929 0152 (international)
Website: *www.hmce.gov.uk*
Status: Non-ministerial department

Responsible to the Chancellor of the Exchequer
for collecting and accounting for UK customs and
excise duties (including value added tax). Also
responsible for the prevention of smuggling and
of the import or export of illegal goods; and for
compiling overseas trade statistics.

Department for Constitutional Affairs (DCA)

Selborne House
54–60 Victoria Street
London SW1E 6QW
Tel: 020 7210 8500
Website: *www.dca.gov.uk*
Status: Ministerial department

UK-wide: reform of the constitution; freedom of information; privacy and data sharing; human rights; reform of the House of Lords; the constitutional relationship with the Channel Islands and the Isle of Man; royal, church and hereditary issues; electoral law and policy; referendums; and party funding.

In England and Wales: the administration of justice; reform of civil law; appointment and training of the judiciary; provision of legal aid and legal services.

DCA brings together most of the Lord Chancellor's Department, the Advocate General for Scotland's office and, for administrative purposes only, the staff of the Scotland Office and the Wales Office – both of which retain their separate identities and continue to report to the Secretaries of State for Scotland and Wales respectively.

Executive agencies
Court Service*
HM Land Registry*
The National Archives*
Public Guardianship Office

Department for Culture, Media and Sport (DCMS)

2–4 Cockspur Street
London SW1Y 5DH
Tel: 020 7211 6000
Website: *www.culture.gov.uk*
Status: Ministerial department

Overall responsibility for the arts, public libraries and archives, museums and galleries, tourism, sport and the built heritage in England. DCMS also has overall responsibility for the film industry and for alcohol and public entertainment licensing in England and Wales, and UK-wide responsibility for broadcasting, press regulation, creative industries, public lending rights, gambling and the National Lottery, censorship and video classification. However, the devolved administrations also have some operational responsibilities in these areas.

Executive agency
Royal Parks Agency

Department for Education and Skills (DfES)

Sanctuary Buildings
Great Smith Street
London SW1P 3BT
Tel: 0870 000 2288
Website: *www.dfes.gov.uk*
Status: Ministerial department

Overall responsibility for policies relating to children, young people and families; school, college and university education; youth and adult training and programmes (England); student support and teachers' pay and conditions (England and Wales).

Department for Environment, Food and Rural Affairs (Defra)

Nobel House
17 Smith Square
London SW1P 3JR
Tel: 08459 33 55 77
Website: *www.defra.gov.uk*
Status: Ministerial department

Sustainable development and the environment; agriculture, horticulture, fisheries and food; rural development; the countryside; animal welfare and hunting. This remit is broadly confined to England, but Defra also has a UK coordinating role on some aspects of environmental affairs.

Executive agencies
Central Science Laboratory
Centre for Environment, Fisheries and
  Aquaculture Science
Pesticides Safety Directorate
Rural Payments Agency
Veterinary Laboratories Agency
Veterinary Medicines Directorate

Department of Health (DH)

Richmond House
79 Whitehall
London SW1A 2NS
Tel: 020 7210 4850
Website: *www.doh.gov.uk*
Status: Ministerial department

Responsible for the National Health Service,
personal social services provided by local
authorities and all other health issues in England,
including public health matters and the health
consequences of environmental and food issues.
Represents UK health policy interests in the EU
and the World Health Organisation.

Executive agencies

Health Protection Agency
Medicines and Healthcare products
  Regulatory Agency
NHS Estates
NHS Modernisation Agency
NHS Pensions Agency
NHS Purchasing and Supply Agency

Department for International Development (DFID)

1 Palace Street
London SW1E 5HE
Tel: 0845 300 4100
Website: *www.dfid.gov.uk*
Status: Ministerial department

Responsible for promoting sustainable
international development and the reduction of
global poverty; managing the UK's programme of
assistance to developing countries; and for
ensuring that government policies affecting
developing countries, including environment,
trade, investment and agricultural policies, take
account of those countries' concerns.

Department of Trade and Industry (DTI)

1 Victoria Street
London SW1H 0ET
Tel: 020 7215 5000
Website: *www.dti.gov.uk*
Status: Ministerial department

Competitiveness; enterprise, innovation and
productivity; science, engineering and technology;
markets; the legal and regulatory framework for
business and consumers. Specific responsibilities

include innovation policy; regional industrial
policy and the Regional Development Agencies,
small businesses, spread of management best
practice, and business/education links in England;
and employment relations, consumer and
competition policy, international trade policy,
energy policy, company law, insolvency, radio
regulation, patents and copyright protection,
import and export licensing, Research Councils
and relations with specific business sectors across
the UK.

See also Office of Science and Technology. UK
Trade and Investment* is a body jointly funded by
the DTI and the Foreign & Commonwealth Office.

Executive agencies

Companies House*
Employment Tribunals Service
Insolvency Service
National Weights and Measures Laboratory
Patent Office*
Radiocommunications Agency
Small Business Service*

Department for Transport (DfT)

Great Minster House
76 Marsham Street
London SW1P 4DR
Tel: 020 7944 8300
Website: *www.dft.gov.uk*
Status: Ministerial department

Policies on roads, local transport and shipping in
England; railways in Great Britain; and aviation,
including the Civil Aviation Authority, across
the UK.

Executive agencies

Driver and Vehicle Licensing Agency*
Driving Standards Agency*
Highways Agency*
Maritime and Coastguard Agency
Vehicle Certification Agency
Vehicle and Operator Services Agency

Department for Work and Pensions (DWP)

Richmond House
79 Whitehall
London SW1A 2NS
Tel: 020 7944 8300
Website: *www.dwp.gov.uk*
Status: Ministerial department

Welfare, pensions, employment and disability issues in Great Britain.

Executive agencies

Appeals Service
Child Support Agency*
Jobcentre Plus*
The Pension Service*

Driver and Vehicle Licensing Agency (DVLA)

Longview Road
Morriston
Swansea SA6 7JL
Tel: 0870 240 0009 (drivers) or
0870 240 0010 (vehicles)
Website: *www.dvla.gov.uk*
Status: Executive agency of the Department for Transport

Registration of drivers and vehicles; collection of vehicle excise duty (Great Britain).

Driving Standards Agency (DSA)

Stanley House
56 Talbot Street
Nottingham NG1 5GU
Tel: 0115 901 2500
Website: *www.dsa.gov.uk*
Status: Executive agency of the Department for Transport

Testing of drivers, motorcyclists and driving instructors in Great Britain; maintaining registers of approved driving instructors and large goods vehicle instructors; and supervising training for learner motorcyclists.

Export Credits Guarantee Department (ECGD)

PO Box 2200
2 Exchange Tower
Harbour Exchange Square
London E14 9GS
Tel: 020 7512 7000
Website: *www.ecgd.gov.uk*
Status: Non-ministerial department

The UK official export credit agency. Insures UK exporters of capital goods against non-payment; guarantees bank loans for buyers of UK goods; provides insurance for UK investors against political risks overseas.

Food Standards Agency (FSA)

Aviation House
125 Kingsway
London WC2B 6NH
Tel: 020 7276 8000
Website: *www.food.gov.uk*
Status: Non-ministerial department

Protection of health and consumer interests in relation to food (UK).

Executive agency

Meat Hygiene Service

Foreign & Commonwealth Office (FCO)

King Charles Street
London SW1A 2AH
Tel: 020 7008 1500
Website: *www.fco.gov.uk*
Status: Ministerial department

Provides the means of communication between the UK Government and other governments and international governmental organisations on all matters of international relations. Responsible for alerting the UK Government to the implications of developments overseas; for promoting UK interests overseas; for protecting UK citizens abroad; for explaining UK policies to, and cultivating relationships with, governments overseas; for the discharge of UK responsibilities to the Overseas Territories; for entry clearance (through UK visas, with the Home Office) and for promoting UK business overseas (jointly with the Department of Trade and Industry through UK Trade and Investment*).

Executive agency

Wilton Park (conferences)

Forestry Commission

Silvan House
231 Corstorphine Road
Edinburgh EH12 7AT
Tel: 0131 334 0303
Website: *www.forestry.gov.uk*
Status: Non-ministerial department

Forestry policy in England, Wales and Scotland, including grant aid for stewardship of existing woodlands and woodland expansion in the private sector; management of the national forests.

Executive agencies
Forest Enterprise England
Forest Enterprise Scotland
Forest Enterprise Wales
Forest Research

Highways Agency

Romney House
43 Marsham Street
London SW1P 3HW
Tel: 08457 504030
Website: *www.highways.gov.uk*
Status: Executive agency of the Department for
Transport

Manages, maintains and improves the motorway
and trunk road network in England.

Home Office

50 Queen Anne's Gate
London SW1H 9AT
Tel: 0870 000 1585
Website: *www.homeoffice.gov.uk*
Status: Ministerial department

In England and Wales: crime and policing; aspects
of the criminal justice system, including the prison
and probation services; race equality and diversity
policies; active communities and volunteering.

UK-wide: Combating terrorism and other threats
to national security; drugs policy; regulation of
entry to and settlement in the UK (see also entry
for the Immigration and Nationality Directorate).

Licensing of the use of animals in scientific
procedures (Great Britain).

Executive agencies
Criminal Records Bureau (England and Wales)
Forensic Science Service (England and Wales)
HM Prison Service (England and Wales)
UK Passport Service*

Immigration and Nationality Directorate (IND)

Lunar House
40 Wellesley Road
Croydon CR9 2BY
Telephone: 0870 606 7766
Website: *www.ind.homeoffice.gov.uk*
Status: A directorate of the Home Office

Regulation of entry to, and settlement in, the UK
including policies on asylum and managed
migration.

Inland Revenue

Somerset House
London WC2R 1LB
Tel: 020 7438 6622
Website: *www.inlandrevenue.gov.uk*
Status: Non-ministerial department and executive
agency, reporting to the Chancellor of the
Exchequer

Administration and collection of direct taxes in
the UK and valuation of property in Great Britain.
Income tax, corporation tax, capital gains tax,
petroleum revenue tax, inheritance tax, stamp
duties, tax credits, National Insurance
contributions and advice on tax and National
Insurance contributions policy. Also enforces the
national minimum wage on behalf of the
Department of Trade and Industry.

Executive agency
Valuation office (GB)

Invest UK

See UK Trade and Investment

Jobcentre Plus

Caxton House
Tothill Street
London SW1H 9NA
Tel: 020 7272 3000
Website: *www.jobcentreplus.gov.uk*
Status: Executive agency of the Department for
Work and Pensions

Helping people into work and employers to fill
vacancies; payment of benefits to people of
working age (Great Britain).

HM Land Registry

Lincoln's Inn Fields
London WC2A 3PH
Tel: 020 7917 8888
Website: *www.landregistry.gov.uk*
Status: Government Department and executive
agency reporting to the Secretary of State for
Constitutional Affairs.

Guarantees the title to, and records the ownership
of, interests in registered land in England and
Wales.

Legal Secretariat to the Law Officers (LSLO)

Attorney General's Chambers
9 Buckingham Gate
London SW1E 6JP
Tel: 020 7271 2422
Website: *www.lslo.gov.uk*
Status: Ministerial department

Supports the Law Officers of the Crown (the Attorney General and the Solicitor General) in their functions as the Government's principal legal advisers in England, Wales and Northern Ireland.

Executive agency
Treasury Solicitor's Department*

Met Office

FitzRoy Road
Exeter EX1 3PB
Tel: 0870 900 0100
Website: *www.metoffice.com*
Status: Executive agency of the Ministry of Defence

Provides meteorological services (including climate advice) to the Armed Forces, government departments, the public, civil aviation, shipping, industry, agriculture, commerce and others.

Ministry of Defence (MoD)

Old War Office Building
Whitehall
London SW1A 2EU
Tel: 020 7218 9000 or 0870 607 4455
Website: *www.mod.gov.uk*
Status: Ministerial department

Defence policy, and control and administration of the Armed Services (UK).

Executive agencies
The MoD has 36 executive agencies including:
Defence Analytical Services Agency
Defence Procurement Agency
Defence Science and Technology Laboratory
Met Office*
Ministry of Defence Police
Veterans Agency*

The National Archives (TNA)

Ruskin Avenue
Kew
Surrey TW9 4DU
Tel: 020 8876 3444
Website: *www.nationalarchives.gov.uk*
Status: Non-ministerial department and executive agency, reporting to the Secretary of State for Constitutional Affairs

Responsible for the public records and national archives of England, Wales and the United Kingdom as a whole; and for historical manuscripts relating to British history. Brings together the work of the Public Record Office and the Historical Manuscripts Commission.

National Savings and Investments (NS&I)

Charles House
375 Kensington High Street
London W14 8SD
Tel: 020 7348 9466
Website: *www.nationalsavings.co.uk*
Status: Executive agency reporting to the Chancellor of the Exchequer

Raises funds for the Government by selling a range of investments to personal savers across the UK.

Office of Communications (Ofcom)

Riverside House
2A Southwark Bridge Road
London SE1 9HA
Tel: 020 7981 3000
Website: *www.ofcom.org.uk*

Becomes the regulator of the UK communications industry at the end of 2003, replacing the Broadcasting Standards Commission, the Independent Television Commission, Oftel, the Radio Authority and the Radiocommunications Agency.

Office of the Deputy Prime Minister (ODPM)

26 Whitehall
London SW1A 2WH
Tel: 020 7944 4400
Website: *www.odpm.gov.uk*
Status: Ministerial department

Policies in England for planning; housing; regeneration; local and regional government; homelessness, urban policy, neighbourhood renewal and social exclusion, and the Fire Service (legislation currently before Parliament will transfer responsibility for the Fire Service in Wales to the Welsh Assembly Government).

Executive agencies

Fire Service College
Ordnance Survey*
Planning Inspectorate*
Queen Elizabeth II Conference Centre
Rent Service*

Office of Fair Trading (OFT)

Fleetbank House
2–6 Salisbury Square
London EC4Y 8JX
Tel: 020 7211 8000 or 08457 224499
Website: www.oft.gov.uk
Status: Non-ministerial department

Administers legislation relating to competition and consumer protection; promotes competition and consumer awareness (UK).

Office of Gas and Electricity Markets (Ofgem)

9 Millbank
London SWIP 3GE
Tel: 020 7901 7000
Website: www.ofgem.gov.uk
Status: Non-ministerial department

Regulates the gas and electricity industries across England, Scotland and Wales.

Office for National Statistics (ONS)

1 Drummond Gate
London SW1V 2QQ
Tel: 0845 601 3034
Website: www.statistics.gov.uk
Status: Executive agency and non-ministerial department reporting to the Chancellor of the Exchequer

Collects, compiles and provides a wide range of statistical information, including the UK National Accounts, UK Census of Population, and population estimates and projections. Also carries out research studies on behalf of other government departments concerned with social and economic issues. The Director of ONS is the National Statistician and Registrar General of England and Wales.

Office of the Rail Regulator (ORR)

1 Waterhouse Square
138–142 Holborn
London EC1N 2TQ
Tel: 020 7282 2000
Website: www.rail-reg.gov.uk
Status: Non-ministerial department

Independent regulation of Network Rail's stewardship of the national rail network infrastructure (track, signalling, bridges, tunnels, stations and depots); economic regulation of the monopoly and dominant elements of the rail industry (Great Britain).

Office of Science and Technology (OST)

1 Victoria Street
London SW1H 0ET
Tel: 020 7215 5000
Website: www.ost.gov.uk
Status: Department of the DTI

Supports the Secretary of State for Trade and Industry and the Minister for Science on issues of science, engineering and technology (SET). Headed by the Government's Chief Scientific Adviser (who reports directly to the Prime Minister), the OST is responsible for policy on SET, both nationally and internationally, and coordinates SET policy across government departments. Through the Director General of Research Councils, the OST also has responsibility for the Science Budget and for the government-financed Research Councils.

Office for Standards in Education (Ofsted)

Alexandra House
33 Kingsway
London WC2B 6SE
Tel: 020 7421 6800
Website: www.ofsted.gov.uk
Status: Non-ministerial department

Inspection of schools, 16–19 education, teaching training institutions, local education authorities and youth work in England; also regulation of early years childcare, including childminders.

Office of Telecommunications (Oftel)

50 Ludgate Hill
London EC4M 7JJ
Tel: 020 7981 3000
Website: *www.oftel.gov.uk*
Status: Non-ministerial department

Independent regulatory body for the
telecommunications industry. From 29 December
2003 Oftel will be merged into the Office of
Communications (Ofcom), the new regulator for
television, radio, telecommunications and the
radio spectrum.

Office of Water Services (OFWAT)

Centre City Tower
7 Hill Street
Birmingham B5 4UA
Tel: 0121 625 1300
Website: *www.ofwat.gov.uk*
Status: Non-ministerial department

Economic regulator of the water and sewerage
industry in England and Wales.

Ordnance Survey (OS)

Romsey Road
Maybush
Southampton SO16 4GU
Tel: 08456 050505
Website: *www.ordnancesurvey.co.uk*
Status: Executive agency and non-ministerial
department reporting to the Office of the Deputy
Prime Minister

Official surveying and mapping of Great Britain,
and associated scientific work.

Patent Office

Concept House
Cardiff Road
Newport
Gwent NP10 8QQ
Tel: 08459 500505
Website: *www.patent.gov.uk*
Status: Executive agency of the Department of
Trade and Industry

Administers patents, trade marks, registered
designs and copyright (UK).

The Pension Service

Ground Floor
Trevelyan House
30 Great Peter Street
London SW1P 3BY
Tel: 0845 301 3011
Website: *www.thepensionservice.gov.uk*
Status: Executive agency of the Department for
Work and Pensions

Payment of state retirement pensions, Pension
Credit and winter fuel payments (Great Britain).

Planning Inspectorate

Temple Quay House
2 The Square
Temple Quay
Bristol BS1 6PN
Tel: 0117 372 6372
Website: *www.planning-inspectorate.gov.uk*
Status: Executive agency of the Office of the
Deputy Prime Minister and the National Assembly
for Wales

Appeals and other casework under planning and
environmental legislation relating to England and
Wales.

Prime Minister's Office (No 10)

10 Downing Street
London SW1A 2AA
Tel: 020 7930 4433
Website: *www.pmo.gov.uk*
Status: Part of the Cabinet Office, which is a
ministerial department

Provides support to the Prime Minister and works
with the Cabinet Office to provide central
direction for the development, implementation
and presentation of government policy.

The Rent Service

5 Welbeck Street
London W1G 9YQ
Tel: 020 7023 6000
Website: *www.therentservice.gov.uk*
Status: Executive agency of the Office of the
Deputy Prime Minister

Makes fair rent evaluations for regulated and
secure tenancies, and determines whether Housing
Benefit claimants (and prospective claimants) are
being asked to pay more rent than their landlords

might reasonably expect in open market conditions (England).

Royal Mint

Llantrisant
Pontyclun
Mid-Glamorgan CF72 8YT
Tel: 01443 623060 or 01443 623061
Website: *www.royalmint.com*
Status: Executive agency of HM Treasury

Production of coins for the United Kingdom and for overseas customers. Also military and civilian decorations and medals, commemorative medals, and royal and official seals.

Scotland Office

Dover House
Whitehall
London SW1A 2AU
Tel: 020 7270 6754
Website: *www.scottishsecretary.gov.uk*
Status: Office within the Department for Constitutional Affairs

The Scotland Office is a distinct office within the Department for Constitutional Affairs. It supports the Secretary of State for Scotland who is a member of the UK Cabinet and represents Scottish interests within the UK Government in matters that are reserved to the UK Parliament under the terms of the *Scotland Act 1998*. He sustains the devolution settlement by encouraging co-operation, between both Parliaments and between the UK Government and the Scottish Executive, or otherwise intervenes as required by the Act.

Small Business Service (SBS)

66–74 Victoria Street
London SW1E 6SW
Tel: 0845 001 0031
Website: *www.sbs.gov.uk*
Status: Executive agency of the Department of Trade and Industry

Provides guidance and services for small and medium-sized enterprises (SMEs) in England, and works in partnership with similar organisations in the rest of the United Kingdom.

Treasury Solicitor's Department

Queen Anne's Chambers
28 Broadway
London
SW1H 9JS
Tel: 020 7210 3000
Website: *www.treasury-solicitor.gov.uk*
Status: Government department and executive agency, reporting to the Attorney General.

Provides litigation and advisory services to Government departments and other publicly funded bodies in England and Wales.

Trade Partners UK (TPUK)

See UK Trade and Investment

HM Treasury (HMT)

1 Horse Guards Road
London SW1A 2HQ
Tel: 020 7270 5000
Website: *www.hm-treasury.gov.uk*
Status: Ministerial department

Financial and economic policy; overseeing the framework for monetary policy; tax policy; planning and control of public spending; government accounting; the quality and cost-effectiveness of public services; increasing productivity and expanding economic and employment opportunities; promoting international financial stability and UK economic interests; the regime for supervision of financial services; management of central government debt; and supply of notes and coins across the United Kingdom. The Office of Government Commerce (OGC) is an independent office of the Treasury.

Executive agencies
UK Debt Management Office
National Savings and Investments*
Office for National Statistics*
OGCBuying.Solutions
Royal Mint*
Valuation Office

United Kingdom Passport Service (UKPS)

Globe House
89 Eccleston Square
London SW1V 1PN
Tel: 0870 521 0410

Website: *www.passports.gov.uk*
Status: Executive agency of the Home Office

Issues new, replacement and amended passports
to British nationals living in the United Kingdom.

UK Trade and Investment

Kingsgate House
66–74 Victoria Street
London SW1E 6SW
Tel: 020 7215 5444
Website: *www.tradeinvest.gov.uk*
Status: Non-ministerial department

Invest UK and Trade Partners UK will be renamed
UK Trade and Investment in November 2003.

Responsible for promoting inward investment;
supporting new and established businesses from
overseas; and helping companies based in the UK
to trade and invest overseas.

Veterans Agency (VA)

Tomlinson House
Government Buildings
Norcross
Blackpool FY5 3WP
Tel: 0800 169 2277
Website: *www.veteransagency.mod.uk*
Status: Executive agency of the Ministry of
Defence

Provides financial and welfare support to war
disabled pensioners and war widows, and advice
to all veterans via a free helpline and website.

Wales Office (WO)

Gwydyr House
Whitehall
London SW1A 2ER
Tel: 020 7270 0583
Website: *www.walesoffice.gov.uk*
Status: Office within the Department for
Constitutional Affairs

The Secretary of State for Wales is the member of
the UK Cabinet who represents Welsh interests
within the UK Government and takes the lead in
matters connected with the *Government of Wales
Act 1998*. The Secretary of State is responsible for
consulting the National Assembly for Wales on the
Government's legislative programme. The Wales
Office is part of the Department for
Constitutional Affairs for administration

purposes, while retaining its separate identity and
continuing to report to the Secretary of State for
Wales.

Wales

Welsh Assembly Government
Llywodraeth Cynulliad Cymru

Cathays Park
Cardiff CF10 3NQ
Tel: 029 20 825111
Website: *www.wales.gov.uk*
www.cymru.gov.uk (yn Gymraeg)

The Welsh Assembly Government is accountable
to the National Assembly for Wales and develops
and implements policy on issues that have been
devolved: most aspects of agriculture, forestry,
fisheries and food, including animal welfare, the
Forestry Commission in Wales, payments to Welsh
farmers, and a role in the negotiations and
implementation of EU policy in Wales; culture,
including the arts, ancient monuments and
historic buildings, sport and the Welsh language;
economic development, including running the
Welsh Development Agency and Wales Tourist
Board, and administering European Structural
Funds; education and training, including setting
and monitoring school standards, the content of
the National Curriculum, funding further and
higher education, and overseeing and funding
training; the environment, including controlling
water quality and flood defence, and determining
policies on town and country planning; some
areas of health, including running the National
Health Service in Wales; local government and
housing, including deciding on overall funds for
local authorities, and overseeing the council tax
system in Wales; social services, including care in
the community, social services for children, and
adoption; the promotion of trade and inward
investment; and some aspects of transport.

National Assembly for Wales
Cynulliad Cenedlaethol Cymru

Cardiff Bay
Cardiff CF99 1NA
Tel: 029 20 825111
Website: *www.wales.gov.uk*
www.cymru.gov.uk (yn Gymraeg)

The National Assembly for Wales has powers to
make secondary legislation to meet distinctive

Welsh needs in areas that have been devolved, sets the budget for those areas and holds the Welsh Assembly Government to account for its policies and operational decisions. It approves the overall policy framework within which the Welsh Assembly Government operates, and its committees work collaboratively with Welsh Assembly Government Ministers to develop new policies.

Agencies
The Welsh National Assembly is responsible for over 50 public bodies including:
Welsh Development Agency
Higher Education Funding Council for Wales
Sports Council for Wales
Welsh Language Board

Scotland

Scottish Parliament
Edinburgh
EH99 1SP
Tel: 0131 348 5000
Website: *www.scottish.parliament.uk*

The Scottish Parliament is responsible for most health issues; education and training; local government, social services, housing and planning; inward investment and promotion of trade; economic development and tourism; most aspects of law and home affairs, including prisons, the prosecution system and the courts; the police and the fire services; the road network, bus policy, ports and harbours; agriculture, the environment, fisheries, forestry and food; the natural and built heritage; sport, culture, the arts and language; and statistics, public registers and records.

Scottish Executive
St Andrew's House
Edinburgh EH1 3DG
Tel: 0131 556 8400
Website: *www.scotland.gov.uk*

The Scottish Ministers and Scottish Executive are responsible in Scotland for a wide range of statutory functions. These are administered by six main departments (see below). Along with Corporate Services, Finance and Central Services Department, Legal & Parliamentary Services, and the Crown Office and Procurator Fiscal Service,

these departments are collectively known as the Scottish Executive. In addition, there are a number of other Scottish departments for which Scottish ministers have some degree of responsibility: the department of the Registrar General for Scotland (the General Register Office), the National Archives of Scotland and the department of the Registers of Scotland. Other government departments with significant Scottish responsibilities have offices in Scotland and work closely with the Scottish Executive.

Scottish Executive Development Department
Victoria Quay
Edinburgh EH6 6QQ

Housing and area regeneration, social justice (including equality, voluntary and social inclusion issues); transport and local roads, National Roads Directorate; land-use planning; building control.

Executive agency
Communities Scotland

Scottish Executive Education Department
Victoria Quay
Edinburgh EH6 6QQ

Administration of public education; science and technology; youth and community services; the arts, libraries, museums and galleries; Gaelic; broadcasting, sport and tourism; protection and presentation to the public of historic buildings and ancient monuments.

Executive agencies
Historic Scotland
Scottish Public Pensions Agency
Student Awards Agency for Scotland

Scottish Executive Enterprise Transport and Lifelong Learning Department
Meridian Court
5 Cadogan Street
Glasgow G2 7AB
and
Europa Building
450 Argyle Street
Glasgow G2 8LG
Tel. 0141 242 5703
and
Victoria Quay
Edinburgh EH6 6QQ

Industrial and economic development: responsibility for selective financial and regional development grant assistance to industry; the promotion of industrial development; urban regeneration and training policy; administration of European Structural Funds programmes for Scotland; and matters relating to energy policy, including renewables. Sponsorship of Scottish Enterprise and Highlands and Islands Enterprise. Transport: public transport, cycling and walking; trunk road construction and maintenance; Clyde Hebrides and Northern Isles ferry services; devolved aspects of rail; Highlands and Islands Airports Ltd. Lifelong learning: further and higher education; science; student support; youth and adult training; transitions to work; Modern Apprenticeships; Careers Scotland. Sponsorship of the Scottish Further and Higher Education Funding Councils and development of the Scottish University for Industry (Scottish Ufi/learndirect scotland).

Scottish Executive Environment and Rural Affairs Department

Pentland House
47 Robb's Loan
Edinburgh EH14 1TY

Agriculture and food; safeguarding of plant, animal health and welfare; land use and forestry; CAP subsidies and commodities. Coordination of the Executive's policy on the promotion of rural development and overall responsibility for land reform. Environment, including environmental protection, nature conservation and the countryside; water and sewerage services; waste management, sustainable development, biodiversity, and climate change. Fisheries and aquaculture; control of sea fishing under the CFP; protection of the marine environment. Agricultural and biological research; support of the agricultural and biological science base and funding of related research.

Executive agencies
Fisheries Research Service
Scottish Agricultural Science Agency
Scottish Fisheries Protection Agency

Scottish Executive Health Department

St Andrew's House
Regent Road
Edinburgh EH1 3DG

Executive leadership of NHSScotland and the development and implementation of health and community care policy, in particular: improving, protecting and monitoring the health of the people of Scotland, implementing policies which address health inequalities, prevent disease, prolong life and promote and protect health; developing and delivering modern primary care and community care services; providing hospital and specialist services; encouraging collaboration and joint working between health and other partner organisations; and promoting and monitoring consistent standards of performance throughout NHSScotland.

Scottish Executive Justice Department

St Andrew's House
Regent Road
Edinburgh EH1 3DG

Law and order issues. Police, fire and emergency planning. Criminal Law and criminal justice; community justice services and parole; civil law, and jurisdiction and procedure; access to justice, legal aid and the legal system generally. The European Convention on Human Rights. Courts and judicial appointments.

Executive agencies
The Accountant in Bankruptcy
The Registers of Scotland
The Scottish Court Service
The Scottish Prison Service

Corporate Services

S1/5 Saughton House
Broomhouse Drive
Edinburgh EH11 3XD

Human resources, including personnel policy, propriety, recruitment, staff appraisal and interchange, pay, employee relations, training and development, equal opportunities and welfare; estate management, accommodation services, internal communications, IT facilities and security matters.

The Crown Office and Procurator Fiscal Service

25 Chambers Street
Edinburgh EH1 1LA
Tel: 0131 226 2626
Website: *www.crownoffice.gov.uk*

The Crown Office and Procurator Fiscal Service provides Scotland's independent public prosecution and deaths investigation service. Although it is a Department of the Scottish Executive, the independent position of the Lord Advocate as head of the systems of criminal prosecution and investigation of deaths in Scotland is protected by the *Scotland Act 1998*.

Finance and Central Services Department

St Andrew's House
Edinburgh EH1 3DG

Matters relating to local government; finance; public service delivery; Europe and external relations (including relations with Whitehall); analytical services; media and communications; public bodies and public appointments; and development of Scotland's cities.

Legal & Parliamentary Services

25 Chambers Street
Edinburgh EH1 1LA

Policy on constitutional issues, devolution settlement and electoral matters. The Scottish Parliament's powers and procedures, coordination of the Scottish Executive's legislative programme, liaison with the Scottish Parliamentary Ombudsman, freedom of information policy and legislation. Provision of legal advice and services for the Scottish Executive through the Office of the Solicitor to the Scottish Executive (OSSE). Also responsible for drafting Bills to be put before Parliament by the Executive and handling associated work.

Executive agency
National Archives of Scotland

Northern Ireland

Northern Ireland Office

Castle Buildings
Stormont
Belfast BT4 3SG
Tel: 028 9052 0700
Website: *www.nio.gov.uk*
11 Millbank
London SW1 4PN
Tel: 020 7210 3000

The Northern Ireland Office is headed by the Secretary of State for Northern Ireland, a Cabinet minister who has direct responsibility for matters not devolved to the Northern Ireland Assembly, including political and constitutional matters, law and order, security, criminal justice and electoral matters. If the Northern Ireland Assembly is suspended, the Secretary of State for Northern Ireland also assumes responsibility for the direction of the Northern Ireland departments.

Executive agencies:
Compensation Agency for Northern Irelan
Forensic Science Northern Ireland
Northern Ireland Prison Service
Youth Justice Agency
The Northern Ireland Court Service is an executive agency reporting to the Secretary of State for Constitutional Affairs

Northern Ireland Assembly

Parliament Buildings
Stormont
Belfast BT4 3XX
Tel: 028 9052 1133
Website: *www.niassembly.gov.uk*

When it is sitting, the Northern Ireland Assembly has the power to make laws on all domestic matters that have been devolved by the Westminster Parliament: agriculture, forestry, fisheries and food; culture, media and sport; economic development; education and training; most areas of employment legislation; environment; making agreements for cross-border co-operation with the Republic of Ireland through the North-South Ministerial Council; the National Health Service; local government; social security; social services; some areas of trade and industry, including inward investment, promotion of trade, exports and tourism, and some elements of company regulation; and most areas of transport.

Northern Ireland Executive and Departments

Website: *www.northernireland.gov.uk*

Office of the First Minister and Deputy First Minister

Castle Buildings
Stormont
Belfast BT4 3SR
Tel: 028 9052 8400

Economic policy; equality; human rights; executive secretariat; liaison with the North-South Ministerial Council, British-Irish Council, British-Irish Intergovernmental Conference and Civic Forum. Liaison with the Northern Ireland Office on excepted and reserved matters. European affairs; international matters; liaison with the International Fund for Ireland; the Executive Information Service; community relations; Programme for Government; public appointments policy; honours; freedom of information; victims; Nolan standards; women's issues; policy innovation; public service improvement.

Department of Agriculture and Rural Development

Dundonald House
Upper Newtownards Road
Belfast BT4 3SB
Tel: 028 9052 0100

Food; farming and environment policy; agri-food development; veterinary matters; Science Service; rural development; forestry; sea fisheries; rivers.

Executive agencies
Forest Service
Rivers Agency

Department of Culture, Arts and Leisure

Interpoint, 20–24 York Street
Belfast BT15 1AQ
Tel: 028 9025 8825

Responsible for the arts, culture, sport, museums, public libraries, inland waterways, inland fisheries, language diversity, visitor amenities and matters relating to the National Lottery and the Northern Ireland Events Company. It also has responsibility for two agencies and two cross-border implementation bodies that deal with inland waterways and language issues.

Executive agencies
Ordnance Survey
Public Record Office

Department of Education

Rathgael House
Balloo Road
Bangor BT19 7PR
Tel: 028 9127 9279

Control of the five education and library boards and education from nursery to secondary education; youth services; and the development of community relations within and between schools.

Department for Employment and Learning

39–49 Adelaide House
Adelaide Street
Belfast BT2 8FD
Tel: 028 9025 7777

Higher education; further education; vocational training; employment services; employment law and labour relations; teacher training and teacher education; student support and postgraduate awards; training grants.

Department of Enterprise, Trade and Investment

Netherleigh House
Massey Avenue
Belfast BT4 2JP
Tel: 028 9052 9900

Economic policy development, energy, tourism, mineral development, health and safety at work, Companies Registry, Insolvency Service, consumer affairs, labour market and economic statistics services. It also has a role in ensuring the provision of the infrastructure for modern economy.

Executive agencies
General Consumer Council for Northern Ireland
Health and Safety Executive for Northern Ireland
Invest NI
Northern Ireland Tourist Board

Department of the Environment

Clarence Court
10–18 Adelaide Street
Belfast BT2 8GB
Tel: 028 9054 0540

Most of the Department's functions are carried out by executive agencies. These include: planning; protection and conservation of the natural and built environment; and driver and vehicle testing and licensing. Core departmental functions include: the improvement and promotion of road safety and supporting a system of local government that meets the needs of citizens and taxpayers.

Executive agencies
Driver and Vehicle Licensing (Northern Ireland)
Driver and Vehicle Testing Agency
Environment and Heritage Service
Planning Service

Department of Finance and Personnel

Rathgael House
Balloo Road
Bangor BT19 7NA
Tel: 028 9127 9657

Control of public expenditure; personnel
management of the Northern Ireland Civil
Service; provision of central services and advice.

Executive agencies
Business Development Service
Construction Service
Government Purchasing Agency
Land Registers of Northern Ireland
Northern Ireland Statistics and Research Agency
Office of Law Reform
Rates Collection Agency
Valuation and Lands Agency

Department of Health, Social Services and Public Safety

Castle Buildings
Stormont
Belfast BT4 3SJ
Tel: 028 9052 0500

Health and personal social services; public health
and public safety; health promotion; Fire
Authority.

Executive agency
Health Estates Agency

Department for Regional Development

Clarence Court
10–18 Adelaide Street
Belfast BT2 8GB
Tel: 028 9054 0540

Main functions include: strategic planning;
transport strategy; transport policy and support,
including rail and bus services, ports and airports
policy; provision and maintenance of roads; and
water and sewerage services.

Executive agencies
Roads Service
Water Service

Department for Social Development

Churchill House
Victoria Square
Belfast BT1 4SD
Tel: 028 9056 9100

Departmental functions include: urban
regeneration; voluntary and community sector;
housing; social policy and legislation; child
support; state, occupational and personal
pensions; social security policy and legislation.

Executive agencies
Northern Ireland Child Support Agency
Northern Ireland Social Security Agency

Appendix B Significant dates in UK history

55 and 54 BC: Julius Caesar's expeditions to Britain

AD 43: Roman conquest begins under Claudius

122–38: Hadrian's Wall built

c.409: Roman army withdraws from Britain

450s onwards: foundation of the Anglo-Saxon kingdoms

597: arrival of St Augustine to preach Christianity to the Anglo-Saxons

664: Synod of Whitby opts for Roman Catholic rather than Celtic church

789–95: first Viking raids

832–60: Scots and Picts merge under Kenneth Macalpin to form what is to become the kingdom of Scotland

860s: Danes overrun East Anglia, Northumbria and eastern Mercia

871–99: reign of Alfred the Great in Wessex

1066: William the Conqueror defeats Harold Godwinson at Hastings and takes the throne

1086: *Domesday Book* completed: a survey of English landholdings undertaken on the orders of William I

1215: King John signs Magna Carta to protect feudal rights against royal abuse

13th century: first Oxford and Cambridge colleges founded

1301: Edward of Caernarvon (later Edward II) created Prince of Wales

1314: Battle of Bannockburn ensures survival of separate Scottish kingdom

1337: Hundred Years War between England and France begins

1348–49: Black Death (bubonic plague) wipes out a third of England's population

1381: Peasants' Revolt in England, the most significant popular rebellion in English history

c.1387–c.1394: Geoffrey Chaucer writes The *Canterbury Tales*

1400–c.1406: Owain Glyndŵr (Owen Glendower) leads the last major Welsh revolt against English rule

1411: St Andrews University founded, the first university in Scotland

1455–87: Wars of the Roses between Yorkists and Lancastrians

1477: first book to be printed in England, by William Caxton

1534–40: English Reformation; Henry VIII breaks with the Papacy

1536–42: Acts of Union integrate England and Wales administratively and legally and give Wales representation in Parliament

1547–53: Protestantism becomes official religion in England under Edward VI

1553–58: Catholic reaction under Mary I

1558: loss of Calais, last English possession in France

1558–1603: reign of Elizabeth I; moderate Protestantism established

1588: defeat of Spanish Armada

c.1590–c.1613: plays of Shakespeare written

1603: union of the crowns of Scotland and England under James VI of Scotland

1642–51: Civil Wars between King and Parliament

1649: execution of Charles I

1653–58: Oliver Cromwell rules as Lord Protector

1660: monarchy restored under Charles II

1660: founding of the Royal Society for the Promotion of Natural Knowledge

1663: John Milton finishes *Paradise Lost*

1665: the Great Plague, the last major epidemic of plague in England

1666: the Great Fire of London

1686: Isaac Newton sets out his laws of motion and the idea of universal gravitation

1688: Glorious Revolution; accession of William and Mary

1707: Acts of Union unite the English and Scottish Parliaments

1721–42: Robert Walpole, first British Prime Minister

1745–46: Bonnie Prince Charlie's failed attempt to retake the British throne for the Stuarts

c.1760s–c.1830s: Industrial Revolution

1761: opening of the Bridgewater Canal ushers in Canal Age

1775–83: American War of Independence leads to loss of the Thirteen Colonies

1800: Act of Union unites Great Britain and Ireland (came into effect 1 January 1801)

1805: Battle of Trafalgar, the decisive naval battle of the Napoleonic Wars

1815: Battle of Waterloo, the final defeat of Napoleon

1825: opening of the Stockton and Darlington Railway, the world's first passenger railway

1829: Catholic emancipation

1832: first Reform Act extends the franchise (increasing the number of those entitled to vote by about 50 per cent)

1833: abolition of slavery in the British Empire (the slave *trade* having been abolished in 1807)

1836–70: Charles Dickens writes his novels

1837–1901: reign of Queen Victoria

1859: Charles Darwin publishes *On the Origin of Species by Means of Natural Selection*

1868: founding of the Trades Union Congress (TUC)

1907: Henry Royce and C S Rolls build and sell their first Rolls-Royce (the Silver Ghost)

1910–36: during the reign of George V, the British Empire reaches its territorial zenith

1914–18: First World War

1918: the vote given to women over 30

1921: Anglo-Irish Treaty establishes the Irish Free State; Northern Ireland remains part of the United Kingdom

1926: John Logie Baird gives the first practical demonstration of television

1928: voting age for women reduced to 21, on equal terms with men

1928: Alexander Fleming discovers penicillin

1936: King Edward VIII abdicates

1936: Jarrow Crusade, the most famous of the hunger marches in the 1930s

1939–45: Second World War

1943: Max Newman, Donald Michie, Tommy Flowers and Alan Turing build the first electronic computer, Colossus I, which was used for breaking enemy communications codes in the Second World War

1947: independence for India and Pakistan: Britain begins to dismantle its imperial structure

1948: the National Health Service comes into operation, offering free medical care to the whole population

1952: accession of Elizabeth II

1953: Francis Crick and his colleague James Watson of the United States discover the structure of DNA

1965: first commercial natural gas discovery in the North Sea

1969: the vote is extended to all over the age of 18

1969: first notable discovery of offshore oil in the North Sea

1971: decimal currency is introduced

1973: the UK enters the European Community (now the European Union)

1979–90: Margaret Thatcher is the UK's first woman Prime Minister

1994: Channel Tunnel opened to rail traffic

1999: Scottish Parliament, National Assembly for Wales and Northern Ireland Assembly assume their devolved powers

2001: for the first time, the Labour Party wins a General Election with sufficient MPs to govern for a second full five-year period

2002: the Queen celebrates her Golden Jubilee

Appendix C Obituaries

Lord Aberconway (Charles McLaren; 3rd baron)
Industrialist and horticulturist
Born 1913, died February 2003

Frank Allaun
Labour MP, 1955–83 and campaigner for left-wing
causes
Born 1913, died November 2002

Sir Hardy Amies, KCVO
Fashion designer
Born 1909, died March 2003

Professor Michael Argyle
Psychologist
Born 1925, died September 2002

Theo Aronson
Writer
Born 1929, died May 2003

Lawrence Batley, OBE
Wholesaler, creator of the cash-and-carry
Born 1911, died August 2002

Duke of Bedford (John Robert [Ian] Russell; 13th
duke)
Owner of Woburn Abbey (Bedfordshire) who
opened it to the public
Born 1917, died October 2002

Duke of Bedford (Henry Robin Ian Russell; 14th
duke)
Custodian of the Woburn Abbey estate
Born 1940, died June 2003

Sir Basil Blackwell
Aero engineer
Born 1922, died May 2003

Lord Boardman, MC, TD (Thomas Gray
Boardman)
Former Conservative minister and chairman of
National Westminster Bank, 1983–89
Born 1919, died March 2003

Christopher Brasher, CBE
Athlete and founder of London Marathon
Born 1928, died February 2003

Peter Bromley
Racing commentator
Born 1929, died June 2003

Air Chief Marshal Sir Ivor Broom, KCB, CBE, DSO,
DFC and 2 bars, AFC
Wartime bomber pilot
Born 1920, died January 2003

Sir John Brown, CBE
Publisher, Oxford University Press, 1956–80
Born 1916, died March 2003

Barry Bucknell
Television do-it-yourself expert
Born 1918, died February 2003

Ronald Butt, CBE
Journalist and author
Born 1920, died December 2002

Phyllis Calvert
Actress
Born 1915, died October 2002

Professor Malcolm Cameron
Forensic pathologist
Born 1930, died June 2003

Dame Elizabeth Chesterton, DBE
Architect
Born 1915, died August 2002

Sir Michael Clapham, KBE
President of CBI, 1972–74
Born 1912, died November 2002

Pattie Coldwell
Broadcaster
Born 1952, died October 2002

Lady Georgina Coleridge
Magazine editor
Born 1916, died March 2003

Dame Diana Collins, DBE
Campaigner against nuclear weapons and
apartheid
Born 1917, died May 2003

Donald Coxeter
Mathematician and geometer
Born 1907, died March 2003

Hugh Crutwell
Principal of RADA, 1966–84
Born 1916, died August 2002

Jennifer d'Abo
Businesswoman
Born 1945, died April 2003

Lord Dacre of Glanton (Hugh Trevor-Roper)
Historian
Born 1914, died January 2003

Alec Dakin
Cryptographer and code-breaker
Born 1912, died June 2003

Professor Glyn Davies
Economist
Born 1919, died January 2003

Michael De-la-Noy
Writer
Born 1934, died August 2002

Lonnie Donegan
'King of Skiffle'
Born 1931, died November 2002

John Dreyfus
Typographer
Born 1918, died December 2002

Sir George Edwards, OM, CBE
Aircraft designer and engineer
Born 1908, died March 2003

Mary Ellis
Actress and singer
Born 1897, died January 2003

Michael Elphick
Actor
Born 1946, died September 2002

Adam Faith
Pop singer, actor and businessman
Born 1940, died March 2003

James Alan Ferman
Chairman of British Board of Film Classification, 1975–99
Born 1930, died December 2002

Mickey Finn
Percussionist with T. Rex
Born 1947, died January 2003

Louis FitzGibbon
Author
Born 1925, died January 2003

Monica Furlong
Author
Born 1930, died January 2003

Sir Paul Getty, KBE
Philanthropist
Born 1932, died April 2003

Maurice Gibb, CBE
Musician and singer
Born 1949, died January 2003**Ron Goodwin**
Composer
Born 1925, died January 2003

Winston Graham, OBE
Author
Born 1910, died July 2003

Sir John Habbakuk, FBA
Economic historian and Vice-Chancellor of Oxford University 1973–77
Born 1915, died November 2002

Lord Hambro (Charles Eric Alexander Hambro)
Banker
Born 1930, died November 2002

Brigadier J.R.E. Hamilton-Baillie, MC
Persistent prisoner-of-war camp escaper in Germany
Born 1919, died April 2003

Richard Harris
Actor
Born 1930, died October 2002

Lord Haslam (Robert Haslam)
Former chairman of British Steel (1983–86) and British Coal (1986–90)
Born 1923, died July 2002

Jocelyn Herbert
Designer
Born 1917, died May 2003

Philip Heslop, QC
Financial barrister
Born 1948, died July 2003

Sir Reginald Hibbert, GCMG
Diplomat
Born 1922, died October 2002

Christopher Hill, FBA
Historian
Born 1912, died February 2003

Professor David Hill, FRS
Biophysicist
Born 1915, died August 2002

Dame Wendy Hiller, DBE
Actress
Born 1912, died May 2003

Dame Thora Hird, DBE
Actress
Born 1911, died March 2003

Peter Hunt
Film editor and director
Born 1925, died August 2002

Baroness Hylton-Foster, DBE (Audrey Clifton Brown)
Convenor of the crossbench peers, 1974–95
Born 1908, died October 2002

Edna Iles
Pianist
Born 1905, died January 2003

Peter Jackson
Artist and illustrator, historian of London
Born 1922, died May 2003

Tom Jackson
General Secretary of the Union of Post Office Workers, 1967–82
Born 1925, died June 2003

Lord Jenkins of Hillhead, OM (Roy Harris Jenkins)
Labour and Liberal Democrat statesman and author
Born 1920, died January 2003

Rt Hon. Aubrey Jones
Former Conservative minister and chairman of the National Board for Prices and Incomes, 1965–70
Born 1911, died April 2003

Professor Sir Bernard Katz, FRS
Biophysicist
Born 1911, died April 2003

Rachel Kempson (Lady Redgrave)
Actress
Born 1910, died May 2003

Professor Geoffrey Stephen Kirk, DSC
Classicist; Professor of Greek, Cambridge, 1974–82
Born 1921, died March 2003

Colin Legum
Journalist
Born 1919, died June 2003

Norman Lewis
Traveller and writer
Born 1908, died July 2003

Joan Littlewood
Visionary theatre director
Born 1914, died September 2002

Countess of Longford, CBE (Elizabeth Pakenham)
Author
Born 1906, died October 2002

Gavin Lyall
Journalist and writer
Born 1932, died January 2003

Val McCalla
Newspaper proprietor
Born 1943, died August 2002

Archer Martin, CBE, FRS
Chemist and Nobel prizewinner (1952)
Born 1910, died August 2002

Sir Bert Millichip
Chairman of the Football Association, 1981–96
Born 1914, died December 2002

Anthony Milner
Composer
Born 1925, died September 2002

George Mitchell, OBE
Musical arranger and conductor
Born 1917, died August 2002

Sir William Mitchell, CBE, FRS
Physicist
Born 1925, died October 2002

Professor Rosalind Mitchison
Historian
Born 1919, died September 2002

Mickie Most (John Michael Hayes)
Record producer
Born 1938, died May 2003

Yfrah Neaman, OBE
Violinist
Born 1923, died January 2003

Vivien Neves
Model
Born 1947, died December 2002

Max Nicholson, CB, CVO
Environmentalist and author
Born 1904, died April 2003

Desmond Norman, CBE
Aircraft designer
Born 1929, died November 2002

Michael Oliver
Music critic and broadcaster
Born 1937, died December 2002

Viscount of Oxfuird (George Hubbard Makgill;
13th viscount)
Deputy Speaker of the House of Lords
Born 1934, died January 2003

Terence Parkes ('Larry')
Cartoonist
Born 1927, died June 2003

Dame Felicity Peake, DBE
First Director of the WAAF (1946–49); first
Director of the WRAF (1949–50)
Born 1913, died November 2002

Ted Perry (Edward George)
Record producer and founder of Hyperion
Records
Born 1931, died February 2003

Lord Perry of Walton, OBE, FRS (Walter Laing
Macdonald Perry)
Founding Vice-Chancellor of Open University
Born 1921, died July 2003

Lord Porter of Luddenham, OM, FRS (George
Porter)
Chemist and Nobel prizewinner (1967)
Born 1920, died August 2002

Sir Philip Powell, CH, OBE, RA
Architect
Born 1921, died May 2003

Kathleen Raine, CBE
Poet
Born 1908, died July 2003

Max Reinhardt
Publisher
Born 1915, died November 2002

Karel Reisz
Film and theatre director
Born 1926, died November 2002

Beti Rhys
Promoter of Welsh language
Born 1907, died April 2003

John Michael Roberts, CBE
Historian
Born 1928, died May 2003

Bryan Robertson, OBE
Director of Whitechapel Art Gallery, 1952–68
Born 1925, died November 2002

Derek Robinson
Director, EURATOM/UKAEA fusion programme
and Culham Science Centre
Born 1941, died December 2002

Arthur Rowley
Footballer, who scored a record 434 League goals
between 1946 and 1965
Born 1926, died December 2002

Lord Ryder of Eaton Hastings (Sydney Thomas
Ryder)
Journalist and industrialist
Born 1916, died May 2003

Marquess of Salisbury (Robert Edward Peter
Gascoyne Cecil; 6th marquess)
Owner and developer of Hatfield House
(Hertfordshire) and Cranborne Manor (Dorset)
Born 1916, died July 2003

George Salt, FRS
Entomologist
Born 1903, died March 2003

Jeremy Sandford
Writer
Born 1930, died May 2003

Sir Peter Saunders
Theatre manager and producer
Born 1911, died February 2003

John Schlesinger, CBE
Film, TV, theatre and opera director
Born 1926, died July 2003

Baroness Serota, DBE (Beatrice Katz)
Deputy Speaker of the House of Lords
Born 1919, died October 2002

Lord Shawcross, GBE, QC (Hartley William Shawcross)
Attorney-General, 1945–51, UK Chief Prosecutor at Nuremberg War Crimes Tribunal, 1945–46
Born 1902, died July 2003

Barry Sheene, MBE
Motorcycle racer
Born 1950, died March 2003

Renée Short
Labour MP for Wolverhampton East, 1964–87
Born 1919, died January 2003

Carmen Silvera
Actress
Born 1922, died August 2002

Fritz Spiegl
Musician, writer and broadcaster
Born 1926, died March 2003

Very Reverend David Steel
Moderator of the General Assembly of the Church of Scotland, 1974–95
Born 1910, died November 2002

Joe Strummer (John Graham Mellor)
Rock singer and lyricist
Born 1952, died December 2002

Sylvia Tait
Biological scientist
Born 1917, died February 2003

Arnold Taylor, CBE, FBA
Chief Inspector of Ancient Monuments in Great Britain, 1961–72
Born 1911, died October 2002

Sir Denis Thatcher, Bt, MBE, TD
Businessman
Born 1915, died June 2003

Graham Stuart Thomas, OBE
Horticulturist
Born 1909, died April 2003

Peter Tinniswood
Comedy writer
Born 1936, died January 2003

Meriel Tufnell, MBE
Champion jockey
Born 1948, died October 2002

Richard Wainwright
Liberal and Liberal Democrat MP for Colne Valley, 1966–70 and 1974–87
Born 1918, died January 2003

Alexander Walker
Film critic
Born 1930, died July 2003

Elisabeth Welch
Singer and cabaret artist
Born 1904, died July 2003

Dee Wells (Alberta Constance Chapman; Lady Ayer)
Journalist and author
Born 1925, died June 2003

Mary Wesley, CBE (Mrs Mary Aline Siepmann)
Writer
Born 1912, died December 2002

Professor Sir Bernard Williams, FBA
Philosopher
Born 1929, died June 2003

Malcolm Williamson, CBE
Composer; Master of the Queen's Music since 1975
Born 1931, died March 2003

Professor Sir Robert Wilson, CBE, FRS
Astrophysicist and space scientist
Born 1927, died September 2002

Baroness Young (Janet Mary Baker)
Conservative politician and Leader of the House of Lords, 1981–83
Born 1926, died September 2002

Commander Edward Young, DSO, DSC and bar
Submarine captain, author and publisher (creator of the Penguin logo and cover design)
Born 1913, died January 2003

Viscount Younger of Leckie, KT, Bt, KCVO, TD
(George Kenneth Hotson Younger; 4th viscount)
Secretary of State for Scotland 1979–86
Born 1931, died January 2003

Appendix D Abbreviations

AONB Area of Outstanding Natural Beauty

BAP Biodiversity Action Plan

BBC British Broadcasting Corporation

BBSRC Biotechnology and Biological Sciences Research Council

BCS British Crime Survey

bfi British Film Institute

BL British Library

BNFL British Nuclear Fuels

BNSC British National Space Centre

boepd Barrels of oil equivalent per day

BSE Bovine spongiform encephalopathy

BTI British Trade International

C&AG Comptroller and Auditor General

CAA Civil Aviation Authority

CAP Common Agricultural Policy

CBI Confederation of British Industry

CCGT Combined cycle gas turbine

CCLRC Council for the Central Laboratory of the Research Councils

CCTV Closed circuit TV

CCW Countryside Council for Wales

CFCs Chlorofluorocarbons

CFP Common Fisheries Policy

CFSP Common Foreign and Security Policy

CGT Capital gains tax

CHAI Commission for Healthcare Audit and Inspection

CHD Coronary heart disease

CITES Convention on International Trade in Endangered Species

CO Carbon monoxide

CO$_2$ Carbon dioxide

CPS Crown Prosecution Service

CRE Commission for Racial Equality

CSA Child Support Agency

CSCI Commission for Social Care Inspection

CSIW Care Standards Inspectorate for Wales

CTC Child Tax Credit

DARD Department of Agriculture and Rural Development (Northern Ireland)

DATs Drug Action Teams

DCAL Department of Culture, Arts and Leisure (Northern Ireland)

DCMS Department for Culture, Media and Sport

Defra Department for Environment, Food and Rural Affairs

DEL Department for Employment and Learning (Northern Ireland); Departmental Expenditure Limits

DETI Department of Enterprise, Trade and Investment (Northern Ireland)

DfES Department for Education and Skills

DFID Department for International Development

DfT Department for Transport

DH Department of Health

DNA Deoxyribonucleic acid

DoE Department of the Environment (Northern Ireland)

DPP Director of Public Prosecutions

DRC Disability Rights Commission

DRD Department for Regional Development (Northern Ireland)

DSD Department for Social Development (Northern Ireland)

DTI Department of Trade and Industry

DWP Department for Work and Pensions

EC European Community

ECGD Export Credits Guarantee Department

EEA European Economic Area; Exchange Equalisation Account

EHS Environment and Heritage Service (Northern Ireland)

ELWa National Council for Education & Training in Wales

EMU Economic and monetary union

EOC Equal Opportunities Commission

EP English Partnerships

EPSRC Engineering and Physical Sciences Research Council

ERDF European Regional Development Fund

ESA Environmentally sensitive area; European Space Agency

ESRC Economic and Social Research Council

EU European Union

EUROPOL European Police Office

FCO Foreign & Commonwealth Office

FSA Financial Services Authority; Food Standards Agency

FSBR Financial Statement and Budget Report

FSCS Financial Services Compensation Scheme

G7 Group of seven leading industrial countries

G8 Group of eight leading industrial countries (the G7 members plus Russia)

GCE General Certificate of Education

GCSE General Certificate of Secondary Education

GLA Greater London Authority

GNVQ General National Vocational Qualification

GOs Government Offices (for the Regions)

GP General practitioner

HSE Health and Safety Executive

ICT Information and communications technology

ILO International Labour Organisation

IMF International Monetary Fund

ISA Individual Savings Account

IT Information technology

ITC Independent Television Commission

JNCC Joint Nature Conservation Committee

JSA Jobseeker's Allowance

km/h Kilometres per hour

kW Kilowatt

LEA Local Education Authority

LEC Local enterprise company

LFS Labour Force Survey

LSC Learning and Skills Council

LTPs Local Transport Plans

MEP Member of the European Parliament

MHRA Medicines and Healthcare products Regulatory Agency

Ml Megalitre

MoD Ministry of Defence

MP Member of Parliament

mph Miles per hour

MRC Medical Research Council

MSP Member of the Scottish Parliament

mtc Million tonnes of carbon

mtoe Million tonnes of oil equivalent

MW Megawatt

NAO National Audit Office

NATO North Atlantic Treaty Organisation

NAW National Assembly for Wales

NCSC National Care Standards Commission

NERC Natural Environment Research Council

NGLs Natural gas liquids

NHS National Health Service

NI Northern Ireland; National Insurance

NICs National Insurance contributions

NIE Northern Ireland Electricity

NIHE Northern Ireland Housing Executive

NITHC Northern Ireland Transport Holding Company

NO_x Oxides of nitrogen

NQ National Qualification

NRU Neighbourhood Renewal Unit

NS&I National Savings and Investments

NSF National Service Framework

NVQ National Vocational Qualification

ODPM Office of the Deputy Prime Minister

OECD Organisation for Economic Co-operation and Development

Ofsted Office for Standards in Education

OFT Office of Fair Trading

OGC Office of Government Commerce

ONS Office for National Statistics

OPAS Office of the Pensions Advisory Service

OPRA Occupational Pensions Regulatory Authority

ORR Office of the Rail Regulator

OSCE Organisation for Security and Co-operation in Europe

OST Office of Science and Technology

OTs Overseas Territories

PFI Private finance initiative

plc Public limited company

PM_{10} Particulate matter

PPARC Particle Physics and Astronomy Research Council

PPG Planning Policy Guidance

PPP Public-private partnership

PSA Public Service Agreement

R&D Research and development

RCUK Research Councils UK

RDAs Regional Development Agencies

RDPs Rural Development Programmes

RSA Regional Selected Assistance

RSL Registered social landlord

SAC Scottish Agricultural College

SBS Small Business Service

SCRC Scottish Commission for the Regulation of Care

SDR Strategic Defence Review

SE Scottish Executive

SEERAD Scottish Executive Environment and Rural Affairs Department

SEN Special educational needs

SEPA Scottish Environment Protection Agency

SET Science, engineering and technology

SEU Social Exclusion Unit

SMEs Small and medium-sized enterprises

SNH Scottish Natural Heritage

SO_2 Sulphur dioxide

sq km Square kilometre

SRA Strategic Rail Authority

SSI Social Services Inspectorate

SSSI Site of Special Scientific Interest

StHAs Strategic Health Authorities

SVQ Scottish Vocational Qualification

TAC Total allowable catch

TME Total Managed Expenditure

TOCs Train Operating Companies

UDP Unitary development plan

UK United Kingdom of Great Britain and
Northern Ireland

UKCS United Kingdom Continental Shelf

UKSI United Kingdom Sports Institute

UN United Nations

UNCTAD United Nations Conference on Trade
and Development

US United States

VA Veterans Agency

VAT Value added tax

VED Vehicle excise duty

VOCs Volatile organic compounds

WDA Welsh Development Agency

WSSD World Summit on Sustainable
Development

WTC Working Tax Credit

WTO World Trade Organisation

Appendix E Bank and public holidays in 2004

Thursday 1 January	New Year's Day	UK
Friday 2 January	Bank Holiday	Scotland
Wednesday 17 March	St Patrick's Day	Northern Ireland
Friday 9 April	Good Friday	UK
Monday 12 April	Easter Monday	England, Wales and Northern Ireland
Monday 3 May	Early May Bank Holiday	UK
Monday 31 May	Spring Bank Holiday	UK
Monday 12 July	Orangemen's Day	Northern Ireland
Monday 2 August	Summer Bank Holiday	Scotland
Monday 30 August	Summer Bank Holiday	England, Wales and Northern Ireland
Saturday 25 December	Christmas Day	UK
Sunday 26 December	Boxing Day	UK
Monday 27 December	Substitute Bank Holiday in lieu of Boxing Day	UK
Tuesday 28 December	Substitute Bank Holiday in lieu of Christmas Day	UK

Note: In addition, there are various traditional local holidays in Scotland that are determined by the local authorities there.

Glossary

Additional Member System
Used in elections for the Scottish Parliament and the Welsh and London assemblies, this system combines the election of constituency members on a first-past-the-post basis with additional members elected from a party list in each electoral region. In the United Kingdom, the additional members are elected using the **d'Hondt** system.

Adoption Order
Gives parental responsibility for a child to the adoptive parent(s). The order is made on application to an authorised court.

Alcohol-related deaths
Includes only those causes regarded as being most directly due to alcohol consumption. Does not include other diseases where alcohol may be a contributory factor, such as cancer of the liver. Also excludes road traffic deaths and other accidents.

Basic prices
Prices excluding taxes and subsidies on products.

Biodiversity
This covers the whole variety of living things, including the habitats that support them, the different arrays of species and the genetic variation within species.

Carers
In the 2001 Census, unpaid care was defined as unpaid help, looking after or supporting family members, friends, neighbours or others because of long-term physical or mental ill-health or disability or problems related to old age.

Children
In surveys, children are never-married people of any age who live with one or both parents. The category also includes step-children, adopted children (but not foster children) and also grandchildren (where the parents are absent).

Communal establishment
In the 2001 Census, a communal establishment was defined as an establishment providing managed residential accomodation. Managed means full-time or part-time supervision of the accomodation.

Constant prices
Prices that have been adjusted for the effects of inflation – the values for a time period are expressed in terms of the prices in a chosen base period. In the National Accounts, this is currently 1995.

Couple
The Labour Force Survey definition includes both married and cohabiting couples.

Current account
In the Balance of Payments, this is an account of transactions in respect of trade in goods and services, income, and current transfers.

Current prices
Actual prices for the time period in question, without adjusting for inflation.

Decent home standard
This is measured against the following criteria:
- whether the home meets the current statutory minimum for housing, which at present is the **fitness standard**;
- whether it is in a reasonable state of repair;
- whether it has reasonably modern facilities; and
- whether it provides a reasonable degree of thermal comfort through effective insulation and efficient heating.

Dependent children
In the Labour Force Survey and the General Household Survey, dependent children are childless never-married children in families who are aged under 16, or aged 16 to 18 and in full-time education. In the 1971 Census the definition was slightly different: never-married children in families who were either under 15 years of age, or aged 15 to 24 and in full-time education.

DERV
Diesel engined road vehicle fuel used in internal combustion engines that are compression-ignited.

Detection of crime
A crime is 'detected' (or in Scotland 'cleared up') if a suspect has been identified and interviewed and there is sufficient evidence to bring a charge. There does not have to be a prosecution: for example, the

offender may accept a caution or ask for the crime to be taken into consideration by the court, or the victim may not wish to give evidence.

d'Hondt system
A form of proportional representation used in England, Wales and Scotland for elections to the European Parliament, and as part of the **Additional Member System** used in elections to the Welsh Assembly, Scottish Parliament, and London Assembly.

The party with the most votes in an electoral region receives the first seat. The votes for that party are then divided by two and this new figure compared with votes for the other parties. The party that now has the most votes receives the next seat. Each time a party wins a seat, its total vote is divided by a number equal to the number of seats it has already been allocated, plus one, and the process is repeated until all seats are allocated.

Downstream
Used in oil and gas processes to refer to the part of the industry after the production of the oil and gas. For example, it covers refining, supply and trading, marketing and exporting.

Drug classifications
In the United Kingdom, illegal drugs are classified under the *Misuse of Drugs Act 1971* into:
- **Class A** drugs, which include opiates (such as heroin and morphine); hallucinogens (such as LSD and magic mushrooms); ecstasy and cocaine.
- **Class B** drugs, which include amphetamines and barbiturates.
- **Class C** drugs, which include cannabis, most anabolic steroids and benzodiazepine tranquillisers.

Economically active
Those in **employment** plus those who are **unemployed**.

Employment
Those in employment include employees, self-employed people, participants in government employment and training programmes, and people doing unpaid family work.

Energy use of fuel
Energy use of fuel mainly comprises use for lighting, heating or cooling, motive power and power for appliances.

Family
In household surveys, this is a married or cohabiting couple, with or without any of their never-married children (of any age) or a lone parent with his or her never-married children. A family could also consist of grandparent(s) and grandchildren if the parents of the children are not usually resident in the household.

Feedstock
In the refining industry, this is a product or a combination of products derived from crude oil, destined for further processing (other than blending).

Final consumption expenditure
Spending on goods and services that are used for the direct satisfaction of individual or collective needs, as distinct from purchases for use in a productive process.

Final energy consumption
Energy consumed by the final user, as opposed to energy which is being used for transformation into other forms of energy.

Financial account
In the Balance of Payments, this records transactions in external assets and liabilities of the UK. It consists of direct investment, portfolio investment, other investment and reserve assets.

Fitness standard
The fitness standard in England and Wales is set out in section 604 of the *Local Government and Housing Act 1989* and in guidance issued to local authorities. A property is fit for human habitation if it meets all of the following requirements:
- it is structurally stable;
- it is free from serious disrepair;
- it is free from dampness prejudicial to the health of any occupants;
- it has adequate provision for lighting, heating and ventilation;
- it has adequate supply of wholesome, piped water;
- it has satisfactory facilities for preparing and cooking food including a sink with supplies of hot and cold water;
- it has a suitably located WC;
- it has a bath or shower and basin, each with supplies of hot and cold water; and
- it has an effective system for draining foul, waste and surface water.

There is a separate fitness standard for houses in multiple occupation.

Fuel poverty
A fuel poor household is one that needs to spend more than 10 per cent of household income to achieve a satisfactory heating regime (21°C in the living room and 18°C in the other occupied rooms).

Gigawatt hour (GWh)
A 1 Gigawatt power station running for one hour produces 1 GWh of electrical energy.

Gross domestic product
The total value of economic activity in a region. It is measured in either **current** or **constant prices**.

Gross fixed capital formation
Investment in assets, primarily by businesses, which are used repeatedly or continuously over a number of years to produce goods, such as machinery used to create a product.

Gross value added (GVA)
The difference between the value of the output of goods and services produced by an industry or sector, and its **intermediate consumption** – that is, the difference between the value of the goods and services produced and the cost of raw materials and other inputs which are used up in production.

Household
A person living alone or a group of people who have the address as their only or main residence and who either share one meal a day or share the living accommodation.

Household final expenditure
Spending by the household sector on products or services to satisfy immediate needs or wants.

Household reference person (HRP)
The person who owns the household accommodation, is legally responsible for the rent or has the accommodation by virtue of some relationship to the owner, where the latter is not a member of the household. If this should apply to one or more person in the household, then the HRP is taken to be the person with the highest income.

Household sector
This covers all residents of the UK as receivers of income and consumers of products. It includes families, residential homes, and one-person businesses where the household and business accounts cannot be separated.

Index
A number giving the value of a quantity relative to a base year, where the value in the base year is set at 100. Index numbers are used to indicate trends in prices, production and other economic variables.

Intermediate consumption
The cost of raw materials and other inputs which are used up in the production process.

Incidence
The frequency of occurrence in a specific period, for example the number of notifications of an infectious disease in a calendar year.

Indigenous production
For oil this includes production from the UK Continental Shelf, both onshore and offshore.

Life expectancy
This is the average total number of years which a person of a given age could be expected to live, if the rates of mortality at each age were those experienced in that year. 'Healthy life expectancy' is defined as the expected number of years of life in good or fairly good self-assessed general health.

Limiting long-term illness
A self-assessment of whether or not a person has a long-term illness, health problem or disability which limits their daily activities or the work they can do, including problems that are due to old age.

Lone parent family
In the Labour Force Survey, a lone parent family consists of a lone parent, living with his or her never-married children, provided these children have no children of their own living with them.

Low income
Households living below 60 per cent of median equivalised household disposable income. This can be calculated before or after deducting for housing costs – both are equally valid. Household incomes are equivalised in order to adjust for variations in household size and composition.

Magnox
A type of gas-cooled nuclear fission reactor developed in the UK, so called because of the magnesium alloy used to clad the uranium fuel.

Market prices

The prices actually paid by the purchaser for goods and services, including transport costs, trade margins and taxes.

Offences in England and Wales

- Indictable-only offence – a category of criminal offence that can only be tried in the Crown Court. This includes serious offences such as murder and manslaughter.
- Either-way offence – an offence that can be tried in either the magistrates' court or in the Crown Court. Magistrates' courts can decline to hear an either-way offence if they consider they do not have the power to sentence appropriately. A defendant has a right to elect a Crown Court trial for either-way offences.
- Summary-only offence – an offence that can only be tried in a magistrates' court. Most traffic offences are summary-only, as are minor offences against public order.

Owner-occupied

Includes accommodation that is owned outright, owned with a mortgage or loan, or on a shared ownership basis (paying part rent and part mortgage)

Pensionable age

State pension age is currently 65 for men, 60 for women.

Prevalence

The total number of cases of a disease in a given population at a specific time.

Primary fuels

Fuels obtained directly from natural sources – for example coal, oil and natural gas.

Real household disposable income

The amount of money the household sector has available to spend after taxes and other deductions.

Single Transferable Vote

System used in Northern Ireland, in which voters rank candidates in order of preference. If a voter's first choice candidate does not need their vote (because they can be elected without it, or because they have too few votes to be elected) then the vote is transferred to the voter's second choice.

Social rented accommodation

Accommodation that is rented from a council or registered social landlord, such as a housing association, housing co-operative, charitable trust, or non-profit housing company.

Total Fertility Rate

Total fertility rate is the number of children that would be born to a woman if current patterns of fertility persisted throughout her childbearing life.

Trade in services

The provision of services between UK residents and non-residents, and transactions in goods which are not freighted out of the country in which they take place – for example, purchases by tourists.

Trip

In the National Travel Survey, this is a one-way course of travel having a single main purpose.

Unemployed

Those aged 16 and over who are without a job, are available to start work in the next two weeks, who have been seeking a job in the previous four weeks, or are out of work and have accepted a job that they are willing to start in the next two weeks. This definition is recommended by the International Labour Organisation and is used in the Labour Force Survey.

Unemployment rate

Percentage of the **economically active** who are unemployed.

Index

D

S